THE WORD IS WORTH A THOUSAND PICTURES

THE WORD IS WORTH A THOUSAND PICTURES

Preaching in the Electronic Age

A Resource for Preaching in the Twenty-first Century

Gregory Edward Reynolds

Wipf and Stock Publishers
150 West Broadway ◆ Eugene OR 97401

2001

The Word Is Worth a Thousand Pictures

By Reynolds, Gregory
Copyright © 2000 by Reynolds, Gregory
ISBN:1-57910-638-2

Wipf and Stock Publishers
150 West Broadway • Eugene OR 97401

Cover design by Gregory Reynolds and James Tedrick
Page design and typesetting by Gregory Reynolds and James Tedrick

Cover picture: William Tyndale [c.1494-1536], stained glass window at Hertford College, Oxford, UK [erected 1994]

*To Robin for being my faithful soulmate and best critic;
Rebekah for being my creative and sympathetic daughter;
Thomas for persevering as my scholar-athlete;
Christopher for being my brightest computer consultant;
My mother for praying like Monica for her son;
Elena for being the best sister a brother could have.*

Contents

Foreword	v
Preface	viii
Introduction: The Thesis	xi

PART I TOOLS OF ENGAGEMENT: THE APOLOGETIC APPROACH

1. No Other Gods: Idolatry in the Bible — 1
  Idolatry in the Old Testament — 2
  Idolatry in the New Testament — 14
  Summary: The Concept of Idolatry — 23

2. The Apologetics of Fire: Idolatry as a Critical Paradigm — 26
  The Place of Idolatry in Biblical Apologetics — 31
  A Paradigm for Cultural Understanding — 46
  A Paradigm for Communication — 54

PART II TOOLS OF HISTORY: THE HISTORY OF COMMUNICATION STUDY

3. Second Thoughts (Part I): Progressive and Scientific Theorists — 65
  European Intellectual Roots — 68
  Progressive Theorists — 81
  Scientific Theorists — 86

4. Second Thoughts (Part II): Critical Theorists — 101
  Critical Communication Theorists: The Founders of Media Ecology — 103
  Contemporary Voices: The Emergence of Media Ecology — 126
  Landmarks in Communication Study — 138
  The Development of the Electric Media — 139

PART III TOOLS OF ASSESSMENT: CHRISTIAN MEDIA ECOLOGY

5. Third Thoughts: A Christian View of Media Theory and Criticism — 151
  The Gist of the Debate — 152
  Religious Presuppositions among the Critical Theorists — 159
  Christian Perspectives — 172
  An Outline for Future Development — 179
  Conclusion — 203

CONTENTS

6. Modernity/Postmodernity: The Culture of Idolatry	**204**
Philosophical Idolatry	208
Cultural Idolatry	214
Conclusion	236
7. Twilight of the Gods: Benefits and Liabilities of Electronic Media	**241**
Media and Common Culture	243
Recreation, Imagination and Edification	244
A Critical Look at Three Key Media	248
Critical Concerns for All Media	264
Cultivating a Counter Environment	271
8. The Fourth Temptation: The Compromise of the Church	**278**
The Church Transformed by the Electronic Media	279
The Church Consecrating the Electronic Media	296
The Church as a Counter Environment	298
Conclusion	309

PART IV TOOLS OF COMMUNICATION: AN ECOLOGY OF PREACHING

9. Tongues of Fire: God's Chosen Medium	**313**
The Primacy of Preaching: A Biblical Overview	315
The Primacy of Preaching: A Church Historical Overview	323
The Excellencies of Preaching as a Medium	333
Hearts of Flesh: The Committed Hearer	345
10. Trumpeter of God: The Effective Preacher	**354**
Remember Your Office	356
Take Heed to Yourself	361
Remember Your Medium	366
Cultivate Your Preaching	375
Coda: Keep Yourselves from Idols	399
Appendix: Principles For Preachers	401
Annotated Bibliography	402
Index of Subjects	461
Index of Authors and Persons	488
Index of Scripture References	502

Foreword

Gregory Reynolds has done us a service by reminding us of the fundamental and pervasive issue that confronts the people of the covenant today: the issue of idolatry. Idolatry is worshipping a creature rather than the Creator who is over all, God blessed forever.

It would be accurate to declare that the Bible has but one purpose: the destruction of idolatry. Its very first chapters are a majestic taunt directed against the frivolous, demeaning religion of the fertile crescent that overspread the world of Moses' day. As a catechumen in Pharaoh's court, Moses had learned that religion well (Acts 7:22). Paul the apostle was appalled by idolatry's overpowering allure, with its orgiastic sexuality, and when he saw it strike into Christ's fledgling church, he warned of hideous snakes that would bring God's inevitable response (1 Corinthians 10:1-13). Virtually the last words to come from an apostolic pen, the closing sentence of John's first catholic epistle, expresses one final warning: "Dear children, keep yourselves from idols."

Much of the Old Testament is a dismal report of the losing battle the covenant nation waged with the detestable idolatry that had brought Canaan its debauchery. And when the people of the covenant were finally purged of idolatry's grossest forms, they transformed the holy law into a merciless taskmaster. The New Testament corrects all this with the appearance of our Savior Jesus, God's ultimate "Son language," the radiance of God's glory and the exact representation of his being...." (Hebrews 1:3).

The covenant people must now be characterized by an unremitting preoccupation with idolatry; they must have a kind of brooding paranoia with regard to idols. The church must be the staging area where the covenant people are equipped to recognize and oppose idolatry. But, alas, the very idea of idolatry is considered somewhat quaint, and, if it is considered at all, it is approached with an historical curiosity, as if this were an ancient problem or the problem of those followers of non-Christian religions who set up house idols in their kitchens. There is virtually no sense that the Scriptures are providing us with information about idolatry so that we can understand the times in which we are living now.

The pages that follow alert us to the idolatry of this age, an idolatry that differs from Canaan's only in the fact that it is much, much more vicious and powerful. Canaan was bad, but Canaan did not have television. We do. And this medium, along with a welter of other electronic technology, has created a world wide web few can escape.

What David Sarnoff and other television pioneers could not foresee when they became ecstatic over television's promise in the thirties was that ultimately television would be joined in a hideous marriage with a godless worldview that considered man exclusively in economic terms. Television cannot be separated from the powers that control it and that use it to achieve the creation of a very specific kind of human being: man the consumer.

The idolatry that now defines our culture is so pervasive and enveloping, we are scarcely aware of what has happened to us. The Chinese are credited with saying that if you want to find out something about water, you should not ask a fish. They cannot view it from a distance; they have no objectivity with regard to this subject. Those who allow themselves to be influenced by television are so modified by the experience, they are scarcely capable of perceiving that they are being influenced by an idolatrous worldview.

The people of God's covenant are in a most precarious situation. The very church that should equip them to discern and withstand the cultural debacle seems to have lost its ability to respond; in fact, it has succumbed to the enormous power of the modern worldview. It is infected with the same marketing mentality that has overtaken the general culture. It seldom speaks of idolatry as the primary concept with which to understand the degeneration of this age.

What it all comes down to is this: the church doesn't seem to know what's going on.

It really doesn't. In many instances, it is willing to surrender the divinely given tools that make it uniquely the church and ape the idol mode itself. It is impossible to exaggerate the depth of this folly. It is one of the primary manifestations of the masquerading Deceiver's art, as masterfully effective as it is because of his intense skill in these years in which he knows, he knows, his time is very short.

In the face of the overwhelming idolatry of this age, there is but one antidote: the preaching of the Word of God. This is a preposterous and audacious statement, but it is a faith statement. Reynolds shows the dominance of the preaching mode within the Bible and calls the church to focus its attention on this fleeting oral event. The preaching that is needed is not that which fills the time slot in a worship service that is so designated (for that could be just about anything these days), but it must be the preaching of Jeremiah's hammer and the fire in his stomach, the compulsive and compelling apostolic announcement that the Kingdom of God is at hand, and we had better repent before we tumble into the abyss.

FOREWORD

No folly is more pernicious than to seek to design preaching so that it will be more user friendly. Don't even think about that. To do that is like trying to strengthen your marriage by having an affair. Preaching is corrupted by our creativity, our cleverness; it must express the content of the Scriptures and that alone. Nothing else! And preaching is fundamentally an oral event. Reynolds is bold in suggesting that it should even be prepared for in oral mode—committing it to manuscript will create a barrier between the Bible's message and the people of the covenant. Preaching is simply the voice of one crying in the wilderness—a voice crying.

The church is desperately in need of abject slaves of Christ and his Word who are willing to burn themselves out in order to make their proclamation truly the Word of God and not the word of man. They must eschew eloquence and excellence and willingly do whatever is necessary to get the message across. They must understand that the message is not simply conveying information, but it is a message that must shatter and crush and restore hapless sinners within the church and those outside it. They can do this only if they have been shattered and crushed and restored themselves.

When Gregory Reynolds and I first met and talked about the impact of the media, especially television, on our age, I already sensed that something of world historical importance was coming about, an event that, as it was turning out, was going to confront the church with an enormous crisis, a persecution as intense and effective as any that has ever happened. During that decade since our first conversations, my pessimism has deepened, not only because I have seen the growing power of these Neo-pagan forces but also because I see the church so naïve in its response. If we were to construct an equation designed to capture what is now happening, it would seem undoubted that the forces of evil have never been more effective, and they are winning.

But there is another factor in all this that cannot be figured into any equation of human making: it is the supernatural, the divine. None of this is happening outside the control of the Creator and Director of the Universe. Toppling idols is his specialty. And this great God, Triune and Holy, has ordained that he will use a preacher's words to do the toppling. The voice of the preacher is the weaponry of God. We must confess our grievous neglect of this weaponry, repent and pray that God will send us preachers. We need them urgently!

Dr. Joel H. Nederhood
Lansing, Illinois, 2000

Preface

In connection with the subject of Christian education, I have often heard people assert that we must not shelter our children from *reality*. This response has made me ask: "Just what is the reality to which our children need to be exposed?" If cultivating a wide and varied knowledge of human life, thought and literature is what is meant, I wholeheartedly agree. In fact, the idea of a liberal education involves just such an exposure in a formal setting.

However, more often than not, I think the assertion is an excuse based on a defective view of what constitutes *reality*. It is an *excuse* because it usually involves a retreat from parental control over the influences of our culture on their children. Popular media culture, in particular, is so pervasive in our lives, that it represents a daunting challenge to the average parent. Abdication is the path of least resistance. Exposure to *reality* is the excuse. As sympathetic as I am with the difficulty of the challenge, I cannot condone such a lack of involvement in the lives of this and the next generation.

The defective view of what constitutes *reality* is equally disturbing. Secular culture, in as much as it lives and thinks independently of its Creator and Sustainer, is engaged in a massive denial and suppression of reality. In place of the truth modern culture constructs a lie which the Bible calls idolatry. The modern electronic media culture simply exacerbates that engagement. Idolatry, of course, is not new. But the forms and power of the image and electronic media give new meaning to the worship of images. Witness tennis star (read idol) Andre Agassi's commercial sound bite for The Rebel camera: "Image is everything." Recent ads have offered a counterpoint: "Image is nothing." This, of course, is just another kind of image which fails to appreciate the McLuhanesque pun in the original.

In the final chapter of his epoch making critique of American image culture, *The Image: Or What Happened to the American Dream*, published in 1962, Daniel Boorstin concludes with a poignant exhortation: "We should try to reach outside our images. We should seek new ways of letting messages reach us; from our own past, from God, from the world which we may hate or think we hate."[1]

---

[1] Daniel J. Boorstin, *The Image: Or What Happened to the American Dream* (New York: Atheneum, 1962) 260.

PREFACE

As a preacher of the Word of God I have become painfully aware, over two decades of regular preaching, of the enormous influence of the electronic and image media on my hearers and on me. The electronic media represent a challenge to the preacher unlike any in the church's history. The challenge is one that needs to be faced by preachers and hearers alike. It is not only the preaching event that is being challenged, but the Christian mind and the Christian way of life which preaching is designed to cultivate.

"We must first awake before we can walk in the right direction" warns Boorstin.[2] The live pastoral preaching of the Word of God is the principal way by which God awakens us from our idolatrous illusions. It is God's chosen way of addressing His people directly. This is the impetus for this book.

The complete record of the debt I owe to many individuals would fill an entire chapter. Chief among my debts is the unwitting gift of the initial idea for the book from Dr. Joel Nederhood in his lectures "Effective Preaching in a Media Age" delivered at Westminster Theological Seminary in California in 1990, during the initial phase of the Doctor of Ministry program. Thanks to Dr. Jay Adams for encouraging me to enter the program, and for his contagious enthusiasm for the task of preaching. Neil Postman's *Amusing Ourselves to Death*, combined with his generous interaction with my initial thesis in an interview at NYU in 1990, as well as through correspondence, have been an enormous encouragement.

My thanks also to my advisor Dr. Joseph A. Pipa, Jr. for his tireless, and I am sure tiring, work of reading the entire manuscript several times. Many thanks to Professor John M. Frame for his careful reading and cogent comments on the apologetic portions of the manuscript. Special thanks to my dear friend Dr. T. David Gordon for his excellent detailed and overall criticism of my manuscript, without which the book would never have been completed in its present form. The enthusiasm of these two men for my thesis kept me going when completion seemed impossible.

Two excellent listserv media discussion groups have proved an incomparable intellectual stimulus: Mark Stahlman and his Non-Linear Circle; Lance Strate and the Media Ecology Association list. Many thanks to Eric McLuhan for his many helpful comments on his father's religious views and his provision of electronic copies of many sections of *The Medium and the Light*. Thanks also to Professor Joshua Meyrowitz for his "media metaphors" and taking time to discuss his book *No Sense of Place* and my thesis over a very long lunch at the University of New Hampshire. I also want to thank the present director of the doctor of ministry program, Dr. Iain Duguid, and Dr. Dennis Johnson for their very insightful interaction with my work. They, along

---

[2] *Ibid.*, 261.

with the faculty and administration of Westminster Theological Seminary in California, made the completion of my program and the defense of my thesis a delightful experience.

Special thanks to my dear wife Robin, who has graciously put with my absent mindedness, especially during the last years of intense study and writing; but especially for her constant encouragement and excellent insights into my thesis. She has been my greatest human inspiration. Thanks to my mother, who prayed me into the kingdom many years ago, and has provided a an example of Christian piety, creativity, and hard work over a lifetime. I am also very grateful to Tony and Hissy Van Brakel for their continued generous support since seminary days. Finally, a hearty thanks to the congregation of Amoskeag Presbyterian Church for their continued prayer and encouragement. Having such friends in Christ makes writing a book and getting a doctor's degree seem very insignificant in comparison with their incomparable fellowship.

Gregory Edward Reynolds
Manchester, New Hampshire, 2001

Introduction: The Thesis

Most books on homiletics focus, as they must, on the preparation and delivery of sermons. Some elaborate on the primacy of preaching. This is especially true in more recent history as the relevance of preaching has been attacked from all sides. The orthodox message of the Christian Gospel has been attacked for not being scientifically acceptable to the modern mind. Recently the exclusivity of the Christian message has been assailed for its intolerance. More to the point of the present thesis: the method of speaking to a large audience has been assaulted for lacking the intimacy of dialogue, the visual interest of television and movies, and the immediacy of electronic communication. We are told that preaching fails to deliver the personal interaction that people crave. It is further asserted that preaching is grossly outdated and simply cannot compete with the electronic media. Preaching simply does not meet the needs of people in the Electronic Age.

In its quest for relevance much of the church has responded by radically altering both its message and its method. As we shall see even just altering the method, i.e. the medium of communication, subtly transforms the message in ways which compromise the Gospel itself. The content of many evangelical sermons has been reduced to a moralistic, anecdotal homily loosely related to a Biblical text. The sermon itself has been shortened to accommodate reduced attention spans. At its worst the sermon has been augmented or even replaced by more entertaining media, such as drama, sacred dance, overhead projectors and films. There is even an alternative to the entire worship service in the form of television worship services and The First Church of Cyberspace, both of which are attempts to transcend space and time.

In light of these developments, the discipline of homiletics is in desperate need of some serious critical reflection on the nature of media, the electronic and visual media in particular. This reflection needs to focus on the peculiar excellence of preaching as God's chosen medium. Along with this, it is necessary for the church to consider the positive use of other media in fulfilling its mandate to spread the Gospel. I will only hint at the latter in the following pages, since my focus is on the defense of live pastoral preaching.

It is my intention to help pastors meet the challenge that modern electronic media have presented to preaching as a medium. As western culture has moved from oral to print media, and now to visual and electronic media, for public discourse, confidence in preaching as a medium to communicate

God's Word has been eroded dramatically. Hence alternatives such as drama, dance and film are being used by evangelicals in evangelism and worship, because these visual media are considered equal to or superior to live preaching. The average pastor, even in denominations that believe in the importance of preaching, often finds himself discouraged in his task, because the culture in which we live has marginalized what he spends his life's energy doing.

Based on the supposition that an all-wise and sovereign God has chosen live, pastoral preaching in his infallible Word as the best and primary means of communicating that word, it is important at this point in history for someone to articulate the characteristics of that superiority from Scripture, with a corroborating analysis of theology, history, sociology, rhetoric, media criticism and the electronic media themselves. Growing out of the two century-old anti-intellectual tendency of Evangelicalism is the assumption that "the foolishness of preaching" referred to by Paul indicates an intentional inferiority of the medium of preaching. I intend to compare and contrast preaching with its visual and electronic competitors in order to vindicate that divinely ordained superiority.

Since the pursuit of excellence in a given task depends in no small degree on confidence in its value and effectiveness, I intend to convince preachers of the superiority of the live medium as a medium that God has chosen for excellent reasons and will therefore bless. I also intend to show how grasping these reasons will improve preaching. In short, preachers need to be gripped with the inexorable spiritual force of Paul's rhetorical question: "How shall they hear without a preacher?" (Romans 10:14). The means of grace are, as they must be, perfectly suited to the message of grace for which they are the vehicles. Preaching is no exception. It is the primary exemplar of this vital theological connection.

Douglas Kelly, in his compelling account of the powerful preaching of four southern stalwarts, astutely observes:

Perhaps this shift of focus (from preaching to entertainment) comes from the valid concern to hold the attention of their audience, which, according to several studies, is increasingly conditioned by frequent television watching to expect rapidly changing scenes of exciting action, rather than a sustained development of thought. Of course no-one should go into the pulpit who is not intensely concerned to gain a hearing with the people, 'for faith cometh by hearing' (Rom. 10:17). And the incarnation of Christ itself teaches us that it is always necessary to take the surrounding culture into account as we present the unchanging truth to it in terms that it can understand. Thus it would be unwise *not* to be aware of the effects on our hearers of the shift from traditional reading to visual media.[1]

The assumption of the average Evangelical preacher is that media are "neutral" tools, which are mere vehicles for the message. As in many things "the children of this world are in their generation wiser than the children of light" (Luke 16:8). So media critics such as Marshal McLuhan and Neil Postman, have warned us that every medium effects the way in which we think about and interact with the message and with reality itself. Several perceptive Protestants such as Jacques Ellul and Malcolm Muggeridge have alerted us to this subtlety. These reflections, however, have gone largely unappreciated in the church at large. As far as the church is concerned, I believe the most important place to begin such reflection is in the discipline of homiletics.

The logic of this book may at first appear to have little to do with preaching. Only the last several chapters actually deal with preaching directly. I am not attempting to repeat or popularize the tried and true classics of homiletics, such as Broadus's *A Treatise on the Preparation and Delivery of Sermons* or, more recently, Haddon Robinson's *Biblical Preaching: The Development and Delivery of Expository Messages.* I propose, rather, to supplement the standard concerns of homiletics in an area of thought which has not been systematically dealt with in the homiletical disciplines. What I wish to accomplish as I approach homiletics proper is to develop and understanding of the new situation faced by the preacher and the church in an electronic age. In doing so I want to equip the preacher with critical tools by which to assess this situation. I have chosen to begin with a chapter on an aspect of apologetics which I believe has been neglected: idolatry. Chapter 2 seeks to place the critical paradigm of idolatry in a more prominent position in presuppositional apologetics, cultural criticism and most specifically media criticism. Chapters 3 and 4 outline the history, of which most Christians and preachers are entirely unaware, of the academic development of communication study. The theoretical analysis of human communication will help us understand and identify the issues which need to be addressed by the thoughtful Christian, as well as alert us to weaknesses in the theories and critical positions of non-Christians. This history also calls the Christian thinker to work on a Christian theory of communication. The theoretical discussion and the extensive annotated bibliography are meant to be tools for future scholarly work, as well as a resource for preachers and thoughtful Christians. Thus, chapter 5 lays the groundwork for future theoretical development. Chapter 6 surveys the idolatrous tendencies of our culture, applying the paradigm of idolatry to

---

[1] Douglas Kelly, *Preachers With Power: Four Stalwarts of the South* (Edinburgh: The Banner of Truth Trust, 1992), pp. 171,2.

several major themes of modernity, and demonstrating their relationship to the electronic environment. Chapter 7 assesses electronic media in particular, especially in relation to preaching. Chapter 8 demonstrates the need for the church to be better informed about the current situation of electronic culture, showing how present naiveté has negatively effected preaching and worship. Chapter 9 deals with the primacy of preaching in the Bible and church history, with observations about the unique excellencies of live pastoral preaching. The end of this chapter contains a section for the worshipper as a sermon listener, pointing out dangers to avoid, and recommending ways to cultivate good listening attitudes and habits in light of the electronic situation. The final chapter deals with the preacher's conception of his office as a minister of the Word, and recommends ways to improve his preaching in light of the challenge of the electronic media.

One thing is certain: the electronic revolution is here to stay, and as one reformed critic has observed, we are only at the beginning of a cultural shift more dramatic than the industrial revolution. "The computer is in the 'horseless carriage' stage of its existence."[2] The question for the Christian minister of the Word is: How will I respond to this revolution? Will I stubbornly ignore it, uncritically accept it, simply cave in to the pressure and abandon my task as a preacher, or will I face the challenge, donning the whole armor of God, with renewed confidence in God's chosen means to spread the Gospel and build the church?

---

[2] James R. Hughes, *The Church in Cyberspace: The Coming Impact of the Computer on the Church*. [WWW document] URL http://www.reformed.com/pub/cyber.htm [9 September 1999].

PART I

TOOLS OF ENGAGEMENT: THE APOLOGETIC APPROACH

1

No Other Gods: Idolatry in the Bible

I fled Him, down the nights and down the days;
I fled Him, down the arches of the years;
I fled Him, down the labyrinthine ways
Of my own mind; and in the mist of tears
I hid from Him, and under running laughter.

—Francis Thompson, *The Hound of Heaven*[1]

Facing the electronic environment the preacher must have effective critical weapons in his arsenal in order to understand his task as an oral communicator and the audience he is addressing. Idolatry is the most comprehensive Biblical concept by which to understand people in their fallen situation. Along with presuppositional apologetics this concept will be used to develop a distinctively Christian approach to the electronic media. Along with a survey of the study and criticism of communication in the Electronic Age we will look at the broad cultural effects of electronic communication and its narrower influence on the church. Only then will we be prepared to look at the place of preaching and its effectiveness in the present environment. The purpose of this chapter is to survey the biblical teaching on idolatry in order to better understand the concept of idolatry as a critical tool.

Idolatry is literally as old as Adam. It is a major theme in both Old and New Testaments.[2] The absence of the concept of idolatry in the church's current thinking indicates a major weakness in its understanding of the covenantal nature of the Bible; and compromises the church's critical understanding of contemporary culture. The evolutionary tendency in modern thought has inclined the church to think of idolatry as a superstitious habit of primitive peoples which has no place in the scientifically sophisticated modern mind. A lack of technological development is often mistakenly equated with a

---

[1] Francis Thompson, *The Hound of Heaven* (New York: Dodd, Mead and Company, 1954) 45.
[2] Os Guinness and John Seel, eds. *No God But God: Breaking with the Idols of Our Age.* (Chicago: Moody Press, 1992). "Idolatry is the most discussed problem in the Bible and one of the most powerful spiritual and intellectual concepts in the believer's arsenal" (p. 23).

lack of intellectual and spiritual subtlety. Thus it is believed that ancient peoples worshipped only the physical object which the Bible refers to as an "idol" or an "image".

A survey of the Bible discloses both its extensive treatment of idolatry as well as the centrality of idolatry to a proper understanding of the mindset of fallen human nature. The following analysis focuses on what I have identified as the *loci communes* of this doctrine. It is important to keep in mind that a biblical concept is larger than any word or group of words such as "image", "idol" or "idolatry" which a study of the concordance may yield. It is significant, however, that the words ordinarily associated with idolatry, even by themselves, lead to an extensive study of the concept in both Testaments.

IDOLATRY IN THE OLD TESTAMENT

Genesis: The Native Instinct of Fallen Man

The historical record of Adam's fall in Genesis 3 confronts us with the first instance of idolatry in the Bible. This is highly significant since this passage forms the basis for our understanding of man's essential covenant breaking inclination. The historic fall sets the course of world history. The visual appeal of the forbidden fruit lies at the heart of the temptation. "So when the woman saw that the tree was good for food, that it was pleasant to the eyes, and a tree desirable to make one wise, she took of its fruit and ate" (v. 6).[3] The underlying assertion of autonomy in Eve's act forms the basic motive of idolatry. She "worshipped and served the creation rather than the Creator" (Rom. 1:25). The God-given beauty of the tree and its fruit became a seductive image through the perception of a rebel. Visual appeal became a medium for deceit. Created reality became the locus of man's devotion. What was created to reflect the glory of God became the object of worship in an effort to usurp God's sovereignty. Man as the "image" (צֶלֶם, Gen. 1:26, 27) of God turned his creative and interpretive powers into an evasion of the truth (Rom. 1:18). This endeavor has polluted all of his cultural activities ever since.

Idolatry is man's religious alternative to the worship of the true and living God. It forms the transcendental ground of his suppression of God's revelation in the natural order. In Genesis 4 we encounter the murderous Lamech's bold poetic rejection of God's protection (vs. 23, 24). In the context we are told that he is in the line of covenant breakers who excel in the earliest developments of

---

[3] *The Holy Bible, New King James Version.* Thomas Nelson, Inc. 1982. All biblical quotations are made from the NKJV, unless otherwise noted. Note that the words "idol" and "image" are not used in this passage.

human culture. They were farmers, musicians, craftsmen and poets. The self-exalting quest of pre-lapsarian mankind comes to a tragic climax in Genesis 6. The often misunderstood references to "the sons of God or the gods" and "giants" has been demonstrated by Meredith G. Kline to refer to kings, men of power and authority (v. 4 "mighty men" הַגִּבֹּרִים "great ones" הַנְּפִלִים), as in Psalms 82:6 and 138:1 (Cf. Exod. 21:6; 22:8, 9, 28), who sought a name for themselves (v. 4, "men of the name" אַנְשֵׁי הַשֵּׁם). These members of the "Cult of Divine Kings" named themselves as deity, the essence and principal agenda of idolaters, and presaged the Anti-Christ in the pre-deluvian world (Cf. Dan. 11:36, 37).[4] The flood judgment foreshadowed the ultimate elimination of idolatry in the final "Day of the Lord." These pretenders to deity met an ignominious end.

The Tower of Babel (Gen. 11) represents another tragic culmination of these early expressions of idolatrous man's creative abilities. By contrasting the two humanities which resulted from the fall in Eden, Moses highlights the goal and motivation of the covenant breaking line in his record of the Babel project. The intention of the idolatrous heart is clear: "Come, let us build ourselves a city, and a tower whose top is in the heavens; let us make a name for ourselves, lest we be scattered abroad over the face of the whole earth" (v. 4). This audacious architectural challenge to the dominion of God indicates the insecurity of autonomous man in his vain, but beguiling effort to escape the claims of his Creator.

The naming activity of the builders in the Babel episode (Gen. 11:4) recalls Adam's Edenic use of God's gift of interpreting and manipulating the creation for God's glory and man's benefit as God's vice-gerent (Gen. 1:19). The spoken word has tremendous recreative power. In the hands of men seeking their independence from God this gift of naming becomes a powerful tool for creating meaning apart from the self-sufficient God who defines everything. God's very name is "I am that I am" (אֶהְיֶה אֲשֶׁר אֶהְיֶה Exod. 3:14). The Psalmist picks up on this theme in describing the godless "who trust in their wealth and boast in the multitude of their riches, ...Their inner thought is that their houses will continue forever, and their dwelling places to all generations; they call their lands after their own names" (Ps. 49:6, 11). The naming of their estates gives them the illusory hope of eternal life. But the ultimate Definer has the last word in His imposition of the reality of death: "Man who is in honor, but does not understand, is like the beasts that perish" (v. 20).

The first actual mention of idols in the Bible is found in the account of Jacob's life in Genesis 31:19. It is difficult to determine the exact nature of

---

[4] Meredith G. Kline, *Kingdom Prologue* (South Hamilton, MA: Meredith G. Kline, 1993) 114-117.

Laban's "household" idols. What is clear is that idols and idolatry had been an intrinsic part of human culture since the fall of Adam.

Mosaic Legislation: Facing the Problem

The Mosaic legislation addresses the problem of idolatry in a unique and emphatic way. The Second Commandment directly challenges ancient idolatry: "You shall not make for yourself any carved image, or any likeness of anything that is in heaven above, or that is in the earth beneath, or that is in the water under the earth; you shall not bow down to them nor serve them. For I, the LORD your God, am a jealous God, visiting the iniquity of the fathers on the children to the third and fourth generations of those who hate Me, but showing mercy to thousands, to those who love Me and keep My commandments" (Exod. 20:4-6). As the sum of the moral law the Decalogue, though couched in terms of the Mosaic covenant, is normative for all postlapsarian covenant epochs. Furthermore, the Second Commandment itself is an essential feature of the first section of the law, which deals with the exclusive allegiance required by the LORD of his people. The First Commandment defines, in negative terms, the object of worship; while the Second Commandment negatively defines the means of worship. Both forbid idolatry, although the second is usually the commandment associated with it. The media used in worship are central to the LORD's concern.

"The second commandment was unique in the world of its day."[5] No other ancient law code expresses this concern for images. Media critic Neil Postman has found this commandment to be formative in his own exploration of the nature and uses of media: "In studying the Bible as a young man, I found intimations of the idea that forms of media favor particular kinds of content and therefore are capable of taking command of a culture. I refer particularly to the Decalogue, the Second Commandment......It is a strange injunction to include as part of an ethical system *unless its author assumed a connection between forms of human communication and the quality of a culture.*"[6] While Postman, viewing the commandment in terms of cultural criticism, does not deal with idolatry *per se*, he puts his finger on a crucial point. The form in which God's character and the nature of his relationship with his people is communicated plays a critical role in determining the content of that communication. McLuhan observed a similar connection in Psalm 115: "The concept of 'idol' for the Hebrew Psalmist is much like that of Narcissus for the Greek

---

[5] J. D. Douglas, *The New Bible Dictionary* (Grand Rapids: William B. Eerdmans Publishing Company, 1962). S.v. "Idolatry," by J. A. Motyer.

[6] Neil Postman, *Amusing Ourselves To Death: Public Discourse in the Age of Show Business*. (New York: Viking Penguin, Inc., 1985), 9 (emphasis in original).

mythmaker. And the Psalmist insists that the *beholding* of idols, or the use of technology, conforms men to them. 'They that make them shall be like unto them.' This is a simple fact of sense 'closure.'"[7]

The point of both Postman and McLuhan is not to comment on the nature of idolatry, but rather to demonstrate the formative power of media. It should not be inferred from their statements that the visual is inherently idolatrous. The Second Commandment deals specifically with the means or media of worship, thus while Postman deals with culture formation, the Biblical commandment deals with cultic formation, that is a connection between the forms of divine communication and the quality of the worship and community which they affect. Although the forms of media in common culture are not divinely prescribed, that does not mean that their is not a connection between those forms and the culture they form.

Central to the biblical concern with idolatry is the danger of diminishing God to a manageable creaturely size and nature. This diminution renders God acceptable to autonomous man because God can be located and controlled. In a foolish and tragic role reversal autonomous man seeks to make God after his own fallen image. The modern view of ancient idolatry assumes the superstitious adoration of a physical object. There is an equally fallacious idea and opposite error often found in the Christian attempt to have a profounder appreciation for the nature of idolatry. That idea is that the god behind the idol is really quite separate from the physical image or representation of the god. The modern reduction of reality to the observable seems to have informed this particular Christian understanding of idolatry more than the reality depicted in the Old Testament. Biblical theologian Geerhardus Vos observed that the "distinction between the god and his image is a thoroughly modern idea. The idolatrous mind forms a far more realistic concept of the image than that of a symbolic representation of the deity. In some way, not always comprehensible to us, the image and the god are seen as one; through the image control is exercised over the deity."[8] C. Trimp sums up Vos's insight nicely: "In pagan worship, a bare image is central. With centuries-old magical rituals people seek to wrest blessing or wisdom from their deity, and the image guarantees the nearness of that deity."[9]

---

[7] Marshall McLuhan, *Understanding Media: The Extensions of Man* (New York: McGraw-Hill Book Company, 1964) 45. McLuhan wrongly attributes this quote to Psalm 113. It may be a typographical error.

[8] Geerhardus Vos, *Biblical Theology: Old and New Testaments*. (Grand Rapids: William B. Eerdmans Publishing Company, 1948), 255.

[9] C. Trimp, *Preaching and the History of Salvation*. Translated by Nelson D. Kloosterman. (Dyer, IN: Dr. Nelson D. Kloosterman, 1996), 15.

This interpretation of idolatry accords more fully with the prophets' idea that the connection of pagan gods with matter is a disgrace.[10] "To the pagans the magically divine presence in the image exists."[11] Idols are linked directly to the forces that they supposedly govern. The Hebrew word *ba'al* (בַּעַל) means "master," "lord," "husband" or "possessor."[12] Thus the Baals were the local deities or lords who controlled their own territories and powers, such as fertility and warfare. For example, the pole of Asherah in the Baal sanctuaries of Palestine was the sacred evergreen, a symbol of eternal life. Creator and creature are confused. Thus Isaiah chides the idols of the nations with biting sarcasm by calling them "godlets" (אֱלִילִים, Isa. 2:8) or "good-for-nothing-ones."[13] Ezekiel calls them "dung pellets" (גִּלּוּלֵיכֶם, Eze. 6:4).[14] The fact that idols are fashioned by men's hands renders them powerless in the presence of the true God. "The idols of Egypt will totter at His presence" (Isa. 19:1). The idols of the prophets of Baal under Ahab and Jezebel are impotent in the face of Elijah's challenge (1 Kings 18:20 ff.). God is living and, therefore speaks, whereas idols are dead (Lev. 26:30) and cannot speak, see, hear, smell, move or think (Ps. 115:4-7; 135:15-17; Isa. 44:18). There is no god who can compare with the majestic God of Israel (Isaiah 40:18; 44:8; 46:6). He alone is separate from his creation and thus has complete dominion over it. He is the Lord.

It must be remembered that while these prophecies are indirectly addressed to the nations, they were *directly* addressed to Israel. The temptation of idolatry was *the* chief threat to the Old Covenant people of God.[15] The apparent power and sophistication of covenant breaking cultures seduced Israel to imitate their idolatry. Thus in the face of abandonment by Moses when he failed to return from atop Mount Sinai, Aaron is beguiled into making a golden calf to assure Israel of God's presence and favor. The image of the ox played a key role in the Egyptian pantheon. The ox-god Apis was a symbol of fertility and wealth, celebrated by wild feasting. Israel longed for the familiar culture of Egypt in the absence of the man who had lead them out of it (Exod. 32:1, 23). Despite their ill conceived attempt to worship the LORD through this familiar image, Israel is characterized by the LORD as "stiff necked" due to their stubborn refusal to acknowledge that He, not a man, redeemed them out of

---

[10] *Ibid.*, 256.
[11] *Ibid.*
[12] Douglas, *The New Bible Dictionary*, S.v. "Baal," by D. F. Payne, 115. Cf. fn. 13.
[13] *Biblical Theology.*, 255. The Hebrew word for "idols" is אֱלִילִים, cf. Isa. 2:8,18,20; 10:10ff; 19:1,3; 31:7.
[14] Douglas, *The New Bible Dictionary*, 553.
[15] It may be argued that idolatry was not a problem for Israel after the exile. I would argue, however, that though the precise forms of idolatry developed along with the structure of the church and the surrounding culture, the spiritual nature of idolatry is a problem for the church in both Old and New Covenants.

Egypt (Exod. 32:9). It is not accidental that the golden calf incident (Exod. 32-34) is sandwiched between the revelation of the plan for the tabernacle and its service (Exod. 25-31) and the details of the execution of the plan.[16] This demonstrates that God's gracious covenant purposes will not be thwarted by idolatry and that His redeeming presence in Christ is the only antidote to idolatry. The tabernacle is God's way of dealing with the pervasive problem of idolatry.

The Exodus: A Declaration of War on Idolatry

The Exodus from Egypt is the central redemptive historical act of God in the Old Testament. At the heart of redeeming Israel from the bondage of the premier pagan culture of the day was the LORD's destruction of the idols of Egypt in the judgment of the plagues. In Numbers 33:4 Moses gives us this summary of that event: "On their gods the LORD had executed judgments." Each of the plagues corresponded to an Egyptian idol.[17] The apotheosis of the powers of nature characterized the earliest forms of idolatry. In the face of the destructive power of God's judgment of their idolatrous culture the gods of Egypt proved impotent, because the LORD of Israel is both Creator and Master of the powers of nature. Their dualistic religion made it imperative to live a life of order, or *ma'at* (Egyptian), in order to keep chaos at bay. In the face of their Creator their would-be mastery over nature was turned into chaos. Enjoyment of God's blessings in his creation without worship of the Creator is short-lived.[18]

Later in Israel's history the rebel king Jeroboam set up alternative sanctuaries at Dan and Bethel. Again golden calves were used to symbolize God's presence. The books of Kings record the constant refrain of the LORD's disapproval of these manmade alternatives (1 Kings 12 ff.). Similar to the ox-god of Egypt they were well-known Canaanite symbols of deity and were thought by the northern tribes to imitate the cherubim in the Holy of Holies of the true temple in Jerusalem, anticipating a dogged history of syncretism in both Israel's and the church's history.[19]

The pervasiveness of the biblical emphasis on this problem is evinced by the command given in pursuing the "holy war"[20] (חֵרֶם) upon entering the

---

[16] David Alexander and Patricia Alexander, *Eerdmans' Handbook to the Bible* (Grand Rapids: William B. Eerdmans Publishing Company, 1973) S.v. "The Tabernacle," by Alec Motyer.
[17] John Currid, "The Message of Egypt's Plagues: Worshipping Idols Doesn't Pay." *RTS Reformed Quarterly*, Fall 1996, 12, 13.
[18] *Ibid.*
[19] *Ibid.*, 552.
[20] הַחֲרֵם Hiphil imperative, "ban" Deut. 13:15; v. 16 in Hebrew.

Promised Land: "Destroy all their engraved stones, destroy all their molded images, and demolish their high places" (Numb. 33:52). The plagues of the Exodus are being extended to Palestine, which like Egypt had reached its apex in the development of idolatrous culture. Moses rehearses the central concern of God's covenantal interests in Deuteronomy on the eve of Israel's entrance into the promised land: Do not allow the idols of the nations to corrupt you so that you forsake the "Rock of your salvation" (Deut. 32:15 ff.). You will be tempted by images of man, woman, animals, and heavenly bodies to worship the creation which God has given to mankind as a "heritage" (Deut. 4:15 ff.). Idolatry is a covenant with death. The spiritual reality behind idols is demonic (Deut. 32:17). God alone has graciously spoken to you. Therefore, pay attention to his Word. He will establish a place of true worship uncorrupted by the deceptions of the nations (Deut. 12).

Of special interest is the Mosaic warning not to heed false prophets just because they produced dazzling signs (Deut. 18:9-22). The power of humanly conjured visible realities is now a major source of religious corruption within the covenant community. False messages often come *impressively* packaged. Visible "happenings" and images have enormous persuasive power over the fallen mind. They focus attention on the immediate potencies of the created order. This is the genius of witchcraft and sorcery as well as of Madison Avenue. As we shall see visible reality and the visual symbols created by man, even in his fallen state, are not *per se* idolatrous, only potentially so.

Subsequently in Israel's history, wherever the revival of true religion occurs it is accompanied by the destruction of idols and their images. The forbidden means of religious communication are destroyed in order to revive the God-ordained means. Gideon highlights the book of Judges with his iconoclasm (Judg. 6). Samson concludes the heroic portion of the book by renouncing his own idolatry in pulling the temple of Dagon to the ground at the cost of his own life (Judg. 16:28-31). The remainder of the book is a testimony to the spiritually and morally degrading nature of the idolatry epitomized by the shrine worship of Micah (Judg. 17:5).

King Saul becomes an example of compromise as he willfully refuses to execute God's judgment on idolatrous Agag and intrudes on the priestly functions of Samuel. In a revealing statement Samuel equates stubborn rebellion with witchcraft and idolatry (1 Sam. 15:23). Witchcraft and idolatry are the means or media which express the controlling agenda of would-be autonomous man. Dying at the hands of the idolatrous Philistines the autonomous king Saul fittingly has his head and armor placed in the Temple of the Ashtoreths (1 Sam. 31:9; 1 Chron. 10:9). In dramatic reversal, David's inaugural victory over the Philistines leaves their idols strewn helplessly over the field of battle (2 Sam. 5).

While First and Second Kings focus on the prophetic dimension and First and Second Chronicles focus on the priestly dimension of Israel's dynastic history; the history of Israel's kings in both places is viewed uniformly from the perspective of idolatry. The Former Prophets [Joshua, Judges, Samuel, Kings] form a court brief, used by the prophets in prosecuting God's Covenant lawsuit against idolatrous Israel.[21] Asa, Jehoshaphat, and especially Joash, Hezekiah and Josiah stand out as heroes by destroying idolatry in varying degrees. Josiah's revival is notable both in its extent and motivation. His reading of the *Book of the Covenant* (2 Chron. 34:14) stirs his devotion and causes him to thoroughly eradicate idolatry from the land. David exemplifies proper royal obedience to the Second Commandment when he sings at the restoration of the ark from the Philistines to the tabernacle: "For all the gods of the people are idols (lit. "worthless things" אֱלִילִים),[22] but the LORD made the heavens (1 Chron. 16:26).

Tabernacle and Temple: Antidote to Idolatry

It is important to note that not every image or symbol is excluded by the LORD from the religious rites and cultus of the Old Covenant, or the New Covenant for that matter. The problem of imagery is not located in material representations of religious truth as such, but rather in the *source* of those representations. The God of Israel goes to great lengths to prescribe the architecture, furnishings, clothing, personnel and rites of the tabernacle and temple. The Author of all meaning precisely chose material representations suited to his redemptive purposes.[23] God chose a medium suited to His message. The means of worship are expressly prescribed by God himself. Knowing man's propensity to idolatry the tabernacle and temple were designed to communicate the redemption given by the God of the Covenant of Grace. Calvin insists that God uses signs of His own choosing to be symbolic of heavenly glory.[24]

---

[21] Meredith G. Kline, *The Structure of Biblical Authority*. Revised Edition (Grand Rapids: William B. Eerdmans Publishing Company, 1975), 57ff.

[22] John Calvin, *Commentary upon the Acts of the Apostles*. vol. 1, 1540-1563. Translation and reprint. Edinburgh: Calvin Translation Society. 1847. Reprint (vol. 18). Grand Rapids: Baker Book House, 1969. "The idol is properly so called reproachfully, as it were a thing nothing worth, because no reason doth suffer man to make God ('Deum...fabricari,' to fabricate a god)," 293.

[23] Meredith G. Kline, "Investiture with the Image of God." *Westminster Theological Journal* 40 (No. 1, Fall 1977): 41.

[24] John Calvin, *Institutes of the Christian Religion* (1559. Reprint (1 vol. in 2). The Library of Christian Classics, vol. XX. Edited by John T. McNeill. Translated by Ford Lewis Battles. Philadelphia: The Westminster Press, 1960) 102.

Thus even as the original creation was designed by the Eternal Word to communicate the creative glory of God (Ps. 19; Rom. 1:18 ff.); so the redemptive creation of the temple was designed to communicate the redemptive glory of God in the incarnate Word (Matt. 2:19-22; Eph. 2:19-22; Rev. 21:22).[25] The magnificence of the temple imitates the magnificence of the creation: "the house that is to be built for the LORD must be exceedingly magnificent, famous and glorious throughout all countries" (1 Chron. 22:5). The temple is a revelation of God's name as the One who defines creation and redemption (Deut. 12:11; 1 Chron. 22:19). Thus, upon entrance into the land of Palestine Israel is commanded to destroy the names of idols, the would-be definers of reality. Idolaters seek to imitate the original heavenly temple by creating idol temples which assert their dominion over creation. Instead the LORD promised to choose a place to establish *His* name (Deut. 12) as a revelation of the true heavenly temple, "an antitype of the greater archetypal tabernacle (Heb. 9:11)."[26] Tabernacle and temple establish the Lord's dominion over the cosmic temple of His creation and anticipate the incarnation of the Son who establishes the Spiritual temple for His people who are the dwelling place of God, who in turn is the dwelling place of His people (Pss. 90, 91). Any distortion of the medium of the revelation of his redemptive purposes undermines His agenda for history. Thus, idolatry becomes the chief enemy of the God of Israel, and the greatest threat to the spiritual health of His people, who are the Temple made without hands by the Master Builder (Gen. 49:24; Exod. 20:25; Prov. 8:30; Isa. 28:16; Mark 14:58).

The presence of the cherubim positioned over the ark of the Covenant and the mercy seat in the Holy of Holies serves as a pointed example of the contrast between the temples of idols and the Temple of the LORD. The two cherubim, fashioned by carving and overlaid with gold (2 Chron. 3:10 ff.), whose wings overshadowed the ark of the covenant, signalized the invisible presence of the LORD between the worshipping cherubim. The winged cherubim were guardians of the divine Glory.[27] "As the Omega-point of the creative cloning of the archetypal Glory-temple, the divine design contemplated a living temple of created spirits."[28] The temple is his chosen location for heavenly redemptive contact with his covenant people. Thus the mercy seat placed on the ark of the Covenant is the footstool of the Great King, where the blood of mediation is remembered. Here in his throne room the LORD establishes dominion over the

---

[25] Kline, "Investiture with the Image of God," 43ff.
[26] *Ibid.*
[27] Meredith G. Kline, "Creation in the Image of the Glory-Spirit," *Westminster Theological Journal* 39 (No. 2, Spring 1977): 251. Cf. Kline, "Investiture with the Image of God," *Westminster Theological Journal* 40 (No. 1, Fall 1977): 44.
[28] *Ibid.*, 258.

earth through his redeemed people. The two golden cherubim point at once to the glory and grace of the King. While the counterfeit golden calves, prescribed by the idolatrous Jeroboam, distorted and compromised the Creator-creature distinction; the divinely prescribed cherubim defined and accentuated that distinction by not reducing God Himself to a visual image.[29]

Solomon's prayer of dedication for the temple indicates this essential contrast. "LORD God of Israel, there is no god in heaven or on earth like You, who keep Your covenant and mercy with Your servants who walk before You with all their hearts. ... But will God indeed dwell with men on the earth? Behold, heaven and the heaven of heavens cannot contain You; how much less this temple which I have built" (2 Chron. 6:14, 18). The temple is a testimony of God's transcendent glory as the Creator and his immanent mercy as Redeemer. Idol worshipers create gods after their own images in order to control the forces of creation according to their own autonomous agendas. "Those who make them are like them; so is every one who trusts in them" (Ps. 115:8).

Likewise, when Israel was taken into captivity by the idolatrous Assyrians, the punishment fit the crime. Israel had "walked in the statutes of the nations whom the LORD had cast out from before the children of Israel. ...they followed idols, became idolaters, and *went* after the nations who *were* all around them, *concerning* whom the LORD had charged them that they should not do like them" (2 Kings 17:8, 15). What might easily be overlooked is the public nature of idolatry, the socio-cultural dimension of media. The media of the cultus set up by Jeroboam, in order to promote political unity, in Bethel and Dan, created a pervasive environment for the northern tribes. They "re-imagined" the Covenant God, after their own rebellious images. This syncretistic distortion in turn cultivated a Pagan view of God's identity.

The Prophets: The Folly of Idolatry

The prophets recall the teachings of the Mosaic Covenant on idolatry and call Israel to account for forsaking the living and true God. "The peculiarly prophetic task was the elaboration and application of the ancient covenant sanctions ... prosecuting Yahweh's patient covenant lawsuit with his incurably wayward vassal people."[30] Like their originator, the Evil One, idols are a lie and the promoters of lies, deception and delusions. They are "teachers of lies", whom their makers trust, yet they do not speak (Hab. 2:18-20). They embody the sin of their makers (Isa. 31:7) who choose their own sinful way in defiance

---

[29] Calvin, *Institutes*, 102.
[30] Kline, *The Structure of Biblical Authority*, 58, 59.

of the LORD (Isa. 66:3). Because idols make promises that they cannot keep (Isa. 48:5) their followers are lost like sheep without a shepherd (Zech. 10:2). Their teachings are empty and useless (Isa. 57:1-13; Jer. 10:8), "wind and confusion" (רוּחַ וָתֹהוּ, Isa. 41:21-29). Idols are an intolerable burden because they cannot save from sin and death (Isa. 45:20; 46:1-7). Therefore, they bring only shame and judgment (Isa. 2:18, 20; 17:8; 44:9-20; 45:16). Because God will not tolerate this ungrateful rebellion he will destroy all idols and their worshipers (Isa. 10:10, 11; Jer. 51:17, 47, 52). No one can hide from his presence (Jer. 23:23, 24). He will brook no rivals, for there is none like him. He alone is God. "I am the LORD, that is My name; and My glory I will not give to another, nor My praise to graven images" (Isa. 42:8).

Ezekiel grieves over the compromise of the Old Testament church: "These men have set up their idols in their hearts, and put before them that which causes them to stumble into iniquity" (Ezek. 14:3; cf. Deut. 29:14-19). Idolatry is a matter of the heart and with deadly consequences. Especially culpable for this tragic state of affairs are the Levites. "And the Levites who went far from Me, when Israel went astray, who strayed away from Me after their idols, they shall bear their iniquity. ... Because they ministered to them before their idols and caused the house of Israel to fall into iniquity, therefore I have lifted up My hand in an oath against them" (Ezek. 44:10, 12). The Levites were to protect the revelation of God in the temple and its worship rites; and to teach the law to the people (Neh. 8). In the revivals under kings such as Hezekiah and Uzziah great emphasis is given to the ministry of the written Word. "And Hezekiah gave encouragement to all the Levites who taught the good knowledge of the LORD" (2 Chron. 30:22). All foreign media were completely removed by the Levites who were guardians of God's media of revelation (2 Chron. 29). All was to be done according to the written commandments of the covenant (2 Chron. 29:25). The revival of Temple worship under Josiah is notably connected, as we have seen with the discovery of the *Book of the Law* by the Levitical high priest Hilkiah (2 Chron. 34:8 ff).

The account of the ensuing restoration is filled with the importance of the written Word. Josiah commands Hilkiah and his retinue: "Go, inquire of the LORD for me, ... concerning the *words of the book* that is found; for great is the wrath of the LORD that is poured out on us, because our fathers have not kept the *word of the LORD*, to do according to all that is *written* in this book" (2 Chron. 34:21, emphasis added). The entire *Book of the Covenant* was read aloud by the King in the Temple in the hearing of all the inhabitants of Jerusalem (2 Chron. 34:29-33, emphasis added). The renewal of the sacrament of Passover was carried out according to what was *written* in *The Book of Moses* (2 Chron. 35:4,12).

The tragedy of idolatry is poignantly recorded in the concluding chapter of the Chronicler. The holy articles of the Temple are co-opted by Nebuchadnezzar, king of Babylon, the epitome of idolatrous power, for use in his idol temple (2 Chron. 36:7,14). The house of God is destroyed by fire (2 Chron. 36:19). Triumph and tragedy are recorded as a revelation of God to his church concerning the danger of idolatry (2 Chron. 35:26; 36:21). Ministers of the Word are responsible to warn the church against idolatry and its perils, and to lead them in true worship. Even the imagery used in the Temple and its rites is known only through God's primary medium, the Word.

Idolatry enslaves its devotees like wine and adultery. Hosea likens Israel's unfaithfulness to the LORD to adultery. Idolatry is spiritual adultery, just as adultery is a form of idolatry (Col. 3:5). Daniel reveals that all of world history is characterized by idolatry. The golden image of Daniel 2 is a picture of world history with its feet of clay. The consummation of history will spell the doom of the idolatrous project of the Evil One and his covenant breaking seed. Nebuchadnezzar's ninety foot golden image epitomizes the would-be autonomy of the political powers of this present evil age. Daniel and his friends in true covenant fashion refuse to cower before the rage of the nations and worship the image, trusting rather in the LORD and his Anointed One (Daniel 4; Ps. 2).

Particularly illuminating is Jeremiah's description of idolatry in chapter 10 of his prophecy. The LORD warns Israel: "Do not learn the way of the Gentiles" (Jer. 10:2). After a description of the practices of idolaters (vs. 2-5) Jeremiah ascribes incomparable greatness to the LORD. No one is like the King of the nations (vs. 6, 7). Then his telling indictment of the foolishness of idolaters: "A wooden idol *is* a worthless doctrine." (v. 8). His use of the word "doctrine" (מוּסָר) in this context reveals the essence of the danger of idolatry. The Old Testament uses the word to mean *teaching* that is effected by discipleship, i.e. instruction (Prov. 1:3, 8). Thus the dimension of "chastisement" or "correction" is included in the definition (Prov. 5:12; 6:23; 13:24). The picture is one of discipleship. The father disciples his son by word and example. Jeremiah early records the LORD's frustration with discipling Israel, who refuses correction (2:30; 5:3; 7:28). God Himself is the chief Discipler of His people (32:33). The point of 10:8 is that idols are the sinner's vain attempt to replace God's discipleship. They are a "worthless doctrine". Idols disciple sinners in fruitlessness and emptiness. It should be noted that the image itself ("a wooden idol") does the discipling. But the soil in which idolatry is born and nourished is the "evil" heart of stone inherited from Adam. Jeremiah refers to idolaters as those who follow the "dictates" (KJV "imaginations"; Jer. 3:17, 9:13, 16:12, 18:12) of their own hearts. The Hebrew word (שְׁרִרוּת) refers to hardness, firmness or stubbornness. Idolaters ironically create "masters" who suit their purposes. In Jeremiah 9:13 the Baals are directly associated with the dictates of the rebel heart. Here the KJV captures an important concept by using *imaginations*. The sin hardened heart conceives images which embody the impulses of the autonomous agenda. They enable him to harness the powers of the creation for his own glory. Idols confirm man in his worship of the creation in place of the Creator. The educational or discipling power of the image media must not be underestimated.

The Old Testament ends with a remnant of Israel awaiting the promised Messiah. They have been exiled and returned to a temple from which the glory had departed; all because of their idolatry. The Christ of Scripture is the only antidote to idolatry. Only the grace of the Mediator, God incarnate, can overcome idols. "In that day a fountain shall be opened for the house of David and for the inhabitants of Jerusalem, for sin and for uncleanness. 'It shall be in that day,' says the LORD of hosts, '*that* I will cut off the names of the idols from the land, and they shall no longer be remembered'" (Zech. 13:1,2).

IDOLATRY IN THE NEW TESTAMENT

The Gospels and Acts: A Subtle Form of Idolatry

It is often thought that after the exile Israel had learned its lesson and forsaken its compromise with idolatry. Actually idolatry was still a problem; it simply took on a different, subtler form. Although the gospels do not make direct reference to idolatry as such, the characteristics of idolatry appear in Jesus' encounters with the Pharisees, who had made an idol of their religious privileges in seeking to establish their own righteousness (Rom. 10:3). As we shall see in the next chapter this is the *broad* concept of idolatry, which is implicit in light of Paul's broad view of idolatry in Romans 1.

In the Sermon on the Mount Jesus makes a sharp distinction between two kinds of ultimate loyalty: "No one can serve two masters; for either he will hate the one and love the other, or else he will be loyal to the one and despise the other. You cannot serve God and mammon" (Matt. 6:24). In the context Jesus is addressing the basic human concern about the needs of daily life. "Mammon" or money represents the created power to meet those needs. Idolaters trust these means as ultimate powers. Thus the Old Covenant model of the two humanities of idolaters and believers is reiterated by Jesus as a basic paradigm for the New Covenant community, as well as the basis for His final judgment of the Old Covenant people.

In a classic encounter with the Pharisees (Matt. 22:15-22) Jesus is asked a loaded question about ultimate loyalties: "Is it lawful to pay taxes to Caesar, or not?" He responds by pointing to the image of Caesar on a Roman coin with the pointed rejoinder: "Render therefore to Caesar the things that are Caesar's, and to God the things that are God's." The Pharisaic commitment to the idol of Mammon (Luke 16:14; 20:47) denied the ultimate loyalty which they pretended to assert and defend. The judgment of God on the covetousness of postexilic Israel in Zechariah 5 reminds us that actual visible depictions of gods are not necessary to idolatry. Commercial dishonesty characterized by theft and perjury is symbolized by the establishment of an idol temple in Shinar in Zechariah's vision. Idolatry is a matter of the heart and its ultimate attachments.

The first specific reference in the New Testament to idolatry is found in Stephen's rehearsal of Israel's history in Acts 7. Stephen is accused of undermining the Mosaic Covenant by speaking "blasphemous words against this holy place and the law; for we have heard him say that this Jesus of Nazareth will destroy this place and change the customs which Moses delivered to us" (Acts 6:13, 14; cf. Mark 14:58; John 2:19). In defending himself against this charge he sets forth the gospel by reminding his accusers that Israel "made a calf in those days, offered sacrifices to the idol, and rejoiced in the works of their own hands. Then God turned and gave them to worship the host of heaven, as it is written in the book of the Prophets: 'Did you offer Me slaughtered animals and sacrifices during forty years in the wilderness, O house of Israel? Yes, you took up the tabernacle of Moloch, and the star of your god Remphan, images which you made to worship; and I will carry you away beyond Babylon'" (Acts 7:42, 43, quoting Amos 5:25-27, LXX).

Stephen goes on to remind his hostile audience that the tabernacle/temple was never meant as an end in itself. The Pharisees had made an idol of the very thing meant to reveal the Christ, whom they had crucified. "The Most High does not dwell in temples made with hands, as the prophet says: 'Heaven is My throne, and earth is My footstool. What house will you build for Me? says the LORD, or what is the place of My rest? Has My hand not made all these things?'" (Acts 7:48-50, quoting Isa. 66:1,2, LXX). Theirs was the spirit of the ancient idolaters, from whom, ironically, the Pharisees had so proudly distanced themselves. Stephen's indictment is bold and clear: "You stiff-necked and uncircumcised in heart and ears! You always resist the Holy Spirit; as your fathers did so do you" (Acts 7:51; cf. Exod. 32:9; Isa. 6:10; Lev. 26:41). Idolatry was at the heart of their false accusation of Jesus regarding the destruction of the temple. Calvin puts his finger on this tendency of the visible church: "God passeth not for those frivolous imaginations; but he complaineth that men put strange gods in his place, so soon as they depart even a very little from his word."[31]

---

[31] Calvin, *Commentary on Acts*, vol. 1, 292.

The instruction given by God through the tabernacle/temple is referred to by Stephen as a "pattern" (Acts 7:44, NKJV, lit. "figure," "type," or "image," τύπον). God condescends to the earthly perspective of humanity by using images as a medium to communicate His grace. The Lord's Supper is a primary New Covenant example.[32] The same word, *pattern*, is translated "images" in verse 43 because the reference in Amos is to the idols that corrupted Israel. In the case of the tabernacle/temple the Pharisees were worshipping the temple "made with hands," and made according to the specific direction of divine prescription, instead of the crucified and resurrected Messiah, whom the temple was designed to reveal.

The rest of Acts deals with the idolatry of the pagan world in which Paul preached the gospel. The miraculous healing of the man at Lystra, who could not walk from birth, causes the people to identify Paul and Barnabas with the Greek gods Hermes (Roman god Mercury) and Zeus (Roman god Jupiter) (Acts 14:12). To prevent them from offering sacrifices Paul quickly corrects their misunderstanding by asserting that he is a mere man just like them. Then he boldly calls them to turn from their idols to the "living God" (v. 15). The word he uses to refer to their idols is ματαίων, the Greek word for "worthless."[33] He recalls the prophetic denunciation of idols as impotent and dead. Paul goes on to explain that the living God is the Creator of the things they wrongly worship. Creation and its blessings are meant to be a witness to the glory and goodness of the true God (v. 17).

Later on, in dealing with the transition from the Old to the New Covenants, the Jerusalem Council is careful to condemn the Judaizing demand that Gentile converts must be circumcised. The four prohibitions issued by the council were meant to keep peace with Jewish Christians without adding a requirement to faith in the crucified Christ. While three out of the four appear to be ceremonial in character, the fourth, to abstain from fornication (Acts 15:29) may also be related to the practices of pagan idol temples. The first prohibition, to "abstain from things offered to idols" (ἀπέχεσθαι εἰδωλοθύτων, v. 29) seems to be the theme of them all. Significant for the present thesis is the fact that the church's witness against the specific practices of idolaters was central to the discipling of the nations.

---

[32] *Ibid.*, 291,2; "They are tokens of heavenly truth," 299, 300; the temple is a "sign and pledge of his (God's) presence, 304.
[33] NKJV "worthless things," singular ματαίος.

Paul Confronts the Idols of the Nations

The most significant of the *loci communes* on idolatry in the historical portion of the New Testament is Acts 17:16-34, relating Paul's ministry in Athens. Romans 1 gives us Paul's theological understanding of idolatry, while on Mars Hill he demonstrates how this is to be applied in spreading the gospel in an idolatrous world, especially in the public proclamation of the Word of God. Christian apologist Cornelius Van Til tersely observes: "Paul knows only two classes of people, those who worship and serve the Creator and those who worship and serve the creature more than the Creator."[34]

It should be remembered that, though the philosophical ascendancy of Athens was already past history in Paul's day, its citizens were still among the most intellectually and culturally sophisticated in the ancient world. While Paul took their learning into account, he did not in any way either compromise his message or fail in his mission, as some have alleged. Paul challenges Athenian idolatry on their own ground because he knows that it is God's ground. "Now while Paul waited for them at Athens, his spirit was provoked within him when he saw that *the city was given over to idols*." (κατείδωλον οὖσαν τὴν πόλιν). The Athenians had committed themselves to idols. His opening statement that the Athenians were very "religious" is not a compliment, for compliments were forbidden by the rhetorical protocol of the Areopagus.[35] Paul asserts at the outset that their God-given worshipping instinct is directed toward the wrong object because they are evading God. Instead of accommodating himself to their philosophy he finds a giant hole in their argument against the true God. Their altar to the "Unknown God" is a way of at once keeping God at a distance and controlling him (Acts 17:23).

Paul preaches the great theme of the prophets: "God, who made the world and everything in it, since He is Lord of heaven and earth, does not dwell in temples made with hands. Nor is He worshipped with men's hands, as though He needed anything, since He gives to all life, breath, and all things" (v. 24, 25). God is immanent as well as transcendent, and thus "He is not far from each one of us" (v. 27). Because He is the Sovereign of history He is not to be confused with His creation. He has no need of His creatures. He is self-existent (Lat. *aseitas*). "We ought not to think that the Divine Nature is like gold, or silver, or stone, something shaped by art and man's devising" (v. 29). Nor is God impressed with man's sense of racial superiority (v. 26).[36] The resurrected Christ is God's final word against all forms of idolatry. One day he will come

---

[34] Van Til, *Paul at Athens*. unidentified booklet, 1956, 1.
[35] F. F. Bruce, *Commentary on the Book of the Acts* (Grand Rapids: William B. Eerdmans Publishing Co., 1979), 355.
[36] Bruce, *Acts*, pp. 358, 9.

and judge all men (vs. 31, 32). The image of God in Christ is the ultimate challenge to the worship of created images. All idols are counterfeit mediators. But now the True Mediator has invaded history.

One final passage in Acts reveals an important feature of the response of unbelievers to the Gospel's challenge to their idolatry. In Ephesus "the Word of the Lord grew mightily and prevailed" (Acts 19:20). Occult books of great value were burned by new converts. The threat to the power structure to which idolatry is connected was tremendous. Demetrius the silversmith reveals two significant aspects of the response of the threatened idolaters. Sounding very contemporary Demetrius expresses vehement concern for the profits which his idol-crafting trade brought (v. 24, 25). His livelihood was threatened. Secondly, he has a disingenuous rationale for his work. Everyone worships the great goddess Diana (v. 27). Social stability is at stake. The grip that idolatry has on men's souls is extraordinary. Their idolatry is woven into the very socio-economic fabric of fallen culture. Their motivations and rationales are adroitly fabricated. We live in the same historical era relative to the cross. Only the images have changed.

Epistles: Idolatry Is No Minor Issue

As we move to the epistles we immediately encounter the foremost *locus classicus* on idolatry: Romans 1:18-32. This passage is as important to a biblical understanding of idolatry as Genesis 3. In setting forth the complete sufficiency of the righteousness of God in Christ for salvation Paul begins with a prophetic indictment of the whole world. God's just anger is revealed from heaven because, despite all the evidence that God is the glorious Creator of all things, men have turned to worship the creation more than the Creator (ἐσεβάσθησαν καὶ ἐλάτρευσαν τῇ κτίσει παρὰ τὸν κτίσαντα, Rom. 1:25). God continually reveals the truth of who He is to the very consciousness of man. Calvin explains: "man was created to be a spectator of this formed world, and that eyes were given him, that he might, by looking on so beautiful a picture, be led up to the Author himself. ... God is in himself invisible; but as his majesty shines forth in his works and in his creatures everywhere, men ought in these to acknowledge him, for they clearly set forth their Maker: and for this reason the Apostle in his Epistle to the Hebrews says, that this world is a mirror, or the representation of invisible things."[37]

---

[37] John Calvin, *Commentaries on the Epistle of Paul to the Romans*, 1540-1563. Translation and reprint (Edinburgh: Calvin Translation Society. 1847. Reprint (vol. 19). Grand Rapids: Baker Book House, 1969), 70. Cf. the discussion of idolatry in John Owen, *The Works of John Owen*. Vol. 1. Edited by William H. Goold. 1850-53. Reprint (Edinburgh: The Banner of Truth Trust, 1965), 65-79.

Man, motivated by his idolatrous heart, is continually suppressing (κατεχόντων) his knowledge of this clear revelation and is thus inexcusable for his ignorance (Rom. 1:18, 20). His blindness is willful and therefore he is entirely culpable, though he is blind by nature. Instead of thankfully worshipping God as He has clearly revealed Himself, men have resorted to creating gods out of their own empty minds (Rom. 1:21). "They befouled the majesty of God by forming him in the likeness of corruptible (mortal) man," concludes Calvin.[38] What fallen man calls wisdom is foolishness from God's perspective. Having evacuated God of His true glory fallen man has conceived of Him as "an empty phantom"[39] and sought to replace him making created beings and powers the object of worship. Due to their confusing the creation with the Creator, God has given them over to their own lawless desires from which all kinds of moral perversion emanate (Rom. 1:24, 26-32). Idolatry and immorality are inseparable.[40]

Idolatry is at the heart of the thought forms and moral habits of fallen culture. Images and other media of communication, give earth-bound coherence to the idolatrous perspective on life. Paul sums up this idolatrous commitment by stating that they "exchanged the truth of God for the lie, and worshipped and served the creature more than the Creator who is blessed forever. Amen" (Rom. 1:25). Paul hearkens back to the origin of idolatry in Eden. The attempted substitute of the creature for the Creator is *the* lie. It is the fundamental lie that undergirds and informs all idolatry and all postlapsarian history. Exchanging the truth of God for a lie is the fundamental transaction of the idolatrous mind. Thus all of the media developed in fallen culture are corrupted in varying degrees by the lie of which idolatry is the primary expression. The suppressing activity of the fallen mind is positively expressed in its attitudes toward created reality. All media become potential modes of communicating the great denial of God's glory. As we shall see God's common grace holds this tendency in check, so that images and other media of communication are used in common culture in positive ways as well.

In exposing the hypocrisy of the Jew, Paul points to the irony of at once claiming to hate idols and yet robbing idol temples. That Paul was vindicated by the town clerk of Ephesus of the charge of robbing temples (Acts 19:37) indicates that this may be taken literally.[41] While the law's prohibition of this practice (Deut. 7:25, 26) shows the inconsistency of the Jew, the sin of theft

---

[38] *Ibid.*, 74.
[39] *Ibid.*, 72.
[40] John Murray, *The Epistle to the Romans* (Grand Rapids: William B. Eerdmans Publishing Co., 1968) 36. Murray's entire discussion of this passage is most illuminating.
[41] *Ibid.*, 84.

reveals an idol which the Jew would not have considered part of the pantheon of idols to be abhorred.

The imaging function of the Mediator, Jesus Christ, is central to the New Testament, especially in Paul's thinking. In Romans 8:29 he indicates this centrality: "For whom He foreknew, He also predestined *to be* conformed to the image of His Son, that He might be the firstborn among many brethren." "But we all, with unveiled face, beholding as in a mirror the glory of the Lord, are being transformed into the same image from glory to glory, just as by the Spirit of the Lord" (2 Cor. 3:18). "Put on the new *man* who is renewed in knowledge according to the image of Him who created him" (Col. 3:5,10; cf. 2 Cor. 4:4; Col. 1:15). The incarnate Son is the medium (εἰκόνος image, likeness, form) of the revelation of God's glory by which His people are transformed to be like Him. The writer of Hebrews indicates that the Son is the *final* medium (πολυτρόπως) of God's self-revelation (ἐλάλησεν ἡμῖν ἐν υἱῷ) in this the final epoch (ἐπ' ἐσχάτου τῶν ἡμερῶν τούτων) of redemptive history. The eternal Son now united inseparably to His human nature by virtue of the hypostatic union (ὑποστάσεως αὐτοῦ Heb. 1:3) is the "express image" (χαρακτὴρ Heb. 1:3) of God, such that he who has seen the Son has seen the Father (John 14:9; cf. 1:14). The Creator-Son has made Himself *visible* in history to draw our attention away from the worship of created things (εἰκόνος Romans 1:23) to which we are so powerfully attracted by our fallen natures. Jesus the Christ is the full and final speech of God to lost humanity. In Him the brightness of God's glory consummately shines (ἀπαύγασμα τῆς δόξης Heb. 1:3). He is the original Image (αὐτὴν τὴν εἰκόνα Heb. 10:1) of which the Old Covenant law, in its prescribed forms, is but a dim shadow (Σκιὰν Heb. 10:1). He is the only antidote to idolatry.

In this historical-theological context comes the urgent mandate that the Christian "flee idolatry" (φεύγετε ἀπὸ τῆς εἰδωλολατρίας 1 Cor. 10:14; Col. 3:5,10). The centrality of this imperative to the Gospel cannot be overestimated. John sums up all that he has to say about assurance of faith in his first epistle with the comprehensive pastoral plea: "keep yourselves from idols" (φυλάξατε ἑαυτὰ ἀπὸ τῶν εἰδώλων 1 John 5:21). Idolatry at its heart represents a demonic alternative to the Covenant of Grace. This underlies Paul's exhortation to the Corinthian church as he compares Pagan idol feasts with the Lord's Table (1 Cor. 10:14-22). They both involve communion with the lord or host of a covenant relationship.

Paul sums up the essence of Christian conversion when he reminds the Thessalonian church of the fruit of the apostolic message: "you turned to God from idols to serve the living and true God" (1 Thess. 1:9). The object of their devotion had been radically altered. Idolatry is the visible expression of the covetousness (πλεονεξίαν) that plagues the sinner's heart (Col. 3:5,10). It has often been observed that while the First Commandment refers to the proper *object* of devotion that the Tenth Commandment refers to the *source* of devotion, thus encompassing the meaning of the Ten Words. The heart redirected by the redemptive work of the Spirit of the Son turns from every aspect of the worship of the creation in place of the Creator; "Therefore put to death your members which are on the earth: fornication, uncleanness, passion, evil desire, and covetousness, which is idolatry" (Col. 3:5).

The church must inhabit the world of idolaters (1 Cor. 5:10, 11). Common grace provides the context for sanctification. However, Christians must be careful not to associate themselves with the practices of idolaters in any way which would suggest a compromise with their new devotion (1 Cor. 10:28, 12:2; 2 Cor. 6:16). While idols are nothing in themselves (1 Cor. 8:4, 7, 10), because they are the constructs of the sinful imagination, none-the-less they are the medium by which the Satanic minions hold sway over the hearts of unbelievers (1 Cor. 10:20). Because idolatry is the work of the flesh (Gal. 5:20), idolaters will not inherit the kingdom of God (1 Cor. 6:9, 10). Those who will bear the image of the heavenly (εἰκόνα τοῦ ἐπουρανίου 1 Cor. 15:49) in resurrection glory must not return to the bondage of the "elements of the world" (στοιχεῖα τοῦ κόσμου Gal. 4:3). This is the way of unbelief for Jew and Gentile alike.

Revelation: The End of Idolatry

The book of Revelation is itself loaded with inspired imagery which communicates the unfolding of the last epoch of redemptive history through the mediation of the Lamb, who has won dominion over the created order through His suffering and glory. The original Liar and his disciples are brought to their logical destination, the "lake of fire" (Rev. 21:8), separate from the New Jerusalem, and filled with each person throughout history "whoever loves and practices a lie" (Rev. 22:15). Drawing from the Old Testament prophetic denunciation of idols, John depicts them as unable to save their worshipers from the judgment of the sixth trumpet: "But the rest of mankind, who were not killed by these plagues, did not repent of the works of their hands, that they should not worship demons, and idols of gold, silver, brass, stone, and wood, which can neither see nor hear nor walk. And they did not repent of their murders or their sorceries or their sexual immorality or their thefts" (Rev. 9:20,21).

Daniel's vision of the Son of Man in Daniel 7 highlights the contrast between the true image of God and false idol image depicted by the statue constructed by Nebuchadnezzar on the plains of Dura. His own descent into beast-like existence, as God's judgment for his idolatry, reveals the true nature of the Satanic project. Revelation 1 begins with the glorious image of the risen Christ as the Son of Man, the true image of God who invades history to establish the final triumphant eschatological kingdom. He is depicted in Daniel 2 as a stone, which emerges supernaturally in the midst of the fourth kingdom of the Roman Empire, and becomes a great mountain, a fifth and final kingdom, which rises up in history to destroy and completely replace the idolatrous kingdoms of this world.[42]

The close connection between idolatry, sorcery, sexual immorality and theft is notable in Revelation, as it is in the Prophets. "Sorceries" (φαρμάκων Rev. 9:21, 18:23, 21:8, 22:15) are the manipulations by fallen man of the powers and potentialities of creation. Thus the vast and world encompassing unity of the Babel-like project which characterizes this final epoch of history highlights the use of technology to create a culture independent of God. The fall of Babylon the Great (Rev. 18:23), which represents world culture allied with an apostate church, united against the Christ and His true church, is depicted as a just conclusion to a history of seduction and deception. The "image of the beast" (εἰκόνα τῷ θηρίῳ Rev. 13:14,15) is the consummate idol of world culture. The image of the beast evokes the decadence of fallen humanity, wild and voracious, earth-bound in all of its propensities. Thus was Nebuchadnezzar humbled to become a beast for his idolatry (Dan. 4). In the end the beast turns on his own world project and destroys it under the sovereign direction of God the Judge (Rev. 17:16; Mark 3:26).[43]

Thus, sexuality and wealth are potent forces harnessed by idolaters to bring salvation through the "works of their hands" (Rev. 9:20 τῶν ἔργων τῶν χειρῶν αὐτῶν). The church in Thyatira warns us of the danger of compromising with the idolatrous tendencies of this present evil age. The One who commends the church for its love, service, faith and patience is described: "These things says the Son of God, who has eyes like a flame of fire, and His feet like fine brass" (Rev. 2:18). Here is the incarnate Son, feet firmly planted in control of history, directing His all-penetrating gaze upon His beloved church, with a critical warning. Meredith G. Kline has demonstrated the connection between the woman named "Wickedness" leading the reversed exodus of Zechariah 5, and the Mother of Harlots, Babylon the Great in Revelation 14 to 18. "Wickedness" is the queen of the idol temple in Shinar, full of idols made of wood and stone (Deut. 28:36), enshrining the worship of Mammon. She brings God's curse, symbolized by the flying ephah and talent,

---

[42] I owe this insight to Meredith G. Kline.
[43] G. K. Beale, *The Book of Revelation: A Commentary on the Greek Text*, (Grand Rapids, MI and Cambridge, UK: Eerdmans, 1999) 884ff.

on thieves and perjurers, focusing on the commercial corruption of apostate postexilic Israel. So the Mother of Harlots seduces the kings of the earth with power and the merchants of the earth with wealth and luxury (Rev. 18:3).[44]

Jezebel, the original radical feminist, is present in the church. This Old Testament character epitomizes the idolater, and the church's seduction by her. Jezebel was the daughter of Ethbaal, king of the Sidonians (1 Kings 16:31ff), a Baal worshiper. Ahab, king of Israel (the 10 northern tribes) continues the idolatrous tradition of Jeroboam by marrying an idolater. Ahab set up a wooden image and a temple in Samaria to please her. She upends godly order by exterminating the prophets and manipulating her husband to embrace greed and murder (1 Kings 21:25, 26). After the failure of her own ministers at Carmel (1 Kings 18:1 ff) she comes to an ignominious end with dogs appropriately licking up her blood (2 Kings 9:30 ff). Idolatry is always dehumanizing because it denies the Creator of humanity.

The Son promises those who resist Jezebel's guile, dominion over the nations. In the interim they must "hold fast" to the Son and His ways and not give in to the temptation to join idolaters in their world dominating agenda, mediated by idolatry. God's just anger against idolatrous culture and its purveyors (Rev. 14:9, 11) guarantees His ultimate victory over the Beast and his Image (Rev. 15:2). All who resist the seduction of idolatry reign with Christ in heaven during this ultimate era of history (Rev. 20:4).

Having only scratched the surface of the Scripture's teaching on idolatry I hope at least to have convinced the reader of the importance of the theme to its Author.

SUMMARY: THE CONCEPT OF IDOLATRY

The Heidelberg Catechism sums up the biblical concept of idolatry succinctly in Lord's Day 34, Question #95: "What is idolatry? A. It is, instead of the one true God who has revealed Himself in His Word, or besides Him, to devise or have something else on which to place our trust."[45] Idolatry is the substitution of an element in God's creation for Him. Idolatry is the worship of a substitute for the true and living God. True worship is the ascription of worth to the Lord as the ultimate source of reality, meaning, and redemption. False worship is the ascription of ultimate worth to a lesser, created object. "Idolatry is the ultimate sin. It is also, in a sense, the root of all other sins."[46]

---

[44] Meredith G. Kline, "Anathema," *Kerux* 10 :3 (Decemaber 1995) 10-19.
[45] G. I. Williamson, *The Heidelberg Catechism: A Study Guide* (Phillipsburg, NJ: Presbyterian and Reformed Publishing Company, 1993) 95.
[46] *Ibid.*, 165.

Creation Is The Medium of General Revelation

The original creation was designed to be a medium of revelation of the glory of God the Creator. Man was designed to cultivate and develop the potential of the created order to glorify God as his Creator. All that man experiences, perceives, and sees is a revelation of the invisible attributes of His eternal power and divine nature (Rom. 1:20). But as a rebel man cultivates and develops the potential of the created order, seeking dominion over the creation without God and glorifying himself in opposition to God. He seeks to "be like God" in harnessing the powers of creation for his own rebellious purposes. Thus, culture is corrupted by the worship of the creation in place of the Creator. Rebel man creates God-substitutes known as idols, which function as media to communicate, cultivate and legitimize his rebellion. Idolatry is an effort to assert autonomy by diminishing God to a manageable size, thus seeking to control Him. Calvin observed that idolaters "wish to reduce God, who is immeasurable and incomprehensible, to a five foot measure."[47]

The Seductive Power of the Visual

The power and immediate presence of the visual lend themselves to the purposes of idolatry. In the hands of sinful men the visual image becomes a means of defining reality independently of God and controlling the powers of His creation. Idols impressively package various forms of the lie that the true and living God is not who He says He is in His Word. The medium is closely associated with the message. Visual images are used by idolaters to give form to their idolatry. The fallen imagination thus names and controls the objects of its affections in forms which embody their own sinful agendas. In reality idolaters are controlled and discipled by their idols in a covenant with emptiness and death, because they live in God's world which is cursed due to idolatry. Images give earth-bound coherence to the idolatrous perspective on life. By giving a sense of historical concreteness the idol lends credibility to the beliefs and practices of the idolater. The suppressing activity of the fallen mind is positively expressed in its attitudes toward created reality. All media become potential modes of communicating the great denial of God's glory. Idolatry and immorality are inseparable. As we shall see in the next chapter man's ultimate ethical commitment determines the objects of his affections and devotion. His rebellious stance is both reflected in and cultivated by the idols he constructs. "Those who make them are like them; *So is* everyone who trusts in them." (Psalm 115:8). Idolatry dehumanizes. Idolatry is at the heart of the thought

---

[47] Calvin, *Institutes*, 104.

forms and moral habits of a fallen culture. Media, especially electronic media, create a pervasive environment. Thus, the vast and world encompassing Babel-like project of modernity highlights the use of technology to create a culture independent of God.

God Chooses His Own Media of Special Revelation

God has designed His own media to communicate, cultivate and assert His Lordship over His creation. He has entrusted these to His chosen people, the church. In the Old Testament these consisted of the Tabernacle-Temple, their rites, priestly order and the Word. In the New Testament these consist of the Mediatorial presence of the Son through His Word and Spirit, prayer and the sacraments. In choosing the media of worship the Lord re-orients the idolatrous misuse of the visual for his creational/redemptive purposes. The Word is central in reasserting this control. In common culture the restrictions of the Second Commandment do not apply in the same way. While idolatry is forbidden for all people, God has allowed fallen mankind to develop media of communication as part of His common order and blessing. The Christian is called to consecrate these media to God's glory in his everyday cultural endeavors.

Idolatry Is the Chief Temptation of the Church

Idolatry is the central means by which the church is tempted and corrupted. Thus, ministers of the Word in Old and New Testaments are called to teach and warn God's people of the nature and dangers of idolatry so that they can develop a paradigm, or pattern of spiritual perception, to understand and resist the idolatrous elements of fallen history and culture. The use of this paradigm is central to the church's task of discipling the idolatrous nations.

The Incarnate Mediator Is the Only Antidote for Idolatry

The image of God in Christ is the ultimate challenge to the worship of created images. All idols are counterfeit mediators. But now the true Mediator has invaded history. The Creator-Son has made Himself *visible* in history to draw sinners from among all nations away from idols. The powerful grip of idolatry on men's souls is evident in the very socio-economic fabric of fallen culture. The sum of true religion is turning from this idolatry to God. Thus the church needs an apologetics of fire on the front lines of spiritual and intellectual warfare in order to thrive in the twenty-first century.

2

The Apologetics of Fire: Idolatry as a Critical Paradigm

If we as Christians today see idolatry only at life's margins, we will be ill-equipped to use this powerful critical tool as the apostles and prophets did—to understand and challenge the surrounding world.

—Richard Keyes, *No Gods But God* [1]

Suaviter in modo, fortiter in re
—*gentle in presentation, powerful in substance.*

—Cornelius Van Til[2]

The twentieth century has challenged mankind with cultural revolutions so profound and swift that all other periods of history seem tame in comparison. Such a Copernican Revolution has inspired a plethora of cultural and historical criticism. Much of this has been brilliant analysis; some has even been apocalyptic, looking at the end of the century with a sense of ominous dread. The nightmarish scenarios of two well-known post-war writers stand out for their prescience and insight in this regard. They also prophesy very different visions of what the future holds. In 1946 Aldous Huxley wrote *Brave New World* and George Orwell wrote *Animal Farm*. Orwell followed in 1949 with his famous *1984*; while Huxley followed in 1960 with *Brave New World Revisited*. Neil Postman succinctly summarizes the difference: "In *1984*, Huxley added, people are controlled by inflicting pain. In *Brave New World*, people are controlled by inflicting pleasure. In short, Orwell feared that what

---

[1] Richard Keyes, "The Idol Factory," in Os Guinness and John Seel, eds. *No God But God: Breaking with the Idols of Our Age* (Chicago: Moody Press, 1992) 30.
[2] John M. Frame, *Apologetics to the Glory of God: An Introduction* (Phillipsburg, NJ: Presbyterian and Reformed Publishing Company, 1994) f.n. 192. "Gentle in our presentation, powerful in the content or substance of what we say."

we hate will ruin us. Huxley feared that what we love will ruin us."³ Postman wrote *Amusing Ourselves to Death* in the belief that Huxley's paradigm is "probably" correct, and that the visual media, especially television, will be the major purveyor of pleasure.

In searching for an overarching paradigm for cultural criticism it is clear that the paradigms of Orwell, Huxley and Postman lack the comprehensive explanatory power of the Biblical model of idolatry. Both the Orwellian totalitarianism of state and the Huxlian totalitarianism of pleasure are compelling, because they give us insight into the sinful propensities of humanity in history. But they are not comprehensive enough because they each have elements of truth, which, taken by themselves, seem contradictory. The Biblical concept of idolatry as a critical paradigm, however, gathers these and other interpretive insights into a larger and more penetrating perspective. Herbert Schlossberg has contended that "idolatry and its associated concepts provide a better framework for us to understand our own society than do any of the alternatives."⁴ The Huxlian totalitarianism of pleasure really goes hand in hand with the Orwellian totalitarianism of state. For as men idolize personal pleasure, peace, and prosperity they tend to look to the state, as a transcendent institution, to provide their overall security in a risk-free environment. Modern technology, especially the electronic media, offers a pervasiveness of control from both of these cultural trajectories, unknown to previous generations.

Cultural criticism as a discipline has both an academic and pastoral function. Criticism involves the careful analysis and evaluation of an area of concern, for example literature, education and politics. Cultural criticism focuses broadly on the phenomena of culture and involves the disciplines of history, literature and the various institutions, aspirations and habits of a given people. The American church has tended to leave this field largely to academics like Henry Adams, Daniel Boorstin, and Jacques Barzun.

At its best the church should share its concern for culture with men like those in the tribe of Issachar *"which were men* that had understanding of the times, to know what Israel ought to do."⁵ They understood the culture of the Philistines and the ethos of Israel under Saul's rule. Their concern was for the welfare of the church. They went to David in the wilderness and supported the true king. Their covenant consciousness moved them to understand their situation in order to provide guidance for God's people in a time of crisis. In the New Covenant era Paul was chosen by God to be the Apostle to the nations

---

[3] Neil Postman, *Amusing Ourselves To Death: Public Discourse in the Age of Show Business* (New York: Viking Penguin, Inc., 1985) viii.

[4] Herbert Schlossberg, *Idols For Destruction: Christian Faith and Its Confrontation With American Society* (Nashville: Thomas Nelson, 1983).

[5] 1 Chronicles 12:32.

because he understood the cultures of the Jews and of Hellenism in the Roman Empire of his day which prepared him to spread the gospel in diverse settings.

In post-apostolic times the Lord has always provided His Ireneaus's. In the electronic age the church needs them as never before. We must be careful not to belittle the work of academics, both secular and sacred, who can help to provide the careful analysis and evaluation of culture needed by the troops on the front lines of battle. Secular academics, like Barzun, are more helpful to the Christian in the area of analysis than they are in evaluation. Along with popular apologists like Francis Schaeffer and Os Guinness every pastor should be conversant with the best apologetics and cultural criticism available, in order to bring this discernment into the pulpit to guide God's people who live in the midst of a bewildering complex of cultural phenomena.

The church has been slow to avail itself of the concept of idolatry as a critical tool. We may well inquire into the reasons for this perilous omission. Certainly the American evangelical church's anti-intellectualism has undermined the possibility of searching for, or even perceiving a need for such a tool, either for apologetics or cultural criticism. Arminian assumptions about the primacy of man's will, and the rejection of the doctrine of total depravity with its attendant minimizing of the noetic effects of the fall, have given the church a mindset friendly to compromise. Coupled with these problems is the constant temptation to dull the edge of the antithesis between the church and the world. Since the church shares the same cultural context with the unbelieving world it is easy to baptize secular attitudes and methods (anti-intellectualism being a prime example) in the name of "being all things to all men" and in the hope of being legitimized by the dominant culture. The uncritical assumptions of consumerism and progress serve as poignant examples. We shall explore these in chapter 6.

An equal, and opposite error, is the assumption by some Christians, that the church and the preacher do not need to understand the world and may not learn anything from it. Only the Reformed doctrine of common grace,[6] combined with the Biblical understanding of idolatry and unbelief, will correct these unbiblical attitudes toward common culture. Thus, for a variety of reasons, the church has failed to appreciate the profoundness of the Biblical concept of idolatry in understanding its cultural situation. As we enter the new millennium the pressure of the Pagan perversion of the virtue of tolerance is causing the church to compromise its identity on every side. Never was the bride of Christ in greater need of an apologetics of fire.

---

[6] Cf. Cornelius Van Til, *Common Grace and the Gospel* (Nutley, NJ: Presbyterian and Reformed, 1977).

IDOLATRY AS A CRITICAL PARADIGM

Cornelius Van Til (1895-1987), Professor of apologetics at Westminster Theological Seminary in Philadelphia, has offered the most compelling philosophical-theological apologetic in the twentieth century. In principle Van Til's Presuppositionalism provides the only cogent way to argue for the Christian faith in light of the contemporary dominance of Immanuel Kant's epistemology. Van Til's critique has laid the groundwork for all future apologetics, and thus I will rely heavily on his insights in this chapter. Much work, however, remains to be done in building on this foundation. Van Til developed his thought in the context of the philosophical and theological disciplines. His audience is limited to scholars, students, and laymen, who are acquainted with these disciplines. Thus, important attempts to summarize his vast corpus, and articulate his thought in more accessible popular language are under way. For cogent, comprehensive summaries the reader should consult: Greg Bahnsen's *Van Til's Apologetic: Readings and Analysis* (1998), and John Frame's *Cornelius Van Til: An Analysis of His Thought* (1995).[7] Of equal importance is Frame's own contribution to Christian epistemology, titled *The Doctrine of the Knowledge of God*,[8] which builds on Calvin's seminal discussion of this topic in *The Institutes of the Christian Religion* (1559), and Van Til's concept of Christian epistemology.

As a seminal thinker Van Til not only needs to be summarized and corrected in the details of his approach, but his thought also needs to be developed in areas such as cultural apologetics and criticism, disciplines for which his apologetic is only suggestive. The late Francis Schaeffer (1912-1984), founder of L'Abri Fellowship in Switzerland, sought to apply Van Til to the irrationalist culture of the twentieth century.[9] Kenneth A. Myers, National Public Radio producer, and founder of Mars Hill Audio, without explicitly acknowledging Van Til, has taken a presuppositional approach to popular culture.[10]

---

[7] The complete works of Van Til are available on CDRom *The Works of Cornelius Van Til*, (New York: Labels Army Co.) 1997. Major works to be consulted by the student are: *The Defense of the Faith* (1967); *A Survey of Christian Epistemology* (1969); *An Introduction to Systematic Theology* (1974).

[8] John M. Frame, *The Doctrine of the Knowledge of God* (Phillipsburg, NJ: Presbyterian and Reformed Publishing Company, 1987).

[9] Schaeffer and Van Til had some fundamental theoretical differences which may be fruitfully explored. My intention here is to capture the fundamental strengths of the presuppositional approach without entering into the intramural debate among reformed apologists, as valuable in its place as that debate may be. Schaeffer's trilogy will acquaint the reader with the best of his work: *The God Who Is There* (1968); *Escape from Reason* (1968); *He Is There, and He Is not Silent* (1972). Egbert Schuurman laments the lack of cultural criticism within Reformational Philosophy, "A Confrontation with Technicism as the Spiritual Climate of the West." *The Westminster Theological Journal* 58, no. 1 (spring 1996) 75.

[10] Kenneth Myers, *All God's Children and Blue Suede Shoes: Christians and Popular Culture* (Westchester, IL: Crossway Books, 1989). Myers was graduated from Westminster Theological

The application of idolatry as a paradigm for apologetics and cultural criticism first appeared in 1983 with the appearance of Herbert Schlossberg's ground-breaking book, *Idols For Destruction: Christian Faith and Its Confrontation With American Society*.[11] Since then David Powlison has used the model of idolatry in developing a theory of Christian counseling.[12] Most recently in 1992 Os Guinness, John Seel, and especially Richard Keyes, et. al. in their *No God But God: Breaking with the Idols of Our Age*,[13] have challenged the church to consider the importance of the paradigm of idolatry in apologetics and cultural criticism.

Unfortunately, Schlossberg offers only a brief description of "Idolatry as a Framework for Understanding," in his introduction. In essence he presents the critical framework of idolatry as a key element in a Christian philosophy of history, and a Biblical alternative to secular philosophies of history. The Bible does not describe societies as rising or declining, progressing or regressing in a quantitative and deterministic fashion. Rather, societies come to their end as a result of turning to idolatry and incurring God's judgment. Hosea 8:4 tells us that "they made idols for their own destruction." Secular historiography's use of the concept of *secularization* ignores the object of loyalty which replaces for a culture what it has rejected. It also minimizes the correlation between belief and action. Citing McLuhan, Schlossberg notes that in the present electronic environment beliefs go unnoticed because they are so much a part of the entire cultural environment.[14]

Building on Schlossberg's insight we may fruitfully turn to Meredith G. Kline's conception of the pattern of history revealed in the predeluvian portion of the book of Genesis. In the battle between the seeds of the woman and the serpent, common grace provides the arena of conflict. Within that arena is a pattern of cultural development, followed by the apotheosis of idolatry, culminating with the intervention of Divine judgment.[15] This pattern reproduces itself throughout the postdeluvian period and may be taken as an eschatological pattern for the entirety of history, which reaches its denouement in the final epoch of history between the two comings of the Christ. It is in this epoch that the church finds itself most in need of a cogent philosophy of history, a trenchant apologetic, and an incisive cultural critique.

Seminary where Van Til taught for most of his career. He currently produces the Mars Hill Audio Tapes.

[11] Schlossberg, *Idols For Destruction*.

[12] David Powlison, "Idols of the Heart and Vanity Fair," photocopy.

[13] Os Guinness and John Seel, eds. *No God But God: Breaking with the Idols of Our Age* (Chicago: Moody Press, 1992).

[14] Schlossberg, *Idols for Destruction*, 5-10.

[15] *Kingdom Prologue* (South Hamilton, MA: Meredith G. Kline, 1993) 132ff.

What follows will assume much of the work mentioned above. I will suggest the application of some major themes of Van Til to my subject. My focus will be on developing a critical understanding of the electronic media. In doing so I believe that the critical lens of idolatry needs to be expanded to play a more prominent role in Christian apologetics, especially as its focuses on cultural discernment. The prominence of idolatry in the Bible is set in the context of the culture of unbelief. Thus I think that viewing culture through the lens of the pattern of idolatry together with the lens of Biblical doctrines of creation and common grace will afford the Christian thinker, and most importantly, the preacher, a well-focused view of a prominent aspect of modern culture, the electronic media.

THE PLACE OF IDOLATRY IN BIBLICAL APOLOGETICS

Elijah posed the ultimate challenge to idolatrous compromise in the church at Carmel when he declared: "How long will you falter between two opinions? If the LORD *is* God, follow Him; but if Baal, follow him. ...Then you call on the name of your gods, and I will call on the name of the LORD; and the God who answers by fire, He is God" (1 Kings 18:21, 24). The baals were as silent as the people in the face of Elijah's challenge. The true and living God acts in history in behalf of His chosen people. He is the ultimate context for all of creation and history, of all thought and culture. He is the starting point and the goal of an apologetics of fire. In thought, word and deed the Christian, and especially the preacher, is called to demonstrate that the Lord, who reveals Himself redemptively in the Bible, is the only true and living God. An apologetics of fire will at once strengthen the church in its antithetical position in the world environment, and challenge the idols of the nations with the truth and power of the Gospel.

Idolatry and Presuppositionalism

The concept of idolatry does not play a large, explicit role in the theoretics of Christian apologetics, either in the classical approach of Warfield, *et. al.* or in the presuppositional approach of Van Til, Gordon Clark or Francis Schaeffer. Recently, however, as we have seen above, the concept of idolatry has begun to play a more significant role in apologetics. Schlossberg, Powlison, Guinness, Seel and Keyes have brought this paradigm to the church's attention.

The excellent popular treatment of presuppositional apologetics, by John Frame, treats idolatry as a central theme in the "offensive" arsenal of the apologist. But his treatment still presents a less comprehensive concept than I think the Bible warrants.[16] In his chapter titled "Apologetics as Offense: Critique of Unbelief"[17] Frame uses two paradigms for criticism of the unbeliever's position: "Atheism" and Idolatry." While he clearly uses the two as "twins," the distinction hinges on his definition of idolatry: "giving one's ultimate allegiance to some *being* other than the God of Scripture."[18] Since atheism denies an ultimate *being* it becomes a separate category. However, if, as Paul says, the essence of man's rebellion is "worshipping the creation more than the Creator," then the atheist has constructed an idol similar to the one found by Paul in Athens, "to an unknown god." Atheism then, in my view, is a form of idolatry. Frame even acknowledges that among idols may be an abstract principle like Plato's Good. Thus the abstract principle which gives coherence to the atheist is that there is no god. Schlossberg asserts: "Even atheisms are usually idolatrous, as Niebuhr said, because they elevate some 'principle of coherence' to the central meaning of life and this is what then provides the focus of significance for that life."[19] This is the object of his allegiance. All idolatry is anthropocentric. Idols are the constructions of fallen man designed to suit his own rebellious purposes. Atheism is simply more explicit in defining the object of his allegiance in terms of a radical anthropocentrism.

On the other end of the spectrum is the view that idolatry is not a comprehensive paradigm at all. Darryl Hart has argued that idolatry is confined to Pagan worship rituals and icons.[20] It is certainly clear, as we have seen in the last chapter, that Old Testament idolatry is just this kind of concrete or explicit worship of the creation of men's hands. Hart is also justly concerned about the simplistic uses of the concept of idolatry by many Christian counselors. I agree wholeheartedly. However, it seems to me that Paul points us to a broader definition of idolatry in Romans 1. As Richard Keyes observes: "As the main category to describe unbelief, the idea is highly sophisticated, drawing together the complexities of motivation in individual psychology, the social environment, and also the unseen world. Idols are not just on pagan altars, but in well-educated human hearts and minds."[21] Schlossberg insists: "Idolatry in its larger meaning is properly understood as any substitution of what is created for the creator. People may worship nature, money, mankind,

---

[16] *Apologetics to the Glory of God: An Introduction* (Phillipsburg, NJ: Presbyterian and Reformed Publishing Company, 1994). William Edgar's *Reasons of the Heart* is also an excellent popular presentation of a presuppositional approach.
[17] *Ibid.*, 191-202.
[18] *Ibid.*, 195, emphasis added.
[19] Schlossberg, *Idols for Destruction*, 6.
[20] Darryl Hart, "Putting the Idol Back in Idolatry," *Nicotine Theological Journal* 3/3 (July 1999) 6, 7.
[21] Keyes, "The Idol Factory," 31.

IDOLATRY AS A CRITICAL PARADIGM 33

power, history, or social and political systems instead of God who created them all.

"The New Testament writers, in particular, recognized that the relationship need not be explicitly one of cultic worship; a man can place anyone or anything at the top of his pyramid of values, and that is ultimately what he serves."[22] Calvin considered idolatry in the broader brushstrokes of Paul in Romans 1:25: "For what is idolatry if not this: to worship the gifts in place of the Giver himself."[23] Commenting on the Second Commandment he distinguished the "outward idolatry" as a gross fault, implying an idolatry of the heart not necessarily expressing itself in a form of cultus. The idolater is guilty for "daring to subject God, who is incomprehensible, to our sense perceptions or to represent him by any form."[24] Powlison asserts: "Idolatry becomes a tool to comprehend the intricacies of both individual psychology and social conditioning. ...[It] is a fertile and flexible conceptual category which stays close to the data of life, unlike the speculative abstractions of alternative and unbiblical explanations."[25]

Biblically we find that the language of service is used in terms of the essential turning of the heart's allegiance (repentance) as Paul declares to the Thessalonians: "For they themselves declare concerning us what manner of entry we had to you, and how you turned to God from idols to serve (δουλεύειν) the living and true God." The language of servitude (δουλεύοντες) is used both of service to the Lord (τῷ κυρίῳ δουλεύοντες Rom. 12:11, cf. Eph. 6:7) and as well as to "serving various lusts and pleasures" (δουλεύοντες ἐπιθυμίαις καὶ ἡδοναῖς ποικίλαις Titus 3:3). In Romans 16:17, 18 we read: "Now I urge you, brethren, note those who cause divisions and offenses, contrary to the doctrine which you learned, and avoid them. For those who are such do not serve our Lord Jesus Christ, but their own belly, and by smooth words and flattering speech deceive the hearts of the simple." More generally such servitude is used regarding sin in Romans 6:6: "knowing this, that our old man was crucified with *Him,* that the body of sin might be done away with, that we should no longer be slaves (δουλεύειν) of sin." Paul chides the Galatian Christians for returning to worship the creation rather than the Creator through the liberty of Jesus Christ: "But now after you have known God, or rather are known by God, how *is it that* you turn again to the weak and beggarly elements, to which you desire again to be in bondage? (Galatians 4:9)" Bondage is

---

[22] Schlossberg, *Idols for Destruction,* 6.
[23] John Calvin, *Institutes of the Christian Religion* (1559. Reprint (1 vol. in 2). The Library of Christian Classics, vol. XX. Edited by John T. McNeill. Translated by Ford Lewis Battles. Philadelphia: The Westminster Press, 1960) 1413.
[24] *Ibid.,* 383, 384.
[25] Powlison, "Idols of the Heart and Vanity Fair," 4, 5.

servitude (δουλεύειν) to the elements (στοιχεία) of the created world, to lords and masters molded by the sinful world.[26] This language of servitude indicates that idolatry is central to the fallen condition of man who lives covenantally either by trusting the true God in true faith or trusting some aspect of His creation in idolatry.

It may be helpful to distinguish between a *broad* (implicit) and a *narrow* (explicit) concept of idolatry. Idolatry in its broad conception is the allegiance of the unbeliever to ideas, ideals and concepts which he holds to be ultimate, along with the specific ways in which he expresses these in his own life and cultural setting. Idolatry in its narrow conception is the allegiance of the unbeliever to a personal god(s) who is worshipped with certain rites and ceremonies and is mediated by depictions of that deity in sculpture or other iconography. Perhaps this distinction will help to correct the facile descriptions of idolatry used by the counselors with whom Hart has a quarrel.

While idolatry in its concrete historical expression is the invention of the fallen human heart, it is never the creation of an individual, but always of groups and cultures in which individuals live and learn. "Rarely if ever is the condition of a culture the product of deliberate decision, either by the society as a whole or by a group of social engineers, whether elected or self-appointed. Cultural development is something that occurs naturally rather than artificially."[27] Culture is a communal enterprise achieved through social cooperation and interaction.[28] "Many of the shades and colors of our idolatries are socially shaped by the opportunities and values that surround us, and so constrain the particular forms our idols take."[29]

We shall now discuss the relationship of the concept of idolatry to the central tenets of a presuppositional apologetic along the lines of Van Til, Frame and Bahnsen.

Rationalism and Irrationalism

Postmodernism has developed in sharp antithesis to the Enlightenment. The central epistemological challenge posed by Postmodernism is to the validity of Cartesian logic. The repudiation of the Enlightenment exaltation of reason finds its consummation in the postmodern mindset. Christians who are sanguine about this shift have perhaps been engaged too long in the battle on the Western front to be aware of the threat on the Eastern front. Both Postmodernism and its putative foe the Enlightenment are children of the same

---

[26] *Ibid.*, 6.
[27] Myers, *All God's Children and Blue Suede Shoes*, 32.
[28] Henry R. Van Til, *The Calvinistic Concept of Culture* (Grand Rapids: Baker Book House, 1959) 32.
[29] Powlison, "Idols of the Heart and Vanity Fair," 18.

philosophical father: man seeking epistemological independence of his Creator. The Enlightenment has waged a war using Reason to seek independence from the Creator, as a sufficient alternative to the self-revelation of God in Scripture. Those who exalt mystery and freedom have been waging an equally virulent war since Adam asserted himself against the revelation of God in the Garden. The greatest problem of philosophy and religion is the coordination of unity and diversity.[30] Enlightenment rationalism has sought the universal application of empirical science to unify culture through technology. Postmodernism seeks on the other hand to abandon this quest as impossible and illegitimate, idealizing the diversity of human culture and experience.

Cornelius Van Til's presuppositional apologetic points to the solution (of course, the very idea of a "solution" is anathema to Postmoderns). "Would-be autonomous man" is at once a rationalist and an irrationalist. For the Christian the dilemma between rationalism and irrationalism is understood to be false at the outset. The problem with rationalism is not the use of reason, but its exaltation of reason to the status of ultimacy. So irrationalism exalts freedom and mystery. The Christian affirms both, but from an entirely different perspective, as aspects of creaturely reality and perception. While the unbeliever vacillates between the equal ultimacy of rationalism and irrationalism, the Christian understands that only the Triune God who has revealed Himself in the Bible is ultimate. There is no mystery for God. He has given man the ability to think His thoughts after Him, knowing truly but not exhaustively, in a world filled with mystery because that world is the revelation of God's majestic glory. It can be said that Christianity is "absolute rationalism" in that God has absolutely comprehensive understanding.[31] The right use of reason for the Christian acknowledges that the law of non-contradiction, which states that A cannot equal non-A, is simply a recognition of the finiteness of the human thought process, as well as the finiteness of creation. The law of non-contradiction is a characteristic of creaturely epistemology by which we are able to distinguish among finite realities. It also enables us to distinguish between the creation and the Creator.

The pantheon of idols is a multifarious construct of the fallen human imagination, seeking control over various forces, potentialities, and ideals through particular visual forms. The Pythagorean views the universe as ruled by number, a mosaic of formulae. The Existentialist worships the god *Libertas*,

---

[30] Cornelius Van Til, *The Defense of the Faith*. 3rd edition (Nutley, NJ and Philadelphia: Presbyterian and Reformed Publishing Company, 1967) 10. Cf. Rousas John Rushdoony, *The One and the Many*. Cf. William Edgar, "No News Is Good News: Modernity, The Postmodern, and Apologetics," *Westminster Theological Journal* 57, no. 2 (fall 1995): 359-82. This is an excellent discussion of the Van Til "rationalism-irrationalism" dialectic critique of Modernity.
[31] *Ibid.*, 41.

absolute freedom. Radical feminists in the mainline Presbyterian church worship a revivified and renamed ancient goddess Sophia. The latter perceptively depict themselves as "re-imagining God." This is classic idolatry. The composition of the pantheon of idols reflects the dilemma of fallen man as he asserts both rationalism and irrationalism. Research into the nature of the human brain indicates that the two hemispheres (bi-cameral) each represent the rational (quantitative) and intuitive (qualitative) functions of human thought. The two are necessarily complementary aspects of what it means to think humanly as imagers of God.

Transcendence and Immanence

Closely related to the rationalism-irrationalism dilemma is the transcendence-immanence dilemma. For the unbeliever transcendence is used, as in Deism, to distance God from the concerns of history. Neo-Orthodoxy in the modern, and Platonism and Neo-Platonism in the ancient, world have posited an utterly transcendent god, who is known through climbing the rungs of created phenomena to arrive at the ultimate One. On the other hand, Liberalism, Process Theology, and much of modern science have opted for various forms of immanentism, creating a god of manageable historical proportions. Each extreme position on the spectrum of the transcendence-immanence dilemma is left without being able to account for the reality on the other end of the spectrum. The transcendentalist cannot account for the particulars of creation and history; the immanentist cannot account for the unknown. Only with the existence of the God of the Bible is true knowledge possible, because without "comprehensive knowledge somewhere" there cannot "be true knowledge anywhere."[32]

What characterizes both Modernism and Postmodernism is their affirmation of immanence. As William Edgar has so tersely stated: "The human horizon replaces the divine as the basic ordering principle."[33]

Idol Making: The Great Denial

Since the Enlightenment man's intentions have been more clearly revealed and he has self-consciously placed himself, where he has always been as a sinner, at the center of the pantheon of gods. Idolatry is autonomy writ large and vice versa. Idols are at once reflections of the sinful aspirations, and practices of fallen man as well as purveyors of the same (Rom. 1:18-32). The idolater's

---

[32] *Ibid.*, 41. Cf. Frame, *The Doctrine of the Knowledge of God*, 13-15.
[33] William Edgar, "No News Is Good News: Modernity, The Postmodern, and Apologetics," *Westminster Theological Journal* 57, no. 2 (fall 1995): 368.

God-replacements are rationalizations of his "would-be autonomy." The Puritan Stephen Charnock observed: "Man hath a boundless appetite after some sovereign good...The natural inclination to worship is as universal as the notion of a God; idolatry else had never gained footing in the world."[34]

There are several ways in which to distinguish among the idols. Keyes distinguishes between *near* and *far* idols.[35] Near idols are accessible and offer power and control over everyday life, such as a particular business. Far idols are distant or transcendent, offering meaning, coherence and legitimacy, such as money or power. These components in the lives of idolaters correspond to the fallen instinct to dominate and control (near idol), on the one hand, and to depend on, as a slave (far idol), on the other hand. They exist in the fallen heart together in varying degrees. As we have seen above this tension in fallen man lies between the poles of rationalism and irrationalism, and transcendence and immanence. The former is the *epistemological* tendency of the idolater and the latter is the *ontological* tendency of the idolater.

In creating substitutes for the true God the idolater at once creates idols of immanence and idols of transcendence; idols of rationalism and idols of irrationalism. The near idol is a substitute for the immanence of God. The prophet Jeremiah describes such idols: "They *are* upright, like a palm tree, and they cannot speak; they must be carried, because they cannot go *by themselves.* Do not be afraid of them, for they cannot do evil, nor can they do any good. Inasmuch as *there is* none like You, O LORD (You *are* great, and Your name *is* great in might) (Jer. 10:5,6)."

Van Til observed: "In paradise God walked and talked with man. Man needs God near to himself. Even in the state of sin man has realized something of the need of a god who is near him. In fact, the sinner has brought God too near to him; he has identified the creator with the creature. In idolatry we have an expression on the part of the sinner which points to his need of a god who is near."[36] "It is of special importance to keep all these matters related to one another in order to see what the real distinction is between true prophecy and false prophecy. We have noted that idolatry is the caricature of true theophany and that divination or mantic is the caricature of true prophecy. False prophecy came in forms similar to the forms of true prophecy. False prophets arose who said they had had dreams and visions of the Lord. These false prophets demanded a hearing, and said that they were entitled to it just as well as were

---

[34] Stephen Charnock, *The Existence and Attributes of God.* 1797. Reprint (Minneapolis, MN: Klock and Klock Christian Publishers, 1977) 55, 67.

[35] Keyes, "The Idol Factory," 35-38.

[36] Cornelius Van Til, *An Introduction to Systematic Theology (In Defense of the Faith,* vol. 5, Nutley, NJ: Presbyterian and Reformed Publishing Company, 1976) 119, in CDRom *The Works of Cornelius Van Til,* (New York: Labels Army Co.) 1997.

the others. Thus the problem became very acute for those who listened."[37] The nearness required by the idolater is a distortion of the immanence of God. The visual and tactile nature of images becomes a means of control as we noted in the last chapter. The far idol is a substitute for the transcendence of God. The prophet Isaiah speaks on behalf of the LORD: "But you *are* those who forsake the LORD, who forget My holy mountain, who prepare a table for Gad, and who furnish a drink offering for Meni. (Isa. 65:11)." Epistemologically the far idol corresponds to the irrationalism and the near idol to rationalism. Only in Jesus Christ, the incarnation of the transcendent-immanent God, can fallen man, bring these elements into proper relationship, and find his place as a servant-master, subduing the earth for God's glory.

Another way of distinguishing among the idols is between *passionate* and *presumptuous*, roughly corresponding to C. S. Lewis's distinction between *warm* and *cold* sins. This distinction takes into account an important epistemological insight of Van Til. Ethics (axiology) is always at the bottom of fallen man's epistemology. Man's problem is not his finitude but his sin.[38] His sinful rebellion shapes his modes of thought and their objects. Passionate idols are the immediate objects of devotion which bring a sense of control, while presumptuous idols shore up man's position in a mysterious and unpredictable world, giving him confidence and feeding his pride. The presumptuous idols give rationale to the sinful practices personified by the idols of passion.

We observe these distinctions in Paul's encounter with the Epicureans and Stoics in the marketplace of Athens. These two rival schools of ancient philosophy really cover the spectrum of philosophy in Paul's day. "Stoicism and Epicureanism represent alternative attempts in pre-Christian paganism to come to terms with life, especially in times of uncertainty and hardship, and post-Christian paganism down to our own day has not been able to devise anything appreciably better."[39] Epicurus (341-270 BC) taught an ethical theory based on the atomic physics of Democritus, known as "Atomism." The logic of his system lead to the ultimacy of mystery and irrationalism, despite his defense of reason against the Sophists and traditional religions.[40] In the end, blind chance rules history. The life of the soul is extinguished at death. Epicureans worship the idol of pleasure, although for Epicurus the pleasures of the mind were superior to the pleasures of the body. Perfect composure is the wisest course. But again, in the end, pleasure is the chief end of life.[41] Cypriote Zeno

---

[37] *Ibid.*, 127, 128.
[38] Van Til, *The Defense of the Faith*, 15.
[39] F. F. Bruce, *Commentary on the Book of Acts* (Grand Rapids: William B. Eerdmans Publishing Company, 1979) 351.
[40] I owe this observation to John Frame.
[41] *Ibid.*, 350-51.

(340-265 BC) was the founder of Stoicism, so named for the portico (stoa) on which he taught in Athens. He believed in the ultimacy of order and reason, borrowing heavily from Heraclitus's doctrine of the logos. Stoics worship the idol of control. By the proper use of reason man can attain self-sufficiency. Stoicism is a pantheistic form of monism, positing God as the world-soul. Participation in the world-soul leads politically to a pure democracy of world-state (*cosmopolis*). Mankind is a brotherhood and looks forward to life after death, all independent of the God of the Bible.[42]

In both philosophies man is in control. For Epicurus pleasure is achieved by careful control over pain and discomfort. For Zeno happiness is achieved by perfect control over thought by reason. Both Epicureans and Stoics had their near and far idols. The Athenian altar to the "unknown god" is an overarching all-purpose far god, which asserts the ultimacy of mystery, more compatible with Epicureanism than with Stoicism. Reason is the far idol of the Stoic. For the believer the God who reveals Himself in His covenant Word is thereby known, and He is the God for whom there is no unknown. He is also intimately involved in history and is thus near and far at once, a position in which no one but the Creator can be. Paul identified the near and far idols of the Athenians with the assertion that the true God is both near and far.[43]

When Calvin described the fallen soul as "an idol factory" he was identifying the tendency to counterfeit the attributes of God. Man's idol constructing activity assumes original creativity, when in fact he is a counterfeiter. "Man's nature is a perpetual factory of idols. ...man tries to express in his work the sort of god he has inwardly conceived. Therefore, the mind begets an idol; the hand gives it birth." The flesh, as we have seen in the incident of the golden calf, is uneasy without an image, "a presence."[44] Moses exhorts the people of Israel on the eve of their entrance into the Promised Land: "You shall make no covenant with them, nor with their gods" (Exod. 23:32). It is man's tendency as fallen to construct an alternative description of reality in which the objects of devotion bless and curse their worshippers in terms of a complex and hierarchy of values established by the sinner.

Powlison's analysis of idolatry in the discipline of Biblical psychology focuses on the existential ramifications of idolatry. "Idols counterfeit aspects of God's identity and character," thereby lending an earthbound locus of control through the idol's definition of good and evil.[45] At the psychological level the idol is what motivates behavior and makes life worth living. The "tri-

---

[42] *Ibid.*, 349-50.
[43] Keyes, "The Idol Factory," 47.
[44] Calvin, *Institutes*, 108, 110.
[45] Powlison, "Idols of the Heart and Vanity Fair," 12.

perspectival" motivation of the world, the flesh and the devil form the total psychodynamic environment of idolatry.[46]

At bottom the sense of deity (*sensus deitatis*) is present in every sinner.[47] His suppressing activity, however subtle, is not to be naively overlooked, as if he were on some neutral ground, waiting receptively to accept the gospel. By nature he is dead set against the Gospel. On the other hand, his sure knowledge, according to Paul in Romans 1, not only leaves him without excuse but assures the evangelist/apologist/preacher that the sinner is painfully aware of living in God's world as a vagrant and a rebel, for all of his efforts to deceive himself into believing otherwise. The evidence as Paul asserts in Romans 1:20 is crystal clear. "The whole world is like a looking glass, which whole and entire represents the image of God..."[48] For this clarity man is responsible. The evidence is not like the signature of an artist on his painting or "footprints in the sands of time." The evidence is the continual existential presence of the Artist Himself in every fact and experience of man's existence. The Artist gives life to His artwork; "for in Him we live and move and have our being." The fallen human artist, with the recreative instinct of his Creator, uses his own brush, provided by God, to paint with the colors of his own fallen imagination, images in a vain attempt to blot out the revelation of the true God. It is this suppressed knowledge in people as image bearers of God which forms the point of contact between the ambassador and the one to whom the message of the gospel is foreign.

Toppling the Idols: Unmasking the Sham

Like Elijah the Christian thinker will seek to unmask the idols for what they are in terms of the discipline or discussion in which he is engaged. In 1 Kings 18:27 "Elijah mocked them and said, 'Cry aloud, for he *is* a god; either he is meditating, or he is busy, or he is on a journey, *or* perhaps he is sleeping and must be awakened.'" He declared the futility of idolatry. They cried out to their baals and cut themselves, but all to no avail. Then with an ominous note of tragedy we read this: "But *there was* no voice; no one answered, no one paid attention." Philosophy since Kant has declared the voices of all the gods, as well as the true and living God, to be silent. Ingmar Bergman's film *The Silence* bears eloquent testimony to the plight of modern man. The movement from the Enlightenment rationalism of Kant to the nihilism of Nietzsche is a movement from man asserting the sufficiency of reason to the assertion of the sufficiency of will, all with the same futile result. The apotheosis of reason is

---

[46] *Ibid.*, 2.
[47] Van Til, *The Defense of the Faith*, 94.
[48] Charnock, *The Existence and Attributes of God*, 28.

replaced by the apotheosis of volition or choice. The ancient pagan has reappeared in reaction to the Cartesian rationalism of Newtonian physics and Modern Science. But the gods of reason and of will, the gods of numbers and of mystery are all members of the same pantheon. They all elevate an element of created reality in the place of the glorious God of Scripture. Elijah demonstrated the bankruptcy of the presupposition of the Baal worshipers. So must we unmask the idols of our age.

Maintaining the distinction between God and His creation; and the antithesis between the Seed of the woman and the seed of the Serpent; the redemptive revelation of God in Scripture and the counsel of the ungodly, is the task of the church. This requires exposing and toppling the idols which stand opposed to the redemptive recreative work of God. Like Gideon we must tear down the idols of our age. Because there is no neutral ground the Christian understands that opposition to God distorts the ethics, epistemology and the ontology of the unbeliever. Because the existence of God and His creation are what they are, however wrongly they may be perceived epistemologically or however vitiated the motives shaping such perception may be, all of those made in God's image live in God's world and are, therefore, continually confronted with the revelation of God in the created world, their own consciousness and consciences.

Thus the Christian apologist must not answer a fool according to his folly (Prov. 26:4), that is by allowing him to define the terms of the engagement. The "fool" in the Bible is not stupid, but a rebel against the wisdom of God. In this sense the more intelligent and articulate the unbeliever the more foolish. God the Creator is the only one in the proper position to define reality. Admit the fool's presuppositions and you become like an unbeliever. This position does not, however, permit a careless disregard for the unbeliever and his thought. We must seek to understand him on his own terms, all the while recognizing what he is up to as an idolater. The next proverb (26:5) seems to give the opposite advice when it instructs us to "answer the fool according to his folly, lest he be wise in his own eyes." Here we are to reveal the inconsistency of his thought as a creature of God. He cannot live in God's world, made in God's image, on his "misguided presuppositions."[49] The revelation of God in every aspect of creation leaves him defenseless.

Exposing and toppling idols requires the thoughtful engagement of the Christian with the culture of our time. The Gospel preacher must demonstrate the futility of idolatry. The media critic must analyse the nature of this idolatry in the various media of the modern world. As Van Til maintains, the

---

[49] Greg L. Bahnsen, *Always Ready: Directions for Defending the Faith*. Edited by Robert R. Booth. Atlanta, GA: American Vision,1996.

presuppositions of the unbeliever are utterly incapable of maintaining the very meaning which the unbeliever has sought to construct.[50] Because he lives in God's world only Christian presuppositions are adequate to establishing rationality itself, and as well all meaning and values. Because no one can live without these, all rationality, meaning and values are surreptitiously introduced by the unbeliever. Media, as we shall see, can only be properly assessed and appropriated (L. *appropriare*, to make one's own) on Christian presuppositions. We shall also see that every valid insight of unbelievers who have studied and evaluated communication is possible only on Biblical presuppositions. The preacher meets the world at the intersection of apologetics and culture, in terms of the concrete expressions of unbelief constructed by the idolater. Through the power of the Gospel message he uses spiritual weapons "for pulling down strongholds, casting down arguments and every high thing that exalts itself against the knowledge of God, bringing every thought into captivity to the obedience of Christ, and being ready to punish all disobedience when your obedience is fulfilled (2 Cor. 10:4-6)." The negative aspect of this task is found in exposing the true nature of idols.

One of the most effective methods of doing this is to demonstrate, as the Old Testament prophets did, the futility and emptiness of idolatry, as we have seen in the last chapter. The plotting of the people against the Lord and His Christ is characterized by the Psalmist in Psalm 2 as "vain," empty and useless. The futility of idolatry comes into its own with the Incarnation, as the Messiah invades the nations to establish the consummate meaning of history in His own person as the Word made flesh. Paul warns the Ephesians not to "walk as the rest of the Gentiles walk, in the *futility* of their mind (Eph. 4:17)." He lays the foundation for this assessment in describing the nature of man's fallenness in Romans 1:21-23, "although they knew God, they did not glorify *Him* as God, nor were thankful, but became *futile in their thoughts*, and their foolish hearts were darkened. Professing to be wise, they became fools, and changed the glory of the incorruptible God into an image made like corruptible man—and birds and four-footed animals and creeping things." When Paul went to Athens as an ambassador of Christ he took careful note of the specific ways in which the Athenians worshipped the creation more than the Creator. Their empty philosophies are internally incoherent, and do not meet the exigencies of life in God's world, that is to say, their philosophies do not correspond to reality as God sees it.

The desire of the Athenians to "know what these things [Paul's gospel] mean" in the hope that they would hear something "new" was met head on by Paul. The "new" thing which God had done, however, did not meet the

---

[50] Van Til, *The Defense of the Faith*, 4.

criterion of intellectual novelty required by the philosophers. This was the heart of Paul's challenge. The God who made the world has now entered history. A new epoch of the Spirit of Christ has been inaugurated. This God is not to be confused with your idolatrous creations. The one in whom "you live and move and have your very being" has come to conquer the hearts of thankless rebels and commands you to turn to Him now for soon He will come as Judge. You have always been without excuse but now you are utterly so.

Paul took on the media of idolatry with the message of the gospel. He challenged the futile constructs of sinners with the true communication of God through His Son. So must the Christian thinker and preacher "deconstruct" the idolatrous world of our day, and announce, not a new idea, but a new era of the world's history of which Jesus Christ is the center. It is not then simply the failure of the internal coherence of the pagan philosophy, or its futility in failing to deal with sin and death, which will topple the idols. It is the heavenly news release that God has entered history in the person of Jesus the Messiah, that topples the idols. Only the Good News of God's grace can deconstruct the idols of the nations. We must topple the idols by presenting their replacement with the Christ of Scripture, who is the Christ of history. The Incarnation is the final blow to idols.[51]

I am not attempting here to set forth the proofs or defense aspects of the apologetic enterprise. I am focusing on the offensive dimension with an eye toward developing a Christian perspective on Media Ecology. In dealing with unbelievers we must appreciate the "person-variable" dimension of apologetics. It is one thing to say that the Christian position is a coherent system or unit. It is quite another to insist that there is only one argument needed to establish that position or convince someone else of its validity. Frame's discussion of Van Til's transcendental argument is very helpful on this point.[52] It is one thing to say that the evidence is certain because it is *in itself* absolutely clear. It is quite another thing to assert that any argument will evoke absolute certainty in a person. It is humbling to observe the variety and often the simplicity of the thoughts, words, arguments, and experiences which the sovereign Spirit of God uses to topple the idols in people's lives, and bring them to bow before the grace of God. The humility and compassion of the Christian in using his intellect as a gospel witness is one of the best "arguments" for the truth of the gospel. It is certainly an essential ingredient, often sadly lacking in all of us.

---

[51] Keyes, "The Idol Factory," 48.
[52] Frame, *Apologetics to the Glory of God*, 69-77.

Replacing the Idols: The Healing Power of the Good News

The focus of repentance in the Bible is described by Paul in his first letter to the Thessalonian church "you turned to God from idols to serve the living and true God (1:9)." The task of the preacher is to replace the toppled idol with the only proper object of ultimate devotion: the Lord who sent His own Son to save mankind from his misplaced devotion. Paul's call to repentance in Athens was met with rejection and acceptance. "Some joined him and believed." The others were offended by God's dramatic installation of Jesus as the Lord of lords. As *Media*tor He is the Lord of all media. He is the essence of authentic communication, and, therefore, the Judge of every medium created by man. He is the Liberator who sets men free from their entanglement and bondage in the media of idolatry. He set Dionysius the Areopagite free from his enslavement to the unknown god of Athens and the lust of his peers for the novel creations of thinkers who entertained their audiences to death.

Paul did not offer the Athenians a "user friendly" gospel, padding their pews with an image boosting "positive" message. He did not cater to their self-indulgent intellects. He gave them the medicine they needed, the Christ of history, Who is the Christ of Scripture. On the other hand, he did not quote Scripture as he would in the synagogue. He began with general revelation as it was known and expressed by his Athenian audience. In this sense we might call his approach "user friendly." While that term carries a lot of commercial baggage, at least we can say he did not go out of his way to be unfriendly. He sought to communicate the message of the Gospel in terms that the Athenians understood. He sought to win them to the Christ of Scripture, but in an uncompromising way.[53] To those who refused to believe, this message was an aroma of death leading to death, and to those who believed and were being saved, the message was an aroma of life leading to life in Jesus Christ.

We must never forget the place of the regenerating and illuminating power of the Holy Spirit in the salvation of dead and blind sinners. Since He is both the Author of the Word of God and the Creator of all human powers and media of communication "he normally works through the word."[54] Prayerfully the Christian should expect the Spirit to use his reasoning power to win people to Christ. Biblically there is no dichotomy between prayer and reasoning. Paul always did both with gusto.

At the center of apologetics is the task of giving an answer or a reason for the hope we possess (1 Peter 3:15). Hope is viewed by most moderns as a purely psychological state, what we call "wishful thinking." In the Bible it is a

---

[53] I owe this insight to John Frame. Cf. Van Til's motto under the title of this chapter.
[54] Frame, *Apologetics to the Glory of God*, 16.

psychological state, to be sure, but it is a state of mind based on historical fact, and the divine interpretation of the meaning of that fact. Peter makes this clear in verse 18: "For Christ also suffered once for sins, the just for the unjust, that He might bring us to God, being put to death in the flesh but made alive by the Spirit." Paul concluded his Mars Hill defense with the same message: "Truly, these times of ignorance God overlooked, but now commands all men everywhere to repent, because He has appointed a day on which He will judge the world in righteousness by the Man whom He has ordained. He has given assurance of this to all by raising Him from the dead" (Acts 17:30, 31). God has an overwhelmingly positive solution to the desperate situation of the idolater. While our pluralistic age does not take kindly to the Gospel claim of being the *only* way of salvation, the preacher must present the glorious uniqueness of this claim. While every other religion and hope is groping vainly toward God, here we have God rescuing man. Is there any other message like this in all the earth? The glorious hope of the Christian is rooted in the magnificent person and work of Jesus Christ. Set Him before sinners and their idols appear to be the distorted and insufficient gods which they are. Our focus is on the *goodness* of the Good News.

A Matter of the Heart

The heart of the matter is a matter of the heart. Many in our day would understand this to be a matter of feeling and emotion, but the Biblical concept of "heart" is much richer than that. When Jesus summed up the commandments He gave us an all inclusive statement: "You shall love the LORD your God with all your heart, with all your soul, with all your strength, and with all your mind" (Luke 10:27). The whole person is depicted by the string of inter-related terms used by Jesus. They are meant to paint a picture of every aspect of what it means to be made in God's image. Rather than strict terms they overlap and interconnect.

The "word study" mentality is often more a product of scientific rationalism than sound exegesis. Important Biblical concepts are rarely communicated by a single word. The nature of the human soul is no exception. While it is useful and necessary to define elements of God's creation, definitions are always incomplete due to the profundity of what God has made, and the finiteness of man as His creature. The four terms used by Jesus in the above quote, and by other Biblical writers, each has a unique accent or emphasis. *Soul* emphasizes the sentient aspect of man as a living, feeling creature. *Heart* emphasizes the center of spiritual life in man as the seat of spiritual convictions or covenantal commitment. *Mind* refers to the intellectual aspect of man as a thinking creature. *Strength* refers more to the volitional aspect of man, as it relates to his various powers of body and soul. In the three synoptic accounts of Jesus' summary of the law two different words are used to describe man's intellectual capacities. Matthew and Luke use διανοίᾳ, while Mark uses συνέσεως. The latter refers to the power of comprehension or insight, and the former means mind or attitude. Furthermore, the word for heart, καρδία, usually has some reference to the thought life of a person. In Mark 7:21 "evil thoughts (οἱ διαλογισμοὶ οἱ κακοί)" come from the heart. Jesus tell us in Matthew 12:34 that "out of the abundance of the heart the mouth speaks." Luke 1:51 "He has scattered *the* proud in the imagination of their hearts." In Luke 9:47 we are told, "And Jesus, perceiving the thought of their heart." "Hard hearts" are those who are adamantly opposed in the seat of their ultimate commitments to the Lord.

1 Peter 3:15 commands us to: "sanctify the Lord God in your hearts, and always *be* ready to *give* a defense (ἀπολογίαν answer) to everyone who asks you a reason (λόγον) for the hope that is in you, with meekness and fear." In humility, and with a keen sense of unworthiness, the Christian, and especially the preacher, must be ready with answers. "Sanctifying the Lord God" in our hearts is not merely a matter of committing ourselves to moral purity, or the result of some devotional experience, though it certainly involves these. It is first of all a matter of cultivating our intelligent allegiance. It means not being "conformed to this world, but be transformed by the renewing of your mind, that you may prove what *is* that good and acceptable and perfect will of God (Rom. 12:2)." The preacher must be clear in doctrine and life as to his own allegiance, and then make plain the significance of that allegiance in comparison with the idolatry of his hearers.

The purpose of this brief excursus is to demonstrate that service to God involves the thought life, and to suggest that the heart-head dichotomy espoused by many Christians is not Biblical. The heart is the intelligent seat of ultimate covenant allegiance. The corollary of this is that we need to appreciate the centrality of the thought life of the unbeliever as we engage people with the gospel. While few are "intellectuals," all have intellects. All have ultimate commitments and use their thoughts and imaginations to serve those commitments.

A PARADIGM FOR CULTURAL UNDERSTANDING

Francis Schaeffer has done more than any popular apologist to intersect philosophical apologetics with cultural criticism. Despite some of the weaknesses of his theoretical framework in apologetics and culture,[55] he has inspired a generation of students to follow his lead into this important arena, and to seriously pursue intellectual disciplines neglected for decades by evangelicals.

The problem of relating Christ and Culture is as old as the church itself. H. Richard Niebuhr's classic *Christ and Culture* identifies and discusses the five approaches to this relationship.[56] T. S. Elliot has wrestled fruitfully with this problem in his *The Idea of a Christian Society* (1939) and *Notes toward the Definition of Culture* (1949).[57] J. Gresham Machen simplified the discussion long before either of these works appeared by distinguishing among three approaches in his opening address to the one hundred and first session of Princeton Theological Seminary in 1912.[58] The first, Christianity subordinated to culture, reduces Christianity to merely a cultural phenomenon. The second, Christ against culture, views culture as essentially inimical to the interests of the gospel. Machen's proposed solution is culture "consecrated" by Christianity.[59] In his critique of popular culture Ken Myers calls for "culture of transcendence" in which culture is consecrated in a way that is beneficial and constructive.[60] This is the only avenue open to the Christian, unless he wants to compromise the gospel by accommodating culture or rejecting culture altogether. Only the Christian is in a proper position to engage in cultural and media criticism. Sin is the problem, not culture *per se*. In redemption the whole man is to be transformed into service of God in the whole of life, including all of the media, electronic and otherwise, which God has enabled him to develop. Van Til has observed:

> So man can never escape having knowledge of good and evil. He cannot do wrong without his moral consciousness within him rebuking him. He cannot do any good without his moral consciousness approving of his doing it. Thus what is sometimes called the image of God in the wider sense, man's rationality and morality, must still be viewed as God speaking to man in the imperative voice. God speaks in the imperative voice to man because he cannot speak otherwise. And man cannot be

---

[55] Cf. Van Til's critique of Schaeffer's apologetic, *A Letter to Francis Schaeffer*, March 11, 1969 in CDRom *The Works of Cornelius Van Til*, (New York: Labels Army Co.) 1997. Cf. Mark Edwards, "How Should We Then Think: A Study of Francis Schaeffer's Lordship Principle," *Westminster Theological Journal* 60 (1998): 193-223.
[56] H. Richard Niebuhr, *Christ and Culture* (New York: Harper and Row, Publishers, 1951).
[57] Thomas Stearns Eliot, *Notes toward the Definition of Culture* (New York: Harcourt, Brace and Company, 1949); *Christianity and Culture: The Idea of a Christian Society and Notes Toward the Definition of Culture* (New York: Harcourt Brace Jovanovich, 1968).
[58] J. Gresham Machen, "Christianity and Culture," *Princeton Theological Review* (1913) 11:1-15.
[59] Ibid.
[60] Myers, *All God's Children and Blue Suede Shoes*, xvi.

otherwise spoken to than by authority. The whole of the created universe is the means by which the I-thou relationship of God and man is effected. ...When the matter is approached in some such form as this then we are frankly taking the Christian position for granted as true. We are not first starting from experience in order to prove the truth of the Christian religion from experience. If we did that then our position would ultimately fall into the same pit of rationalism-irrationalism in which modern thought is in its death gasp. In other words, it is the frankly authoritarian position of the triune God of Scripture from which we start in order then to show that unless we thus start there is no possible intelligibility in the scientific procedure. ...Such then, broadly speaking, is the philosophy of fact which the non-Christian scientist today assumes to be the only available view. It is composed of the two ingredients of utter meaningless contingency and of complete exhaustive rationalization. On both counts such a philosophy of fact would be destructive of the most basic concepts of the Christian religion. The idea of utter contingency means that God together with man is confronted with, or rather is immersed in, a bottomless and shoreless ocean of pure meaningless darkness. To use an expression from F. H. Bradley, we might say that on such an assumption there would be no positive character in any one fact in distinction from any other fact. Nor would there be any possibility of distinguishing any fact from any other fact. Only a Calvinist can account for the fact of counting. That is only a Calvinist can offer a basis on which counting makes any sense. And on the other hand, the matter of exhaustive rationalism means that man is in no sense dependent upon God for his knowledge; all knowledge is 'in' from all eternity. ... 'Nobody knows, but your hypothesis is wrong and ours is right.' That is the thing many a modernist says, in effect, if not in words, to the Christian believer. ...Modern science has to live from that which in its assumptions it negates. The Christian doctrine of revelation, of special and general revelation as interdependent, shows itself to be the only foundation of the possibility of science.[61]

There is no cogent and comprehensive explanation of culture apart from Christian presuppositions.[62]

While it is first of all necessary that the Christian and the preacher appreciate the proper place of culture in the Christian life, we must also appreciate the proper position of the unbeliever in culture. Despite his

---

[61] Cornelius Van Til, "Christianity and Scientific Effort," Address given to the Calvin College Alumni of the Chicago area, March 27, 1953 in CDRom *The Works of Cornelius Van Til*, (New York: Labels Army Co.) 1997.
[62] Cf. Van Til in Frame, *Apologetics to the Glory of God*, 70, 71, 89.

inconsistency with his presuppositions his cultural accomplishments are a gift of God, and must be appreciated as such. This does not mean, however, as the church has tended to do in our day, that these gifts are to be *uncritically* appreciated.

The Cultural Enterprise: God's World, God's Culture

In the beginning God created man to subdue the earth to His glory. The presence of sin introduced at the fall does not negate or diminish man's cultural calling. However vitiated his motives or distorted his cultural creations, he is by nature a cultural being. Every activity involved in exploring and exploiting the potentialities of the creation is a cultural activity. Culture "is regarded by Scripture as an extension of creation."[63] Ken Myers demonstrates the richness and complexity of this enterprise when he describes culture as "a dynamic pattern, an ever changing matrix of objects, artifacts, sound, institutions, philosophies, fashions, enthusiasms, myths, prejudices, relationships, attitudes, tastes, rituals, habits, colors, and loves, all embodied in individual people, in groups and collectives and associations of people (many of whom do not know they are associated), in books, in buildings, in the use of time and space, in wars, in jokes, and in food."[64] Henry Van Til offers a more distilled definition: "Culture, then, is any and all human effort and labor expended upon the cosmos, to unearth its treasures and its riches and bring them into the service of man for the enrichment of human existence unto the glory of God."[65]

In all of culture making the religious impulse is central. Where there is culture there is cultus. Since culture making *per se* is a human instinct rather than obedience to a command, since the fall, the term "cultural mandate" may be misleading. "Common cultural instinct" might be better. In Genesis 9:1-17 we see the Rainbow Promise of God to Noah of a continual Providential blessing on all people until the end of history. The theater of blessing and curse is common to all, until the redemptive program of God is fulfilled. Since the fall, only the believer understands his responsibility to engage in every activity in life for God's glory. For the believer the cultural mandate is still a command (Gen. 1:28). Only the Christian can take God's original design into account. "Although a given culture does form the individual man, nevertheless, man as cultural being precedes his culture and is the creator of culture. But religious faith is necessary to understand human destiny. And man in his faith is covenantally related to a Being that is transcendent, and, because of this covenantal relationship, which constitutes true religion, man has an eternal

---

[63] Myers, *All God's Children and Blue Suede Shoes*, 35.
[64] *Ibid.*, 34.
[65] H. Van Til, *The Calvinistic Concept of Culture*, 30.

destiny, which transcends culture. The meaning of life does not lie in culture as such, but culture derives its meaning from man's faith in God; it is never an end in itself, but always a means of expressing one's religious faith. ...Culture, then, may be either godless or godly, depending on the spirit which animates it."[66]

Cornelius Van Til has made a distinction that is crucial to our understanding of the interaction between the Christian and the fallen world in which God has placed him. "The absolute contrast between the Christian and the non-Christian in the field of knowledge is said to be that of *principle*. Full recognition is made of the fact that in spite of this absolute contrast in principle, there is relative good in those who are evil in principle and relative evil in those who are good in principle."[67] The presence of the Holy Spirit in all of the creative and cultural activities of fallen man accounts for what Reformed theologians have termed "common grace." In his commentary on Genesis 4:19 ff, Calvin notes that "the invention of arts, and of other things which serve to the common use and convenience of life, is a gift of God by no means to be despised, and a faculty worthy of commendation. ...Let us then know, that the sons of Cain, though deprived of the Spirit of regeneration, were yet endued with gifts of no despicable kind; just as the experience of all ages teaches us how widely the rays of divine light have shown on unbelieving nations, for the benefit of the present life; and we see, at the present time, that the excellent gifts of the Spirit are diffused through the whole human race."[68] This restraining influence in turn accounts for the continuation of history for the redemptive purposes of God.

"Common grace whose mercies are real while they last, provides the field of operation for redemptive grace, and its material too."[69] While the "holy culture" of Eden no longer exists, at the heart of redemptive revelation is the assertion of "holy culture" in the redemptive-historical acts of God. The Exodus produced a "holy nation." "The culture of Israel was intended to demonstrate the holy eschatological reality of God's rule, but human culture *as such* cannot do that because human beings *as such* do not submit to the rule of God."[70] The church is commanded to abandon this national project and disperse among the nations as ambassadors from the King who claims the whole earth as His dominion. In the mixed situation, we are called to

---

[66] *Ibid.*, 28, 23.
[67] Van Til, *The Defense of the Faith*, fn. 50, emphasis added.
[68] John Calvin, *Commentaries* (1540-1563. Translation and reprint. Edinburgh: Calvin Translation Society. 1847. Reprint (22 vols.). Grand Rapids: Baker Book House, 1969) vol. I:218, 219..
[69] Meredith G. Kline, *The Structure of Biblical Authority*. Revised Edition (Grand Rapids: William B. Eerdmans Publishing Company, 1975) 155.
[70] Myers, *All God's Children and Blue Suede Shoes*, 50.

appreciate the good cultural gifts of God and demonstrate their consecration to Him in Christ.

Fields of Conquest: The Academic Disciplines

As in every area of culture the Christian must engage in intelligent reflection on his/her participation. Those who are academically gifted should seek to bring every thought in their particular discipline(s) into captivity to Christ. Those without academic propensities or callings must beware of denigrating the place of academic work in the church. "What is today matter of academic speculation begins tomorrow to move armies and pull down empires."[71]

The propensity of modern scientific rationalism is to limit the use of the intellect to empirical investigation, whereas the tendency of Postmodernism is to denigrate the importance of rational thought and discourse altogether. The Christian mind has certainly fallen on hard times, as a number of recent pleas among Evangelicals indicate. Mark Noll has traced the marginalizing of the Evangelical mind in American academia, and wondered if there is an evangelical mind.[72] Imitating Allan Bloom's classic *The Closing of the American Mind*,[73] Ronald Nash has written *The Closing of the American Heart*, intimating a Biblical understanding of the word "heart."[74] Finally, Os Guinness in *Fit Bodies Fat Minds: Why Evangelicals Don't Think and What to Do about It*, lovingly lambastes the church for its folly in sanctifying its anti-intellectualism, and its failure to "think Christianly."[75] The church apes the very culture to which it is supposed to be an embassy.

In the seminary we would do well to heed the words of Machen: "Instead of making our theological seminaries merely centers of religious emotion, we shall make them battlegrounds of the faith,, where, helped a little by the experience of Christian teachers, men are taught to fight their own battle, where they come to appreciate the real strength of the adversary and in the hard school of intellectual struggle learn to substitute for the unthinking faith of childhood the profound convictions of full-grown men. Let us not fear in this a

---

[71] Machen, "Christianity and Culture."
[72] Mark A. Noll, *The Scandal of the Evangelical Mind* (Grand Rapids, MI: William B. Eerdman Publishing Co., 1994).
[73] Allan Bloom, *The Closing of the American Mind: How Higher Education Has Failed Democracy and Impoverished the Souls of Today's Students* (New York: Simon and Schuster, 1987).
[74] Ronald, Nash, *The Closing of the American Heart: What's Really Wrong With America's Schools* (Dallas, TX: Probe Books, 1990).
[75] Os Guinness, *Fit Bodies Fat Minds: Why Evangelicals Don't Think and What to Do About It* (Grand Rapids: Baker Books, 1994).

loss of spiritual power. The Church is perishing today through the lack of thinking, not through an excess of it."[76]

The Idols of Modernity: God's World, Full of Idols

The sociologist Peter Berger has made some helpful distinctions in seeking to defend the place of religion in sociology. In *A Rumor of Angels*[77] he describes the church in the context of secularization as a "cognitive minority". Such minority experiences "cognitive dissonance" as it encounters a general culture which does not share its assumptions about reality. The church either adjusts to the cognitive majority by revising its ideas or it defends itself against the general assumptions. The sociology of knowledge, which became familiar to the English speaking world as a discipline through the writing of Karl Mannheim in Germany in the 1920s, seeks to identify "plausibility structures" in terms of the "social networks and conversational fabrics" which reinforce ideas of what is credible and thereby legitimize them.

Berger maintains that the "pluralism of the twentieth century represents a competition among worldviews.[78] This, Berger asserts, is "the most important cause of the diminishing plausibility of traditional religions."[79] Thus sociologists who seek to relativize everyone but themselves need to take some of their own medicine. Unfortunately, Berger's own solution of seeking "signals of transcendence" capitulates to the very relativism he attempts to avoid. His arguments from: the propensity for order, play, hope, damnation, and humor suggest transcendent realities which should lead us in our everyday experience to an "openness to the mystery that surrounds us on all sides."[80] His "inductive faith" seeks to discover meaning in the particulars of experience. Here is the nub of the problem: "I would prefer an emphasis on 'discovery' as against 'revelation'."[81] "I see Christ as historically manifested in Jesus but not historically given ..."[82] Christ becomes a construct developed from the data of the history of religion as the "christian" moves forward in an evolution of self-understanding.

Thus Berger's diagnostic construct is more helpful for the Christian than his solution. He helps us to understand the hidden agenda of sociologists who claim to be objective observers of sociological realities, while surreptitiously

---

[76] Machen, "Christianity and Culture."
[77] Peter L. Berger, *A Rumor of Angels* (Garden City, NY: Doubleday-Anchor, 1969). What follows is a summary of the basic conceptions articulated by Berger.
[78] *Ibid.*, 53.
[79] *Ibid.*, 55.
[80] *Ibid.*, 94.
[81] *Ibid.*, 103.
[82] *Ibid.*, 115.

assuming the correctness of their own positions. In our sociological milieu it is important to appreciate how we are being perceived. Portius Festus, who was largely ignorant of Judaism and emerging Christianity, describes the dispute between the Jews and Paul's belief in the resurrection of Christ as "some questions against him about their own religion and about a certain Jesus, who had died, whom Paul affirmed to be alive" (Acts 25:19). Resurrection was completely outside of Festus's plausibility structure. Paul understood this when he preached in Athens. On the other hand when he spoke to the Jewish King Herod Agrippa II he asked "Why should it be thought incredible by you that God raises the dead?" (Acts 26:8).

Unlike the Fundamentalist who repudiates the entire cultural enterprise, the Reformed apologist seeks to understand culture, not because it makes good marketing sense, but because it is a God-given activity in God's world. The separatist ghetto approach is a tacit denial of God the Creator and of the cultural mandate he has clearly given man, and by which we are called to glorify God..

As Machen pointed out at the beginning of our century the "chief obstacle" to Christianity in our day "lies in the sphere of the intellect."[83] By this he meant something similar to Berger's "plausibility structures." It is not that the majority think things through, but their indifference to Christianity is "due to the intellectual atmosphere in which men are living." While removing the obstacles in that atmosphere is not in itself sufficient to convert people, "[u]sually He [God] exerts His power in connection with certain conditions of the human mind." "Yet the culture of today cannot simply be rejected as a whole. It is not like the pagan culture of the first century. It is not wholly non-Christian. Much of it has been derived directly from the Bible. There are significant movements in it, going to waste, which might well be used for the defense of the gospel. The situation is complex. Easy wholesale measures are not in place. Discrimination, investigation is necessary. Some of modern thought must be refuted. The rest must be made subservient. But nothing in it can be ignored. He that is not with us is against us. Modern culture is a mighty force. It is either subservient to the gospel or else it is the deadliest enemy of the gospel. For making it subservient, religious emotion is not enough, intellectual labor is also necessary. And that labor is being neglected. The church has turned to easier tasks. And now she is reaping the fruits of her indolence. Now she must battle for her life."[84] The Christian media critic must be willing to assess the atmosphere created by the electronic media and to discern to what degree the media themselves make Christianity implausible.

---

[83] Machen, "Christianity and Culture."
[84] *Ibid.*

This was precisely Paul's tack in Athens. He turned their own weapons against them.

A PARADIGM FOR COMMUNICATION

The paradigm articulated in this section will be considerably amplified in chapter 5. Here we will outline only the apologetic foundation. Let me clearly assert that whatever insights are gained from observations outside of the Scriptures, their validity must always be judged by criteria exegeted from the Scripture itself. The fundamental framework of Christian media understanding and criticism must arise from the text of Scripture. This is not to minimize the place of and importance of natural revelation, only to say that all knowledge based on a correct interpretation of that revelation must be in line with the standard of God's Word. With Calvin we look at nature through the "spectacles of Scripture."[85]

Idols for Destruction: No Neutral Ground

Man knows himself in relation to his environment. But God is pervasive in that environment. "God is man's ultimate environment..."[86] Man's very rational processes depend on the continual presence of the Divine Logos, who enlightens every person who exists (John 1:9). Man's rationality is at heart communicative. His development of modes of communication such as writing, printing, film and the Internet reflect his God-given instinct to be a communicator. Within the Trinity there is eternal communication among the three Persons. Adam was created to "receptively reconstruct" God's thoughts as a servant ruler in God's world. In sin man seeks to independently or "creatively construct" his own interpretation of God's world.[87] Thus all of his inventions are distorted by his rebellious intentions. The "Tower of Babel is a monument to man's use of culture to serve his idolatrous ends."[88] This "stairway to heaven" (Ziggurat) symbolizes his quest for meaning independent of God.

In assessing technology, especially communication technology, we are foolish to assume neutrality either in the use *or in the creation of* them. As we shall see, Marshall McLuhan's dictum "the medium is the message" points in the direction of criticizing the medium as well as its use. The tower of Babel

---

[85] Frame, *Apologetics to the Glory of God*, 23.
[86] Van Til, *The Defense of the Faith*, 42, 43.
[87] *Ibid.*, 48, 49.
[88] Myers, *All God's Children and Blue Suede Shoes*, 45

was in its essence idolatrous, and while all tower building is not idolatrous *per se*, that particular architectural creation was. Media of communication are not merely containers of messages but are messages in themselves, as they alter our perception of God and His world.

The *figure/ground* distinction in McLuhan is central to Van Tilian presuppositionalism. The *figure* is the content (visual, written) which is perceived by the right brain in "visual space". It is linear and sequential. This was the focus of the one-way Shannon Weaver model of communication. The *ground* is the medium (background) itself as a shaper of perception, and is simultaneous (auditory, electronic), synthetic, and is perceived in "Acoustic space."[89] The tendency of the latter is "discarnate man."[90] McLuhan observed: "The 'Laws of the Media' have been shaped by studying the effects of media, so there is always a hidden *ground* upon which these effects stand, and against which they bounce. That is, the law of a medium is a *figure* interplaying with a *ground*."[91]

Van Til's statement above that "idolatry is the caricature of true theophany and that divination or mantic is the caricature of true prophecy," is pregnant with significance for the Christian media critic. Idols and their divination, or the transcendent communication connected with them are media for communication, which distort the actual situation in God's world. If all technologies are "extensions of man" then they amplify his powers of lordship over creation. In sin every extension amplifies his potential for idolatry. While the idols of the pre-technological world were the handiwork of the metallurgist and lapidary craftsman, they extended man no less, both as images of their own would-be autonomous humanity and as cultivators of that humanity. Truly the medium was an essential aspect of the message. Man seeks to create his own meaning out of the materials and potentialities of creation. He is ultimate, and yet cannot live consistently with that benighted presupposition.

It is important to distinguish between the technology of a given medium from the medium itself. For example the technology of sculpting is itself not idolatrous. But it has its own spatial visual bias. When sculpting is used to fashion a golden calf as a medium of worship the intention of the sculptor and the group or culture for which he does his sculpting makes his creation a medium of idolatry. As we have said idolatry is a matter of the heart, a matter of intention. A sculptor may even create golden calves without the intention of idolatry, but in the hands of idolaters the sculpture becomes a medium of

---

[89] McLuhan, Marshall, "The Brain and the Media," in George Sanderson and Frank Macdonald, eds., *Marshall McLuhan: The Man and His Message* (Golden, CO: Fulcrum, Inc., 1989) 184.
[90] *Ibid.*, 185.
[91] McLuhan, Marshall, "The Laws of the Media," in Sanderson and Macdonald, eds., *Marshall McLuhan: The Man and His Message*, 206.

idolatry. As well someone may discover a golden calf which was originally created as a medium of idolatry and use it as a door stop. If he is living in a culture which might misunderstand his "innocent" use of the calf, Scripture directs him to be sensitive to the implications of his otherwise non-idolatrous use of the image. Paul instructs the Corinthians in 1 Corinthians 10 not to compromise with the idolatry of their culture. He lays down this principle: "All things are lawful for me, but not all things are helpful; all things are lawful for me, but not all things edify" (v. 23). If you buy food offered to idols in the marketplace, or eat the same at someone's house, don't ask questions, just enjoy it as unto the Lord (vs. 25-27). If someone tells you it was offered to idols then do not eat it for their sake, as a witness against idolatry (v. 28). Whatever you do it for God's glory (v. 31).

The "world," which in the Johannine sense is humanity dead in sin, lives in God's world as interlopers. The old dictum that Christians are "in the world but not of it" may leave the false impression that the created world has been abandoned by God and Christians are simply here waiting for the end, at which time we will become disembodied spirits. The eschatological picture is rather one in which we are preparing for the "new heavens and the new earth" by consecrating every human activity in anticipation of an eternity of service in our coming glorious bodily, historic state. The epistemology, the axiology and the ontology of the unbelieving media theorist and everyone effected by the media must be challenged by the Christian. Only the infinite, personal Trinitarian God of Scripture can give us true knowledge, meaning and an understanding of existence. Every other perspective lives from the "borrowed capital" of Biblical truth and must be exposed as such, in order to construct a Christian view of media and effectively preach the gospel in the Electronic Age.

The Gnostic Tendency: An Escape with a Twist

Throughout its history the church has been threatened by a competitor which claims to be Christian, but actually ends up subsuming Christianity under a very alien religion: Gnosticism.

Gnosticism (with a capital "G") of the second century represents a specific kind of philosophical religion with specific concepts. *Webster's New World Dictionary and Thesaurus* gives a succinct definition: "an occult salvational system, heterodox and syncretistic, stressing gnosis as essential, viewing matter as evil, and variously combining ideas derived especially from mythology, ancient Greek philosophy, ancient religions, and, eventually, from Christianity." The same dictionary defines *gnosis* (with a small "g") as "knowledge of spiritual things; especially, an esoteric, syncretistic, allegedly superior spiritual knowledge gained by self-illumination and limited to an elite few, like that the Gnostics claimed to have." What I shall call the *gnostic impulse* is the more general tendency characterized by the immanentism of post-Kantian thought. In his idolatrous tendency post-Kantian man seeks transcendence by creating a mental pseudo-transcendence.

The quest to escape reality as well as the quest to redeem it by the imposition of a Utopian scheme are both the outworking of the gnostic impulse. While the results of the escapist version, such as the Heaven's Gate cult, may be troubling, it is the latter expression which effects us more pervasively. The self anointed seek to impose schemes like Marxism on the benighted masses. The quest for perfection through a plan other than the historical plan of salvation revealed by God in His Word is the tendency of gnosticism. This is a quest to overcome the finite limits of creatures in space-time history. Never was a technology more suitable to such aspirations than Cyberspace.

The Electronic Revolution displays a strong tendency toward what Os Guinness calls "Cybergnosticism."[92] McLuhan feared that the great tendency of the global village would be "discarnate man. ...The discarnate TV user, with a strong bias toward fantasy, dispenses with the real world..."[93] In *Understanding Media* McLuhan observes: "Language as the technology of human extension, whose powers of division and separation we know so well, may have been the 'Tower of Babel' by which men sought to scale the highest heavens. Today computers hold out the promise of a means of instant translation of any code or language into any other code or language. The computer, in short, promises by technology a Pentecostal condition of universal understanding and unity."[94] "This reminds me of cyber-guru John Perry Barlow's keynote presentation a few years back in which he told an audience of on-line music marketing execs that 'If you want to understand what is really going on with the Internet, it's the transformation from monotheism to pantheism, almost overnight. The whole problem started with Abraham and we are only now in a position to overcome the destruction which he and his followers have wrought.'"[95] While we ought to balk at the blanket statement that the Internet is pantheistic, the tendency of the "medium of media" should be duly noted. There are recent examples within mainline Protestantism, as well as in the general culture, of the resurgence of ancient Gnosticism, with the "re-imagining" of God in the form of a woman and the popularity of the

---

[92] Guinness, *Fit Bodies Fat Minds*, 129.
[93] Marshall McLuhan, "A Last Look at the Tube," Sanderson, George and Macdonald, Frank, eds. *Marshall McLuhan: The Man and His Message* (Golden, CO: Fulcrum, Inc., 1989) 197.
[94] Marshall McLuhan, *Understanding Media: The Extensions of Man* (New York: McGraw-Hill Book Company, 1964) 80.
[95] Mark Stahlman, "Infinity," mediaecology@ube.ubalt.edu (14 Apr 1999).

writings of Elaine Pagels's *Gnostic Gospels* (1979). I do not think it is accidental that *The First Church in Cyberspace* is an invention of the Presbyterian Church in the USA, in which much of this re-imagining is going on.

Plundering Egypt: Just Tools

James Hughes in *The Church in Cyberspace* has stated that media are just tools. I have taken issue with that general idea. However, there is a sense in which media are "just tools." Hughes asserts: "We must resist 'silicon idolatry' and see the computer as only a tool, and not as our savior."[96] Media are not simply tools in that, while they are not inherently good or evil, they do change the way we interpret the world and relate to others, including God. However, they are tools in the sense that they are used in culture building. They are limited means to achieve certain tasks and goals. It may be better to say that media are finite means of asserting lordship over the creation.

Thus, by virtue of common grace, technology is created and developed by unbelievers. The Christian must neither accept these "tools" without understanding their tendencies nor reject them as "tools of the devil." He will rather "consecrate" them, not merely by using them for "Christian purposes," but by assessing and using them critically with awareness of the consequences as well as the results. In conceiving of media as tools there is also the danger of loving them as the works of our hands instead of fulfilling our mandate to cultivate the earth and communicate the glory of God through our technology.[97]

A key passage for our consideration at this point deals with the spiritual nature of the church's warfare. 2 Corinthians 10:3-6 teaches: "For though we walk in the flesh, we do not war according to the flesh. For the weapons of our warfare *are* not carnal but mighty in God for pulling down strongholds, casting down arguments and every high thing that exalts itself against the knowledge of God, bringing every thought into captivity to the obedience of Christ, and being ready to punish all disobedience when your obedience is fulfilled." In the previous verses Paul sets the tone of this warfare by calling the proud Corinthians to imitate the "meekness and gentleness of Christ." They were impressed by the wisdom of the world and needed to understand that the wisdom of God in the crucified and resurrected Christ is the only wisdom that can penetrate the "fortresses" (ὀχυρωμάτων) of idolatry. It is the truth of the Scriptures which demolishes the (λογισμοὺς) false reasoning and every proud

---

[96] James R. Hughes, *The Church in Cyberspace: The Coming Impact of the Computer on the Church*. [WWW document] URL http://www.reformed.com/pub/cyber.htm [9 September 1999].
[97] H Van Til, *The Calvinistic Concept of Culture*, summarizing Schilder, 61.

obstacle (ὕψωμα ἐπαιρόμενον) of the unbeliever which exalts itself against the knowledge of God. By constructing Babels with modern technological prowess, fallen mankind believes it can outsmart God. The Christian is to bring every thought (νόημα, design or plot), into captivity (αἰχμαλωτίζοντες) as a prisoner. This is the consecrating activity of the believer of which Machen spoke. Living in the flesh, that is in this fallen world, we are to bring every element of culture to the feet of Christ and use it in His service. This involves intellectual activity, thinking God's thoughts after Him, applying Scripture in a thoughtful way to every new invention, every technology, and every medium.

Paradigms are for People: Apollo and Dionysius

The organization of life and culture has been greatly aided by the Cartesian mentality. Rationality is ultimate. Mathematics and empirical science have worked technological wonders in the modern world. Newtonian physics viewed everything as mechanism, and, because there is divine order in God's world, the royal office of man may properly use this dimension of his image-bearing capacity to bring marvelous control to the created order. The recent modern/postmodern reaction to the Enlightenment and its rationality, however inaccurate its assessments or misguided its proposals, indicates the insufficiency of rationalism. Apollo is being radically challenged by Dionysius; Reason by Irrationality. The wise Christian thinker will choose neither and yet affirm aspects of each.

One of the great challenges to philosophy throughout its history has been to relate the world to our knowledge; to relate the particulars of experience to transcendent universals. Plato posited the ideal realm, but could not connect it with the particulars of creation. Aristotle constructed an elaborate system for understanding the particulars of the world, but ended with an Unmoved Mover. However, if we begin with God as He has revealed Himself in Scripture we may assume that he has made us as His image to interpret His creation, and that He has made His creation intelligible. Historically philosophers have constructed two basic theories in response to this problem of subject and object. *Coherence theory* seeks the logical consistency of the theory itself. Rationalism has used this theory to support its system. Philosophers such as Spinoza, Leibniz, Berkeley, Hegel have espoused various forms of this theory. Rationalists have properly recognized that without a prior interpretive structure of thought there can be no meaning to experience. Rationalists have failed to relate their internally coherent theory to the particulars. Empiricists, on the other hand, have sought to construct a *theory of correspondence* between the mind and the world by which all knowledge is based on experience. The problem with this theory is that the interpretive assumptions necessary to understanding cannot come from experience itself.[98]

Without entering the philosophical debate over this important issue, the Christian must assume some form of *coordination theory* which includes both correspondence and coherence. "God furnishes the rational structure of the world and of the human mind, so that the two structures are adapted to one another."[99] Ultimately perfect coherence is found only in the mind of God, and correspondence is the gift of His Spirit to Everyman (John 1). The covenantal nature of the relationship which God has established between Himself and man lies at the heart of our understanding of His world. As Francis Schaeffer has often said, we may know truly but not exhaustively. Since God has created and called mankind to cultivate the rich resources of His world to His glory, He has gifted us with the ability to discover the wondrous complexity of His world in order to develop its rich potential. Thus, we discover patterns or paradigms in order to make sense out of the world and manipulate it for the benefit of ourselves and others. Because of sin, this culture-creating instinct is perverted to bring glory to man, and thus much of what man does with God's creation is deeply destructive and alienating. We need to develop patterns of understanding in every endeavor of life. The thoughtful Christian must develop them through the lens of God's Word as he seeks to perceive the revelation in the structures of creation and culture in the fallen situation.

Paradigms are for Preachers: God's Word for His People and the World

The Christian apologist should be a joyful iconoclast like G. K. Chesterton, turning the weapons of unbelief back on the critics themselves. Several classic examples of this are noted in the observation of Richard Keyes: "Like someone held at gunpoint with his own pistol, Christians have been threatened and attacked for two hundred years on the basis of their own view of idolatry, turned against them. Such celebrated critics of the gospel as Karl Marx and Sigmund Freud based their debunking of religion on the insights that originally came from the Biblical notion. They claimed that religion was not true, but merely a projection of the believer. Curiously, however, now that these critics and their philosophies are themselves in bad shape, Christians have been surprisingly slow in reclaiming their own best weapon."[100]

---

[98] For an excellent discussion of this problem cf. John Frame, *Apologetics to the Glory of God: An Introduction* (Phillipsburg, NJ: Presbyterian and Reformed Publishing Company, 1994) Chapter 2, pp. 62-75; 133-144.
[99] Frame, *Apologetics to the Glory of God*, 24.
[100] Keyes, "The Idol Factory," 29.

The preacher who would serve his Lord wisely as a guide of the church will challenge unbelief in all of its dimensions. The world is the situation in which idols are constructed and in which the church is called to be a witness lamp (Rev. 1-3). The flesh is the internal problem of sinful rebellion and idolatrous allegiance. The devil is the master deceiver who coordinates the world and the flesh to achieve dominion over God's creation.

The Biblical perspective on unbelief and the preaching of the whole counsel of God, based on careful exegesis of Scripture, are the weapons of the wise preacher, who like Paul studies his audience at every level, out of a passionate desire to see God's Word penetrate to the center of ultimate allegiance. Paul understood the chief medium of classical communication: classical rhetoric. The wise preacher will expose the idols of his time by bringing them under the searching light of Scripture, and topple them with the preaching of Christ and Him crucified. He will understand the means of communication as a critical element in exegeting his culture. He will believe in the power of God to speak to this generation, and use the medium of live pastoral preaching in the historical presence of people made in God's image to bring sinners to repentance, and build a new servant-humanity after the glorious image of the Incarnate Son.

PART II

TOOLS OF HISTORY: THE HISTORY OF COMMUNICATION STUDY

3

Second Thoughts (Part I): A Brief History of Communication Study
Progressive and Scientific Theorists

> *Whether or not it draws on new scientific research,*
> *technology is a branch of moral philosophy, not of science.*
>
> —Paul Goodman, *New Reformation*[1]

Media theory and criticism is a relatively new academic discipline. Thus, recording and analyzing its development in a definitive way will be the task of future historians. The purpose of this chapter is to provide an overview of the intellectual roots of communication study, and the major communication theorists and critics, and the gist of their thinking in order to aid Christians in developing a more articulate and coherent view of the electronic media which are currently engulfing our culture at an astonishing pace. Furthermore, the historical perspective will lay the groundwork for my own assessment of the electronic media. First, however, we must seek to appreciate the thinking of the figures who make up this history on their own terms. Then, and only then, are we in a position to analyze and criticize them through the *paradigm of idolatry* and an *apologetics of fire*. I understand my contribution to this task as only a small beginning. Furthermore, I claim no originality in this historical summary. It is heavily referenced because much of the information comes from secondary sources. However, my interpretive perspective places this history in a new light. While not exhaustive, my representative approach is meant to give a fairly full picture to future students of this critical subject. I am aware of the number of thinkers omitted here. To

---

[1] Neil Postman, *Technopoly: The Surrender of Culture to Technology* (New York: Vintage Books, 1993) epigraph.

cover the entire history in an exhaustive way will be the lifelong work of a historian who is prepared to write a multivolume set.

Two important histories of communication study are Daniel Czitrom's *Media and the American Mind: From Morse to McLuhan* (1982), and Everett M. Rogers' *A History of Communications Study: A Biographical Approach* (1994). The latter is written from a perspective which minimizes what to my mind is the most important dimension of media studies: the context of humane learning, specifically the historical, sociological, epistemological and theological context of the media. Thus Rogers gives cursory and dismissive accounts of two giants: Harold Innis and Marshall McLuhan. Five pages are devoted to "The Technological Determinists" in the final part of the history which covers the establishment of communications study in the university. Jacques Ellul, Walter Ong and Neil Postman do not even merit passing reference. Rogers focuses on the scientific study of communications as it developed in American academia and the intelligence community during World War II. He admits as much in the introduction: "The history of communication study is the story of the social sciences, with important contributions from biology, mathematics and electrical engineering."[2] For Rogers the early history of communication study begins and ends with the consummate scientific theorist, Wilbur Schramm.[3] The obvious weakness of this history is that it almost totally ignores the place of communication study within the disciplines of the universities in which he accounts for them. Thus men like Ellul, Ong and Postman, who were not trained as scientists, but as liberally educated thinkers and teachers, have no place.

Czitrom's *Media and the American Mind* is a stimulating intellectual history which covers the contemporary response (essentially nineteenth century) to three seminal modern media: the telegraph, the cinema, and the radio. Czitrom goes on to chronicle three periods of theoretical assessment of modern communication (pioneers, empirical, and radical). In contrast to Rogers, Czitrom devotes over a quarter of his history to Innis and McLuhan. Czitrom was a student and disciple of Innis, as well as a student of James Carey. Carey's book *Communication as Culture*, while not a history, provides the foundation for much of Czitrom's work.[4]

Similar to the proper study of Biblical Theology we must read the text from the conclusion. So in Rogers's history he elucidates his bias in the final section: "The Communication Discipline Today". He opines, "Communication scholarship today is mainly empirical, quantitative, and focused on determining

---

[2] Everett Rogers, *A History of Communication Study: A Biographical Approach* (New York: The Free Press, 1994) xiii.
[3] *Ibid.*, xv.
[4] James W. Carey, *Communication as Culture* (Boston, MA: Unwin Hyman, 1989).

the effects of communication."[5] Critical of the limits of the statistical social science paradigm of communication study, due to its imitation of true science, Rogers sees the shift from qualitative to quantitative empirical research as a boon to the discipline. He does, however, note the existence of a small number of what he labels "critical communication scholars," who "do not buy into the dominant perspective of Schramm-type communication study."[6] Then Rogers make a perceptive distinction: "While mainstream communication scholars look mainly at 'what is,' critical scholars are more interested in 'what should be.'"[7] While acknowledging the existence of "a variety of theoretical and methodological perspectives," he concludes: "Nevertheless, the heart of communication study is still characterized by quantitative studies of the effects of communication."[8] It is telling that from the beginning of media study in this century the instinct was more critical than purely scientific. As technical science gained hegemony in academia the autonomous, atomistic bent of the rationalist mind gained temporary ascendancy. The Postmodern climate, it seems to me, may foster greater respect for the more global assessments of the likes of Ellul, Ong, McLuhan and Postman.

My approach in this historical survey unashamedly favors the global thinkers who self-consciously seek to understand the nature and effects of media in the context of humane studies, cultural criticism, and especially theological studies. The epistemological and historiographical issues at stake here are central to my thesis. An epistemology which defines reality or the discipline of communication study so as to exclude all but physical, psychological and limited sociological reality is unacceptable to the Christian. While many, if not most, of the media theorists and critics in this survey may not be personally committed to historic Christianity, they have cultivated their insights in the soil of humane learning, whether they acknowledge this or not, a soil which has been made fertile by Western Christianity for two millennia.

The individuals and schools which make up this history may be roughly distinguished among three groups of theorists: progressive, scientific, and critical. Unfortunately these three groups do not coincide with the three historical periods of the development of communication study. As was noted above there are several important thinkers who are not mentioned by Rogers. This is also true of Czitrom, who omits thinkers like Ellul and Ong, and because he ends his study with McLuhan (1982), does not cover the last several decades of history. I have chosen to proceed chronologically within each of the three thematic categories. The progressive and critical communication

---

[5] Rogers, *A History of Communication Study*, 491.
[6] *Ibid.*, 492.
[7] *Ibid.*, 493.
[8] *Ibid.*

theorists developed their thinking in the humane context, while the scientific theorists developed their thinking with the narrower purview of the physical and psychological sciences. These also tend to fall mainly within the period between 1930 and 1960.

EUROPEAN INTELLECTUAL ROOTS

The story of modern communication begins with the European Renaissance (1450-1600). The revival of learning, spawned by the rediscovery of the Greek philosophers, opened up an age of multidimensional discovery. Nothing was more monumental than Johannes Gutenberg's invention of movable type in 1457. Significantly the Bible was the first book printed by this new printing press. Hence McLuhan's *Gutenberg Galaxy*, a revolution in communication media equal to that caused by the astronomer Copernicus and his heliocentric universe. Through exploration, the expansion of trade and the rise of the middle class, learning spread throughout Europe at an unprecedented pace. The printed text individualized and nationalized learning thus undermining the Medieval ecclesiastical hegemony of Rome.

Carl Mitcham makes a strong case for Francis Bacon being the first to philosophize on the importance of science and technology in mastering nature.[9] Perhaps the first to use the term "philosophy of technology" was the German philosopher Ernst Kapp (1808-1896), who wrote *Philosophy de Technik*. Upon immigrating to Texas he saw the possibilities of technology overcoming "dependence on raw nature" by transforming time via linguistic linking power of "universal telegraphics" into "a global transfiguration of the earth and a truly human habitat."[10] Kapp was also the first to conceive of man's inventions as "organ projections", anticipating McLuhan's "extensions of man."[11]

The rise of the university within the Medieval Roman church provided the foundation for the development of learning during the Renaissance period. Rogers distinguishes among three "models" of university education: 1) *liberal arts university*, emphasizing undergraduate study as exemplified in Padua, Bologna, Göttingen, Berlin, Frankfurt, Heidelberg, Paris, Oxford, Cambridge, Harvard, the American Ivy League, and other early American universities; 2) *German research university*, emphasizing graduate study as exemplified in the University of Göttingen (founded in 1737), University of Berlin (founded in

---

[9] Samuel Ebersole, "Media Determinism in Cyberspace." http://regent.edu/acad/schcom/rojc/mdic.html (12 July 1999) noting Carl Mitcham, *Thinking Through Technology: The Path Between Engineering and Technology* (Chicago: University of Chicago Press, 1994).
[10] *Ibid.*, noting Mitcham, *Thinking Through Technology*, 23.
[11] *Ibid.*, 24.

PART I: PROGRESSIVE AND SCIENTIFIC THEORISTS   69

1820), and Johns Hopkins University (founded in 1876); 3) *vocational university*, emphasizing agricultural and engineering studies as exemplified in the land grant colleges established in America by the Morrill Act of 1862, such as the universities of Illinois, Wisconsin, Minnesota, Michigan State, Cornell and the University of New Hampshire. The latter category, especially in the Midwest, "played a key role in the diffusion of communication study in the United States."[12]

The more immediate European roots of communications study are found in the three thinkers who have been most influential in the twentieth century: Darwin, Freud and Marx. This nineteenth century trio may be seen as reductionists after the ancient Greek philosophical pattern which sought to explain reality by positing its simplest or most essential element after the formula: "All is ..." For example, for Thales, the first philosopher, all is water. As with these Greeks each of the Europeans was a monist, believing that created reality is ultimate. For Darwin all is natural selection: biology is ultimate. For Freud all is sexual repression: psychology is ultimate. For Marx all is class struggle: economics is ultimate. Each had an enormous impact on the social sciences as they developed in the late nineteenth century, and, therefore, on communication study as it emerged within the social sciences in America after 1900.[13] Each ultimately failed to find a unifying philosophy because they worshipped one aspect of the creation more than the Creator.

Charles Darwin (1809-1882)

Grandson of the famous English evolutionist and naturalist Erasmus Darwin, and the son of a physician, Charles came well by his love of natural science. Inherited wealth, a Cambridge education and the inspiration of his professor of botany, John Henslow, conjoined to make Darwin a "serious naturalist".[14] His theory of natural selection was not formulated until after his famed voyage on the *Beagle*. Intellectually he was influenced dramatically by Thomas Malthus's *Essays on the Principle of Population* (1797), which he read two years after his return on the *Beagle*. Adam Smith's *Wealth of Nations: An Inquiry into the Nature and Causes of the Wealth of Nations* (1776) taught Darwin the place of the "invisible hand" in the free enterprise theory of economics and the survival of the most industrious. Along with the well known influence of Sir Charles Lyell's evolutionary geology and Jean-Baptiste de Monet de Lamarck's theory of the inheritance of acquired characteristics, Darwin was influenced by the Belgian statistician Adolphe Quetelet who helped him understand Malthus's

---
[12] Rogers, *A History of Communication Study*, 38, 39.
[13] *Ibid.*, 34.
[14] *Ibid.*, 41, 42.

theoretical principle that while population grows geometrically the food supply only grows arithmetically.[15]

Most significant for our study is the influence of Auguste Comte (1798-1857), the French Pragmatist philosopher, known as the father of sociology. As early as 1839 he argued that sociology was a science.[16] Eliminating the metaphysics of Hegel he applied the Hegelian idea of historical development to the history of human understanding. Theological explanation for the particulars of experience was necessary in the nascent stage of this development. The adolescent stage of intellectual development was metaphysical abstraction. Finally, the human mind came to full evolutionary maturity by abandoning the empty quest for absolutes and affirming positive scientific law, hence, the term used to describe Comte's philosophy: Positivism. Due to the complexity of social phenomena, sociology is the last discipline to arrive at this stage.[17]

Comte's thought was the most global of the thinkers Darwin read as he was formulating his theory of evolution. It would appear that Positivism had a unifying effect on Darwin's thinking. Darwin's scientific theorizing took place in the context of a wide variety of disciplines. "Key to the formulation of Darwin's evolutionary theory were his wide reading and his ability to identify the analogies to biology from other scientific fields. Creating his theory was a highly social process, involving its gradual construction through interaction with the ideas of others, both through reading and extensive correspondence with scientific colleagues."[18] Certainly, then, part of the reason that Darwin's theory came to dominate every discipline within the western academy over the two decades after the publication of *On the Origin of Species* is the fact that he had gathered elements of his theory from a wide variety of disciplines. His extensive correspondence with some of the best minds of his day helped lay the groundwork for the acceptance of his ideas.

It was not until over two decades after the initial development of his theory that the reticent Darwin published the book which he knew would cause a furor: *On the Origin of Species, by Means of Natural Selection: Or the Preservation of Favored Races in the Struggle for Life* (1859). Despite Rogers's egregious omission of intelligent Christian responses to Darwin (he only refers to Wilberforce anecdotally and Bryant as the dupe of that great publicity stunt known as the Scopes Trial), perceptive theologians did not miss

---

[15] *Ibid.*, 53.
[16] *Ibid.*, 132.
[17] Gordon H. Clark, *Thales to Dewey: A History of Philosophy* (Boston: Houghton Mifflin Company, 1957) 498, 499.
[18] Rogers, *A History of Communication Study*, 53.

PART I: PROGRESSIVE AND SCIENTIFIC THEORISTS 71

the implications of Darwin's Positivism.[19] Charles Hodge (1797-1878), professor of Exegetical, Didactic and Polemic Theology at Princeton Theological Seminary, devoted thirty pages to Darwin's theory in his monumental three volume *Systematic Theology* (1872) under the rubric "Anthropology".[20] In "Theology Proper" Hodge spends eight pages dealing with the "Positivism" of Comte, which made up part of the philosophy at the foundation of Darwin's theory.[21] "The fundamental principle of the 'Positive Philosophy' is ... that the senses are the only source of our knowledge, hence nothing exists but matter. There is no mind distinct from matter; no such thing as efficiency; no causes, whether first or final; no God; no future state of existence for man."[22] Comte's claims for sociology as a science include not only the apodictic certainty of its conclusions but its eventual social dominance. Hodge quotes Thomas Huxley's pithy characterization of Positivism's aspirations: Positivism is "Catholicism *minus* Christianity".[23]

Sadly Hodge dismissed Comte's influence as a passing fad. Little did he realize the pervasive influence of scientific rationalism in the twentieth century. While he did recognize the strong influence of Darwin's theory on the public mind of his day, this too, he thought, was "for the time being".[24] Hodge expressed great respect for Darwin as "in the first rank of naturalists ... respected not only for his knowledge and his skill in observation and description, but his frankness and fairness."[25] But this did not change his assessment of Darwin's system as "thoroughly atheistic".[26] "The mere naturalist, the man devoted so exclusively to the study of nature as to believe in nothing but natural causes, is not able to understand the strength with which moral and religious convictions take hold of the minds of men. ...This is atheism to all intents and purposes, because it leaves the soul as entirely without God, without a Father, Helper, or Ruler, as the doctrine of Epicurus or of Comte. Darwin, moreover, obliterates all the evidences of the being of God in the world. ... Professor Huxley says that when he first read Darwin's book he

---

[19] *Ibid.*, 56-58. Rogers states that "According to the Book of Genesis, the earth was created in six days, and humans were created on the seventh day (sic)." Rogers needs to read his sources more carefully. Rogers also fails to record the intellectual unrest among scientists caused by genetic discoveries in biochemistry, which is presently resulting in a trenchant critique of Neo-Darwinism (Cf. Behe, *Darwin's Black Box*, Denton, et. al.).

[20] Charles Hodge, *Systematic Theology*, 3 vols. 1872 Reprint (Grand Rapids: William B. Eerdmans Publishing Company, 1975) vol. 2, 12-41.

[21] *Ibid.*, vol. 1, 254-262.

[22] *Ibid.*, 254.

[23] *Ibid.*, 261.

[24] *Ibid.*, vol. 2, 12.

[25] *Ibid.*

[26] *Ibid.*, 15. Hodge is quick to note that his assessment of Darwin's system as "atheistic" is not to say that Darwin is an atheist.

regarded it as the death-blow of teleology, i.e., of the doctrine of design and purpose in nature."[27] Hodge goes on to examine the theory in the details as an hypothesis.

To say that Darwin's thought was no passing fad is an understatement of huge proportions. "The Darwinian revolution constituted a radical restructuring of natural science that has had major repercussions outside the narrow confines of evolutionary biology, especially in the social sciences."[28] In a forgotten book, which was a best seller in its day, published soon after *The Descent of Man and Selection in Relation to Sex* (1871), *The Expression of the Emotions of Men and Animals* (1873), Darwin expounded a theory of nonverbal communication.[29] "Karl Pearson (1857-1936) and Darwin's first cousin Sir Francis Galton (1822-1911), key founders of the field of statistics, developed the techniques of chi-square test and correlation, respectively, in order to test Darwin's theory of evolution."[30] Galton went on to propound the Draconian theory of eugenics, "the improvement of the human race by encouraging reproduction by the most capable individuals and discouraging reproduction by the least capable individuals."[31] Despite the current rejection of Sir Herbert Spencer's (1820-1903) Social Darwinism he managed to put sociology on the intellectual and popular map, and fostered the application of evolution to social problems.[32] Rogers maintains that the relatively new discipline of "population ecology" (1970s) was developed along evolutionary lines in terms of the interrelatedness of groups in a larger system.[33] Most important in the direct line of the development of communication study the Chicago school of sociology was directly influenced by Darwin's thought.[34]

Thus for Darwinism, rooted as it was in Comte's Positivism, it is not so much a matter of explaining reality, but controlling it. If God has not spoken, because there is no one to speak, then man is on his own. Put in a more Pauline way, because man *wishes* to be on his own, i.e. autonomous, he will define God out of existence, or at least define Him in a way which will attempt to render Him powerless. All is natural evolutionary process.

---

[27] *Ibid.*, 15, 16.
[28] Rogers, *A History of Communication Study*, 59.
[29] *Ibid.*, 62.
[30] *Ibid.*, 59.
[31] *Ibid.*, 60.
[32] *Ibid.*, 62.
[33] *Ibid.*, 63.
[34] *Ibid.*, 64.

PART I: PROGRESSIVE AND SCIENTIFIC THEORISTS

Karl Marx (1818-1893)

No one has cast a longer or darker shadow over the present century than the German social theorist Karl Marx. He studied law at the University of Bonn and the University of Berlin, where he imbibed the Idealism of G. W. F. Hegel (1770-1831). At the University of Jena Marx earned his Ph.D. in philosophy, majoring in political economy.[35] With his assistant Friedrich Engels (1820-1895) he wrote *The Communist Manifesto* in 1848. The three volume *Das Kapital*, the first volume of which was written in 1867, was dedicated to Darwin.[36] Later on as Darwin's ideas became known throughout Europe, Marxists adopted Darwinism as a "sort of antidote to organized religion."[37] In reaction to Spencer's social Darwinism, which upheld the *status quo* of *laissez-faire* capitalism, Marx believed that social evolution needed revolutionary help from the underdogs of the working class. In Berlin Marx had abandoned his Lutheran religious background after studying the materialist Hellenistic philosopher Epicurus.[38] Ludwig Feuerbach (1804-1872) taught Marx to turn Hegel upside down, while retaining his dialectical historical method of analysis. Instead of the dialectical development of Universal Mind or Absolute Spirit Marx enunciated the dialectical development of class conflict. History is the dialectic of economic forces. Religion for Feuerbach, as with Marx, was a dangerous delusion, which disguises man's wishes in the face of uncontrollable natural forces. "Feuerbach regarded religion as a gigantic projection of man's own being, that is, as essentially man writ large. He, therefore, proposed reducing theology to anthropology..."[39] Thus Marx's famous assertion: "religion is the opiate of the people." Therefore, political power must be used to eradicate the church, and replace God with Humanity.[40] Anthropology and sociology become the central concerns of history. For Marx all is economic energy and conflict.

As a critical philosophy which sought to understand the present system of things in order to propose an alternative, Marxism proved a powerful force. At the center of that critique was the belief that "mass media belong to the superstructure of society, and that mass media content is dominated by social class relationships. The media reinforce the dominant values of society and are mainly antirevolutionary and antichange."[41]

---

[35] *Ibid.*, 104.
[36] *Ibid.*, 105.
[37] Koster, *The Atheist Syndrome*, 170.
[38] *Ibid.*, 163.
[39] Peter Berger, *A Rumor of Angels* (Garden City, NY: Doubleday-Anchor, 1969) 57.
[40] Clark, *Thales to Dewey*, 476, 477.
[41] Rogers, *A History of Communication Study*, 108.

Friedrich Nietzsche (1844-1900)

Raised in the home of a Lutheran pastor, Nietzsche rejected his Christian roots in a more radical way than anyone of his day. During his education in a Prussian boarding school, and at the universities of Bonn and Leipzig he was strongly influenced by the post-Kantian romantic philosophy of Arthur Schopenhauer (1788-1860). Along with Schopenhauer's misogyny Nietzsche imbibed his theory of the will. In reaction to the materialistic science of his day Schopenhauer posited the activity of will as the incomprehensible vital force of the universe.[42]

From 1869 to 1879 Nietzsche was professor of classical philology at Basel. Prior to his mental breakdown in 1889 he wrote several virulent attacks on orthodox Christianity and all traditional religious systems. *Thus Spake Zarathustra* (1883) sets forth his alternative gospel. As the "philosopher of evolution" he called man to reach beyond himself by asserting his will and becoming superman (*Übermensch*). More consistently atheistic than Darwin he challenged the notion of progress in humanity and the survival instinct as vestiges of Victorian Christianity. It is the creative *will to power* that is manifested in the random appearance of geniuses and supermen that makes nature worthwhile. While repudiating the romanticism of his former heroes Schopenhauer and Wagner, Nietzsche's concept of the *superman* is itself highly romantic and anti-intellectual. Germany will never be great until she repudiates Darwin's materialistic mistake and reaffirms the importance of "spirit".[43] Caesar and Napoleon imposed themselves on the chaos of history and are thus to be admired. Polytheism offers a relativism which cultivates the development of the individual.[44] In *Thus Spoke Zarathustra* Nietzsche proclaims:

> Behold, I teach you the overman. The overman is the meaning of the earth. Let your will say: the overman *shall be* the meaning of the earth! I beseech you, my brothers, *remain faithful to the earth*, and do not believe those who speak to you of otherworldly hopes! Poison-mixers are they, decaying and poisoning themselves, of whom the earth is weary: so let them go.
>
> Once the sin against God was the greatest sin; but God died, and these sinners died with him. To sin against the earth is now the most

---

[42] Clark, *Thales to Dewey*, 470.
[43] Walter Kaufmann, editor and translator, *The Portable Nietzsche* (New York: The Viking Press, 1954) 505ff, 522ff.
[44] Clark, *Thales to Dewey*, 492-498.

PART I: PROGRESSIVE AND SCIENTIFIC THEORISTS

dreadful thing, and to esteem the entrails of the unknowable higher than the meaning of the earth.[45]

With God dead the distinction between good and evil is meaningless and becomes a hindrance to the will to power. The title of Nietzsche's book *Beyond Good and Evil* (1886) says it all. The superman rises above the suffocating and arbitrary standards of nineteenth century Europe. In *The Gay Science* (1887) he boldly asserts:

> The greatest recent event—that "God is dead," that the belief in the Christian God has ceased to be believable—is even now beginning to cast its first shadows over Europe. For the few, at least, whose eyes, whose *suspicion* in their eyes, is strong and sensitive enough for this spectacle, some sun seems to have set just now. . . . In the main, however, this may be said: the event itself is much too great, too distant, too far from the comprehension of the many even for the tidings of it to be thought of as having *arrived* yet, not to speak of the notion that many people might know what has really happened here, and what must collapse now that this belief has been undermined—all that was built upon it, leaned on it, grew into it; for example, our whole European morality. . . .[46]

Nietzsche's ethics, as expounded in *The Twilight of the Idols* (1888), demonstrate his clear understanding of what was at stake and why a cultural sea change was coming "Christian morality ...stands and falls with faith in God."[47] The ethics of the superman are Dionysian:

> For it is only in the Dionysian mysteries, in the psychology of the Dionysian state, that the basic fact of the Hellenic instinct finds expression—its 'will to life.' What was it that the Hellene guaranteed himself by means of these mysteries? *Eternal* life, the eternal return of life; the future promised and hallowed in the past; the triumphant Yes to life beyond all death and change; true life as the over-all continuation of life through procreation, through the mysteries of sexuality.[48]

While not commenting on media *per se* Nietzsche's prescience regarding the autonomy of man the manipulator of every medium, sets the stage for the modern world, positing his god(s) within the framework of creation in the true spirit of ancient Paganism. That Adolph Hitler should find inspiration here is no surprise, since a deceased God leaves us only *The Will to Power*. And *The Will to Power* is only achievable by moving the masses. In *Mein Kampf* Hitler set forth his own theory of mass media: "Since the masses have only a poor

---

[45] Kaufman, *The Portable Nietzsche*, 125.
[46] *Ibid.*, 447.
[47] *Ibid.*, 516.
[48] *Ibid.*, 561.

acquaintance with abstract ideas, their reactions lie more in the domain of feelings, where the roots of their positive as well as their negative attitudes are implanted. ...Whoever wishes to win over the masses must know the key that will open the door to their hearts. It is not objectivity, which is a feckless attitude, but a determined will, backed up by power where necessary."[49]

Furthermore, he correctly valued the spoken word over the written or printed word, and thus he used the latter with great effect. Again in *Mein Kampf* he opines: "The force which ever set in motion the great historical avalanches of religious and political movements is the magic power of the spoken word. The broad masses of population are more amenable to the appeal of rhetoric than any other force." Sounding very much like a teacher of homiletics he goes on to say: the speaker "will always follow the lead of the great mass in such a way that from the living emotion of his hearers the apt word which he needs will be suggested to him and in its turn this will go straight to the hearts of his hearers." Emotional resistance is overcome not by argument, but by an appeal to the "hidden forces" in the audience.[50]

Otto Strasser, one of Hitler's most bitter critics, described the secret of his extraordinary power as a speaker: "I can only attribute it to his uncanny intuition, which infallibly diagnoses the ills from which his audience is suffering. ...His words go like an arrow to their target, he touches each private wound on the raw, liberating the mass unconscious, expressing its innermost aspirations, telling it what it most wants to hear."[51]

For Nietzsche all is will. In the hands of a superman with the right ideal to impose this can be a very dangerous concept, especially in the absence of truth. Modern communication study was born as a reflection on the enormity of Fascism, as we shall see.

Sigmund Freud (1856-1939)

Born in Freiberg, Moravia in 1856, Freud's family moved to Vienna in 1860 in order to escape the anti-Semitism ushered in by the revolution of 1848. His education took place in a Vienna full of new ideas. The Bauhaus movement of Walter Gropius sought an architectural aesthetic reflective of the new technology introduced by the Industrial Revolution. Arnold Schoenberg's twelve-tone music sought to revolutionize the classical music world. Moritz Schlick and Otto Neurath's famous Vienna Circle of Logical Positivists, which

---

[49] Alan Bullock, *Hitler: A Study in Tyranny*, revised edition (New York: Harper and Row, Publishers, 1962) 69.
[50] *Ibid.*, 71.
[51] *Ibid.*, 373, 374.

was heavily influenced by Ludwig Wittgenstein's *Tractatus Logico-philosophicus*, focused philosophy on the epistemology of language and logic.[52]

Freud studied medicine at the University of Vienna and in 1886 he began his own private practice in Vienna. The arch-materialist Prussian physiologist Ernst Brücke influenced Freud's rejection of the existence of soul and spirit in scientific investigation. Freud studied hypnotism and female hysteria with the Parisian physician Jean Martin Charcot for six months from 1885 to 1886.[53] As a specialist in neurology Freud, after several years in practice, began to see neurotic patients. He began to develop his theory of the unconscious. In 1896 he coined the term "psychoanalysis" as he developed his method of treating neurotic patients.[54]

Freud's most important book, *The Interpretation of Dreams*, published in 1899, most fully develops his idea that the repression of sexual desire is at the root of most emotional disturbances. The famous Swiss psychiatrist Carl G. Jung (1875-1961) was a friend and colleague of Freud's until their famous break over the theory of the unconscious caused by the publication of Jung's *The Psychology of the Unconscious* in 1912.[55] Jung, like Nietzsche, insisted that there is a spiritual dimension to life which Freud, who intensely rejected the Judeo-Christian *weltanshauung*, rejected. Freud reduced religious experience to wish fulfillment, and ended his writing career by writing *Moses and Monotheism* (1938), in which he sought to undermine the veracity of the Biblical account of Moses in the Exodus.[56]

Apart from powerfully contributing to the intellectual atmosphere which formed the foundation of the twentieth century western intellect, Freud contributed more directly to communication study through the influence of his theory of the unconscious on the University of Chicago sociologist Harold D. Laswell, the critical school through Frankfurt in the 1930s and 1940s, and to a lesser degree Carl I. Hovland.[57] The Palo Alto Group, influenced by its founder, Gregory Bateson, reacted to the individualist approach of Freud and developed a systems theory of epistemology based on cybernetics, which emphasized the centrality of individual and group interaction and its effect on behavior.[58] Bateson's *Communication: The Social Matrix of Psychiatry* (with Ruesch 1951) and *Steps to an Ecology of Mind* (1972) evince the

---

[52] Rogers, *A History of Communication Study*, 65. Cf. *The Encyclopedia of Philosophy*, 1st ed., reprint 1972, s.v. "Logical Positivism."
[53] John P. Koster, Jr. *The Atheist Syndrome* (Brentwood, TN: Holgemuth and Hyatt, Publishers, Inc., 1989) 110, 111.
[54] Rogers, *A History of Communication Study*, 71.
[55] *Ibid.*, 83.
[56] Koster, *The Atheist Syndrome*, 114, 118, 119.
[57] Rogers, *A History of Communication Study*, 65, 83ff.
[58] *Ibid.*, 87ff.

interdisciplinary influence on communication study, especially of the more critical kind.

Freud's severely materialistic approach to the human psyche reduced reality to impulses. Like Feuerbach and Marx he inverted the Hegelian dialectic and concluded that all is sexual energy. Though the particulars of his theories may be largely rejected today, his radical rejection of revealed religion in favor of empirical science has cast a long shadow over twentieth century psychology, anthropology, sociology and communication study.

The Critical School

This intellectual movement took its cue from the critical social theory of Marx and combined it with the psychology of Freud. It also dealt with avant-garde art and literature. It was established as the Institute for Social Research in Frankfurt, Germany in 1923. In the 1960s it was referred to as the Frankfurt School. Max Horkheimer, who became its director in 1930, advanced the "theoretical program now called 'materialism'." Scholars associated with this movement were: Theodor Adorno, Leo Lowenthal, Herbert Marcuse, Eric Fromm, Walter Benjamin, and Jürgen Habermas. The most important scholarly research publication, written by Adorno et.al., to come from this school was *The Authoritarian Personality* (1950), "a large-scale survey of prejudice funded by the American Jewish Committee." Their most famous publication was Marcuse's *One Dimensional Man* (1964). The latter made the school, especially Marcuse, popular in the American student movement of the 1960s.[59]

The critical school rejected Positivism as a reduction of social theory to a "value neutral" scientific observation of the facts, thus endorsing the status quo. As neo-Marxists the critical school deplored Stalinist tyranny and the idea that the proletariat would inevitably achieve a worker's paradise. Finally they critiqued capitalist society for its human exploitation.[60] From 1933 to 1950 the Frankfurt School moved to Manhattan to escape Hitler's Fascism, and became loosely affiliated with Columbia University. Thus they sought to explain the roots of Fascism through the critical apparatus of Freud and Marx. Eric Fromm used Freud's psychology to complement Marx's sociology and went on to write *Eros and Civilization* (1955), *The Art of Loving* (1956) and *Zen Buddhism and Psychoanalysis* (1960).

The critical school brought a very important distinction into focus. "Critical scholars think that the mass media are used by the establishment to

---

[59] *Ibid.*, 108-111.
[60] *Ibid.*, 113.

control society, while empirical scholars see the media as able to help ameliorate social problems..."[61] The interdisciplinary approach of critical scholars, is evinced by the fact that several of them have engaged in literary criticism. Thus the trajectory of the critical approach is toward assessing the effects of communication and our responsibility for those effects, whereas the empirical approach is more scientifically descriptive and progressive in its goals. Rogers notes that "the critical-empirical split is the strongest cleavage within the communication field today."[62] Czitrom claims that the exiled Frankfurt Institute for Social Research issued "the most developed critique of the empirical research approach."[63]

Albert Einstein (1879-1955)

Born German, Albert Einstein became a Swiss citizen in 1894. After professorships in Prague and Zurich he was invited by the Prussian Academy of Sciences to Berlin as a professor in the University of Berlin in 1914. The rise of National Socialism caused him to immigrate to the United States in 1933 and take up a lifelong position at the Institute for Advanced Studies in Princeton. In 1934, after the Nazis deprived him of German citizenship and confiscated his property, he became an American citizen.

The modest theoretical physicist little dreamed that his theories of Special (1905) and General Relativity (1915) would have such an enormous effect on the *Weltanschauung* of the twentieth century. "The modern world began on 29 May 1919 when photographs of a solar eclipse, taken on the island of Principe off West Africa and at Sobral in Brazil, confirming the truth of a new theory of the universe."[64] The well ordered world depicted by Newton's cosmology, with its straight Euclidean lines and Galileo's concept of absolute space, which formed the theoretical foundation the Enlightenment and the Industrial Revolution, was altered irrevocably. No verification of a scientific theory had ever had such a worldwide impact or influenced the general public as Einstein's concept of Relativity. Of course, never had there been such influential media. The newspaper, and the instant telegraphic information upon which it depended, had gained worldwide readership by the end of the nineteenth century. Philosopher Karl Popper of Vienna University was impressed by Einstein's insistence that his theory would be untenable should it fail certain

---

[61] *Ibid.*, 122.
[62] *Ibid.*, 123.
[63] Daniel Czitrom, *Media and the American Mind: From Morse to McLuhan* (Chapel Hill: University of North Carolina Press, 1982) 142.
[64] Paul Johnson, *Modern Times: The World from the Twenties to the Eighties* (New York: Harper and Row, Publishers, 1983) 1.

tests, and was not valid until verified by experimentation. Popper would become famous for his own insistence that unless a theory was open to falsification it was not following the proper scientific method.[65]

Einstein came to epitomize another of Popper's principles: "the law of unintended consequences." While his theory referred strictly to physical phenomena, in the thinking of most people "mistakenly but perhaps inevitably, relativity became confused with relativism. No one was more distressed than Einstein by this public misapprehension. ... Einstein was not a practicing Jew, but he acknowledged a God. He believed passionately in absolute standards of right and wrong."[66] What he hadn't reckoned with was the tidal wave of anthropocentric modernity which was overwhelming the new century. For all of his theoretical brilliance he was no theologian, and thus allied himself, perhaps unwittingly, with the major purveyors of the rising worldview. In 1933 he wrote *Why War?* with Sigmund Freud. In his latter years he was dismayed at the use which had been made of his theorizing: moral relativism and the atomic bomb. His example stands as a warning at the beginning of the electronic century, that "the law of unintended consequences" must be taken seriously, especially in communication study.

"Marx, Freud, Einstein all conveyed the same message in the 1920s: the world is not what it seems." After the First World War "The old order had gone. ...There were ...disquieting currents of thought which suggested the image of a world adrift, having left its mooring in traditional law and morality. ... Of the great trio of German imaginative scholars who offered explanations of human behavior in the nineteenth century [Marx, Freud, and Nietzsche] ...Marx described a world in which the central dynamic was economic interest. To Freud, the principal thrust was sexual. Both assumed that religion, the old impulse which moved men and masses, was a fantasy and always had been. Friedrich Nietzsche, ...was also an atheist. But he saw God not as an invention but as a casualty, and his demise as in some important sense as an historical event, which would have dramatic consequences." If the Christian God is dead then the vacuum must be filled. "The Will to Power" is the most likely candidate.[67] How prescient! We shall see as we continue our survey, how communication study can both foster and prevent the totalitarian instinct of our time. The Postmodern penchant to focus on surface structures as the ultimate and only reality, combined with the consequent "Will to Power" being the only ultimate authority left to fill the vacuum, requires the Apologetics of Fire to expose what lies beneath the surface.

---

[65] *Ibid.*, 3.
[66] *Ibid.*, 4.
[67] *Ibid.*, 11, 47, 48.

PROGRESSIVE THEORISTS

The larger American historical context of this survey is found in the intellectual developments of key movements and individuals as well as the establishment of several schools of communications study. The individuals selected below are related in different ways to these movements and institutions. European, and especially German, universities account for the largest intellectual influence up to the 1930s. Graduate study in Germany was an unspoken requirement for academic success, especially during the last three decades of the nineteenth century.[68] Hitler's rise to power meant the migration of the best European intellectuals to America. Nearly fifty percent of all academics left German universities, including forty eight percent of all social scientists.[69]

Especially important for communication study were Kurt Lewin, Paul Lazarsfeld and the entire Frankfurt School. The majority of social scientists settled in New York City. The Frankfurt School settled near Columbia University, and farther downtown the New School for Social Research became a haven for European scholars.[70] In sum this meant that the ideas of European theorists in the social sciences was transferred to North America. Among these were Auguste Comte (1798-1857) and his philosophy of Positivism; Emile Durkheim (1858-1917) and his pioneering work in sociological method *The Rules of Sociological Methods* (1895) considered the co-founder of modern sociology; George Simmel (1858-1918), the other co-founder of modern sociology, and very influential in the Chicago School; Gabriel Tarde (1843-1904), whose *Laws of Imitation* (1900) expounded diffusion and social learning theory; Max Weber (1864-1920), whose *The Protestant Ethic and the Spirit of Capitalism* (1930) posited the relationship between Protestant religious values and the rise of capitalism, and gave us the concepts of bureaucracy, role playing, ideal types, and charisma; and Wilhelm Wundt (1832-1920), who pioneered experimental psychology.[71]

The Chicago School

Due to its Baptist founders the University of Chicago was at its inception a typical late Victorian reformist institution. It was also a beachhead for the influence of German research institutions on American academia. Thus it is central to the development of communication study in America during that institution's golden era (1915-1935). Here social science was studied

---

[68] Rogers, *A History of Communication Study*, 129, 130.
[69] *Ibid.*, 131.
[70] *Ibid.*, 131, 132.
[71] *Ibid.*, 132-135.

empirically for the purpose of solving social problems. The Chicago theorists believed that "to be social and to be human was to communicate." Simmel's theorizing on the influence of the newspaper on public opinion was taken up by the Chicago School and paved the way for future mass communication research on the effects of media.[72]

Albion W. Small was recruited from Colby College in Waterville, Maine to found the department of sociology at the University of Chicago. He had pioneered the teaching of the subject and written an introductory textbook while at Colby. He studied at the universities of Berlin and Leipzig and purposed to promote the works of Simmel in order to build an outpost of German sociology. While Simmel's concept of urban ecology focused on fundamental intellectual analysis from a sociological perspective, later American sociology tended in the empirical direction of Durkheim and Weber.[73]

Charles Horton Cooley (1864-1929), under the influence of John Dewey theorized that "the mass media of communication could restore a sense of community." Cooley transformed Adam Smith's idea of the "looking glass self" into the concept that the individual mirrors and thus interacts with his environment: "I am what I think you think I am."[74] He sought to blend the understanding of the individual with his social context by promoting the idea of "primary groups" in order to influence "organized intelligence." For Cooley the history of communication is the foundation of all of history. His books *Human Nature and the Social Order* (1902); *Social Organization: A Study of the Larger Mind* (1909); and *Social Process* (1918); set forth the idea that that mass communication is the key to solving social problems. Cooley believed that mass media are capable of creating a democratic utopia because they are universal; they overcome the constraints of space and time; and they carry ideas and feelings to the masses.[75]

John Dewey (1859-1952) brought comprehensive theoretical power to the University of Chicago. Pragmatist Emile Durkheim (1858-1917), who reduced the categories of human thought to the sociological, influenced Dewey. William James (1842-1910), who helped import experimental psychology from Germany, and reduced religious experience to empirical reality, was a strong factor in Dewey's thought.[76] Both Dewey and James studied with the founder

---

[72] *Ibid.*, 137, 138.
[73] *Ibid.*, 149, 150.
[74] *Ibid.*, 153.
[75] Czitrom, *Media and the American Mind*, 93, 97-99.
[76] Clark, *Thales to Dewey*, 501. For James's influence cf. *The Encyclopedia of Philosophy*, 1st ed., reprint 1972, s.v. "John Dewey."

of Pragmatism, C. S. Peirce. Dewey, "the philosopher of democracy," chaired the Department of Philosophy, Psychology and Pedagogy. For him "the processes of science are the most obvious and successful methods of knowing."[77] Like his colleague, Mead, he rejected the mind-body dualism in favor of experience as the locus of meaning.[78] Science is the search for relations.[79] Value is the consequence of intelligent action, and as science discovers the proper means it may also establish the goals and norms, which are never fixed.[80]

Dewey opined, "Communication can alone create a great community." Dewey hoped that modern mass media, such as the newspaper, would provide the necessary glue to hold urbanized society together.[81] As a social activist, involved in the reformist enterprise of Hull House,[82] he believed that enlightened social workers and educators could create the "Great Community".[83] The experiential continuum is central to Dewey's democratic faith. In *Education and the Social Order* (1936) he opines, "Social planning can be had only by means approaching dictatorship unless education is socially planned."[84] The public school is the institution of social transformation. It will bring about a new social order "by making the method of intelligence, exemplified in science, supreme in education."[85] It comes as no surprise then that Dewey's 1928 visit to Russia left him impressed with the Marxist experiment. For Dewey the Christian belief in God as supernatural represented a surrender of true human endeavor. The distinction between saints and sinners is inimical to the process of democratization.[86] His egalitarian instinct would inform the next several generations of educators and sociologists. Dewey's thought had a powerful impact on communication study. Unifying the public in community requires the power of media. In *The Public and Its Problems* (1930) Dewey declared, "Our Babel is not one of tongues but of signs and symbols without which shared experience is impossible."[87] For Dewey the great society replaces the individual, and education is not a matter of content but of method.

---

[77] *Ibid.*, 519.
[78] *Ibid.*, 523.
[79] *Ibid.*, 525.
[80] *Ibid.*, 529.
[81] Rogers, *A History of Communication Study*, 158-164.
[82] *Ibid.*, 160.
[83] *Ibid.*, 163.
[84] Rousas John Rushdoony, *The Messianic Character of American Education* (Nutley, NJ: The Craig Press, 1979) 148, 150.
[85] John Dewey, *Experience and Education* (New York: The Macmillan Company, 1938) vi, 99, 100.
[86] Rushdoony, *The Messianic Character of American Education*, 157.
[87] Rushdoony, *The Messianic Character of American Education*, 159.

George Herbert Mead (1863-1931), son of a Massachusetts Congregational minister, studied at Harvard with William James (1842-1910) and Wilhelm Wundt (1832-1920) before spending thirty seven years teaching at the University of Chicago. His theory of "symbolic interactionism" posited the development of mind as purely a product of social interaction. Following the Pragmatism of James, Mead asserted that meaning is formed through interacting with and modifying the communication of others.

Robert E. Park (1864-1944) "best exemplified the Chicago School and can be considered the first academic student of mass communication."[88] Dewey's grand scheme for social reform was embraced with enthusiasm by his protégé. Park explored communication as an instrument of integrating society, especially the newspaper and telephone.[89] At Harvard he studied under William James and in Berlin under George Simmel. His doctoral dissertation entitled "The Crowd and the Public" (1904), distinguishes between *the crowd* and *the public*.[90] He began teaching in Chicago in 1913 and "elevated the Chicago department into international prominence, forging a new type of empirically based social science.[91] His "mapping" of social problems came to be known as "human ecology", and was conducted along Darwinian lines of thought.[92] Park altered the aims of the school by focusing on objective research, and separating it from the applied field of social work.[93] Such empirical research should be done independent of the researcher's personal moral values.[94]

As the "first theorist of mass communication" Park wrote his only book, *The Immigrant Press and Its Control* (1922). Mass communication is a "social-psychological process" in which humans connect on the basis of instinct rather than moral reason.[95] *The Introduction to the Science of Sociology* (1924), written with Ernest W. Burgess, became the Bible of early American sociologists.[96] Park distinguished between *referential* and *expressive* forms of communication. *Referential* communicates ideas and facts, while *expressive* communicates attitudes, emotions and sentiments. Park found the *expressive* use of modern media troubling, and especially found the cinema "demoralizing". His hope was founded on his dialectical approach to

---

[88] Rogers, *A History of Communication Study*, 156.
[89] *Ibid.*, 174.
[90] Czitrom, *Media and the American Mind*, 114, 115.
[91] Rogers, *A History of Communication Study*, 179.
[92] *Ibid.*, 180.
[93] *Ibid.*, 186.
[94] *Ibid.*, 187.
[95] *Ibid.*, 189, 190.
[96] *Ibid.*, 195, 196.

communication development, by which after a period of competition and conflict, accommodation and assimilation took place.[97]

The Chicago School declined as sociologists tended to focus more on the positive social phenomena of social status and work, rather than on social problems. Furthermore, the method of sociology began to imitate the natural sciences as quantitative and statistical.[98] However, Chicago provided a framework for future communication study which is relevant today. It maintained that communication is more than the exchange of information. Communication creates and maintains society. Thus the interrelationship of public opinion and the mass media was cultivated by the Chicago School to be a fertile field for exploration.[99]

The interdisciplinary character of the Chicago school helped foster the "Interpretive" approach in communication study since the 1960s. Rather than view the receiver of communication as merely passive as a subject of manipulation, the Interpretive School explores the nature of the active participation of the receiver as a constructor of meaning—"a full partner in the communication process."[100] This approach has provided a healthy corrective to the more mechanistic methodology of the quantitative scientific theorists, who developed their technique in the milieu of wartime propaganda study as we shall see.

Lewis Mumford (1895-1988)

While not a communication scholar, Lewis Mumford has contributed significantly to the larger context of communication study as an historian of technology and as a cultural critic. The perspective of the cultural historian which he brought to bear on the development and use of technology was ground breaking in the thirties, but naturally follows from the learned interdisciplinary context from which communication study arose. I have placed Mumford among the progressive theorists because Mumford believed technological advance, including media, would lead to a better society.

Born in Flushing, Long Island, New York, Mumford became a lecturer at the New School for Social Research in New York City in 1925, and at Dartmouth College from 1931 to 1935. During his tenure at Dartmouth, Mumford wrote his classic history and assessment of technology *Technics and Civilization*. This work established Mumford's reputation as a major cultural

---
[97] Czitrom, *Media and the American Mind*, 116-119.
[98] Rogers, *A History of Communication Study*, 192, 193.
[99] *Ibid.*, 196.
[100] *Ibid.*, 200, 201.

historian. As an editor he worked on *Dial* and *The Sociological Review* and *The American Caravan*. As an educator he was a member of the Board of Higher Education in the City of New York in the thirties and the Commission on Teacher Education of the American Council on Education from 1938 to 1944.

In *Technics and Civilization* Mumford divides the historical development of technology into three epochs: eotechnic (middle ages), paleotechnic (industrial revolution), neotechnic (present day with emphasis on science). Although Mumford warned of the regressive possibilities of mechanized culture, his evolutionary view of history, "leading to a 'kind of superior *machina sapiens*',"[101] together with his democratic ideals,[102] lead to a sanguine assessment of man's ability to harness the powers of technology for the good of civilization.

Written over thirty years after *Technics and Civilization*, *The Myth of the Machine* (1966) is more pessimistic in light of the military use of atomic energy. Mumford distinguished between two types of technology: polytechnic and monotechnic. Polytechnic is a diversity of technologies serving mankind in various capacities. Monotechnic is the domination of mankind by technology. The megamachine is a "rigid, hierarchical social organization" whereby large numbers of human beings are organized to perform a task with the precision of a machine, as in the building of the pyramids and the fighting of the two World Wars.[103]

Mumford's reflection on the history and uses of technology provides a helpful context in which to consider the specific development of communication technologies.

SCIENTIFIC THEORISTS

"The shift from the philosophical approach and subjunctive mood of the Progressive media theorists coincided with a larger trend toward empirical analysis within American social science."[104] The focus shifted from studying the use of media to effect society to studying the effects of media on society and the individual. Czitrom identifies four areas of research by the empirical researchers. 1. Propaganda research emerged after World War I as a reflection

---

[101] W. Rybczynski, *Taming the Tiger: The Struggle to Control Technology* (New York: Penguin Books, 1983) 16, in Ebersole, "Media Determinism in Cyberspace."
[102] James W. Carey, *Communication as Culture* (Boston, MA: Unwin Hyman, 1989) 186, in Ebersole, "Media Determinism in Cyberspace."
[103] C. Mitcham, *Thinking Through Technology: The Path Between Engineering and Technology* (Chicago: University of Chicago Press, 1994) 43, in Ebersole, "Media Determinism in Cyberspace."
[104] Czitrom, *Media and the American Mind*, 122.

PART I: PROGRESSIVE AND SCIENTIFIC THEORISTS   87

on the massive propaganda efforts of both sides in that conflict. 2. Public opinion research grew out of the larger concern for the effects of mass media on society at large. 3. Social psychology was used for the first time in studying the effects of modern media. 4. Marketing research emerged as a powerful new discipline using consumer surveys to determine market response and need.[105]

Harold Lasswell (1902-1978) - *Propaganda Analysis*

Born in Donnellson, Illinois, his father was a Presbyterian minister and his mother a high school teacher. While trained as a political scientist Lasswell's wide ranging intellect explored psychoanalysis, social psychology, sociology, history and communication.[106] His eclectic approach was not well received during his early career, as he attempted to integrate Marx and Freud. In *Psychopathology and Politics* (1930) he explored two types of political leader: the agitator and the administrator, thus founding the field of political psychology.[107]

Lasswell cut his teeth on the discipline which became his métier, propaganda analysis, when he did his doctoral dissertation on World War I propaganda, under his mentor at the University of Chicago, Charles Merriam. The definition of propaganda was reduced, as a result of its manipulative use during the war, to its pejorative connotation. Public disillusionment with use of propaganda by both sides prompted scholarly investigation into its effects during the 1920s and 30s.[108] Lasswell defined *propaganda* as "the management of collective attitudes by the manipulation of the significant symbols." He concluded that "propaganda is one of the most powerful instrumentalities in the modern world."[109]

Lasswell came into his own with his appointment as chief of the Experimental Division for the Study of War-Time Communication in the U.S. Library of Congress during World War II. This project had grown out of the Rockefeller Foundation Seminar on Mass Communication (1939-1940).[110] During the war Lasswell both analyzed and created propaganda.[111] His *content analysis* proved to be his most lasting and memorable contribution to communication study. While his analysis of World War I was quantitative, his

---

[105] *Ibid.*, 123-125.
[106] Rogers, *A History of Communication Study*, 204, 206.
[107] *Ibid.*, 207, 208.
[108] *Ibid.*, 210, 211. The original meaning of propaganda was to propagate an idea (Latin "to sow"). Thus persuasion in a positive sense. Preaching is a form of persuasion which intends the good of its hearers, while propaganda is mass persuasion which intends the good of the persuader.
[109] *Ibid.*, 213.
[110] *Ibid.*, 219.
[111] *Ibid.*, 224.

technique in World War II was decidedly more quantitative and statistical.[112] This objective approach is summed up in his epigrammatic formula for one way communication: "*Who* says *what* in *which channel* to *whom* with *what effects*?" "This became the dominant paradigm defining the scope and problems of American communications research."[113] The obvious weaknesses of this model are: the absence of the question "why"; and its focus only on the effects of communication.[114] "The omission of the 'why' from the series of questions reflected an unwillingness to investigate issues concerning which social groups controlled the messages communicated through the media."[115] The epistemological and hermeneutical dimensions of communication became the concerns of the next generation of theorists.

As a project consultant for the Stanford University think-tank the Hoover Institution on War, Revolution, and Peace, Lasswell promoted the development of policy sciences as a means of resolving political and social problems unique to modern society. Lasswell acknowledged John Dewey's inspiration on this subject.[116] The integration of sociological knowledge with public action should alert us to the dangers noted throughout this historical sketch along Orwellian lines.

Walter Lippmann (1889-1974) is a figure closely associated with Lasswell's work. Rogers asserts that "Lippmann is undoubtedly the most influential non-academic intellectual influence on communication study."[117] If not *the* most influential, he was certainly *one of the most*, especially early in this century. He was urbane, a world traveler, and the confidant of kings and presidents. The consummate journalist, he was editorial writer for the influential liberal *New York World* from 1921 to 1931, and a nationally syndicated columnist from 1931 until his retirement in 1967. Lippmann, like many of his intellectual peers, studied under William James at Harvard and was deeply impressed by Freud's *The Interpretation of Dreams*. He was an active Socialist in his early years, sharing Lasswell's interest in Marx. During World War I he wrote many of the front-line propaganda pamphlets which Lasswell analyzed.[118]

Lippmann's most significant book, *Public Opinion* (1922), distinguishes between an event ("the world outside") and the mass media depiction of the event ("pictures in our heads"). James Carey considers this book to be the

---

[112] *Ibid.*, 213.
[113] *Ibid.*, 221.
[114] *Ibid.*, 221, 223.
[115] Czitrom, *Media and the American Mind*, 132.
[116] Rogers, *A History of Communication Study*, 228, 229.
[117] *Ibid.*, 233.
[118] *Ibid.*, 234, 235.

founding text for communication study.[119] Lippmann should really be counted among the *Critical Theorists* (see below). Propaganda results from the efforts of a group to create an intended barrier between an event and the public. *Stereotypes* help organize and simplify complex realities for public consumption. Mass media gatekeepers thus create a *pseudo-environment*. Daniel Boorstin was the first to use the term "pseudo-event" to describe the intentional creations of the mass media.[120] Lippmann's concept, no doubt, grew out of Freud's influence.[121] Lippmann's sense of responsibility for this insight led him to believe that "experts could serve as the saviors of American democracy by conveying their expert knowledge widely, so as to inform public opinion." His 1925 book *The Phantom Public* was not sanguine about the possibility of the public's salvation.[122]

More recent research, which grew out of Lippmann's notion of the media's *agenda setting*, has yielded McCombs-Shaw content analysis. Moving from the earlier idea that media informs to its persuasive intention McCombs (1938-) and Shaw (1936-) discovered that media set the agenda for what people think about. Content analysis of media presentation combined with polls and surveys to determine public perception demonstrated a +.98 correlation.[123] Hence the politics of consensus follows from the formula: Media agenda setting → Public agenda setting → Policy agenda setting.[124] This research has proved a Copernican Revolution in mass media communication study.[125] Thomas Kuhn in his epoch making (1970) work *The Structure of Scientific Revolutions* states that "science employs paradigms as organizing concepts in guiding research."[126] When enough scientists observe enough evidence that doesn't fit the conventional wisdom a "crisis" occurs. As crisis gives way to a new or revised paradigm it again takes on the characteristics of what Kuhn calls *normal science*. Thus Lippmann moved beyond the one-sided paradigm of Lasswell and helped create the revolution in communication study that gave birth to Media Ecology.

Paul F. Lazarsfeld (1901-1976) - *Mass Communication Effects*

Born in Vienna, Lazarsfeld was raised in a home which was a center for Viennese intellectuals, socialist politics and Freudian thought. Another eclectic

---

[119] *Ibid.*, 233.
[120] *Ibid.*, 236, 237.
[121] *Ibid.*, 234.
[122] *Ibid.*, 236, 237.
[123] *Ibid.*, 237-243.
[124] *Ibid.*, 239.
[125] *Ibid.*, 240, 243.
[126] Phillip E. Johnson, *Darwin on Trial* (Washington, DC: Regnery Gateway, 1991), 118.

intellect, he became the founder of modern communication research and created the idea of the university research institute. He earned his Ph.D. at the University of Vienna in mathematics, writing his dissertation on the relationship between Einstein's theory of gravitation to the movement of the planet Mercury. He used his love of mathematics to develop a quantitative sociological methodology.[127] Lazarsfeld placed himself within the European humanistic tradition of the analysis of "action" (*handlung*). But unlike pure behaviorism this tradition took human consciousness, motivation and external influences into account.[128]

In 1925 Lazarsfeld founded the Research Center for Economic Psychology in Vienna. In 1936, fleeing Hitler's rise, he founded the Research Center of the University of Newark in New Jersey. In 1937 he directed the Office of Radio Research at Princeton University. In 1939 the Office of Radio Research moved to Columbia and later became the Bureau of Applied Social Research. He eventually became the chair of the department of sociology and Quetelet Professor of Social Science. Lazarsfeld pioneered radio audience investigations of human response by developing "question-and-interviewing" design along with "cross-tabulation." He used market research as a means of funding his methodological research, and thus became a friend of government and business alike. He influenced Theodor Adorno's important study of prejudice, *The Authoritarian Personality* (1950).[129]

Lazarsfeld's work in radio research is most important to our subject. He began his investigation fifteen years after the first commercial radio station, KDKA in Pittsburgh, was founded by Westinghouse Corporation in 1920. Hitler's minister of propaganda, Josef Goebbels, used radio effectively for the Nazi cause. American advertising agencies and Roosevelt's use of radio during the Great Depression, all fostered the development of mass communication research in the 1930s. Rockefeller Foundation official John Marshall (1903-1980) spearheaded the Radio Research Project and coined the term "mass communication" in 1939. He viewed radio as an instrument for cultural improvement.[130] Lazarsfeld brought his expertise to the interpretive dimension of radio research, in the methodology of studying the effects of radio on the audience. With Frank Stanton he developed the Lazarsfeld-Stanton Program-Analyzer, with which "like-dislike" responses were electronically recorded. Along with this device reaction, questionnaires were filled out and focus group discussion regarding the reasons for likes and dislikes were held.[131] The

---

[127] Rogers, *A History of Communication Study*, 246-250.
[128] Czitrom, *Media and the American Mind*, 127.
[129] Rogers, *A History of Communication Study*, 253-255.
[130] *Ibid.*, 265-270.
[131] *Ibid.*, 275.

development of focus groups is perhaps Lazarsfeld's most enduring legacy. David Sills observes, "The Lazarsfeld Radio Research Project virtually created the field of mass communication research."[132]

Another important dimension of Lazarsfeld's contribution is his quest to engage theorists in the problem defining stage of applied research. While he failed in his attempt to collaborate with the cultural intellectual Theodor Adorno, he both influenced Adorno's work on prejudice, and established a long working relationship with the social theorist Robert Merton. This combination of inductive theoretical rigor and systematic empirical investigation went a long way to ameliorate the disdain of theorists for applied research.[133]

In 1944 Lazarsfeld published his first famous book, *The People's Choice*, in which he investigated the impact of radio broadcasts on voters in Erie County, PA during the 1940 presidential election. Conceptually, this book was important because it upended the old idea of the one-sided influence of mass media. The "refined survey approach revealed the complexities of the persuasion process as it operated in society."[134] It was discovered that people persuaded other people, and the effect of mass media was almost nil.[135] In the end Lazarsfeld framed future research in his book, co-authored by Elihu Katz, *Personal Influence: The Part Played by People in the Flow of Mass Communication* (1955). This discovery "lead researchers to construct the 'two-step flow' model of communication effects."[136] Lazarsfeld observed what he discovered, while critics, such as sociologist C. Wright Mills, author of *The Power Elite* (1956), were interested in theoretical criticism as a means of effecting radical social change.[137]

In another critical area Lazarsfeld's research uncovered an important thread in the nature of media effects. The Kate Smith War Bond drive, promoted by CBS in 1943, demonstrated the power of feigned personal concern in identifying with, and manipulating a mass audience. From this research Merton developed the concept of pseudo-Gemeinschaft (feigned personal concern), which is related to the idea of "para-social interaction," "the degree to which an individual perceives a mass medium as being like an interpersonal relationship."[138] More recent research on soap operas has confirmed this insight.

---

[132] *Ibid.*, 279.
[133] *Ibid.*, 280-284; 304-308.
[134] Czitrom, *Media and the American Mind*, 134, 135.
[135] Rogers, *A History of Communication Study*, 285-289.
[136] Czitrom, *Media and the American Mind*, 135.
[137] Rogers, *A History of Communication Study*, 296-298.
[138] *Ibid.*, 307, cf. fn.

In 1940 Lazarsfeld published *Radio and the Printed Page*. This book consolidated the field of market research as it dissected the radio audience according to demographics, income, education, income, etc. Lazarsfeld was candid in stating the motivation for radio broadcasting: "Broadcasting in America is done to sell merchandise."[139]

"The Lazarsfeld-Merton team became one of the most effective and important collaborations in the history of their field, raising Columbia sociology to a dominant status in the nation."[140] While Lazarsfeld concentrated on research into the one-way effects of mass communication at the micro-level, it would be left to another generation to consider the two-way interactive effects of media like the telephone, as well as the privatized dimension of that medium. Even more important would be exploration at the macro-level of the context(s) in which media function.[141]

Kurt Lewin (1890-1947) - *Group Dynamics*

Born in Mogilno, East Prussia (now Poland) Lewin earned his Ph.D. at the Royal Friedrich-Wilhelms University of Berlin in 1914. Under the influence of Gestalt psychology, he studied individual perception and learning, seeking to understand the forces which lead to individual action. The Gestalt emphasis on the context of perception led Lewin to focus on the dynamics of group behavior, the group being the field or context of individual action in that group. "Field Theory" in his psychology was borrowed from physics.[142] This change in focus came about after Lewin's migration to America in 1933 due to the anti-Semitism in Nazi Germany. Hitler's rise caused him to have an intense interest in prejudice, authoritarian leadership and group influence. He left Germany earlier than most due to scholarly contacts made beginning at the International Congress of Psychology at Yale in 1929. Pavlov, Piaget and Clark Hull were among those early acquaintances. In his new land he would become one of the founders of social psychology. Group dynamics was based on the idea that "Membership in a group is part of the 'ground' upon which a person stands."[143] After a stint at Cornell, Lewin became a member of the faculty at Iowa in the Iowa Child Welfare Research Station. Eventually the Psychology Department chairman Kenneth Spence's behavioristic preferences moved Lewin to MIT in 1945 to head the Research Center for Group Dynamics within the Department

---

[139] Czitrom, *Media and the American Mind*, 130, 131.
[140] *Ibid.*, 245, 246.
[141] *Ibid.*, 314.
[142] *Ibid.*, 317-321.
[143] *Ibid.*, 323, 324.

PART I: PROGRESSIVE AND SCIENTIFIC THEORISTS   93

of Economics and Social Sciences.[144] His carefully-constructed and controlled experiments in leadership style reinforced his natural tendency to the democratic. Divided into three main groups, authoritarian, democratic and laissez-faire, the experiments demonstrated that the low degree of control of democratic leadership was the most productive, with the authoritarian style being the least productive.[145]

Lewin viewed his own field theory of group dynamics as an alternative to the prevailing S-R (stimulus-response) theory of behaviorist Clark Hull of Yale. Hull in turn was influenced by Pavlov. His concept of "gatekeepers" has proved seminal in communication theory. The one who controls the flow of information through a medium ("channel") dictates the shape and content of messages. This concept has been particularly fruitful in mass communication study.[146] His long-standing interest in business management led to his criticism of Taylor's "time-and-motion" theory of factory management in his book *The Socialization of the Taylor System* (1920). He argued for worker participation as a means of humanizing the factory system and thus increasing production. In 1939 he was able to verify his "worker participation" theory at the Harwood Pajama Factory.[147] Lewin's group psychology research centered around the concept of *cohesion*. He discovered that group expectations often strengthen individual achievement. The negative effect of groupthink, which leads to negative results, was not explored by Lewin.[148] Lewin's group dynamics has lead to the study of communication networks.[149]

Leon Festinger (b.1919), a Lewin student, is considered by some to be the father of experimental psychology. While at Stanford's Center for Advanced Study in the Behavioral Sciences he wrote his famous book, *Cognitive Dissonance* (1956) in which he developed the idea that *dissonance* is "the degree to which an individual faces to conflicting cognitive elements." The concept arose from the study of a doomsday cult.[150] Sociologist Peter Berger has made helpful use of this concept in assessing the marginalization of transcendence in modern thought.[151]

Group dynamics became a trendy social movement in the sixties with its "T-groups" (training groups), "encounter groups" and "sensitivity training".[152]

---

[144] *Ibid.*, 326, 327.
[145] *Ibid.*, 330, 331.
[146] *Ibid.*, 335-337.
[147] *Ibid.*, 339-341.
[148] *Ibid.*, 343.
[149] *Ibid.*, 344, 345.
[150] *Ibid.*, 350-352.
[151] Cf. Peter Berger, *A Rumor of Angels* (Garden City, NY: Doubleday & Company, Inc., 1969).
[152] Rogers, *A History of Communication Study*, 353, 354.

Carl Hovland (1912-1961) - *Persuasion Research*

Born in Chicago in 1912, Hovland received his Ph.D. from Yale under the behaviorist scholar Clark Hull (1884-1952). The Institute of Human Relations had been developed with Rockefeller Foundation funding, in order to provide a unified theory of behavior as the basis for legal and medical training. Hull focused the interdisciplinary approach of the Center on human motivation. His own training in Pavlov's theory of conditioning and the functional behaviorism set the tone of the school.[153] Hovland drew upon Hull's behaviorism and Freudian psychoanalytic theory to develop his intentional communication theory of persuasion.[154] During World War II he did extensive controlled research on the effects of the film series *Why We Fight* on soldiers' motivation. Out of this work Hovland pioneered the MLA (message-learning approach).

Due to his highly controlled experiments, the application of this approach is not as effective in mass communication. In addition, Hovland continued to promote the one-way communication idea, one which has obvious limitations in two-way situations.[155] Hovland's persuasion theory yielded several important insights. High-credibility sources tend to greater immediate attitude change, except as the source is forgotten over time (the "sleeper" effect). Messages which present only one side of an argument are more effective with less educated audiences. Strong group attachment makes persuasion less likely. Stating a conclusion at the end of an argument is more persuasive than leaving it implicit. When persuasion involves those who are being persuaded they are more likely to be convinced.[156]

Norbert Wiener (1894-1964) - *Cybernetics*

Born in Missouri in 1894, Wiener was raised in the intense intellectual atmosphere of a Cambridge, Massachusetts home dominated by his father, who was a professor in the Department of Slavic Languages and Literature at Harvard University. A child prodigy, young Norbert went to Tufts at age eleven and received his Ph.D. from Harvard at the age of eighteen in 1913. He went on to Cambridge University on a two-year fellowship to study mathematical philosophy with Bertrand Russell, who had just co-authored *Principia Mathematica* with Alfred North Whitehead. He also became interested in types, paradox, and Einstein's theory of relativity. After study in the University of Göttingen, he studied with John Dewey at Columbia University. In 1919 he

---

[153] *Ibid.*, 358-361.
[154] *Ibid.*, 361, 362.
[155] *Ibid.*, 384, 385.
[156] *Ibid.*, 380, 381.

PART I: PROGRESSIVE AND SCIENTIFIC THEORISTS 95

began teaching mathematics at MIT, remaining there for the remaining forty-five years of his brilliant career.[157]

Wiener developed his interest in the concept of *feedback* and systems design during his World War II research on improving the timing of antiaircraft fire. The theoretical result would become his famous *Cybernetic Theory*, the theory of self-regulating systems. "Feedback allows a source gradually to self-correct the effectiveness of a series of messages, making them closer and closer to what is needed to accomplish their intent."[158]

Cybernetics theory is a holistic view of systems, focusing on the interrelationship of the many parts. It presents a paradigmatic alternative to the reductionist linear approach of classic physics. However, Wiener was skeptical about the application of cybernetics from machine-machine or human-machine relationships to the social sciences. Human relations are more complex than these. Nonetheless Systems Theory came to pervade all fields of science, mass media, and popular jargon within a decade. German biologist Ludwig von Bertalanffy, who wrote the influential *General Systems Theory: Foundations, Development, Applications* (1968), founded the Society for General Systems Research with economist Kenneth Boulding in 1954. Systems theory applied to living beings shows that they are interrelated to other systems and thus considered open (negentropic), as opposed to closed systems (entropic) whose energy gradually dissipates.[159]

The ten Macy Foundation Conferences (1946-1953) on cybernetics allowed Wiener's influential theory to affect a wide number of disciplines within the social and biological sciences. Gregory Bateson took what he learned and developed the "interactional communication" viewpoint in the Palo Alto group. Watson and Crick would use cybernetics to discover the structure of DNA molecule. Anthropologist Margaret Mead and mnemonics expert Heinz von Foerster were among the key participants in the conferences.[160]

Wiener himself was multidisciplinary in his interests. Along with his classic *Cybernetics: Or Control and Communication in the Animal and the Machine* (1948) he wrote *The Human Use of Human Beings: Cybernetics and Society* (1950); *God and Golem, Inc.: A Comment on Certain Points Where Cybernetics Infringes on Religion* (1964); along with two autobiographies.[161]

As America's most famous mathematician Wiener single-handedly transformed MIT from a technological to a theoretical mathematical institution,

---

[157] *Ibid.*, 388-391.
[158] *Ibid.*, 394-399. *Cybernetics* is from the Greek meaning "steersman".
[159] *Ibid.*, 406-410.
[160] *Ibid.*, 401-405.
[161] *Ibid.*, 399, 405.

and thus one of America's most important research universities.[162] Wiener has had a considerable influence on Media Ecology. "*The Human Use of Human Beings* (1950) was required reading in the first year (1971) of Postman and Nystrom's Media Ecology doctoral program."[163]

Claude E. Shannon (1916-2001) - *Information Theory*

Born in 1916 in Petosky, Michigan, Shannon cut his teeth on the technological toys of his day: erector sets and radio kits. After earning undergraduate degrees at the University of Michigan in electrical engineering and mathematics, he earned his Ph.D. in mathematics, assisting Vannevar Bush with his mechanical computer, the differential analyzer machine, at MIT in 1940.[164] He integrated his knowledge of Russell's symbolic logic and Boolean mathematics and applied it to electric circuitry for his Master's thesis. Then at Bell Labs, while studying postdoctoral mathematics at Princeton, Shannon realized that the thermodynamic formula for *entropy* (the degree of uncertainty or disorganization of a system) was identical to the formula he had developed to quantify information. During World War II he continued at Bell Labs and turned his attention to cryptography (an early interest inspired by Edgar Allen Poe's *The Gold Bug*, 1843); and antiaircraft gunfire.[165]

In 1948 Shannon was encouraged by his colleagues to publish his formulations, which he did in the *Bell System Technical Journal*. This was the first publication of information theory. A year later Warren Weaver convinced Shannon to publish his two journal articles with Weaver's non-mathematical explanation as part II. The resulting *The Mathematical Theory of Communication* "is one of the most widely selling academic books published by a university press."[166]

"From the beginning he [Shannon] claimed that his model did not apply to human communication, the type of information exchange in which an individual interprets the meaning of a message." Shannon insisted, "The semiotic aspects of communication are irrelevant to the engineering aspects."[167]

---

[162] *Ibid.*, 391,392.
[163] Strate, Lance. "Norbert Wiener." owner-mediaecology@ube.ubalt.edu (26 Feb. 1999). It should be noted that the 1954 edition of *The Human Use of Human Beings* is considerably revised.
[164] Rogers, *A History of Communication Study*, 419, 420.
[165] *Ibid.*, 420-423.
[166] *Ibid.*, 425.
[167] Cf. Pennings, Anthony. "Norbert Wiener." mediaecology@ube.ubalt.edu (26 Feb 1999) "Weaver was with the Ford Foundation and helped pushed the publication of Shannon's ideas. As with many scientific breakthroughs, it was taken up by all kinds of laymen as a simplistic panacea to complex social problems. It's seemingly non-ideological stance made it quite popular at a time when researchers wanted a research strategy with non-political research problems on one side of the research equation and minimal interpretation of results on the other.

Weaver, however, "invited the wide application of Shannon's information theory to all types of intentional communication."[168]

Bell Labs, where the revolutionary transistor had been invented in 1949, was principally interested in electronic systems, especially telephonic. Shannon developed the concept of the "bit" (short for "binary digit") which is the basis for all computer programming since the Hollerith (IBM) card. He was "concerned with increasing the channel capacity of communication systems, specifically of telephone systems."[169] Shannon's model of SMCR (source-message-channel-receiver) provided a common set of concepts to a new generation of students and scientists, known as the "transmission model of communication." David K. Berlo's *The Process of Communication* (1960) became the standard university textbook to convey these concepts during the 1960s and early 1970s. "The theory became a milestone in communication research and marked the transition from an industrial to an information society."[170]

Thus Popper's law of unintended consequences took theorists far beyond Shannon's theory of *"signal* transmission" to make it a full blown *communication* theory, providing a fundamental paradigm for emerging communication study. Shannon's work became part of the impetus for the development of the first communication research institutes and doctoral degree granting programs in American universities.[171]

The self-acknowledged limits of Shannon's information theory, which, with few exceptions, have pervaded academia's communication study departments, need to be re-evaluated along lines which only the discipline of Media Ecology can provide.

Wilbur Schramm (1907-1987) - *Communication Study*

Wilbur Schramm was born in Marietta, Ohio. He was graduated summa cum laude from Marietta College in history and political science in 1928.[172] He

---

Shannon was aware of this which was why he was hesitant to publish. But I guess it was an idea whose time had come (or was allowed). Shannon made an impressive contribution to the analysis and optimization of relay switching circuits. His statistical communication theory allowed the separation of noise from the information carrying signals, creating a system to evaluate communication channel efficiency.

Although a truly outstanding contribution to the telecommunication networks we all use today, his ideas are less impressive outside the engineering field. In human communication systems, 'noise' is generally a good thing. It's sometimes called 'democracy'."

[168] Rogers, *A History of Communication Study*, 426-428.
[169] *Ibid.*, 412-414.
[170] *Ibid.*, 416-418.
[171] *Ibid.*, 438-442.
[172] *Ibid.*, 3.

received his MA from Harvard University in American Civilization in 1930. His favorite professor was the philosopher, Alfred North Whitehead. He went on to earn his Ph.D. at the University of Iowa in English literature in 1932. His problem with stuttering motivated him to pursue postdoctoral work in the Psychology Department on the emerging field of communication study. He studied with Carl Seashore, who had been impressed first hand by the work of Wilhelm Wundt at the University of Leipzig.[173]

As an assistant professor of English from 1935 to 1942 he directed the Iowa Writers' Workshop, as part of a growing interest in journalism as a means of communication. He participated in Kurt Lewin's regular informal discussion group known as "the "Hot Air Club".[174] His interest in writing put him in touch with poet Archibald MacLeish, who lectured at the University of Iowa. As Librarian of Congress, MacLeish was appointed director of the Office of Facts and Figures. Soon after the bombing of Pearl Harbor, Schramm wrote to MacLeish and volunteered his services, anticipating the importance of communication in the war effort. MacLeish appointed him as OFF's educational director.[175]

Schramm became part of a fortuitous connection of social scientists which would launch the field of communication study. European immigrant scholars Lewin, Lazarsfeld and Adorno, were thrown together with U.S. scholars Hovland, Lasswell, Wiener and Shannon. The war effort precipitated the government creation of three research agencies loaded with social scientists: Research Branch of the Division of Information and Education of the U.S. Army; the Surveys Division of the Office of War Information; and the Division of Program Surveys of the U.S. Department of Agriculture. Consultants like Lazarsfeld worked among them. Schramm wrote speeches for Roosevelt's radio broadcasts.[176] The need for public information, foreign intelligence and propaganda created the soil out of which the new field of communication study grew after the war. "Mass communication research began in the Library of Congress in 1942."[177]

After the war Schramm returned to the University of Iowa with a vision to found a new field of communication study. He began as director of the School of Journalism to fulfill his vision. He initiated the first Ph.D. program in a school of journalism. Because Schramm was forced by circumstances to develop the communication field within an extant department, communication study has ever since been divided into mass communication and interpersonal

---

[173] *Ibid.*, 5-7.
[174] *Ibid.*, 8-10.
[175] *Ibid.*, 13, 14.
[176] *Ibid.*, 10-13.
[177] *Ibid.*, 16.

communication. The latter was inaugurated later, separately in the Department of Speech and Dramatic Arts at the University of Illinois.[178]

The teaching of journalism was born at the dawn of the twentieth century at the University of Wisconsin under the auspices of Willard G. "Daddy" Bleyer (1873-1935). He sought to establish this new discipline by aligning it with sociology, so that reporters would understand the context of what they were reporting.[179] The University of Iowa School of Journalism was established in 1924. One of its early instructors was George H. Gallup (1902-1984), who founded the Quill and Scroll Society. Journalism was becoming a respected academic discipline.[180] It is intriguing that although the prestige Ivy Leaguer universities were forerunners of communication study in conducting the first research, they refused to institutionalize the emerging discipline at the doctoral level. The first Ph.D. programs in mass communications were established at the large land-grant universities in the Midwest and at Stanford in the 1940s and 1950s. The only exception to this is the school of journalism at Columbia, endowed by Joseph Pulitzer. Most of these had been students of Bleyer.[181] The establishment of research institutes along with most of these departments insured interdisciplinary flexibility.[182]

George Stoddard (1897-1981) invited Schramm to found the first degree granting academic unit called "communication" at the University of Illinois in 1947, the Institute of Communications Research. Schramm was also the first to write textbooks for the new field; the first to award Ph.D. degrees in communications; and the first "professor of communication."[183] Stoddard's interest in world government and Keynesian economics lead to his dismissal in 1953. This caused Schramm to move to Stanford in 1955 and become the chairman of the newly formed Department of Communication and Journalism. He was also appointed director of the Institute for Communication Research. This "highly interdisciplinary" institute dominated the field of the study of mass communication effects until 1970.[184]

It is important to note that this emerging scientific theoretical approach to communication study was not immediately well received by many journalists, who emphasized the skills of reporting, writing and editing. Ultimately, however, the quantitative statistical approach won out with the advent of

---

[178] *Ibid.*, 17, 18, 450.
[179] *Ibid.*, 18-20.
[180] *Ibid.*, 23.
[181] *Ibid.*, 25, 26, 477.
[182] *Ibid.*, 26, 27.
[183] *Ibid.*, 444-448.
[184] *Ibid.*, 455-460.

polling and market research. Journalists realized that polls results were themselves news.[185]

Schramm's most influential books reveal the bias of his research emphasis on the effects of mass communication rather than on the nature of the media themselves: *The Process and Effects of Mass Communication* (1954); *Mass Media and National Development* (1964). His most influential book, written with Jack Lyle and Edwin Parker, was *Television in the Lives of Our Children* (1961). Schramm's gifts as a scholar, organizer, motivator and writer put the field of communication study on the map in academia, bringing psychology, sociology and political science into a new and powerful interrelationship. Communication study transformed speech departments from the "humanistic study of rhetoric toward a scientific analysis of interpersonal communication."[186] By the 1990s almost every major university had a school or department of communication.[187] Due to its continued alignment with journalism and speech departments, however, communication study remains largely an applied field, with little purely theoretical research; and it remains divided between mass communication and interpersonal communication.[188] Rogers maintains that consequently "A doctoral student who wishes to study communication, rather than mass communication or interpersonal communication, has almost no place to go ..."[189]

Almost, but not quite. Rogers has not accounted for the school which combines mass communication and interpersonal communication studies, and places them on a new and more comprehensive theoretical footing: The Critical Communication Theorists known as Media Ecologists.

---

[185] *Ibid.*, 460-463.
[186] *Ibid.*, 477, 478.
[187] *Ibid.*, 479.
[188] *Ibid.*, 480, 481.
[189] *Ibid.*, 494.

4

Second Thoughts (Part II): A Brief History of Communication Study
Critical Theorists

> *Today, in the electronic age of instant communication, I believe that our survival, and at the very least our comfort and happiness, is predicated on understanding the nature of our new environment, because unlike previous environmental changes, the electric media constitute a total and near instantaneous transformation of culture, values and attitudes.*
>
> —Marshall McLuhan, "A McLuhan Mosaic"[1]

Just as mass communication study emerged from departments of journalism, and interpersonal communication study emerged from departments of speech and drama, so Media Ecology emerged from departments of English literature. Media Ecology, however, never transformed or replaced a department and thus has struggled to find its place in the American academy. As we shall see the unique perspective which literary criticism, and humane studies in general, bring to communication study demands a very different account of media: their nature, place and value in our culture, as well as our relation to and responsibility for them. Czitrom uses the label "radical theorists." This is certainly accurate because Media Ecologists such as Innis and McLuhan probed the *root* (Lat. *radix*) of the matter. I prefer McLuhan's term *ecologists*, however, because, while it includes dealing with the *why* of media, it also includes the larger idea of managing our discoveries of

---

[1] in George Sanderson and Frank Macdonald, eds., *Marshall McLuhan: The Man and His Message* (Golden, CO: Fulcrum, Inc., 1989) 1.

the nature and effects of media. Media Ecology deals with the all-important homiletical question: "So what?" *Stewardship* of what we discover is the issue. Furthermore, Media Ecology assumes the broader cultural and historical criticism which make up not only the context in which media function, but the context for their ecology as well. This was the vision of Marshall McLuhan, to whom we owe the coining of the term.[2]

During the entire development of communication study from 1930 to 1960, the dominant ideas of mass-society and mass-communication were challenged by numerous critics, who were then like voices crying in the wilderness. Even among Progressive and Scientific theorists there was evidence that the concepts of mass-society and mass-communication were suspect. Charles Horton Cooley's Hawthorne studies in the 1930s demonstrated the importance of interpersonal relationships within social groups.[3] Paul Lazarsfeld's study of the 1940 presidential election demonstrated the power of personal influence over mass media. In 1953 Eliot Friedson argued that the use of media is usually part of group activity. In 1960 Joseph Klapper set forth a series of "emerging generalizations" based on his review of empirical research in *Effects of Mass Communication*. Klapper maintained that mass communication is not a necessary and sufficient cause of audience effects. Media function in the context of many other mediating influences. In 1961 Leon Bramson traced the history of the theory of mass society in European and American social thought, challenging its scientific basis and its socio-political assumptions.[4] As far back as 1939 sociologist Robert Lynd had asked the unsettling question: "Where are our institutions taking us, and where do we want them to take us?"[5]

The Frankfurt Institute for Social Research, as we have seen in chapter 3, maintained a sustained critique of the empirical approach, by insisting on the study of the cultural matrix of communication and the duty of giving direction to social change. Social research must be done within a moral and historical context. Theodore Adorno's failed attempt to work with Paul Lazarsfeld illustrates the fundamental theoretical split between the empirical and critical approaches. "Adorno resisted the pressure to transform cultural phenomena into quantitative data." Adorno reflected: "When I was confronted with the demands to 'measure culture,' I reflected that culture might be precisely that

---

[2] Marshall McLuhan, "At the Moment of Sputnik...," in Sanderson and Macdonald, eds., *Marshall McLuhan: The Man and His Message*, 71.
[3] Daniel Czitrom, *Media and the American Mind: From Morse to McLuhan* (Chapel Hill: University of North Carolina Press, 1982) 136.
[4] *Ibid.*, 136-139.
[5] *Ibid.*, 141.

condition that excludes a mentality capable of measuring it."[6] In its general concern for social context, value and meaning this school paved the way for Media Ecology. In the context of these concerns Media Ecologists turned their attention to the nature of the media themselves, rejecting the dominant theory that media are mere conduits of information, and insisting that media change patterns of communication and thus are themselves a "hidden ground" or environment.

THE CRITICAL COMMUNICATION THEORISTS: FOUNDERS OF MEDIA ECOLOGY[7]

Martin Heidegger (1889-1976)

Born in Baden, in Germany's Black Forest, Heidegger, the son of a Roman Catholic sexton, enrolled in the University of Freiburg to study theology with the intention of becoming a priest. Soon, however, he became passionate about philosophy, and that became his lifework.[8] As a student of Edmund Husserl he adopted the phenomenological methodology. He became Privatdozent at the University of Freiburg in 1915, professor at Marburg in 1923, and finally professor at Freiburg in 1928. His major work, *Sein und Zeit* (1927) was translated into English in 1962 by J. Macquarrie and E. S. Robinson as *Being and Time*,[9] in which he famously asserted, in good Post-Kantian fashion, "Ontology is possible only as phenomenology."[10] Heidegger was profoundly influential on twentieth century philosophy. His work laid the foundation for theologians Paul Tillich and Rudolph Bultmann, and inspired existentialist Jean-Paul Sartre. Heidegger "firmly denied that he was an existentialist."[11] He believed that the question of "being" was the central philosophical problem. Few, he maintained, profit from the *Angst* caused by the contemplation of their nothingness. Mass-man (*Massenmensch*) "is so entrenched in the banalities of

---

[6] *Ibid.*, 142-146. Theodor Adorno quote, "Scientific Experiences of a European Scholar in America." In *The Intellectual Migration: Europe and America, 1920-1960*. Donald Fleming and Bernard Bailyn, eds., (Cambridge: Harvard University Press, 1969) 347.

[7] It should be noted that my use of the category of "Critical Communication Theorists" is not the same as Rogers' category of the "Critical or Frankfurt School" as summarized above. I have used Roger's category "Critical Communication Theorists" to help distinguish the two; I have not used his more limited, and I think somewhat pejorative, category "Technological Determinists" which he applies to Innis and McLuhan.

[8] Merrill Sheils, "Being's End," *Newsweek* (7 June 1976).

[9] *The Encyclopedia of Philosophy*, 1st ed., reprint 1972, s.v. "Heidegger, Martin."

[10] Cornelius Van Til, *The New Modernism: An Appraisal of the Theology of Barth and Brunner*, in *The Works of Cornelius Van Til*, (New York: Labels Army Co.) 1997.

[11] Sheils, "Being's End," *Newsweek*.

everyday life that he is doomed to mediocrity, and will never understand the real roots of his being."[12] Later in his career he focused on language and literary criticism.

Of greatest moment to the Media Ecologist is Heidegger's *The Question Concerning Technology and Other Essays*, published in English in 1977. The book is the result of four lectures delivered in 1949 which apply his ontological concerns on the problems of the Post-War Europe.[13] In it he focuses on one of his major themes: "darkening of the world." We live in the age of research in which every endeavor is carefully planned to solve a specific well-packaged problem. Technology producing gadgets, beings, which produce a haze that prevents us from paying attention to "Being".[14]

Technology for Heidegger is not "defined by things or processes. ... *Gestell*, literally 'framing' [Heidegger uses the hyphenated *Ge-stell* to suggest 'Enframing'], is an all-encompassing view of technology, not as a means to an end, but as a mode of human existence."[15] Heidegger's fear was that human being, actions and aspirations, are distorted by technology, "transforming the way we know and think and will."[16] This idea that media create an environment is central to the thinking of Media Ecologists.

"Innis and McLuhan, rejecting the behavioral model and eschewing the standard empirical techniques, advanced versions of the most holistic and radical media theory yet propounded. ... They represent two wings of a body of speculation that locates the formal characteristics of communications media as the prime mover behind the historical process, social organizations, and changing sensory awareness."[17] The Canadians came south to confront American culture, especially its communication media.

Harold Innis (1894-1952)

Harold Adams Innis was born on a small farm in Ontario into a poor family known for its religious faith and industriousness. He completed his undergraduate work at McMaster University in 1916. After serving in World War I, he received his MA from McMaster and went on to earn his Ph.D. in economics from the University of Chicago during the teaching careers of

---

[12] *Ibid.*
[13] Samuel Ebersole, "Media Determinism in Cyberspace." http://regent.edu/acad/schcom/rojc/mdic.html, 1995.
[14] *The Encyclopedia of Philosophy*, 1st ed., reprint 1972, s.v. "Heidegger, Martin."
[15] Ebersole, "Media Determinism in Cyberspace." summarizing Michael Heim, *The Metaphysics of Virtual Reality* (New York: Oxford University Press, 1993) 57.
[16] *Ibid.*
[17] Czitrom, *Media and the American Mind*, 146, 147.

PART II: CRITICAL THEORISTS   105

Robert E. Park and George Herbert Mead when the Chicago School of communication study was in full flower. At Chicago he was strongly influenced by Thorstein Veblen, author of the influential sociological classic *Theory of the Leisure Class* (1926), even though Veblen had left Chicago several years earlier.[18]

From Chicago Innis went to the University of Toronto where he taught political economics from 1920 until his untimely death in 1952. His first book, *The History of the Canadian Pacific Railroad* (1923), reveals the influence of Veblen. Innis demonstrated the connection between technological development and cultural institutions as he explored the change that the land-borne transportation of the railroad had on a culture that had depended on a water-borne system.[19]

It was only in the last decade of his life that Innis turned his attention to an analysis of communication. "By 1940 Innis drastically reoriented his reading and research, beginning an intensive study of the history of printing, journalism, advertising, censorship, and propaganda." He concluded that economic growth is directly related to modes of communication.[20] *Empire and Communications* (1950), and *The Bias of Communication* (1951) placed the study of communication technology in its historical context. The latter work has become a classic in communication study. Undergirding his work during this period was research which traces the history of communication from 4,000 BC to the 1940s. The unfinished manuscript, "A History of Communication," remains unpublished. The gist of both books is nicely summed up by Czitrom: "Systems of communication, that is, modes of symbolic representation, were the technological extensions of mind and consciousness. They therefore held the key to grasping a civilization's values, sources of authority, and organization of knowledge."[21] Rogers assesses Innis as "one of the most influential media determinists. Media determinists contend that the dominant communication technology of a civilization is central to the culture and the social structure of that society."[22] His work was uniquely interdisciplinary at a time when no one in North America was studying communication technology in its humane

---

[18] Everett Rogers, *A History of Communication Study: A Biographical Approach* (New York: The Free Press, 1994) 485. See also Czitrom, *Media and the American Mind*, 149. Rogers maintains that Innis "enrolled in courses" with Veblen, whereas Czitrom says the influence was "in absentia" since Veblen left Chicago years before. Veblen was a critic of "neoclassical economics" and coined the term "conspicuous consumption", which he opposed along with "conspicuous leisure", "conspicuous waste", "speculation" and "wasteful competition". His thought helped Innis look for the unique impact of technological development on Canadian geography, resources and institutions.
[19] *Ibid.*
[20] Czitrom, *Media and the American Mind*, 153.
[21] *Ibid.*, 155.
[22] Rogers, *A History of Communication Study*, 486.

context as an aspect of cultural criticism in connection with history, economics and sociology.

Innis distinguished between two essential types of communication media: *time-biased* and *space-biased*. All civilizations exist through control of space and time, and thus may be understood by identifying the predominant communications media.[23] *Time-biased* media, such as clay, parchment, and the spoken and hand written word used in ancient cultures, were "durable but difficult to transport," and thus enabled control over time, engendering stable, traditional societies. *Space-biased* media, such as papyrus, paper and print, were "less durable and easily transportable," and thus enabled control over space, facilitating empire building.[24] Classical Greece, Renaissance Italy and Elizabethan England were ideal times in which the two biases were balanced. "Innis made no secret of his own bias toward oral tradition," and thus time-biased communication.

One of the principal historical concepts of Media Ecologists is the strongly stated idea expressed by Innis that the development of writing, the phonetic alphabet, and finally printing tilted the balance toward space biased culture. This spatial bias, according to Innis, lead to bureaucratic control, and ultimately the "modern obsession with present-mindedness."[25] The electronic media have dramatically empowered government and business to grow in ways that threaten liberty and humanity. Innis viewed Canada as a last bastion of the oral tradition.[26] Innis recognized and lamented what he referred to as the mechanization of knowledge. The dominance of the sciences in the interests of state and commercial interests is subversive of the traditional role of the university. The great problem of modern civilization, for Innis, is to counteract this dominant bias through intelligent assessment of communication media.[27]

Space-biased media dominate the present and presumably the future of modern culture.[28] The move from temporal to spatial control, epitomized by the electronic media, dramatically effects metaphysical, community and ethical concerns. Innis was pessimistic because of the potential of space controlling media being used to tyrannize cultural and political institutions, secularize culture and idolize commercialism. He wrote: "The oral dialectic is overwhelmingly significant where the subject matter is human action and feeling, and it is important in the discovery of new truth but of very little value in disseminating it. The oral discussion inherently involves personal contact

---

[23] Czitrom, *Media and the American Mind*, 156.
[24] *Ibid.*, 156.
[25] *Ibid.*, 157-158.
[26] *Ibid.*, 159-160.
[27] *Ibid.*, 162-163.
[28] Rogers, *A History of Communication Study*, 486, 487.

and a consideration of the feelings of others, and it is in sharp contrast with the cruelty of mechanized communication and the tendencies which we have come to note in the modern world."[29]

Innis had an important seminal influence on his younger and decidedly more famous colleague, Marshall McLuhan. The centrality of media technologies in culture formation, the interdisciplinary approach to media criticism, and a certain bias toward oral tradition, became foundational in the pioneering and popularizing work of the media mentor of the sixties.[30] Innis focused more on the influence of media in socio-political organization, whereas McLuhan explored the nature of media themselves as extensions of man, especially they influence the balance of the sensorium.[31]

Eric Havelock (1903-1988)

Born in London, Havelock became a U.S. citizen in 1955. He received his BA from Cambridge University in 1926, and his MA in 1929. He taught classics at Acadia University in Nova Scotia from 1926 to 1929, and at Victoria College in Toronto from 1929 to 1947. From 1946 to 1951 he taught classics at Harvard, where from 1951 to 1963 he was professor of Greek and Latin. He went on to become Sterling Professor of Classics in Yale University from 1963 until his retirement in 1971.[32]

Havelock is considered by many to be one of the founders of Media Ecology. *Preface to Plato* (1963) was his first significant book. In it Havelock explores new territory in asserting his hypothesis that Plato's entire philosophy was constructed as an attack on the oral tradition of Greek poetry. Greek culture had been stored in the oral memory of the bardic tradition. The invention of the phonetic alphabet radically altered the storage system and laid the basis for Western education and literacy. The eye replaced the ear as "the chief organ employed for this purpose."[33] His *Origins of Western Literacy* (1976) continue to amplify this theme. Most important to Media Ecology, according to Fordham professor Lance Strate, is *The Greek Concept of Justice*

---

[29] Harold Innis, *Empire and Communications* (London: Oxford University Press, 1950) 57, in *Czitrom, Media and the American Mind*, 157.
[30] Claude T. Bissell, "Herbert Marshall McLuhan" in George Sanderson and Frank Macdonald, eds., *Marshall McLuhan: The Man and His Message* (Golden, CO: Fulcrum, Inc., 1989) 7.
[31] Rogers, *A History of Communication Study*, 487.
[32] *Contemporary Authors–Permanent Series*, Clare D. Kinsman, ed. (Detroit: Gale Research, 1975, vol. 1) s.v. "Havelock, Eric A. 1902-." Cf. Thomas Farrell, *Walter Ong's Contributions to Cultural Studies: The Phenomenology of the Word and I-Thou Communication* (Creskill, NJ: Hampton Press, 1999).
[33] Eric Havelock, *Preface to Plato* (Cambridge: Harvard University Press, 1963) "Foreword," vii.

(1978).[34] In it Havelock "traces shifts in word use and meaning (i.e., from more concrete to abstract) as reflections of the shift from orality to literacy."[35] *The Muse Learns to Write: Reflections on Orality and Literacy from Antiquity to the Present* (1986) is Havelock's most recent contribution. In the foreword he acknowledges his debt to Walter Ong's *Orality and Literacy* (1982) as the foundation for his attempted "synthesis."[36]

Havelock was a frequent lecturer in Toronto during McLuhan's tenure there. He often visited and corresponded with McLuhan. McLuhan mentions *Preface to Plato* frequently in his correspondence from 1964 to 1974 when McLuhan introduced Havelock to a University of Toronto audience.[37] The shift from oral to written culture was central to McLuhan's assertion that the electronic media are reversing this shift, and that cultural memory is once again being stored in the pithy slogans and sound bites of the modern world. The individualism fostered by the phonetic alphabet is now being absorbed by the new tribalism, which is cultivated by the ear. Havelock, perhaps to a lesser degree than Ong, idealizes orality. His insistence on the Greek origin of the phonetic alphabet and literacy is highly questionable. Alphabetic texts from the Syrian town of Ugarit, modern Ras Shamra, from the fourteenth and fifteenth centuries BC, indicate Canaanite and Phoenician origins of the phonetic alphabet.[38] Clearly Greek culture and its alphabet are a latter development, pushing the origins of literacy back at least a millennium prior to Havelock's assertion.

Marshall McLuhan (1911-1980)

Herbert Marshall McLuhan was born in Edmonton, Alberta of Scottish-Irish lineage. He was raised by gifted parents, the traits and propensities of whom he imitated with all the energy of a first born son. His mother Elsie was raised in a Baptist family in which daily Scripture reading and prayer played a vital part. Her association with Miss Josephine Goodspeed and later with Miss Alice Mitchell, both trained in Boston's Emerson School of Oratory, taught her the Emersonian art of "elocution." "Elsie's grounding in elocutionary craft ...converged with the performance-based aspect of literary New Criticism that

---

[34] Tom Farrell. "Ong." Personal Email (24 May 1999).
[35] Lance Strate. "Havelock." mediaecology@ube.ubalt.edu (Feb 1999).
[36] Eric Havelock, *The Muse Learns to Write: Reflections on Orality and Literacy from Antiquity to the Present* (New Haven: Yale University Press, 1986) "Acknowledgments."
[37] Marshall McLuhan, *Letters of Marshall McLuhan*. Edited by M. Molinaro, C. McLuhan, and W. Toye (Toronto: Oxford University Press, 1987) 495.
[38] Moshe Greenberg, *Introduction to Hebrew* (Englewood Cliffs, NJ: Prentice-Hall, 1965) 14, 15. Johanna Drucker, *The Alphabetic Labyrinth: The Letters in History and Imagination* (London: Thames and Hudson, 1995) 47, 54.

her son Marshall would learn at Cambridge University."[39] McLuhan's father Herbert came from a line of fine intellects. Although young Marshall did not display the scholarly bent which would dominate his adult life, in his teens he loved to build, and showed enormous practical intelligence as a boat builder.[40]

He began his undergraduate work in engineering at the University of Manitoba in Winnipeg in 1928. His early interest in English literature did not find a welcome home among engineers. Thus he changed his degree program in 1929 and went on to complete his undergraduate degree in English, history and philosophy in 1933, receiving his MA in English literature in 1934. Already his voracious reading led him far beyond his course requirements.[41] He spent the next six years earning his Ph.D. in English literature at Trinity Hall in Cambridge University, which he received in 1942. After finishing his BA he returned to America in 1936.[42] During this time McLuhan's study of literature "inaugurated a lifelong concern for the study of rhetoric." His fascination with Elizabethan rhetoric led to his dissertation on Thomas Nashe titled *The Place of Thomas Nashe in the Learning of his Time*, "a history of the verbal arts in Western culture from antiquity to the sixteenth century."[43] From professors I. A. Richards and F. L. Leavis he learned to analyze texts in their cultural context, and was thus initiated into the school of the New Criticism.[44]

McLuhan returned to America to teach English at the universities of Wisconsin (1936-37) and Saint Louis (1937-44). McLuhan's first encounter with American university students initiated his interest in popular culture. "I was confronted with young Americans I was incapable of understanding. I felt an urgent need to study their popular culture in order to get through."[45] While teaching in his first post at the University if Wisconsin in 1937 McLuhan was baptized and became a devoted member of the Roman Catholic Church. He had been raised in the conservative Baptist religion of his parents. His brother

---

[39] W. Terrence Gordon. *Marshall McLuhan: Escape into Understanding, A Biography* (New York: BasicBooks, 1997) 8.
[40] *Ibid.*, 12f.
[41] *Ibid.*, 16.
[42] *Current Biography* (June 1967), "McLuhan, (Herbert) Marshall," in Raymond Rosenthal, ed. *McLuhan: Pro and Con* (Baltimore: Penguin Books, 1968) 16.
[43] Tom Farrell. "Ong." Personal Email (24 May 1999). "Toward the end of his dissertation, McLuhan mentions Ramism, so he was at least familiar with this movement. As the story goes, McLuhan at some juncture (presumably around 1939-1941) called Ong's attention to Perry Miller's *The New England Mind: The Seventeenth Century* (1939), in which Miller documents that almost all of the teachers at Harvard considered themselves to be Ramists. At the time when Miller's book was published, the scholarly world knew relatively little about Peter Ramus (1515-1572) and the movement known as Ramism."
[44] Bissell, "Herbert Marshall McLuhan" in Sanderson and Macdonald, *Marshall McLuhan: The Man and His Message*, 5. Cf. Czitrom, *Media and the American Mind*, 166.
[45] *Current Biography* in Rosenthal, ed. *McLuhan: Pro and Con*, 17.

went on to become an Episcopal minister.[46] His adult conversion to Catholicism at the height of his early intellectual development means that his Catholicism was not nominal and must be taken seriously as an important aspect of the backdrop of his reflections on media. This aspect of McLuhan's life and thought will be explored more fully in the next chapter. In 1939 Marshall eloped with Fort Worth socialite Corinne Lewis. They were married in St. Louis Cathedral, much to the chagrin of the Protestant Lewis's. The newlyweds arrived at Cambridge just as England declared war on Germany. Having completed his doctoral residency the McLuhans returned to St. Louis in 1940.

In 1944 he returned to Canada and taught English at Assumption College (now the University of Windsor) in Windsor, Ontario. In 1946 he joined the Department of English at Saint Michael's College in the University of Toronto, becoming a full professor in 1952, and where he continued to be a faculty member throughout his career until his death on the last day of 1980. During this period his interests moved from Renaissance to Modern literature. It was in Toronto that his lifelong interest in communication blossomed. In 1963 the university created the Centre for Culture and Technology as the academic foundation for McLuhan's work.[47] He was appointed its first director.

McLuhan's literary criticism is *the* most important influence on his media criticism. With it he developed the epistemology and the hermeneutic of his media criticism. During his years as a professor of English, T. S. Eliot, Ezra Pound, Gerard Manley Hopkins, W. B. Yeats and Wyndham Lewis commanded his attention. James Joyce, however, became the dominating influence.[48] He strongly favored the generalist approach of the "Ciceronian ideal" by which the whole man cultivates his mind and soul in liberal studies in order to be a well informed and responsible citizen, i.e. the wise man, as opposed to becoming a creature of the state along the lines of the liberalism of his day. For McLuhan *liberal* education represented *liber*ation from the conventional wisdom. The Ciceronian ideal placed the humanistic studies of grammar and rhetoric prior to the study of dialectics. The scientific focus on methodology becomes dangerous when it seeks to dominate the entire educational curriculum.[49] His growing perception of the centrality of rhetorical patterns in reader involvement, inspired by his investigation of literary symbolism,[50] would become a dominant

---

[46] *Ibid.*, 16.
[47] *Ibid.*, 9.
[48] *Ibid.*, 6.
[49] McLuhan, "An Ancient Quarrel in Modern America."
[50] *Current Biography* in Rosenthal, ed. *McLuhan: Pro and Con*, 6. Cf. McLuhan's 1946 article in *Classical Journal* titled "An Ancient Quarrel in Modern America: Sophists vs. Grammarians." Cf. Czitrom, *Media and the American Mind*, 168.

force in his later media study, reflected in his assertion that "All media are active metaphors in their power to translate experience into new forms."[51] Richards had taught him not to separate the meaning of words from the words themselves.[52] The word is the message. And so he would discover is every medium of communication. McLuhan left Cambridge having been trained to perceive, critic of the word; critic of the world.[53]

McLuhan's first book, *The Mechanical Bride* (1951), was in his own words, "an extremely moralistic approach to all environmental technology. I loathed machinery. I abominated cities, I equated the Industrial Revolution with original sin and mass media with the Fall."[54] McLuhan's early affinity with English Populism is expressed in his first published essay: "G. K. Chesterton: A Practical Mystic." He was full of praise for "Mr. Chesterton's inspiriting opposition to officialdom and bureaucracy. The cynical social legislation of today, undertaken in supposed accord with unyielding economic circumstance, is often light-headed because it is not light-hearted. And Mr. Chesterton is a revolutionary, not because he finds everything equally detestable, but because he fears lest certain infinitely valuable things, such as family and personal liberty, should vanish."[55] He goes on to uphold the importance of agriculture and private property in the maintenance of liberty. As noted in the last chapter, Chesterton's classic *What's Wrong with the World* (1910) played a role in McLuhan's conversion, although Chesterton did not enter the Roman Catholic Church until 1922. McLuhan admired the same virtues in the Southern Agrarians.[56] He was ever the curmudgeon, iconoclast, *contra mundum*.

During the 1940s McLuhan was engaged in the debate surrounding the "Great Books" program developed at the University of Chicago. While sympathetic with the hope that humanist studies might strengthen its students to confront the folklore of the new age, in which advertising was setting the cultural agenda, McLuhan expressed his radical reservations about the effectiveness of the project in *The Mechanical Bride* (1951).[57] "In the matter of insistence on the supremacy of technique at the expense of nutriment, The

---

[51] Marshall McLuhan, *Understanding Media: The Extensions of Man* (New York: McGraw-Hill Book Company, 1964), 57.
[52] W. Terrence Gordon, *Marshall McLuhan: Escape into Understanding, A Biography* (New York: BasicBooks, 1997) 49.
[53] *Ibid.*, 66.
[54] Sanderson and Macdonald, eds., *Marshall McLuhan: The Man and His Message*, 2.
[55] Marshall McLuhan, "G. K. Chesterton: A Practical Mystic," *The Dalhousie Review* (January 1936), in Eric McLuhan, *The Medium and the Light* (Toronto: Stoddart Publishing Co. Limited, 1999).
[56] Czitrom, *Media and the American Mind*, 167.
[57] *Ibid.*, 170, 171. Cf. McLuhan, "An Ancient Quarrel in Modern America," in *The Interior Landscape: The Literary Criticism of Marshall McLuhan, 1943-1962*, edited by Eugene McNamara (New York: McGraw-Hill Book Company, 1969) 223-234.

University of Chicago is the child of Harvard, as Harvard is the child of German know-how. ... Why has it not occurred to Dr. Hutchins that the only practical answer to the 'storm of triviality and propaganda' is that it be brought under control by being inspected. Its baneful effects are at present entirely dependent on its being ignored."[58] The "unofficial" education of the media cannot be counteracted by "official education". The book itself (*The Mechanical Bride*) was McLuhan's first effort at "inspection." The subliminal effect of the visual media is reversed so that, like the sailor in Poe's "A Descent into the Maelstrom," the whirlpool may be observed and a thread through the Labyrinth may be found.[59] It was his immersion in Yeats, Pound, Joyce, Eliot and Gerard Manley Hopkins, however, that awakened him from his dogmatic slumbers, and enabled him to discover "a totally different approach, based on the identity of the processes of cognition and creation. I realized that artistic creation is the playback of ordinary experience—from trash to treasures. I ceased being a moralist and became a student."[60] Despite the transformation in outlook and approach, McLuhan never ceased to be deeply concerned about the human situation in the electronic age. Surely the seeds of all that followed may be found in *The Mechanical Bride*. The simultaneity announced in the introduction, "the circulating point of view," which allows the reader to read the essays in any order they wish, already sets the agenda for a new approach. The "somnambulist public" must be awakened! He became an "intellectual detective,"[61] and the consummate iconoclast.

McLuhan's shift in strategy is clearly stated in his June 22, 1951 letter to Ezra Pound: "This is not set down in pique, nor extenuation. I am an intellectual thug who has been slowly accumulating a private arsenal with every intention of using it. In a mindless age every insight takes on the character of a lethal weapon. Every man of good will is the enemy of society. [Wyndham] Lewis saw that years ago. His 'America and Cosmic Man' [London, 1946] was an H-bomb let off in the desert. Impact nil. We resent or ignore such intellectual bombs. We prefer to compose human beings into bombs and explode political and social entities. Much more fun. Lewis clears the air of fug. We want to get rid of people entirely. And it is necessary to admire the skill and thoroughness with which we have made our preparations to do this. I am not of the 'we' party. I should prefer to de-fuse this gigantic human bomb by starting a dialogue somewhere on the side-lines to distract the trigger-men,

---

[58] Marshall McLuhan, *The Mechanical Bride: Folklore of Industrial Man* (Boston: Beacon Press, 1951) 43, 45.
[59] *Ibid.*, v.
[60] Sanderson and Macdonald, eds., *Marshall McLuhan: The Man and His Message*, 2.
[61] T. W. Cooper, "The Unknown McLuhan," in Sanderson and Macdonald, eds., *Marshall McLuhan: The Man and His Message*, 42.

or to needle the somnambulists. In London in 1910 [Pound's early days with Lewis leading up to 'Blast' and the Vorticism movement] you faced various undesirable states of mind. Since then the word has been used to effect a universal hypnosis. How are words to be used to unweave the spell of print? Of radio commercials and 'news'-casts? I'm working on THAT problem. The word is now the cheapest and the most universal drug."[62]

The influence of Innis on McLuhan remains the subject of some debate.[63] Clearly Innis's work on communication in the last decade of his life (1940-1952) contributed to McLuhan's media analysis. Czitrom maintains that "McLuhan borrowed from Innis the tools with which to extend an aesthetic doctrine into an all-encompassing theory of social change. Innis's historical and economic studies provided the intellectual legitimacy for McLuhan's grand leap from investigating the forms of transmitted messages to the forms of transmission themselves."[64] Others refer to Czitrom's perspective as the "Innis mythology". Donald Theall, author of *The Medium is the Rear View Mirror: Understanding McLuhan* (1971), says, "Not only my personal contact with Marshall and the University of Toronto over a period of sixteen years and my close association with him [McLuhan] as a doctoral student in the first half of the 1950s assures me that the Innis' influence has been considerably over-stressed (I say this in full awareness of such statements as his own Introduction to the Second Edition of Innis' *The Bias of Communication*). ...While McLuhan was interested in Innis in the 1950s (he first began reading Innis seriously in 1950), Innis had little presence in McLuhan's approach to the early Culture and Communication Seminars [which McLuhan chaired from 1953 to 1955, sponsored by the Ford Foundation]...While McLuhan learned much from Innis, Innis did not have a privileged position in his work."[65] McLuhan's letters also reveal the fact that he had reservations about some aspects of Innis's ideas, and Innis was not entirely comfortable with McLuhan's thought.[66]

---

[62] McLuhan, *Letters of Marshall McLuhan*, 227.
[63] For McLuhan's views on Innis's work cf. Czitrom, *Media and the American Mind*, 172; Marshall McLuhan, "The Later Innis," Queen's Quarterly 60 (Autumn 1953); McLuhan's introduction to Innis's *The Bias of Communication*.
[64] Czitrom, *Media and the American Mind*, 172.
[65] Theall, Donald. "Tom Wolfe Lecture." owner-mediaecology@ube.ubalt.edu (26 Feb. 1999). "Innis's work was mainly introduced into the seminar through Marshall's lifelong friend, Tom Easterbrook, who was a member. It should be noted that in Explorations 3, while there is an article by Innis (the only one), that McLuhan merely introduced a series of comments from graduate essays by Walter Kenyon, Robert Dailey, Endel Tulving and Donald Theall. ...This is further confirmed by the recently published reminiscences of his friend from the 1950s until his death, the co-founder of his original seminar and the founder of Explorations E. S. ("Ted") Carpenter. An abridged version of Ted's comments can be found in *Canadian Notes and Queries*, No. 46 (Spring 1992) 3-14. Incidentally, there is still much to be noted about Carpenter's very significant influence on McLuhan's interests during this period."
[66] *Ibid.*, "McLuhan's critical stance towards Innis at the time can be confirmed by the one published letter he wrote to Innis (March 4, 1951, 220-4). That his reservations continued is confirmed by a letter

Among other influences was the cybernetic theory of MIT mathematician Norbert Wiener. McLuhan first read his book *Cybernetics* (1948) in 1950.[67] Theall remembers: "When his first Culture and Communication seminar began, there were a number of books related to cybernetics and information theory in its library. I can confirm this since I was academic secretary to the seminar at that time and had charge of the library. It included Shannon and Weaver, some of the Macy material, Reusch and Bateson's *Communications: The Social Matrix of Psychiatry* and later Karl Deutsch's book. Marshall's penciled notes are still in my copy of Reusch and Bateson, which is when he first read it. But Marshall never was comfortable with cybernetics and/or information theory as conceived in the Shannon-Weaver-Wiener paradigms."[68] One aspect of cybernetics which certainly did appeal to McLuhan was the concept of patterns. What he objected to in the Shannon-Weaver model was the insistence that media are conduits of information or messages.

During the early years at Toronto McLuhan was perhaps most influenced by his friend and colleague, anthropologist Edmund S. Carpenter. McLuhan and Carpenter founded a periodical called *Explorations*, which provided a forum for Culture and Communication seminar members. They co-edited an anthology of these articles in *Explorations in Communications* (1960).[69] McLuhan's interest in history and especially the history of invention and technology was initially fostered by the work of Sigfried Giedion, author of *Mechanization Takes Command: A Contribution to Anonymous History* (1948), and Lewis Mumford who wrote *Technics and Civilization* in 1934. "His interest in the history of communication arises in a very large part from his still unpublished Cambridge Ph.D. work on the history of the trivium, *The Place of Thomas Nashe in the Learning of his Time*."[70]

---

years later to Claude Bissell, his friend and president of the University of Toronto (March 23, 1971, 429). ...For Innis' attitude towards McLuhan and a general sense of the University of Toronto sense of the encounter, see Graeme Patterson, *Harold Innis, Marshall McLuhan and the Interpretation of History* (Toronto: University of Toronto Press, 1990)."

[67] *Ibid.*, "Wiener plays an important role in the interests of McLuhan in the early 1950s. He did not encounter *Cybernetics*, which was published in 1948, until 1950. Having just reviewed *Cybernetics* for the *Yale Scientific Magazine* in the spring of 1950, I happened accidentally to bring Wiener's *Cybernetics* to his attention when we first met in the Summer of 1950. Naturally he was fascinated and borrowed my copy. ..."

[68] *Ibid.*, "That library also contained many items from communication study of the time such as Schramm; some of the work of William Stephenson; many psychological texts; and perhaps most strikingly, material from the Culture and Personality, and Culture and Language areas of anthropology, such as Sapir, Boas, Whorf, and later Hall, of course."

[69] *Current Biography* in Rosenthal, ed. *McLuhan: Pro and Con*, 17, 18.

[70] Theall, "Tom Wolfe Lecture," "His interest in history and artifacts had been sparked off earlier by the work of Giedion and Mumford, reinforced by writers on contemporary art such as Gyorgy Kepes and Moholy-Nagy. His interest in the history of communication arises in a very large part from his still

The charge that McLuhan sought credibility as a scientist may be understood not as a desire to become something he was not, but rather to dress his thinking in a way that would gain a hearing in a culture which values nothing unless it is dressed in scientific garb. Barzun's *Science: The Glorious Entertainment* give testimony to the culture dominating power of science and its vocabulary. The simplest products, such a shampoo and toothpaste, are now billed as "systems". Despite criticism on this point it was as a generalist in the humanities that McLuhan made his mark as an ecologist of media.

It is ironic that the staunchly anti-Marxist, orthodox Catholic, McLuhan should become the "guru" of a generation of anti-Vietnam War protesters, who mistook his "probes' for a blanket ap*prob*ation of the electronic media. Becoming a "student" did not mean that McLuhan stopped being a critic. It meant that he recognized the centrality of understanding the nature of media, the water in which we swim, in order to be aware of our involvement with media and if possible to take control of its future development. After his transformation his criticism took an entirely different tack. Even while at Cambridge "McLuhan learned to think in terms of environments that needed, above all, to be understood, to be controlled, to be broken through—not broken into—particularly if they were nothing more than cults. And he learned to do this with what he called a 'bland acceptance of the contemporary world as a scene,' an acceptance his future critics were to misinterpret as endorsement."[71]

The counterculture identified with McLuhan's probes because it was a searching, not so much a probing, generation which like spoiled children had to experience the world for themselves in reaction to all their establishment elders said and did. They lacked the critical understanding which McLuhan had developed over many decades. For all of its callowness this new generation proved attractive to McLuhan because of its iconoclasm. Perhaps he thought that they more than anyone would be open to his insights. If they had only realized how conservative McLuhan really was, they would never have thought him to be avant-garde. He was happy to be labeled "conservative, if by conservative I mean that he wishes to conserve what is worthwhile at all costs." In McLuhan's 1934 essay on Chesterton he showed his appreciation for him as one who "is concerned to maintain our endangered institutions."[72] He also said, "I want to understand everything, then neutralize it. Turn off as many buttons as you can. I am resolutely opposed to all change and innovation, but I

---

unpublished Cambridge Ph.D. work on the history of the trivium, *The Place of Thomas Nashe in the Learning of his Time.*"

[71] Gordon, *Marshall McLuhan*, 65.

[72] Marshall McLuhan in Eugene, McNamara, ed. *The Interior Landscape: The Literary Criticism of Marshall McLuhan, 1943-1962.* New York: McGraw-Hill Book Company, 1969) vi.

am determined to understand what's happening."[73] In a 1966 *Newsweek* interview he was asked why he did not attend the "happenings" attributed to his insights into the simultaneity of the electronic environment he commented: "I'm not inclined to favor these things ...Temperamentally, I'm a stodgy conservative."[74]

Rogers's label, "*technological determinist*", for Innis and McLuhan is misleading. Certainly he is not the first to use this label. John Wilkinson, the translator of Ellul's *The Technological Society*, maintains that Thorstein Veblen was the first to use the term "technological determinism".[75] Daniel Chandler and Samuel Ebersole uses the distinction, first made by William James, between "hard" and "soft" determinism to posit a range between "libertarianism and hard determinism". The "hard" variety posits communication technology as the sufficient condition to effect inevitable cultural change, while the "soft" variety posits communication technology as an "enabling or facilitating factor."[76] The problem is that James viewed "soft" determinism as a sophistry.[77] Rogers defines *technological determinism* more simply, and I think accurately, as "the belief that changes in technology cause social changes in society."

Rogers goes on to note that critics of *technological determinism* argue that it does not take social context into account in its assessments.[78] This presents two problems. First, the word "*determinism*" suggests *fatalism*, i.e. people and cultures are at the mercy of media. For McLuhan nothing could be further from the truth. His agenda was to awaken people from their technological slumbers, in order to take charge of their media involvement and perhaps their media environment. "There is absolutely no inevitability as long as there is a willingness to contemplate what is happening."[79] "Consequently, in practice, everyone is intellectually and emotionally a patchwork quilt of occupied and unoccupied territory. ... All the more, then, is it urgent to foster habits of

---

[73] "A McLuhan Symposium," in Sanderson and Macdonald, *Marshall McLuhanThe Man and His Message*, 120.
[74] "Understanding McLuhan," *Newsweek*, 18 February 1966, p. 57. Quoted in Joshua Meyrowitz, "Taking McLuhan and 'Medium Theory' Seriously: Technological Change and the Evolution of Education." Chapter 4 in *Technology and the Future of Schooling: Ninety-Fifth Yearbook of the National Society for the Study of Education*. Part II. Chicago: University of Chicago Press, 1996.
[75] John Wilkinson, in Jacques Ellul, *The Technological Society*. Translated by John Wilkinson(New York: Alfred A. Knopf, 1964) xviii.
[76] Daniel Chandler, (1995, rev. 1998): "Technological or Media Determinism" [WWW document] URL http://www.aber.ac.uk/~dgc/tecdet.html [13 July 1999]; Ebersole, "Media Determinism in Cyberspace."
[77] *The Encyclopedia of Philosophy*, 1st ed., reprint 1972, s.v. "Determinism."
[78] Rogers, *A History of Communication Study*, 484.
[79] Marshall McLuhan and Quentin Fiore, *The Medium Is the Massage: An Inventory of Effects* (New York: Bantam Books, 1967) 25.

inspection until workable standards of securely civilized judgment emerge from those habits."[80] Finally, Claude Bissel, former president of the University of Toronto, asserts that McLuhan "was unhappy ...at the criticism that he had revealed a deterministic world in which man was at the mercy of his technology. He maintained that, by understanding the effects of the media, we could control them, 'even as the Greeks chose to alter the Dionysian fury with Apollonian detachment.'"[81] Ellul agreed, as we shall see below.[82]

Secondly, McLuhan's focus on the nature of media does not necessarily imply denial of the influence of the social context in which media are invented, developed and used. Meyrowitz observes that McLuhan "claims that electronic technology was bypassing traditional boundaries and making *global* phenomena the key unit of analysis."[83] Rogers does concede: "During his lifetime McLuhan did more than any other individual to interest the general public in communication study."[84] In *Understanding Media* McLuhan, commenting on Hans Seyle's contribution to media awareness, asserts, "the latest approach to media study considers not only the 'content' but the medium and the cultural matrix within which the particular medium operates."[85] Furthermore, it should be noted that while individuals may make choices within a given culture, the culture itself is a given which individuals must work and choose within. Freedom has boundaries, even at a sociological level. As we shall see, Meyrowitz has a proper appreciation for this aspect of McLuhan.

Central to McLuhan's understanding of media is the polarity between "visual space" and "acoustic space." Based on his reading of Havelock he came to understand the tremendous shift which took place when the phonetic alphabet was invented and the eye orientation gained dominance over ear orientation. The tribal and epoch nature of earlier culture was transformed into nation-states and democratic institutions based on hierarchical control. The dawning of the printing press exacerbated this tendency and gave birth to the Gutenberg Galaxy with its attendant "new cult of individualism." The electronic age, however, is reverting to ear oriented culture, which presages a new global tribalism, hence the "Global Village." Media change the balance in the sensorium and "patterns of perception" in ways unseen, i.e. "subliminally."

---

[80] McLuhan, *The Mechanical Bride*, 144.
[81] Bissell, "Herbert Marshall McLuhan," in Sanderson and Macdonald, *Marshall McLuhan: The Man and His Message*, 11.
[82] Jacques Ellul, *The Technological Society*. Translated by John Wilkinson. (New York: Alfred A. Knopf, 1964) xxviii.
[83] Meyrowitz, "Taking McLuhan and 'Medium Theory' Seriously," 77.
[84] Rogers, *A History of Communication Study*, 489.
[85] Marshall McLuhan, *Understanding Media: The Extensions of Man* (New York: McGraw-Hill Book Company, 1964) 11.

The focus on the use and "content" of media causes distraction from the medium itself, and the media, thus numbs the culture into sleep walking.[86]

The Gutenberg Galaxy: The Making of Typographical Man (1962) is "a great synthetic work, a *tour de force* of humanist scholarship."[87] The man of letters and literary critic, was, after all, a product of the written and printed word. Like *The Mechanical Bride*, *The Gutenberg Galaxy* is a montage used to explore his subject by awakening the "somnambulist" reader from his print-induced slumbers. Without "normal" chapter headings the arrangement of the text is itself a message about the change in perception introduced by electronic media. The new revolution, which follows the one brought about with the advent of moveable type, is a revolution in consciousness, but one which is a dilemma or "plight" in which modern man is already completely involved. McLuhan uses his lengthy discussion and analysis of the ramifications of the printed word to demonstrate the means and the need of looking at the environment created by the media themselves rather than the supposed content they carry. The ground is more important than the figure. It is the background of the message to which the critic must pay attention.

Understanding Media: The Extensions of Man (1964) "was his educational guide for easing the psychic conversion into the new age."[88] "An intellectual explorer, McLuhan intends to probe, expose, and provoke, rather than to explain or prove, and even the more skeptical of his critics recognize the heuristic importance of his controversial *Understanding Media*."[89] This work analyses the nature of a host of particular technologies as media, as an application of the historical perspective unfolded in *The Gutenberg Galaxy*. The introduction and first seven chapters lay out the McLuhan paradigm for media criticism. The next twenty-six chapters move in a subtle historical progression from the spoken word to automation. The detective does his work. McLuhan begins by boldly asserting: "Today, after more than a century of electric technology, we have extended our central nervous system itself in a global embrace, abolishing space and time as far as our planet is concerned. Rapidly, we approach the final phase of the extensions of man—the technological simulation of consciousness, when the creative process of knowing will be collectively and corporately extended to the whole of human society, much as we have already extended our senses and our nerves by the various media."[90] The first chapter is "The Medium Is the Message."

---

[86] Czitrom, *Media and the American Mind*, 173-179.
[87] *Ibid.*, 176.
[88] *Ibid.*, 177.
[89] *Current Biography* in Rosenthal, ed. *McLuhan: Pro and Con*, 15.
[90] McLuhan, *Understanding Media*, 3, 4.

McLuhan is to Media Ecology what Luther was to the Reformation. While he never established an academic institution he was a pioneer who influenced a host of brilliant men. McLuhan directed Ong's master's thesis on Gerard Manley Hopkins while teaching English at St. Louis University in the early 1940's. He did the same with Donald Theall who wrote his doctoral dissertation in the early 1950's at Toronto. The Centre for Culture and Technology in McLuhan's day was McLuhan. It was left to others to establish an institutional presence. During the school year of 1967 and 1968 McLuhan spent a year at Fordham teaching with his Toronto colleague, anthropologist Edmund Carpenter.[91] After McLuhan returned to Toronto in 1968 John Culkin, who had first met McLuhan in 1963 and was responsible for bringing McLuhan to Fordham, resigned his post as Director of the Center for Communications at Fordham University and founded a not-for-profit organization to carry on McLuhan's work called The Center for Understanding Media. "Within three years we had founded a graduate school program in Media Studies based on Marshall's ideas. It is at the New School for Social Research in New York City. As far as I know, it is the only school with such a lineage with Marshall's thinking." In 1988 the Marshall McLuhan Chair of Communications was established.[92] While Neil Postman never studied formally under McLuhan, it was at McLuhan's suggestion that Postman set out to establish a university department at New York University, which he did in 1971. Postman now directs New York University's Department of Culture and Communication in the School of Education.

At the University of Toronto McLuhan's legacy lives on in the graduate program: The McLuhan Program in Culture and Technology. A host of communication study departments continue to develop McLuhan's insights. Professor Joshua Meyrowitz, who received his doctorate under Postman's direction at NYU in 1978 is the guiding light of the undergraduate Department of Communication at the University of New Hampshire. Media Ecologists throughout the world bear witness to the pervasiveness of McLuhan's influence by disseminating his fundamental insights in a variety of academic and professional contexts. Beyond this the Media Ecology Association, formed in 1998, has generated interest in scholarly discussion with the initiation of an annual convention, a newsletter, and an electronic discussion list. Surely, as McLuhan student Donald Theall suggests we may refer "metaphorically" to "a Toronto School of Communications."[93] Media Ecologists await a chronicler of this growing movement.

---

[91] Czitrom, *Media and the American Mind*, 105.
[92] John Culkin, "Marshall's New York Adventure," in Sanderson and Macdonald, *Marshall McLuhan: The Man and His Message*, 109.
[93] Donald Theall. "Some questions." mediaecology@ube.ubalt.edu (9 Jan 1999)

In the end, we may well wonder if McLuhan finally found his way through the Poe's Maelstrom. At times it seems that he was caught in the swirl. But then that is both the strategy of and the danger faced by the detective. When all is said and done, McLuhan was a man of letters, an artist, yes, but an artist of the printed word, who understood the *Zeitgeist* of the last half of the twentieth century as few others have. On the front lines he avoided the triggermen by appearing to be caught in the swirl of the whirlpool; back stage he was one of the most literate men of our time, a potential Chesterton for the electronic age. But I do not believe he achieved what we see in the trilogy of the early McLuhan. As a popularizer McLuhan exhibited the strength of leaving us with a number of pithy, memorable and insightful sayings; he also seems to have fallen prey to the anti-dogmatic tenor of our times.

McLuhan's failure to develop a cohesive theoretical foundation, in the name of "suspended judgment," and his insistent anti-institutionalism constitute his greatest weakness just because he came to see resistance to a "point of view" as a virtue. In a 1953 letter to Walter Ong he stated "We need somebody to do a Thomistic Theory of Communication."[94] As Meyrowitz observes: "he was more interested in being consistently provocative than in being consistently right or logically consistent."[95] The combination of this style, along with confusing his description and predictions for advocacy, account for the neglect of his thought by the scholarly world.[96] Ironically, the ideas, especially about education, which he *did* advocate, were dismissed as radical in his day. The idea that instruction would shift toward discovery, increasing student participation, has now become a common place among educational reformers.[97]

"At times in *Understanding Media* and elsewhere he seems to simply be describing the tendency of the electronic media, as an observer of the *Maelstrom*. At other times he appears to have been caught in the swirl. 'My approach to the media is never from a point of view but is in fact a *swarming*.'"[98] As a self-confessed "prophet" of the new media he never made his fundamental Christian assumptions about God, Christ and the church explicit. Sometimes a *modus operandi* can be a man's undoing. One would hope that the very man who perceived that the medium is the message would have seen the folly of claiming a "neutral" stance.

---

[94] McLuhan, *Letters*, 236.
[95] Meyrowitz, "Taking McLuhan and 'Medium Theory' Seriously," 76.
[96] *Ibid.*, 74-78.
[97] *Ibid.*, 77.
[98] Gordon, *Marshall McLuhan*, 253. Cf. Theall's insightful comments on McLuhan's lack of a clearly articulated theoretical foundation in *The Medium is the Rear View Mirror: Understanding McLuhan*. (Montreal: McGill-Queens University Press, 1971) 199-219, especially 205-207.

Walter J. Ong (1912-)

Ong was born in Kansas City, Missouri, of stock dating back to the Massachusetts Bay Colony in 1631. Attending Roman Catholic schools from the fourth grade on, he completed his undergraduate work at Rockhurst College in 1933. In 1935 he entered the Society of Jesus as a novice at St. Stanislaus Seminary in Florissant outside St. Louis. There he studied the humanities, going on to St. Louis University to study philosophy at the Jesuit philosophate from 1938 to 1940 and receiving his MA in English in 1941. His Masters thesis on the sprung rhythm of the Jesuit Victorian poet Gerard Manley Hopkins was directed by Marshall McLuhan, who taught at St. Louis from 1937 to 1944.[99] After being ordained to the priesthood in 1946, Ong went on to Harvard for doctoral studies in English in 1948. His dissertation was a voluminous 1700 pages titled *Ramus, Method, and the Decay of Dialogue*, which was published in two volumes by Harvard in 1958. During part of his Guggenheim Fellowship in Europe he lived at the Jesuit house of *Etudes* in Paris, across the hall from Père Pierre Teilhard de Chardin (1950). After completing his dissertation he returned to St. Louis University in 1954 to begin a long and distinguished career teaching English and humanities.[100]

From 1963 to 1964 Ong gave the Terry Lectures at Yale University. These were published in 1967 as *The Presence of the Word*. This and *Orality and Literacy* (1982) are the most significant for the preacher in considering the oral nature of his task. Ong's nuanced reflection on the nature of orality is incomparable. Ong's emphasis on orality often suggests that writing and print are an inferior form of communication. In reviewing Graham's *Beyond the Written Word: Oral Aspects of Scripture in the History of Religion* he asserts: "Graham's searching examination of orality in the scriptures of major world religions is more than welcome in today's print-bound, book-bound world, where reading ordinarily suggests silence, without even movement of the lips."[101] However, he does balance this by observing in the same review: "Writing does have an incalculable value. ...Yet writing is inextricably intertwined with orality."[102] His plea is for the recovery of "the sense that language is (and always will be) basically oral."[103]

---

[99] Tom Farrell, "Reducing Religion." Personal E-mail (25 May 1999).
[100] Randolph Lumpp. "Walter Jackson Ong, S. J.: A Biographical Portrait." *Oral Tradition* 2/1 (1987):13-18.
[101] Walter Ong, Review: *Beyond the Written Word: Oral Aspects of Scripture in the History of Religion* (William A. Graham) in *America* (Mar. 4, 1989): 204.
[102] *Ibid.*
[103] *Ibid.*

Unsettling, from a theological perspective, is the influence of Teilhard de Chardin on Ong's thinking. Teilhard's *The Phenomenon of Man* (1959) is cited with approval in *The Presence of the Word*. "As material being develops higher forms interiority increases. This has been spelled out in great detail by Pierre Teilhard de Chardin. ...And in an even more sweeping fashion [than the work of phenomenologists], Pierre Teilhard de Chardin has undertaken in *The Phenomenon of Man* and elsewhere to relate the interior consciousness of individual human beings to the history of the cosmos. ...McLuhan is quite right in relating our present sense (Teilhard's noosphere) to the electronic revival of sound and to the generation of something like a preliterate global village."[104] Thomas Farrell points out that Ong was one of the first writers to bring Teilhard's writings to the attention of American Catholics.[105] McLuhan's references to Teilhard in *The Gutenberg Galaxy* (1962)[106] focus on Teilhard's insights into the evolution of culture and technology, not necessarily implying McLuhan's approbation of Teilhard's Gnostic scheme of cosmic evolution.

Ong's propensity to elevate "the mystery of sound" above the written Word/word reminds the Protestant reader of the Neo-Orthodoxy of Barth's God of "utter transcendence." Both Barth and Ong, in a serious and often profound effort to counteract the "silent God" of immanentistic theological Liberalism, existentialism, and phenomenology, undermine the integrity and historical concreteness of God's written speech. Ong's religious perspective will be discussed in the next chapter.

Jacques Ellul (1912-1994)

Ellul was born in Bordeaux, France and studied at the universities of Bordeaux and Paris. He held degrees in Sociology, Law, and the History of Law. In 1937 he was married and became lecturer at the University of Montpellier. From 1938 to 1946 he taught at the University of Strasbourg. From 1946 until his retirement he was professor of History and Contemporary Sociology at the University of Bordeaux. During World War II he was a leader of the French

---

[104] Walter J. Ong, *The Presence of the Word* (New York: Simon and Schuster, 1967) 120, 179, 260.
[105] Thomas Farrell. "Tom Wolfe on Teilhard," owner-mediaecology@ube.ubalt.edu (2 July 1999). Ong was one of the first writers to call Teilhard's thought to the attention of American Catholics: see Ong's *Frontiers in American Catholicism* (Macmillan, 1957, pp. 1, 37), *American Catholic Crossroads* (Macmillan, 1959, pp. 22, 110-111), and *The Barbarian Within* (Macmillan, 1962, pp. 49, 239-240). Ong also edited and contributed a selection to the collection *Darwin's Vision and Christian Perspectives* (Macmillan, 1960), in which we find Teilhard being mentioned on pages 11 (by Alexander Wolsky of Fordham University) and 90 and 100-102 (by James Collins of St. Louis University).
[106] Marshall McLuhan, *The Gutenberg Galaxy: The Making of Typographical Man* (Toronto: University of Toronto Press, 1962) 47, 174, 179.

resistance movement. At age nineteen, in 1931, Ellul became a Marxist; but three years later became a Christian. "His religious faith evolved out of the Death of God movement and the response of the Neo-orthodox theologians Bultmann, Barth, Niebuhr and Tillich. ... As a theologian, Ellul drew from the dialectical theology of Kierkegaard and Barth, and as a sociologist, from Marx and Weber."[107]

The dominant theme of Ellul's thought is "'the threat to human freedom and Christian faith created by modern technology.' Ellul's constant theme has been one of technological tyranny over humanity. As a philosopher and theologian, Ellul explored the religiosity of the technological society."[108] The Barthian dialectic helped shape Ellul's view of history as under the blessing and judgment of God. Modern technology for him has a secularizing power so that "that which desacralizes a given reality, itself in turn becomes the new sacred reality."[109] "Fasching offered the following examples. Christianity desacralized nature, after which Christianity became sacred. The Reformation desacralized the church in the name of the Bible, and the Bible became the sacred book. Science and reason desacralized the scriptures, and since that time Science has become sacred. Today, argued Ellul, it is the technological society that we hold sacred."[110]

Ellul's magnum opus is *The Technological Society* (1964), first published in French in 1954 as *La Technique: L'enjen du siegravecle*, "the stake of the century." Ellul defines technique as "the *totality of methods rationally arrived at and having absolute efficiency* (for a given stage of development) in *every* field of human activity."[111] In answer to the charge of "rigorous determinism" Ellul maintains: "As to rigorous determinism, I should explain that I have tried to perform a work of sociological reflection, involving analysis of large groups of people and of major trends, but not of individual actions. I do not deny the existence of individual action or of some inner sphere of freedom. ...I believe that there is a collective sociological reality, which is independent of the individual. ...We are conditioned by something new; technological civilization." Fatalism regarding technology is not inevitable unless each person "abdicates his responsibilities with regard to values... Awareness of the dangers and divine intervention offer the only hope for mankind. ...At stake is our very life, ... each of us, in his own life, must seek ways of resisting and transcending technological determinants. ... We must look at it dialectically, and say that

---

[107] Ebersole, "Media Determinism in Cyberspace." quoting D. Fasching, *The Thought of Jacques Ellul: A Systematic Exposition.* (New York: Edwin Mellen Press, 1981) 2, x, 7.
[108] *Ibid.*, 1.
[109] *Ibid.*, 35.
[110] Ebersole, "Media Determinism in Cyberspace."
[111] Ellul, *The Technological Society*, xxv (emphasis in original).

man is indeed determined, but that it is open to him to overcome necessity, and that this *act* is freedom. ... In the modern world, the most dangerous form of determinism is the technological phenomenon. It is not a question of getting rid of it, but, by an act of freedom, of transcending it."[112] In sum, we must resist the new god of "efficiency". The more we worship it the more our humanity is eroded and threatened.

In *Propaganda: The Formation of Men's Attitudes* (1965), Ellul takes issue with the definitions of propaganda proposed by American propaganda and mass media scholars from Lasswell to Reisman.[113] Propaganda is more pervasively effective as a sociological phenomenon than these theorists have surmised. "Not only is propaganda itself a technique, it is also an indispensable condition for the development of technical progress and the establishment of a technological civilization. ...The force of propaganda is a direct attack on man." This attack exists regardless of the ideology of the propagandist. Thus it must be studied in the context of the technological society.[114]

The Humiliation of the Word (1985) was first published as *La Parole Humiliée* in 1981. Walter Ong observes: "There is no mistaking that Ellul favors the spoken word over the visual image as the conveyor of truth."[115] Ellul goes so far as to advise his readers not to have pictures of "dear ones."[116] More profoundly Ellul warns of the dangers of the apotheosis of the visual maximizing the visualization of reality and thus undermining the spoken word. Even writing is suspect. The irony of this is not lost on Ong: "The book takes no note of the fact that writing (not to mention print) itself is a technology that is absolutely essential to generate the philosophical and scientific speculation in which Ellul excels."[117]

Most of what Ellul wrote on the subject of technology and media is really commentary on the doctrine stated in *The Technological Society*. This represents a profound contribution to Christian cultural criticism and communication study.

---

[112] *Ibid.*, xxviii-xxxiii.
[113] Jacques Ellul, *Propaganda: The Formation of Men's Attitudes*, translated by Konrad Kellen and Jean Lerner (New York: Vintage Books, 1965).
[114] *Ibid.*, x, xiv, xvi, xvii.
[115] Walter Ong, Review: *The Humiliation of the Word* (Jacques Ellul) in the *Journal of Communication* (1986): vol. 36, no. 1, pp. 156-158.
[116] *Ibid.*
[117] *Ibid.*

Daniel Boorstin (1914-)

Born in Atlanta and raised in Oklahoma, Boorstin received his BA with highest honors from Harvard in 1934 and was graduated with a "double-first" from Balliol College as a Rhodes Scholar, Oxford with a BA in 1936. He was admitted as a barrister-at-law of the Inner Temple, London. He received his Ph.D. from Yale and a Litt.D. as Pitt Professor of American History and Institutions and Fellow of Trinity College, Cambridge University. He was also the first incumbent of the chair of American History at the Sorbonne. From 1944 to 1969 he taught at the University of Chicago and became Preston and Sterling Morton Distinguished Service Professor of American History. From 1969 to 1973 he was senior historian of the Smithsonian Institution and director of The National Museum of History and Technology. He went on to become the Librarian of Congress where he served for twelve years until his retirement in 1985.

As a premier American historiographer Boorstin is best known for his Pulitzer Prize winning trilogy *The Americans: The Colonial Experience* (1958); *The National Experience* (1965); *The Democratic Experience* (1973). His insights into unique aspects of American culture provide a rich background resource for the Media Ecologist. Of most immediate interest, however, is his ground breaking critique of American advertising and celebrity: *The Image or Whatever Happened to the American Dream?* (1962). This book was revised in 1964 and 1971 with the subtitle *A Guide to Pseudo-Events in America*. It is a foray into the world of the technologically created illusions of electronic culture, from the pseudo-events of news making to the pseudo-persons of celebrity making. Madison Avenue admen are the P. T. Barnums of the Graphic Revolution. The American public is the willing participant in the culture of self-deception. Boorstin uses all of the critical tools of the historian to analyze the present situation in our "new civilization." Unfortunately, as one might expect from a historian, Boorstin's brilliant discovery of the disease is not matched by any compelling cure. In good relativistic fashion he concludes: "There is no cure. There is only the opportunity for discovery."[118] For the Christian Media Ecologist his plea to awaken ourselves to new ways of receiving messages from the past, God and the world, beyond the images of the mass media, is suggestive of the trajectory on which our study should send us.

Boorstin was deeply influenced by Walter Lippmann's critique of the Utopian views of the early Chicago School. Lippmann is truly a *Critical*

---

[118] Daniel J. Boorstin, *The Image or Whatever Happened to the American Dream?* (New York: Athenaeum, 1962) 260, 261.

Theorist and should perhaps be considered the first *Media Ecologist*, the school of scholars to which we shall now turn.

CONTEMPORARY VOICES:
THE EMERGENCE OF MEDIA ECOLOGY

Working with the insights of the founders are a host of contemporary thinkers in an ever expanding field of study and concern. The following is only a sample of several of the most noteworthy.

Neil Postman (1932-)

Neil Postman received his BA from the State University of New York in Fredonia in 1953, his MA from Columbia in 1955, and his Doctor of Education from Columbia in 1958. Early in his career he taught in elementary and secondary schools.

Postman first met Marshall McLuhan at Columbia University. In an interview in 1990 Postman reminisced: "I wasn't ever formally a student of his, but I was a graduate student at Columbia when I first came in contact with him. He gave a lecture there, and he and I became friends, and he actually encouraged me to develop this department because he didn't have any abilities as an administrator at all, nothing. And his Center of Culture and Technology at the University of Toronto was not really a program; it was just McLuhan. ...So he urged me many years ago. He said, what we need, what we have to do here, is develop an academic program that gives degrees and has a research agenda that pursues these questions. So I did that. I mean, there were a lot of things that McLuhan was talking about that made no sense to me whatsoever, but he was a pioneer, and of course Lewis Mumford, and Gerbner, and Walter Ong, and Ellul, and these people were all kind of getting at the same thing. As a matter of fact, in the introduction to the book I'm writing now (*Technopoly*, 1992), I try to make this point very explicit: that there has been a sort of conversation going on, in recent times I mean. It has its antecedents back in the Old Testament. But in modern times, you know, the people from the Frankfurt School, like Adorno and Hannah Arendt and so on who started to write about this, and then you get up to Mumford and Boorstin and then on to McLuhan, and then all I'm doing is continuing. This is my contribution to the conversation."[119]

---

[119] Interview by Gregory E. Reynolds. Transcript. New York University, 18 April 1990, 28, 29.

PART II: CRITICAL THEORISTS   127

In 1970 Dr. Postman founded the Media Ecology Program at New York University. This was the first of its kind in the communication study academic landscape. NYU was founded in 1831 as a private liberal arts university. It is comprised of seven undergraduate colleges including the School of Education, of which Postman's department is a part.[120] Postman is University Professor of Communications Arts and Sciences and the Chair of the Department of Culture and Communications in which the Media Ecology Program is taught. This program, according to Dr. Postman is "based on the assumption that the forms of human communication are fundamental in shaping psychological, social, and even political consciousness. ...our focus is on how 'extensions of man' create unique environments, and I am happy to say that more university communication departments than ever accept this project."[121]

As a critic, writer, educator and communications theorist Neil Postman has written almost two dozen books, including, *Language in America* (19??), *Teaching as a Subversive Activity* (1969, with Charles Weingartner), *Teaching as a Conserving Activity* (1979), *The Disappearance of Childhood* (1983), *Amusing Ourselves to Death* (1985), *Conscientious Objections* (1988), *Technopoly* (1992), and *The End of Education* (1995).

Postman has lectured around the world, and his articles have appeared in *The New York Times Magazine*, *The Atlantic*, *The Saturday Review*, *The Harvard Education Review*, *The Washington Post*, *The Los Angeles Times*, *Stern* and *Le Monde*. For ten years, he was editor of *Et Cetera*, the journal of General Semantics. Postman is recipient of the George Orwell Award for Clarity in Language by the National Council of Teachers of English, the Christian Lindback Award for excellence in teaching and the Distinguished Professor Award by New York University. He was the Laurence Lombard Visiting Professor of The Press and Public Policy at the John F. Kennedy School of Government at Harvard University in 1991.

Postman maintains that each significant media theorist has one book which sets forth the main thesis or doctrine of his thought. The rest, he maintains, is commentary. Among the most significant books of this kind, Postman has students read: Ellul, *The Technological Society*; McLuhan, *Understanding Media*; Mumford, *Technics and Civilization*.[122] He also requires first year doctoral students to read classics such as: Wiener's *The Human Use of Human Beings* (1950).[123]

Postman clearly departs from the McLuhan *modus operandi* in advocating the primacy of traditional text oriented education. He has no interest in

---

[120] *Barron's Profiles of American Colleges*, 16th ed., 1988.
[121] Dr. Neil Postman to Gregory E. Reynolds, letter, 13 July 1998.
[122] Interview by Gregory E. Reynolds. Transcript. New York University, 18 April 1990, 31.
[123] Lance Strate, "Norbert Wiener." owner-mediaecology@ube.ubalt.edu (26 Feb. 1999).

swimming through the Maelstrom. His trenchant modern classic, *Amusing Ourselves to Death* (1985), is a penetrating critique of the pervasive cultural influence of television. While avoiding the Luddite position, Postman advocates media education, which understands the proper place and use of each medium according to its uniqueness, and thus "demystifies" them.[124] Thus television and the computer need to be properly understood and then used to serve the purposes of education rather than dictate them. That purpose is as Cicero stated: "to free the student from the tyranny of the present."[125] As a medium for entertainment television is excellent; as a medium for education television is a problem, not part of the solution.

In *Technopoly* Postman takes on the cultural monopoly of technology itself. Postman applies the McLuhan insight of questioning the way in which computing and television change the entire educational and cultural enterprise. Education is always uppermost in Postman's thinking. Having moved from tools to technocracy in the Industrial Revolution, we are now entering Technopoly in which every aspect of human life is reduced to machinery and technique.[126] "The milieu in which Technopoly flourishes is one in which the tie between information and human purpose has been severed."[127] The deification of technology which characterizes Technopoly effects every institution in our culture. This is most dangerously true of education, which is the one institution that should offer a defense against Technopoly.[128] Postman digs down to the foundational questions. "Lacking a lucid set of ethics and having rejected tradition, Technopoly searches for a source of authority and finds it in the idea of statistical objectivity."[129] In the end the scientific view of the world rules and defines not only words to describe its functions and goals, but the very idea of what is meaningful. Thus ensues the "great symbol drain." Postman's solution is development of an army of "loving resistance fighters." Many of Postman's specific suggestions for educational reform are conceptually useful. His ten commandments for the resistance are perceptive. But his own affirmation of the ultimate relativity of the "great narratives" and the "conversation" of Western intellectual tradition leaves us with humanity as the final locus of meaning.

---

[124] Neil Postman, *Amusing Ourselves To Death: Public Discourse in the Age of Show Business* (New York: Viking Penguin, Inc., 1985) 161. In a personal letter in May 1996 Postman expressed having ":no interest" in the Internet, even though students have created a Neil Postman website since then.
[125] *Ibid.*, 146.
[126] Neil Postman, *Technopoly: The Surrender of Culture to Technology* (New York: Vintage, 1993) 52.
[127] *Ibid.*, 70.
[128] *Ibid.*, 71ff.
[129] *Ibid.*, 132.

Postman's Second Commandment critique of media doesn't go far enough theoretically, because he has rejected the normativity of the context of that commandment and its assessment of idolatry. Furthermore, he is interested in culture, not cultus. In many particulars, both of his media criticism and his proposed pedagogical remedies, Postman is pointing in the right direction. His own theoretical relativism, which we shall discuss more fully in the next chapter, radically undermines any hope for the effectiveness of his proposals.

Two Articulate Near Luddites

Sven Birkerts (1951-)

Born in Pontiac, Michigan, Birkerts completed his liberal arts degree at the University of Michigan in 1973. He then spent a number of years in the "book business". His passion for writing grew as he read and became more enthralled with the world of books. He worked in a number of "Used and Antiquarian" bookstores, such as Charring Cross in Ann Arbor and Boston's famed Brattle Book Shop. Eventually he would teach expository writing at Harvard, and writing, literature, and publication at Emerson College. While his initial attempt at writing a novel was never published, he found his niche as a literary critic. In the well worn tradition of communications studies he is part of the core faculty of the Bennington Writing Seminar, loosely connected with Bennington College in Vermont. Since 1997 Birkerts has been a lecturer in non-fiction writing at Mount Holyoke College in South Hadley, Massachusetts. Birkerts has written three books of criticism and been recognized with several awards for the excellence of his work. He has also been awarded the Lila Wallace-Reader's Digest Foundation and Guggenheim fellowships. His essays and reviews have appeared in the *New York Times Book Review*, the *Atlantic Monthly*, *Harper's*, and the *New Republic*.

As a literary critic Birkerts is profoundly aware of the insights of Havelock, McLuhan, Ong and Postman. "The medium shapes the message."[130] Birkerts is presently one of the most articulate apologists for the unique genius and benefit of reading, and the beauty of writing, or for what Ong refers to as *chirographic man*, the penman. His *The Guttenberg Elegies: The Fate of Reading in an Electronic Age* (1994), is an unashamed apology for the written, printed and read word. As the electronic media spread our sensibilities over the surfaces of life and culture, the "vast lateral connectedness," and thus rob us of the interiorizing strength of reading and writing, the human presence is

---

[130] Sven Birkerts, *The Guttenberg Elegies: The Fate of Reading in an Electronic Age* (Winchester, MA: Faber and Faber, Inc., 1994) 215.

seriously diminished. Depth is replaced with shallowness. "Our postmodern culture is a vast fabric of competing isms; we are leaderless and subject to the terrors, masked as freedoms, of an absolute relativism."[131]

Clifford Stoll (ca. 1952-)

Stoll is valuable to the media critic, not for theoretical reasons, but as a testimony of an insider to the reality of the modern problem of *cyber-hype*. His wittily written *Silicon Snake Oil: Second Thoughts on the Information Highway* (1995) is the confession of a computer-Internet addict.[132] As a true iconoclast Stoll explodes myths left and right with all the credibility of an early user. While acknowledging the benefits of the on-line and computer worlds, as an astronomer, he articulates grave reservations concerning the overblown claims of techies and cyberspace promoters. He challenges conventional assumptions at a pragmatic level, especially debunking myths about vaunted educational uses of computing and the Internet. Stoll used the emerging computer network as a scientist in the seventies, writing software and using his connection for research and recreation.[133]

"What started out so various, so beautiful, so new, now appears to be less than meets the eye."[134] Stoll went on to discover that "[l]ife in the real world is far more interesting, far more important, far richer, than anything you'll ever find on a computer screen."[135] In short nothing can replace personal presence and interaction. We might add that the problem with virtual reality is that it lacks virtue. The virtue it lacks is discovered in examining its many claims to enhance the virtues of our civilization. It claims to promote reading, education, personal communication, community, empowerment and democracy. In reality it undermines all of these, claims Stoll. His conclusion is simple and profound: stop grossly overestimating the information highway and its entrance ramp the personal computer. "For all the promises of virtual communities, its more important to live a real life in a real neighborhood."[136]

---

[131] *Ibid.*, 228.
[132] Clifford Stoll, *Silicon Snake Oil: Second Thoughts on the Information Highway* (New York: Doubleday, 1995).
[133] *Ibid.*, 12.
[134] *Ibid.*
[135] *Ibid.*, 13.
[136] *Ibid.*, 235.

Daniel Chandler (ca. 1950-)

Dr. Chandler teaches in the Education Department of the University of Wales in Aberystwyth. In his first year course, "Introduction to Media Theory," Chandler explores two major themes: first, the active ways we interpret "reality, the world, meaning and information"; second, the extent to which we are influenced by the media themselves.[137] Chandler is critical of the "transmission model of communication" known as the Shannon-Weaver Model, SMCR (source-message-channel-receiver), due to its failure to adequately deal with both the nature of media themselves and the nuances of message content.[138] Chandler is also critical of "cultivation theory," an "approach developed by Professor George Gerbner, dean of the Annenberg School of Communications at the University of Pennsylvania. Chandler began the 'Cultural Indicators' research project in the mid-1960s, to study whether and how watching television may influence viewers' ideas of what the everyday world is like." Chandler maintains that "[o]ver-reliance on content analysis" tends to overlook the influence of the medium itself as well as the active interpretation of the viewer.[139]

Chandler's main thrust, however, is a critique of "technological determinism" and its offspring "media determinism." In his discussion of this topic we learn his own greatest strength, and thus value for the Christian Media Ecologist. Chandler is a professor bent on asking the right questions as he challenges his students to deal with the central issues of communication theory. The negative is that for all of his criticism of McLuhan and Postman, he does not offer a cogent alternative. However, he does raise concerns about Media Ecology which ought to be addressed by every serious student and theorist.

In "Technological or Media Determinism," Chandler asks the global question which lies at the interface between media theory and cultural criticism. "A central controversy concerns how far technology does or does not condition social change."[140] "Technological determinism" is the belief that technology is the "prime mover" of history. Chandler cites Sigfried Giedion, Leslie White, Lynn White Jr, Harold Innis and Marshall McLuhan as examples of this theory. His problem is with any "mono-causal" explanation of history, which reduces historical cause to a single force, whether it be Cartesian

---

[137] Daniel Chandler, (1994, Rev. 1998): "Introduction to Media Theory," [WWW document] URL http://www.aber.ac.uk/~dgc/ed30410.html [13 July 1999].
[138] Daniel Chandler, (1994, Rev. 1998): "The Transmission Model of Communication" [WWW document] URL http://www.aber.ac.uk/~dgc/trans.html [13 July 1999].
[139] Daniel Chandler, (1994, Rev. 1998): "Cultivation Theory" [WWW document] URL http://www.aber.ac.uk/~dgc/cult.html [13 July 1999].
[140] Daniel Chandler, (1995, rev. 1998): "Technological or Media Determinism" [WWW document] URL http://www.aber.ac.uk/~dgc/tecdet.html [13 July 1999].

quantification or Ellul's autonomy of "technique." Chandler's practical concern is that such determinism leaves people with a sense of helplessness in the face of technological autonomy. Chandler points out that both positive and negative technological determinists assume this autonomy. The positive, progress oriented determinists, like Lewis Mumford, posit a linear evolution which is headed inevitably toward better and better control over our environment. The negative determinists, like McLuhan and Postman, forecast the doom of man enslaved to the machine.

Chandler fails to take into account a dimension of the McLuhan/Postman/Ellul Media Ecology which we will discuss in the next chapter. They all believe in an irreducible center to man which enables him to "resist" the determining power of technology/media.

Chandler reminds us of two areas to which the Christian Media Ecologist must pay attention. First, we must not reduce cultural formation, and hence criticism, to a single force. Culture is formed under a matrix of influences. I believe we may assert this without minimizing the centrality of communication as a distinguishing characteristic of man as God's image. Second, however powerful the influence of any aspect of culture may be it is neither inevitable in itself, nor is its affect on us in particular inevitable. What Chandler fails to take into account are sin and the existence and presence of the true and living God. Just here the Christian affirms at once that God is absolutely sovereign and that we are absolutely responsible.

Joshua Meyrowitz (1949-)

Born in New York City, Meyrowitz completed his undergraduate degree in mass communication and drama at Queens College of the City University of New York in 1972. After finishing a masters degree at Queens in 1974, he went on to receive his doctorate in media theory at New York University, in the program directed by Neil Postman, in 1978. Since 1979 Meyrowitz has been teaching in the undergraduate Department of Communication at the University of New Hampshire. In 1998 he was awarded the Class of 1938 Professorship. He has been widely acclaimed for both his scholarship and his teaching ability. For *No Sense of Place* he was awarded the Book of the Year Award by the National Association of Broadcasters and the Broadcast Education Association. He also won the Lindberg Award for Outstanding Scholar-Teacher in the College of Liberal Arts in the University of New Hampshire. His articles have been published in scholarly journals such as the *Journal of Communication*, as well as popular publications such as *Psychology Today, Newsweek,* the *Boston Globe,* and *USA Today.*

In 1985 Meyrowitz published his ground breaking book *No Sense of Place: The Impact of Electronic Media on Social Behavior*. This is a synthetic work of great scope and insight combining the "medium theory" of Marshall McLuhan with the sociological "situationist" paradigm of Erving Goffman. "The situational analysis offered here describes how electronic media affect social behavior—not through the power of their messages but by reorganizing social settings in which people interact and by weakening the once strong relationship between physical place and social 'place.'"[141] "The situationists suggest how our particular actions and words are shaped by our knowledge of who has access to them, and the medium theorists suggest that new media change such patterns of access."[142] Meyrowitz explores the social implications of the shift from "print situations" to "electronic situations."[143] McLuhan's observation of this change was summed up in his concept of "retribalization" caused by the pervasiveness of electronic media. It is the mechanism of this change which is not clear in McLuhan. Changes in "sensory balance" do not in themselves account for changes in behavior. Meyrowitz proposes a link between face-to-face interaction and media in the "structure of social 'situations.'"[144]

Goffman distinguished between "backstage" and "onstage" social settings as necessary aspects human life. What is appropriate in one setting may not be appropriate in the other. Television offers a concrete example of this link. It tends to blur social boundaries such as public and private, masculine and feminine, adult and child. Children "overhear" the adult world which used to function "backstage" and now the boundary between childhood and adulthood is removed. It is not the message of television but its change of the "'situational geography' of social life" which is producing a "new social order."[145] "Electronic media have undermined the traditional relationship between physical setting and social setting." Thus we live in a "placeless" culture of electronic nomads.[146] Television "frees us from the constraints of our isolated physical locations, but flies us to a place that is no place at all."[147] Meyrowitz advocates an awareness of boundary changes in the situational pattern of social behavior.

In response to the common criticism of Meyrowitz's approach, that it is deterministic, he asserts that we are both limited and free. "I argue, ...that once

---

[141] Joshua Meyrowitz, *No Sense of Place: The Impact of Electronic Media on Social Behavior* (New York: Oxford University Press, 1985) ix.
[142] *Ibid.*, 33.
[143] *Ibid.*, 3.
[144] *Ibid.*, 4.
[145] *Ibid.*, 4-6.
[146] *Ibid.*, 7-9.
[147] Joshua Meyrowitz, "The 19-Inch Neighborhood," *Newsweek* (22 July 1985): 8.

invented and used, media affect us by shaping the type of interactions that take place through them. We cannot play certain roles unless the stages for those roles exist." We are both controlled and controlling. We are born with physical and social constraints, but also have the freedom to analyse our situation and act accordingly.[148]

Meyrowitz offers the media critic a helpful synthetic approach to media criticism, by combining the metaphors used historically by others to analyse media in the history of communication study. Media are viewed as *conduits* in which the content of messages are analyzed, as *languages* in which the grammar (unique variables or production techniques) of a medium is analyzed, and as *environments* in which the environment created by a medium is analyzed.[149] His experience in film production at Queens College makes his analysis all the more compelling. We shall consider this analytical paradigm in chapter 5.

The negative in Meyrowtiz's account is similar to that of Postman. The absence of the normative element in his critical apparatus will leave the Christian Media Ecologist unsatisfied. The extent to which his observations have enabled him to develop a paradigm of analysis consistent with a Christian worldview will determine the use of his work to the Christian thinker. Like Postman, Meyrowitz's Jewish heritage gives him certain covenantal assumptions about the family and other mediating institutions, which may be inconsistent with his own ultimate commitments, but leave the Christian critic with excellent tools and insights for which to be grateful.

In conclusion we should note the impetus of sociology in communication study. Postman observes the contrast between two types of totalitarianism embodied in Orwell's and Huxley's future scenarios. Postman opts for Huxley. I would prefer to look at both as a kind of polarity describing the temptation or "test" of our culture. Lazarsfeld (as an illuminated detail of the history of communication study) courted and did market research for both the Federal government and Madison Avenue. In both institutions their knowledge, ala the elitist sociological assumptions of Auguste Comte (cf. p. 51), comes from sociology as translated and applied by Lasarsfeld (with the help of Merton his theorist, not to be confused with Merlin the Magician). All of these early sociologists were heavily influenced by Pragmatist William James and Reformist Educator John Dewey. Lasswell's government policy studies thrust was inspired, he said, by Dewey. In the absence of the Christian hope in the

---

[148] Meyrowitz, *No Sense of Place*, 328, 329.
[149] Joshua Meyrowitz, "Images of Media: Hidden Ferment—and Harmony—in the Field." *Journal of Communication* 43, no. 3 (summer 1993): 55-66; "Multiple Media Literacies." *Journal of Communication* 48, no. 1 (winter 1998): 96-108.

City of God, modernity has spawned a host of "Paradise projects," which seek a man-made heaven on earth. This is the gnostic tendency writ large.

Czitrom concludes his history *Media and the American Mind* by positing a dialectic, which he sees reflected in the American mind he has explored. The dialectic is the tension between the progressive instinct which looks at the Utopian possibilities of new communications technologies, and their sinister use as instruments of tyranny.[150] From a Christian perspective this analysis falls short because it places the tension on only one side of the larger dialectic between the City of Man and the City of God, between those who succumb to the tyrannies of state or self, and those who manage media, technology and culture as a stewardship before the Creator and Sustainer of history. Czitrom's ultimate message is "power to the people." He sees the present proliferation of media as an opportunity for individuals to wrest back power from the commercial giants who have controlled mass media for business purposes for so long.[151] The "dream of transcendence through machines," which Czitrom properly understands to be ancient,[152] will move toward a Tower of Babel on either side of his dialectic. The nightmares of Orwell and Huxley seem to be two perspectives on the same tragic human project. Once one has denied the existence of Original Sin the true conflict is ignored.

An important connection exists between the development of communication study in the soil of Federal interests during the war effort and the broader humanistic interest in controlling society and culture in the hope of making a Paradise on earth.[153] The problems of the human condition, as political and social engineers believe, especially as those conditions have been exacerbated by urbanization, industrialization, immigration, and secularization, can be solved by scientific analysis and governmental solutions. One particularly notable theme of Rogers' history is the influence of Rockefeller money and social theory on communication study. He lists thirteen major Rockefeller contributions between 1891 and 1955. $35 million was given to the founding of the University of Chicago between 1891 and 1910. Baptist

---

[150] Czitrom, *Media and the American Mind*, 184.

[151] *Ibid.*, 194-196.

[152] *Ibid.*, 187.

[153] Cf. Christopher Simpson, *Science of Coercion: Communication Research & Psychological Warfare 1945-1960* (Oxford University Press, New York/Oxford, 1994). "For the first decade after 1945 -- which is to say, the decade in which communications studies crystallized into a distinct academic field, complete with colleges, graduate degrees, and so on -- U.S. military, propaganda, and intelligence agencies provided the large majority of all project funding for the field. The earliest cumulative data concerning government funding of social science is provided by the National Science Foundation (NSF) in 1952; that report shows that over 96 percent of all reported federal funding for social science at that time was drawn from the U.S. military . . . Social science funding rooted in national security missions totaled $12.27 million that year, the NSF reported, while comparable 'civilian' funding totaled only $280,000.", 52.

president Harper turned to devout Baptist John D. Rockefeller for funding for this new kind of urban university, which would seek scientific answers to the social problems of the new urban society represented by Chicago. From 1923 to 1932 Rockefeller gave $3.4 million to the social sciences at Chicago. The Rockefeller Foundation went on to fund Lasarsfeld's fellowship to the United States from 1933 to 1935; Lasarsfeld's Radio Research Project; Hull, Hovland and other Yale faculty in the founding of the Yale Institute of Human Relations; Hovland's Yale Communication Research Project on persuasion; Kurt Lewin's work at the University of Iowa; the ten meetings of the Rockefeller Communication Seminar; Lasswell's War-Time Communications Project on propaganda analysis; Schramm's communication research symposium, and a conference on educational television at the University of Illinois; Wiener's research on the cybernetics of brain physiology at MIT; and Gregory Bateson's cybernetic research and interactional communication.[154]

Rockefeller's vision for social improvement was not limited to higher education and communication study. The Rockefeller Foundation funded a study which led to the publication of *Rethinking Missions: A Layman's Inquiry* in 1932. This study was part of a concerted effort among Liberal naturalists within the Presbyterian Church in the USA to radically challenge the spiritual nature of the church along lines of social improvement through government, educational and ecclesiastical institutions.[155] Theirs was an ecumenical project of worldwide proportions, a quest to bring human potential to its fruition, and scale to the heights of heaven by human endeavor. The most notable opponent of the Liberalism within the PCUSA was Princeton Theological Seminary professor J. Gresham Machen. He deplored both the syncretistic impulse of the liberals within the church, as well as the "tyranny of experts" outside the church. Machen's Reformed Protestant, as well as Southern Agrarian instincts moved him to oppose the Utopian goals of the anti-metaphysical pragmatism of the social sciences.[156] In 1933 Machen wrote:

> What will be the end of European civilization, of which I had a survey from my mountain vantage ground - of that European civilization and its daughter America? What does the future hold in store? Will Luther

---

[154] Rogers, *A History of Communication Study*, 143, 144.

[155] Cf. John Patton Galbraith, *Why the Orthodox Presbyterian Church?* (Philadelphia: Committee on Christian Education of the OPC, 1939) *Rethinking Missions* was a report by an interdenominational committee about foreign mission work, led by Prof. Hocking of Harvard, which "favored an eclectic religion composed of the good parts of all religions." The report insists that "the missionary "will look forward not to the destruction of these religions (of Asia), but to their continued coexistence with Christianity, each stimulating the other's growth toward the ultimate goal, unity in the completest religious truth."

[156] D. G. Hart. *Defending the Faith: J. Gresham Machen and the Crisis of Conservative Protestantism in Modern America* (Baltimore: Johns Hopkins University Press, 1994), 102, 103.

prove to have lived in vain? Will all the dreams of liberty issue into some vast industrial machine? Will even nature be reduced to standard, as in our country the sweetness of the woods and hills is being destroyed, as I have seen them destroyed in Maine, by the uniformities and artificialities and officialdom of our national parks? ....Will some dreadful second law of thermodynamics apply in the spiritual as well as in the material realm? Will all things in church and state be reduced to one dead level, coming at last to an equilibrium in which all liberty and all high aspirations will be gone? Will that be the end of all humanity's hopes? I can see no escape from that conclusion in the signs of the times; too inexorable seems to me to be the march of events. No, I can see only one alternative. The alternative is that there is a God - a God who in His own good time will bring forward great men again to do His will, great men to resist the tyranny of experts and lead humanity out again into the realms of light and freedom, great men, who above all, will be the messengers of His grace. There is, far above any mountain peak of vision, a God high and lifted up who, though He is infinitely exalted, yet cares for His children among men.[157]

Is not this danger, of which Machen warns, the vaunted freedom of self-reflection independent of the Trinity, the gnosis, of which McLuhan warned us as well? Does not such autonomous reflection inexorably proceed from and lead to the worship of the creature rather than the Creator? These are issues that Christian thinkers must address as they consider the Electronic Revolution in which we live, worship, serve and preach.

As a movement Media Ecology offers a perspective on media which, *mutatis mutandi*, is compatible with a Christian worldview. It can also be argued, as we have seen above, that the intellectual and spiritual frame of reference among founders, such as McLuhan, Ellul and Ong, and among contemporary thinkers such as Postman and Meyrowitz is Judeo-Christian implicitly, and at times explicitly, although never consistently. Media Ecology is inherently opposed to the tyranny of experts, and is so because it places its critical endeavor squarely in the context of the Western intellectual tradition. This was clearly the *esprit fort* of McLuhan and Ellul, and must be the attitude of the Christian Media Ecologist.

However, the lack of a unified theoretical foundation leaves Media Ecology on a insubstantial footing which will not withstand the tidal wave of the Electronic Revolution and the culture it is inexorably bringing with it. For the Christian the Word of God, and the exalted Christ, provide the only

---

[157] J. Gresham Machen, "Mountains and Why I Love Them" (Reprint from *Christianity Today*, August 1934), 11, 12.

protection and the only the only hope of ultimate conquest of the new Tower of Babel agenda, which is building a stairway to heaven, one which will one day collapse in Final Judgment.

LANDMARKS IN COMMUNICATION STUDY

1922 - Walter Lippmann publishes *Public Opinion*.
1934 - Lewis Mumford publishes *Technics and Civilization*.
1943 - Wilbur Schramm founds first doctoral program in mass communications in the world at the University of Iowa.
1947 - Wilbur Schramm founds Institute of Communications Research at the University of Illinois.
1948 - Sigfried Giedion publishes *Mechanization Takes Command: A Contribution to Anonymous History*.
1948 - Norbert Wiener publishes *Cybernetics: Or Control and Communication in the Animal and the Machine*.
1949 - Claude Shannon publishes *The Mathematical Theory of Communication*.
1950 - H. A. Innis publishes *Empire and Communication*.
1951 - H. A. Innis publishes *The Bias of Communication*.
1951 - Herbert Marshall McLuhan publishes *The Mechanical Bride: Folklore of Industrial Man*.
1953 - Institution for Communication Research at Stanford University founded.
1954 (1st French ed.) 1964 (English) - Jacques Ellul publishes *The Technological Society*.
1956 - Erik Barnouw publishes *Mass Communication*.
1957 - Vance Packard publishes *The Hidden Persuaders*.
1960 - David K. Berlo publishes *The Process of Communication*.
1960 - Merrill R. Abbey publishes *Man, Media and the Message*.
1961 - Kenneth E. Boulding publishes *The Image*.
1962 - Daniel J. Boorstin publishes *The Image or Whatever Happened to the American Dream?*
1963 - Centre for Culture and Technology established at the University of Toronto for McLuhan's work.
1964 - Marshall McLuhan publishes *Understanding Media: The Extensions of Man*.
1966 - Lewis Mumford publishes *The Myth of the Machine: Technics and Human Development*.
1967 - Walter J. Ong publishes *The Presence of the Word*.

1967 - Marshall McLuhan and Quentin Fiore publish *The Medium Is the Massage: An Inventory of Effects.*
1968 - Marshall McLuhan and Quentin Fiore publish *War and Peace in the Global Village.*
1971 - Neil Postman founds the Media Ecology Program at New York University at the suggestion of Marshall McLuhan.
1977 - Malcolm Muggeridge publishes *Christ and the Media.*
1977 - Marie Winn publishes *The Plug-in Drug.*
1982 - Walter J. Ong publishes *Orality and Literacy: The Technologizing of the Word.*
1985 - Jacques Ellul publishes *The Humiliation of the Word.*
1985 - Neil Postman publishes *Amusing Ourselves To Death: Public Discourse in the Age of Show Business.*
1986 - Theodore Roszak publishes *The Cult of Information.*
1993 - Neil Postman publishes *Technopoly: The Surrender of Culture to Technology.*
1994 - Sven Birkerts publishes *The Guttenberg Elegies: The Fate of Reading in an Electronic Age.*

AN HISTORICAL SKETCH OF
THE DEVELOPMENT OF THE ELECTRIC MEDIA

As a backdrop to media studies it is important to have an overview of the history and development of technology and the media themselves. Lewis Mumford provides a valuable resource in *Technics and Civilization*, though one must be careful of his accuracy in dates and details. His "List of Inventions" covers from 999 AD to 1933. Jacques Ellul gives a helpful overview in *The Technological Society*. Czitrom's *Media and the American Mind* focuses on the criticism of electric media, and gives a helpful background of their early development.

Telegraph, Movies and Radio

The sea change in which we are presently engulfed began technically with the first electric communication between Baltimore and Washington, DC on May 24, 1844. After battling disbelief and ridicule Samuel Finley Breese Morse (1791-1872), who had begun investigating telegraphy as early as 1832, finally convinced Congress to appropriate $30,000.00 to build the experimental line. Morse's famous first message is unwittingly prescient: "What hath God wrought!" By 1852, just eight years later, 23,000 miles of line, referred to as "lightning lines," had been laid.[158] Public reaction was almost universally optimistic. On January 15, 1846 the *Philadelphia North American* heralded the telegraph's revolutionary effect to be the "annihilation of time." As part of a minority of dissenters, Boston minister Ezra S. Gannett, after quoting Job 38:35, called electricity "the swift winged messenger of destruction."[159] But most saw the new means of instant communication as a "wonderful vehicle" for Christian world unity.[160] Technology would enable civilization to advance to new heights in subduing nature. Postmillenial eschatology provided an optimistic view of the future which knew no bounds, given the energy of the new nation, the city set on a hill. Morse convinced Congress to fund his experiment by prophesying that the telegraph would make "one neighborhood of the whole country..." and unify the intelligence of America. He anticipated the "global village."[161] As can readily be imagined newspapers quickly availed themselves of the new instant information and the "wire service" was born.[162] So the modern newspaper was born, too.

Henry David Thoreau was one of the few intelligent critics to point out the most significant negative consequence of the new wonder. In the seclusion of Walden Pond (1845-1847) he opined: "We are in great haste to construct an magnetic telegraph from Maine to Texas; but Maine and Texas, it may be, have nothing important to communicate ...We are eager to tunnel under the Atlantic and bring the old world some weeks nearer to the new; but perchance the first news that will leak through into the broad flapping American ear will be that Princess Adelaide has the whooping cough." By decontextualizing information the new medium would change the nature of discourse, trivializing the profound and making the irrelevant relevant.[163] Not everyone was thrilled with the idea of a national village either. In 1889 *The Spectator* mused over "The Intellectual Effects of Electricity": "The world is for purposes of intelligence reduced to a village." The incompleteness of information as well as the lack of time to reflect on its significance causes "perpetual dissipation of the mind."[164] The problem of "information overload" and its concomitant lack of teleology was already being noticed by our grandfathers.

As for the rest, even the most thoughtful men of letters, such as Whitman, Emerson and Van Wych Brooks set their eyes on a glorious future in which the

---

[158] Czitrom, *Media and the American Mind*, 3-6.
[159] *Ibid.*, 7, 9.
[160] *Ibid.*, 10.
[161] *Ibid.*, 11, 12.
[162] *Ibid.*, 67. Cf. Czitrom, 14ff.
[163] Postman, *Amusing Ourselves To Death*, 65-69. Cf. Thoreau's *Walden*.
[164] Czitrom, *Media and the American Mind*, 19.

democratic ideal would be realized in the universal dissemination of the best knowledge.[165]

Then came the movies. In 1892 the first moving picture camera was invented and used. By 1900 there were four hundred theaters in New York City alone. Almost one quarter of the population attended. This caused The Rev. Richard H. Edwards to lament: "Why has the love of spontaneous play given way so largely to the love of merely being amused?"[166]

The third great electric medium, radio, was the first to bring the outside world into the homes of Americans. Marchese Guglielmo Marconi (1874-1937) of Bologna, successfully experimented with wireless telegraphy as early as 1895. In 1897 he founded the Marconi Wireless Telegraph Co., Ltd. in London. The first signal was sent across the Atlantic in 1902. Czitrom titles his chapter on radio "The Ethereal Hearth."[167]

Television

The first attempt to transmit an image via wire was by the German Paul Nipkow in 1884. Laying the groundwork for television in 1887 Heinrich Hertz identified the photoelectric effect and in 1906 Lee De Forest invented the vacuum tube. In 1925 American Charles Francis Jenkins broadcast a silhouette picture in Washington, DC. In 1926 John L. Baird applied the vacuum tube to amplify the image, the cathode ray replaced the perforated disk for receiving, and he publicly demonstrated his shadow pictures. On September 11, 1928 General Electric presented the first televised dramatic production.

Then Vladimir Zworykin developed the ionoscope for electronic scanning, producing a partially electronic television system in 1923. It was an Idaho farm boy, Philo T. Farnsworth, who invented a completely electronic television, suitable for home viewing in 1930. Allen B. Du Mont developed the first commercially available television sets in 1939. RCA president David Sarnoff began experimental broadcasting from the Empire State Building through his subsidiary, National Broadcasting Company, in 1932. In 1935 the British Broadcasting Corporation began experimental broadcasting. In 1936 the Columbia Broadcasting System began installing its own system in the Chrysler Building. The first notable public event, the coronation procession of George VI, was broadcast in 1937. 1939 witnessed a host of firsts: NBC began its regular broadcasting with the opening ceremonies of the New York World's Fair, at which President Roosevelt became the first televised president; and the first broadcast of a major league baseball game. On February 1, 1940 the first

---

[165] *Ibid.*, 35, 36.
[166] *Ibid.*, 38, 43.
[167] *Ibid.*, 60.

network broadcast from NBC was rebroadcast by General Electric's WRBC in Schenectady, NY.

In 1941 the standard code for commercial telecasting was established in the United States, requiring 525 scanning lines in the picture with a minimum of 30 pictures per second. Commercial broadcasting began in the summer of 1941 with WNBT broadcasting 15 hours of programming per week in New York City. By 1945, after a hiatus in development due to the war, NBC began network broadcasting connecting New York with Philadelphia and Schenectady. By 1948 there were 36 stations servicing 1 millions sets. By 1953, 125 stations were broadcasting from 77 cities, with the three networks, NBC, CBS, and ABC firmly established; and by 1956 there were 38 million televisions in the United States. By 1970 118 countries had television, with 880 stations on the air in the United States, in 59.4 million homes watching 6.5 hours per day.[168]

The Personal Computer and the Internet

Blaise Pascal (1623-1662) invented the first mechanical adding machine in 1642, although Mumford attributes this invention to another Frenchman of the same place and era, John Napier (1550-1617), in 1620.[169] So much for Mumford's precision with dates. Suffice it say that mechanical devices for computing were invented in France in the early seventeenth century. This invention laid the basis for the modern electronic computer.

Beginning in 1822 English inventor Charles Babbage developed the first calculating machine. By 1834 he had developed a "programmable machine that became the forerunner of the modern computer." This proto-computer was controlled by punch cards adapted from the device used by French weavers to control thread sequences. He became aware of the power of his invention to classify, store and retrieve information through the manipulation of non-numerical symbols. Postman maintains that this discovery is comparable to the Greek invention of the phonetic alphabet. The modern computer had to await the discovery of the telegraph, the telephone, and the application of Boolean algebra to relay-based circuitry.[170]

Claude Shannon, as we have seen in chapter 3, developed the concept of the "binary digit" or "bit," at the Bell Labs in 1949, which became the basic

---

[168] *Compton's Pictured Encyclopedia*, 1957 ed., s.v. "Television." *The Encyclopedia Americana International Edition.* Danbury, CT: Grolier Incorporated, 1997, s.v. "Television."
[169] Douglas Groothuis, http://www.gospelcom.net/ivpress/groothuis/truthincyber.htm. Mumford, Lewis. *Technics and Civilization* (New York: Harcourt, Brace and World, 1934) 440.
[170] Neil Postman, *Technopoly: The Surrender of Culture to Technology*, (New York: Vintage, 1993) 109.

building block (digital logic circuitry) for computer programming. The first programming used the Hollerith (IBM) card as the memory unit of computing. Herman Hollerith, a statistician and the founder of the Tabulating Machine Company in 1896 (now IBM), developed the first electromechanical machine to read and sort the data entered on punch cards. He conceived this machine during the 1880 census and used it on the 1890 census, completing the tally in one third the time it had taken a decade earlier. During the 1940s John von Neumann invented the first version of what we now refer to as the "computer," which as Postman asserts, was the beginning of the idea that a machine, and not a person, does the calculating.[171] George R. Stibitz, a physicist at the Bell Telephone Laboratories, was the first to use telephone lines for his Complex Number Calculator. The first large-scale automatic digital computer, the Mark I, was conceived by Howard H. Aiken of Harvard in 1937, and produced by IBM. It was also the first commercial computer with eight sales. The Mark II was a relay computer which weighed 5 tons and contained 23,000 relays and 13,000 vacuum tubes, making about one computation per second. The first successful experimental all-electronic binary computer was built by John B. Atanasoff at Iowa State University in 1939. In 1946 the first general-purpose electronic digital computer was built at the University of Pennsylvania by J. Presper Eckert and John W. Mauchly. Known as ENIAC (Electronic Numerical Integrator and Computer), it was used in the Manhattan Project. It was 1,000 times faster than its electromechanical predecessor.

Between 1952 and 1958 the first-generation computers were manufactured with vacuum tube circuits, individual processors and electromagnetic memories, and used by large scientific customers and government sponsored laboratories. In 1953 IBM delivered its first Defense Calculator, the IBM 701. In 1955 the 702 was marketed to take advantage of the growing commercial data processing industry. The 1947 invention of the transistor began to replace the vacuum tube in second-generation computers developed in cooperation with defense related applications. Along with improved magnetic-core memory the transistor was capable of executing over 100,000 instructions per second. Between 1964 and the mid seventies the silicon chip, combined with IBM's recognition that compatibility among various computers was commercially important, lead to IBM's introduction of the System/360 series in 1964, for scientific and commercial customers.

In 1959 Ken Olsen of Digital Equipment Corporation began to develop the first commercial "minicomputer," known as the PDP-1 (Programmed Digital Processor). In 1965 the PDP-8 was the first to use integrated circuits.

---

[171] *Ibid.*, 110.

It fit in a packing case and cost $18,000.[172] Beginning in 1975 an advanced version, known as DEC VAX, became very popular in academic circles because it provided multiple terminals allowing many students to use it at once. The fourth-generation computers were launched with the micro-processor, invented by Intel inventor Marcian "Ted" Hoff, Jr. in 1971 as the 4004 and sold for $1,000.[173] By 1980 IBM introduced the 8086 16-bit Intel chip as the industry standard. This central processing unit (CPU) combined with the development of random access memory (RAM) and semiconductor memory laid the groundwork for a communications revolution with the advent of the personal computer and the Internet. Soon mainframe capabilities would be available on a desk top.

The personal computer became popular in the 1970s. In the early 1970s Xerox Corporation began to develop the microchip at its Xerox PARC site near Stanford University.[174] This allowed for the transition from the bulky room sized computers of the 1960s, with their cathode tubes and punch cards, to the high tech personal computers which went on sale in the early 1980s. The first personal computer, replete with monitor and floppy disks, developed by Xerox PARC was called the Alto. Xerox invented the first graphic user interface (GUI) with mouse, icons, and overlapping windows and word processor. "In January 1975 the first microprocessor-based computer, the Altair 8800, was announced on the cover of *Popular Electronics*." Altair 8800 was a hobbyist's do-it-yourself kit and had 256 bytes of memory with no keyboard and no display, all for $397.[175] "In 1977, Ken Olsen, president of Digital Equipment Corporation, proclaimed, 'There is no reason for any individual to have a computer in their (sic) home.'"[176] Meanwhile the Commadore PET and Radio Shack's Tandy were marketed, and along with the Altair 8800, sold well.

But it was left for a more savvy group of techies, who formed Microsoft and Apple, to recognize the market and take the ball. The producer of the Altair 8800, Micro Instrumentation Telemetry Systems (MITS), entered into a licensing agreement with Bill Gates and Paul Allen, who had produced a BASIC software programming system for MITS in 1975.[177] Meanwhile Apple Computer Inc. (1976) founder Steve Jobs and his partner Steve Wozniak were also among the first to develop a commercial personal computer with the advent of Apple II series and Macintosh. Unlike Olsen, Jobs envisioned the

---

[172] Martin Campbell-Kelly, and William Aspray, *Computer: A History of the Information Machine* (New York: BasicBooks, 1996) 224.
[173] *Ibid.*, 236
[174] R. Emmett Tyrrell, Jr., "The Internet Turns Thirty," *The American Spectator* 32:10 (October 1999): 14, 16, 75.
[175] Campbell-Kelly, *Computer: A History of the Information Machine*, 240.
[176] Stoll, *Silicon Snake Oil*, 12.
[177] Campbell-Kelly, *Computer: A History of the Information Machine*, 242.

PART II: CRITICAL THEORISTS 145

personal computer as a home appliance.[178] By then IBM had marketed the first desktop computer (model 5100) for the scientific market in 1975 and by 1980 was marketing a microprocessor based word processor.[179] In 1980 Gates entered an agreement with IBM for an operating system. Gates did not have one actually developed, so he purchased one from Seattle Computer Products, and MS-DOS was launched. As the interface between hardware and software, it became an indispensable part of every IBM typePC by 1983.[180] In 1981 the original IBM Acorn was marketed as the IBM Personal Computer with 64 Kilobytes of memory, an Intel 8088 microprocessor and a floppy disk for $2,880. Almost overnight it became the industry standard. Clones, like Compaq, called IBM-compatibles, flooded the market and *Time* nominated the PC "Man of the Year."[181] Meanwhile, Steve Job sought his market niche by producing better software.[182] "By the end of 1981 the affordable, reliable personal computer was routinely available to anyone who wanted one."[183]

The problem was that only Macintosh, which made up 10% of personal computers, was "user-friendly." The rest had to rely on the Disk Operating System (DOS), usually MS-DOS, which relied on the old mainframe technology of the efficient but intimidating UNIX system. Only techies were comfortable with this operating system, which functioned off of a single line command on a black screen. The graphic user interface (GUI) was designed to enable anyone to intuitively use the PC, through a system of icons, pull down menus and windows.[184] Pioneering work had been done on developing a GUI by Doug Engelbart and J. C. R. Licklider ("man-computer symbiosis") at the Stanford Research Institute (SRI) and David Evans's and Ivan Sutherland's graphics research group at the University of Utah in the 1960s. The use of the standard typewriter keyboard and the mouse pointer came from the SRI research in 1965. Xerox was the first to develop the GUI, as noted above. After its Alto "workstation" was used in the White House and Congress in 1975, the Xerox Star was launched in 1981, but proved to be a failure due to poor marketing and high retail price.[185]

Meanwhile in late 1979 Steve Jobs was invited by Xerox PARC to enter into a marketing agreement which gave Apple access to Xerox PARC's technology. Xerox's Larry Tesler was recruited to develop the Lisa to replace the Apple II. It, too, proved to be a commercial failure in 1983 for the same

---

[178] *Ibid.*, 248.
[179] *Ibid.*, 253.
[180] *Ibid.*, 263.
[181] *Ibid.*, 257.
[182] *Ibid.*, 258.
[183] *Ibid.*, 264.
[184] *Ibid.*, 264, 265.
[185] *Ibid.*, 266-269.

reasons the Xerox Star had failed before it. This left Jobs with the task of creating the Macintosh to compete with IBM.[186] In January 1984 the Mac was launched in a Super Bowl ad. But once again its cost ($2,500) kept it from being a home appliance. The publishing and media industries, along with educators, however, viewed it as the machine of choice, allowing Apple to survive.[187]

Meanwhile Microsoft entered a program writing agreement with Apple, allowing it to gain knowledge of Xerox's GUI, and use Apple's most valuable asset to develop the first Microsoft Windows operating system. Because MS-DOS already existed in most IBM-type PCs, Microsoft was forced to develop its system with a second layer of software between the user and the hardware. It used the Intel 80286 processor and thus became known as the 286 with a Windows 1.0 operating system. Its slowness forced the development of the 386 and the 486. In 1987 IBM and Microsoft joined to develop a new operating system, which by year's end was marketed as Windows 2.0. In 1990 Windows 3.0 was launched and assured Microsoft of its future success. Apple and IBM lawsuits have failed, but the competition continues.[188] Windows 95 and 98 have become the industry standard, leaving IBM OS/2 in the dust. Only Apple continues to be a competing platform for most software. Amidst a sea of change one thing is certain: the pervasive presence of the PC in office, industry, school and home.[189] Enter the Internet.

It was Vanevar Bush, the developer of the analogue computer, who first proposed the information storage machine, called the *memex*, which would access microfilm, prior to WW II. By 1962 J. C. R. Licklider, head of ARPA's Information Processing Techniques Offices, who was working on a project called Libraries of the Future, came up with the idea of computer linkage. Shortly after this Ted Nelson coined the term *hypertext*. Douglas Engelbart of SRI was working on a similar project. Both Nelson and Engelbart acknowledged that their ideas came from Bush.[190] The Internet was invented in 1969 by UCLA professor Leonard Kleinrock, et. al., as part of a Defense Department research on a project known as Arpanet (Advanced Research Projects Agency Network),[191] under the leadership of Licklider and Larry Roberts. Computers began to communicate with each other with the invention and installation of the IMP (Interface Message Processor). By 1970 the

---

[186] *Ibid.*, 270-271.
[187] *Ibid.*, 274-275.
[188] *Ibid.*, 276-281
[189] For general information in this section cf. *The Encyclopedia Americana International Edition.* Danbury, CT: Grolier Incorporated, 1997, s.v. "Computers and Computer Science." *The New Encyclopædia Britannica*, Chicago: Encyclopædia Britannica Incorporated, 1997 s.v. "Computers."
[190] Campbell-Kelly, *Computer: A History of the Information Machine*, 286-289.
[191] Tyrrell, "The Internet Turns Thirty."

PART II: CRITICAL THEORISTS 147

original network, linking UCLA, SRI in Stanford, CA, the University of California at Santa Barbara, and the University of Utah, was operational.[192] By 1971 twenty-three hosts were on the network. In 1983 the military connection with Arpanet was severed and it became Milnet, so that the Arpanet could grow on its own with less restraint.[193]

Soon the invention of Ethernet by Robert Metcalfe and LAN made the present Internet and World Wide Web possible.[194] Meanwhile other networks, such as CSNET (Computer and Science Network), and BITNET ("Because it's Time"), were formed. Vint Cerf and Bob Kahn developed the gateway and network packets concept which allowed the various networks to be interconnected, hence the Internet.[195] By 1980 Arpanet was widely used by scientists and academics. Data files and electronic mail were sent at lightning speed through modems. Usenet brought news from around the world, and by 1991 had 35,000 nodes and millions of subscribers. Various networks proliferated largely because electronic mail (E-mail) became an important force as early as the mid seventies. As an advanced personal form of the telegraph it became popular for its administrative efficiency.[196]

Used initially by the Defense Department and research scientists the Internet did not become public until the late 1980s, along with the proliferation of the PC. In 1980 there were fewer than two hundred hosts on the Internet. As late as 1984 there were only a thousand. In 1988 there were over 50,000 hosts, a number which tripled in 1989. The first successful retrieval system was the University of Minnesota's "gopher" in 1991. The first electronic publishing, known as the World Wide Web (WWW), was developed by the CERN High-energy Physics Laboratory in Geneva in 1989. It remained for emerging companies such as CompuServe, Prodigy, Genie and America On-line to provide access to the general public, bringing the Internet and the WWW to half a million homes by 1991, one million by 1992, and 3.8 million by 1994 and a million each quarter in 1995.[197] The explosion had begun and became a visible cultural force in the last half of the 1990s with the help of the presidential slogan the "information super highway." By 1993 most of the world, with the exception of large portions of central and northern Africa, was connected.[198] The most optimistic proponents of the Internet and the World

---

[192] Daniel P. Dern, *The Internet Guide for New Users* (New York: McGraw-Hill, Inc., 1994) 8, 9.
[193] Campbell-Kelly, *Computer: A History of the Information Machine*, 293-294.
[194] Tyrrell, "The Internet Turns Thirty."
[195] Dern, *The Internet Guide for New User*, 11,12.
[196] Stoll, *Silicon Snake Oil*, 2; Campbell-Kelly, *Computer: A History of the Information Machine*, 295.
[197] Campbell-Kelly, *Computer: A History of the Information Machine*, 297-300.
[198] Dern, *The Internet Guide for New User*, 17.

Wide Web hope to offer the general public the fruition of the Enlightenment dream of encyclopedic knowledge for Everyman.

Such is the Electronic Revolution, in the midst of which we enter bravely into a new millennium.

Key Dates in the Electronic Revolution

Telegraph:
May 24, 1844 - first electric communication between Baltimore and Washington, DC By 1852 23,000 miles of line had been laid.

Movies:
1892 - first moving picture camera invented and used. By 1900 there were four hundred theaters in New York City alone.

Radio:
1902 - first wireless signal was sent across the Atlantic.

Television:
September 11, 1928 - General Electric presented first televised dramatic production. February 1, 1940 the first network broadcast from NBC.

Computer:
1953 - IBM delivered its first Defense Calculator, the IBM 701.

Personal Computer:
January 1975 - first microprocessor-based computer, the Altair 8800, announced on cover of *Popular Electronics*.
1981 - first IBM Personal Computer.

Internet:
1970 - first Defense Department network operational.
1980 - first internetwork, known as Arpanet, linked a number of scientific and academic networks.
1990 - first commercial public links make the Internet and World Wide Web household realities.

PART III

TOOLS OF ASSESSMENT: CHRISTIAN MEDIA ECOLOGY

5

Third Thoughts: A Christian View of Media Theory and Criticism

> *The media have, indeed, provided the devil with perhaps the greatest opportunity accorded him since Adam and Eve were turned out of the Garden of Eden. ...the only antidote to the media's world of fantasy is the reality of Christ's kingdom proclaimed in the New Testament. ...our amazing technology has a built-in reductio ad absurdum, whereas the Word that became flesh, and dwelt among us, full of grace and truth, in the most literal sense, speaks for itself. ...That almighty Word was the medium, and the message was Christ.*
>
> —Malcolm Muggeridge, *Christ and the Media*[1]

> *This Life's dim windows of the soul*
> *Distorts the Heavens from Pole to Pole,*
> *And leads us to believe a lie*
> *When we see with, not through, the eye.*
>
> —William Blake "Camera Obscura"[2]

Media Ecology offers a perspective on media which, *mutatis mutandi*, is compatible with a Christian worldview. Now it remains to be demonstrated just how this compatibility works. This requires an analysis of the theoretical perspective of several key Media Ecologists, along with an investigation of how their religious convictions affected their theory.

---

[1] Malcolm Muggeridge, *Christ and the Media* (Grand Rapids: William B. Eerdmans Publishing Company, 1977) 15, 24, 42, 59.
[2] William Blake, in Malcolm Muggeridge, *Christ and the Media* (Grand Rapids: William B. Eerdmans Publishing Company, 1977) 62.

We will conclude with the integration of our findings with a consistently Christian perspective.

Let us begin with a general definition. Media Ecology is the study of the relationship of media to their cultural environment. *Ecology* is from the Greek οἶκος for house, and deals with the management of households and other realms as interconnected environments or systems. Media Ecology focuses on the critical analysis of media as environments and as part of the larger environment or cultural context. Secondly, Media Ecology deals with management or stewardship which the analysis of media warrants. I will offer a distinctively Christian definition in the last section of this chapter.

In order to focus the concerns of Media Ecology we will now turn to various ways of assessing technology and media in terms of several polarities which have emerged in the recent history of communications theory. Since we are discussing a subject in the realm of common grace I will suggest that the Christian seek what is true among these various spectra. Using the image of a graph with vertical and horizontal axes the Christian will tend to locate coordinates around the center of the graph, but should look for insights at the poles as well.

THE GIST OF THE DEBATE

As an aid to analysis, to help us hone in on a Christian perspective, we will use the image of a graph to plot perspectives covering ranges of media theory concerns. We will look at perspectives (axes or spectra) on technology in general and then zero in on the narrower foci of communication technologies. The vertical axis covers a range of general attitudes toward technology between two extremes: *technophobes* (those who fear/hate technology) and *technophiles* (lovers of technology). The horizontal axis has to do with attitudes regarding the media in determining culture from *progressive* to *conservative*. Along with these we will observe several diagonal axes. *Soft* and *hard* determinism deal with the relative influence of media on culture, and is closely linked to the horizontal axis. Finally two similar axes cover the range of theories about the nature of technology and media themselves between *instrumental* and *substantive* theories; and between *transmission* and *ritual* theories.

Technophobes and Technophiles: Attitudes toward Technology

Those opposed to technology, or at least to technological advance, are often referred to as *Luddites*, after Ned Lud. Lud was born in Leicestershire, England, in 1789. In early nineteenth century, during the Regency period, he and his followers smashed labor saving textile machinery, due to the threat it posed to their weaving guild. Thus, ever since, those who are opposed to technology have been labeled as his followers. Historically, in the church, this tendency has been manifested in the Anabaptist impulse to build a culture entirely separate from the world of common grace. Anabaptists have in varying degrees been suspicious of cultural, and especially technological, development. The Mennonites and the Amish have chosen, somewhat arbitrarily, to arrest development at certain points in history, notably in the middle of the nineteenth century as the Industrial Revolution was changing America. I shall refer to this general cultural and technological attitude as *technophobia*.

On the other end of the spectrum are the *technophiles*, who embrace every new technology with almost uncritical enthusiasm and Utopian aspirations. Every new advance is a sign of progress in the evolutionary development of culture. Put in its most extreme and crudest form this view asserts that whatever is technologically possible should be pursued. Technology has the potential for solving all human problems. Postman and other Media Ecologists, as we have seen, oppose this euphoria and the *technopoly* which it tends to create.

Conservatives and Progressives: Attitudes toward Cultural Determinism

The horizontal axis provides us with another dimension of the debate and helps us chart the coordinates of a variety of media criticism. In terms of media's connection with culture, communications theorists and sociologists ask the question: "Does media determine culture or vice versa?" *Media determinists* such as McLuhan, Ellul and Postman emphasize the pervasive determining effect of media on culture. In the previous chapter I have alerted the reader to several serious misconceptions promulgated by the label *media determinist*.

Among media determinists, however, we discover what Nancy Kaplan calls *conservatives* and *progressives*. *Conservatives* are strongly critical of the effects of the electronic media on traditional cultural institutions. *Progressives*, on the other hand, assess those same effects in a positive light. Thus, a *media determinist* may be either a *technophobe* or a *technophile*. On the other end of the axis or spectrum are those who propose a more sociological account of the cultural assumptions that give rise to various technologies. Thus we may refer to these as *cultural determinists*.

Hard and Soft Determinism: Media's Influence on Culture

Samuel Ebersole and Daniel Chandler use the distinction between *hard* and *soft* determinism to posit a range between "communication technology determining social organization and development," and technology shaping the structure of culture along with other "mediating factors" which form culture.³ *Hard determinism* posits communication technology as *the*, or at least the central, factor determining culture formation. *Soft determinism* posits communication technology as one among a number of factors determining culture formation.

While I think Samuel Ebersole has not argued properly for using the label "technological" or "media determinist," he asks the right questions: "Those who fear the impact of technology (*technophobes*) are often the most ardent believers in technological determinism and are outspoken about our need to promote our humanity while at the same time subjecting technological progress to rigorous critique. Critics of technological determinism counter that the technology is not the sole determinant of change. Rather, it is the technology working within a complex social structure. ...If indeed culture is shaped by technological developments, and more specifically by media technology, how might the World Wide Web impact society as we know it? What philosophical underpinnings are inherent in this new form of computer-mediated communication? And how might an individual's world-view impact one's decision to participate, and determine the level at which one participates, in this revolution?"⁴

One of the great dangers of the deterministic approach is to fall into the monistic reduction of Thales and his colleagues, and conclude: "all is technology." Daniel Chandler calls this tendency "technocentrism."⁵ All of human culture is accounted for in terms of technology. As we shall see, Joshua Meyrowitz offers a synthetic approach to this debate by asserting that media affect social structures by changing the situational settings of a culture. Media are determinative of these structures, but within the given culture the individual may both change the settings and make decisions about how to interact within the given situation(s). Furthermore, media are not the only forces at work in cultural formation. Economic, political, sociological, psychological, historical, and religious forces all play a part.

Instrumental and Substantive Theories: The Nature of Technology

Ebersole gives a very helpful and full description of these two theories:
> Andrew Feenberg, in *Critical Theory of Technology* (1991), argued that theories of technology fall into one of two major categories: the

---

³ Samuel Ebersole, "Media Determinism in Cyberspace." http://regent.edu/acad/schcom/rojc/mdic.html, 1995. Daniel Chandler, (1995, rev. 1998): "Technological or Media Determinism" [WWW document] URL http://www.aber.ac.uk/~dgc/tecdet.html [13 July 1999].
⁴ Ebersole, "Media Determinism in Cyberspace." My parenthetic insertion of *technophobes*.
⁵ Chandler, "Technological or Media Determinism."

instrumental theory, and the *substantive theory.* The *instrumental theory,* "offers the most widely accepted view of technology. It is based on the common sense idea that technologies are *tools* standing ready to serve the purposes of their users. Technology is deemed *neutral,* without valuative content of its own" (p. 5). Technology is not inherently good or bad, and can be used to whatever political or social ends desired by the person or institution in control. Technology is a "rational entity" and universally applicable, thus allowing similar standards of measure to be applied in diverse situations. Given these propositions, the only response is unreserved commitment to its employment. One may make exceptions on moral grounds, but one must also understand that the "price for the achievement of environmental, ethical, or religious goals...is reduced efficiency" (p. 6). Arnold Pacey (1992) described the person who holds to an instrumental theory of technology. For such a person, when technology fails them or when it has negative consequences, it is not the technology but the improper use of it by "politicians, the military, big business, and others" (p. 2).[6]

In contrast to the instrumental theory is the *substantive theory* of technology. Best known through Ellul and Heidegger, the substantive theory "argues that technology constitutes a new type of cultural system that restructures the entire social world as an object of control" (Pacey, p. 7). Heidegger (1977) claimed that we are engaged in the transformation of the world and ourselves into "standing reserves," raw materials waiting to be used up in the process (p. 17). According to Feenberg (1991), "Heidegger asserts that the technical restructuring of modern societies is rooted in a nihilistic will to power, a degradation of man and Being to the level of mere objects" (p. 7). Feenberg continued, "The issue is not that machines have *taken over,* but that in choosing to use them we make many unwitting cultural choices. Technology is not simply a means but has become an environment and a way of life: this is its *substantive* impact" (p. 8). While acknowledging the apparent neutrality of a basic machine, Pacey (1992) said that we must look further, at the "web of human activities surrounding the machine, which include its practical uses, its role as a status symbol....Looked at in this second way, technology is seen as a part of life, not something that can be kept in a separate compartment" (p. 3). According to Pacey, "a technocratic value system...gives rise to what is often called a *technocratic* outlook that is single-mindedly insistent on an unambiguous view of progress, of problem-solving, and of values" (p.

---

[6] Ebersole, "Media Determinism in Cyberspace."

127). Those intolerant of ambiguity see only one course for technology, one that leads to greater progress and efficiency (p. 127).[7]

Whether one accepts the neutrality of technology depends on one's valuing philosophy—whether one tends toward the pragmatic and situational, or the absolute and authoritarian. Those who believe that technology is neutral argue that "guns don't kill people, people do," or that a knife can be used to "cook, kill, or cure." Those who believe the opposite counter with evidence that technology cannot be evaluated in a vacuum. Monsma (1986) argued for the "value-ladenness" of technology (chapter 3). He based his premise on two traits that he believed are common to all technological developments: (1) technological objects are unique; they are designed to function in a particular and limited way, and (2) technological objects are intertwined with their environment; they interact in unique ways with the rest of reality.[8]

Transmission and Ritual Theories: The Nature of Media

James Carey distinguishes between the *ritual* (transformation) and *transmission* (transportation) theories of communication. Prior to electronic communication, i.e. the telegraph, communication was identified conceptually with transportation. Thus communication was identified with the transmission of messages through space. With the advent of electronic media, and the new theoretical reflection on the nature of communication that came with it, this definition continued to hold sway, as we have seen in the development of communication study, with the result that the *transmission* view has, until recently, dominated communications theory. Transmission views communication media as mere *conduits* of information. The *ritual* view seeks to put *communion* back into the word communication, capturing the personal and symbolic interaction which has always been central to communication.[9] Boorstin reminds us that the ancient meaning of the word "communicate" refers to God sharing His grace in the Eucharist.[10] Communication has to do with a communion of persons, and not simply with the transmission of information.

---

[7] *Ibid.*
[8] *Ibid.*
[9] James W. Carey, *Communication as Culture* (Boston, MA: Unwin Hyman, 1989) 13-23.
[10] Daniel Boorstin, *Democracy and Its Discontents: Reflections on Everyday America* (New York: Random House, 1971) 4.

The Rest of Us: A Christian Response

We might quickly conclude that, however frustrated we may get with our computers on a given day, we are certainly not going to follow the Anabaptist tendency, which appears to be a Christian version of the Luddites. However, as an example of the thoughtfulness required by the Christian thinker in assessing the graph of spectra which we have outlined above, we should consider a community of people considered to be Luddites, the Amish. They have sought to view every technology in terms of submission to God and His authority structure, albeit in a separate culture, which tends to have stopped its development in the nineteenth century. Observing the tendency of the telephone to isolate the individual from the family and the community, they restricted the use of telephones to community locations, to be used only when necessary.[11] This was their way of knowing where the off button was and using it. Hence, we may learn things even from those with Luddite tendencies.

McLuhan's idea of being aware and taking control, especially of electronic media, is undergirded by an eminently Christian view of God, man and things. As stewards we must recognize the inherent nature of a particular medium, note how it tends to change us either for good or ill, and take appropriate steps to control or even change that medium. Christians are called to analyse and manage every medium, from the tongue to the television. In analyzing we must determine the environmental tendency of each media, noting the positive and the negative affects. The book, for example, tends to individualize or privatize the experience of the reader. On a very basic level (McLuhan has explored the general historical and cultural implications) a person may spend all his time reading, and cut himself off from his family, church and community. Much of the anti-institutionalism which has undermined the church is closely related to this privatizing tendency of print. "All I need is my Bible." On the other hand, the same mental environment fostered by print, with its social consequences, may be viewed positively as Birkerts does, when he refers to the *interiority* cultivated by reading. Print tends toward deep reflection and cultivates the interior, or the soul of the reader. Hence it may empower the reader in important ways which enhance social involvement.

I have noted that a thoughtful study of the nature of media and culture will tend to lead Christians to a coordinate near the center of these axes. At the center of the horizontal axis the Christian will be neither *technophobe* nor *technophile*. Neither the outright rejection of media or technology nor the uncritical embrace of the same are Biblical options. Using the Biblical

---

[11] Ebersole, "Media Determinism in Cyberspace." quoting Diane Zimmerman Umble, "The Amish and the Telephone: Resistance and Reconstruction." in R. Silverstone and E. Hirsch, eds. *Consuming Technologies*. (London: Routledge, 1992) 184-192.

paradigm of idolatry to critique media helps the Christian to come to an intelligent appreciation and use of all of God's cultural gifts. We should find ourselves at points of critical concern appreciating the insights of the *technophobe*. On other points we will have an optimistic appraisal of new technology.

At the center of the horizontal axis the Christian will be neither a *media determinist* nor a *cultural determinist,* neither a *conservative* nor a *progressive*. The Covenant of Common Grace, the cultural calling of the Christian and a Biblical anthropology point clearly to an interaction between culture and technology. We should recognize the centrality of communication technology in cultural development without failing to account for all of the other mediating elements, such as family, state, church, man as the image of God, sin, and God Himself, which contribute to making culture what it is. The Christian will tend more toward *soft* determinism, since this position takes other cultural factors into account, along with communication media. While I am not convinced that Ellul, McLuhan and Postman are *hard* determinists, we must be aware of and avoid that tendency wherever it appears in their writings.

In viewing historical development we are never to be fatalists, but we also recognize that history and cultural development as totalities are beyond our control. At the same time we believe that God is sovereign over this development of common grace culture, as the context in which the history of redemption unfolds (Eph. 1:10). We are responsible for our part in that development. As central as communication technologies are in culture we must understand that the influence is not one way, but rather interactive. Human choice is not only involved in responding to technological givens, but are also central in their creation, development and use. A failure to recognize this is tantamount to abdication of human responsibility, which is never an option for the Christian. The Bible has too many imperatives. On the eve of the strike of the so-called "Millennium Bug" a commentator in *Newsweek* observed: "I have come to believe that the Y2K apocalypse is a myth. The truth is not that civilization will come to an end, but rather that civilization as we know it has ended already. We are no longer in complete command of our creations."[12] The assumption that we have ever been in control of our cultural creations is false. The rapid advance of electronic communication simply puts us in touch with this reality in a new way, with a simultaneous intensity never experienced before. For Christians, who know Who *is* ultimately in control, this new intensity, while calling us to responsible watchfulness and action, will not unsettle us.

---

[12] Danny Hillis, "Why Do We Buy the Myth of Y2K?" *Newsweek* (31 May 1999) 12.

The Christian should also tend strongly toward the *substantial*, as opposed to the *instrumental*, theory of technology; and thus tend strongly toward the *ritual*, as opposed to the *transmission*, theory of media. The *substantial* and *ritual* theories are the legacy of the critical theorists, who sought to correct the mathematical, rationalistic reduction of the scientific theorists. In positing modern technology as a way of life, a culturally pervasive environment, these theorists give the Christian fertile soil in which to explore the idolatrous tendencies of communication technologies.

RELIGIOUS PRESUPPOSITIONS AMONG THE CRITICAL THEORISTS

At this point we will explore some of the ways in which the Judeo-Christian intellectual and religious traditions of several Media Ecologists have influenced their media theories. I have encountered some resistance, even among Media Ecologists, to the idea that religion and theology are central to the task of media criticism. Many are content to live off of the "borrowed capital" of Western Christian presuppositions, while relegating the presuppositions themselves to matters of personal religion. This mindset is perhaps the greatest obstacle which the Christian thinker encounters in the academy and in the world. To presuppositional apologists this should come as no surprise. This spiritual opposition must be engaged with the whole armor of God, prayer and thoughtfulness, as well as compassion.

Jacques Ellul: *Neo-Orthodox Critic of the Technological Society*

At age nineteen, in 1931, Ellul became a Marxist, as we have seen in the previous chapter; but three years later became a Christian. "His religious faith evolved out of the Death of God movement and the response of the Neo-orthodox theologians Bultmann, Barth, Niebuhr and Tillich. ...As a theologian, Ellul drew from the dialectical theology of Kierkegaard and Barth, and as a sociologist, from Marx and Weber."[13]

Ellul's deep distrust of technology combined with his Neo-Orthodox theology ends up at points in his writings seeming to deny the value of life in this world. Ellul's belief in the present as "eschatological time" in which the risen Christ is alive suprahistorically, moves him in a dialectical direction

---

[13] *Ibid.*, quoting D. Fasching, *The Thought of Jacques Ellul: A Systematic Exposition*. (New York: Edwin Mellen Press, 1981) 2, x, 7. Fasching's reference must refer to a precursor, probably Nietzsche, of the movement which Americans refer to by the name Death-of-God, created by Altizer, Hamilton, and van Buren in the mid sixties.

which makes redemption a universal reality.[14] At bottom, however, his faith in Christ always leads him to sound a note of hope.

Ellul's essential concern with the deterministic tendency of technology is insightful. For Ellul fatalism regarding technology is not inevitable, as we have seen in chapter 4. Each person is responsible for his assessment and stewardship of technology. In other places there is a kind of fatalistic conclusion in Ellul's thought. "Ellul even went so far as to claim that whether one believes the technological system to be a good or bad influence is immaterial. The nature of technology, for Ellul, was so encompassing that it defied being judged. Whether we believe in it or not, and whether we think it is good or bad, technology continues on its course doing what it always does—subjugating our humanity."[15] Christianity places man at the point of intersection between the material and eternal worlds.[16]

Dr. Raymond Gozzi, author of *The Power of Metaphor in the Age of Electronic Media*, has observed: "Ellul's most direct book dealing with media-generated visual imagery is *The Humiliation of the Word*. Ellul felt that visual images ultimately formed a closed world, reinforcing things as they are. They portray 'reality' as the entirety of existence. Against visuals, Ellul posits the Word, which is from the realm of 'truth' (and falsity). The Word can open up the closed systems of 'reality' to other possibilities, in particular, a transcendent, invisible God."[17]

"In all of this Ellul continued to place his understanding of technology and its proper role in this present society in a context that recognizes a faith in the eternal. Mitcham (1994) posits that his vantage point allowed Ellul to 'propose a more explicit alternative to the technology of the technician' (p. 61) than those provided by some of his contemporaries, e.g., Heidegger. To throw this wager or secular faith into the boldest possible relief, Ellul places it in dialectical contrast with biblical faith. As a dialectical contrast to *La Technique*, for instance, Ellul writes *Sans feu ni lieu* (1975, although written much earlier). Whereas technology is the attempt of human beings to create their home in this world, the Bible denies that they are truly at home here (p. 60)"[18] At his best Ellul encourages the Christian to transcend the historically inevitable by exercising pilgrim faith. But given his Neo-Orthodoxy, this faith is not necessarily the same as Biblical faith. Rather than assessing, resisting and consecrating culture, Ellul opts for a transcendental escape. This should

---

[14] Walter Ong, Review: *The Humiliation of the Word* (Jacques Ellul) in the *Journal of Communication* (1986): vol. 36, no. 1, pp. 156-158.
[15] Ebersole, "Media Determinism in Cyberspace."
[16] Wilkinson, "Introduction," in *The Technological Society*, by Jacques Ellul, xx.
[17] Raymond Gozzi, "Hidden Religious Ground," mediaecology@ube.ubalt.edu (10 Dec 1998).
[18] Ebersole, "Media Determinism in Cyberspace."

not deter the Christian Media Ecologist from appreciating the profoundness and depth of his scholarly critique and insight. More often than not one will be moved to consider him to be on the side of the angels. The careful student of Ellul will be moved to a high regard for the magnitude of his scholarship, and the depth and precision of his insight. His discernment of the dangers of the image as well as the importance of the word/Word are a salutary counterpoint in the modern context.

Marshall McLuhan: *Catholic Media Prophet*

McLuhan's religious convictions have been largely overlooked (perhaps in certain cases even avoided) by media theorists. That McLuhan himself was very serious about his religion, and its relationship to his thought, cannot be doubted.

Conversion: Life and Intellect

His conversion to Roman Catholicism at the age of twenty six was closely connected with his immersion in the intellectual British Catholicism of writers like G. K. Chesterton, Gerard Manley Hopkins, James Joyce, and T. S. Eliot.[19] It was especially to Chesterton, and his book of essays *What's Wrong with the World*, that McLuhan attributed his conversion to the Roman Catholic Church. In an interview with his son Eric in the mid seventies he recalled: "I know every word of him: he's responsible for bringing me into the church."[20] However, the idea that McLuhan's upbringing was secular, or even only nominally Protestant, is erroneous.[21] McLuhan's interest in Christianity was

---

[19] *Current Biography* (June 1967), "McLuhan, (Herbert) Marshall," in Raymond Rosenthal, ed. *McLuhan: Pro and Con* (Baltimore: Penguin Books, 1968) 17. In the early 1950s McLuhan "was interested in Charles Williams' novel, *The Greater Trumps*, a novel about the Tarot and the occult, and since C. S. Lewis shared an interest in Anglicanism with Williams, McLuhan looked into works such as *The Screwtape Letters*-. In any case, he would have read C. S. Lewis earlier since Lewis wrote the major scholarly history for *Oxford University Press* on sixteenth century English literature, a period in which McLuhan had expertise." Donald Theall, "Some questions." mediaecology@ube.ubalt.edu (9 Jan 1999).

[20] W. Terrence Gordon, *Marshall McLuhan: Escape into Understanding, A Biography* (New York: BasicBooks, 1997) 54.

[21] Liss Jeffrey, "Some questions." mediaecology@ube.ubalt.edu (7 Jan 1999), emphasis mine.
"McLuhan was raised a secular Protestant in Winnipeg, and chose Roman Catholicism at Cambridge. He was not a cradle Catholic (as he himself said) and the consequence in my view is that he retained an independence of mind engendered by the JUXTAPOSITION of his think-for-yourself boyhood and the deeply committed faith of his adult life. NO doubt about his piety, and in fact most evidence that I have seen would indicate that the rock of faith may have allowed him to some degree to calm his tempestuous intellect. However, he did inspire many of us in the next generation to the idea that it is necessary to

not new when he went to England. W. Terrence Gordon's authorized biography of McLuhan documents the deeply religious nature of his family and of his own early convictions. "Years of religious training from early childhood produced reflexes in Marshall. If it was Sunday morning, he was in Bible class at Winnipeg's Nassau Baptist Church, even in his university years. If a friend confided a personal problem, he prayed for him."[22]

McLuhan's demand that the same intellectual rigor and comprehensiveness which he applied to other subjects be applied to religion left him unsatisfied with the teaching and sermons he found in his Baptist context.[23] For McLuhan Christianity and the humanities were to be studied hand in hand. No wonder it took a Chesterton to give his faith intellectual foundations: "had I not encountered Chesterton I would have remained agnostic for many years at least."[24] The Roman Catholicism he encountered at Cambridge was highly intellectual, lending a perfect logic to his conversion. One can only wonder what exposure to contemporary Calvinism and Reformed apologetics would have done to his thinking. Was his impatience with dogma, which we often encounter in interviews and letters, due to his never seeing it intelligently applied to all of life, or was his intellectual creativity too all absorbing to be submitted to the creeds of Christendom? His love of Chesterton, who was never afraid to assert his ideas or the dogma of the church, would lead me to believe it was the former. In the end, after voluminous reading, McLuhan confessed (in 1977): "I came into the church on my knees. That is the only way in. ...You don't come into the church through ideas and concepts."[25] But is the humility of faith really opposed to "ideas and concepts"?

It was the summer of 1931, prior to entering his third year in the humanities in Manitoba, in which McLuhan first encountered Gilbert Keith Chesterton. After reading *What's Wrong with the World* he wrote in his diary: "Few writers, yes I can say, no other writer, has ever been able to arouse my

---

understand media before pronouncing whether it is a good or a bad thing. In this he departed from the premature moralizers of all faiths."

[22] Gordon, *Marshall McLuhan*, 25.
[23] *Ibid.*, 25ff.
[24] Marshall McLuhan, *Letters of Marshall McLuhan* (Edited by M. Molinaro, C. McLuhan, and W. Toye. Toronto: Oxford University Press, 1987) 73. "Perhaps I can help here. Marshall had--owned--a great deal of GKC's books and had also read a good number of the articles (including CK's Weekly) in the occasional press. He had read all of the basic books, like Orthodoxy and Heretics, The Everlasting Man, The Thing, the Father Brown stories and books and a good number of the novels and collections of essays (such as The Defendant). He did not try to read all of the lighter things, but was quite familiar with the rest--and that is quite a corpus. He was similarly acquainted with Belloc's writing. " Eric McLuhan, "MM's GKCs," mediaecology@ube.ubalt.edu (27 August 1999).
[25] Gordon, *Marshall McLuhan*, 74.

enthusiasm for ideas as has G.K."[26] Later from Cambridge he revealed the essence of his attraction to Chesterton's thought as he referred to his work as "the writings of a thinker and a poet with a serious and comprehensive belief about the nature of life." This accounts for McLuhan's attraction to Thomism with its Aristotelian concreteness.[27] In Thomas and Aristotle he encountered "ideas and concepts" with a vengeance. Chesterton dealt with the world as it is but from a distinctly Christian perspective. In a letter written in 1935 McLuhan wrote: "It is the whole bias of the mind that it seeks the truth, and of the soul which inspires our very life, that it seek that which gave it. The great difficulty about the Truth is that it is not simple except to those who can attain to see it whole."[28]

The intellectual substance and scope McLuhan had failed to find in the Baptist church of his youth was present in a persuasive way in Chesterton. McLuhan's conversion, then, was not so much to Christian faith, as to the Roman Catholic Church, and at a time in his life when his mind would not have been satisfied with anything less than a Chestertonian defense. A faith which faced all of life squarely was what he had sought.

Protestantism

McLuhan's antipathy to Calvinism is reflected in a letter from Cambridge: "Plato was, of course, a Puritan in his artistic views, and his philosophy when fully developed as by the 15th century Augustinian monks (of whom Luther was one) leads definitely to the Calvinistic position."[29] For McLuhan Roman Catholicism was the original from which all the sects derived. The progressive, commercial legacy of the sect of Protestantism is the one the modern world lives with. "Catholic culture produced Don Quixote and St. Francis and Rabelais ...Everything that is especially hateful and devilish and inhuman about the conditions and strains of modern industrial society is not only Protestant in origin, but it is their boast (!) to have originated it."[30] McLuhan certainly perceived one of the major flaws, particularly of American Protestantism. "It implies that the map of the universe was not radically altered by the Incarnation and the Resurrection."[31] Aligning itself uncritically with the commercial interests of the Industrial Revolution the Protestant church is partly responsible

---

[26] Ibid., 32.
[27] *Ibid.*, 42. In another letter McLuhan stated, "Aristotle is the soundest basis for Christian doctrine." 53.
[28] Marshall McLuhan, *Letters of Marshall McLuhan*, 72-76.
[29] Gordon, *Marshall McLuhan*, 51.
[30] *Ibid.*, 55.
[31] *Ibid.*, 56.

for the state of American Evangelicalism. McLuhan saw this as the cause of its cultural sterility.

The Place of Christian Theology in Media Study

Former McLuhan doctoral student Donald Theall describes the intellectual atmosphere of his own student days: "Within the Toronto milieu of the late 1940s and early 1950s theology was an all important aspect of the nature of that university and gnosticism, as represented in Northrop Frye's fascinating work on Blake, a powerful presence, and McLuhan's historic dissents from Frye were a significant factor in his work. When we try to write religion and theology out of the picture we do not realize that theology was a vital and living issue at the University of Toronto throughout the 1950s and 1960s and impacted it in a variety of ways. Three of Toronto's four colleges had one or more theological schools affiliated with them and there were others affiliated with the university. Besides, St. Michael's where McLuhan was based, also encompassed the Pontifical Institute of Medieval Studies, which also gave rise to other works relevant to Media Ecology, such as Brian Stock's books."[32]

McLuhan's perception that culture is "ultimately determined by religion" makes one wonder why his religious convictions played no *explicit* role in his media theory or criticism. We have seen in the last chapter that after publication of *The Mechanical Bride* he changed his tack and went incognito. But even his "undisguised" criticism assumed, rather than disclosed, his beliefs. His son Eric has stated that while McLuhan never hid his religion, or failed to apply his media criticism to the church, he was a "private" and not as some of his colleagues "public Catholics."[33] Since McLuhan did not view his religion as an individual matter, in the contemporary sense which renders religion as subjective and thus irrelevant to the concerns of life, we must view McLuhan's

---

[32] Donald Theall, "Some questions." mediaecology@ube.ubalt.edu (9 Jan 1999).
[33] Eric McLuhan. "McLuhan and Catholicism," mediaecology@ube.ubalt.edu (28 Dec 1998). "My father did not try to hide his religion but also he shunned any attempt to make it a public matter. Some of his colleagues were 'public Catholics'; he was a private one, that is, a man who believed that some matters are properly held private(ly). Consequently, he was careful to keep his religion and his public affairs (teaching and lecturing) quite separate. On the other hand, he did not shun the opportunity to point out how media had affected or were affecting ANY public or any audience or speaker/audience dynamic, past or present--including congregations." Tom Farrell, "Not So Hidden?" mediaecology@ube.ubalt.edu (16 Dec 1998). "McLuhan converted to Roman Catholicism as a young man, at a time when anti-Catholic bias meant that he was limiting his career prospects by converting to Roman Catholicism. Except for teaching one year at the University of Wisconsin, McLuhan devoted himself to teaching in Catholic institutions of higher education--nothing hidden about that. In 1936, he published an article praising G. K. Chesterton, the well-known Catholic writer. Nothing hidden about that. Later, he published an introduction to Hugh Kenner's book about Chesterton. Nothing hidden about that. Did he ever try to hide his religion?"

"privacy" as a matter of method. Even as he sought to penetrate environments, so his thought must be approached. The perceptive student will seek to draw out McLuhan's veiled assumptions. Like the existentialist McLuhan sought authenticity, but found it rather in the unchangeable institution of the Roman Catholic Church. Unlike the existentialist he saw the necessity of grounding authenticity in the perception of "infinitely valuable things."

That McLuhan's religious convictions were essential to his Media Ecology is clear from his own correspondence. In a 1973 letter to Allen Maruyama McLuhan observed: "At one time, when I was first becoming interested in the Catholic Church, I studied the entire work of G. K. Chesterton and the entire group from the pre-Raphaelites and Cardinal Newman through to Christopher Dawson and Eric Gill. *All of this really is involved in my media study, but doesn't appear at all.*" To Joe Keogh he wrote in 1970: "Am enclosing Father Johnstone's piece. He's the first to notice that my approach to media is metaphysical rather than sociological or dialectical."[34]

God

Regarding McLuhan's preference for percepts over concepts he said, "The thingness of Christianity has always been a scandal to the conceptualist." According to McLuhan God and Christianity only die when they become concepts. "As long as they remain 'percept', directly involving the perceiver, they are alive."[35] Marshall McLuhan seems to wish to capture the essence of what Paul says on Mars Hill: "In Him we live and move and have our being." His rejection of concepts is in the interest of preserving the uniqueness of God's omnipresence. In the same interview quoted above, Hoskins tries to get Marshall McLuhan into the comparative religions corner by calling Christianity a 'myth'. Marshall McLuhan agrees but with a poignant twist: "I see myth as the super-real. The Christian myth is not fiction but something more than ordinarily real." World religions, such as Buddhism and Hinduism "were rendered obsolete at the moment of the Incarnation and they remain so." Some concept this! McLuhan appreciated the historical concreteness of Christianity.

Marshall McLuhan's lack of philosophical precision regarding percept and concept doesn't negate the force of what he is saying. Paul teaches that God's omnipresence is the necessary ground of all reasoning: percepts and concepts. The "thingness" of God impinges on every element of human

---

[34] Gordon, *Marshall McLuhan*, 75, emphasis added, cf. fn. 373
[35] Hubert Hoskins, "Electric Consciousness and the Church," in George Sanderson and Frank Macdonald, eds., *Marshall McLuhan: The Man and His Message*, (Golden, CO: Fulcrum, Inc., 1989) 161, 166.

experience. McLuhan's objections to theology were rooted in his viewing it as a kind of anachronism which became an obstacle to "personal and direct confrontation."[36] He viewed theology as contemplation of the "thingness" of God and His mysterious nature. Theoretical constructs are the games of conceptualizers, Scribes and sophisticates with "too many theories to perceive anything." That "Christ is the medium and the message" is a percept only "visible to babes, but not to sophisticates."[37]

McLuhan's anti-gnosticism was central to his aversion to theological formulation. In a letter to Ong McLuhan stated:

As fallen spirits or devils men have their intellect which is of the earth earthy, presided over by the Earth Mother, the White Goddess of Robert Graves etc. The intellect is the dark principle. But the imagination is mode of divine union for the 'uncreated' divine spark hidden in our corrupt clay etc. You are familiar with this aspect of the Old Religion, Gnosis, Neo-Platonism theosophy et al?

I don't see how it is possible to teach English literature, or any European lit. without full knowledge of the 'secret doctrine' for which the arts are the sole means of grace. I realize now that my own rejection of philosophy as a study in my pre-Catholic days was owing to the sense that it was a meaningless truncation. Not that my present interest is due to any conviction of truth in the secret doctrine. Quite the contrary. It is rather to a sense of it as the fecund source of lies and misconceptions, e.g. Puritan Inner Light.

Can you think of any reason why Catholic students of philosophy and lit. today should not be given the facts about these 'secrets'? I can find nobody here who can or will discuss the question.[38]

McLuhan identified all "concepts" with gnosticism, because they mediated knowledge. His quest was for immediate contact with the "thingness" of God. Thus he would appear to reject the Biblical doctrine of the illumination of the Holy Spirit, which he identifies with "Puritan Inner Light." He even criticized Aquinas's assertion that Scripture uses figures of "sensible things" in order to teach us divine truth and enable us to "mount up to such as are invisible."[39]

In commenting on one of Teilhard de Chardin's statements in *The Phenomenon of Man*, McLuhan says, "The computer promises, in short, by technology, a Pentecostal condition of understanding and unity." McLuhan, in a

---

[36] *Ibid.*
[37] *Ibid.*, 162.
[38] Marshall McLuhan, *Letters of Marshall McLuhan*. Edited by M. Molinaro, C. McLuhan, and W. Toye. (Toronto: Oxford University Press, 1987) 243-244 (letter to Walter Ong, October 14, 1954).
[39] *Ibid.*, 237.

veiled way, understands Teilhard's cosmic evolutionary optimism in a negative way. The electronic extension of human consciousness is creating universal gnosticism.[40]

In *The Mechanical Bride* McLuhan comments on an ad from the *New York Sun* (5 Jan 1948), which displays a dialogue between the Bill of Rights and the Stars on an American flag. The caption says 'I am Liberty, more than a principle, a passion.' McLuhan observes: "But a passion is much *less* than a principle. For passions are private emotions and appetites, or combinations of such, whereas a principle binds all men and all things. Therefore principles must be superseded in this scheme of utilitarian mechanism. Principles are intelligible and abiding aspects of reality. They bind men in mutual social obligations deriving from the very nature of man and his dignity as a rational creature. The grasp of principles assists men to resist private passions and order them to a rational good that is both private and social. .....'God' is no longer outside the machine. He is now inside. He is seen as trying to develop his personality by big dynamic efforts at extroversion in the domain of matter, energy, and industry. ...At this point God gets the Hegelian brush-off. Merged in the cosmos, He is now felt only as a pulse in the big vibrating organism of matter and energy. ...It is not by any means plain that there is a lack of good faith in all this. There is only evidence of a painful confusion of mind and exuberant incoherence. The stereotypes to which such ads appeal are now embedded in the popular dreams of success and opportunity for all."[41] McLuhan makes a plea for the Creator-creature distinction.

The Church

McLuhan had a lifelong concern for the welfare of the Roman Catholic Church. The recently published book titled *The Medium and the Light*[42] is a collection of McLuhan's religious writings, including twelve letters, ten articles, and five interviews. McLuhan addressed the problems faced by the church in the new electronic environment. He was troubled by the church's general lack of awareness of this environment, and the consequences of this ignorance for its future. The "high speed" situation means that "religion undergoes tremendous changes under these conditions." "[O]ld private identities of centuries of cultural heritage" are being wiped out. When there is no cultural basis for the individual "in the technological culture, then Christianity is in trouble. When you have a new tribal culture confronting an individualist religion, there is

---

[40] Hoskins, "Electric Consciousness and the Church," 168.
[41] Marshall McLuhan, *The Mechanical Bride: Folklore of Industrial Man* (Boston: Beacon Press, 1951) 140.
[42] Eric McLuhan, ed., *The Medium and the Light*. Toronto: Stoddart Publishing Co. Limited, 1999.

trouble." This means that the massive centralized bureaucracy is "passé" but that is no loss. But as long as the church has the "the divine fact" and the sacraments are available the church will not die.[43]

The Eucharist

In consistent Roman Catholic fashion McLuhan saw the sacraments as central to Christian faith. This accounts for his neglect of the place of the Bible in the life and piety of the Church. It also gives us insight into his aversion to concepts and ideas. "Yes, some people did notice that he had made pejorative-sounding statements about print culture in *The Gutenberg Galaxy* (he doesn't sound so pejorative about print culture in *Understanding Media*). Because it was well-known that he was a Catholic, some people did view his pejorative-sounding comments as signaling that he was engaging in another round of Catholic anti-Protestant polemic."[44]

The freedom which he felt intellectually upon conversion to the Roman Catholic Church was due to the fact that the metaphysical ground of his thought was established and connected him with great Catholic writers of the past (such as Cervantes and Rabelais). In the end McLuhan ended up being more the artist than the "prophet". The preacher of the Word of God, however, cannot afford to veil his message either in his philosophy of communication or in his pulpit.

The Christian View of Man

As we have noted in chapter 4 McLuhan was not a fatalist who believed that we are simply victims of technology. Interpreters have latched onto McLuhan's statements which stress the powerful nature of media as an environment which functions subliminally. Poe's whirlpool is deadly unless negotiated after careful observation and with great wisdom in proceeding. In the late seventies McLuhan observed, "It needs to be noted that the strategies for saving literacy, or the Western way of life, are always pointed to the *content* of specific programs. No heed is given to the effects of the new man-made environments in reshaping the perceptual life of the young. It is obvious that if man-made

---

[43] Hoskins, "Electric Consciousness and the Church," 164-166.
[44] Tom Farrell, "Not So Hidden?" mediaecology@ube.ubalt.edu (16 Dec 1998). "While Walter Ong did not sound quite so pejorative about print culture, he did not make print culture sound exactly like an unqualified good development; since he also was a Catholic, certain people at that time even went so far as to refer to McLuhan's and Ong's work as a Catholic conspiracy, a charge I've seen in print. As you may know, Ong mentions this particular charge in his article "McLuhan as Teacher," which appeared after McLuhan's death in the *Journal of Communication*, along with other articles about McLuhan by James Carey, Bruce Gronbeck, and James Curtis."

environments are destroying the institutions of American society, then these environments can also be altered in such ways as to restore and to sustain the desired way of life. This desired effect actually calls for a suspension of the simultaneous structures that are eating out the heart of American institutions. Should this appear to be too great a sacrifice to demand, there would at least have been confrontation. Would not a deliberate decision be preferable to the current mood of absentmindedness and drift?"[45] As an example of his concern he wrote: "It is not easy to get these readers to see that the use of print creates modes of thought and space that are quite alien to other cultures, and even alien to our own earlier culture."[46]

In an unpublished paper, titled "Educational Effects of the Mass Media of Communication," written in 1955 as part of the celebration of the inauguration of a new president in the Teachers College at Columbia University, McLuhan says: "Yes, we must substitute an interest for the media for the previous interest in subjects. This is the logical answer to the fact that the media have substituted themselves for the older world. Even if we should wish to recover the older world we can do so only by an intensive study of the ways in which the media have swallowed it. And no matter how many walls have fallen the citadel of individual consciousness has not fallen nor is it likely to fall. For it is not accessible to the mass media."[47] "Christianity definitely supports the idea of a private, independent metaphysical substance of the self..."[48] Sounding like Ellul he asserts: "There is absolutely no inevitability as long as there is willingness to contemplate what is happening."[49]

Marshall McLuhan's Christianity caused him to hold to an irreducible soul within man characterized by the *imago dei* which is not subject to perception, but has the power to interpret and even withstand the percepts of experience, especially the mass media. "At the speed of light all the physical factors disappear. Naturally churches tend to become extremely spiritualized places. The theology of discarnate man, I should think, is going to be extremely transcendental and gnostic. It's not going to have much place for the human being as an incarnate spirit."[50]

---

[45] Marshall McLuhan, "Inside on the Outside, or the Spaced-out American," in Sanderson and Macdonald, eds., *Marshall McLuhan: The Man and His Message*, 148.
[46] Marshall McLuhan, *Counterblast* (London: Rapp & Whiting, 1969) 75.
[47] *Ibid.*, 135.
[48] Hubert Hoskins, "Electric Consciousness and the Church," in George Sanderson and Frank Macdonald, eds., *Marshall McLuhan: The Man and His Message*, 165.
[49] Marshall McLuhan, "McLuhan Probes," in Sanderson and Macdonald, eds., *Marshall McLuhan: The Man and His Message*, 219.
[50] Marshall McLuhan, *The Review of Books and Religion* (Belmont, Vermont), Vol. 3, #9, Mid-June 1974

McLuhan declared: "Christianity proclaims its communication theory loud and clear. Every aspect of the Christian thing is communication and change and transformation."[51] Catholic Media Ecologist John Maguire explains: "As a Catholic, apparently an intensely practicing one, he was steeped in the Gospels and the Epistles. (He would have to be, if he attended Mass every day, since in the course of a year, the Catholic liturgy covers a great deal of the New Testament.) The subtext of the New Testament epistles is, more or less, 'Christ came and revealed God to all of us, and now you, fellow Christians—in your new form of humanity—are the Message.'"[52]

Taking McLuhan's ecclesiology, and sacramental theology into account, along with the Roman Catholic *ex opera operatum* view of the means of grace, we must be cautious of the tendency in McLuhan to diminish the centrality of the written Word of God in the life of the church. However, with this caveat in mind, the Christian Media Ecologist will not find a more insightful and stimulating thinker in the field of cultural, media, and literary criticism.

Walter Ong: *Catholic Apologist for Orality*

The influence of Pierre Theilhard de Chardin has been discussed, along with his diminishment of the written word, in the previous chapter. In 1960 Ong wrote *Darwin's Vision and Christian Perspectives*.[53] As noted in the last chapter Ong was instrumental in introducing Theilhard de Chardin to American Catholics. In 1977 he wrote *Interfaces of the Word: Studies in the Evolution of Consciousness and Culture*. This is especially problematic for the theologian/preacher who trusts the Scripture's own testimony to its infallibility. "And in thinking of the Son as the divine Word, the Christian is conceiving of the divine Word by analogy with the human spoken word, certainly not by analogy with the written word. God's Son is not thought of as a text. With Him is associated not a quill and parchment but the Holy Spirit—*spiritus* or *pneuma* means breath, on which human beings' spoken words ride."[54]

Within his evolutionary framework literacy is sometimes portrayed by Ong as a prison from which to escape.[55] Writing is an aid to memory but not the original habitat of the word, as sound is.[56] Speech, as truth itself, is an

---

[51] Marshall McLuhan, *Letters of Marshall McLuhan*. Edited by M. Molinaro, C. McLuhan, and W. Toye. (Toronto: Oxford University Press, 1987) 467-468 (letter to Barbara Ward, February 9, 1973).
[52] John Maguire, "Not So Hidden?" mediaecology@ube.ubalt.edu (16 Dec 1998).
[53] Walter Ong, ed. *Darwin's Vision and Christian Perspectives* (New York: Macmillan, 1960).
[54] Walter Ong, Review: *Beyond the Written Word: Oral Aspects of Scripture in the History of Religion* (William A. Graham) in *America* (Mar. 4, 1989): 204.
[55] Walter Ong, *The Presence of the Word* (New Haven: Yale University Press, 1967. Reprint, Minneapolis, MN: University of Minnesota Press, 1981) 19.
[56] *Ibid.*, 22ff.

event.[57] It is committed to time and may not be housed in space.[58] For all of this Ong in other places, as we shall see, defends the written and printed word as a blessing and a necessary stage in the development of culture and communication. In our discussion of orality at the end of the present chapter we will interact with Ong's view, and demonstrate the usefulness of several important themes in his work.

Neil Postman: *Jewish Enlightenment Media Critic*

In describing his place in the "conversation" among media critics and theorists Postman asserts that the discussion has "its antecedents in the Old Testament."[59] Furthermore, as has been noted in chapter 1, Postman's initial interest in media criticism was sparked by the Second Commandment. Forms of communication effect both the content of the communication and the culture in which they are communicated.[60] As a Liberal Jew, however, he places more emphasis on the sacredness of space, rather than the content of a sermon. "The most important spiritual messages communicated to people when they go to church ... is the sacred space of the church itself, which includes all of the icons and symbols and even rituals that one is required to observe when entering this space."[61] Postman is not interested in the heart and soul of the Second Commandment, because he is not interested in the cultus, or worship *per se*, but in culture. The Decalogue, for Postman is, after all, a product of human culture. As would be expected, Postman also confuses the contemporary situation of the church with the theocratic, geo-political, kingdom of the Mosaic Covenant. Jesus' encounter with the Samaritan woman in John 4 makes the new situation of the church plain: "Woman, believe Me, the hour is coming when you will neither on this mountain, nor in Jerusalem, worship the Father. You worship what you do not know; we know what we worship, for salvation is of the Jews. But the hour is coming, and now is, when the true worshipers will worship the Father in spirit and truth; for the Father is seeking such to worship Him" (John 4:21-23).

The most troublesome aspect of Postman's critical work lies at the foundation of his position. During my 1990 interview we touched on the subject of absolute truth. Then in 1996 I challenged Postman's presuppositions in a letter. He suggested I read *The End of Education*. In that book he deals

---

[57] *Ibid.*, 33f.
[58] *Ibid.*, 42ff.
[59] Interview by Gregory E. Reynolds. Transcript. New York University, 18 April 1990, 29.
[60] Neil Postman, *Amusing Ourselves To Death: Public Discourse in the Age of Show Business*. (New York: Viking Penguin, Inc., 1985), 9.
[61] Interview by Reynolds, 4.

with the importance of "the great narratives" in a true education. The problem is that, according to Postman, these narratives are all in some sense "true". He wishes that we would "cure ourselves of the itch for absolute knowledge."[62] But then he makes a plea for "standards to which civilized people adhere."[63] I suspect that he is living off of the "borrowed capital" of his Judaism. He believes in "self-evident truths."[64] Ultimately Postman is happy to be considered a Post-Kantian thinker. We must, according to Postman, act "as if" our narrative is true.[65] This is nothing less than Kant's "heuristic principle" of ethics. "I am uncertain as to whether God has spoken, but I am going to live life as if God spoke, in part because if I don't believe this, I will lose my way."[66] Postman's most recent book, *Building a Bridge to the Eighteenth Century*, clarifies his commitment to Enlightenment epistemology. Thus Postman's position as a media critic is inconsistent with his presuppositions. He has built his house on the shifting foundation of relativism. Yet, because he cannot live with his presuppositions he surreptitiously imports "standards," because he lives in God's world. Despite the weakness of his foundation the discerning Christian Media Ecologist will find much helpful insight in the building itself, precisely because he assumes so much of a Judeo-Christian view of men and things.

CHRISTIAN PERSPECTIVES

The following Christian thinkers are only a choice sampling. Among others, not mentioned below, who have made significant contributions to Christian thinking about media, are the following. Douglas Groothuis, author of *The Soul in Cyberspace* (1997), teaches in the Philosophy of Religion Department at Denver Seminary, and has been a visiting instructor in apologetics at Westminster Theological Seminary in California. Samuel Ebersole, who has done his doctorate at Regent College, has produced a thoughtful hypertext titled: "Media Determinism in Cyberspace" (1995). Stephen V. Monsma, who teaches at Calvin College, has edited: *Responsible Technology: A Christian Perspective* (1986). Of course other apologists and cultural critics such as Os Guinness have addressed the problem of electronic media from a Christian perspective. What is absent from this entire section is a Christian scholar who has focused almost exclusively on media criticism. Quentin Schultze comes the

---

[62] Neil Postman, *The End of Education* (New York: Alfred A. Knopf, 1995) 70.
[63] *Ibid.*, 81.
[64] Interview by Reynolds, 12, 13.
[65] *Ibid.*, 13.
[66] *Ibid.*, 14.

closest. There is also a Dutch Dooyeweerdian scholar, Egbert Schuurman, at the Technological Universities of Delft and Eindhoven who has written several excellent books: *Reflections on the Technological Society* (1977); and *Technology and the Future* (1980).

Malcolm Muggeridge (1903-1990) *Anglo-Catholic Journalist*

Muggeridge was not a media theorist. He was a journalist and an unintentional media celebrity. As a Moscow correspondent for the *Manchester Guardian* in the thirties his enchantment with the Soviet Union came to an abrupt end. He witnessed the tragic failure of central policy in the Ukranian famine. In the fifties Muggeridge was the editor of the British magazine *Punch*. Having forsaken his Socialism in the thirties he forsook his vocal agnosticism in the sixties by becoming a Christian. As a television journalist for the BBC almost since its inception, he offers a scathing critique of the medium. As an ardent anti-Communist he was disposed to view Orwell's scenario of the future as the most accurate. In *Christ and the Media* he asserts that the BBC was his model for the Ministry of Truth in *1984*.[67] Of course, unlike American television, British television is in fact government controlled.

By 1975 Muggeridge no longer owned a television, and participated in television interviews only with great reluctance.[68] He describes television journalism as "fraudulent," because it presents the public with what he calls "newsak," (the journalistic counterpart to Musak) which seeks a consensus based on a very skewed presentation of news events. In so doing the reality of absolute truth is muted and people view news as a form of entertainment. "The people producing the news are not really thinking of informing people but of exciting them."[69]

Muggeridge's most cogent objections to television are articulated in his only book on the subject, *Christ and the Media* (1977). The book consists of three lectures delivered in 1976 at the London Lectures in Contemporary Christianity, along with questions and chairmen's' speeches at the end of each. Muggeridge maintains that the media (usually synonymous with television for Muggeridge) are playing a major role in the disintegration of Western civilization by undermining traditional standards and values. He goes on to assert that "the only antidote to the media's world of fantasy is the reality of Christ's Kingdom proclaimed in the New Testament."[70] He does not mince words: "Not only *can* the camera lie, it always lies. ...News is ten million

---

[67] Muggeridge, *Christ and the Media*, 105.
[68] Malcolm Muggeridge, "Muggeridge on Media," Interview by Steve Turner. *Radix* (May 1975): 7.
[69] *Ibid.*
[70] Muggeridge, *Christ and the Media*, 23, 24.

people induced to think the same thing."[71] The Second Commandment reminds Muggeridge of the "sinister overtones of narcissism" evoked by the television image. As a fabricator of fantasy "it is almost invariably *eros* rather than *agape* that provides all the excitement; celebrity and success rather than a broken and a contrite heart that are held up as being pre-eminently desirable; Jesus Christ in lights on Broadway rather than Jesus Christ on the cross who gets a folk hero's billing."[72] Its corrupting power has created a "cult of consumption," mystified with sex.[73] The most dangerous aspect of television is that it purports to be reality, and yet is drawing people away from reality.[74] Muggeridge recalls his confusion upon seeing himself on television. It was not actually him, he discovered.[75] Muggeridge perceptively notes that in this shadowland the universality of its audience undermines all values and traditions.[76] "In the beginning was the *Word*, and the Word was made flesh, not celluloid."[77]

Because of his commitment to the word, as opposed to images, as the chief purveyor of Christian faith, Muggeridge believed that Christians who work with television must labor to overcome its propensity toward fantasy.[78] Answering a question after the final lecture Muggeridge betrays his unfortunate ignorance of McLuhan's understanding of the nature of media. The questioner wondered if Muggeridge would have given similar lectures after the invention of the printing press. Muggeridge emphatically denied a similarity between television and the printing press. Printed words, he claims, are connected to thought, whereas images are not.[79] Like Clifford Stoll, Muggeridge has the credentials of the consummate insider, and thus should be listened to with care. We must also be careful not to reject television as inherently evil, which is the tendency of near Luddites like Muggeridge and Stoll. If Muggeridge errs on the side of the technophobes, our next thinker tends to err more on the side of the technophiles.

Quentin Schultze (1952-) *Reformed Media Scholar*

Born in Chicago, Schultze earned the Ph.D. in communication from the University of Illinois. Remember that it was at the University of Illinois that

---

[71] *Ibid.*, 30, 32.
[72] *Ibid.*, 46, 47.
[73] *Ibid.*, 54, 57.
[74] *Ibid.*, 60.
[75] *Ibid.*, 47.
[76] *Ibid.*, 86.
[77] *Ibid.*, 88.
[78] *Ibid.*, 92, 93.
[79] *Ibid.*, 105, 106.

Wilbur Schramm founded the first communication study program offering the Ph.D. Schultze taught at Illinois and at Drake University, where, in addition to serving as Assistant and then Associate Professor of Journalism and Mass Communication, he was chair of the graduate program in mass communication and Lecturer in Sociology. In 1982 he joined the faculty of Calvin College, where he is now Professor of Communication Arts and Sciences. He has worked as a copywriter in radio and television, an advertising salesman, scriptwriter, and media critic. He has written *Television: Manna From Hollywood?* (1986); *Dancing in the Dark: Youth, Popular Culture and the Electronic Media* (1991); *Televangelism and American Culture: The Business of Popular Religion* (1991); *Redeeming Television: How TV Changes Christians - How Christians Can Change TV* (1992); and edited *American Evangelicals and the Mass Media* (1990). He is also author of the forthcoming *Communication through the Eyes of Faith* (Baker Book House).

Dr. Schultze's scholarly publications have appeared in several dozen journals, including the *Journal of Communication*, the *Journal of Broadcasting & Electronic Media, Qualitative Sociology, Journalism Quarterly, Critical Studies in Mass Communication* and *The Journal of Communication Inquiry*. Dr. Schultze has won three book awards and was nominated in 1982 by the Newcommen Society of North America for the best article published by a junior scholar in *Harvard's Business History Review*. He has lectured at over 30 colleges and universities, including as a Staley Distinguished Lecturer at seven institutions.

Professor Schultze is former president of the Religious Speech Communication Association, now called the Religious Communication Association. He also co-founded the Gospel Communications Network, the most popular religious Web site in the world, and founded and served as Executive Editor of the *Internet for Christians Newsletter*, which is read by over 100,000 people around the world.

Schultze is at his best in analyzing the narrative power of television as a master teacher of our culture. "Television is the most significant medium for mythologic storytelling in contemporary American society."[80] His plea for television producers to take more advantage of the narrative power of television by creating "illuminative" programming which deals with substantive themes is well taken. "Masterpiece Theatre" is used as an example of television at its best. Intelligent viewing and "visual literacy" are enjoined by Schultze. He encourages content criticism which rises above the usual Christian moralism found in much of the church's outrage over programming. Schultze's

---

[80] Quentin Schultze, *Redeemimg Television: How TV Changes Christians - How Christians Can Change TV* (Downers Grove, IL: InterVarsity Press, 1992) 49. Cf. all of Chapter 2, 37-60.

distinction between *portrayal* and *point of view* is an important consideration which takes context and motivation into account.[81] He quotes Gene Edward Veith and Kenneth Myers to the effect that we must distinguish between moral and aesthetic goodness, and that both unite to make worthwhile art.[82]

Schultze's doctoral training at the University of Illinois is evident throughout his writings. He has essentially baptized the Progressive and Scientific theories of media influence, viewing media essentially as conduits of information. His own production experience leads him to occasionally mention the grammar of media. He calls Christians to pursue excellence in broadcasting technique, as well as motivation. Schultze is properly critical of both a totally negative and a naively positive assessment of media technology.[83]

In his criticism of negative assessments of television, and the image media, Schultze oddly lumps Muggeridge, Ellul, Postman, Virginia Stem Owens, and Jerry Mander into the same category as "Christian Critics."[84] Postman, for one, is a Jew. By combining the entirely negative assessments of image media of Muggeridge and Ellul with Postman, Schultze fails to appreciate Postman's seriously positive view of television *as* entertainment. Worse is the lack of any substantive interaction with McLuhan or Meyrowitz, both of whom appear in end notes. While rightly warning of the "Gnostic Impulse" of viewing television as inherently evil, he fails to recognize that as an orthodox Roman Catholic McLuhan was self-consciously anti-gnostic. His only concession is to say: "no medium is neutral with respect to its effects on both messages and the people who use it." In an end note Schultze expresses his disagreement with McLuhan: "I do not agree with McLuhan that the fundamental effects of a medium are psychological—that each media technology merely rearranges the priority of the human senses in perception. Nevertheless, the technology does carry its own bias."[85] It is difficult to imagine a less accurate understanding of McLuhan from a media scholar. He makes the classic mistake of imagining every technology, in itself, as merely a tool: "The technology is inherently neither good or bad." He maintains that both critics and "celebrators" make a common mistake: failing "to distinguish between the *technology* and the *social institution* of television."[86] It is the institutions of which technologies become part that determine the values and beliefs which guide the use of the consequent medium. Schultze does concede

---

[81] *Ibid.*, 133ff.
[82] *Ibid.*, 139.
[83] *Ibid.*, 26-29.
[84] *Ibid.*, 23, 24.
[85] *Ibid.*, 197, 198.
[86] *Ibid.*, 31

to Postman that television is not well suited for philosophical argument.[87] But even after somewhat favorably quoting Postman's assessment of the problem being not *what* we watch, but *that* we watch, Schultze fails to understand the environmental aspect of the problem.

Despite Schultze's plea that in order to "redeem" television we must understand the "inherent nature of the technology and the human nature of the institutions that use it," what is totally absent from Schultze's work is the Media Ecology focus on media as environment(s). His work is reminiscent of Shramm's mass media influence approach. Thus he is able to deal with mass media effects on a sociological and spiritual level. His lack of a coherent theory of communication, along with his content oriented analysis, causes him to propose remedies which treat the symptoms rather than the disease.

Joel Nederhood (1930-) *Reformed Preacher-Broadcaster*

Born in Grand Rapids Joel Nederhood was graduated from Calvin College in 1952. He served in the U. S. Army in the Korean War and returned to graduate from Calvin Seminary in 1957. Nederhood went to Free University of Amsterdam as a Fulbright Scholar from 1957 to 1959, receiving the Th.D in 1959. His dissertation was titled: "The Church as Mission and the Educated American," and later published by Eerdmans as *The Church's Mission To the Educated American* in 1960.

For the next thirty-six years Nederhood focused on his life work as director of the Christian Reformed Church's radio ministry, the *Back To God Hour*. His passion to communicate the gospel clearly, cogently and intelligently has characterized his work as a minister of the Word. Along with coordinating the ministries in Arabic, French, Spanish, Chinese, Portuguese, Japanese, Indonesian and Russian, writing and producing the weekly *Back to God Hour* program, he broadcast the daily *Insight* program and the daily *Faith 20* television program. *Faith 20* began in 1981 and continued in production until 1997, when *Primary Focus* took its place. He was editor of *TODAY*, a devotional guide, from 1965 to 1997. Dr. Nederhood is presently pastor of preaching and worship at the Cottage Grove, Christian Reformed Church in South Holland, Illinois, and continues to broadcast the daily *Insight* program.

Dr. Nederhood taught in the homiletics department of Trinity Evangelical Divinity School in 1997 and 1998. He has also lectured in the homiletics department of Westminster Theological Seminary in California occasionally over the past several decades. It was his course, taught at the latter school in 1990, titled "Effective Preaching in a Media Age" which inspired the present

---

[87] *Ibid.*, 32-36.

book. Most pertinent to the Christian Media Ecologist are two of Nederhood's publications: *Christian Reformed Church Synod Report,* "The Back to God Hour: Mission Television Report" (1977), and "Communication: Is it Possible," in *The Evangelical Roundtable* (1987).[88] The synodical report in 1977 is a carefully articulated approach to the church's use of television for evangelistic purposes.

Dr. Nederhood maintains that preaching is the only "bridge" between Scripture and our age. God is a great user of media. His creation is a great medium. Jesus Christ as the Mediator bridges the gap between the infinite and the finite. Due to sin man perverts media. The television has created a pervasive environment which threatens the content orientation of print. As a careful student of McLuhan and Postman, Nederhood distinguishes between the use of television as a "technique" and a "medium." Preachers should only use television as a technique or "delivery system."[89] "I am one who favors something that is not prize winning television but that tells people about Christ very explicitly and virtually every time."[90]

Nederhood distinguishes five "categories of influence" or television impact: neurological, epistemological, experiential, modalistic, and sociological. Thus he concludes that the television alters brain function to a non-sequential "dream state." It alters our perception of reality. It mediates experience. It defines life as entertainment. It is the primary socializing force in our culture. The powers which control television are essentially "anti-Christian" and commercial in their motivation. Its tendency toward idolatry is enormous.

Thus, if the church uses television it should be as a "delivery system," with full understanding of its negative potential as a medium.[91] In his "Mission Television Report," Nederhood warned the church: "television has immense power not only as a communication tool, but also as a modifier of those who use it."[92] Thus the church must use television with a recognition of the tension between the nature of the church's mission and the nature of television, and a "high degree of cultural awareness—of cultural realism."[93] It is the church's responsibility to "assess the effect of this presence."[94] "Because of the intensity and extent of television's impact on culture, the effect of this

---

[88] Joel Nederhood, Personal Email (10 November 1999).
[89] Joel Nederhood, "Effective Preaching in a Media Age," class notes, Westminster Theological Seminary in California, 1990.
[90] Nederhood, Personal Email.
[91] Nederhood, "Effective Preaching in a Media Age."
[92] Joel Nederhood, "The Back to God Hour: Mission Television Report," in *Christian Reformed Church Synod Report.* Report 1:A, Supplement, 1977, 168.
[93] *Ibid.,* 169.
[94] *Ibid.,* 170.

A CHRISTIAN VIEW OF MEDIA THEORY AND CRITICISM 179

medium must be considered whenever we attempt analyses of the environment in which we conduct our mission."[95]

In our preaching, Nederhood asserts, we must emphasize that salvation is not "personalistic," but rather church oriented, covenantal, and counter cultural. The Bible is the "alternative environment" to the pseudo-environment of television. The preacher may take heart because idolatry is vulnerable to the universal truth of Scripture. The cross of Jesus Christ must, therefore, be central to the message of the preacher. The authenticity of the preacher is at the center of the power of the gospel to unmask an inauthentic world.[96]

Although Nederhood is not a media scholar in a school of communications, he is a media scholar in the school of the prophets. His thoughtful assessment of television as a medium for evangelism should serve as a model for the Christian Media Ecologist.

AN OUTLINE FOR FUTURE DEVELOPMENT

A Definition of Communication

How shall we define communication? Carey suggests: "communication is a symbolic process whereby reality is produced, maintained, repaired, and transformed."[97] The fatal flaw in this definition is found in the word "reality." As we noted in chapter 2 man in sin considers his thought, and consequently his expression of thought in language, to be "creatively constructive," that is originating in human consciousness. The Christian rightly understands all meaning and reality to originate in the Triune God, and man's thinking to be "receptively reconstructive."[98] The Christian seeks to think God's thoughts after Him, while the unbeliever is vainly seeking to create his own reality with words and actions. He must, of course, deal with created reality as he finds it. However, he distorts it by interpreting it for his own ends. Still he must deal with reality and meaning as God has created it. The Christian Media Ecologist will use this concept in his definition. Communication originates in the eternal intra-Trinitarian communion of thought, and is imitated by His image-bearing creature man, in the construction of verbal symbols, and the means of propagating them, which enable him to fulfill the cultural mandate before the fall, and his cultural instinct after the fall, and for the Christian his cultural

---

[95] *Ibid.*, 171.
[96] Nederhood, "Effective Preaching in a Media Age."
[97] Carey, *Communication as Culture*, 23.
[98] Cornelius Van Til, *The Defense of the Faith*. 3rd edition (Nutley, NJ and Philadelphia: Presbyterian and Reformed Publishing Company, 1967) 48, 49.

calling, in the various spheres of human life and society. Augustine's *De Magistro* is fruitful reading at this point. The rule of language assumes that "when signs are heard the attention is directed to the realities signified."[99]

The most egregious omission of Media Ecologists lies within the boundaries of metaphysics, or, more properly, theology. James Carey's definition of "communication" explicitly grounds reality in the existence of communication itself. After defining "communication" as we have seen above, Carey comments, "I want to suggest, to play on the Gospel of St. John, that in the beginning was the word ...Reality is not given, not humanly existent, independent of language and toward which language stands as a pale refraction. Rather, reality is brought into existence, is produced, by communication—by, in short, the construction, apprehension, and utilization of symbolic forms."[100] What a subtle, dangerous twist this gives to the truth that reality is in fact brought into existence, not man's communication, which is derivative, but by God's communication when He said "Let there be...and it was so." Thus, communication is first a divine reality, and only then may it be considered a human one. Augustine found the certainty of human knowledge in the fact that all truth is grounded in the ontological reality of God.[101] Man's communicative ability then is recreative.

Communication Is Essentially Trinitarian and Covenantal

While brilliant secular theorists may "discover" many true and important things about communication and media, their theory of communication is always inadequate when it comes to foundational or ultimate things. The Christian theorist must begin with God Himself. He is the Original Communicator and the Creator of all human communication and all media of communication.

We must not fail to add the most essential element of our worldview to the definition of Media Ecology as "the study of the relationship of media to their cultural environment." Because the Christian community is God's dwelling or "house" then Christian Media Ecology is a stewardship of the media of communication *before God*. It may never then be merely a study. It is a study with an all-consuming purpose: to bring glory to God. Thus, Christian Media Ecology is the study and stewardship of all media in their relationship to God, the church, and its cultural environment for God's glory. This quest is inherent in *being* the church. Biblical reflection on the specifics of our task is a mandate

---

[99] Saint Augustine, *The Greatness of the Soul; The Teacher*, in *Ancient Christian Writers*, translated and edited by Joseph M. Colleran (Westminster, MD: The Newman Press, 1964) 115.
[100] James W. Carey, *Communication as Culture*. Boston, MA: Unwin Hyman, 1989.
[101] Augustine, *The Greatness of the Soul; The Teacher*, 122.

motivated by this larger purpose. Prior to a concern which will be expressed below regarding anthropology, should be an alertness to the ways in which electronic media tend to eclipse the true and living God.

Communication is essentially Trinitarian. In the Biblical text our knowledge of the Trinity is embedded in the history of redemption. Thus we are given only hints of the eternal "before the beginning," so far is it beyond the ken of human understanding. Yet the glimpses were sufficient to produce the magnificent formulation of the doctrine of the Trinity at Nicea. The most significant declaration of Scripture is the startling statement with which John begins his gospel: "In the beginning was the Word, and the Word was with God, and the Word was God" (John 1:1). The phrase "In the beginning" hearkens back to Genesis 1:1. There, as the name of the Son (Word) implies, was communication par excellence. In John 5:20 we read "For the Father loves the Son, and shows Him all things that He Himself does." The verb "shows" (δείκνυσι) means reveal, explain, and in the present tense indicates a continuous activity. In Christ's high priestly prayer in John 17 we are told that there was a covenant made in eternity between the Father and the Son to save His elect people. "I have glorified You on the earth. I have finished the work which You have given Me to do" (v. 4). Here is communication of the profoundest sort in the Covenant of Redemption. In verse 8 Jesus says "For I have given to them the words (τὰ ῥήματα) which You have given Me." The inter-Trinitarian love and glory is shared through eternal communication in the mysterious interpenetration of the divine Persons.

Communication is also essentially covenantal. From the beginning human communication was not only imitative of Trinitarian communication, but it was covenantal in nature as God spoke to Adam in the Garden. The very first human experience of communication was not social, but between God and man; and God was the first to speak. His speech was always by way of the sovereignly initiated and defined arrangement of His relationship with man, which the Bible calls a *covenant* (OT בְּרִית NT διαθήκη). When Adam named the animals he was using language recreatively to fulfill the cultural mandate and assert his God-given lordship over creation. Since the fall, language is used either in covenant keeping or covenant breaking activity. Interestingly, in the Common Grace Covenant with Noah after the flood, God communicated His covenant verbally to His people, but visually to everyone else. "The rainbow shall be in the cloud, and I will look on it to remember the everlasting covenant between God and every living creature of all flesh that *is* on the earth" (Gen. 9:16). This was a sign for all to see.

The perversion of language is nowhere more poignantly depicted than in the Tower of Babel incident in Genesis 11. Human language was used to make the Cult of Man out of the culture given by God. Fallen humanity sought solidarity through communication in defining (naming) itself above God. "Come, let us build ourselves a city, and a tower whose top *is* in the heavens; let us make a name for ourselves, lest we be scattered abroad over the face of the whole earth" (Gen. 11:4). This is the awful tendency of human culture. The final apotheosis of this project is depicted at the end of history in connection with the deification of man. "He was granted *power* to give breath to the image of the beast, that the image of the beast should both speak and cause as many as would not worship the image of the beast to be killed" (Rev. 13:15). Idolatry degrades man, and thus the metaphor of "beast" reveals this dehumanizing tendency, as we have seen in chapter 1. *Speaking* and thus communicating is his most important means of asserting the Tower of Babel agenda. Communication always has reference to God. The act and mental environment of speech is a revelation of God's existence and omnipresence as Paul pointed out to the Athenians, "for in Him we live and move and have our being" (Acts 17:27, 28). All nominalistic tendencies in secular communication and linguistic theory, which seek to divorce meaning from metaphysics are an evasion of the existence and continual revelation of God to man (Rom. 1:18-20).

The Christian doctrine of the Trinity is utterly unique, and is the only metaphysical basis for communication. "God cannot be self-contemplating, self-cognitive, and self-communing, unless he is trinal in his constitution."[102] Communication is of the essence of the Godhead, and central to the *opera ad intra* of the Trinity. The whole creation reveals His name and thus His omnipresence "Your wondrous works declare *that* Your name (שם) is near" (Ps. 75:1). His name is the sum of all His revealed attributes: "He has sent redemption to His people; He has commanded His covenant forever; Holy and awesome *is* His name" (Ps. 11:9). He is as good as His Word. His covenantal Word expressed in Scripture and preached by His prophets is placed on a par with His own glory. "You have magnified Your word above all Your name" (Ps. 138:2). The naming power He has given man is derivative, but powerful; with it comes awesome responsibility.

Thus we may define Christian Media Ecology as the study of the relationship of media to their cultural environment, which is a stewardship of the God-given gift of communication.

Percept and Concept Are Complementary in a Biblical Anthropology

To accept the best insights of Media Ecology is to affirm that media have a profound effect on the way that we look at the world. But as *imago dei* we want

---

[102] William G. T. Shedd, *Dogmatic Theology*, vol. 1, Reprint, 1888, 2nd ed., (Nashville: Thomas Nelson Publishers, 1980) 251.

to affirm that man is not a constantly evolving being. McLuhan and Ellul understood that the changeless heart of man's identity was a source of hope in the Electronic Age. Ong's concept of an evolving sensorium does not adequately account for that changeless center. While the conceptual structure which interprets perception is altered by the various media, the ontological nature of man remains the same. His essential ability and need to communicate and to receive communication from God and his fellow man is an inviolable part of his identity as God's unique creation. His essential need for transcendent reality as a source of meaning, whether it be the true and living God or an idol of his or his culture's own creation, is ever present. His essential instinct for culture building can never be obliterated.

Augustine distinguished between "audibles" and "visibles," in which "things written are to things spoken as signs of signs." "[A]ll things uttered by the articulate voice are called word."[103] Words are not the only signs. Gestures may also signify something else. Word-signs are heard while gestures and written words are seen. Written words are signs of heard words, which, when presented to the eye, bring the heard word to mind.[104] Speech teaches us by reminding us and learning takes place by remembering. Even thinking involves pondering words within the mind. "[S]o, too, speech serves only to remind us, since the memory in which the words inhere, by recalling them brings to mind the realities themselves, of which the words are signs."[105] The meaning of a word is "hidden in the sound."[106] Reality is prior to verbal communication, not created by it.[107] Thus the Augustinian dictum: *Nisi crediteritus, non intelligetis*, based on Isaiah 7:9 "unless you believe you shall not understand." Everyman consults the Wisdom of God in the act of knowing and speaking. "He it is who teaches—Christ—that is, *the unchangeable Power of God and everlasting Wisdom* (1 Cor. 1:23). This Wisdom every soul does, in fact, consult. But to each one only so much is manifested as he is capable of receiving because of his own good or bad will."[108] Mere words do not teach anything apart from the inner light of God's revelation. God alone is the Teacher, *Magistro*.

In McLuhan we have seen the failure of developing a theoretical foundation for his insight. He claimed to be a Thomist, and although he shunned the publicity of his theological assumptions we may glean a general outline of a Biblical view of man from his work. Donald Theall suggests that:

---

[103] Augustine, *The Greatness of the Soul; The Teacher*, 141.
[104] *Ibid.*, 139.
[105] *Ibid.*, 131.
[106] *Ibid.*, 174.
[107] *Ibid.*, 175.
[108] *Ibid.*, 177.

"It could be instructive to re-examine McLuhan with the assumption that his work depends on a prior acceptance of Thomistic philosophy. This immediately provides a 'view of man' as implicit behind his work, though it is quite likely that in sociologizing this view he has actually removed much of its integrity within the neo-Thomist position."[109] While it is not within the scope of this book to address the differences between the Augustinian and Thomistic epistemologies, which ultimately involves their dependence at points with Plato and Aristotle, I am not suggesting that traditional Reformed objections to the Thomistic anthropology, especially as they bear upon soteriology, should be abandoned. It is only at the point of stating that man is not purely the product of his culture that I think all Christians can agree with McLuhan. In chapter 4 and above we have discussed the weakness in McLuhan's dichotomizing of percept and concept.

Another of McLuhan's ideas which is certainly Christian is that our tools are extensions of ourselves. The hammer is an extension of the fist. The wheel is an extension of the feet.[110] The ability to create such tools is God's gift in developing common culture, but also implies and even mandates wise stewardship of those tools for the Christian. "Ordinary life-work demands that we harness and subordinate the media to human ends."[111]

While there is much to be explored both in the anthropology of McLuhan as well the development of the relation of Biblical anthropology to Media Ecology, what is clear at this point is that man the communicator is both dependent on God for the gift of communicating, and responsible before Him for the ways in which he uses this extraordinary gift (James 3:1-12).

A Medium and Its Content Must Be Understood Together

In seeking to parse McLuhan's proverbial dictum "the medium is the message" we must understand two things. First, McLuhan used hyperbole in order to probe or cause others to think critically about something they had never considered. Secondly, the medium cannot be the entire message or else there would be no point in trying to communicate anything with any medium. McLuhan's point is that the medium affects the message and the user(s) of the medium dramatically. We must reckon on this effect in our interaction with all media, especially those which are new to us. Media are not simply channels or containers of messages, but themselves affect the way we receive and interpret the message. The medium is a critical aspect of the content of every mode of

---

[109] Donald F. Theall, *The Medium is the Rear View Mirror: Understanding McLuhan*. (Montreal: McGill-Queens University Press, 1971) 207.

[110] McLuhan, *Counterblast*, 42.

[111] *Ibid.*, 53.

communication, which by its nature is least obvious to users of the medium, and thus requires special attention.

Thus the distinction which we encountered in chapter 2 between *figure* and *ground* is all important. McLuhan observed: "The fatal flaw of the Graeco-Roman thing has always been specialism and unrelatedness.... Communication theory for any figure requires the including of the ground for that figure and the study of the interplay between the figure and its ground. Graeco-Roman, or visual man, has consistently studied the figure minus the ground....whereas the Graeco-Roman, from Plato to the present, has no theory of communication at all (what is called 'communication theory' today is merely the transportation of data from one machine to another machine), Christianity proclaims its communication theory loud and clear. Every aspect of the Christian thing is communication and change and transformation."[112] The word *content* itself implies a container (Lat. *continere*). Consider the modern idea of "packaging." This a tacit concession to McLuhan. The package radically effects our view of what is in it. The medium and the message are inextricably interrelated.

This is not to diminish the importance of content analysis. Nor was that the point McLuhan was making. It is only to focus on an almost universally ignored dimension of media study. As Meyrowitz points out, this environmental aspect of media helps us understand the ways in which social structure is changed by media. He goes on to express his preference for the label "medium theory" because such analysis asks: "What are the relatively fixed features of each means of communicating and how do these features make the medium physically, psychologically, and socially different from other media and from face-to-face interaction."[113]

Meyrowitz offers the media critic a helpful synthetic approach to media criticism, by combining the metaphors used to analyse media in the history of communication study. Media are viewed as *conduits* in which the content of messages are analyzed, as *languages* in which the grammar of a medium is analyzed, and as *environments* in which the environment created by a medium is analyzed.[114] In this way the media critic will foster an awareness that no single way of viewing media is sufficient to understanding communication.

---

[112] McLuhan, *Letters*, 467-468 (letter to Barbara Ward, February 9, 1973).
[113] Joshua Meyrowitz, "Taking McLuhan and 'Medium Theory' Seriously: Technological Change and the Evolution of Education," Chapter 4 in *Technology and the Future of Schooling: Ninety-Fifth Yearbook of the National Society for the Study of Education*. Part II (Chicago: University of ChicagoPress, 1996) 79.
[114] Joshua Meyrowitz, "Images of Media: Hidden Ferment—and Harmony—in the Field." *Journal of Communication* 43, no. 3 (summer 1993): 55-66; "Multiple Media Literacies." *Journal of Communication* 48, no. 1 (winter 1998): 96-108.

3 Media Metaphors (Meyrowitz) - to Analyse a Particular Medium of Communication[115]

#1. *Medium as a Conduit* - This aspect of media analysis accesses, interprets and evaluates messages in different genres, such as "cultural, institutional and commercial." Wilbur Schramm insisted, "The message is the message, and the medium is the medium."[116] This most obvious and, therefore, most discussed dimension of media is not specific to particular media, but crosses "easily from medium to medium and between mediated and unmediated interaction," and deals with "behaviors, themes, and topics."[117] Assessing the impact of sex and violence on television is a classic example of this kind of analysis.

#2. *Medium as a Language* - This aspect of media analysis focuses on the "unique 'grammar' of each medium and the ways in which the production variables of each medium ...interact with content elements..." and are used to "shape perception and response to mediated communications."[118] This form of analysis "demands some understanding of the specific workings of individual media..." such as the television's camera-ability to make close-up and personal shots and distance shots, which focus more on social roles.[119] Clear comparison among grammatical elements of a medium or media requires the content to remain constant, such as a murder shown from the perspective of the victim or from the perspective of the murderer. Unlike content, the more effective the grammar is the less obvious it is to the audience.[120] Such analysis might discover that a producer favored a political candidate in a televised debate by having the camera zoom in for close-ups at favorable moments in the debate, and from the best perspective, and perhaps more frequently than with the opposing candidate. Close-ups of the opposing candidate might be done when the candidate is blowing his nose or looking confused.

#3. *Medium as an Environment* - This aspect of media analysis focuses on "the particular characteristics of each medium. ...The nature of the medium shapes key aspects of the communication on both the micro-, single-situation level and

---

[115] Joshua Meyrowitz, "Multiple Media Literacies," *Journal of Communication* 48, no. 1 (winter 1998): 96-108.
[116] Wilbur Schramm, *Men, Messages, and Media: A Look at Human Communication* (New York: Harper and Row, 1973) 128, quoted in Meyrowitz, "Multiple Media Literacies," 98
[117] Meyrowitz, "Multiple Media Literacies," 98.
[118] *Ibid.*, 99.
[119] *Ibid.*, 100, 101.
[120] *Ibid.*, 102.

the macro-, societal level."[121] Macro-level analysis assesses the social changes effected by a medium, in terms of social boundaries, situations, and institutions. It also takes into account the contextual social, political and economic forces which foster media development. This form of analysis is most difficult, because it is the least obvious of the three aspects, especially after a medium becomes culturally pervasive.[122] The fact that television, as a medium, discourages rational discourse, and encourages "all-at-onceness" may explain why Johnny has difficulty reading because print is linear and logical in its essence. At the macro-level this will lend insight to discussion of the failure of the traditional curriculum, which is based on a literary model.

Meyrowitz holds out the ideal of integrating these metaphors in media analysis, while at the same time recognizing that most media critics and theorists use only one most of the time. Furthermore, "Any communication through media encompasses all three simultaneously."[123]

McLuhan developed several other themes of media analysis. The "rear-view mirror" is a metaphor for his observation that with the advent of each new medium we tend to notice qualities of the medium which it is replacing. For example the movie called attention to the narrative structure of the novels it adapted. Furthermore, looking back brings new appreciation for older content, exemplified by the reruns of some of the best 1950s television.[124] The danger of the "rear-view mirror" is that it may distract us from seeing what is ahead. Calling the first automobile a "horseless carriage" focused attention on the carriage, and distracted us from recognizing the unique ways in which the high speed travel of the automobile would affect culture.

McLuhan's work, as we have said, focused on the third metaphor of Meyrowitz: medium as environment. In the 1970s he and his son Eric developed the "four laws of media."[125] Known as the *tetrad* four essential questions are asked of each medium to enhance our understanding of their environmental effect. 1) *Extension* asks "What aspect of man or his culture does the medium amplify?" For example television amplifies sight and sound and extends the central nervous system. 2) *Closure* asks "What does the medium make obsolete or less prominent?" Television makes the newspaper less prominent as a news source. 3) *Reversal* asks "What characteristics does

---

[121] *Ibid.*, 103.
[122] *Ibid.*, 105, 106.
[123] Joshua Meyrowitz, "Understandings of Media." *ETC* 56 (Spring, 1999): 51.
[124] Paul Levinson, "Millennial McLuhan: Clues for Deciphering the Digital Age," [WWW document] URL http://chronicle.com/weekly/v46/i08/08b01001.htm (14 October 1999).
[125] Marshall McLuhan and Eric McLuhan. *Laws of Media: The New Science* (Toronto: University of Toronto Press, 1988).

the medium reverse to, or 'flip into,' when it reaches its limits?" Television "flipped into broadcasts of both sounds and images." These are ancient pre-electronic percepts. 4) *Retrieval* "Asks how does the medium recast old forms as the content of the new medium?" Television recast Vaudeville as the variety show (e.g. Ed Sullivan).[126]

Each Medium Must Be Understood in Its Context

Communication does not take place in a vacuum, but in a social context. Meyrowitz, as we have seen in chapter 4, has suggested the link between "medium theory" and culture through understanding the structure of social situations. He is simply fleshing out the point McLuhan often made when he said: "For the 'message' of any medium or technology is the change of scale or pace or pattern that it introduces into human affairs."[127] Meyrowitz maintains that social identity is linked to social situations through patterns of access to information. Our knowledge of who knows what about whom makes the difference between what we do in private and what we do in interacting with others. Media alter patterns of access among social situations and roles, and thus alter those roles and the boundaries of social place and structure.

Meyrowitz's "role triad" covers all social roles in three general categories: socialization, group identity, and hierarchy. Each depends on a different "pattern of access to information." New media change these patterns. *Socialization* depends on gradual access to information from the group of which they are becoming a part. College students must begin with introductory material before they can enter into the discipline of a department. *Group identity* is defined by the information which is unique to a particular group, and not shared with outsiders. Thus lawyers, who have passed the bar exam, share special knowledge with other lawyers. *Hierarchies* depend on unique access to information which only the authority may have. Thus the president of a company depends on information which no one else has.[128] The hidden tape recorder in Nixon's office is a poignant example of this.

When new media change, blur or eliminate these boundaries the roles of individuals in their various social settings changes, sometimes dramatically. Whereas print media tended to create and maintain more boundaries, electronic media, especially television, tend to blur the boundaries by providing

---

[126] Eric McLuhan, "The Genesis of the Laws of Media," in George Sanderson and Frank Macdonald, eds. *Marshall McLuhan: The Man and His Message* (Golden, CO: Fulcrum, Inc., 1989) 202. Levinson, "Millennial McLuhan."
[127] Marshall McLuhan, *Understanding Media: The Extensions of Man* (New York: McGraw-Hill Book Company, 1964) 8.
[128] Meyrowitz, "Taking McLuhan and 'Medium Theory' Seriously," 85.

knowledge across the boundaries, and integrating once separate "informational worlds."[129] A most obvious example of this is the change in childhood, effected by access to adult information via television, even before children are able to read. The resultant "blurring of childhood and adulthood" alters the behavior of both children and adults.[130]

The Christian, however, will not agree with Meyrowitz's definition of social identity. He argues that "Social identity does not rest *in* people, but in the network of social relations."[131] He asserts that "'childhood' and 'adulthood' were invented in Western culture in the sixteenth century, and their spread follows the spread of schooling."[132] Such a reduction of mediating institutions is not acceptable to the Christian, who takes the Bible seriously. The family was instituted by God with the *ex nihilo* creation of Adam and Eve. The church as we know it, and the state were instituted by God after the fall as means, along with the family, of providing the essential structure of the common grace situation until the end of history, as we have seen in chapter 2.

To part company with Meyrowitz at this fundamental point does not, however, mean that much of what he says about the influence of communication media on social structure and behavior is inaccurate. Nor does it mean that within the context of the God-given structure of society that there is no development. It does mean that the essential God-given structure is normative for the Christian thinker. Meyrowitz's insight will at least help us enormously in structurally assessing the impact of electronic media on the people and institutions we cherish.

More than this, several suggestions for institutional change, which both Meyrowitz and McLuhan make, for example, in education, should be carefully considered by Christians: teaching young people how to think about media; encouraging the development of exploration and logical skills in critical thinking. It will not do to seek a return to the traditional classroom, without thinking through strategies for dealing with the electronic media and the changes it has wrought in culture as a whole. We should be asking ourselves questions such as, are there better ways to motivate students to learn than traditional grading? Does the motivational scheme which works for one age group work for all ages? What is the goal of education? How do we teach media awareness? What role should electronic media themselves play in education?

---

[129] *Ibid.*, 86, 91.
[130] Joshua Meyrowitz, *No Sense of Place: The Impact of Electronic Media on Social Behavior* (New York: Oxford University Press, 1985) Chapter 13, 226-267.
[131] Meyrowitz, "Taking McLuhan and 'Medium Theory' Seriously, 84.
[132] *Ibid.*, 93, 94.

Ong laments the secularization which he maintains is fostered by the shift from orality to literacy. "Acoustic space implies presence far more than does visual space. ...It is essentially inhabited space."[133] However, his vision of the ideal is as we have seen informed more by Theilhard de Chardin than by the Bible. Biblically, common culture is desacralized by God Himself, since the fall of Adam, especially according to the terms of the Noahic covenant as we have seen in chapter 2. It is in the redemptive community of the church that sacredness exists. The means of grace indicate that when God speaks He brings a perfect balance between space and time, acoustic and visual. Ong wants to suggest that the Trinity is conceived of as communicating "in a world of sound rather than in a world of space and light."[134] This founders on the Biblical conception of God from the beginning of His self-revelation. The Trinity is not bound inherently by either time or space, both of which are the necessary context for sound.

Innis, as we have seen, distinguished between two essential types of communication media: *time-biased* and *space-biased*. Communication media shape the institutions of a culture in terms of their control of space and time.[135] *Time-biased* media, such as the spoken word, tend to foster traditional societies, whereas *Space-biased* media, such as print and electronic media, tend to promote global communities of interest and control.[136] Innis pointed to periods when the two media biases were held in harmony: Classical Greece, Renaissance Italy and Elizabethan England. It would seem that a balance between the two would serve the Christian best in the space-time world in which God has placed him.

Joel Nederhood has developed five categories to analyse the effects of television on people which include both analysis of the medium and the social context of the medium.

5 Categories of Influence (Nederhood) - to Analyse the Effect of a Medium on People[137]

#1. *Neurological* - Television causes modification of brain function. Brain wave patterns are similar to the dream state, and work in the non-analytical right hemisphere. Advertisers employ neurophysiologists because the "quick flash technique" stimulates the brain much like brainwashing. Many believe

---

[133] Ong, *The Presence of the Word*, 164.
[134] *Ibid.*, 180.
[135] Czitrom, *Media and the American Mind*, 156.
[136] *Ibid.*, 156.
[137] Nederhood, "Effective Preaching in a Media Age," class notes.

that this neurological escape from reality promotes addictive behavior and decreases educational progress among watchers.

#2. *Epistemological* - Television's ubiquity as a medium, as well as the nature of the medium itself, changes the epistemology of culture. It alters the way in which we know; and thus changes the way in which we think about reality, ourselves, others and God. It changes perception by altering the grid through which we view and interpret reality.

#3. *Experiential* - Television defines experience as the ultimate reference point, by authenticating the reality of life. It is normative for all experience. It defines what is important in human life. Television mediates reality, and when seen this is idolatrous.

#4. *Modalistic* - Television defines life in the entertainment mode. All is entertainment. It takes one mode of experience and reshapes every other mode to itself. Television trivializes everything, and makes everyone less serious.

#5. *Sociological* - Television is the primary socializing force in America. It defines identities and social situations.

Since the ultimate goal of this book is to help preachers preach more effectively in the electronic environment, we need to focus especially on the Word of God as a medium, or as I am now proposing as media.

The Word of God Is a Multimedia Triad

Media Balance

General and special revelation refer to God's communication as *non-verbal* and *verbal*. The multimedia triad begins with God's communication to His people, and is thus also verbal and non-verbal. The fact that writing is a relatively recent mode of verbal communication (third millennium BC) means that essentially speaking and seeing are *natural* to man. However, since writing and reading represent an interface between speaking and seeing I have chosen to refer to these as a triad of *primary media*.[138] While writing and printing favor sequential, linear, logical thought, I do not believe that rationality came about

---

[138] For the distinction between primary and secondary orality cf. Walter Ong, *Orality and Literacy: The Technologizing of the Word* (New York: Methuen, 1982); Eric Havelock, *The Muse Learns to Write: Reflections on Orality and Literacy from Antiquity to the Present* (New Haven: Yale University Press, 1986).

due to writing and print, however much they may accentuate that aspect of man's consciousness, but rather that writing and print developed because man *is* a rational creature. Even in oral cultures stories have a beginning and an end. Thus the intuitive and rational aspects of man are inherent in man as God's image, and both are reflected in his creation, development and use of communication media. Thus oral, written, and visual are *primary* in the sense that they are fundamental to most of man's pre-electronic situation, especially in the history of special revelation. Each of these reappear in the secondary forms of electronic communication, which are *secondary media*.. Walter Ong and Eric Havelock were the first to identify pre-literate cultures in terms of *primary orality*. Radio, since it was developed in a literate culture, is referred to as *secondary orality*. So also is all orality in a literary context.

Meyrowitz observes: "Electronic media bring back a key aspect of oral societies: simultaneity of action, perception, and reaction. Sensory experience again becomes a prime form of communicating. Yet the orality of electronic media is far different from the orality of the past. Unlike spoken communication, electronic communication is not subject to the physical limitations of time and space."[139] Primary orality was a time-biased medium, whereas secondary orality is space-biased. The dramatic shift changes the way we think, and the questions we ask. "The major questions are no longer 'Is it true?' 'Is is false?' Instead, we ask 'How does it look?' 'How does it feel?'"[140] Therein lies the real danger of the electronic environment. Its relativising tendency is immense. Its potential for undermining stability of every institution is enormous. The epistemology of critical thought and the boundaries of all of the essential mediating institutions of common grace are radically threatened. Since secondary orality is the only kind of orality we can experience in the electronic situation, the Christian, and especially the preacher, must distinguish between the *mediated orality* of the electronic media and *unmediated orality* of face-to-face personal encounter. The unmediated orality of the preacher in the *local* church brings a time-bias to the medium, as we shall see, which is no small matter in preserving the identity of the church itself.

Here I take issue with the tendency of the "orality" school to dichotomize orality and literacy. In Ong we see the tendency to glorify the primitiveness of orality, especially in his earlier work. In *The Presence of the Word* he speaks of the Christian "addiction to literacy." "The word is not an inert record but a living something, like sound, something going on." "We are the most abject prisoners of literate culture." Again, "Speech in its original state has nothing at all to do with writing." "Speech at its oral optimum must

---

[139] Meyrowitz, "Taking McLuhan and 'Medium Theory' Seriously, 96.
[140] *Ibid.*, 97.

be free from all this sense of hindrance or pressure that is inseparable from print." Ong attributes "more reality" to the spoken, as opposed to the written word. He goes on to assert: "Sound is a special sensory key to interiority." The "book takes the reader out of the tribe." Finally, Ong insists that the written word "devitalizes the universe."[141] Actually, the first words in Scripture are God's creative fiats, which were first *visible* to man. In reviewing Graham's *Beyond the Written Word: Oral Aspects of Scripture in the History of Religion* Ong contends: "Graham's searching examination of orality in the scriptures of major world religions is more than welcome in today's print-bound, book-bound world, where reading ordinarily suggests silence, without even movement of the lips."[142]

On the other hand, even in *The Presence of the Word*, Ong shows some appreciation for the "endurance and stability" of the written Word.[143] In his later work *Orality and Literacy: The Technologizing of the Word* (1982),[144] written a decade and a half after *The Presence of the Word*, Ong goes so far as to state: "Orality is not an ideal, and never was. To approach it positively is not to advocate it as a permanent state for any culture. Literacy opens possibilities to the word and to human existence unimaginable without writing. ...Both orality and the growth of literacy and the growth of literacy out of orality are necessary for the evolution of consciousness."[145] However, the dichotomy between written and spoken, which is often evident in Ong's thinking, is contrary to what the Bible clearly teaches about the complementary relationship between the two. David's meditation on the Word in Psalm 1, among dozens of other similar passages, demonstrates that private reading may also be a powerful vehicle for interiorizing, as Sven Birkerts has pointed out of reading in general. Furthermore, the public reading and preaching of the written Word seals what is written on the corporate consciousness and memory of the church, which has been entrusted with the deposit of the written Scriptures (2 Tim. 3:15).

It is highly significant that the importance of God's Word taking written form, as Scripture, appears in the history of redemption precisely at the time when the body of revelation became mnemonicly impossible to handle. Since writing, or the codification of cultural realities, had been developed in common culture at least a millennium prior to Moses, it was in the Providence of God, a perfect medium for the design and promotion of the typological kingdom of

---

[141] Ong, *The Presence of the Word*, 14, 12, 19, 21, 97, 111, 117, 135, 162
[142] Walter Ong, Review: *Beyond the Written Word: Oral Aspects of Scripture in the History of Religion* (William A. Graham) in *America* (Mar. 4, 1989): 204.
[143] Ong, *The Presence of the Word*, 191.
[144] Walter Ong, *Orality and Literacy: The Technologizing of the Word* (New York: Methuen, 1982).
[145] *Ibid.*, 175.

Israel, the nation. It is also an open question whether or not there are any purely oral cultures open to our historical inspection. One thing is certain: the Greeks were not the first literate culture, as Havelock and Ong assert. Brandeis archeologist Cyrus Gordon has spent his career demonstrating the common origin of Greek and Hebrew cultures in a common Mediterranean civilization, as well as the presence of phonetic literacy long before Greek civilization.[146]

Also, the presence of sin is entirely overlooked by the "oralist school." Sin itself gives no small reason for the revelation of the Mosaic Covenant to be in written form. Thus, for the church awaiting the consummation of the kingdom, and in the midst of the development toward the apothcosis of the deification of human culture as the cult of man, it is critical to seek the proper balance between the written and the oral, as well as the appropriate place of the visual in culture and the church.

The Incarnate Son Embodies the Balance among Media

The Incarnate Son provides us with *the* model for media criticism. Ellul points in a helpful direction when he observes that in Christ the word and the creation are united. Space, time, sight and sound would have always been united in perfect balance were it not for the Fall.[147] McLuhan maintained that the Medieval failure to understand the Gutenberg technology could have been avoided had they "created a new synthesis of oral and written education."[148] A synthetic approach will avoid the Scylla of the Luddite and the Charybdis of the technophile.

The Word of God is at once a written/read, an oral/heard, and a visual/seen medium. Any one of these isolated from the others leads to idolatry. The threefold Mediatorial office of the Firstborn of the New Humanity is replicated in his people. The richness of this threefold office can only be properly appreciated and implemented as the Word of God is understood as a multimedia triad. God's world of space-time, created reality is all of these at once for creatures made in His image, but only a proper understanding of the means of grace will enable the Christian to maintain the necessary balance among the three, and hence in relationship to all other media in our culture.

---

[146] Cyrus H. Gordon, *Ugarit And Minoan Crete; The Bearing of Their Texts on the Origins of Western Culture* (New York: W. W. Norton, 1966); *Homer and Bible: The Origin and Character Of East Mediterranean Literature* (Ventnor, NJ: Ventnor Publishers, 1967); *Before the Bible; The Common Background of Greek and Hebrew Civilizations* (Plainview, NY: Books for Libraries Press, 1973).

[147] Walter Ong, Review: *The Humiliation of the Word* (Jacques Ellul) in the *Journal of Communication* (1986): vol. 36, no. 1, pp. 156-158.

[148] Marshall McLuhan, *Understanding Media: The Extensions of Man* (New York: McGraw-Hill Book Company, 1964) 51.

The three media or modes of communication given to us in speaking/hearing, reading/writing, and seeing/touching/tasting are the *primary* media of communication. They are fundamental to being created in or as God's image. If we learn to keep the balance in the means of grace, and which the means of grace are meant to cultivate, we will be prepared to deal with all of what we might call the *cultural* or *technological* media. Because of sin, even when the three aspects are held in harmonious relationship, there will be cursing and blessing present. In the worship of the church the primary media are set apart or sanctified to be a unique blessing to God's people.

The visual, which is locked in space, demands the spoken and written words to give it meaning. The written, and especially the printed word, provides a transition between the visual and the oral. The written must be read by sight, but the meaning transcends sight. The spoken word gives special effect to the written, and is prior to the written historically.

The incarnate Lord embodies this triad. Augustine understood that the eternal Second Person of the Trinity, the Word, is the "cause and pattern of all created truth and the light of all created intellects."[149] He comes in history for all to see. He is seen dying on the cross and raised from the dead on the third day. He is the eternal Word made visible. His ministry is a teaching ministry. He preaches from the day of his baptism and installation as the Messiah until he breathes His seven last sayings on the cross. Then He preaches through His apostles, as He had spoken through His servants the prophets in the Old Covenant. All that He declares and accomplishes is a fulfillment of His inviolable written Word in the Old Testament. "You search the Scriptures, for in them you think you have eternal life; and these are they which testify of Me." (John 5:39). And all that He declares and accomplishes is written as His final revelation to mankind in the pages of the New Testament. In His incarnation the Mediatorial Son "exegetes" (ἐξηγήσατο) the Father. John 1:18 "No one has seen God at any time. The only begotten Son, who is in the bosom of the Father, He has declared *Him*." In Him we find visual, oral and written communication in perfect harmony.

Epistemological Perspectives

The perspectival epistemological model of John Frame is helpful in distinguishing three perspectives which are dimensions of the single human experience of knowing. The written, visual, oral triad relates to the *normative, situational,* and *existential* perspectives of knowledge.[150] These three

---

[149] Augustine, *The Greatness of the Soul; The Teacher*, 120.

[150] John M. Frame, *The Doctrine of the Knowledge of God* (Phillipsburg, NJ: Presbyterian and Reformed Publishing Company, 1987) 73-75.

correspond to the law, the world and the self. All human knowing involves these three dimensions or "perspectives."

The same is true of communicating human knowledge. The written Word of God is normative, and thus written communication takes on the form which has normative significance in human experience. The fixity of writing and print lends authority to it as a medium for good or ill. Apart from the absolute normativity of God's written Word everything that is written takes on the normative characteristic by the very fact of being written. The negative aspect of this normativity is accented by McLuhan's question in a letter to Ezra Pound: "How are words to be used to unweave the spell of print? ...The word is now the cheapest and most universal drug."[151] Printing and mechanization, especially as electric media have accelerated their effect, have lulled people into accepting them as authoritative. However there is a certainty attached by God Himself to the written Word which functions in perfect harmony with the power of the voice in catechizing the church. Luke begins his gospel by stating his purpose in writing to Theophilus: "that you may know the *certainty* of those things in which you were instructed" (Luke 1:4, emphasis added). *Instructed* is the word catechize, or sound in the ear. Thus ink and voice are friends not enemies.

The general revelation of God in the visible world is the situation in which all knowledge and communication takes place. Created to reveal the invisible glory of the Creator in His "eternal power and Divine nature,"[152] the visible world is both a medium of God's communication to man, and a medium of man's communication to man. Used as a primary medium of culture building, when it is used as a tool to assert autonomy the visible it becomes a medium of idolatry. This covenant-breaking mode of existence is reversed by the counter environment of the visible revelation of the Covenant of Grace. Redemptive recreation of the visible world is central to the Tabernacle and Temple of the Old Covenant and the sacraments of Baptism and the Lord's Supper in the New Covenant. Closely related to the visual is the tactile and olfactory perception of the created world. Thus the visible world is restored to its original intention in the eyes of the believer.

The person or self provides the third perspective of epistemology and communication. Existentially man is addressed by the oral Word of God. God conversed with Adam in the Garden of Eden, and has spoken directly to His people throughout the history of revelation after the fall. The immediacy of the oral *affects* man existentially. The power of the oral is revealed throughout Scripture. Gossip is like a sword and words of encouragement and truth are

---

[151] McLuhan, *Letters*, 227.
[152] Romans 1:20.

like ripe fruit. In sin the oral has enormous destructive potential. Preaching is the primary medium for restoring speech to its original intention: to express God's thoughts after Him.

In Jesus Christ we find the perfect balance of communication media. In Jesus Christ we find the perfect model for the preacher and the media critic. The media triad provides a structural reminder of the importance of a balanced sensorium in the service of God. Walter Ong observes: "Christian revelation has survived vast changes in the sensoria of the cultures in which Christians have lived."[153] He further opines:

> Indeed, the fact that the focal point of Hebrew and, even more, of Christian belief is found in a culture which for historical reasons makes so much of the word should be thoroughly reassuring for the believer: God entered into human history in a special fashion at the precise time when psychological structures assured that his entrance would have greatest opportunity to endure and flower. To assure maximum presence through history, the Word came in the ripeness of time, when a sense of the oral was still dominant and when at the same time the alphabet could give divine revelation among men a new kind of endurance and stability. The believer finds it providential that divine revelation let down its roots into human culture and consciousness after the alphabet was devised but before print had overgrown major oral structures and before our electronic culture further obscured the basic nature of the word.[154]

Is it not the threefold balance among written, oral and visual which accounts for this resiliency?

The Written Word

The written word is the incarnation of thought, an imitation of the Trinity and the Incarnation of the Word. It is, as we have seen, an exercise of lordship. The fact of God's writing the ten words with His own finger in Hebrew at Sinai (Exod. 31:18), and that He wrote words of judgment on the wall of Belshazzar's royal dining hall in the diplomatic language of Aramaic (Dan. 5:5ff), demonstrates that writing is not an evolutionary cultural development, as many Media Ecologists claim. They too have been tainted by the social science hegemony of the Enlightenment. In support of the primacy of the oral it is often asserted that Jesus taught but never wrote a book or even a word, as far as we know. What is missing in this simplistic observation is the place of the

---

[153] Ong, *The Presence of the Word*, 11.
[154] *Ibid.*, 190, 191.

written Word in the ministry of Jesus. All of the events of His birth fulfilled what was *written* by the Old Covenant prophets. He battled the Devil in the temptation in the wilderness with what was *written* in Moses and the Prophets.[155] He viewed His entire life and ministry as a fulfillment of what is *written*. "The Son of Man indeed goes just as it is *written* of Him."[156]

Most important of all the Word Incarnate is the Author of all that is *written* in both testaments of the Bible. "Of this salvation the prophets have inquired and searched carefully, who prophesied of the grace *that would come* to you, searching what, or what manner of time, the Spirit of Christ who was in them was indicating when He testified beforehand the sufferings of Christ and the glories that would follow. To them it was revealed that, not to themselves, but to us they were ministering the things which now have been reported to you through those who have preached the gospel to you by the Holy Spirit sent from heaven—things which angels desire to look into."[157] Furthermore, Jesus told the Apostles in the upper room that they would be the instruments of written revelation after the resurrection. Peter received Paul's letters as Scripture during Paul's lifetime.[158]

For David the written Word of God was fundamental as he demonstrated in giving the plans and specifications for the Temple to Solomon as David turned the throne over to him: "'All *this*' said *David*, 'the LORD made me understand in writing, by *His* hand upon me, all the works of these plans.'" (1 Chron. 28:19).

As with the triad of epistemological perspectives the triad of media perspectives are always interrelated. Thus what is written is also always both oral and visual. We are to think of them separately only to understand their interrelationship. In reality they are never separate. The first written portion of Scripture is an account of the most astounding oral event in history, the creation out of nothing by the spoken commands of God. The preacher is always preaching to readers of the word. When he reads the Word publicly he speaks and is heard. When readers read privately they hear the voice of the preacher. This why it is dangerous to forsake the church and the means of grace, living in isolation from the public ministry of the Word.

What is written is also always visual. The reader of Scripture always brings his eyes to the text, not only as he sees the letters, but as he brings his visual memory to the text. Genesis 1 is a feast for the eyes as the reader is confronted with the majestic power of *ex nihilo* creation. The created world is the context of his vice gerency as the image of God. Scripture is filled with

---

[155] Matthew 4:1-10.
[156] Matthew 26:24, emphasis added.
[157] 1 Peter 1:10-12.
[158] 2 Peter 3:15,16.

metaphors which are rooted in our experience of God's world and the history and culture developed by His image bearers. Chapter 12 of Revelation is a striking example of how all of the history of redemption is viewed through several powerful and evocative visual images. Archeology is always pushing the date of writing back further and further. Languages such as Proto-Sumerian and Egyptian hieroglyphics use pictographs, which picture the visual reality or a symbol of it.

Written words are an incarnation of speech, just as spoken words are an incarnation of thought. The invention of the phonetic alphabet simply drew out the implications of language, i.e. that each distinct set of sound has meaning. Phonetics codifies this meaning in an efficient storage and transmission system. This is part of cultural development for which man was created in God's image.

I would argue that The Written is *Foundational* to the life and worship of the church and informs the other two media. The oral and visual found in preaching, teaching and the Sacraments ingraft and seal the Word to the church in Public Worship. The Fixity of print is essential to the Covenant Document of Scripture in a fallen world. This comports well with the aseity and eternity of God. Fixity and permanence communicate the faithfulness and immutability of God and His inviolable promises. "Writing is fixed in space, confined, bound, unvarying, subject to inspection and reinspection, and thus firm, controlled. ... *Scripta manent*."[159] Furthermore the written Scripture liberates the church from the possible tyranny of the oral, what we might call the "heard" mentality seen in tribal cultures.

The nature of second millennium BC suzerainty treaties placed a strong emphasis on written documents (tablets). Exod. 24:12 "Then the LORD said to Moses, 'Come up to Me on the mountain and be there; and I will give you tablets of stone, and the law and commandments which I have written, that you may teach them'" Deut. 30:10 "if you obey the voice of the LORD your God, to keep His commandments and His statutes which are written in this Book of the Law, *and* if you turn to the LORD your God with all your heart and with all your soul." This list could be a very long one since the entire Bible exemplifies this balance of oral and written. Especially interesting in this last quotation is the juxtapositioning of the Lord's "voice" and what is "written."

It is eschatologically significant that the first written revelation established the typological kingdom of the Mosaic Covenant. The completed writings of the canonical Scriptures now foreshadows and assures the arrival of the consummation kingdom at the end of history. "The medium of the Word ...relates to eschatology. Inscripturation marks the Word with a permanence and constancy that reflects eternity. In fact, the transition from the oral to the

---

[159] Ong, *The Presence of the Word*, 94.

written Word proclaims the transition from this age to the age to come. In this regard it would be well to take exception to the 'historicistic' claim for the primacy of the oral tradition. Not that the Scripture itself ever divides the speaking and writing of God's Word in the manner some critics do. Still, the written Word bears a distinct eschatological stamp that grants it an elevated and even incomparable position for the people of God."[160] In God's providence printing, as the "first mass medium," ushered in a new are of gospel preaching which has spread throughout the world, as the church sojourns toward the promised eschatological consummation of history.

The immediacy of the oral is fixed and bounded by the written Word of God. Scripture as a medium promotes the concept of history. It is linear moving from beginning to end. It is also essentially a narrative, the historical genre being primary. The poetry, wisdom literature, and epistolary literature are all rooted in the narrative of redemption. "In the beginning ..." signals the primacy of the historical perspective. The linear approach to history, the very idea of history itself, is rooted in the book. The Linear nature of the written/printed word is appropriate to the historical movement of Redemptive History.

While this characteristic of writing and print is often criticized by Media Ecologists, such criticism does not comport with a Biblical viewpoint. The dehistoricising tendency of Postmodernism idealizes the right-brain intuitive function. While it is certainly true that the institutionalizing and privatizing, or isolating tendency of print can be a monumental problem in an idolatrous world, it is patently unbalanced to declare as Ong does that writing and print are "permanently decadent" compared with the oral medium. Quoting 2 Corinthians 3:6 "The letter kills but the spirit gives life," only exacerbates the imbalance. Paul is distinguishing between the Mosaic and the New covenants, and not on the contrast between oral and written communication. Linearity and logic need not lead to Cartesian rationalism or its child, scientific materialism. If in fact the human brain reflects a polarity between linear and intuitive thought, it would seem wise to see the two, at best, as working in harmony to perceive and communicate the truth of God's Word and the meaning of His world.

The privacy of print is important for the deep, meditative reading of God's Word by His people in imitation of David (Ps. 1). This kind of reading cultivates reflection and thus expansion of the soul in relation to God, His church, and one's culture. Ultimately God seeks residence in the hearts of His people and thus He communicates inwardly. Private reading helps foster this.

---

[160] Charles G. Dennison, "Thoughts on the Covenant," in *Pressing toward the Mark*, eds., Charles G. Dennison and Richard C. Gamble (Philadelphia: The Committee for the Historian of the Orthodox Presbyterian Church) 12.

But this privacy is not meant to function to isolate the individual or to be used in isolation from the other media or the church.

The reading of Scripture aloud publicly forms a kind of covenantal juncture between private reading and preaching. The text of Scripture is a corporate document. Thus the negatives of print, such as the its privatizing, and democratizing effect are corrected by a Biblical place of the preaching and public reading of God's Word. The written word links the oral and the visual.

The Oral Word

The oral Word, bounded by the *foundational* written Word, is *central* to the life and worship of the church. The primary means of grace is not the Word alone, but the *preached Word*. It applies the written Word as the living voice of God with all of the immediacy and power unique to the spoken word. God is the God of the living and not the dead. On the Lord's Day the living and true God addresses His people directly through His chosen servant the minister of the Word. While the prophetic voice is silent in the sense of providing fresh revelation, it is not silent in terms of God speaking to His people. McLuhan went so far as to say that orality "insures fixity" more than writing.[161] Surely writing tends to be easily forgotten if it is not read and reread. We shall see the need to balance this with the *foundational* position of the written Word of God in the covenantal arrangement of God. But that we cannot do without the oral Word is the assumption of every preacher who takes his calling seriously.

Since we will expand on the oral medium of preaching extensively in the last two chapters, we will not go further here.

The Visual Word

The visual, which is locked in space, demands the spoken and written words to give it meaning. The written, and especially the printed word, provides a transition between the visual and the oral. The written must be read by sight, but the meaning transcends sight. Ong often pits the oral against the visual. A Jesuit disciple of Ong, who is also a leading Ong scholar, Thomas Farrell, asserts, "Now, what did the visual analogues for intellection contrast with? For Ong, they contrasted with biblical expressions about 'hearing' the word of God. Because of the visual analogues in Greek philosophy, Ong inferred that Greek philosophic thought manifested the impact of the written word (more so than biblical thought did). Ong worked all of this out before the publication of

---

[161] McLuhan, *Counterblast*, 81.

Havelock's *Preface to Plato*."[162] The Bible, however, is full of visual analogues for intellection. Gen. 2:19 "Out of the ground the LORD God formed every beast of the field and every bird of the air, and brought *them* to Adam to see what he would call them." Ps. 34:8 "Oh, taste and see that the LORD *is* good; Blessed *is* the man *who* trusts in Him!" Ps. 36:9 "For with You *is* the fountain of life; In Your light we see light." John 3:3 "Jesus answered and said to him, 'Most assuredly, I say to you, unless one is born again, he cannot see the kingdom of God.'" Rom. 7:23 "But I see another law in my members." The Bible reflects a perfect balance among the God-given media of visual, oral and written.

The sacraments are the visual Word which are signs and seals of the written and oral Word in the life and worship of the church. They are informed by the written and preached Word. The presence of the preached Word along with the sacraments was a hallmark of the Reformation as over against the Roman Catholic tendency to place the visible at the center of public worship. The tendency toward idolatry is exacerbated by isolation of the visible Word.

The sacraments remind the church that it is redeemed in history in space and time through the Incarnation and presence of the Spirit of the risen Lord. Jesus ate fish with the twelve, reminding them that He who had eaten the last supper with them was the same person who was now resurrected as the Heavenly Lord in His glorious body. He was not an apparition, but the Lord of history and the first born from among the dead. The Apostle John testified: "That which was from the beginning, which we have heard, which we have seen with our eyes, which we have looked upon, and our hands have handled, concerning the Word of life—the life was manifested, and we have seen, and bear witness, and declare to you that eternal life which was with the Father and was manifested to us—that which we have seen and heard we declare to you, that you also may have fellowship with us; and truly our fellowship *is* with the Father and with His Son Jesus Christ." So participants in the Lord's Supper see, smell, taste, and handle the elements of bread and wine. They see and feel the waters of baptism. Protestants have often been too hesitant to affirm the importance of the sacraments as sentient experience. As visual the sacraments represent a critical dimension of the environment which counters idolatry. The "neglect of the Lord's Supper may be responsible for a dangerous individualism that weakens its [the church's] witness."[163]

As we shall see in chapter 8 the importance of the visual in the sacrament does not imply the use of other visual elements, such as drama, dance or overhead projectors. The elements of worship, according to the Regulative

---

[162] Thomas Farrell, "Visual Epistemologies?" Personal E-mail (18 March 2000).
[163] R. William Franklin and Joseph M. Shaw, *The Case for Christian Humanism* (Grand Rapids: Eerdmans, 1991) 174.

Principle, are only those prescribed by express warrant in the written Word. As in the Mosaic Covenant the visual means of worship are clearly prescribed by God in opposition to the idolatry of surrounding nations. The preaching of the Word is the medium prescribed for communicating the Word in public worship. While it may be debated whether or not bulletins, hymnals and over-head projectors are elements or circumstances or worship, at least the Second Commandment calls us to consider the effect of the medium upon an element. If we learn nothing from McLuhan and Postman we should affirm their insight that the media of communication form a vital aspect of the message. Thus the importance of the Second Commandment in the life of the worshipping community.

There is a visual dimension to preaching. The appearance and gestures of the preacher are an aspect of the medium. A picture is worth a thousand words only if the Word is primary, prescribing and defining the image.

CONCLUSION

As we step back from this discussion it would seem that the task of Media Ecology was defined by Marshall McLuhan in terms of man's unique ability to reflect on his involvement with every medium, and in so reflecting taking responsibility for that involvement. We are not ultimately determined by media. Only when we fail to understand the environmental power of media do we become victims.

By keeping the primary media in balance through worship, we will be habitually reminded to duplicate that balance in the use of all other artificial media, especially the electronic media. By keeping the focus of communication on the communion of persons, we will be alert to the ways in which each medium either promotes or undermines: personal relationships with God and others; and our commitments to the church, the family and the community. The written, preached and visible Word are the antidote to idolatry and cultivate the atmosphere of thought and life, which is the only anti-environment capable of withstanding the onslaught an idolatrous culture.

6

Modernity/Postmodernity: The Culture of Idolatry

*In the world of advertising
there's no such thing as a lie.
There's only expedient exaggeration.*

—Roger Thornhill in *North by Northwest* [1]

*The bias of each medium of communication
is far more distorting than the deliberate lie.*

—Marshall McLuhan, *Counterblast* [2]

*Things fall apart; the center cannot hold;
Mere anarchy is loosed upon the world,
The blood-dimmed tide is loosed, and everywhere
The ceremony of innocence is drowned;
The best lack all conviction, while the worst
Are filled with passionate intensity.*

—William Butler Yeats, *The Second Coming* [3]

Presently there is a spate of analysis distinguishing Modernism from Postmodernism. I suspect that future historians of our times will distinguish these, not so much as distinct movements, but rather as species of the same genus. Perhaps, however, only Christian thinkers will be able to do this, for reasons alluded to in chapter 2. Francis Schaeffer was focusing on the themes of Postmodernism, without using that label, back in the sixties. The *avante garde* in philosophy, the arts and literature, especially in

---

[1] Alfred Hitchcock, *North by Northwest*, Metro Goldwyn Mayer, 1959.
[2] Marshall McLuhan, *Counterblast* (London: Rapp & Whiting, 1969) 119.
[3] in Gene Edward Veith, Jr., *Loving God with All Your Mind: How to Survive and Prosper as a Christian in the Secular University and Post-Christian Culture* (Westchester, IL: Crossway Books, 1987) 149.

the counter culture, have been the harbingers of Postmodernism throughout the better part of this century. The difference which began to surface in the late seventies and eighties is that what was once isolated at the center of the circle of Western culture now pervades the entire circle; the elite purveyors of Postmodernism have come of age and have largely succeeded in their project. As Kenneth Myers observes: "It is in Romanticism that we see the beginnings of what was later called the 'adversary culture,' ...so Liberalism's individualism and rationalism provided the social freedom for a movement that shook its fist in the face of Liberalism. Liberalism created the demon that would threaten to destroy it."[4] I remember how odd it seemed for a counter-cultural friend in the sixties to read Whitman's "Song of Myself," since I had had to read it in high school English, the quintessence of the establishment. Now it is so perfectly clear.

The apologetic approach of Cornelius Van Til delineated in chapter 2 helps the Christian cultural critic to go beneath the surface. One of the hallmarks of Postmodernism is its singular attention to the open-ended *surface structures* of culture. For Postmoderns these particulars *are* reality; there is no other. This in part explains why some have analyzed the distinction between the Modern and the Postmodern too sharply. Beneath the surface of both the Modern and the Postmodern lies the Enlightenment commitment to the autonomy of man expressing itself in both rationalism, which seeks to order life by unaided reason and build civilization apart from God, and irrationalism which seeks open-ended experience of the particularities of existence in personal freedom. As we have seen in chapter 2 both the Modern and the Postmodern display each of these poles, while the Modern emphasizes the rational and the Postmodern emphasizes the irrational. At bottom both deny the relevance of the God of the Bible to history, life and culture, and thus pay the dear price of all affirmations of immanentism: the ultimate loss of meaning logically ending in solipsism.[5] Postmodernists and Modernists play different notes in the same score. The autonomous individual, experiencing and structuring reality according to unaided human reason or intuition, is the problem of both. They are enemies on the same team. As cultural critic Jacques Barzun has stated, "the antinomian passion ...is the deepest drive of the

---

[4] Kenneth M. Myers, *All God's Children and Blue Suede Shoes: Christians and Popular Culture* (Westchester, IL: Crossway Books, 1989) 109.
[5] William Edgar, "No News Is Good News: Modernity, The Postmodern, and Apologetics," *Westminster Theological Journal* 57, no. 2 (fall 1995): 359-82. This is an excellent discussion of the Van Til rationalism-irrationalism dialectic critique of Modernity.

age. ...The rage for absolute freedom is virulent."[6] Nietzsche's apotheosis of the will has taken center stage in the form of "choice."

A critical overview of contemporary culture logically follows. This is the larger context of preaching. Criticism must done from philosophical-theological and socio-cultural perspectives. This chapter explores modern culture and its transcendental assumptions through the critical lens of the Biblical paradigm of idolatry. In light of what we discovered about the cultural calling of the Christian, and the cultural instinct of the non-Christian, in chapter 5 we should remember that "Culture ...may be godless or godly, depending on the spirit which animates it."[7] Our analysis will focus on idolatrous tendencies, especially as they impinge on electronic media and the task of preaching. The preacher who is unaware of what is going on in contemporary culture will not be as effective a preacher of the Word, either inside or outside of the church. For example, the person who thinks that because he turns off his television he has escaped its baleful effects is naively mistaken. He must live in a culture in which television is a pervasive in every institution, and in the lives of every individual. He cannot escape television culture.

Culture, with all of its mediating institutions, is a gift of God re-established for us in the postdeluvian world through His covenant with Noah. The City of God is developed in the context of the City of Man. Thus the Christian is called by God to live as a pilgrim in a mixed situation. This requires the discernment of distinguishing between good and evil. We must analyse culture in terms of the inherent nature of its concrete historical institutions, technologies, and aspirations. Then we must determine how the Christian may consecrate his activities in the given situation, alter the situation for the temporal betterment of his neighbor, and be a consistent witness to his heavenly hope. This must be the practice of the preacher as well as a part of the subject matter of his preaching.

The insight of Meyrowitz regarding the relationship between media and social settings is important at this point. Looking now at the cultural context of electronic media from a global viewpoint, we will zoom in on particular media in the next chapter. Were we to skip this chapter we would make a fatal mistake and be tempted, as so many critics have been, to view media, as isolated phenomena, and as mere conduits of information. Using the situationist sociology of Goffman, Meyrowitz has alerted us to the interaction between media and social settings, as well as the threefold perspective for

---

[6] Jacques Barzun, *The Culture We Deserve*, edited by Arthur Krystal (Middletown, CT: Wesleyan University Press, 1989) 169.
[7] Henry R. Van Til, *The Calvinistic Concept of Culture* (Grand Rapids: Baker Book House, 1959) 23.

viewing and analyzing the media themselves. The movement from print situations to electronic situations has altered the entire structure of human relationships, especially its institutions, tending to diminish our "sense of place." William Edgar has pointed out that Neo-Conservatives are often blind to the structural links, like capitalism, technology, electronic communication, and urbanization, which undergird Modernity.[8] The Christian will understand the Modern/Postmodern tendency to seek some form of transcendence for our creaturehood, which is central to the *modus vivendi* of idolatry. This is true of those who cling to the rational project of the Enlightenment, as they posit metanarratives, as well as those who embrace the new openness of Postmodern micro-narratives. In our next chapter we will see how each medium is at once a conduit, a language, and an environment. The latter two really cannot be understood without grasping their socio-cultural context.

David Altheide and Robert Snow have posited the relationship between media and culture in terms of "media formats."[9] They observed: "Throughout these pages we have argued that American society is ordered largely through the sense-making strategies developed in mass media, particularly television. In part, this argument draws from the work of sociologist Georg Simmel, who observed at the turn of the century that people create their culture within the strategies of abstract social forms, such as work, play, art, and institutions, such as the family, education, and religion. To this category we add modern mass media, and argue that it is the dominant social form in American society today...."[10] Electronic media are an intrinsic part of every cultural institution.

In 1973 George Gerbner explained: "The mass media are a major social influence because their logic and formats have become incorporated within the logic of social institutions. Media logic and the formats it has created are important because they are nondiscursive and taken for granted. They precede the discourse and communication content usually associated with 'mass communication'...."[11] and later Robert Snow further noted: "In 1979 we argued that mass media have risen to a dominant position in the institutional network of society primarily because various institutions follow a media logic

---

[8] Edgar, "No News Is Good News," 376.
[9] Raymond Gozzi, Jr., "Methodologies." mediaecology@ube.ubalt.edu (2 August 1999). Altheide and Snow "look at media 'formats' (which are somewhat intermediate between media forms and media content, being repetitive patterns in media) and study institutional changes in government, politics, and other social institutions, looking for related patterns. ...I think this process of discovering media logics at work in different parts of the environment rests upon a sensitivity to analogy, pattern, metaphor, as I mentioned at NCA in NYC last year."
[10] Altheide, David and Robert Snow. *Media Worlds in the Postjournalism Era* (New York: Aldine de Gruyter, 1991) 241. Quoted in listserve message noted above.
[11] *Ibid.*, quoted from George Gerbner and W. H. Melody, eds. *Communications Technology and Social Policy.* New York: John Wiley, 1973. 560ff.

in the definition and solution of problems. This process has resulted in the construction of a media culture—a cultural content that emerges from acting through specific media formats. The entire process is best understood as an interaction between the various participants rather than as a one-way form in which media dictate definitions of reality. However, existing media logic is so incorporated into contemporary urban society that media professionals and the public take for granted that 'seeing' social phenomena through media logic is 'normal'. To this extent media logic 'cultivates' a media consciousness as well as a media culture."[12]

In *Communication as Culture* James Carey observed: "Technology, the hardest of material artifacts, is thoroughly cultural from the outset: an expression and creation of the very outlooks and aspirations we pretend it merely demonstrates."[13] We now turn to those outlooks and aspirations which animate concrete cultural realities, both in their formation *by* and in their influence *on* its participants. I am not pretending to anything like a comprehensive treatment. Cultural analysis, especially in our time, is a highly complex business, because the situation is complex, and because being in the midst of the situation, makes it difficult to gain critical perspective. I am attempting to present an overview of philosophical assumptions and their several key cultural manifestations, in order to help the preacher understand what he is up against, so that he may face his responsibility to help build a consciousness in the church by which it may grow in more wisely structuring its experience through the grid of Biblical, covenantal thinking.

PHILOSOPHICAL IDOLATRY

The philosophical notions of one generation of academics, formulated in the "ivory tower," have a nasty way of permeating the culture of the subsequent generations. Our penchant for underestimating what goes on in the world of influential thinkers is dangerous, because it wrongly assumes that such thinking bears no relationship to the everyday world. Idolatry resides in the presuppositions of cultures and their participants. What becomes "plausible" to one generation of thinkers gets passed on through our educational institutions to become the "plausibility structures" of society. We shall look at only two philosophical assumptions. These are what we might call "presuppositional idolatry," from which the lesser gods spring. Thomas Oden has identified four "key motifs" which characterize "deteriorating modernity." They are:

---

[12] *Ibid.*, quoted from Robert Snow, *Creating Media Culture*. Newbury Park, CA: Sage, 1983.

[13] Carey, James W. *Communication as Culture*. Boston, MA: Unwin Hyman, 1989, 9.

"autonomous individualism, narcissistic hedonism, reductive naturalism, and absolute moral relativism."[14] I will look at the same motifs through somewhat different categories in terms of philosophical epistemology and its sociological expression.

Relativism: Perspective on Truth

As early as 1968 Dr. Francis Schaeffer alerted the church to the problem of relativism. While it is true that thinkers like Cornelius Van Til had been exposing the problem of relativism long before the sixties, it was Schaeffer who presented the issue to the church at large through his more popular writing and his work with people from the sixties Counterculture at L'Abri Fellowship in Switzerland. What other had earlier detected in the academy had moved into the streets in the sixties. In dealing with the students of the sixties generation Schaeffer recognized that philosophical relativism, which undermines the very concept of truth, was a problem the church had not adequately addressed. Schaeffer's early books, *The God Who Is There* (1968); *Escape from Reason* (1968), grew out of the concerns of his ministry for a generation which had often unwittingly accepted a relativism which is inimical to Biblical faith. Schaeffer focused on the emerging tendency of the Enlightenment toward irrationalism, which is now called Postmodernism.

A change in the concept of truth is the hallmark of Modernity [Modernity = Modernism + Postmodernism] according to Schaeffer. The old framework, which assumed the existence of absolute truth, began to erode as a result of the philosophy of Immanuel Kant and G. W. F. Hegel. They marked the "line of despair" which set the epistemological framework for modern man in the twentieth century. Although I have historical and apologetical problems with some of Schaeffer's analysis, his conclusion is unassailable. "*So this change in the concept of the way we come to know and truth is the most crucial problem, as I understand it, facing Christianity today.*"[15] By the 1990s this problem had become a staple of Christian apologetics and cultural criticism, as relativism had moved from the Counterculture into the mainstream. Gene Edward Veith, Jr.'s *Postmodern Times* (1994), begins with a chapter titled "There Are No Absolutes."[16] Charles Colson's *Against the Night* (1989) has a chapter titled:

---

[14] Thomas A. Oden, "On Not Whoring after the Spirit of the Age," in *No God But God: Breaking with the Idols of Our Age*, edited by Os Guinness, and John Seel (Chicago: Moody Press, 1992) 195.
[15] Francis A. Schaeffer, *The God Who Is There: Speaking Historic Christianity into the Twentieth Century* (Downers Grove, IL: Inter-Varsity Press, 1968) 12 (Schaeffer's emphasis).
[16] Gene Edward Veith, Jr., *Postmodern Times: A Christian Guide to Contemporary Thought and Culture* (Wheaton, IL: Crossway Books, 1994) 15-24; cf. Veith's excellent treatment of Deconstruction as a new form of relativism, 43-70.

"The Reign of Relativism."[17] Most recently D. A. Carson's *The Gagging of God* (1996) begins with a section titled: "Hermeneutics," with a thirty five page section "The Taming of Truth: The Hermeneutical Morass."[18]

More significant for the preacher is the present dominance of relativism at the level of popular culture. This is evident not only in what people say, i.e. the "content" of communication, but in the very nature of media themselves. Mass media, for example, have a pluralizing tendency. In exposing people to a wide range of religions and viewpoints mass media reveals the diversity of the world. Encyclopedias and newspapers have done this for some time. Electronic media enhance this exposure and tend to democratize the world. Reality becomes a menu of choices. This is not, as we have seen, a one way affair. The creation of these media reflect as well as promote the attitudes and aspirations of a culture obsessed with "choice." This, I would argue, in turn springs from a more basic view of truth, which insists that all values are "person variable." Mass media tend to cultivate this view of truth. Many of those like Neil Postman and Allan Bloom who oppose relativism seek to reaffirm metanarratives, which are relativistic in a different way: all values are "culture variable." Theirs is a relativism of ultimates, or *transcendental relativism*. Relativism is a problem, no less, for Enlightenment Modernists as well as Anti-Enlightenment Postmodernists.

It is not my intention to explore the philosophical roots of this tendency more than I have already done in chapter 2. Edgar rightly indicates that architecture was the first discipline to witness a shift from the Modernist International Style of architects like Walter Gropius to the Postmodern style of architects like Robert Venturi as far back as the late sixties and early seventies.[19] The second great juncture at which Postmodernism made a dramatic appearance was with the English edition of Jean-François Lyotard's *The Postmodern Condition: A Report on Knowledge* (1984).[20] Lyotard brought many disciplines into the debate, especially focusing on the epistemology of science and technology, and announcing the end of the validity of the metanarratives.[21]

The New Hermeneutic, which was developed by Heidegger and his student Hans-Georg Gadamer, along with the linguistic philosophy of the later Wittgenstein, in the first half of the last century, forms the interpretive

---

[17] Charles Colson and Ellen Santilli Vaughn, *Against the Night: Living in the New Dark Ages* (Ann Arbor: Servant Publications, 1989), chapt. 4.
[18] D. A. Carson, *The Gagging of God: Christianity Confronts Pluralism* (Grand Rapids: Zondervan, 1996); cf. Carson's excellent treatment of Deconstruction, 57-92.
[19] Edgar, "No News Is Good News," 371f.
[20] Jean-François Lyotard, *The Postmodern Condition: A Report on Knowledge* (Minneapolis: University of Minnesota Press, 1984).
[21] Edgar, "No News Is Good News," 373f.

foundation of the contemporary Postmodern attitude toward texts. Derrida, Foucault, Barthes and de Man developed a theory of literary criticism based on the New Hermeneutic. This relativistic literary criticism has been promulgated in American university English departments by Stanley Fish and the Duke University literary critics, along with other American Postmodern scholars like Richard Rorty. Postmodernism as an academic discipline has largely developed among a school of literary critics known as "Deconstructionists,"[22] and now pervades nearly every discipline in the Western academy as its new hermeneutic.

Deconstruction: Perspective on Texts

Media critic and professor Daniel Chandler gives a useful description of the range of theories regarding the relationship between reader and text. On one pole the *Objectivist* finds meaning entirely in the text as something "transmitted" by the author. On the other end of the polarity the *Subjectivist* finds meaning entirely in its interpretation by the reader as something "re-created." Chandler's own view lies midway between the two extremes: the *Constructivist* finds meaning in the interplay between the text and the reader as something "negotiated" between the two.[23] Practically this is probably where the average student presently ends up in their attitudes towards texts. However, as D. A. Carson points out: "The result is what Stephen Carter calls a 'culture of disbelief.'" In 1991 a Barna Poll showed 64 percent of Americans agree that "there is no such thing as absolute truth."[24] Deconstruction is only one of many cultural threads, which contribute to the overall fabric of unbelief. While few have ever heard of Jacques Derrida or Stanley Fish, theoretically Deconstruction proper is a very radical, and in my opinion, dangerous notion, one which affects every preacher and every worshiper. It taps into the broader notion that the individual consciousness is the ultimate locus of meaning. This idea of radical autonomy must be continually confronted by the preacher.

Literary critic Allan Bloom comments: "Comparative literature has now fallen largely into the hands of a group of professors who are influenced by the post-Sartrean generation of Parisian Heideggerians, in particular Derrida, Foucault and Barthes. The school is called Deconstructionism, and it is the last, predictable, stage in the suppression of reason and the denial of the possibility of truth in the name of philosophy. The interpreter's creative

---

[22] Veith, *Postmodern Times*, 51.
[23] Daniel Chandler, (1995): "Texts and the Construction of Meaning" [WWW document] URL http://www.aber.ac.uk/~dgc/act.html [13 July 1999]
[24] Carson, *The Gagging of God*, 23.

activity is more important than the text; there is no text, only interpretation."[25] It is a wonder that Deconstructionists are such prolific writers, when their theory undermines their very enterprise. Unfortunately it undermines a whole lot more than that. It has contributed substantially to providing a rationale for rebellion against the Word of God.

Heidegger and Gadamer correctly challenged Modernism's claim to "objective" knowledge. No fact is uninterpreted. Thus far every presuppositionalist would agree. The problem is that the New Hermeneutic ends with no subject-object distinction whatsoever, and thus no Creator-creature distinction. All we are left with is the "phenomena of being" or at best the "context of a form of life."[26] Along these lines French Structuralist linguistics, epitomized by Ferdinand de Saussure assumed that linguistic meaning resides in the structure of language and bears no necessary connection with what it signifies.[27] Jacques Derrida took this logic one step further, asserting that Structuralism was not deconstructive enough, and claimed that "all meaning [is] bound up irretrievably with the knower, rather than with the text," and furthermore that "words themselves never have a referent other than other words and even then with an emphasis on irony and ambiguity—the 'plain meaning' of the text subverts itself."[28]

Every aspect of culture according for Derrida is a "text." There are no universal values or meanings; everything is *difference*. Stanley Fish, along with being far more accessible than the enigmatic and philosophically technical Derrida, is less radical when he posits meaning as residing in the "interpretive community," rather than in text or reader.[29] But this more palatable approach is no less inimical to Biblical truth or preaching. It is actually more sinister just because it is more plausible. In the end, truth and meaning are merely human social constructs without any ultimate immutable referent, that is the Referent in Whom all meaning resides. At a human level, or course, language is apparently arbitrary, with a variety of words both within and among various languages referring to a single "reality." The point is that God has given His image bearers the ability to construct and develop language to communication the human experience of living in God's world. He also controls and interacts with every aspect of cultural development in His Providence. When God's presence in the reality of human language is not taken into account, analysis of

---

[25] Allan Bloom, *The Closing of the American Mind: How Higher Education Has Failed Democracy and Impoverished the Souls of Today's Students* (New York: Simon and Schuster, 1987) 379.
[26] Carson, *The Gagging of God*, 68-70.
[27] Ibid., 72.
[28] Ibid., 73.
[29] Ibid., 75.

meaning becomes a tool in the suppression of the general and special revelations of God.

At its worst, Deconstruction is a surreptitious power grab. When anarchy takes over someone steps in to rule as a tyrant. It is not philosophically accidental that Heidegger and Derrida's protégé Paul de Man, who came to teach at Yale, openly supported the Third Reich. Such tyranny is inherent in the relativism of Deconstruction.[30] Deconstructionists are notorious for "uncovering" the "oppressive agendas" of the authors in the Western canon, only to replace them with their own version of the way reality "ought" to be. Never mind that their own epistemology forfeits the right to declare any "ought" at all. Academia has in many instances been reduced to a political battleground on which shrill sloganeering wins the day, and political correctness is the surreptitiously affirmed standard. Dinesh D'Souza shrewdly reports and analyses the situation on the American campus in *Illiberal Education: The Politics of Race and Sex on Campus*.[31] Ronald Nash concludes that "Deconstruction means the end of human learning."[32]

One of the tendencies of electronic media is Deconstruction. Take the most textually oriented medium of word processing. The text is ephemeral. It exists only in bits and bites, flashes of light and electricity. It may be changed at will. On the Internet it may be altered by multiple author/readers. We read "into" rather than "out of" the text. Electronic texts give free reign to the Deconstructive movement already present in late modern epistemology. Consider the practical implications of this in a major institution. Recent decisions of the Supreme Court, claim to find a "right to privacy" in the text of the Constitution.[33] On the everyday level of the pastor I have experienced numerous encounters with Christians and unbelievers who both respond to quotations form the Bible with: "That's your interpretation." They are deconstructing the Bible.

When texts no longer have any intrinsic meaning or objective referent the preacher is in trouble. Postmodernism has become mock-culture; all assertions, all texts are reduced to a choice of game plans. Worse, if taken seriously by everyone, Deconstruction means the end of all communication, especially God's communication. Thankfully the Deconstructionists and their disciples must live in the reality God has created. They assume all kinds of "borrowed

---

[30] Dinesh D'Souza, *Illiberal Education: The Politics of Race and Sex on Campus* (New York: The Free Press, A Division of Macmillan, Inc., 1991) 191-193.

[31] *Ibid.*, cf. chapt. 6, 157-193.

[32] Ronald Nash, *The Closing of the American Heart: What's Really Wrong With America's Schools* (Dallas, TX: Probe Books, 1990) 158.

[33] Cf. Robert H. Bork, *Slouching towards Gomorrah: Modern Liberalism and American Decline* (New York: HarperCollins Publishers, Inc., 1996).

capital" as they write, teach, and live their lives. William Edgar points out that the Christian should not be comforted by the proposals of Neo-Conservatives who at worst rely on the autonomous reason of the Enlightenment, or at best rely on natural theology as a universal ground for its rational project. "Must we choose between dogmatic universalism and anarchy?"[34] The preacher must challenge this inconsistency in both Modernists and Postmodernists, and face it squarely and compassionately with the absolute truth of the knowledge of God which is assumed in their denial, and suppressed in their epistemology; and with the absolute truth of the Gospel.

Now we shall observe several important examples of the ways in which philosophical idolatry manifests itself in the lesser gods of our culture. These are the concrete expressions of the assumptions emanating from the alter of the greater philosophical idols, who provide the dominant atmosphere of the world's pantheon. These lesser gods are the creations of Modernism: both Modernity and Postmodernity. They are the unbelieving world's alternatives to the God of the Bible, who, in His goodness as their Creator, provides the very materials and gifts by which they assert their would-be independence of Him, treasuring up for themselves wrath on the Day of Judgment.[35]

CULTURAL IDOLATRY

Powlison asserts: "Idolatry becomes a tool to comprehend the intricacies of both individual psychology and social conditioning."[36] The world is a realm of covenantal commitments. Everyone, who is dead in sin is a covenant breaker. In place of Biblical covenantal allegiance through and to the Christ of Scripture, every covenant breaker engages in a covenant with idols in idolatrous devotion, not only rooted in the sinful heart, but "powerfully impinging on us from our social environment."[37] We now turn to a summary analysis of the latter phenomena. These elements of modern cultural reality are what concretely provide the "plausibility structures" of modern people. One of the main tasks of the preacher is to expose and challenge these rationalizations for rebellion against God, as Paul did, for example, in Lystra, Athens, and Corinth.

---

[34] Edgar, "No News Is Good News," 377-379.
[35] Rom. 2:5.
[36] David Powlison, "Idols of the Heart and Vanity Fair," (photocopy) 4.
[37] *Ibid.*, 5.

Narcissism: The Culture of Self

Narcissism is the logical outworking of sin in its most extreme form. Enamored of his own image in a fountain, Narcissus died of despair and frustration in his vain attempt to connect with the ephemeral object of his affections. The "Me Generation" has unwittingly imitated this ancient god. In 1979 American historian Christopher Lasch published an alarming book, *The Culture of Narcissism: American Life in an Age of Diminishing Expectations*. He begins: "This book ...describes a way of life that is dying—the culture of competitive individualism, which in its decadence has carried the logic of individualism to the extreme of a war of all against all, the pursuit of happiness to the dead end of the narcissistic preoccupation with the self. ...Liberated from the superstitions of the past, he doubts even the reality of his own existence."[38] Barzun observes: "Throughout our culture, the most visible trait is concentration on what is owed to the self."[39]

Early in our nation's history Tocqueville noted a troubling characteristic of American culture: "The woof of time is every instant broken, and the track of generations effaced."[40] Individualism, slowly loosed from a framework of Christian tradition, eventually ends in narcissism. The self without heritage, without purpose, without transcendence or transcendent values, is left with only a self. We are left with self-analysis, self-discovery, self-awareness, searching for the "child within," an endless quest to figure out one's feelings and get "in touch" with oneself. In school "values clarification," no fault grading, and self-image propaganda, teach children that they are number one, and should "feel" good about what once would have been called "selfishness."

The self-fulfillment and self-awareness movement focuses on the self to the exclusion of an objective referent, and thus leads to "privatizing" as opposed to the healthy self-reflection encouraged in Christian tradition. As we shall see in the next chapter many aspects of electronic media encourage "privatizing," thus isolating the self from its context in the world and before God. The self-reflection of "individualizing," on the other hand, deepens the self in relationship to the God and world. As Lasch points out, not all psychological therapies tend toward narcissism.[41] However, given the relativism of the contemporary setting, it is difficult to see what convincing objective reasons therapists can offer for relating to the world, which will effectively counter the narcissistic bent of our times.

---

[38] Christopher Lasch, *The Culture of Narcissism: American Life in an Age of Diminishing Expectations* (New York: Warner Books, 1979) xv, xvi.
[39] Barzun, *The Culture We Deserve*, 105.
[40] In *Ibid.*, 9.
[41] Lasch, *The Culture of Narcissism*, 31ff.

"The mass media, with their cult of celebrity and their attempt to surround it with glamour and excitement, have made America a nation of fans, of moviegoers. The media give substance to dreams of fame and glory, encourage the common man to identify himself with the stars, and to hate the 'herd,' and make it more and more difficult to accept the banality of everyday existence."[42] I once imagined how glorious it would be to be the Man from Uncle, until I realized that in the real world of espionage there is no audience. Such are the aspirations cultivated by television. The very existence of photography has a tendency to be self-conscious about how we look. The increase in medical labels for character disorders combined with a dizzying array of medical examination technologies tend to make us think about our physical and psychological well-being in a self absorbed way.[43]

Deconstruction reflects and cultivates narcissism by viewing the text chiefly as a means of reflecting the self, like the reflection in the pool of Narcissus. This is the way in which most Christians read their Bibles. They treat the text of Scripture as a mirror, rather than a picture, or a window.[44] While seeking what the text asks as a response from the reader is essential to a true reading of the Bible, it is not the proper place to begin. By seeking personal guidance first and only, the reader misses almost entirely the objective meaning of the text itself (the picture) in its context of the history of redemption (the window), and our situation in relation to God's world. The danger in this omission is multiplied by the fact that the personal application is often distorted, and sometimes even contradictory to the meaning intended by the Primary Author, the Holy Spirit. Is it any wonder the church is filled with "need" and "feeling" oriented people, when they look in the Bible for *themselves*? That is sadly just what they find, only the self, and not the Word of God. An equal and opposite error lies in discarding the mirror, and failing to give in to the Divine pressure of the text.

A typical example of narcissism is given in Bellah's *Habits of the Heart*. Nurse Sheila Larson, after much therapy to overcome an obsessively conformist upbringing, describes her faith as "Sheilaism." While claiming to believe in "God", she describes her belief: "It's just try to love yourself and be gentle with yourself. You know, I guess, take care of each other."[45]

---

[42] *Ibid.*, 21.
[43] *Ibid.*, 49ff.
[44] I owe this hermeneutical metaphor to Richard Pratt and T. David Gordon. Cf. Richard L. Pratt, Jr., "Pictures, Windows, and Mirrors in Old Testament Exegesis," *Westminster Theological Journal* 45 (1983): 156-167. Cf. Lasch, *The Culture of Narcissism*, 10.
[45] Robert N. Bellah, Richard Madsen, William N, Sullivan, Ann Swidler, and Steven, M. Tipton, *Habits of the Heart: Individualism and Commitment in American Life* (New York: Harper and Row, 1985) 221.

Personal choice is another theme of narcissism. The apotheosis of choice is a catch 22 for Modernity. Choice, the unlimited menu of possibilities, is constantly presented as an ideal. Yet along with this comes a dark sense of meaninglessness as standards by which to choose disappear, and as history and meaning are deconstructed. With the loss of meaning comes the sense of not having any *real* choice. Our creations, especially the electronic media, seem to be out of control and overwhelming us with choices which lead nowhere, in a labyrinth of emptiness.

The center of gravity for Postmodern thought is inexorably the self. Given the growing economic, political, and technological, and psychological, investment in narcissism, it would seem that Neo-Enlightenment alternatives will have great difficulty in persuading the self-satisfied of the validity of their agenda. Where the bankruptcy of Liberal rationalism will lead it is difficult to tell. As long as people are sinners in the Electronic Age, the Gospel offers a sufficient and compelling alternative to the preoccupation with self which seems to continue on its ascendancy. Because the self only and always exists in relationship to God and the socio-cultural context in which He has placed us, Postmodernism can only go so far in its attempt to establish difference as the ultimate category. I suspect that the more moderate Postmoderns will strike up a bargain with Neo-Conservatives and agree on a combination of lesser narratives to keep the barbarians at bay.

Each of the remaining categories, except the last, look at culture from different aspects of self worship, which is after all the essence of idolatry.

Therapy: The Redemption of Self

The thrust of the shift to viewing truth as relative, rooted as it is in the immanentism of the Naturalist outlook, has led to the quest for the god within. Eastern mysticism, as well as other forms of New Age thinking, which have entered American culture since the sixties, seeks redemption within the soul of the individual. Every image, every doctrine and technique is designed to seek salvation within. Freud provided a secular version of the inner quest. Now without the pressures of Victorian society to keep up some appearance of being interested in the larger cultural context, the narcissistic tendency of psychotherapy has become evident in a painfully visible way.

Thus in the twentieth century we have witnessed the "triumph of the therapeutic," not only as a discipline but as a worldview.[46] Os Guinness

---

[46] Os Guinness, "America's Last Men and Their Magnificent Talking Cure," in *No God But God: Breaking with the Idols of Our Age*, edited by Os Guinness and John Seel (Chicago: Moody Press, 1992)111, 117.

identifies the therapist as one of the six main "carriers" of modern culture.[47] Many ministers are looked to as therapists, and thus spend much of their time counseling as if this were the chief means of grace. Or they are just simply ignored. "And should true tragedy occur, the psychologists and counselors are there on the front lines, elbowing out the friends and clergy if not the paramedics. No other area of science or medicine so informs our national discussions or perceptions of who we are and who we should be."[48]

Often the "help" which is received is found no matter what the belief system or therapeutic theory of the counselor or therapist, simply because the counselor "cares" enough to listen.[49] The modern world has witnessed the breakdown of all of the traditional mediating institutions which once provided the personal support, empathy and caring now sought in the therapist. Marriage, the family, the church, the neighborhood have all been radically altered by modern technologies, especially means of "communication", in ways that leave people not only without a sense of place, but without a sense of personhood or belonging in relationship to others. The counselor who is unaware of this reality will provide for a reality which needs to be sought elsewhere if long term change is to be implemented. Furthermore, the secular therapist, and many Christian counselors, encourage the quest for the god within only exacerbating the real problem of self-absorption.

Isolated individuals tend to see themselves as victims and seek healing by shifting the blame to external sources. Some are, of course, true victims of the cruelty, selfishness and sin of others. However, with only the self as a resource, the quest for healing ends up being a self-frustrating venture, as any participant in many victim recovery groups will attest. The Puritans used to refer to the minister as a "physician of the soul." The healing he offered, however, was found in looking by faith outside of the self, to the crucified Son of God, by whose wounds the sinner is healed.[50] We should never forget, as we have seen in chapter 3, Freud offered his version of introspective healing not as a handmaid of the church, but as a replacement for the Gospel. Therapy replaces theology.[51] The therapist is the new secular priest.

Guinness maintains that "together with the managerial revolution, the therapeutic revolution is the leading source of contemporary Christian

---

[47] Os Guinness, *Dining with the Devil: The Megachurch Movement Flirts with Modernity* (Grand Rapids: Baker Books, 1993) 69.
[48] Mary McNamara, "Therapy Is All the Rage, But Is It Helping?" *The Union Leader* (22 January 2000) B2.
[49] Paul C. Vitz, "Leaving Psychology Behind," in *No God But God: Breaking with the Idols of Our Age*, edited by Os Guinness and John Seel (Chicago: Moody Press, 1992) 100, 101.
[50] Isa. 53:5, Guinness, "America's Last Men," 112, 113.
[51] Guinness "America's Last Men," 115.

idolatry."[52] We need not look very carefully to observe ways in which the church has been corrupted by this idol. The "Twelve Step" program of Alcoholics Anonymous, and self-esteem philosophy have made inroads into the most conservative Protestant circles.[53] For all of AA's talk of a "higher power" and the importance of acknowledging one's "problem," God is co-opted as a therapist, a tool of wholeness. In the self-esteem movement even the commandment "Love your neighbor as yourself," has been twisted to promote self-esteem as the heart and soul of love.

Addictions, syndromes, and the disease model for human behavior, have all in various ways conjoined to relieve people of responsibility for their actions. The materialist view that all behavior is attributable to chemistry and genetics has proved a boon to the pharmaceutical industry, and the bane of our culture. While the Christian takes the physical aspect of man's being seriously, it should never be taken as an excuse for sin. The mind body interaction is very complex. This means that not only may the body effect the mind, but that the mind also effects the body. Thus, ingrained sinful habits change the body in adverse ways.

The other way in which the therapeutic ideal has worked against responsibility is blameshifting in which individual problems are blamed on family, other groups and society in general. As Guinness points out, when the therapeutic is conceived in this way it moves from being a remedy to a revolution. "At its most challenging, the therapeutic is a more formidable 'alternative gospel' than humanism or the New Age movement can ever aspire to be."[54] Guinness enumerates the categories in which the therapeutic replaces Christianity as an alternative religion. It has an alternative authority, worldview, language of skepticism, priests, pathology, self, faith, and salvation. "'In a way, psychology has replaced religion,' says David Blankenhorn of the Institute for American Values, based in New York. 'It is who we are, the air we breathe. And it can truly help people who suffer and can yield important insights. But the assumptions of the paradigm are so relentlessly centered on self, all other structures of meaning and authority evaporate. 'What do I want?' becomes the governing question.'"[55]

For the preacher the idol of therapy represents a major idol of our culture which must be met head on with a call to repentance and fruit worthy of repentance. The temptation is, as Guinness says, to be a CEO in the study and a therapist in the pulpit. Rather than merely confronting the syndromes and

---

[52] *Ibid.*, 112.
[53] Carson, *The Gagging of God*, 51.
[54] Guinness, "America's Last Men," 120.
[55] Mary McNamara, "Therapy Is All the Rage, But Is It Helping?" *The Union Leader* (22 January 2000) B2.

addictions proffered by the gods of therapy, the minister of the Word needs to bring the healing power of the crucified and risen Christ to bear on the root of all problems: sin.

Consumerism: The Gratification of Self

The world has not been designed around our needs and desires. Consumer culture teaches us that it is. As far back as the 1950s the president of National Sales Executives declared: "Capitalism is dead—consumerism is king."[56] It is the facile assumption of many Christians that capitalism and consumer culture are all one wonderful package. However, belief in the value of a free market economy does not in itself imply consumerism. Divorced from a Christian view of calling and service, however, the enormous prosperity created by capitalism leads ineluctably to the decadent idol of consumption. "Born to shop" brags the bumper sticker. "For Lasch the therapeutic is a key part of the permissiveness of capitalist consumerism."[57] One might even argue that for some consumption is itself the best therapy.

At the heart of Modernism, and exacerbated by many aspects of its cousin Postmodernity, is the technology of consumerism. The meteoric growth of electronic commerce on the Internet, amalgamated with the commercially generated success of print media, radio, and television, have institutionalized consumerism in the communication media of our society. Advertising is part of the warp and woof of our cultural fabric. Personal prosperity, affording increased convenience, and pleasure, is a fundamental aspiration of our world. All nations aspire to come and worship the gods of prosperity in the American pantheon. The American dream has been altered, perhaps irreparably, in favor of these new gods, who promise unlimited happiness and satisfaction in the present world, in place of the original dream of the freedom to worship and serve the God of the Bible, while hoping in the world to come. Consuming is an essential ingredient of amusing ourselves to death.

So tainted with the commercial motive is our culture, that even benevolence is appealed to in terms of self-gratification. Public Broadcasting lures the donor to give by offering gifts. Not long ago the charity itself was a sufficient "gift" to attract donors. The New York Times seeks new subscribers by offering to give to some charity if you will buy their product. Olympic athletes, once amateurs, who participated for love of their sport (the original Latin for *amateur*), now wear the symbols of their godlike sponsors. Can anyone doubt the godlike pretensions of this pantheon? That is not to say that

---

[56] Vance, Packard. *The Hidden Persuaders* (New York: Penguin, 1957) 21.
[57] Guinness, "America's Last Men," 121.

athletes themselves, who love their sport for its own sake, are not capable of godlike pretensions. Public Service Company of New Hampshire bills itself as "supporting your life in every moment." Doubters should see the ad in which an English choir boy sings the motto with all the beauty of a Handel oratorio. These are the powers to which we are beholden. More than half of every piece of mail, e-mail, and telephone calls, are commercially motivated. The most tragic and serious news stories are punctuated by narcissistic advertising. "I love what you do for me, Toyota."[58] "[H]ow contrary the spirit of advertising is to the spirit of Christian communication."[59] This is not to say that all advertising is idolatrous. But the tendency of our times is to make commercial success a god worshipped at any cost. Activities without commercial motives seem to be fast disappearing from our culture. There is no break from business. For all the benefits of free enterprise—and those benefits are enormous—idolatry is its greatest danger. The greatest idols in this world are the greatest blessings of God, elevated to replace Him.

Central to advertising is the image. As the immediacy of the cathode ray images of television bombard the viewer, the intellect is often effectively bypassed and the visual seduces the soul to accept its value without reflection. The most powerful ads are like participation in a Bacchanalian feast, a perfect fit for the Neo-Pagan ethos. The sinful soul is fertile ground for such seduction, albeit responsible for its own willingness to be seduced. As early as 1914 Walter Lippmann observed this seduction: "The eastern sky [is] ablaze with chewing gum, the northern with toothbrushes and underwear, the western with whiskey, and the southern with petticoats, the whole heavens...[are] brilliant with monstrously flirtatious women..."[60] By 1957 the power of advertising was a well established and highly sophisticated business. Vance Packard exposed the "new world of symbolic manipulation and motivational research in his classic *The Hidden Persuaders*. One chapter is titled: "Self-Images for Everyone."[61] The central place of commercial motivational research in the early development of communication study should not be forgotten.

Appealing to the narcissistic tendencies of fallen human nature through mass media is a well-practiced profession, deeply ingrained in the institutional and economic structure of our electronic world. Style has triumphed over substance, and images promise immediate pleasure to the devotee, which, of course, end up being as ephemeral as the idols who promise them. The ascendancy of the image as a chief ingredient in contemporary cultural

---

[58] Os Guinness, *Fit Bodies Fat Minds: Why Evangelicals Don't Think and What to Do About It* (Grand Rapids: Baker Books, 1994) 85.
[59] *Ibid.*, 87.
[60] *Ibid.*, 91.
[61] Vance Packard, *The Hidden Persuaders* (New York: David McKay Company, Inc., 1957) 46ff.

communication, has left the word, as Ellul suggests, humiliated.[62] Propaganda, as Ellul explains it, undermines truth not by telling lies but giving the appearance of truth. "Believable" is the modern word which sums up this legerdemain.[63] Much advertising is designed to create needs along with its products. It tends to cultivate a worshipping public with every form of "expedient exaggeration" imaginable.

That the visual is a gift of God we have established in chapter 5. That the visual is peculiarly suited to idolatry has been established in chapter 1. That the electronic media, when uninformed by literacy, especially the Word of God, are the chief purveyors of idolatry should be a commonplace in the church's spiritual assessment of the modern situation. While we need to be careful not to make sweeping generalizations, or exaggerate the situation, the preacher is chiefly responsible to make it a commonplace. As Guinness points out Paganism, and the church's compromise with it, has always been associated with the predominance of the image. Neo-Pagans like Camille Paglia are quite plain about this connection and their approval of it: "We are steeped in idolatry. The sacred is everywhere. I don't see any secularism. We've returned to the age of polytheism. It's a rebirth of the pagan gods."[64] Nietzsche would be proud. The new Baals have made a place for themselves in the Temple of God. They can only be resisted when the Christian mind is fortified by the careful study of the Word of God, and all other human literature which teaches us how to think, discern, and live before the face of God, as the old Puritans used to say, *coram Deo*.

Professionalism: The Advancement of Self

The Protestant work ethic, which was once connected with a Biblical view of life in this world, was oriented toward the future and rooted in the concept of calling by God to serve Him and one's fellow creatures. Slowly, but surely, the Puritan view of usefulness was replaced by the Unitarian Yankee idea of self-fulfillment.[65] The concept of self-advancement followed close on the heels of this utilitarian view of work. Dale Carnegie promoted the idea of a winning image, and brought the concept of a career into full focus. Enter the images of

---

[62] Jacques Ellul, *The Humiliation of the Word* translated by Joyce Main Hanks (Grand Rapids: Eerdmans, 1985).
[63] Lasch, *The Culture of Narcissism*, 76ff. Cf. *Propaganda: The Formation of Men's Attitudes* (New York: Vintage Books, 1965).
[64] Camille Paglia, "She Wants her TV! He Wants his Book!" *Harpers* (March 1991) 47, in Guinness, *Fit Bodies Fat Mind*, 99.
[65] Lasch, *The Culture of Narcissism*, 54ff.

mass advertising and the growing love of celebrity and you have an idea of work almost entirely divorced from the concept of service.

Both consumerism and professionalism may be seen as reversals of the Christian concept of calling. A general understanding of professionalism as the pursuit of excellence in a given field of endeavor is, of course, commendable. However, the idea, which has achieved wide cultural currency over the past century, represents a radically secular conception of work. The professional pursues a career for his own sake or glory and enjoyment, satisfying the needs of those he "serves" only ultimately to fulfill his own goals. The career is literally the orbit of a life centered in the self. The consumer is the narcissist who devours the goods and services of professionals for their own enjoyment. Since every professional is a consumer, and, as the word "professional" is increasingly attached to every producer of goods and services, every consumer is a professional, an endless cycle of self-gratification is created. Burton Bledstein chronicles the development of "professionalism" in its connection with educational ideals in the nineteenth century in *The Culture of Professionalism: The Middle Class and the Development of Higher Education in America*.[66] Bledstein demonstrates the shift in the meaning of "career" to include the idea of self-advancement, and eventually replace the Christian ideal of calling, which implies following of the will of God in an area of service and usefulness.

Bledstein takes the ministry as a case in point, carefully documenting the emerging shift in ministerial attitudes beginning in the early nineteenth century. As the idea of career slowly replaced the concept of calling; a man's lifework became *his* choice, and not God's. "Far from setting an elevated moral example of clerical detachment, the minister often appeared to be an entrepreneur, privately negotiating the contractual terms of a successful career as he moved upward from congregation to congregation. In the course of an individual's career, every congregation now became a conquest, a stepping-stone to the next challenge."[67] While Bledstein is generalizing in his observation of this tendency in the American Industrial Revolution, the fact that some clergymen embraced this new concept of career is a warning. The preacher had better carefully assess his own motivations for the ministry, if he is to challenge an idol at whose feet he too may be worshipping. The transformation of service into seduction, from Horatio Alger to Moll Flanders,[68] has made the modern world a dangerous place to live, and an especially dangerous place to preach. Of course, in Paul's day similar motivations were

---

[66] Burton J. Bledstein, *The Culture of Professionalism: The Middle Class and the Development of Higher Education in America* (New York: W. W. Norton and Company, 1976).
[67] *Ibid.*, 176.
[68] Lasch, *The Culture of Narcissism*, 53.

present in ministers. Paul was careful to distinguish his own work from such: "For neither at any time did we use flattering words, as you know, nor a cloak for covetousness—God *is* witness" (1 Thess. 2:5).

David Wells cites several televangelists as the most "exaggerated example" of the professionalization of the ministry. Closer to home, however, is the emergence of Doctor of Ministry programs in almost every Evangelical and Reformed theological seminary by the 1980s. With the growing displacement of the ministry as a "respectable" or desirable career, "status anxieties" led to an upgrade of degree nomenclature. "What had been the B.D. became the M.Div. in the early 1970s, and, for those seeking upward mobility, the D.Min. was shortly thereafter added to the arsenal of social tools. ...the D.Min. was a lucrative new product to sell." Three quarters of those interviewed expected more respect and more money for their efforts.[69] Along with the baleful effect of self-advancement the professionalization of the ministry has led to an emphasis on leadership technique and attendant success as opposed to knowledge of the truth and its effective communication.[70] Theology plays second fiddle if it plays any real role at all. The Bible has a lot to say about godly leadership, but the study of this was never the center of the theological curriculum as it often is today. While we need to be careful not to impugn the motives of men who pursue these degrees, or of those who have determined the nomenclature, the evidence points to a real danger, one with which the earnest minister must deal honestly before God.

On the other end of this new concept of the ministry as a career is the congregational consumer. The modern bureaucrat is someone who serves in a position which once-upon-a-time was created to serve others. Now it serves the one who fills it. Of course, corollary is the consumer who demands that everyone in any position meet their needs, especially when paid to do so. The church and the Christian ministry are not exempt from these expectations. "There are those who think in terms of paying the church and minister to meet their needs. If they are disappointed, they quickly look for alternatives, or seek to undermine and replace him. What the consumer looks for most is what the self movement offers, except in evangelical dress."[71] Biblical expectations, which should be demanded by every congregation of its leaders, are often eclipsed by the new managerial emphasis.

The impact of professionalization on the task of preaching is profound. "If preaching, like the ministry, is now defined by the needs of the Church

---

[69] David F. Wells, *No Place for Truth or Whatever Happened to Evangelical Theology?* Grand Rapids: Eerdmans, 1993) 234-236.

[70] *Ibid.*, 248.

[71] David F. Wells, "The D-Min-ization of the Ministry," in *No God But God: Breaking with the Idols of Our Age*, edited by Os Guinness, and John Seel (Chicago: Moody Press, 1992) 187.

rather than the fabric of truth in the Bible, ...the pulpit is little more than a sounding board from which the Church hears itself."[72] The pressure is on to sound "relevant," instead of challenging the idolatry of the modern world. Meanwhile, real needs, identified in Scripture, are often neglected or ignored. An analysis of over two hundred Evangelical sermons covering 1980 to 1991 by David Wells revealed virtually no attempt to account for "the modernity into which the Word was preached." Instead congregations are often left "vulnerable to all of the seductions of modernity precisely because they have not provided the alternative, which is a view of life centered in God and his truth."[73] That there have been some sermons preached in the 1980s which did address the problems of Modernity does not diminish the reality of the problem of which Wells speaks. Perhaps Wells's strong antipathy toward Modernity yields an exaggerated critique. Surely in the face of the naiveté with which most Christians approach Modernity such a critique is necessary. Only after we have appreciated its general validity are we in a position to raise cautions about the particulars of the challenge.

Our self-oriented culture is the context into which the Christian minister must speak. The degree to which he imitates the worst aspects of professionalism is the degree to which his message will be muted. The preacher must insist as Wells frames it: "The Bible is not a remarkable illustration of what we have already heard within ourselves; it is a remarkable discovery of what we have not and cannot hear within ourselves."[74] Only the faithful preaching of the Word by men who understand the times will bring about repentance in a self-absorbed culture.

Novelty and Anti-historicism: The Glorification of Self

One of the downsides of the pioneering spirit of the rugged, and once responsible, individualism, which made America great, is its tendency, disconnected from tradition, to worship the god of novelty. The very word "modern" comes from the Latin *modo*, for just now. Modernity may be characterized as a movement for which "now" is paramount. The "Now Generation" of the sixties made a religion out of happenings, eschewing the past and disdaining the future. The latest product makes what you presently own outmoded. Advertising and your own children will use all the forces of moral suasion to convince you that it is a sin not to be up to date, especially by owning the latest product. "The narcissist has no interest in the future because,

---

[72] Wells, *No Place for Truth*, 253.
[73] *Ibid.*
[74] *Ibid.*, 279.

in part, he has so little interest in the past."[75] Lasch observes that the present phenomenon of "nostalgia" is a consequence of the "poverty of the narcissist's inner life," but does not translate into a genuine interest in history, because the narcissist does not want to face any serious challenge to his self-orientation.[76] "A denial of the past, superficially progressive and optimistic, proves on closer analysis to embody the despair of a society that cannot face the future."[77]

What C. S. Lewis has aptly labeled "chronological snobbery" has helped to cultivate narcissism. Divorced from the past, the self indulges in glorying in its present superiority. Often when history is studied today, it is in one way or another harnessed in the service of the present, rather than being studied for its own sake. History becomes part of the rationale, either by negative example or precedent, for the present. At worst history, along with most of what we think of as "high culture," has become another form of entertainment, rather than a tool for expanding the soul and the mind. As Thomas Oden points out, the rhetoric of novelty appears everywhere, even in the seminary curriculum, yielding "new hermeneutics," "new morality," and heating up the modifiers—"revolutionary breakthroughs."[78] Postmodenism has spawn a host of "new directions" in every conceivable discipline, including homiletics.

The underlying doctrine of novelty is the idea of progress dissociated from a Christian view of history. Divorced from an Augustinian philosophy of history the doctrine of progress tends only to look forward from *now*, and this accepted makes every new invention a step forward. "Gutenberg was a towering genius; his 42-line Latin Bible produced about 1453-5 remains perhaps the most beautiful and technically perfect book ever printed, and printing by hand-press neither required nor received any radical improvements for three centuries to come."[79] The Industrial Revolution changed that. Mechanical progress moved at an ever increasing rate. The Electronic Revolution, building on mechanical mass production and new forms of power proceeds at lightning speed. Computer operating programs are "obsolete" six months after they are installed. Progress in turn fuels consumer culture as every "new and improved" item must be purchased to stay "current." This instinct, of course, is as old as Adam and the Athenians whose ears itched to hear something new.[80]

The International style of architecture, self-consciously divorced itself from the history of architecture. As noted earlier the "collapse" of the pure

---

[75] Lasch, *The Culture of Narcissism*, xvi.
[76] *Ibid.*, xvii.
[77] *Ibid.*, xviii.
[78] Oden, "On Not Whoring after the Spirit of the Age," 195.
[79] George D. Painter, *William Caxton: A Biography* (New York: G. C. Putnam's Sons, 1977) 53.
[80] Acts 17:21.

Utopian rationalism of Modern architecture was the first signal of the emergence of the Postmodern reaction. Ironically, this has lead to the literal "collapse" of several prominent International style buildings. While a renewed interest in historical study has been a fruit of this reaction, the cynicism of Postmodernism is by no means a return to the aesthetic values of the past. "It pilfers various historical styles and works them into a pastiche (the characteristic of postmodernist form), void of coherence or meaning."[81] Much like its grandfather Romanticism, described by Kenneth Myers as the "melancholy half-sister" of "the boisterous boy Industrialism," both children of the Enlightenment, Postmoderns seek relief from the sterile precincts of pure reason.[82] If Modern architecture is U-topian (no place) then the particularism of Postmodern architecture is pan-topian.

When novelty is worshipped everything gets old quickly. Electronic media by their very nature create McLuhan's "all-at-onceness." Innis's distinction between time-biased to space-biased media reminds us that space biased media promote "present mindedness." The televising of the first moon landing evoked historian Daniel Boorstin's observation: "Because television enables us to be there, anywhere, instantly, precisely because it fills the instant present moment with experience so engrossing and overwhelming, it dulls our sense of the past. ...with television we saw that historic event—as we now see more and more of whatever goes on in our country—as only another vivid item in the present. Almost everything about television tempts the medium to a time-myopia—to focus our interest on the here-and-now, the exciting, disturbing, inspiring, or catastrophic instantaneous now."[83]

The rise of narcissism coincides with the rise of the electronic media. As far back as 1971 Boorstin noted that fragmentation, or what he calls "segregation," is the main problem with television. Most modern conveniences have tended to isolate people. Running water keeps people from the town well, and their community. Now the television and telephones make leaving the home even more unnecessary. With a television in every room Americans have withdrawn as isolated individuals.[84] Thus the narcissistic self has only the self in the present moment of viewing. History and community go hand in hand. The self without either has no future, and an identity locked into the moment experienced now. "A denial of the past, superficially progressive and optimistic, proves on closer analysis to embody the despair of a society that cannot face the future."[85] When novelty is worshipped the "cult of youth"

---

[81] Veith, *Postmodern Times*, 115.
[82] Myers, *All God's Children and Blue Suede Shoes*, 138.
[83] Daniel Boorstin, "Television." *Life* (10 September 1971): 38.
[84] *Ibid.*, 36.
[85] Lasch, *The Culture of Narcissism*, xviii.

flourishes and the fear of aging and death go underground. There are no midlife crises in cultures which revere its older and wiser citizens. In our culture everyone is expected to act and dress like a teenager. Isaiah described just such a problem in the corrupt, idolatrous culture of ancient Israel, upon which God pronounced His curse: "I will give children *to be* their princes, and babes shall rule over them. The people will be oppressed, every one by another and every one by his neighbor; the child will be insolent toward the elder, And the base toward the honorable."[86]

Anti-intellectualism: The Protection of Self

Anti-intellectualism is an important theme in American life from its founding era. Richard Hofstadter has chronicled this theme in his monumental *Anti-intellectualism in American Life*.[87] For all of his anti-Christian bias Hofstadter singles out the Puritans as unique in American Christendom for their devotion to the life of the mind. He might have added the Presbyterian intellect exemplified in a century of Reformed scholarship at Princeton Theological Seminary from 1812 to 1929. Os Guinness gives us a succinct definition of anti-intellectualism: "Anti-intellectualism is a disposition to discount the importance of truth and the life of the mind."[88] Today it is a culture-wide phenomenon.

In the postwar era there have been a number of eloquent expressions of concern about the lack of a Christian mind: the failure of Christians to develop a cohesive living intellectual tradition within the church. Joel Nederhood's *The Church's Mission to the Educated American* (1960); Harry Blamires's *The Christian Mind* (1960); Nathan Hatch's *The Democratization of American Christianity* (1989); David Wells's *No Place for Truth or Whatever Happened to Evangelical Theology?* (1993); George Marsden's *The Soul of the American University: From Protestant Establishment to Established Nonbelief* (1994); and Mark Noll's *The Scandal of the Evangelical Mind* (1994), each express a similar concern.[89]

Already crippled by the strong anti-intellectual strain in eighteenth and nineteenth century revivalism, Evangelical Christianity has been ill equipped to face the intellectual challenges of the twentieth and twenty-first centuries. Add to this the problematic spiritual ideal of Pietism, which makes personal

---

[86] Isa. 3:4, 5.
[87] Richard Hofstadter, *Anti-intellectualism in American Life* (New York: Vintage Books, 1966).
[88] Guinness, *Fit Bodies Fat Minds*, 9.
[89] Cf. George Marsden, "The Collapse of American Evangelical Academia," and Grant Wacker, "Uneasy in Zion: Evangelicals in Postmodern Society," in *Reckoning with the Past*, edited by D. G. Hart (Grand Rapids: Baker Books, 1995).

salvation and individual knowledge of God the alpha and the omega of the Christian life. Unwittingly imitating some of the worst traits of the emerging egalitarianism of the new nation, the church has joined the trend toward narcissism. When personal experience is king, the pursuit of intellectual growth based on the intellectual heritage of the church is not only neglected, but ironically becomes a form of worldliness to be shunned. As Oden laments the church is infected by an intellectual AIDS virus, unable to fight off the spiritual diseases attacking it.[90]

As the world is losing its mind in the electronic environment, the church must awaken to the perils of the electronic media. The effect on the intellectual life of our nation has been established by too many diverse sources to be doubted or ignored. Neil Postman has demonstrated the radical deterioration of the substance of public discourse as a result of the entertainment mode of perception promulgated by the ubiquity of television. The next chapter will explore the nature and extent of this problem which David Wells nicely labels the "electronic analgesic." Along with stealing our attention from more worthwhile endeavors, and pummeling the viewer with values and behavior which are decidedly antithetical to Christian faith, the medium itself restructures human consciousness, as McLuhan and Ong have long maintained.[91]

The connection between anti-intellectualism and narcissism is important. I have noticed that educated and uneducated people alike, when presented with a cogent argument for a particular truth or principle, often respond by not responding at all. Why? To protect what is most precious to the sinner—the self. While this tendency may always have been present in human nature, it is exacerbated by the last category of this chapter, Pragmatism. Americans are famous for valuing action over thought, experience over contemplation. The electronic media have amplified this tendency. Many Christians have noted that the questions being asked in the sixties are no longer being asked. We have moved from the last remotely literate generation to a generation firmly committed to anti-intellectualism through thorough immersion in the electronic culture. Those for whom the self is the ultimate reality find their narcissism threatened by intelligent discourse, especially one which challenges their most cherished assumptions and consumptions. The narcissist demands attention without achievement, and is intimidated by anything which diminishes a sense of self-importance. The nature and content of electronic media feed this self-assessment by mirroring the narcissist's self-concern. Entertainment is demanded, and if not received, the channel is turned. The latest technology is

---

[90] Oden, "On Not Whoring after the Spirit of the Age," 196.
[91] Wells, *No Place for Truth*, 200.

seen by many as the solution to educational problems. In most cases it only staves off the boredom. As Postman has demonstrated, in *The End of Education*, without the proper goals, true education is just an illusion, and worse the goal of having a successful career wins out.

Exegetically, this idol has seduced the church into divorcing the heart from the head, leaving it decapitated, and undermining a true Biblical psychology, as has been explained in chapter 2. Creeds have been reduced to a small cluster of "Fundamentals," divorced from the rich tradition of Biblical creedal theology, mimicking Enlightenment Positivism. Most twentieth century efforts at Christian education, focused on "practical" Bible knowledge as it relates to evangelism and missions, displaying little intellectual interest or effort. The quest for relevance in the last half of the twentieth century, has compromised the integrity of the text of Scripture, and its inherent power as the Word of God to transform the minds of God's people (Rom. 12:1,2).

Oden is right on target as he lays out the main thrust of "rediscovering the treasure": "Our first task is to *listen to the Scripture text itself.*"[92] The average Evangelical congregation is hearing everything but the text and the Christ revealed in it. We need to rediscover the import of Paul's statement in Romans 1:16 "I am not ashamed of the gospel of Christ, for it is the power of God to salvation for everyone who believes..." Preachers need to preach the Christ of Scripture, and not the christ of psychology, sociology, and marketing. As we shall see in chapter 10, the text of Scripture is relevant because it *is* God's Word. It is the fallen world which is irrelevant from God's perspective, and it is time for the preacher to use the powerful spiritual-intellectual sword given him by the Spirit of the ascended Christ to bring every thought captive to Him, and topple the idols of our age. The Bible is "the textual center of orthodoxy. But Biblical canon did not drop out of the sky. The canon emerged out of a history."[93] The Bible not only infallibly records God's saving acts, but *is* the voice of the Good Shepherd to His people today.

In conjunction with centering on the text of Scripture the church must recover its knowledge of the classics of Christian faith. The Reformation was as much an intellectual renaissance as a spiritual awakening. It was an awakening of the Christian mind. Historical and linguistic studies flourished in an effort to return to the sources (*ad fontes*) of Christian understanding. As an awakening it was not merely academic; it was study with a homiletical and evangelistic purpose. The common people heard these preachers gladly and became student-disciples of the Risen Lord. As a consequence literacy flourished. Meanwhile, we may hope with Oden that we are in the winter

---

[92] *Ibid.*, 199.
[93] *Ibid.*

season of the "waning of modernity" and awaiting a glorious springtime.[94] However long the winter lasts the church must return to a serious study of its covenantal text and the heritage of interpreting and living out of it. Perhaps our generation will be the harbingers of spring. This task begins with the undershepherds of its Lord.

Impermanence: The Dislocation of Self

The advent of the automobile and the airplane, the telegraph and the telephone, have altered our sense of place in unprecedented ways. The electronic media have rearranged every traditional institution, blurring the boundaries, both of physical and social place, once thought impenetrable. Joshua Meyrowitz has astutely observed: "Although oral and print cultures differ greatly, the bond between physical place and social place was common to both of them. ...Changes in media in the past have always affected the relationship among places. ...But the relationship between place and social situation was still quite strong. Electronic media go one step further: They lead to a nearly total dissociation of physical place and social 'place.' When we communicate through telephone, radio, television, or computer, where we are physically no longer determines where and who we are socially."[95] Social roles and situations are being transformed as the communications media invade these social places in new ways.

For example, the illusion of face-to-face encounter is cultivated by the televised "personality." Thus, people like Johnny Carson are "known for being known." Viewers tend to think of them as friends.[96] People also think of themselves as having *been* somewhere if they have seen it on television. Actually seeing the place may even be disappointing, depending on the experience of the viewer and the expectations created by the visual medium. Information and experience, which were once available only via a "rite of passage," is now available to everyone. Meyrowitz and others have explored the "disappearance of childhood" resulting from the advent and intrusion of the visual media.[97"] The absence of the first stage in the development of adulthood seems to have homogenized our culture into the transitional stage of adolescence. Everything from attire to reading levels in public discourse seem

---

[94] *Ibid.*, 203.
[95] Joshua Meyrowitz, *No Sense of Place: The of Electronic Media on Social Behavior* (New York: Oxford University Press, 1985) 115, cf. 308 for four aspects to the meaning of "sense of place."
[96] *Ibid.*, 118ff.
[97] Cf. Meyrowitz, "The Blurring of Childhood and Adulthood," in *No Sense of Place*; Neil Postman, *The Disappearance of Childhood* (London: Allen, 1983).

to promote a kind of adolescence for all ages.[98] "Place has never been less consequential. ...And television has extended ...transcendence of space mentally and psychologically, making us contemporary observers of the entire world."[99] This is not only a threat to our sense of geographical place, but to social place as well. For all of the benefits of this new cosmopolitanism, created by communication media, we seem to have little awareness of its dangers, what it takes away.

As we have seen in chapter 5 Meyrowitz, along with many fellow Media Ecologists, considers social order to be "based on arbitrary distinctions among social situations," rather than God-given or "natural."[100] Thus he avoids making "value judgments" about the revolutionary changes we are experiencing. Ethics are situational. We only need to be aware of the changes which new media effect. The Christian will consider this conclusion to be part of the problem rather than the solution. The dislocation of physical and social place, while being haled as liberation by some postmoderns, is a problem for the Christian, inasmuch as it threatens the normative character of God's Word. While face-to-face contact is an implication of the resurrection it is not normative to the exclusion of other forms of communication, such as the letters Paul wrote. For example, Christian parents may decide that their teenager will not own an automobile in high school because it will undermine face-to-face interaction with family, church and neighbors, which is an essential ingredient in Christian growth. The mandate for that growth is not a social construct, but a Biblical absolute. The situational dimension of Biblical ethics might lead rural Christian parents to allow their teenager to own an automobile, but restrict its use to travel to and from school and other healthy activities, thus fostering face-to-face experience. This process of applying the Biblical norm demonstrates the wisdom of understanding both the strengths and weaknesses of a given technology.

We have many renters in the buildings on one side of our home. It is impossible to establish many very deep relationships with them because of impermanence. Another neighbor has lived next door much of his life, and for all eight years since we bought our home. Our relationship with him is long lasting, and there is a community of trust in such connections which contributes to the health of our neighborhood. The average person prior to the advent of the automobile stayed in one place for much, if not all, of his life. Thus, he knew a relatively small number of people, and therefore was able to invest a significant part of his life in those around him. Today, in any given area of the

---

[98] I owe the inspiration for this insight to the comments of John Frame. He asked: "Does the modern world displace some identities and create others?"
[99] Wells, *No Place for Truth*, 43.
[100] Meyrowitz, *No Sense of Place*, 313.

country, 20 percent of adults move each year.[101] The health of the community, the extended family, and the nuclear family, has been significantly threatened by the impermanence created by modern technology.

Novelty and impermanence, of course, go hand in hand. C. S. Lewis once asked, "How has it come about that we use the highly emotive word 'stagnation,' with all its malodorous and malarial overtones, for what other ages would have called 'permanence'?" Once the thirst for novelty is ingrained, it finds a vocabulary to suit its aspirations.[102]

People dislocated physically and socially, tend not to know who they are, especially in the relativistic climate of our times. They go from identity crisis to identity crisis, reinventing themselves, hoping against hope that one day they will find themselves. Idolatry enters the picture as we remember that impermanence is not simply a given in many cases. It is a cultural trend which is driven by an increasing desire to escape responsibility or conflict in favor of instant gratification. The relationships which are being undermined by impermanence all take some degree of work and self-denial to establish and maintain. The culture of narcissism has little patience with such efforts. Narcissism is also exacerbated by impermanence because dislocated people look within, more than without for meaning.[103] Anonymity dislocates and desocializes in alarming ways. The self, left to itself, tends to be removed from the God-given constraints on sinfulness, and criminal activity, for which He has designed civil government and common culture in this fallen world. The dislocated self tends to be the disappearing self. Postmodernist Arthur Kroker says, "The disappearing ego is the victory sign of Postmodernism. ...The self is transformed into an empty screen of an exhausted, but hyper-technical culture."[104]

Pastors are among the most "mobile" and impermanent members of the church. Their average stay in one place is now under two years. To this geographical dislocation is added social dislocation as we have seen above. It is certainly true that increased mobility has been an enormous blessing, especially in church planting. Paul used the mobility afforded by the Roman road system to tremendous advantage. So in our day missionary aviation and the automobile have helped spread the gospel to unreached peoples. However, this does not obviate the negative effect which impermanence has had on the settled pastorate in particular and the community in general. How can men who move rapidly from one pastorate to another exemplify stability with respect to God's calling, command respect for His authority structure, cultivate

---

[101] Wells, *No Place for Truth*, 249.
[102] Myers, *All God's Children and Blue Suede Shoes*, 65, 66.
[103] Wells, *No Place for Truth*, 249.
[104] Veith, *Postmodern Times*, 82.

meaningful and long-lasting relationships in the context of such impermanence? What is most troubling about this trend is the church's almost complete lack of awareness of the effects that the structures and media of Modernity are having on the spirituality of God's people.

Pragmatism: The Worship of Technique

Technology worshipped for its own sake unites all of the lesser idols in their grand quest for control of God's creation. Our culture evinces this, in the words of William Edgar: "We celebrate the technological."[105] Technological efficiency has become our ultimate concern. "As one sociologist puts it, we have moved from public morals to parking meters. If life can be regulated by a simple technique, why confuse things with mutual respect."[106] Or as David Wells observes: "We have adapted to our technological world so completely that sometimes we seem to be little more than psychological components in it."[107]

Jacque Ellul has been very insightful in alerting us to the problem of technology and technique, the latter which Ellul famously defines as "any complex of standardized means for attaining a predetermined result."[108] In his introduction to *The Technological Society* John Wilkinson sums up the foundational insight of Ellul by stating: "Ernst Jünger once wrote that technology is the real metaphysics of the twentieth century."[109] It is when technological means become ends in themselves, when human ends become forgotten and swallowed up by the quantitative approach to life, that technology becomes a god. Mass man is mechanically dominated man.[110] "Virtual reality" is symbolic of the quest to create a reality apart from God. Worshipping the means or techniques without the proper ends result is endless means, all seeking fruitlessly to control the world.

This quest erodes the centrality of the personal, and is rooted in the rejection of the tri-personal God of the Bible. Fallen man has attributed to himself the ability to manipulate reality for his own salvation. He ends up ironically and tragically destroying his own humanity. When control and pleasure become ends in themselves, and the standards by which to correct the resultant behavior are disavowed, and Sadism is the ugly result. Radical

---

[105] Edgar, "No News Is Good News," 372.
[106] *Ibid.*, 365.
[107] Wells, *No Place for Truth*, 46.
[108] Robert Merton, "Foreword," in *The Technological Society* by Jacques Ellul, translated by John Wilkinson (New York: Alfred A. Knopf, 1964, first French edition, 1954) vi.
[109] John Wilkinson, "Introduction," in *The Technological Society* by Jacques Ellul, translated by John Wilkinson (New York: Alfred A. Knopf, 1964, first French edition, 1954) ix.
[110] *Ibid.*, xvi, xvii.

individualism repudiates the human.[111] The rationalistic Modernist quest to have human dignity without the God of the Bible has sown the seeds of the destruction of the human in Postmodernism.

Egbert Schuurman has argued that what he calls "*technicism* is the deepest background of our culture."[112] The term *technicism* refers to the Baconian ideal of use of technology to eradicate the effects of sin. Bacon "changes biblically eschatological perspectives into the idea of progress." The redemptive character of *technicism* "entails the pretension of the autonomous man to control the whole of reality..."[113] Theology is subordinated to this reductionist motif in the way Bultmann sought to remove the supernatural from the center of the Biblical text. God is a projection of the consciousness of man, a creation of man. Schuurman understands Postmodernism to a pessimistic reaction to the negative effects of Enlightenment rationalism. However, the Postmodern critique of rationalism is not a critique of *technicism*, rather a democratizing of it, a quest for technological anarchy.[114] This is why many Postmoderns are so optimistic about the multi-media nature of the Internet. It represents the "revenge of the particular."[115] Thus within secular culture, technique is, in one way or another, the means of man's salvation. One exception would be the only genuine Luddites around, the earth worshipping ecologists. Many are literally machine smashers, in the tradition of Ned Lud. They oppose *technicism*, according to Schuurman, by seeking to reclaim the original garden Paradise, instead of creating a technological one.[116] Their Neo-Animism is simply another example of the quest for redemption through the worship of the creation instead of the Creator.

Pragmatism as a formal philosophy emerged at Harvard in the person of C. S. Peirce, as we have seen in chapter 3. His students William James and John Dewey applied Pragmatism to their respective disciplines of philosophy and religion, and education and sociology. The "practical" results are everything. What works is true, and all else is irrelevant. This theoretical idea is the rationale of *technicism*. Technology gets results. Technique makes all the difference. Control of the results of the fall become more imaginable with each new invention. Add a little positive thinking to the mix and you have modern America and all of its imitators throughout the world.

---

[111] Lasch, *The Culture of Narcissism*, 68ff.
[112] Edgar Schuurman, "A Confrontation with Technicism as the Spiritual Climate of the West." *The Westminster Theological Journal* 58, no. 1 (spring 1996): 67.
[113] *Ibid.*, 68, 69.
[114] *Ibid.*, 71.
[115] *Ibid.*, 72.
[116] *Ibid.*, 76, 77.

Ellul was neither a determinist nor a Luddite because he maintained that at his best man uses technique to achieve human ends.[117] The problem is that the technological society is a sociological reality, which cannot be changed by individual action. Thus the Christian is only in a position to resist. "[E]ach of us, is his own life, must seek ways of resisting and transcending technological determinants."[118] Like McLuhan, Ellul is calling the "sleeper to awake" to the technological determinism around him.[119] Technique quantifies everything it encounters. The Industrial Revolution was not a revolution of technology as much as a revolution of applying technique to every area of life. Thus was born the "myth of progress."[120] As the masses saw individual benefit of technique, they subordinated their rights to the state.[121] The problem with technique is that it denies the validity of qualitative, ethical and spiritual concerns. It demands calculation and quantitative perfection.[122]

CONCLUSION

The greater idols of philosophy and the lesser idols of culture which inhabit the pantheon of the world's temple of devotion, are precisely what Paul has in mind when he declared: "For though we walk in the flesh, we do not war according to the flesh. For the weapons of our warfare *are* not carnal but mighty in God for pulling down strongholds, casting down arguments and every high thing that exalts itself against the knowledge of God, bringing every thought into captivity to the obedience of Christ..."[123] As Veith suggests, Christians deal apologetically with idolatry with a kind of deconstruction of our own.[124] In the place of "oppressive agendas" we look for "suppressive agendas" in all of the cultural "texts" of the unbeliever as Paul asserts in Romans 1:18-20. For example, the revelation of "intelligent design" in the startling complexity of the DNA chemistry is explored by men like Francis Crick, who insist on a closed system of evolutionary causation. Such men are suppressing the truth which is clearly revealed in God's general revelation. Their insistence that the God of the Bible does not and cannot exist is a stronghold, defended by arguments which exalt them in their unrighteousness against God. These arguments

---

[117] Wilkinson, "Introduction," in *The Technological Society*, xix.
[118] Jacques Ellul, *The Technological Society*, xxxii.
[119] *Ibid.*, xxxiii.
[120] *Ibid.*, 42, 47.
[121] *Ibid.*, 51-55.
[122] *Ibid.*, 134ff.
[123] 2 Cor. 10:3-5.
[124] Veith, *Postmodern Times*, 63ff.

cannot stand against His truth in revealed in creation and in His covenantal Word, the Bible.

The Deconstructionist insists that we follow their text of political correctness which is totally inconsistent with their denial of absolutes. They are denying the existence of the God without which all meaning and communication are impossible. The preacher must continually deconstruct the idols of our culture, especially as the electronic media tend to cultivate the pantheon we have just observed. The electronic environment lends credence to the Postmodern idea that we are radically deconstructed subjects of continual reinvention. There is no more humanity, there is only the experience of particular structures. Nothing is fixed. Everything is in flux. The text, the reader, and the individual are dead. We live on the surfaces of sense experience. There is no other reality.

In the transition from the idolatrous rationalism of Enlightenment reason to the idolatrous irrationalism of Postmodernism we have noted that the denial of the God of the Bible, and the exaltation of man, are common to both. The self-proclaimed autonomy of man which created electronic technology with the tools of reason, is now using those tools to deny the place of reason in human life.[125] It is an ironic conflict, in which we see a rock group like Rage Against the Machine, using the machine to rage against it. One kind of rebel rages against another. Our culture is filled with such contradictions and ironies because the wisdom of this world is folly. Surfing the tube and the Web is the sport of choice for paddling down the stream of consciousness. A young teenage "techie" being interviewed on a PBS special, titled "The Internet" (fall, 1996), said that he liked the Web because on it no one knows who you really are. The actual is what is sensibly tangible. This is the reality of cyberspace as we shall see in the next chapter.

A Biblical philosophy of history will lead us to two assertions which affect our view of culture, especially *our* culture. First, history has a beginning and an end, which are wrapped up in the covenant purposes of the Alpha and Omega. Thus the cyclical idea of the Greeks and many modern unbelievers, is to be rejected. Postmodernism has rejected the linear view of history largely because this view has been perverted by the Enlightenment secularization of the Augustinian teleology. Without the goal of eschatological glory, progress has no meaning. Second, this *linear*, Augustinian approach does not obviate the presence of cycles. In the pre-deluvian period we see cultural developments with the descendants of Cain, which were in themselves a blessing. In common culture the family and the state are designed to restrain sin.

---

[125] *Ibid.*, 80ff.

However, due to the presence of sin and idolatry, culture tends to develop toward an apotheosis of man's rebellion. Dr. Meredith G. Kline has wisely discerned and expounded upon this historical pattern in Genesis.[126] In Lamech we see just such an apotheosis, as he abuses the power of the state to oppress those under his royal rule, multiplies wives after his own lust, and uses his poetic powers to exalt himself above God.[127] Autonomous mankind reaches an apex of developing culture as an idolatrous alternative to the City of God which can no longer be tolerated by God, since His purposes in establishing the City of Man as a refuge in a fallen world are threatened. The flood judgment is the result. The divine intrusion brings idolatry to a temporary halt. The covenant of common culture is renewed with Noah, only to bring further judgment in the dispersion of mankind at the Tower of Babel, through another divine intrusion.

The New Covenant initiates the final intrusion of God in the person and work of the Mediator, the Second and Last Adam, Jesus Christ. The church now finds itself awaiting the culmination of this final intrusion, the Second Coming of the Lion, who is also the Lamb. The Book of Revelation presents the history between the first and second comings of the Last Adam, clearly pointing to an ecumenical development of the city of man in which a final alternative to the City of God is attempted by idolaters.

Discerning where we are in that final development is a risky business. Dispensationalists have proved to be an embarrassment to the church, with their misunderstanding of the purpose and application of John's Apocalypse. Identifying the symbols and metaphors with specific persons and events is to reduce and undermine the comfort and wisdom intended by the Divine Author for the church throughout this entire final epoch of history. The wise preacher and apologist will discern the elements of idolatry as they appear, warning the church, loving his neighbor, participating in culture in a God glorifying way, and leaving the denouement to the Alpha and the Omega. Meanwhile, at whatever stage Babylon the Great is in her development the preacher will warn his congregation continually not to "drink of the wine of the wrath of her fornication."[128]

Lewis Mumford observed that Genghis Kahn was one of the last to proclaim himself sole ruler of the world. "That boast was at once an aftermath of the myth of divine kingship and a prelude to the new myth of the machine."[129] Unless our culture reaffirms the Augustinian view of history by bowing before Augustine's God, its quest for progress will be toward an

---

[126] Meredith G. Kline, *Kingdom Prologue* (South Hamilton, MA: Meredith G. Kline, 1993).
[127] *Ibid.*, 113.
[128] Rev. 14:8.
[129] Lewis Mumford, *The Myth of the Machine: Technics and Human Development* (New York: Harcourt, Brace and World, 1966) 187.

apotheosis of human power amalgamated with technology, the like of which former tyrants only dreamed. The hubris of Modernity is typified by International Style architectural prophet Walter Gropius, in his *Bauhaus Manifesto*: "Together let us desire, conceive, and create the new structure of the future, which will embrace architecture, sculpture, and painting in one unity and which will one day raise toward heaven from the hands of a million workers like the crystal symbol of a new faith."[130] Though it may appear that our culture is drowning in a sea of subjectivism, it seems rather that given the rational investment of modern man in science and its cultural fruit, autonomous man's quest for Paradise now will only be quenched by the coming of the One who has already won the rights to the only true Paradise which is yet to come in a repristinated new heavens and new earth, inhabited by His new humanity.

The Christian must, therefore beware of such progress, never assume its goodness, disconnected as it is from God's purposes in Christ. Leonardo D'Vinci was astonished at the equation of mechanical invention with human betterment: "O marvel of mankind! What frenzy has thus impelled you?"[131] Jacques Ellul has reminded us that "Propaganda is a manipulation of psychological symbols, having goals of which *the listener is not* conscious."[132] Modern propaganda is inextricably linked to the technological society, whose advocates wish to integrate everyone into the progressive idea and system of civilization. Government and business have a vested interest in propaganda. The New Babel cannot be built without it. Every idol in the Devil's pantheon is a propaganda tool to adjust the world to his lie that God does not exist; that man is the lord of the world. As Yeats has so poetically concluded: "The ceremony of innocence is drowned; the best lack all conviction, while the worst are filled with passionate intensity." The passionate intensity of a self-absorbed world can only be resisted, and in some cases overcome, by a church whose convictions are strong and articulate. That the church is no longer among the central gate keepers of our culture should not be a cause for despair. Now the lines between genuine faith and unbelief are not as clouded by the hypocrisy toward which "Christian civilization" tends. The preacher called by God to cultivate and fortify Christian convictions must be passionate in his mission, like our Savior in Gethsemane, though everyone else may sleep.

It should be noted that each of the defining idols and problematic cultural trends explored in this chapter are mediated in one way or another by mass electronic communication. Cultural trends and electronic media are

---

[130] Ulrich Conrads, ed., *Programs and Manifestoes on Twentieth-Century Architecture* (London: Lund Humphries, 1970) 49, in Edgar, "No News Is Good News," 372.
[131] *Ibid.*, 291.
[132] Jacques Ellul, *Propaganda: The Formation of Men's Attitudes*, translated by Konrad Kellen and Jean Lerner (New York: Vintage Books, 1965) xi.

inextricably linked. The next chapter will observe our culture from the angle of the electronic media themselves.

7

Twilight of the Gods: Benefits and Liabilities of Electronic Media

Now it is still not uncommon to say that images are idols and that idols are dolls. I am content to say here that even dolls are not idols, but in the true sense images. The very word images means things necessary to imagination. But not things contrary to reason; no, not even in a child. For imagination is almost the opposite of illusion.

—G. K. Chesterton, *Autobiography* [1]

Inundated by perspectives, by lateral vistas of information that stretch endlessly in every direction, we no longer accept the possibility of assembling a complete picture ...a big picture that refers to human endeavor sub specie aeternitatis, *under the aspect of eternity.*

—Sven Birkerts, *The Guttenberg Elegies*[2]

Every medium of communication is a unique art form which gives salience to one set of human possibilities at the expense of another set.

—Marshall McLuhan, *The Literary Criticism of Marshall McLuhan, 1943-1962* [3]

The simplistic approach to media dictates either total rejection or naïve acceptance. The thoughtful Christian should be happy with neither of these alternatives. It is helpful to remember Postman's dictum, based

---

[1] Chesterton, G. K. *Autobiography*. In Vigen Guroian, "The Moral Imagination in an Age of Sentiments." *The Intercollegiate Review*, 34, no. 1 (fall 1998) 16.
[2] Sven Birkerts, *The Guttenberg Elegies: The Fate of Reading in an Electronic Age* (Winchester, MA: Faber and Faber, Inc., 1994) 75.
[3] Eugene McNamara, ed. *The Literary Criticism of Marshall McLuhan, 1943-1962* (New York: McGraw-Hill Book Company, 1969) 7.

on McLuhan's critical analysis of media: "The Lord gives and the Lord takes away." Every medium has benefits and liabilities. In this chapter we shall explore both aspects of the electronic media.

The modern world has no trouble with the first part of Neil Postman's dictum regarding the evaluation of media: "The Lord gives..." As a culture we are quick to list the benefits of a given medium, but almost always refuse to even consider the liabilities. Since I have contended in chapter 5 that one of the most serious problems facing the church today is its uncritical use of the rapidly emerging electronic media, it remains to be proved that there are serious liabilities. Thus, in what follows, I will spend more time on the liabilities of media. This is in no way a denial of what has been asserted regarding a Christian view of creation, culture and the media. In 1950 Norbert Wiener warned: "I have said that the modern man, and especially the modern American, however much 'know-how' he may have, has very little 'know-what.' He will accept the superior dexterity of the machine-made decisions without too much inquiry as to the motives and principles behind these."[4]

One of my son's brightest young friends once insisted that the computer makes learning Latin unnecessary. Not only had he uncritically accepted the benefits of the computer, but he also grossly overvalued it by failing to consider the very nature of education, or the nature of the computer. I encountered a similar attitude among adults when I worked as an architectural designer. In the early nineties we were using AutoCAD, release 12, which is a computer assisted architectural drawing program. Contractors and project managers would regularly ask if their drawings were ready before they were scheduled to be completed, thinking that the computer would do all the work in almost an instant. Actually the initial drawings would sometimes take longer than hand drawing. The human factor in such work is often totally underestimated due to the propaganda surrounding computer technology.

An Associated Press release in July of 1999 announced the invention of "molecule-sized switch" which presages "ultra-tiny PCs." This means there will be computers everywhere, unseen, even in the fibers of clothing. UCLA researcher Eric Wong declared, "Imagine millions of tiny computers everywhere in our lives."[5] The assumed premise is that if it is technologically possible it must be good. One final sample combines unlimited trust in technology with its usual corollary, Utopian possibilities. Science fiction writer Sir Arthur C. Clarke in an article for *British Heritage*, which looks ahead to the year 3000, offers this astonishing expectation: "I would like to close with

---
[4] Norbert Wiener, *The Human Use of Human Beings: Cybernetics and Society* (Boston: Houghton Mifflin, 1950) 212. Not that the second edition (1954) is an almost completely different book.
[5] Anne M. Peterson, "Molecule-sized switch promises ultra-tiny Pcs," *The Union Leader*, Saturday, July 17, 1999, front page.

one of the future's most awesome possibilities—that some people alive today may witness the year 3000. This may be through the achievement of biological immortality, downloading the mind into another carrier (probably inorganic), or through suspended animation."[6]

On the other hand there is no shortage of Luddites, literally "technology smashers," who see only doom in the rise of the electronic age. There is a Fundamentalist strain in the church and the world alike. "Eliminate the TV and don't go on line. It's all evil." How is a Christian to respond? In light of our discussion of cultural themes in chapter 6 we should be alert to the power of media to both echo and shape cultural trends.[7] For the preacher, to whom this book is principally addressed, the electronic media represent, not only communication competitors in the church, but also an essential ingredient of the culture in which he lives and preaches. Of these, then, he must be acutely aware.

MEDIA AND COMMON CULTURE

When we consider the liabilities of various media we should distinguish between liabilities and limits. As creatures we are finite or limited. Such is the nature of all of created reality, fallen or not. However, with the fall came the idolatrous propensity to absolutize various elements of creation. In the common culture, inhabited by believers and unbelievers, there is common curse and a common blessing in every area of culture under the terms of the Noahic Covenant.[8] Media are no exception to this covenantal principle of historical reality since the fall. Another way of putting this is that when we fail to understand the limitations of media our failure becomes part of the liabilities. Many of the extravagant claims made for various new inventions are caused by failing to assess the limits of that invention. For example, the computer is not going to solve all of the world's problems. Some educators imagine that the incorporation of the computer into the classroom situation will "revolutionize" education by making the students more "computer literate," or putting more information at their fingertips. As Postman so tersely puts it: "any problems the schools cannot solve without computers, they cannot solve with them."[9]

---

[6] Sir Arthur C. Clarke, "A Thousand Years Hence," *British Heritage*, 20:5 (August/September 1999) 48.
[7] Quentin Schultze, *Redeeming Television: How TV Changes Christians - How Christians Can Change TV* (Downers Grove, IL: InterVarsity Press, 1992) 49.
[8] Meredith G. Kline, *Kingdom Prologue* (South Hamilton, MA: Meredith G. Kline, 1993) 95-99.
[9] Neil Postman, *The End of Education* (New York: Alfred A. Knopf, 1995) 45.

On the other hand, there are also unintended consequences to each new invention. Usually these come from not thinking about the nature of the new invention relative to everything else, especially the human dimension. The automobile, thought of as a mere improvement on the horse and carriage, changed the American landscape both literally and figuratively. The goal of a more efficient carriage, with a team of horses under the hood, blinded most people to the pervasiveness of the changes the automobile would affect. Greater mobility made the suburbs possible, but ruined the village; it made travel to far away places a reality for larger numbers, but undermined the place of the family; it made travel faster, but local streets were no longer seen with pedestrian detail; it made travel safer and more comfortable, but isolated people from their neighbors.

Consider the simple technology of the hammer, as an extension of man's hand. On occasion it ends up unintentionally being used to smack an unsuspecting thumb. At worst it may intentionally be used as a murder weapon. However, few would counsel its elimination. But any wise carpenter quickly learns the negative side of this simple technology. Every technology has its "hammered thumb," and its "murder weapon" problems; these are unintended and intentional negatives. Harnessing atomic power is what many consider the most egregious example of an unintended consequence in the twentieth century. In this case it was unintended by the original discoverer, but intentionally used as a very effective weapon to bring World War II to a rapid close.

As we have noted in chapter 5 understanding media involves investigating each medium from a number of different angles, as well as its connections with the cultural fabric. Only when we have labored at understanding a medium are we in a position to assess its benefits and liabilities. Although the automobile is not a medium of communication the contrast among various benefits and liabilities noted above was based on a prior assessment of the nature of the automobile in terms of several of the categories we have discussed.

RECREATION, IMAGINATION AND EDIFICATION

While it is not my principal aim in this chapter to be an apologist for the electronic media, I want to suggest several important ways in which a Christian may begin to think about various communication technologies in terms of their positive benefits. I heartily concur with Os Guinness's and John Seel's purpose for writing their book *No Gods But God*, "Our purpose in writing is to provide fellow-followers of Christ to be on the lookout for the idolizing of modern myths and be prepared to give a rigorous account of our use of the best insights and powers of modernity."[10] This is our task in the present chapter.

Recreation: A Gift of God and Comfort in a Fallen World

The positive blessings of common culture discussed in chapter 2 impinge on our assessment of electronic media. Along with the need for rest in a fallen world, recreation is a gift of God meant not only to relieve the tedium of work, but to bring glory to Him in the enjoyment of His creation. At the heart of a Reformed view of creation and culture, along with the service of God and man, is the enjoyment of God. Recreational activity mediates His glory, even in a fallen world. I suspect that the dichotomy between work and recreation will no longer exist in the new heavens and the new earth. Interesting and diverting activity is part of what it means to be human. *Recreation* is perhaps a better word than entertainment for the Christian, since it reminds us etymologically that this activity is part of thinking God's thoughts after Him as we live in His world. For the new humanity dominion begins provisionally in this life.

The Fundamentalist view of human activity is seriously truncated, as it almost entirely dismisses the refreshing activity of enjoying God's creation as His creatures. As a young Christian I wrestled with this question of the value of creation and culture. One day I was observing a collection of shells which I had arranged on a book shelf in my study. Each had housed the same kind of organism. Yet each displayed a playfully different arrangement of colors and shapes. I discovered that God the Creator is playful and imaginative. Were this not the case He would have created one efficient type of shell to "get the job done." The Christian is called to reject the pragmatic tendency of Enlightenment Rationalism as it eclipses the delight God has designed into His creation and the development of common culture.

Imagination: A Gift of God for Creativity and Communication

Clives Staples Lewis reminds us of the importance of the imagination as a gift of God: "I think that all things, in their way, reflect heavenly truth, the imagination not least. 'Reflect' is the important word. This lower life of the imagination is not a beginning of, nor a step toward, the higher life of the spirit, merely an image."[11] The image, the visual aspect of being human, is not *per se* problematic for the Christian. G. K. Chesterton properly distinguishes between imagination, as God-given gift, and illusion, which is the stuff of

---

[10] Os Guinness and John Seel, eds. *No God But God: Breaking with the Idols of Our Age* (Chicago: Moody Press, 1992) 26.
[11] C. S. Lewis, *Surprised By Joy* (New York: Harcourt, Brace and World, Inc., 1955) 167.

idolatry, in the quote under the title of this chapter. Quentin Schultze has accurately criticized Jacque Ellul's outright rejection of the image in favor of the word.[12] Many Jews and Protestants have wrongly constructed a dichotomy between word and image, based on a false interpretation of the Second Commandment. The Biblical dichotomy is between idolatry and consecration. The Second Commandment specifically focuses on the *means of worship*. Even in the redemptive revelation of the tabernacle and temple God displays a concern for beauty and craftsmanship using images of various kinds. Bezalel and Aholiab went to great pains to craft the tabernacle in accordance with God's plans and specifications. In Exodus 31:3-5 we read: "I have filled him with the Spirit of God, in wisdom, in understanding, in knowledge, and in all *manner of* workmanship, to design artistic works, to work in gold, in silver, in bronze, in cutting jewels for setting, in carving wood, and to work in all *manner of* workmanship." This included images of pomegranates and cherubim. Thus, even images were not forbidden in the Old Covenant means of worship. They had to be prescribed by God explicitly. While these images were part of the "types and shadows" of the Mosaic economy, the two New Covenant sacraments involve prescribed visual elements. The Puritan "Regulative Principle," as we shall see in the next chapter, clearly forbids the use of images in worship, which form part of the *substance* of worship. This does not apply, nor did the Reformers of the Puritans intend it to apply, to our cultural endeavors.

Imagination is "*a)* the act or power of forming mental images of what is not actually present *b)* the act or power of creating mental images of what has never been actually experienced, or of creating new images or ideas by combining previous experiences; creative power."[13] Imagination is a gift of perception essential to all human activity. Electronic media employ varying combinations of verbal and image-oriented means of perception and communication. As we have seen the verbal interprets the visual, and the visual expresses the verbal. Witness how many words refer to visual realities. Language is full of metaphors. Imagination involves a complex mixture of the verbal and the visual. Reading involves the interpretation of images of letters and words on a printed page. To drive a wedge between words and images is not an option for the Christian Media Ecologist. Electronic media, especially the image media, are not inherently idolatrous. Remember, Calvin's "idol factory" is the fallen human soul, not General Electric or Microsoft. Electronic media are part of the God-given development of human culture. The Christian must critically appreciate them as such.

---

[12] Quentin Schultze, *Redeeming Television: How TV Changes Christians - How Christians Can Change TV* (Downers Grove, IL: InterVarsity Press, 1992) 84.

[13] *Webster's New World Dictionary and Thesaurus*, version 2.0, build #25, s.v. "imagination."

Edification: The Value of Entertainment as Recreation

Amuse is literally to stare stupidly or be distracted from the point at issue.[14] As Neil Postman has warned we are in danger of amusing ourselves to death, especially when it comes to the television. However, the abuse of something legitimate should not divert us from seeing its proper place. Amusement and entertainment have a proper place for humans, especially in a fallen world. Everyone needs a break from the rigors of work, even work which one enjoys. The quality of the entertainment we choose, however, raises many important questions for the Christian Media Ecologist, and the preacher. As we shall see, not only do ethical questions need to be asked, but also epistemological questions. Beyond this, however, aesthetic questions should also be addressed. The dominance of popular culture has blinded our culture to these questions. Just as the forms of communication affect the content, so it is with forms of cultural expression. Popular culture is like the mud room of a grand mansion, in which young people get stuck, not realizing the unexplored treasure they are missing.

Kenneth Myers has demonstrated how many secular assumptions about reality have shaped the forms of popular culture. Christians should be alert to the nature of these forms. To say that diversion from work is not sinful *per se* is not to say that all forms of diversion are of equal value. Much contemporary diversion is part of the suppression of the knowledge of God and an escape from the seriousness of life in God's world. Myers has distinguished among "high, folk, and popular culture." He argues that popular culture is a dangerous hybrid which is uniquely a product of industrialized society.[15] The wise Christian should consider these as he contemplates the value of various forms of entertainment. Further reading on this question should include Myers, *All God's Children and Blue Suede Shoes: Christians and Popular Culture*; C. S. Lewis's *An Experiment in Criticism*; and T. S. Eliot's *Christianity and Culture: The Idea of a Christian Society and Notes Toward the Definition of Culture.*[16]

Thus well done movies, video cassettes, documentaries, searching the Internet to pursue a hobby, may be enjoyed with thanksgiving as each of these activities is consecrated to God.

---

[14] *Oxford English Dictionary*, 1971, s.v. "amuse."
[15] Kenneth M. Myers, *All God's Children and Blue Suede Shoes: Christians and Popular Culture* (Westchester, IL: Crossway Books, 1989) 60ff.
[16] Kenneth M. Myers, *All God's Children and Blue Suede Shoes: Christians and Popular Culture* (Westchester, IL: Crossway Books, 1989); C. S. Lewis, *An Experiment in Criticism* (Cambridge, UK: Cambridge University Press, 1961); T. S. Eliot, *Christianity and Culture: The Idea of a Christian Society and Notes Toward the Definition of Culture* (New York: Harcourt Brace Jovanovich, 1968). See comments in annotated bibliography.

A CRITICAL LOOK AT THREE KEY MEDIA

It is important, as we have argued in chapter 5, to consider each individual medium in terms of its being a conduit, its grammar, and its environment as part of the cultural fabric. While we will make comments along these lines, it is not my intention to give an in-depth analysis. Entire books have been written analyzing each of the communication technologies below. The bibliography should be consulted for further study. The purpose here is to outline an approach in order to stimulate the thinking of the preacher to better inform his congregation through his preaching, and better understand the nature of his competition, especially realizing the temptations which exist for his listeners. This section should also help in counseling people regarding responsible stewardship of the electronic media.

Television

The television, observes Douglass Cater, "arrived so swiftly and so totally: in January 1949 only 2.3 percent of American homes had the box with the cathode-ray tube. Five years later it had penetrated more than half of our homes. Today [1975], 97 percent of them have one or more sets—a distribution roughly matching that of indoor plumbing."[17] Between "1948 and 1952, television ownership in America rose from a few thousand to 15,000,000."[18] Thus the Baby Boomers are the first "television generation," especially those born after 1950.

Using the three media metaphors of conduit, grammar and environment, let us consider the television. Television understood as a *conduit* of information focuses on what the newscaster is saying, as he reads the teleprompter. This could be analyzed as a printed document. The content of the story of the fire in the next town will differ little in the newspaper or on the evening news. We should remember that the modern newspaper is electrically generated, as its information, beginning with the telegraph, comes largely through "the wire." In fact, the newspaper is more like television news than vice versa. When the *grammar* of the medium is accounted for a large difference begins to appear. The same fire may be the lead story on the evening news, and there is nothing else on the "page" (screen) to distract the viewer. This *is* what you see. In the newspaper the story may be on the second page, in the midst of a number of other totally unrelated stories. In this respect there is a similarity between the newspaper and the television, in that there is little

---

[17] Douglass Cater, "The Intellectual in Videoland," *Saturday Review*, 31 (May 1975) 13.
[18] Marie Winn, *The Plug-in Drug*. Rev. ed. (New York: Viking Penguin, 1985) 128.

logical sequence in the order and arrangement of "stories." One story might focus on pictures of burning building, while the other describes conversation with the burned out family. The television will capitalize on the anguished faces, whereas the newspaper will more likely show the burned out building, and focus on statements made by victims and firefighters at the scene. The television report will often be "live," whereas the printed account will always be "old." The *environment* of television is far more complex, and must be considered in terms of both its immediate environmental affects as well as its broader cultural affects.

People are generally naive about these broader affects. Some people have removed the television from their homes, in the hope of totally avoiding its influence. It is easy to forget that removing an intruder may not restore all that he may have stolen. In the case of television the theft has been subtle but dramatic. There is nothing to do except read and talk and ....whatever people have done for most of history. Conversation, social interaction, and the social structure which characterized the free time of the past has largely disappeared. We have moved from the privacy of the printed page, which defined and cultivated the social structures of the past, to the privacy of the image and the electronic impulse, which has totally redefined those structures as well as the ways in which we understand our lives and the lives of those around us. We are truly alone in a new way, whether or not we own a television. This is a reminder that we have much more to do than unplug the "drug." We must consider the total environmental effect of electronic media.

As we have seen, Nederhood distinguishes five "categories of influence" or television impact: neurological, epistemological, experiential, modalistic, and sociological. Thus neurologically the television alters brain function to a non-sequential "dream state." Epistemologically it alters our perception of reality. Experientially it mediates experience. Modalistically it defines life as entertainment. Sociologically it is the primary socializing force in our culture. Let us consider television under these categories.

Neurologically the effect of television is well documented. A recent Associated Press story states: "Study: Bedtime TV prevents kids from sleeping well."[19] According to a recent study by Dr. Judith Owens, professor of pediatrics at Brown University, TV watching seems to stimulate some children so that they have difficulty sleeping. Reading is recommended for "winding down." The article goes on to say that a growing amount of recent research has shown that "heavy TV viewing may be linked to depression, anxiety and violent

---

[19] Tammy Webber (Associated Press writer), "Study: Bedtime TV prevents kids from sleeping well," "The Back Page," *The Union Leader*, September 8, 1999. Postman reports that violent crime perpetrated by children has risen 11,000% since 1950, Postman, *The Disappearance of Childhood*, 134. That is not a "typo."

behavior, as well as obesity." Seventy six percent of parents said that TV viewing was a regular part of the regular bedtime routine. The question is: what causes the violence? Is it imitation of violent behavior on screen, or is there something about the medium itself which engenders violence?

McLuhan referred to the "light through" quality of television as "not merely rear projection. There is also the entire electric mesh—what Joyce calls 'the charge of the light barricade.'"[20] Like a stained glass window the television image is characterized by the "resonant *interval*." It extends the sense of touch and totally involves the viewer, creating a mosaic of suggestions which are immediate, thus extending the central nervous system.[21] Thus, television tends to hypnotize the viewer and may even cause dyslexia, as McLuhan explained to correspondent Claire Booth Luce. Paul Levinson describes "light through" media as tapping "some primordial notion of heaven."[22]

Marie Winn labels one negative result of this hypnotic effect "television addiction."[23] The trance-like state of viewers gives evidence of being mastered by the medium, a classic definition of addiction. A college English instructor, who is a heavy user confesses: "I find television almost irresistible. When the set is on, I cannot ignore it. I feel sapped, will-less, enervated. As I reach out to turn off the set, the strength goes out of my arms. So I sit there for hours and hours."[24] Had he not been trained in a literate culture to express himself verbally, his description would no doubt have been far less cogent. The logical, written and verbal skills of the television generation have declined noticeably since the advent of the box. Marie Winn argues convincingly that "Young people themselves frequently associate drug use and the television experience." A teenager explains his experience on pot being like "...a TV show with a screen so small it goes right into your head so you can feel what it shows on the pictures."[25]

Commenting on TV ratings, Eric McLuhan has suggested: "It might be more to the point—from a media-ecological standpoint—to 'V-rate' the various media according to the degree of psychic and cultural violence they impose on

---

[20] W. Terrence Gordon, *Marshall McLuhan: Escape into Understanding, A Biography* (New York: BasicBooks, 1997) 217.
[21] Marshall McLuhan, *Understanding Media: The Extensions of Man* (New York: McGraw-Hill Book Company, 1964) 308-337; Marshall McLuhan, *Letters of Marshall McLuhan*, edited by M. Molinaro, C. McLuhan, and W. Toye (Toronto: Oxford University Press, 1987) 437, letter to *The Listener*, 11 August 1971.
[22] Paul Levinson, "Millennial McLuhan: Clues for Deciphering the Digital Age," [WWW document] URL http://chronicle.com/weekly/v46/i08/08b01001.htm (14 October 1999).
[23] Marie Winn, *The Plug-in Drug*, 23ff.
[24] *Ibid.*, 25.
[25] *Ibid.*, 133.

their users in a (once-) civilized society. Assume that the user is a private individual and literate and rate the media—telephone, radio, TV, computer, et al—according to the damage prolonged exposure will inflict on that individual's sensory balance. ...It seems that in getting wrapped up in 'violent content' we are missing the *real* violence of new media in willy-nilly transforming culture and society—which ought to be the main preoccupation of Media Ecology. Lots of sociologists out there are willing to hack away at the content disputes, but there are precious few who have the ability to look on the media themselves."[26]

The Columbian government made a bold and unprecedented move in seeking to tone down the television reporting of violence, by altering the medium as opposed to altering the content. In a Reuters news release from Bogota on August 27, 1999 titled: "TV To Transmit War In Black And White" we read, "Colombian television will stop broadcasting color images of its long-running guerrilla war and instead broadcast scenes of political violence in black and white, industry chiefs said Thursday." Eric McLuhan applauded this attention to "reprogramming the environment" of the medium in order to "take the color out of the war," but cautioned, "Probably this particular effort will backfire, not so much for ideological or propaganda reasons as because they don't understand that B&W images on colour screens are in fact more involving than colour images on the same screens. They are hoping to decrease involvement and in that sense 'cool' interest; in fact, they will 'cool' the medium and heighten involvement in the images and in the situations. Otherwise they would have been spot-on: B&W *monochrome* images are indeed less involving than colour-screen images."[27]

Merrelyn Emery's survey of all available studies of the effects of television concludes: "At the short-term level, the picture [of overall effects of television on users and culture] cannot be called final as there is still a dearth of clarifying experimentation. Analyses, however, of television epilepsy and theta-wave activity are confirmatory of the direct testing so far performed; the modal reaction to the CRT (cathode ray tube) is cortical slowing. There is internal consistency between the two levels of analysis."[28] Jerry Mander warns of the danger of "X-radiation emanating from television sets. ...Television light is purposeful and directed rather than ambient. It is projected into our eyes from behind the screen by cathode-ray guns which are literally aimed at us. These

---

[26] Eric McLuhan, "Response to Tom Farrell," mediaecology@ube.ubalt.edu (6 November 1999).
[27] Eric McLuhan, "Media Ecology," mediaecology@ube.ubalt.edu (2 Sept 1999).
[28] Eric McLuhan, "Response to Tom Farrell," and Merrelyn Emery, *The Social and Neurophysiological Effects of Television and Their Implications for Marketing Practice: An Investigation of Adaptation to the Cathode Ray Tube* (Ann Arbor, MI: University Microfilms, 1985).

guns are powered by 25,000 volts in the case of color television, and about 15,000 volts in black-and-white sets."[29]

In his ground breaking sociological analysis Alvin Toffler describes what he calls the "bombardment of the senses." He identifies three levels of "overstimulation:" sensory, cognitive, and decisional. Brainwashing techniques involve "sensory bombardment involving flashing lights, rapidly shifting patterns of color, chaotic sound effects—the whole arsenal of psychedelic kaleidoscopy."[30] The similarity to much television advertising is striking. It also reminds us of the connection Marie Winn makes between television and the drug culture mentality. American advertisers have become technological masters of the "quick flash" technique, based on five decades of motivational research. Rapid movement of images enhances the by-pass of critical reflection, which is already inherent in television. Eye and ear-catching ads wash over the mind like a tidal wave. While no medium can eradicate the humanity of man, the power of each to distort that humanity is always present. With television this is a powerful presence indeed. The evidence for "television epilepsy" and hyperactivity, along with its mesmerizing effect, should cause serious concern in and of itself.

Considering the epistemology of television, Kenneth Myers challenges the Christian: "Even if all of the entertainment on television was inoffensive to Christian ethics and of the highest artistic merit, its form of communication (and form of knowing) encourages the aversion to abstraction, analysis, and reflection that characterizes our culture at all levels. Thinking is often hard work. Television's surfeit of instant entertainment not only provides relief from such hard work; it offers an attractive, alternative 'way of knowing' (as does rock 'n roll) that makes reasoning seem anachronistic, narrow, and unnecessary."[31] Television appeals to the non-analytical hemisphere of the brain.[32] It cultivates an aversion to the more laborious work of logical thought, especially in the mind which has never developed that faculty.

Television has become the interpretive spectacles of our culture. As we shall see below, it is becoming part of a larger electronic environment created by internetworking. Through television we view and interpret life. "[T]elevision is at its most trivial and, therefore, most dangerous when its aspirations are high, when it portrays itself as a carrier of important cultural conversations."[33] Television creates and engenders symbols which give our

---

[29] Jerry Mander, *Four Arguments for the Elimination of Television* (New York: Morrow, 1978) 170ff.
[30] Alvin Toffler, *Future Shock* (New York: Bantam Books, 1971) 348ff.
[31] Myers, *All God's Children and Blue Suede Shoes*, 171.
[32] Winn, *The Plug-in Drug*, 44ff
[33] Neil Postman, *Amusing Ourselves To Death: Public Discourse in the Age of Show Business* (New York: Viking Penguin, Inc., 1985) 16.

culture its significance for good or ill. It is, in this sense, religious. Video icons become mediators of secular values. As Gregor Goethals points out, television as a secular substitute for religious ritual leaves us with "Big Mac and Coca-Cola [as] substitutes for more demanding sacraments."[34] Television and visual media draw us into an unreflective symbolic environment. Ads overwhelm, they do not inform. Their message is: "Don't think. Buy!" Advertising seeks to define who we are for commercial purposes and with religious motives. "Volvo is a car you can believe in." "The new Chrysler 300M has Guts, Brains and a Soul." Miata MX-5 is a soul-stirring roadster: "To stir your soul, use the proper utensil." Gospel-like songs claim that Ford makes you happy: "O how happy you have made me." This is nothing less than the gospel of entertainment and consumption! Or consider: "300 people were killed when a 747 crashed in Tokyo." "Now a word from our sponsors." Television makes entertainment even out of news. The most tragic events are trivialized by the commercial message.

"Disdained though it may be, the TV commercial is the most distinctive icon in our secular culture. ...Like traditional icons, commercials appeal to hope and fear. They even promise miracles."[35] Ads during the Superbowl draw as much of a crowd as the game, and make the game worthwhile as a complete media event in people's lives. Even the baseball stadium is dominated by the presence of the big screen, playing back what you have just seen, and sounding the virtues of Budweiser. "The commercial has become a kind of visual, musical catechism that effects the way persons see themselves and their world."[36] It should remind Christians with catechetical traditions that the original word "catechize" means to sound in the ear. The "audio-tactile" power of television will only be resisted by the sounding in the ear of the truth of the God of the Bible.

As an environment, television has altered traditional social institutions, such as the school. Meyrowitz reminds us that "Television is mostly a presentational analogic system, whereas text information is discursive and digital." Thus, whereas a child once had to learn how to read children's literature before he could slowly work his way toward adult books over time. But now adult and children's television can be watched prior to reading or on the same evening. American education is in a state of "perpetual crisis" because the structure of education is based on the goal of text literacy, not "nontextual media." The schools, however, are attempting to incorporate "nontextual media" education into the old structure and, therefore, failing. Only the environmental understanding of media is able to parse this situation

---

[34] Gregor T. Goethals, *The TV Ritual: Worship at the Visual Altar* (Boston: Beacon Press, 1981) 133.
[35] *Ibid.*, 136, 137.
[36] *Ibid.*, 137, 138.

and at least clarify what is going wrong.[37] This was McLuhan's quest. "Electronic or discarnate man is automatically committed to the primacy of the right hemisphere."[38]

Pleas for "television literacy," besides being an oxymoron to the Media Ecologist, fail to aim at one of the most important things contemporary educators should be doing: teaching the nature and stewardship of media. Using technology without thinking about it does not promote literacy of any kind. As Postman asks, how many of our students know anything about the origin of the alphabet or any other medium of communication?[39] Merrelyn Emery concludes: "Television as educator in both the formal sense and as promoter of well-informed democracies has failed to meet expectations. There is more forgetting than remembering and the a-conceptual knowledge so afforded is testable only by recognition, not recall."[40] Southern Agrarian writer Wendell Berry concludes: "After forty-odd years, the evidence is everywhere that television, far from proving a great tool of education, is a tool of stupefaction and disintegration. Industrial education has abandoned the old duty of passing on the cultural and intellectual inheritance in favor of baby-sitting and career preparation."[41]

Experientially, as Joel Nederhood has observed, television mediates and authenticates reality.[42] It defines what is and is not important in human experience. It does so in a culturally pervasive way, such that people who constantly watch certain soap operas and sit-coms identify with its characters more closely than with anyone else in their lives. They also tend to relate to others who share their viewing experience through that experience, rather than directly. Finally, they tend to view others in terms of television personalities.

Television has become the defining mode of American culture and consciousness, even with the presence of the Internet. "For some marketing purposes, however, television reigns supreme. The dynamics elucidated here to account for its failure in education also account for its success in marketing. These dynamics appear to be inherent in the medium and hence not readily gainsaid. There is also evidence that over a longer time scale heavy viewing has broad dissociative and disadvantaging effects."[43] Actually, the Internet is more

---

[37] Joshua Meyrowitz, "Multiple Media Literacies," *Journal of Communication* 48, no. 1 (winter 1998): 107.
[38] Marshall McLuhan, "A Last Look at the Tube," in *Marshall McLuhan: The Man and His Message*, edited by George Sanderson and Frank Macdonald (Golden, CO: Fulcrum, 1989) 198.
[39] Postman, *The End of Education*, 188ff.
[40] Emery, *The Social and Neurophysiological Effects of Television*, Abstract.
[41] Wendell Berry, *What Are People For?* (New York: Farrar, Straus and Giroux, 1990) 187.
[42] Joel Nederhood, "Effective Preaching in a Media Age," class notes, Westminster Theological Seminary in California, 1990.
[43] Emery, *The Social and Neurophysiological Effects of Television*, Abstract.

pervasive form of televising ads. Almost every site has them everywhere. One might change Postman's versatile title *Amusing Ourselves to Death* to *Advertising* or *Consuming Ourselves to Death*. Indeed, the reason why television is so uniquely suited to marketing is that is does best what Americans have fallen in love with—entertainment. Hollywood, and the powers who shape the content of film and television, have found the perfect media to promote their view of the world. Enjoy the moment! Never has a medium been better designed to shape a message.

One need not look far to see ways in which our culture, even print culture, has been changed by television. Everywhere, including church, as we shall see, people are looking for entertainment. Public discourse is now being transformed by show business, mediated by television. Political campaigns are mounted with sound-bite slogans and flashy engaging images. This is the burden of Postman's *Amusing Ourselves to Death*. Daniel Boorstin, former Librarian of Congress, warns, "Our first assignment is not to allow the published electronic image or the public word deter us from the primary effort of our education. We must raise citizens qualified to choose their experience for themselves, from books past and present, and so secure the independence that only the reader can enjoy."[44] It is doubtful that our constitutional republic can survive without the high level of literacy it assumes. The average person is no longer able to deal with the ideas which lie at the foundation of our freedom.[45] Everything from classical music to the daily newspaper is being billed as fun in the mode of popular culture. Many people now vote on the basis of the face, not the issues.

Sociologically, what we have seen in the areas of epistemology, experience, and modality is summed up by Richard Adler: "If this country has a unifying culture, it is the mass, popular culture: and today, television is the most vital expression of that culture." Adler goes on to quote John Leonard: "Television is now our only way of talking to each other about who we think we are."[46] Of course, that must now include the Internet, which actually enables a kind of conversation, since it is more two way, or interactive than television. The one way tube, however, is still the most culturally pervasive and influential electronic medium.

---

[44] Winn, *The Plug-in Drug*, 95.
[45] Neil Postman, *The Disappearance of Childhood* (London: Allen, 1983) 101ff.
[46] Richard Adler, *Television as a Cultural Force* (New York: Praeger Publishers, 1976) 3, 4, quoted in Joel Nederhood, "The Back to God Hour: Mission Television Report," in *Christian Reformed Church Synod Report*. Report 1:A, Supplement, 1977, 172. Nederhood notes that Leonard calls the television "Cyclops." The Leonard quote is from William Severini Kowinski, "Cyclops: Man with One Eye in the Land of the Blind," *TeleVISIONS* (October/November 1975) 5.

Furthermore, the television tends to short-circuit the normal development of family and other social relationships. The mere act of viewing for hours on end replaces time formally given to building social skills and relationships. As Urie Bronfenbrenner says, "The primary danger of the television screen lies not so much in the behavior it produces—although there is a danger there—as in the behavior it prevents: the talks, the games, the family festivities and arguments through which much of the child's learning takes place and through which his character is formed. Turning on the television set can turn off the process that transforms children into people."[47] In 1971 Daniel Boorstin posed a test, the result of which I think he anticipated: "The great test is whether somehow we can find ways in and through television itself to break down the walls of the new [television induced] segregation—the walls which separate us from one another, from the sources of knowledge and power, from the past, from the real world outside."[48]

The passivity of "watching" exacerbates this problem, especially in children, since they are habituated to not thinking for themselves, not creating their own entertainment, or growing into adult experience and behavior. Add to this the adult information to which they have access, without the traditional rites of passage and wisdom required to deal with adult realities, such as war, crime, violence, sexuality, and you have the disappearance of a very important institution of our civilization—childhood. The former restraint of "shame" has almost disappeared. Adult supervision of the entrance into adulthood, once provided by the reading of the Bible and imaginative children's literature, has been circumvented by television. Every form of experience and knowledge is available to everyone, all the time. Television blurs the boundaries of childhood by blurring the boundaries of ethical norms. "Television has come close to eliminating the concept of sexual aberration altogether."[49]

McLuhan was quite frank in his recommendation regarding television viewing. "As for restricting the use of TV, it surely should be part of a media ecology program. If people became aware that TV watching diseased the young, physically, and independently of programming, there would be no problem about restricting its use. TV is as radioactive as radium." He gave this advice in the context of explaining the problem of dyslexia. McLuhan maintained that it is caused by prolonged television watching during the formative stages of youth, and that much of the unexplained rage present in young people is due to the frustration which this learning disability causes.[50] Joel Nederhood, in his synod report advising the Christian Reformed Church

---

[47] Winn, *The Plug-in Drug*, 141.
[48] Daniel Boorstin, "Television," *Life Magazine* (10 September 1971) 39.
[49] Postman, *The Disappearance of Childhood*, 91.
[50] McLuhan, *Letters*, 534, letter to Clare Booth Luce, 29 August 1977.

on the use of television for religious broadcasting, advises: "Turning off the television is a serious and important act..."[51]

Os Guinness nicely summarizes the dangers of television under five categories. "television discourse has a bias against understanding ...responsibility, ...memory and history, ...rationality, and ...truth and accuracy."[52] He closes with a quote from Ted Koppel, who is troubled by television's being on "the verge of becoming a hallucinogenic barrage of images, whose only grammar is pacing, whose principal theme is energy. We are losing our ability to manage ideas; to contemplate, to think."[53]

Quentin Schultze gives some helpful criteria by which to judge good television in *Redeeming Television: How TV Changes Christians - How Christians Can Change TV.* His general assessment of television is altogether too sanguine, in my opinion, as we have seen in chapter 5. However, I think within the narrow limits of what television does best—entertain—he offers some well thought out advice for discerning the most powerful image on television—the human face; and critically evaluating a variety of television programming.[54] While I would not necessarily agree with his assessment of particular programs, I think Christians need to begin with the principles of evaluation which he enumerates.

According to McLuhan's assessment "movies and TV complete the cycle of mechanization of the human sensorium. With the omnipresent ear and moving eye, we have abolished the dynamics of Western Civilization." History begins with writing and ends with television.[55] Television creates its own context. "The medium has absorbed and eradicated the idea of a pretelevision past; in place of what used to be we get an ever new and ever-renewable present."[56] McLuhan's quest to understand the dynamics of this dramatic electronic change did not leave him optimistic about its effects.

In his excellent discussion of the narrative power of television Quentin Schultze notes that "commercial television sometimes functions like the sacred stories of religion, confirming the myths of secular society."[57] Urie Bronfenbrenner evokes a darker image: "Like the sorcerer of old the television casts its magic spell, freezing speech and action, turning the living into silent

---

[51] Joel Nederhood, "The Back to God Hour: Mission Television Report," *Christian Reformed Church Synod Report* (Report 1:A, Supplement, 1977) 174.
[52] Os Guinness, *Fit Bodies Fat Minds: Why Evangelicals Don't Think and What to Do About It* (Grand Rapids: Baker Books, 1994) 78, 79.
[53] *Ibid.*, 80.
[54] Quentin Schultze, *Redeeming Television: How TV Changes Christians - How Christians Can Change TV* (Downers Grove, IL: InterVarsity Press, 1992) chapters 4-6, 81-145.
[55] Marshall McLuhan, *Counterblast* (London: Rapp & Whiting, 1969) 17, 122.
[56] Birkerts, *The Guttenberg Elegies*, 119.
[57] Schultze, *Redeeming Television*, 51. Cf. all of Chapter 2, 37-60.

statues so long as the enchantment lasts."[58] Gregor Goethals concludes with a sobering challenge to Christians, especially preachers: "Until institutional religion can excite the serious play of the soul and evoke the fullness of human passion, television will nurture our illusions of heroism and self-transcendence."[59] Since television is a "tradition-smashing phenomenon,"[60] we need to know, not only when to turn it off, but we need to have a tradition strong enough to resist its power. In the next chapter we will assess the television's suitability as a medium for worship and preaching.

The Personal Computer

The personal computer, especially when connected to the Internet, is fast becoming a dominant means of communication. In considering the personal computer I have observed that the reason for my frustration over the lack of information found in CD-ROM encyclopedias and atlases is based on the simple fact that they are created in a multi-media technology. They are meant to compete with "mere words," through multimedia audio-visual presentation. At present all but the most expensive CDs are "information lite." The most useful software and disks are based on printed texts which existed as printed texts prior to being scanned onto a disk. "Technological society in the electronic stage cannot exist without vast quantities of writing and print."[61] But the computer has transformed the way we view and use print.

Walter Ong notes the tendency of the written and then the printed word to undermine the oral. The written became the repository of memory, especially since the invention of the phonetic alphabet. Now, despite a restoration of secondary orality with the telephone, radio and television, the computer represents the "word silenced once more, and thought processes pretty completely reorganized by extreme quantification."[62] Hence, McLuhan's reference to the computer as a "two bit machine." Its mechanics are pure Enlightenment rationalism. Its application, however, radically undermines the vision of a predictable universe.

Neurologically we are no better off with the PC than with the television as Merrelyn Emery reminds us: "A check of literature on VDUs (visual display unit) confirms that the maladaptive agent is indeed the CRT (cathode ray tube)

---

[58] Winn, *The Plug-in Drug*, 141.
[59] Goethals, *The TV Ritual*, 143, 144.
[60] Harvey Cox, *Religion in the Secular City: Toward a Postmodern Theology* (New York: Simon and Schuster, Inc., 1984) 67.
[61] Walter Ong, *The Presence of the Word* (New Haven: Yale UniversityPress, 1967. Reprint, Minneapolis, MN: University of Minnesota Press, 1981) 89.
[62] *Ibid.*, 88.

rather than any other dimension of television viewing."[63] Eric McLuhan observes: Emery "concluded that TV was a 'maladaptive medium'—irrespective of program content. Her document [*The Social and Neurophysiological Effects of Television*] thus deserves to be a cornerstone of Media Ecology. Maladaptivity is certainly an ecological concern. What she had to reveal about the CRT applies all the more to the environment of computer monitors we live in."[64] When the orange words "It is now safe to turn off your computer" appear, perhaps we should ask: "Was it ever safe to turn it on?"

Aside from this, word processing requires and even *encourages* literacy. It "produces words, not images, on its video screen."[65] The author of a text is able to manipulate changes and additions in ways which were impossible with a typewriter. I suspect, however, that those best equipped to benefit from word processing are those who have learned to write with the fixed media of pen, paper and typewriter. My experience with AutoCAD demonstrated that those who had never drawn with a pencil and a straight edge did not draw or design as well with the computer. Thus, word processing also *discourages* literacy. Facility with text manipulation is also a liability, since fluidity can lead to laziness, and undermine the precision and logic required of writers in the past. "Words now arrive on the screen under the aspect of provisionality. ...when they are deleted it is as if they had never been. There is no physical reminder of the wrong turn, the failure. ...the consequentiality of bringing forth language has been altered."[66]

The ephemeral nature of pixels on a screen, are similar to images in that they come and go. They actually exist nowhere in accessible space-time form, until they are printed. They exist in digital memory. Such memory storage "has potential, not actual locus."[67] Computers thus exacerbate one of the negatives of the book: they undermine memory by offering almost endless storage space. Only now the accessibility of vast quantities of texts make memorizing anything seem like a waste of time. Scrolling on a screen is very different from turning the pages of a book in space and time. This should remind us of the standard principle of Media Ecology: how "we receive information bears vitally on the ways we experience and interpret reality."[68] Screen reading tends to undermine our sense of history, permanence and place. "The depth of field that is our sense of the past is not only a linguistic

---

[63] Emery, *The Social and Neurophysiological Effects of Television*, 1985, Ph.D. dissertation abstract.
[64] Eric McLuhan, "Response to Tom Farrell," mediaecology@ube.ubalt.edu (6 November 1999).
[65] Winn, *The Plug-in Drug*, 96.
[66] Birkerts, *The Guttenberg Elegies*, 157.
[67] *Ibid.*, 155.
[68] *Ibid.*, 72.

construct, but is in some essential way represented by the book and the physical accumulation of books in library spaces."[69] Veteran book readers tend to print out documents in order to have a sense of truly possessing them; in order to contemplate their content. With computing we tend to spend more time managing and processing information than contemplating its meaning. "Where the electronic impulse rules, and where the psyche is conditioned to work with data, experience of deep time is impossible. No deep time; no resonance, no wisdom. The only remaining oases are churches (for those who still worship) and the offices of therapists."[70] The physical properties of the book support tradition, lineal sequence and logic; every book has a distinct beginning and a definite end.

The impermanence of the digital words radically alters our perception of them, especially when the reader reads exclusively from a screen. Those who once never read from a screen and now only sometimes do are in the best position to retain respect for the permanence and rationality of words. For those who have never read books exclusively, and who now never do, the word will be less absolute. "The difference between words on a page and words on a screen is the difference between product and process, noun and verb."[71] The naiveté of those who claim that the word processor is just a better typewriter is the same as those who thought the automobile to be simply a better horse and carriage.

The complex logical and analytical skills required for computer programming are an educational benefit.[72] Some of the best minds in our culture are devoted to computer development. However, this expertise must not be confused with the kinds of knowledge and education which make lasting differences in our lives. Such skill represents only *one* of the lost tools of learning, and none of the subject matter. Technological problems, after all, are not the most important problems with which we have to deal. And yet in the present climate we are often led to believe that there are really no other problems.

The Internet

Cyberspace represents the final extension of man, which in principle Joyce and McLuhan foresaw in electric communication. It is not a medium, but a connection of all electronic media. Douglas Groothuis asks the right questions of this new multi-media environment: "What is the fate of truth in cyberspace

---

[69] *Ibid.*, 129.
[70] *Ibid.*, 76.
[71] *Ibid.*, 156, 157.
[72] Postman, *The Disappearance of Childhood*, 149.

(the realm of computer-mediated communications)? Will the torrential flow of information overcome crippling ignorance? Will on-line communication become the next great medium for evangelization? Will our increasing connectedness facilitate the sharing of truth to an degree unprecedented in history? What chances does truth have in cyberspace?"[73] In cyberspace the "all-at-onceness" observed by McLuhan takes on new meaning.[74]

Cybernetics is the essential structural model of cyberspace as the name implies. It focuses on the interrelationship of the many parts of a system. Thus the Internet is a network of systems yielding the total interaction of a universal system. Communication is spread over a network of horizontal surfaces, rather than concentrated in focused meaning. The obsolescence of the book has become a predominant prediction. Robert Coover opines: "Indeed, the very proliferation of books and other print based media, so prevalent in this forest-harvesting, paper-wasting age, is held to be a sign of its feverish moribundity, the last futile gasp of a once-vital form before it finally passes away forever, dead as God."[75] The present Librarian of Congress, in stark contrast with the attitude of his predecessor, predicts that his library will become more like a museum.[76] Books will become like the quaint tools of New England farmers, which no one can imagine using today.

The Christian needs to be especially careful in assessing the Internet, both because it is new and because it is becoming rapidly more pervasive than even the television. Even as print changed the medium of writing by mechanizing it, so the telegraph electrified it, and now this powerful new medium, or "medium of media" encompasses print, television, radio, etc. all in one. According to McLuhan, we have shifted from a visual world to an acoustic world.[77] However, the Internet really combines the visual and the acoustic. For those who deal with text on the screen, it is more visual. "A computer connected to a memory bank may have access to a treasure trove of information... There is little doubt that computers may be a valuable resource for advanced students engaged in research, just as they are for scholars, journalists, and others who require swift access to great amounts of categorized information."[78] The availability of large amounts of information covering the entire scope of human knowledge is a clear benefit of the Internet and the World Wide Web. The purposeful use of this resource can be an enormous help on many levels.

---

[73] Douglas Groothuis, http://www.gospelcom.net/ivpress/groothuis/truthincyber.htm
[74] Marshall McLuhan and Quentin Fiore, *The Medium Is the Massage: An Inventory of Effects* (New York: Bantam Books, 1967) 63.
[75] Birkerts, *The Guttenberg Elegies*, 152. Quoted from Robert Coover, "The End of Books," *New York Times Book Review* (21 June 1992).
[76] *Ibid.*, 127.
[77] McLuhan, *Counterblast*, 94.
[78] Winn, *The Plug-in Drug*, 96.

Information should not be confused with communication, which as we have seen involves some level of involvement between or among persons. However, committees exchanging documents such as minutes and position papers, scholars searching the card catalogue of the Library of Congress, can save enormous amounts of time, formerly spent on the "mechanics" of scholarship. On a more practical level getting a map, which hones in on a specific address, can save not only time but perhaps even a life. Finding help for medical problems or resources for a particular project are possible in a way which never existed before the Internet. With the advent of the Internet, everyone who is "on-line" is connected to this treasure trove. This is in essence pure information exchange. Along with this, of course, comes the trash heap, not only of accessible material, but of material which comes uninvited like the paper "junk mail" in your mailbox. Instead it is digital debris. We shall look more at information overload below.

Electronic mail has changed our daily communication in countless ways. It actually combines several media, at least word processing and the Internet. Its efficiency cannot be gainsaid, that is for a certain kind of communication. But the transmission of information seems to be its genius, and that is not, after all, communication at its best. The worldwide distribution of prayer requests, documents, meeting notices, "personal" and group contacts are all a benefit of the medium. Given the limits of this benefit electronic mail may be a useful invention.

However, there are obvious, as well as hidden liabilities. The obvious include the proliferation of junk mail or "spam," and the time often wasted on this "efficient" form of communication. The regular mail, dismissively referred to as "snail mail," still has to be read, and before you know it you are informing yourself to death. Not so obvious is the undermining of literacy, revealed in the sloppy grammar and spelling, and thus one would think, the quality of thought given to messages and posts. Even people who ought to know better, type everything in lower case letters, without paragraph breaks, and with none of the lovely and personal formality of letter writing. I know, it is supposed to be quick. But isn't that just the problem? Not only this, but the author of a text or hypertext recedes and his/her production becomes evanescent in its character. Deleting is very easy in comparison with throwing a piece of paper in the waste basket.

The lack of place is a troubling subtlety of e-mail. After all, cyberspace is nowhere. When do we move among real people? Sure, email is cheaper than a phone call, but it removes us one step farther away from people. My most effective use of email is with people I already know face-to-face. Gestures, histories, images, all connect with the words on the screen. Others are little more than names, evanescent words on a screen. Most troubling of all is the disenfranchisement of those who are not "on-line." You become a social pariah, without having offended anyone. It was suggested at a presbytery meeting that no one who did not have access to email should be elected to a particular important special committee. This eliminated some of the wisest older men present. The norm of novelty and efficiency tends to favor the young and not the wise. The management of information should not be confused with the understanding of it.

Hypertext adds a new dimension to the personal computer. Everything becomes connected to everything else, in no sequential order and with little fixity. Attempts to print out such a document confirm this fluidity. Hence the Postmodern dream of the authorless text is realized; "hypertext can be seen as delivering a mighty blow to the long-static writer-reader relationship." The old view that a text is rooted in and valued for the wisdom and authority of its creator disappears.[79] The wise Christian with his life staked on the authority of the text of Scripture must pay special attention to this critical liability of computing and cyberspace. The preacher of that Word more so. One can only wonder if the "read only" function, and the copyright laws will stem the tide.

If the genius of print is its cultivation of interiority, the genius of the Internet is its universality and interconnectedness. But this very ever-present connectedness makes it a unique vehicle for the deconstructive agenda of Postmodernism, with its "shrugging sense of anarchy."[80] As culture comes loose "from its textual moorings" under Postmodern pressures Birkerts warns: "To challenge oppression is salutary. To challenge history itself, proclaiming it to be simply an archive of repressions and justifications, is idiotic."[81] Cybergnosticism brings the Utopian tendency of fallen mankind into its own, into a new dimension of limitless possibilities. Birkerts worries about the electronic penchant to spread language thin, evacuating it of subtly and depth. True education in the humanities is not a trivial pursuit of data management. Despite misgivings, he hopes that language may flourish, as Joyce prophesied, in the new synthesis of the sensorium: "for language is the soul's ozone layer and we thin it at our peril."[82]

Being in cyberspace is like being dumped in New York City and being able to go to every shop or apartment without having to move. That may be excellent if we know where to go and why we are going there. But I suspect that the range of choices walking down a street is great enough. Beyond this, as sinners, we have a propensity to go to the wrong places. Now we may go there anonymously, or so we think, if we have no sense of a transcendent

---

[79] Birkerts, *The Guttenberg Elegies*, 163.
[80] Ibid., 169.
[81] Ibid., 124.
[82] Ibid., 128-133.

Presence. The reality of pornography, violent occultism, sexual predators, as well as adulterous liaisons, may be obvious, but represent a problem of giant proportions for the preacher and the church.

The best communication will always take place among those who know each other face-to-face. History, gesture, and language all form the context of every message. However the electronic media may threaten our humanity, one thing is certain: it can never eradicate it. God's Rainbow Promise to Noah insures that. Thoughtful Christians must find ways to consecrate the new environment created by the "medium of media" to the redemptive purposes of their Lord.[83]

CRITICAL CONCERNS FOR ALL MEDIA

Images of the Gods: Reality and Virtual Reality

There is a presentness about the image which gives the illusion of being more real than the word. It has been so since the Serpent in his subtlety beguiled Eve with the image of the fruit and the immediate pleasure it seemed to promise. "In images, everything is in the present tense and the indicative mood."[84] The image media present the church with a temptation unlike any the world has ever known. Its being on a screen as opposed to being a real object makes it doubly beguiling. Electronic media create a reality of their own. Our daughter was once beguiled by a toy called "Squirt, Squirt the Animals," in an image-filled action-packed television advertisement. After receiving it for her birthday she was bored with it in less than half an hour. Marie Winn observes that television "fosters the illusion of a varied experience for the viewer."[85] A nineteen year old describes his marijuana experience: "...the first thing you learn is that you can no longer make the value judgment between what is real and what is not. Just like with TV."[86] Lewis Mumford observed the primitive power of the image even in static cave paintings. The picture of an animal

---

[83] A good example of such consecration is reflected in the comments of a friend and colleague who read and critiqued my manuscript. "To be perfectly honest, I think that the effects of TV and computers in my own life and those of my family are almost entirely positive. That of course reflects a somewhat disciplined approach to these media that perhaps most families don't take. We use TV almost entirely for news, public events, educational programs, etc., and computers almost entirely for word processing, etc." John M. Frame, "Chapters 6 & 7." Personal e-mail (7 Feb. 2000).
[84] Myers, *All God's Children and Blue Suede Shoes*, 164.
[85] Winn, *The Plug-in Drug*, 3.
[86] *Ibid.*, 133

"captures" the animal, and is "a higher mode of magic in its own right, as miraculous as the magic of words, yet even more secret and sacrosanct."[87]

As we have stated above, imagination is a God-given gift which enables us to "make sense" out of experience in God's creation. Even as the creation itself is a medium of God's revelation of His own glorious Being, so the imagination observes and constructs images in order to map reality and give it meaning. In turn, the products of the imagination reconstruct the elements of creation to reflect and cultivate human values. Since the fall this creative ability has been used idolatrously by unbelievers. Images in the mind and their recreation in the physical world reflect and cultivate the aspirations and devotions of human beings. Idolaters substitutes various images in created reality for God. And it does so subtly as Richard Keyes warns: "Our hearts' drive to idolatry means that our conscious thinking is inspired and shaped by images from the imagination, of which we are barely aware."[88]

Images are powerful transformers of human consciousness and our perception of God and His world. Occultists and New Age practitioners understand this, but use this knowledge in a way clearly forbidden in the Second Commandment, to eclipse the true and living God, who is a Spirit. "Visualization" is an ancient occult technique whereby the imagination is used to conjure up and manipulate space-time realities. Applied to advertising it yields: "Imagine yourself in a Mercury." The manipulative power of the image is major factor in the visual media. Calvin approvingly quotes Augustine's comment on the power of human sculpture used idolatrously: "Images have more power to bend the unhappy soul."[89] After all, "seeing is believing," and a picture is worth a thousand words. This power is understood by the Media Ecologist.

Properly developed and used, the imagination helps us to deal more effectively with the real world. God's common blessing enables each person to do this to a degree. The disturbing tendency in the electronic environment, however, is that reality and imagination become confused rather than correlating. This is a confusion toward which unbelief and idolatry tend. Take the example several years ago in which a teenager killed another boy for his new Nike sneakers. The image of the sneakers became a source of ultimate devotion for this boy. It transformed his thinking and acting in a dramatic and tragic way. While the image in this case may not have been an idol in the

---

[87] Lewis Mumford, *The Myth of the Machine: Technics and Human Development* (New York: Harcourt, Brace and World, 1966) 119.

[88] Os Guinness and John Seel, eds. *No God But God: Breaking with the Idols of Our Age* (Chicago: Moody Press, 1992) 25.

[89] John Calvin, *Institutes of the Christian Religion* (1559. Reprint (1 vol. in 2). The Library of Christian Classics, vol. XX. Edited by John T. McNeill. Translated by Ford Lewis Battles. Philadelphia: The Westminster Press, 1960) 113

narrow sense, because it lacks traditional ritual and teaching, it surely functioned that way in the broad sense for that young man. As Goethals notes: "both the traditional and the electronic icons render visible the invisible centers of meaning and value."[90]

The idol of novelty which is at the root of C. S. Lewis's "chronological snobbery" has also produced "technological snobbery." The latest technology becomes a status symbol, a locus of meaning and value. Not to be technologically up-to-date is tantamount to a sin in Technopoly. The image media constantly remind us of this, like the preacher reading the Ten Commandments. Whether it is "ring around the collar" or not having the most powerful modem, the iconic pressure is there. Ads become parables for the people. Commercials have a theology and a congregation.[91] Image is everything! Like Proteus, the modern pantheon of images is constantly changing, and thus continually making new demands, creating new needs and hence constructing new realities. In the context of the modern world the image, electronically generated, represents the most powerful opponent of truth. Images, when they dominate the "shared modes of knowledge," work *against* the communication of norms. A culture that is rooted more in images than in words will find it increasingly difficult to sustain any broad commitment to *any* truth, since truth is an abstraction requiring language."[92] Is it any wonder that tolerance has become the ultimate virtue of Postmodernism?

Virtual reality is all around us, or inside of us. But then who can tell the difference? We are told that the stereo system in a Lexus will "make your life like a movie." The "effect is for the media to substitute for reality just in the degree to which they become virtuosos of realistic detail."[93] A cartoon shows a little boy looking forlornly out a car window as his dad fixes a flat tire in the rain. His dad barks at him, "Don't you understand? This is *life*, this is what is happening. We *can't* switch to another channel."[94] Virtual reality mediates experience and may undermine primary experience. Speaking of television Marie Winn concludes, "It renders other experiences vague and curiously unreal while taking on a greater reality for itself." A teenage boy who survived a devastating tornado exclaimed: "Man, it was just like something on TV."[95] What is "real" is reduced to tragic events, terrible disasters, sports heroes, celebrities, and the last episode of a sit-com. Life, to the heavy user, seems

---

[90] Goethals, *The TV Ritual*, 132.
[91] Postman, *The Disappearance of Childhood*, 109, 110.
[92] Myers, *All God's Children and Blue Suede Shoes*, 164.
[93] Mumford, *The Myth of the Machine*, 125.
[94] Drawing by Robert Day; © 1970 The New Yorker Magazine, Inc.
[95] Winn, *The Plug-in Drug*, 25, 105.

unimportant without television.⁹⁶ Gerbner and Gross found that heavy television users tend to overestimate the number of professional jobs, the number of police and the amount of violence in he real world. Television tends to define reality,⁹⁷ like the shadows in Plato's cave.

Ironically the profusion of images on television and the Internet, rather than enhancing imaginative abilities, tend to eliminate them. Everything is done for you, especially on the television. This is one reason why I have always preferred to listen to baseball on the radio, and above all read a book rather than see a movie by the same title. Bruno Bettelheim, author of *The Uses of Enchantment*, notes, "Television captures the imagination but does not liberate it. A good book at once stimulates and frees the mind."⁹⁸ Imagination involves initiative and creativity, mental work which the television does for the viewer. Watching involves no choices, but the choice not to watch or switch to another channel to continue being uninvolved. Playtime—of which television robs many children—is essential to developing creative skills. The absence of playtime in the lives of children is showing up in a variety of ways in the present generation. Notable are the passivity, lack of initiative, and the continual quest to be entertained.⁹⁹ Even in a sport like baseball, Little League—which has developed with the television generation—is designed so that adults do the organizing. As Postman notes, it is not for fun, but for reputation that most parents are involved.¹⁰⁰

"Images themselves are invitations to conformity." To conform means literally "to fit into an image." Boorstin observes that advertising images become ideals when they are public. The passivity of our engagement with them enhances our conformity. They seduce us with their simplicity, as they embody desires and aspirations. An "image must be simpler than the object it represents," in order to captivate our attention. In chapter 1 we saw that the nature of Old Testament idols was precisely this. The simple, sensual and concrete image mediates the ideal or god, which is worshipped.¹⁰¹ Advertising offers idols not facts.¹⁰² Mass media promote images to which the masses conform. The masses become like the objects of their devotion. McLuhan observes: "The primitive witch-doctor had spells which controlled the elements. The modern advertiser concocts spells which compel the customer. What the advertisers have discovered is simply that the new media of communication are

---

⁹⁶ Nederhood, "Effective Preaching in a Media Age."
⁹⁷ Mander, *Four Arguments for the Elimination of Television*, 255.
⁹⁸ Winn, *The Plug-in Drug*, 58, 59.
⁹⁹ *Ibid.*, 111ff.
¹⁰⁰ Postman, *The Disappearance of Childhood*, 4.
¹⁰¹ Daniel J. Boorstin, *The Image or Whatever Happened to the American Dream?* (New York: Atheneum, 1962) 183-193.
¹⁰² Postman, *The Disappearance of Childhood*, 108.

themselves magical art forms."[103] Image media do the thinking and imagining for us in a beguiling way.

The propensity for media to mediate reality in Messianic terms with salvific expectations is growing. In a section of his book *Fit Bodies, Fat Minds* Os Guinness has a section titled, "The Esperanto of Our Time." In it he comments on the specific technology of "Virtual Reality" (VR). These reality-simulating technologies are viewed by its most ardent proponents as having "godlike capacities—the verisimilitude of the simulation, the all-embracing immersion of the environment, and the near-omniscience of the 'hypertext' potential for interpreting any text. ...The calculus of digital information is the esperanto of our time. ...As one critic puts it, human knowledge now approaches the 'omniscient intuitive cognition of the deity.'"[104] Timothy Leary, LSD guru of the sixties, heartily approved of emerging "electronic realities, ...I hope it's totally subversive and unacceptable to anyone in power. I am flat out enthusiastic that it is for the liberation and empowerment of the individual."[105] A more poignant and blatant example of the self-deifying quest of fallen man cannot be imagined.

Voices of the Gods: The Blind Leading the Blind

Electronic media tend to be anti-social. We should thus distinguish between *privatizing* and *individualizing*.[106] Literacy is reflective and strengthens the inner self in ways that enhance social interaction, whereas electronic media tend to isolate the self in non-reflective ways that inhibit and, at times, even oppose healthy social interaction. If we reduce communication to the mere processing of information and images we *privatize*. If we define communication, as we have in chapter 5, as *communicare*, to impart, share, literally to make common, then we have *individualizing*. *Privatizing* is an isolating process in which the self is separated from social interaction through sensory introversion, whereas *individualizing* enhances interiority through reflection and expansion of the soul in relation to one's culture. Literacy helps one take one's place in the context of society and its mediating structures, whereas electronic *privatizing* focuses on the entertainment and immediate

---

[103] Marshall McLuhan, "Catholic Humanism and Modern Letters," in *The Medium and the Light: Reflections on Religion*, edited by Eric McLuhan and Jacek Szlarek (Toronto: Stoddart Publishing Co. Limited, 1999) [midway].

[104] Guinness, *Fit Bodies, Fat Minds*, 127-129. Quoting Michael Heim, *The Metaphysics of Virtual Reality* (New York: Oxford University Press, 1993) 38.

[105] Glenn Emery, "Virtual Reality's Radical Vision," *Insight on the News* (6 May 1991) 25.

[106] I owe the essential idea of the distinction between *Privatizing* and *Individualizing* to James Curtis, "Media Balance," mediaecology@ube.ubalt.edu (17 Aug 1999). In a subsequent post I articulated the distinction in a way that Dr. Curtis found helpful.

gratification of the individual. That is not to say that all electronic media are inherently *privatizing*. But they tend in that direction when used exclusively. Certain media like video games, television, and the Walkman are inherently privatizing.

Electronic media tend to be anti-intellectual. Alvin Toffler warns: "[D]espite its extraordinary achievements in art, science, intellectual, moral and political life, the United States is a nation in which tens of thousands of young people flee reality by opting for drug-induced lassitude; a nation in which millions of their parents retreat into video-induced stupor or alcoholic haze ...Social rationality presupposes individual rationality, and this, in turn, depends not only on certain biological equipment, but on continuity, order and regularity in the environment. It is premised on some correlation between the pace and complexity of change and man's decisional capacities. By blindly stepping up the rate of change, the level of novelty, and the extent of choice, we are thoughtlessly tampering with these environmental preconditions of rationality. We are condemning countless millions to future shock."[107]

The effects of mass media, especially television, due to its one way effect, open the public to what Jacques Ellul calls "modern propaganda." Without "mass media there can be no modern propaganda." Centralized control, either government or private, is necessary. While the complicity of the "propagandee" is required for mass media to effectively propagandize, mass media also have the power to "create their own public." Such a public will form a kind of allegiance to the mass media which reflect their own ideas and aspirations. Ellul is particularly concerned with the "hypnotism of TV."[108] Effective propaganda requires dissociation and restructuring in order to define reality in terms of what it alone communicates. Confuse, then clarify. Enter the "Super-Simplifier." He will put everything in perspective and provide a clear solution. Adolph Hitler effectively mastered this essential technique of propaganda with mass communication in Weimar Germany.[109]

The confusion part of this formula is characterized by the tendency of electronic media to produce "information overload." Toffler has an entire section in *Future Shock* on this problem.[110] Human beings can only handle so much information before they shut down. Thus the average person becomes more and more attracted to the slogan, which gives the illusion of simplifying a problem. The popularity of the game Trivial Pursuit is symptomatic of a general problem with our whole attitude toward information and knowledge.

---

[107] Toffler, *Future Shock*, 366, 367.
[108] Jacques Ellul, *Propaganda: The Formation of Men's Attitudes*, translated by Konrad Kellen and Jean Lerner (New York: Vintage Books, 1965) 102-105.
[109] Mander, *Four Arguments for the Elimination of Television*, 195ff.
[110] Toffler, *Future Shock* 350ff.

As Jacques Barzun reminds us in his witty essay "Look It Up! Check It Out!" "...the age of ready reference is one in which knowledge inevitably declines into information."[111] This is why the interpretive structure of Christian theology and doctrine is so important as the substance of cultivating a counter environment, or antidote to the propagandizing tendency of the electronic media.

If Thoreau was troubled by the aggravation and irrelevance of the communication of the whooping cough of the Princess Adelaide, imagine what his comments on the tidal wave of information crashing over our heads daily would be. "E-mail, Pagers Add to Killer Stress" was a recent front page story in *The Union Leader* (Tuesday, July 6, 1999) from the *London Observer* (wire) Service. The article went on to say that occupational psychologist Cary Cooper of the University of Manchester Institute of Science and Technology "has warned that workers in many companies are close to breakdown because of data overload. ...The consequences could be devastating, says Eric Harth of Syracuse University... 'Technology is cumulative, growing through the addition of many small contributions, while intelligence, the source of this steady growth remains fixed. We may find ourselves overwhelmed by our creations, when the intelligence required to achieve a certain level of technology may be less than that needed to survive it.'"

French philosopher Jean Baudrillard observed: "We live in a world where there is more and more information and less and less meaning."[112] The idea that somehow more information is good is related to the idea that information in and of itself will solve real problems. This information messiah is one of the great myths of the so-called "Information Age." Mass communication has an uncanny way of making the irrelevant relevant, by the mere force of its existence. McLuhan forcefully opined: "Electric information environments being utterly ethereal fosters the illusion of the world as aspiritual substance. It is now a reasonable facsimile of the mystical body, a blatant manifestation of the Anti-Christ. After all, the Prince of this World is a very great electric engineer."[113] But if information and instantaneous communication will not save us what will? Cultivating a Christian counter environment. T. S. Eliot put it eloquently stated our great need in "Choruses from the Rock":

> *Where is the Life we have lost in living?*
> *Where is the wisdom we have lost in knowledge?*

---

[111] Jacques Barzun, *The Culture We Deserve*, edited by Arthur Krystal (Middletown, CT: Wesleyan University Press, 1989) 39.

[112] Jean Baudrillard, *The Transparency of Evil: Essays on Extreme Phenomena*, translated by James Benedict (New York: Verso, 1990) ??.

[113] Marshall McLuhan, Letter to Jacques Maritain, May 6, 1969, in *The Medium and the Light: Reflections on Religion*, edited by Eric McLuhan and Jacek Szlarek (Toronto: Stoddart Publishing Co. Limited, 1999) [midway].

Where is the knowledge we have lost in information?
The cycles of Heaven in twenty centuries
Bring us farther from GOD and nearer to the Dust.[114]

CULTIVATING A COUNTER ENVIRONMENT

McLuhan counsels: "Faced with information overload, we have no alternative but pattern recognition."[115] In order to discern the patterns of the structures of human experience one must have a well defined grid through which to evaluate them. Ultimately, while God's common grace enables the unbeliever to discern enough to remain sane, only the Christian can know the patterns of heaven, which define and encompass all of created reality. As Paul exhorted the Roman church: "Do not conform any longer to the pattern of this world, but be transformed by the renewing of your mind. Then you will be able to test and approve what God's will is—his good, pleasing and perfect will."[116]

What are we to do? Cultivate a counter environment, keeping the sensorium balanced, with an awareness of what we are doing with every medium of communication. A Christian counter environment is the totality of covenantal reality cultivated by the Risen Lord through the means of grace. This alone will effectively counteract the liabilities of electronic media. Indeed, while no single individual can change a culture, we can, with some intelligent reflection, and to a significant degree, control our involvement in that culture. Furthermore the church is not simply an aggregate of individuals, but the body of Christ, a new creation, a new humanity. The preacher should be a model of such control, and a teacher of the various ingredients required to maintain the balance. The word "pattern." is most often used in the Bible to refer to the plan given by God for the Tabernacle and Temple. These in turn were revealed to reflect the archetypal pattern of heavenly reality, of which Jesus Christ is the complete revelation. Christians are called to shed the pattern of this world, its way of thinking and living, and model their lives after the pattern of their heavenly Lord and His Word. This covenantal pattern is a *pattern of teaching* (2 Tim. 1:13); and a *pattern of behavior* (Tit. 2:7). Thus, the counter environment includes the new perception of reality given in the heavenly pattern revealed in the Christ of Scripture and the entirety of His written Word, the canon of Scripture; and that pattern worked out in the heavenly life of His corporate people, the church. Below are several areas in which Christians need

---

[114] Myers, *All God's Children and Blue Suede Shoes*, 66.
[115] Guinness and Seel, *No God But God*, 132.
[116] Rom. 12:2 (*New International Version*).

to cultivate the means of following this heavenly pattern (Eph. 4). Remember the means of communication are central to our concerns.

Reading and Writing: Cultivating the Soul

An illuminating example of a surprising liability of an electric medium was noted in 1930 by James Truslow Adams, when he made a poignant observation about the earliest electronic communication medium: the telegraph. During the American Civil War a Union sea captain, by the name of Wilkes, broke international law by capturing two Confederate diplomats *en route* to Europe on a neutral British ship. Adams observed: "When we so pride ourselves on what we consider the self-evident value of modern inventions, we may be given pause when we realize that, had there been a submarine cable in 1861, it is almost certain that England and the North would have been at war in that December. As it was, the slowness of communication gave both sides time to think, and allowed Seward in America and Palmerston and Russell in England, with Adams as the connecting link, to guide the situation."[117]

"The slowness of communication." Savor that phrase for a moment. Today it is assumed that speed of communication is an absolute virtue. Efficiency has become an end in itself. Combining speed with a lack of context, electronic media radically undermine reflection and criticism. We live in a sea of thoughtlessness, informing ourselves to death. The fact that we may stop a video does not make it an inherently reflective medium, as reading is. Knowing where the off button is, and using it, is only the first step in creating a Christian counter environment. Taking advantage of the change of pace this affords is a major key to cultivating the soul. How many letters, written in angry haste, have not been sent the next day because of time to reflect. That was what the American and English diplomats did with their time which made the difference in the Civil War. They had "time to think."

The business of reading—wide and good reading—provides a fortification against the onslaught of high-speed media, and promotes a healthy balance of the senses and of every aspect of the soul. We are in need of an apologia for reading, writing and print in the new context. Birkerts and Postman have in different ways made such an apologia; Birkerts as a writer and Postman as an educator. But there is in their work a flavor of the monastic, a call to preserve Western literacy until more propitious times arrive. They appeal to the Enlightenment model of rationality, which is inadequate to meet the Postmodern challenge, as we have seen. As to the value and importance of good reading we should approve almost entirely of what they say. What they

---

[117] James Truslow Adams, *The Adams Family* (Boston: Little, Brown and Company, 1930) 280-81.

lack is the transcendental narrative of Covenant religion and the institution of the church founded upon it.

The act of reading deepens and extends the self, because the printed word, at its best, involves a continuing conversation with the great ideas of the past, ideas which connect us with our culture and beyond. Reading expands the soul in its connectedness with creation, culture and cultus. "In reading great literature I become a thousand men and yet remain myself. Like the night sky in the Greek poem, I see with a myriad eyes, but it is still I who see. Here, as in worship, in love, in moral action, and in knowing, I transcend myself; and am never more myself than when I do."[118] Good reading then is more than just reading; it involves being delivered from ourselves; to rid ourselves of the narcissist. "But one of the chief operations of art is to remove our gaze from that mirrored face, to deliver us from that solitude. When we read the 'literature of knowledge' we hope, as a result, to think more correctly and clearly. In reading imaginative work, I suggest, we should be much less concerned with altering our own opinions—though this of course is sometimes their effect—than with entering fully into the opinions, and therefore also the attitudes, feelings and total experience, of other men."[119]

Sven Birkerts emphasizes the importance of "inwardness" or to use Ong's term "interiority." The older definition of sensibility is "of a refinement or cultivation of presence; it refers to the part of the inner life that is not given but fashioned: a defining, if cloudy, complex of attitudes, predilections and honed responses. ...Here is the power, the seductiveness of the act: When we read, we create and then occupy a hitherto nonexistent interior locale."[120] Cultivating inner resources is the business of God's image bearers. Sinners do so solely for their own purposes, and find there a giant God-sized void, which can never be filled even with the best human fashioning.

The Psalmist experienced and even longed for this inwardness in the profoundest way. "You desire truth in the inward parts, and in the hidden *part* You will make me to know wisdom" (Ps. 51:6). "Even though our outward man is perishing, yet the inward *man* is being renewed day by day" (2 Cor. 4:16). "I will also meditate on all Your work" (Ps. 77:12). Meditation is reflection, often done by the Psalmist on his bed in complete quiet, concentrated musing, consideration of the meaning of the text, especially the text of Scripture, and its implications in the wide world. "Commune with your own heart upon your bed, and be still" (Ps. 4:4). This alone builds the interior of the soul. It is one of the great antidotes to the a-musement of the lightning-paced electronic world spreading itself thinner every day on the surfaces of

---

[118] Lewis, *An Experiment in Criticism*, 141.
[119] *Ibid.*, 85.
[120] Birkerts, *The Guttenberg Elegies*, 87.

experience. Good reading exercises the imagination. At the 1988 commencement of Columbia University Professor Barzun told his students, "For to read intelligently and profitably, your imagination must work every minute, reconstructing the lives, events, and emotions depicted in print."[121] There is a priority to the verbal and the written which prevents sinful creatures from being beguiled or stupefied by mere images. The best humanly produced images are dispersed purposefully among the paragraphs of a printed book and dominated by the text. We may think of this as an illuminated detail of our approach to all images in God's world, controlled by the text of Scripture, the pure revelation of the infinite, eternal, and unchangeable God.

In *An Experiment in Criticism* C. S. Lewis deals especially with works of literature. For all kinds of reading the original 1940 edition of Mortimer Adler's and Charles Van Doren's *How to Read a Book* is very helpful. Lest Christians devalue other kinds of reading than the Bible, we should remember that we are first creatures made in God's image and placed in His world. As redeemed sinners we read God's infallible Word in the context of that world. Thus we are called to explore, understand, and enjoy His world for His glory. Unless the Christian is a good reader generally he will not usually be a good reader of Scripture. This is not to deny that many poor readers who become Christians will become good readers by first reading their Bibles; but reading more generally should follow if they wish to be most useful in Christ's service.

Preachers especially must be deep and wide readers. The breadth of Paul's reading stands as an exquisite example. Joel Nederhood counsels ministers to understand the Bible as a "cultural tract," a document with a solitary purpose, divinely inspired to destroy idolatry.[122] Moses was profoundly aware of his culture and blessed by God's Providence with "all the learning of Egypt." The preacher must plumb the depths of Scripture to speak to our times, demonstrating the irrelevance of idolatry and calling people to change by God's grace. "The Bible is our environment." The preacher must be "addicted to reading."[123]

The aversion which the present generation displays toward reading, must be dealt with early in a child's development. The patterns of knowing are established from birth by exposure to various media of communication. A balance and hierarchy of communication should be established by parents. Face-to-face interaction, in the family, church, neighborhood and general culture come first. Good listening and speaking come next. Reading, especially good reading, should be cultivated before much exposure to the visual media is allowed. Then parents should teach their children critical skills

---

[121] Jacques Barzun, "An American Commencement." *Columbia* (June 1988) 50.
[122] Nederhood, "Effective Preaching in a Media Age," class notes.
[123] *Ibid.*

for assessing each medium. Television is "undifferentiated in its accessibility;" it requires no skill to use.[124] Because children tend to take the path of least resistance, the immediate gratification offered by the visual media, will surely lead them down the wrong pathway, left to themselves.

As we have seen, Marshall McLuhan participated little in the electronic environment. He was one of the most literate men of his or any generation. Thus we are not surprised to hear: "For all their obsolescence he himself finds books 'a warm, visceral, tactile medium'..."[125] He eliminated the clutter from his life to read and think and teach face-to-face. His son Eric echoes this effort with simple advice for media ecologizing: "This could also take the form of advisories concerning exposure: e.g., 'no more than three hours per week of e-mail or Internet' without necessitating, say, four or five hours of direct exercise of literacy as counterbalance (by reading a novel printed on paper—or something)."[126] The Christian must order his time so as to master the art of meditation and develop critical intelligence.

Along with this some of the simplest pleasures and activities need to be revived as part of creating a Christian counter-cultural environment. Conversation, pure and simple, informal, with no other agenda needs to be *planned*. Reading aloud is a wonderful way to promote orality and literacy in tandem. It also enhances sermon listening ability. Reading and writing are essential to our humanity. Letter writing stands out as unique in the age of email. The writing of handwritten notes and letters offers an effective counter-environment. With the advent of email, added to the telephone, the art of letter writing has fallen on hard times. Handwriting is no longer taught in most schools. Thus regular mail, or as I prefer to call it "real mail," as opposed to the sneering pejorative, "snail mail," has been reduced to mostly "junk mail." This makes every hand addressed envelope look like a treasure in the mail box. Some organizations have resorted to hand addressing, or what looks like handwriting, to avoid its being discarded without being opened. Listen to what Robert Grudin has to say in *Time and the Art of Living*.

> ...the act of producing a letter, even one which is never mailed, necessitates a form of creative concentration which can improve our lives. Copies of our own letters are useful for our records and memories. If their recipients think them worth saving, they can have value and effect far beyond that of the spoken word. In friendship, the letter is not only a message but a gift, a physical symbol of esteem and affection. In business or politics, the letter can not only express the concerns of the moment but remain as a document of such concerns, available for

---

[124] Postman, *The Disappearance of Childhood*, 79.
[125] Jane Howard, "Oracle of the Electric Age," *Life Magazine* (28 February 1966) 96.
[126] Eric McLuhan, "Response to Tom Farrell," mediaecology@ube.ubalt.edu (6 November 1999).

prolonged scrutiny by more than one reader. Moreover, while speakers and listeners in a debate are vulnerable to emotion and subject to fallacy, the well-written letter remains calm and crisp and is subject to nothing except superior reason. It can convince the open-minded, goad the weak-hearted, give our opponents an exact index of the level and intensity of our commitment, and be quoted by those who agree with us. But perhaps most importantly, our letters are the proof and body of our concern for life in its detail and our conviction that this concern should be shared with others.[127]

The Christian faith is not only threatened by the devaluation of written and printed texts, but is in the best position, indeed the only position, to withstand the worst features of modernity. Our narrative comes in a text which originates in heaven. Our narrative is about the true God who acts in history. Our narrative helps us to begin to understand all other narratives, texts and contexts, and to know that whatever we do not understand, is nonetheless understood by the ultimate Author.

Worshipping and Communing: Connecting with Heaven in the Church

A well balanced sensorium will avail little without the soul being connected to heaven and heaven's glory, God. I have suggested that in the act of worship the oral, the visual and the written are experienced in a healthy balance. The result will be, for the alert worshipper, that the soul is thus best fortified to stand firm in the electronic environment. But the purpose of worship should not be confused with this one great benefit. All balance and all beauty is a reflection of the glory of God Himself. He is the purpose and sole object of worship. In His presence the heart is strengthened to resist the idolatrous temptations of our world. As we shall see in the next chapter it is public worship where the Second Commandment comes into its own. It is just here that the church must protect itself against the incursions of the worst electronic influences of our age. If we are not connected with the text of Scripture, and the God who speaks through it, here then the battle is lost. Here our communion with God begins and ends in the cycle of life in a fallen world. Here we are fortified by our communication, the communion of persons, by the body of Christ, in whose midst our Savior promises to be present (Matt. 18:20).

Preaching, based on the covenanal document of Scriptures, unites the community in the Word of God. McLuhan's characterization of the written word as "a detribalizing force," fails to account for the "tribalizing" power of the Scriptures as a community document. The preaching of God's Word unites

---

[127] Robert Grudin, *Time and the Art of Living* (New York: Tichnor & Fields, 1982) 142, 143.

the people of God, connecting them with it in the present, even as the text itself connects the church with the past and the future. The church, reading and hearing the Word of God, is united in the most powerful way conceivable. It would seem that the tendency of the written and printed word to "detribalize" is as much a function of human sin as it is of the medium itself. Thus it prevents the worst tendencies of both the printed word and the electronic media to individualize. It creates the most powerful counter environment imaginable.

8

The Fourth Temptation: The Compromise of the Church

> *Suppose there had been a fourth temptation*
> *when our Lord encountered the Devil in the wilderness*
> *—this time an offer of networked TV appearances,*
> *in prime time, to proclaim and expound his Gospel.*
> *Would this offer, too, have been rejected like the others?*
> *If so, why?*
>
> —Malcolm Muggeridge[1]
>
> *The prophetic complaint of the Old Testament*
> *seems to preclude any modern attempt at utilizing*
> *the sacred groves of TV and magazine*
> *as basic bearers of the Good News.*
>
> —Duane Mehl[2]

It is the church, and not the world, to which the bulk of the warnings in the Bible against idolatry are addressed. The seductive nature of idolatry requires the vigilance of the church, especially of its preachers, who shepherd the souls of God's people principally through preaching and teaching God's Word. "Confronting idols is the corollary of letting God be God, living by faith alone, and practicing the principle of *ecclesia semper reformanda*—the church always needs reformation."[3] Now we will focus on the church's use of electronic media. We must be careful to distinguish between the use of electronic media by individual Christians or Christians organizations, and the church as an institution. The church as an institution, mandated by our Lord,

---

[1] Malcolm Muggeridge, *Christ and the Media* (Grand Rapids: William B. Eerdmans Publishing Company, 1977) 30.
[2] Duane Mehl, "Mass Media and the Future of Preaching," *Concordia Theological Monthly* 41 (1970): 210.
[3] Richard Keyes, "The Idol Factory," in Os Guinness and John Seel, eds. *No God But God* (Chicago: Moody Press, 1992) 25.

has a narrowly defined mission in this world. Thus certain uses of media may be quite legitimate for individual Christians or Christians organizations, which would not be legitimate for the church *per se*. For example a Christian book distributor, or a Christian business man might take full advantage of the commercial dimension of television or radio, whereas the church must not. The church, as a divinely-instituted society, is the burden of this chapter.

SUCCUMBING TO TEMPTATION:
THE CHURCH TRANSFORMED BY THE ELECTRONIC MEDIA

Marshall McLuhan didn't mince words when he observed: "Our conventional response to all media, namely that it is how they are used that counts, is the numb stance of the technological idiot."[4] The term "idiot," is only *apparently* uncharitable. The original Greek word (ἰδιώτης 1 Cor. 14:24 "unlearned," 2 Cor. 11:6 "untrained in speech") indicated ignorance of a particular language. The point is that, as a culture, we are largely ignorant of what we are doing with media, or more precisely, what the media are doing to us. That too was McLuhan's point—technological ignorance. In a 1977 interview with Edward Wakin, McLuhan clarifies this by saying, "One of the effects of innovation is somnambulism. When people are under a heavy strain psychically they tend to cave in, to turn zombie."[5] Most Christians, and most Americans, are totally unaware of the nature of media. Christian criticism of the electronic media in particular focuses almost entirely on content, rather than on the nature of the media themselves—as grammar and environment. Thus, the average American and, therefore, the average Christian says, "They are just tools." "The problem with TV is all the sex and violence." But, as we have seen, every tool changes the way we think about and experience life. Remember the "horseless carriage" illusion with the automobile. People naively think it simply gets us places faster. Actually it has radically changed the fabric of American life for both good and ill. When it comes to the electronic media it is almost as if the church has taken the advice of Oscar Wilde seriously. When asked what he recommended in the face of temptation, he quipped, "Give in to it."

Communication technologies are even more dramatic in their effect. In *The Disappearance of Childhood*, Neil Postman summarizes the three types of

---

[4] Marshall McLuhan, *Understanding Media: The Extensions of Man* (New York: McGraw-Hill Book Company, 1964) 18.
[5] Marshall McLuhan, "Our Only Hope Is Apocalypse," in *The Medium and the Light: Reflections on Religion*, edited by Eric McLuhan and Jacek Szlarek (Toronto: Stoddart Publishing Co. Limited, 1999) [midway].

changes which such technologies bring into culture, based on Harold Innis's work. They change the "structure of interests," by refocusing what we think *about*. They change the "character of symbols," by altering the visual and linguistic tools *with which we think*. They change the "nature of community," reorganizing *social structure*. Machines are ideas with consequences;[6] consequences with which the church must reckon. We have explored the importance of written communication in the history of the church going back to Mosaic times. In the Reformation era, printing was a powerful means of spreading the gospel. Luther declared printing to be "God's highest and extremist act of grace, whereby the business of the Gospel is driven forward." Postman observes that print made the language of the common man into a mass medium for the first time in history.[7] Printing helped undermine the centralized authority of the Papacy, just as the image media of painting and sculpture had once intensified its iconography.[8]

Lewis Mumford describes the enthusiasm with which the machine was greeted: "Mechanics became the new religion, and it gave to the world a new messiah: the machine. ...The machine came forward as the new demiurge that was to create a new heaven and a new earth."[9] The advent of the electronic media elicited similar encomiums from secular and sacred quarters alike. Morse's question, after the first telegraph message was sent, "What hath God wrought?" seems to have received an almost unanimous answer from Evangelicals—a great blessing! Mid-twentieth century television teacher Bishop Fulton Sheen summed up the naive attitude of the church toward television when he declared, "Radio is like the Old Testament, hearing wisdom, without seeing; television is like the New Testament because in it the wisdom becomes flesh and dwells among us."[10] While we should appreciate the effects of the printing press on culture and the church, there is a vast difference between word based media and the image media. Director of communications for the Chicago Federation of Churches, Gary Rowe, chastises clergymen who resist the use of television for ministry: "It's not news to say that we are living with a new consciousness about reality. Church professionals need to get involved with the miraculous opportunities of telecommunications and match actions to their words." For Rowe, thinking about Guttenberg and McLuhan, during the sixties, was a "pleasant fad." Rowe concludes with breathless optimism: "As the great moments in television attest, there is a vast appetite for

---

[6] Neil Postman, *The Disappearance of Childhood* (London: Allen, 1983) 23.
[7] *Ibid.*, 33.
[8] *Ibid.*, 39.
[9] Lewis Mumford, *Technics and Civilization* (New York: Harcourt, Brace and World, 1934) 45, 58.
[10] Daniel. *Media and the American Mind: From Morse to McLuhan* (Chapel Hill: University of North Carolina Press, 1982) 188.

a larger vision of the world, our connections with each other, and the immediacy of thought and feeling that can bind us together. Surely we have community, drama, symbolism, and information ready for a hungry audience. Let's brighten our ideas and light up the tube."[11]

Covenant religion has always given priority to the Word written, read and preached.[12] Since there are always both benefits and liabilities to every medium, we must look for both in the electronic potpourri. Because the electronic and image media have become the vernacular of our culture, we must consider their potential for communicating the gospel. However, if we accept them uncritically, we will allow the curse to have its way, and the liabilities will outweigh the benefits. Postman has asserted that Morse has been more influential because Darwin's ideas are debatable, whereas Morse's idea of electric communication is not.[13] So words are debatable and images are not. The instantaneousness of electronic words take on the characteristics of images. In the church the nature as well as the messages of electronic media must be debated. Presently there is little substantive discussion on this subject, even in circles where one would expect it.

One example of our dilemma is found in the insightful writing of James Hughes, who is a member of the Reformed Presbyterian Church of North America, a conservative denomination carrying on the Scottish covenanting tradition. At the denominational website his electronic book is available to be downloaded. *The Church in Cyberspace* provides much useful information on the development of current technologies, especially the "Electronic Highway." However, despite having read Marshall McLuhan, Hughes makes a number of statements throughout the book revealing that he has not done much thinking about the nature of the media themselves. "Television, like any other tool of communication, is in itself neither good nor bad."[14] While it is true that *things* are neither good or bad in themselves, in an ethical sense, we have seen that every medium of communication has its inherent benefits and liabilities. Every medium is an idea, a new way of perceiving. The point is that our assessment of "tools" is complicated and must be done from many different angles as we have seen in chapters 5 and 7. The church needs to take this question much more seriously than it has hitherto. Media are *never* just tools, and must never be used as such in communicating the message of the gospel.

---

[11] Gary Rowe, "The Living Room Pew." *The Christian Ministry* 12:3 (May 1981):11-15.

[12] Cf. Hughes Oliphant Old. *The Reading and Preaching of the Scriptures in the Worship of the Christian Church*. 3 vols. (Grand Rapids: Eerdmans, 1998, 1998, 1999).

[13] Postman, *The Disappearance of Childhood*, 69.

[14] James R. Hughes, *The Church in Cyberspace: The Coming Impact of the Computer on the Church*. [WWW document] URL http://www.reformed.com/pub/cyber.htm [9 September 1999].

Marketing the Church: Building an Audience

The ultimate in media naiveté is found in the Church Growth Movement. It differs from the next two examples of compromise in that it is an earnest, if very misguided, attempt to fulfill the Great Commission, and reach our culture for Christ. The founder of the movement, Donald McGavran, was a missionary to India in the 1930s. Os Guinness connects McGavran's experience in Third-World missions with the "fateful sea-change" in American Evangelicalism during the era of Jacksonian populism, when technique began to replace truth, and serving God was eclipsed by "an emphasis on 'serving the self' in serving God."[15] Os Guinness's *Dining with the Devil* (1993) is one of the most insightful and balanced popular critiques of this movement. The title tells it all. Using the analyses of cultural anthropology and the techniques of American marketing, the movement which began in the Institute of Church Growth in Eugene, Oregon in 1961, came into prominence in the 1970s as the Institute moved to Fuller Theological Seminary. By the late seventies Church Growth mounted a formidable challenge to everything traditional in American Evangelicalism.[16]

The phrase "marketing the church" originated with George Barna, who founded the Barna Research Group in 1984. This idea has been planted in the soil of a long history of the American church aligning itself with business technique. The concept is simple. The church is like a business, if not quite actually one. Thus, the formula for success, which is the goal of the church, is to analyse the market and adapt the "techniques" of ministry to meet the needs of that market. Of course, we are always assured that this does not involve doctrinal compromise, but is rather a matter of "packaging." Among the marketing tools to be learned at a seminar in 1991, offered at Reformed Theological Seminary in Jackson, Mississippi, are: "Seven steps involved in Biblically marketing a local church, without compromising the gospel...Identification of 17 traits common to churches that are successful and growing." Effective communication means that "the media, the messages, and the means of measuring their impact" must be analyzed by the local church. Among the lectures given by Dr. Barna are: "User Friendly Churches: Where Ministry Is Working."[17] This is American business at its best, and American

---

[15] Os Guinness, *Dining with the Devil: The Megachurch Movement Flirts with Modernity* (Grand Rapids: Baker Books, 1993) 20, 27. David Eby's *Power Preaching for Church Growth: The Role of Preaching in Growing Churches* (Fearn, UK: Christian Focus Publications, 1996) provides an excellent summary of the Church Growth Movement in chapters 14 and 15.
[16] Eby, *Power Preaching for Church Growth*, 95, 96.
[17] Luder G. Whitlock, Jr., "Marketing the Church," a brochure advertising a seminar held at Reformed Theological Seminary in Jackson, Mississippi, on January 29, 1991. In 1991 Barna wrote *User Friendly Churches: What Christians Need to Know About the Churches People Love to Go To*.

ecclesiology at its worst. The impact of this movement on worship and preaching can hardly be overestimated.

For the present purpose, two problems present themselves in this movement. First, the primacy of preaching is almost totally neglected. After ransacking 48 books on Church Growth, David Eby found that only 20 pages out of 10,000 dealt with preaching. Only one out of 377 Doctor of Ministry dissertations submitted to Fuller Seminary, between 1971 and 1995, were written on preaching.[18] What Eby did find on preaching was not encouraging. Consider this from the 1990 book *The Baby Boomerang*, "Limit your preaching to roughly 20 minutes, because boomers do not have much time to spare. And don't forget to keep your messages light and informal, liberally sprinkling them with humor and personal anecdotes."[19] Powerful proclamation of the gospel, a clear call to repent and believe, take up your cross, deny yourself and follow Jesus Christ, are terrible marketing, according to Church Growth thinking.

Second, the influences of the electronic media are uncritically affirmed as a blessing. While most of the literature of Church Growth does not deal explicitly with the electronic media, the assumption that we should give people what they want is a tacit affirmation of one of the greatest liabilities of the electronic media—its man-centeredness. Rather than challenge the idols of our culture, Church Growth has chosen, perhaps in many cases unwittingly, to invite them to dinner. The lack of a well developed Christian mind and sensibility has allowed the Trojan Horse of Modernity into the church.[20] "Churches are right to seek ways to communicate with and appeal to contemporary society. They must remember, however, that while we need to reach out to postmoderns, they dare not leave them where they found them."[21] While not catering to idolatrous tendencies the church certainly needs to be aware of the idols, identify them for what they are, and gently wean their worshipers away from them. The preacher, as we shall see, must seek ways to overcome the sins, propensities and weaknesses of our culture relative to the way in which he preaches; but to overcome, not to succumb, must be the goal.

The following ad on the religious page of *The Union Leader*, Manchester, NH, Friday, April 9,1999, illustrates how pervasive the Church Growth influence has become.

"This Sunday: 'God's antidote to busyness'

---

[18] Eby, *Power Preaching for Church Growth*, 102-105.
[19] *Ibid.*, 104.
[20] Keyes, "The Idol Factory," 31.
[21] Gene Edward Veith, Jr., *Loving God with All Your Mind: How to Survive and Prosper as a Christian in the Secular University and Post-Christian Culture* (Westchester, IL: Crossway Books, 1987) 227.

When was the last time you had fun at church?"

**** CHAPEL OF CHURCH GROWTH ****
Worship Celebration at 10 am

- fresh gourmet coffee
- practical messages with eye-catching graphics
- loving childcare provided and children's church

Another church advertised in the same newspaper eighteen months later boldly announces: "...meeting Saturday nights for your convenience." The closing line in the ad invites the reader to "Come visit us at New Life and help begin a new church ... *with you in mind.*"

Being "user friendly" has become the controlling goal of the marketing church. Religious correspondent Terry Mattingly describes the Metropolitan Community Church of San Diego: "Greeters handed out 'celebration folders' instead of bulletins. Clergy wore jeans and polo shirts instead of vestments and the faithful sang along to slides projected on a wall, instead of using hymnals. The call to worship became a 'warm up' and the service ended with a 'see you next week' benediction, followed by pizza. The 'action words'—that's the sermon—led into question-and-answer sessions. Often the clergy yielded the floor to 'guest headliners' who sang, spoke on social issues or discussed their latest books."[22] Of course, MCC is essentially a gay and lesbian church. But the "conservative" Evangelicals take the same approach, and nobody has done it better than Bill Hybels.

Pastor of Willow Creek Community Church in South Barrington, Illinois, Hybels has one of the most successful mega-churches in the country—almost 15,000 people per Sunday in 1990. Rejecting much of his Christian Reformed background, Hybels sought to answer the question: How can we make church so it isn't what baby boomers always say: boring, predictable and irrelevant? The answer is "Ask consumers what they want, then let them (as they say at Burger King) have it their way. At non-denominational Willow Creek, that means a slick, show-biz service where drama and soft rock are served up on a stage washed in pink and blue spotlights. A soft-sell sermon is delivered by Hybels from a Lucite lectern. It's been put down as pop gospel, fast-food theology, McChurch. Hybels says his message is rock-solid Biblical principles, only the medium is unorthodox. No one disputes it sells like Big Macs."[23]

---

[22] Terry Mattingly, "Making Churches 'User Friendly,'" *The Union Leader* (21 March 1998).
[23] Cindy Lafavre Yorks, "Gimme That New Time Religion," *U. S. A. Weekend* (13-15 April, 1990): 4-7.

There's the rub: as if unorthodox media will yield orthodox Christians. "Hybels ...wants to remain doctrinally sound but with his dualistic approach this has become entirely impossible. For, as Paul says, the form of the message and its content belong together (1 Cor. 2:13)."[24] Once marketing dominates the church's agenda "the concern is not with 'finding an audience to hear their message but rather with finding a message to hold their audience.' After all, when the audience and not the message is sovereign, the good news of Jesus Christ is no longer the end, but just the means."[25] It has always been the temptation of the church to use the wrong means to achieve God's ends, but it is an even greater temptation to use the right means as ends in themselves. In either case God's glory is diminished, and the purity of His sovereign grace is sullied. The reader controls the text.

The question Christians must ask is: What kind of an audience do we build when we market the church? The tragic answer is that we gather a group of people who are consumer oriented, who may have come to church for the wrong reasons, and who find as Barna attests that "the Christian life-style and belief structure...[are]...impractical and unreasonable for today's world."[26] David Wells sums up the result: "The audience is sovereign, and ideas find legitimacy and value only within the marketplace."[27] The gospel, on the other hand, is not a "marketable product." Sinners do not know what they need.[28] The most important question of all is: What kind of a God are we communicating? Is He the majestic sovereign God who uses means, but doesn't depend on them, to fulfill His purposes, or is he really just a psycho-sociological phenomenon? Despite their best intentions, and I believe many have them, the Church Growth movement relegates God and His truth to second fiddle. Technique is king. A brochure, which I recently received in the mail, highlights the problem. It is titled: "Fail-proof Church Fundraising." Inside we are told: "Fund raising does not happen just because you are doing God's work. ...This remarkable new guide makes the fund raising process less mysterious ...more manageable and useful. ...Low on philosophy, high on nuts-and-bolts, this book fills an urgent void."[29] Whatever happened to prayer and tithing? One can barely imagine a more blatant example of American Pragmatism as it affects the church.

---

[24] Jacobus De Jong, "User Friendly Evangelism," *Lux Mundi* 17:1 (March 1998): 4.
[25] Os Guinness, *Dining with the Devil*, 78.
[26] In Eby, *Power Preaching for Church Growth*, 105.
[27] David F. Wells, *No Place for Truth or Whatever Happened to Evangelical Theology?* (Grand Rapids: Eerdmans, 1993) 207.
[28] David Wells, "Our Culture of Chaos," Lecture notes, July 12, 1996, L'Abri Fellowship, Southborough, MA.
[29] Precept Press, Chicago, IL.

Discarnate Christianity: The First Church of Cyberspace

The ultimate in compromise is revealed in the existence of The First Church of Cyberspace.[30] At www.Godweb.org one can experience a poignant example of contemporary Gnosticism in the church. This "church" offers the complete escape from space and time; it is precisely what McLuhan meant by "discarnate." Its motto is: "Building a Church for the New Millennium Now." That this website is sponsored by the mainline Presbyterian Church in the USA is not surprising for those who are aware of the Postmodern direction this denomination has taken in recent years. Its rejection of Biblical orthodoxy in the 1920s provided the soil for the more recent incursion of radical feminism which has taken to "reimagining" God as Sophia, and giving a prominent voice to the Gay and Lesbian lobby. The Neo-Pagan overtones of this movement are blatant. With this comes the Gnostic impulse toward antinomianism and the transcendence of space and time, which is epitomized at this website.

Enter Cyberspace. In 1998 the PCUSA founded The First Church of Cyberspace. Here is the perfect medium to transcend the nasty imperfections encountered in the real church. One immediately encounters the purported virtues of the "virtual" church upon entrance to the website through the motto: "Building a Church for the New Millennium Now." There is a dogmatic urgency about this motto. Church historian Darryl Hart has noted that the penchant to extol the virtues of the electronic church goes back to the 1950s when "dial-a-prayer" ministry became popular.[31] Since then telemarketing has become a popular vehicle for home missions work in most denominations, liberal or conservative. But nothing equals the opportunities for "electronic" ministry afforded by the Internet. One church website designer makes the extravagant claim that "all elements of congregational life can be experienced through the Internet."[32] Equally serious is the arrogant "trendier than thou" attitude that getting the church on the Internet is keeping pace with the "real world." The "Minister of Technology" of a Presbyterian Megachurch recently opined that a failure to come up to speed technologically will render the church "completely irrelevant."[33] The importunate "now" in First Church's motto is an exhortation to stop being bogged down in the past.

Back to The First Church of Cyberspace (FCC), wherever that may be. The home page is replete with sanctuary, prayers, and sermons. One may listen to everything from J. S. Bach to Jani. There is a special section for "Adult

---

[30] http://www.Godweb.org (17 Aug 1999) © 1999 About.com, Inc. All rights reserved.
[31] Darryl Hart, "No Assembly Required," *Nicotine Theological Journal* 3:3 (July 1999): 1.
[32] *Ibid.*
[33] *Ibid.* I owe the apt phrase "trendier than thou" to the late Charles Dennison, church historian of the Orthodox Presbyterian Church.

Christianity," perhaps in contrast to the adolescence of everything else at the site. There is an art gallery and a large section on "Alternative Religions." New Age spirituality is treated as simply another road to wholeness. Instructions for using the I-Ching are available. The sanctuary has three Eastern Orthodox iconographic screens with a virtual burning flame at the center.

Four ministers "oversee" this church. None is identified as Pastor. They pretend to represent a perfect diversity: two white Anglo-Saxon men, one white Anglo-Saxon woman, and one black man. A sample of the sermons is very revealing. Charles Henderson, presumably the "Senior Pastor," posts a sermon titled "We Would See Jesus."[34] Cyberspace will give the answer we need. "Biblical affirmations, theological statements, creeds and sermons, however effective, still leave us with that elementary desire. We'd like to have a sharper image and a closer knowledge of this man whom we call the Savior of the world. Fortunately, today, on the Internet, there is a profusion of images and artwork which provide us with plenty of material to look at as we pursue this age-old question. As there were no cameras at the time of Christ, as there were no Polaroids, no Nikons, and certainly no video cassette recorders, we'll have to rely upon the imagination of the artists to render an image of what he must have looked like." The text of the sermon is peppered with artistic representations of Jesus. The implication is clear: the question of the Greeks in the Gospel text is about visual images. Henderson goes on to describe the variety of depictions as revealing the artists' background and not an historically accurate picture. Then the author's message: "as Christ was divine, in him we find the very best of all that we aspire to for ourselves." Here is pure Gnosticism: the seed of the divine in Everyman.

Predictably all of his references and quotes cover the range from Byzantine to Russian Orthodox, Carl Sandberg to Salvidor Dali, without once mentioning the historic Presbyterian and Reformed tradition of which he is nominally a part. At bottom Christianity is a socio-psychological reality. "As Christians we find the Christ figure in each other, for Christianity is not a solitary experience, it is something we find in community. Wherever two or three are gathered, there is the Christ. And there, more accurately than any artist can render it, is the face of Jesus. In the end we can locate the Christ figure most meaningfully in each other's eyes." The real irony here is the assumption that somehow the cyberchurch can promote "community." Can the multitudes visiting a website possibly have *anything* to do with the reality which Christ describes as "wherever two or three are gathered"? The First

---

[34] Charles Henderson, "We Would See Jesus." http://www.Godweb.org (17 Aug 1999) © 1999 About.com, Inc. All rights reserved.

Church of Cyberspace is literally "Utopian" from the Greek meaning "no place." Instead of being "where it's at" it is "nowheresville." As Hart perceptively observes: "no assembly required."[35]

Stephen C. Rose's sermon titled "You Are The Temple," based on 1 Corinthians 3:16, also extols the virtues of the Internet: "Cyberspace is offering the world another chance to figure out what the curious advent of one Jesus Christ actually means." He proposes to explain "what religion is finally all about." Then a fatal concession "...this preacher believes Jesus Christ is what religion is about, *but* if you are thinking it is because Jesus beats the competition, think again." Jesus came "to abolish religion as the world has known it. ...the good news of Jesus makes sense right at the cutting edge of the world that is presently evolving. Right here online." How perfectly Postmodern! The authoritative basis for the preacher's assertions: "My reference is available to all: It is the Bible interpreted as Jesus interpreted it—as a living and evolving body of understanding. ..." and the church is just "me and you." Christianity is about life not doctrine: "He gave us Beatitudes which are a way of living, not an invitation to attend the Temple." Consistent with Cyberecclesiology Jesus "eliminated the middle man." The church is ultimately unnecessary. "Reject churches entirely—never go on Sunday? That is not the point. YOU are the temple, so what is a church?" Then the magic of Cyberspace is invoked: "He comes to you NOW in Cyberspace hoping that somehow, through this curious medium, you will understand that you are, in prospect, a temple of God." At its best the church "resources" people to create "Christ people." "You are the pearl of great price."[36] Here is a breathtaking but predictable corruption of the New Testament text. Christ and the message of His redeeming grace is the pearl of great price. But the Gnostic impulse is irrepressible. Man is divinized. Cyberspace is the medium of divinization. Ironically at the bottom of my copy of this sermon, undermining the divinely appointed institution of the church, and minimizing the supernatural work of the Holy Spirit as it does, is the webpage option "Return to Sanctuary."

Katherine R. Henderson's sermon "A Vision of One's Own"[37] presents a highly subjective point of view. In seeking to "explain" the Jacob's ladder passage in Genesis 28 she observes "I realized that it was not so much the words in Gen. 28 that captured my attention.... But the vision. God spoke, yes...there were words...But there was the vision." Here is the epitome of the Postmodern attitude toward Scripture and written texts of all kinds. Words are

---

[35] Hart, "No Assembly Required," *Nicotine Theological Journal*.
[36] Stephen C. Rose, "You Are The Temple." http://www.Godweb.org (16 Aug 1999) © 1999 About.com, Inc. All rights reserved. Emphasis mine.
[37] Katherine R. Henderson, "A Vision of One's Own." http://www.Godweb.org (16 Aug 1999) © 1999 About.com, Inc. All rights reserved.

those nasty concrete things with which Postmoderns are compelled to communicate their disdain for texts. She continues, "I realized for myself this was not a time for words, for articulation, but a more primitive time...a season of the senses, for feeling the coolness of that stone, for hearing the whirring of the wind while swinging on a swing, or feeling the sticky, sweet wetness of a baby's skin in August....A time for images, impressions and visions, not words." Everything is reduced to an experience. All is a stream of consciousness. Genesis 28 teaches us that we are afraid like the traditionalist Jacob to re-imagine God. Rather we should take the tack of the feminists who "speak of the mother God or goddess, or others see God as black or peoples of the third world portray God as standing with the poor in opposition to the policies of our own government." Scripture itself, perhaps especially, is guilty of traditionalism: "But if we filter out every image of God that does not match what we have read about in Scriptures or heard about from others like ourselves, then we disqualify ourselves as a people of vision. ...We are not confined to the visions of God in pages long ago." No, we must look within for vision, where the spark of the divine lives. "If our pictures of God are not alive within us, people will know, they will see right through. ...Is that not what Jesus encourages us to do, for he was the one who encountered the other, the numinous as a daily experience." We are after all a post-Kantian people who must project ourselves into the unknown.

Among the many ironies discovered at this website is the fact that, while the word "now" is used relentlessly, the sermons were posted in the first half of 1998. A return to the site in February 2000 revealed the same sermons—surprisingly out of date for such an up-to-date enterprise. Rose and Henderson begin their "sermons" by identifying where they live, as if to assure us that space and time still have some relevance. This comes across as a kind of "cyber-slip." Ms. Henderson goes into great poetic detail to describe her stone house in the country. There is no redemption, no suffering Savior, no historical death and resurrection of Jesus the Christ. No Incarnation. But if you desire to be a disembodied spirit, cyberspace is the place (sic) to be. Jennifer Cobb's *Cybergrace: The Search for God in the Digital World*, is a classic example of the Gnosticism and Neo-Paganism resurgent within mainline Protestantism. A graduate of Union Theological Seminary in New York, and a disciple of Teilhard de Chardin, Cobb seeks an "alchemical marriage" between technology and spirituality. Exploring Celtic religion in England and France helped her to understand the "sacred dimension of the universe," and find "wholeness in a computational world."[38]

---

[38] Jennifer Cobb, *Cybergrace: The Search for God in the Digital World* (New York: Crown Publishers, Inc., 1998) ix-xii.

Does this mean that there is no appropriate use of the Internet by Christians? Is the Gnostic, Postmodern tendency inherent in the medium, or the medium of media? Certainly not, if, and only if, it is used with great caution, as indeed dis-incarnation is its tendency. The church does not lack examples of the thoughtful use of the Internet. A fine example is the website of the Orthodox Presbyterian Church <www.opc.org>. It functions essentially as an information center. It does not seek to replace the ministry of the church in any way, because its conception and design has been based on a prudent policy, which is in turn rooted in a Biblical conception of the mission of the church. There are hundreds of quality Web sites of this kind, being used fruitfully by Christians and by the church as an institution.

Profitable Spirituality: Beliefnet

A recent article in *USA Today* announced the formation of a new religious website:

> Beliefnet [is] a Web site launched last week that aims to be an on-line spiritual community for people of all religious backgrounds... Waldman and co-founder Bob Nylen are gearing up to sell ads and plan to add an e-commerce section by spring—everything from crosses and meditation cushions to books, music, travel and charity donations on-line.
>
> Beliefnet manages to gracefully walk a fine line, balancing inspiration and practical information, entertainment and spiritual substance. Staffers in New York package news and features on religion, spirituality and culture, as well as family and "milestones," deeper issues raised by births, deaths and the rites of passage in between....
>
> Many of the articles are by a diverse group of more than 50 columnists, top names in religion and spirituality, from orthodox to fringe. They include Episcopal Bishop John Shelby Spong, Jesus scholar Marcus Borg, Catholic priest/sociologist Andrew Greeley, Buddhist Lama Surya Das, Rabbi Joseph Telushkin and Margot Adler, a writer on goddess spirituality.
>
> Even though Beliefnet's scope is broad and inclusive, "our goal is not to create one big, bland amalgam religion," Waldman says. He expects the site to be controversial. "It can't help but be, dealing with death and sex and abortion and God." But in a multicultural society, he adds, "people will tend to disagree, and the Net is a great place to explore our diversity. People are coming from so many different

directions, there's a need for information and help in sorting all this out."[39]

Lance Rose observes that Beliefnet is "A demonstration, as it were, that now we can aggregate religions at a web site as if they were different brands of laundry soap on the supermarket shelf ..."[40] There is a clear connection between the commercial and the inclusive. Just as we have a wide range of products for everyone, so a wide range of religious preferences to suit all needs, and thereby build the market, the bottom line. Every page "outside" the sanctuary of the First Church of Cyberspace is adjacent to a strip of advertising. This, of course, is everywhere on the web and does not stand out as unusual in a commercial environment. The best airfares and books prices are among the ads. Then among the Cyberchurch choices just after "Pagan/Wiccan Religion" is "Stock quotes." It is not accidental that the electronic galaxy is the context in which the commercialization of the church has emerged. As the church naively, and in some cases knowingly, participates in the electronic world, which is driven largely by commercial, not communicative, motives, it is no wonder that narcissism and consumerism are promoted and reflected in the Church itself.

Today, similar to the Middle Ages, when superstitious and subjective expressions of Christianity thrived, the image is the chief means of communicating with the masses. The Charismatic Movement has experienced a revival in tandem with the electrifying of communication. Since images have taken center stage, by mid century, the Charismatic movement has begun to dominate the Evangelical church. This should not be surprising, for at the heart of this movement is the man-centered theology of Arminianism which looks at the reason, will and emotions of man as essentially untainted by sin. Cultural productions are thus considered "neutral." This subjective theology puts a premium on feelings, which in turn emphasizes the "needs" of the Christian, tending toward a kind of Christian narcissism. The purpose of New Testament miracles are inverted, bringing excitement and therapy to individuals, instead of glorifying God as the Author of redemption. In the New Testament Jesus performs miracles as attestations of His divine power: "What manner of man is this that the wind and the seas obey Him?" His authority to forgive sins is verified by His healing of the paralytic in Capernaum.[41]

---

[39] Lance Rose, "<nlc> Heard of Beliefnet?" nlc@bbs.thing.net (13 January 2000), quotes from http://www.usatoday.com/life/cyber/tech/cth139.htm. Leslie Miller, "A Community of Believers of All Faiths: Religious Site Strives to Be Inclusive," *USA Today* (13 Jan. 2000).
[40] Lance Rose, "<nlc> Heard of Beliefnet?" nlc@bbs.thing.net (13 January 2000).
[41] Mark 2:1-12.

Celebrity Preachers: Television Worship

Pastor and homiletics professor Warren Wiersbe boldly states, "When it comes to religious TV, I think evangelicals missed the boat completely because we didn't take time to understand the medium and how it worked... What does TV add to our ministry? I say it adds nothing to our ministry, but it can take a great deal away. TV puts God's people and God's Word into a context that can rob the message of reality."[42] "Television worship" is an oxymoron. Those for whom it is not, should consider the ways in which television distorts the Biblical concept of worship. In his now classic critique of television, *Amusing Ourselves to Death*, Neil Postman presents an overwhelming case, in his chapter on religion titled chapter titled "Shuffle Off to Bethlehem," to support the proposition that television is not a suitable medium for preaching or worship.[43]

First, television is essentially an entertainment medium. Entertainment focuses on what the audience wants, especially what a large, diverse audience wants. Worship focuses on what God wants.[44] Television creates a passive audience which demands to be entertained. "....on television, religion, like everything else, is presented, quite simply and without apology, as an entertainment. Everything that makes religion an historic, profound and sacred human activity is stripped away; there is no ritual, no dogma, no tradition, no theology, and above all, no sense of spiritual transcendence. On these shows (Schuller, Roberts, Swaggart, Falwell, Baker, Robertson) the preacher is tops. God comes out as second banana."[45] Liberal Harvard Divinity School professor Harvey Cox picks up on the irony of Fundamentalists using the tube. "This is a tension between content and form, between message and medium, that occurs when the Old Time Gospel Hour goes out on network television. ...The move from the revivalist tent to the vacuum tube has vastly amplified the voices of defenders of tradition. At the same time it has made them more dependent on the styles and assumptions inherent in the medium itself. ...a set of attitudes and values that are inimical to traditional morality. ...If the devil is a modernist, the TV evangelist may have struck a deal with Lucifer himself, who always appears—so the Bible teaches—as an angel of light."[46]

---

[42] In Douglas Van Allen Heck, "Is TV a Medium for the Gospel?" *These Expository Times* (May and June 1990): 1.
[43] Neil Postman, *Amusing Ourselves To Death: Public Discourse in the Age of Show Business* (New York: Viking Penguin, Inc., 1985) 114ff.
[44] I owe this insight to my dear wife Robin Reynolds.
[45] Postman, *Amusing Ourselves To Death*, 116, 117.
[46] Harvey Cox, *Religion in the Secular City: Toward a Postmodern Theology* (New York: Simon and Schuster, Inc., 1984) 68-70.

The entertainer is the preacher. The preacher is the celebrity who gets help like Johnny Carson from celebrity musical performers and converts. "...on television God is a vague and subordinate character. Though His name is invoked repeatedly, the concreteness and persistence of the image of the preacher carries the clear message that it is he, not He, who must be worshipped. I do not mean to imply that the preacher wishes it to be so; only that the power of a close-up televised face, in color, makes idolatry a continual hazard. Television is, after all, a form of graven imagery far more alluring than a golden calf."[47] "What makes these television preachers the enemy of religious experience is not so much *their* weaknesses but the weaknesses of the medium in which they work. ....not all forms of discourse can be converted from one medium to another."[48] Graham and Robertson have publicly and naively approved of TV as an excellent medium for preaching, overlooking ways in which the "delivery system" effects the message.

Second, television promotes secularism and inclusivism, thus undermining absolute truth. "Television favors moods of conciliation and is at its best when substance of any kind is muted."[49] It caters to the wide audience of the Neilson ratings. The revenues required to program make attracting an audience for advertising purposes the main goal of the program. TV gives people what they want. It is "user friendly" and therefore market driven. In 1990 *Newsweek* provided statistics showing the percentage of airtime devoted by television preachers to "fund raising and promotion": Oral Roberts 53%; Pat Robertson 44%; Jerry Fallwell 37%; Billy Graham and D. James Kennedy 19%.[50] Rex Humbard represents "the infantilization of theology."[51] Anti-doctrinal Evangelicals find television to be the perfect medium because emotion replaces content. Charisma is everything. As Calvin asserted, images distract from the business of the church, which is inculcating Biblical doctrine in the heart, minds, and lives of people.[52] The "television screen itself has a strong bias toward a psychology of secularism. The screen is so saturated with our memories of profane events, so deeply associated with the commercial and entertainment world that it is difficult for it to be recreated as a frame for sacred events. ...The television screen wants you to remember that its imagery is always available for your amusement and pleasure."[53]

---

[47] Postman, *Amusing Ourselves To Death*, 122, 123.
[48] *Ibid.*, 117.
[49] *Ibid.*, 116.
[50] Prof. Stephen Winzenburg, "Vital Statistics," *Newsweek* (9 April 1990): 8.
[51] Postman, *The Disappearance of Childhood*, 116.
[52] John Calvin, *Institutes of the Christian Religion*, 1559, Reprint (1 vol. in 2), The Library of Christian Classics, vol. XX, edited by John T. McNeill, translated by Ford Lewis Battles (Philadelphia: The Westminster Press, 1960) I.11.7, 107.
[53] Postman, *Amusing Ourselves To Death*, 119, 120.

Third, television is an artificial reality and does not establish, but undermines, personal relationships. It especially undermines the covenantal interaction of the congregation. On television there is no congregation. If an actual congregation is being televised it becomes like the seconds on a set, part of the setting for the *real* audience. But, the preacher cannot truly relate to anyone outside of the studio. "...there is no way to consecrate the space in which a television show is experienced."[54] The electronic church "separates the media clergy from their audience, believers from their local communities, and the experience of worship from the problems of daily affairs in the social realm. These are matters of great concern. The services of the historic Reformation churches ...have been pushed off the air. On our screens and radios worship is dominated by preachers, the community is secondary, and the Eucharist is absent."[55]

Because of its focus on faces, television gives the illusion of intimacy, when in fact the preacher does not even know that any individual viewer exists. What the preacher gains in the quantity of presence in the mass audience, he looses in the quality of presence. This is a great loss indeed. The television viewer conforms without belonging, is isolated without a unique identity. In the church each individual is a unique part of a larger corporate whole. He belongs without conforming, he is an individual without being isolated. What a contrast the Biblical picture presents of the church "speaking the truth in love," in order that it "may grow up in all things into Him who is the head—Christ—from whom the whole body, joined and knit together by what every joint supplies, according to the effective working by which every part does its share, causes growth of the body for the edifying of itself in love."[56]

Another dimension of this artificiality is what Walter Benjamin called "the decay of aura." In his 1936 essay "The Work of Art in the Age of Mechanical Reproduction," he says, "the technique of reproduction detaches the reproduced object from the domain of tradition."[57] Image media detach us from the reality of personal presence. In worship this presence is not only of the congregation, but the presence of God Himself, who promises to be present Himself in the congregation of His worshipping people. "I will praise You forever, because You have done *it;* and in the presence of Your saints I will wait on Your name, for *it is* good" (Psalm 52:9). "Let us come before His presence with thanksgiving; let us shout joyfully to Him with psalms" (Psalm 95:2).

---

[54] *Ibid.*, 118.
[55] R. William Franklin, and Joseph M. Shaw, *The Case for Christian Humanism* (Grand Rapids: William B. Eerdmans Publishing Company, 1991) 174.
[56] Eph. 4:15, 16.
[57] In Cox, *Religion in the Secular City*, 68.

Whatever naive notions preachers may have about the use of television, it is clear that "old time religion" is impossible on television. Television transforms Christianity into another religion altogether. Postman concludes: The executive director of the National Religious Broadcasters Association sums up what he calls the unwritten law of all television preachers: "You can get your share of the audience only by offering people something they want." You will note, I am sure, that this is an unusual religious credo. There is no religious leader—from the Buddha to Moses to Jesus to Mohammed to Luther—who offered people what they want. But television is not well suited to offering people what they need. It is "user friendly." It is too easy to turn off. It is at its most alluring when it speaks the language of dynamic visual imagery. It does not accommodate complex language or stringent demands. As a consequence, what is preached on television is not anything like the Sermon on the Mount. Religious programs are filled with good cheer. They celebrate affluence. Their featured players become celebrities. Though their messages are trivial, the shows have high ratings, or rather, *because* their messages are trivial, the shows have high ratings. I believe I am not mistaken in saying that Christianity is a demanding and serious religion. When it is delivered as easy and amusing, it is another kind of religion altogether.[58]

"There is no doubt, in other words, that religion can be made entertaining. The question is, By doing so, do we destroy it as an 'authentic object of culture'?"[59] Here, again, we notice a fundamental mistake in Postman's identifying the church with culture *per se*. More important is the question, By doing so, do we destroy it as "authentic," period? Paul wanted to make sure the Thessalonians understood that the means of communicating the message of the gospel must be suited to the message. "But as we have been approved by God to be entrusted with the gospel, even so we speak, not as pleasing men, but God who tests our hearts. For neither at any time did we use flattering words, as you know, nor a cloak for covetousness—God *is* witness."[60] The medium of television corrupted both the men and the message in the televangelist scandals of the eighties. The beguilement of Madison Avenue is nothing new—only its electric means are new. Just as the first century church identified and resisted the sophistic rhetoric of its day, so must the church today evaluate every medium in terms of its suitability to the glorious message of saving grace in Jesus Christ.

---

[58] Postman, *Amusing Ourselves To Death*, 121.
[59] *Ibid.*, 124.
[60] 1 Thess. 2:4, 5.

RESISTING TEMPTATION: THE CHURCH CONSECRATING THE ELECTRONIC MEDIA

The Heidelberg Catechism Lord's Day 35, Question #98 asks: "But may not images be tolerated in the churches as books for the laity? Answer: No; for we must not be wiser than God, who will not have His people taught by dumb images, but by the living preaching of His word." Samuel Ebersole nicely sums up what Christians ought to think regarding the *progressive* optimism of the world's assessment of technological innovation: "In a world where anything is possible, we cannot accept the conclusion that everything is permissible."[61] If this is true for the individual Christian, more so for the church. In dealing with the question of consecrating electronic media for use in the church's mission, as the church, we must always carefully define the goal of such use. Is it to bring the gospel to those unacquainted with the Bible's message, or for the edification of Christians? Our reflection on these questions must then move toward identifying what the Bible has to say about these areas. Only then may we take our knowledge of the nature of a particular medium and apply it to a particular aspect of the mission of the church. Pragmatism spells the death of truth.

Joel Nederhood has effectively shown how radio and television may be used for gospel witness in limited and thoughtful ways. He begins his "Mission Television Report," by warning, "As we work with this medium, we feel a tension that arises because of the nature of our mission as church and the nature of television itself."[62] He quotes Jesus' counsel to His disciples in Matthew 10:20, as He sends them out to preach the gospel, as model for Christian communication: "Wise as serpents and innocent as doves." Paul's "high degree of cultural awareness" calls us to careful reflection in using the cultural means at the church's disposal. After a survey of the tremendous dangers of television as a tool of "exceptional power," Nederhood concludes: "it is clear that the skillful use of this medium by the church which has the responsibility for communicating the most powerful message of all could have a very strong positive impact."[63] His recommendations include: technical excellence and production of intrinsically interesting material. "The entire program package is designed to communicate important information about the Bible in a way that will appeal to individuals who have only a passing acquaintance with it."[64] He warns of a danger which will be explored below.

---

[61] Samuel Ebersole, "Media Determinism in Cyberspace." http://regent.edu/acad/schcom/rojc/mdic.html, 1995.
[62] Joel Nederhood, "The Back to God Hour: Mission Television Report," *Christian Reformed Church Synod Report* (Report 1:A, Supplement, 1977) 169.
[63] *Ibid.*, 175.
[64] *Ibid.*, 178.

Television amplifies the importance of the preacher. Remember it excels with faces. Thus Nederhood recommends against "worship" programming, and in favor of a "semi-documentary approach."[65]

Nederhood ends his report with a chapter titled "A Word of Caution." The possibly dehumanizing impact of television must be carefully considered by the church. The medium once thought to have enormous potential for drawing society together has fragmented it. Television is largely commercialized and tends to have a "narcotic effect" on viewers. Nederhood leaves as an open question whether or not these effects are inherent in the medium. He concludes by insisting that while the church must not "turn aside from using television," it must not consider it to be "the great instrument that will solve our communication problem once and for all." Among his final recommendations are two which should be taken very seriously by the church. First, the entire body of Christ is responsible to contribute to the assessment of the electronic media. Second, funding must be done through the church's mission giving, and not through commercial solicitation.[66] This report should be a model for the church considering the use of electronic media in connection with the mission of the church. It is at least an excellent place to begin.

Sadly, the very institution which offers the most powerful means of withstanding modernity has so often capitulated both wittingly and unwittingly to some of the worst excesses of the whelming tide of modernity. Jacques Ellul "believes that throughout the West the secular religions are insinuating themselves into the Christian churches, or else they are absorbing Christianity into themselves."[67] In his treatise on propaganda Ellul asserts: "The psychological structures built by propaganda are not propitious to Christian beliefs." This faces the church with a dilemma: to ignore or make propaganda. If the church chooses not to use it, the mass media label the church as irrelevant. If the church uses propaganda it discovers that "people manipulated by propaganda become increasingly impervious to spiritual realities." Christianity becomes one among many myths, fitting into one of the categories created by propaganda, and "reduced to nothing more than an ideology. ...from the moment the church uses propaganda and uses it successfully, it becomes, unremittingly, a purely sociological organization," submitting "to the laws of efficiency in order to become a power in the world. ...At that moment it has chosen power above truth." Propaganda "is one of the most powerful factors of de-Christianization in the world through the psychological modifications that it

---

[65] *Ibid.*, 179.
[66] *Ibid.*, 184-188.
[67] Jacques Ellul, *The New Demons*, translated by C. Edward Hopkin (New York: Seabury Press, 1975) 209, noted in Herbert Schlossberg, *Idols For Destruction: Christian Faith and Its Confrontation With American Society.* (Nashville: Thomas Nelson, 1983) 258.

effects, through the ideological morass with which it has flooded the consciousness of the masses, through the reduction of Christianity to the level of an ideology, through the never-ending temptation held out to the church—all this is the creation of a mental universe foreign to Christianity. And this de-Christianization through the effects of one instrument—propaganda—is much greater than through all the anti-Christian doctrines."[68] The church which fails to understand that the electronic media are doctrines with their own inherent messages and presuppositions, may be very successful in gathering large numbers, but will no longer be what it set out to be.

In the end, the purpose and meaning of worship are what is at stake. Worship is meant to bring us into the very presence of Almighty God. If we wish to do away with the profundities of Christian theology then we really wish to do away with the God who gave us the Book. He is awesomely majestic and means to get our attention and become the all absorbing Reality of our lives. Thus, most of all, we must come to worship prepared to praise and know Him, and listen carefully to what He has to say through His preached Word. The medium here is Jesus Christ the Mediator, who is present through the means of grace, the preached Word, prayers, and the sacraments, as well as the whole church as His living temple, inhabited by His Spirit (Eph. 2:21; 1 Pet. 2:5). When we once understand the true nature and glory of Biblical worship we shall then be able to put the electronic media in proper perspective. Whatever legitimate uses the church may make of the electronic media, as disseminators of information, or in a limited evangelistic way, one thing is clear in the Bible: when it comes to the worship and preaching of the church those media have no place.

RESISTING TEMPTATION:
THE CHURCH AS A COUNTER ENVIRONMENT

Sven Birkerts, author of *The Guttenberg Elegies: The Fate of Reading in an Electronic Age*, raised in a non-religious Midwestern Latvian family, perceptively notes that churches, temples, and ashrams are "places that have traditionally served as repositories of the sacred. Whatever else they may be, our religions are grand stories that make a place for us."[69] Birkerts believes that the church is one of the last outposts, and therefore hopes, for preserving literacy. Our hopes should be considerably more profound and definite. The

---

[68] Jacques Ellul, *Propaganda: The Formation of Men's Attitudes*, translated by Konrad Kellen and Jean Lerner (New York: Vintage Books, 1965) 228-232.
[69] Sven Birkerts, *The Guttenberg Elegies: The Fate of Reading in an Electronic Age* (Winchester, MA: Faber and Faber, Inc., 1994) 196, 197.

church is called to preserve a message, which is true for all people, in all places and in all times. Paul writes to a new generation of preachers, when he tells Timothy: "*I write* so that you may know how you ought to conduct yourself in the house of God, which is the church of the living God, the pillar and ground of the truth. And without controversy great is the mystery of godliness: God was manifested in the flesh, justified in the Spirit, seen by angels, preached among the Gentiles, believed on in the world, received up in glory."[70]

Whatever influence we may have in our world depends on how we conduct ourselves in the church. If we compromise the worship and preaching connected with two millennia of history, if we fail to root our worship and preaching in the text of Scripture, we shall have no message for a lost world. We must take the gospel more seriously; we must take the local church more seriously; and we must take the potential of the mass electronic media for spreading the gospel less seriously. As Wells reminds us, secularization is not the enemy of spirituality, only of true spirituality.[71] Virtual reality can only be challenged by the virtuous reality of the local church. "To be sure, the local church is not exactly an ideal entity. It is full of people with problems. But it is the place where people can come together to confess their problems, their doubts and their sins; where they can remember and celebrate their common spiritual heritage and find forgiveness and hope. ...The local church is the place for realizing, making real, God's work in our lives."[72] It is the ideal place, just *because* it is filled with sinners in the process of sanctification. This is the real historical situation of the church in all ages, living by grace, and dealing with sin in communion with God and one another.

McLuhan insisted that culture in general needs a "counter-environment as a means of perceiving the dominant one."[73] With typical hyperbole he asserts that the "Old Testament from first to last is a counterblast against all technologies."[74] Let me suggest that the church, both as a Biblically ordered institution and as the living body of Christ, and the means of grace constitute the counter-environment and the counterblast, which God has provided for His people. Thus, the use of electronic communication media, especially in public worship, represents a potential threat to the church's very identity. As we have seen in chapter 5 technology must be consecrated to Christ, not rejected out of hand. However, McLuhan's "counterblast" statement sounds a warning against the Babel-like deification of humanity through its technological developments. Worship, public worship, is especially vulnerable at this point.

---

[70] 1 Tim. 3:15, 16.
[71] Wells, "Our Culture of Chaos."
[72] William F. Fore, "The Church and the Electronic Media." *The Christian Ministry* (May 1981): 8.
[73] Marshall McLuhan, *Counterblast* (London: Rapp & Whiting, 1969) 5.
[74] *Ibid.*, 38.

Historic Worship Standing in the Gap

If we have learned anything from the Media Ecologists it is that the forms of communication have everything to do with their content. Our zeal for historic worship should never be confused with an unreflective, act of desperation—clinging to tradition. Rather it must be fueled by the desire to preserve the "pure Word and worship of God," as Calvin loved to call it. That is what the Regulative Principle of worship is all about. Function follows form. This truth has escaped the members of the cult of informality. "The method of worship is determined by its contents. If one then brings in the style of the world (rock and roll) and attempts to weld this style to the gospel message, one ends up losing both the proper form and content of true Christian worship."[75] Alter the forms and the function is changed. That is precisely why God has prescribed both for His church in His infallible Word. The following reflections on worship deal with this relationship between form and content. Electronic media are not the immediate concern. However, the context of proposed innovations in worship within the Evangelical church, is clearly electronic.

Historian Darryl Hart argues that what evangelicals who prefer, what he calls "Praise & Worship (P&W),"

> to older liturgies share with academics who teach Louis L'Amour instead of Shakespeare is an inability to see the value of restraint, habit, and form. Evangelicals and the academic left believe that we need to be liberated from the past, from formalism, and from existing structures in order to come into a more intimate relationship with life or the divine. This is really quite astounding in the case of evangelicals whose public reputation depends upon defending traditional morality. Yet, the effort to remove all barriers to the expression and experience of the individual self is unmistakably present in the efforts to make worship more expressive and spontaneous. This impulse in evangelical worship repudiates the wisdom of various Christian traditions which, rather than trying to liberate the self in order to experience greater intimacy with God, hold that individuals, because of a tendency to sin and commit idolatry, need to conform to revealed and ordered patterns of faith and practice. The traditions which Presbyterians follow, for instance, are not done to throttle religious experience but rather as the prescribed means of communing with God and his people. These means were not arbitrarily chosen by John Calvin and John Knox. Rather Presbyterians have conducted public and family worship in specific ways because they believe worship should conform to God's revealed truth. But just as the

---

[75] De Jong, "User Friendly Evangelism," 4.

academic left has abandoned the great works of Western civilization because of a desire for relevance in higher education, so evangelicals have rejected the various elements and forms which have historically informed Protestant worship, again, because they are boring to today's youth.

Anti-formalism also explains the stress upon novelty and freshness so often found in P&W. The leader of worship planning at one of the dominant megachurches says, for instance, on a video documenting a P&W service, that she is always looking for new ways to order the midweek believer's service so that church members won't fall into a rut. She goes on to say that people are often tired, having worked all day (an argument for worshipping on Sunday) and need something which will arrest their attention and put them in a proper frame of mind. This perspective, however, fundamentally misunderstands the relationship between form and worship. C. S. Lewis had it right when he said that a worship service "'works' best when, through long familiarity, we don't have to think about it." "The perfect church service," he added, "would be the one we were almost unaware of; our attention would have been on God. But every novelty prevents this. It fixes our attention on the service itself; and thinking about worship is a different thing from worshipping... 'Tis mad idolatry that makes the service greater than the god.' A still worse thing may happen. Novelty may fix our attention not even on the service but on the celebrant." But this is precisely what has happened in P&W where the service and elements are designed to attract attention themselves rather than functioning as vehicles for expressing adoration to God. Lewis knew that repetition and habit were better guides to the character of worship than novelty and manipulation. In fact, one doesn't need to be a professor of liturgics to sense that the idiom of Valley Girls is far less fitting for a believer to express love for God than the language of the *Book of Common Prayer.* Such an instinct only confirms the wise comment of the Reformed theologian, Cornelius Van Til, who while preferring Presbyterian liturgy, still remarked that "at least in an Episcopalian service no one says anything silly."

Hugh Oliphant Old, in his fine study of worship, concludes with a reflection about mainline Presbyterian worship that applies well to what has transpired in contemporary evangelical churches. "In our evangelistic zeal," he writes, "we are looking for programs that will attract people. We think we have to put honey on the lip of the bitter cup of salvation. It is the story of the wedding of Cana all over again but with this difference. At the crucial moment when the wine failed, we took matters into our own hands and used those five stone jars to mix up a batch of Kool-Aid instead." Such is the state of affairs in contemporary evangelical worship. The thin and artificial juice of popular culture has replaced the finely aged and well-crafted drink of the church through the ages. Aside from the merits of the instant drink, it is hardly what you would expect defenders of tradition and the family to choose to serve at a wedding, or at the banquet supper of our Lord. And yet, just as evangelicals in the nineteenth century substituted Welches for red wine, so a century later they have exchanged the superficial and trivial for the rich forms and elements of historic Protestant worship.[76]

The following is a thoughtful example of applying McLuhan's observation that "the medium is the message" to contemporary worship.

McLuhan devoted much of his writing to establishing the principle that the medium within which a message is delivered is its own kind of message. More pithily, McLuhan argued that *the medium is the message*. Various media are more or less efficient at communicating certain messages. A handshake communicates the message of friendship better than does a flyer addressed to "occupant." Musically, one could say that there should be a correspondence between the lyrics (the message) of a given work and the musical score itself. Music is affective; it touches the human in ways which written discourse does not. Therefore, if the musical score produces an affective response which is contrary to the conclusions drawn from the lyrics, dissonance results, a troubling experience of incongruity between the message in the lyrics and the "message" in the score. A hymn of trust is most at home in a score which is dignified, resolute, and deliberate (consider, e.g., the Bach tune ordinarily chosen as the vehicle for Luther's "A Mighty Fortress"; or the "Foundation" tune to which "How Firm a Foundation" is ordinarily set). A hymn in which the saints militant commune with those triumphant in praising God, such as W. W. How's "For all the saints," is properly at home in a score which is celebratory, such as R. Vaughan Williams's "Sine Nomine" tune. Hymnists endeavor to "match" the musical score of a given piece of music with its lyrics.

If this is so, then the question may very well be raised as to whether the tunes to which most scripture choruses are set are adequate to the message they carry. As perhaps the most notorious example of one which evidently is inadequate, consider the (somewhat-regrettably) well-known chorus mentioned earlier, "This is the day that the Lord has made." It is set to a simple, peppy, brisk, light-hearted melody. Yet the

---

[76] D. J. Hart, "Evangelicals on the Durham Trail." *Calvin Theological Journal* 30, no. 2 (Nov. 1995).

lyrics, contextually understood, do not fit this tune. Contextually, the psalmist has spoken of that most somber day in Israel's future when "The stone that the builders rejected has become the chief cornerstone. This is the LORD's doing; it is marvelous in our eyes." Such a significant and sobering reality is poorly communicated by such a musical score.

Indeed, it can be generally said that scripture choruses ordinarily do not and cannot carry the theological "weight" of their lyrics. The issue, in such cases, is not whether it is wrong or immoral to sing such; the issue is whether we have something *better* available to us. The actual question is not whether such choruses are categorically prohibited, as being inherently evil; the question is whether such choruses are better or worse than the known alternatives at *conveying those thoughts, sentiments, and feelings appropriate to Christian worship*. It is our opinion that, in the English-speaking world, where our treasure of hymnody is perhaps the richest in the world, very few (if any) of the "top 100" choruses would compare favorably to the "top 100" hymns, if evaluated by this standard.[77]

The challenge to worship will only be met by good teaching on the nature of Biblical worship and by the experience of true participation in it. The Church Growth movement has in many ways capitulated to the pressures of the electronic media, promoting entertainment, immediate gratification, and self orientation, in place of true worship and spirituality. Biblical teaching will help correct false expectations. One of the real challenges will be to overcome the individualism which has become a defining American trait. As we have seen in chapter 6, at its worst this trait degenerates into narcissism. Biblical worship calls us to participation in a corporate reality which connects us not only with the immediate worshipping body, but with the church universal, and triumphant—"we are surrounded by so great a cloud of witnesses."[78] While each electronic medium may be used in various ways as a part of our more general gospel witness no electronic medium is a substitute for the worship, service and witness of the local church.

Electronic Media and the Regulative Principle

The *Westminster Standards* assert that "there are some circumstances concerning the worship of God, and government of the Church, common to

---

[77] Allen Tomlinson and T. David Gordon, "Scripture Songs or Hymns?" n.d.
[78] Heb. 12:1. Cf. Marshall McLuhan, "Liturgy and Media: Do Americans Go to Church to Be Alone?" in *The Medium and the Light: Reflections on Religion*, edited by Eric McLuhan and Jacek Szlarek (Toronto: Stoddart Publishing Co. Limited, 1999).

human actions and societies, which are to be ordered by the light of nature, and Christian prudence, according to the general rules of the word, which are always to be observed."[79] In light of the nature of media and their affect on message content, the media of worship cannot be considered to be part of what the Puritans meant by "circumstances." If we are correct in our conclusion that the live pastoral preaching of God's Word is His chosen medium for public worship, then all electronic media would be forbidden. The elements of worship, which must be explicitly warranted by Scripture, include the media of their expression. While I do not claim to have all of the answers regarding every medium, such a sound amplification, these are the issues and questions with which the church must wrestle. In commenting on the incident of the golden calf in Stephen's recounting of the history of Israel's idolatry, Calvin says, "Not content with the means which God hath appointed, they boldly get to themselves new means. This is no small fault, because their fingers itch always to have new inventions without keeping any mean, and so they are not afraid to pass the bounds which God hath appointed them."[80]

A very important implication of the regulative principle, which is usually overlooked, is the fact that it is *limited* to matters of worship and church government. For example, by prohibiting the solo performance from public worship, the church is not prohibiting the same performance in other contexts. Even then, or course, especially when it comes to the Christian use of electronic media, liabilities, as well as benefits, must be considered. A Christian theater group or musical ensemble could perform for the edifying entertainment of a Christian audience, or anyone else, on a day other than the day of worship. The Internet is a fruitful venue for document and information distribution, as we have seen. Listserv groups and chat rooms might be used fruitfully as adjuncts to the mission of the church, but never as replacements for face-to-face communication.

Radio and television may be used in thoughtful ways, by the church, as a means of evangelism. The Back to God Hour, under the wise leadership of Joel Nederhood is a sterling example of how the church, as the church, may use these two powerful media, without compromising her mission, and under her God-given guidance. Nederhood, as we have seen, has laid a theoretical foundation for the proper use of these media. He has concluded that because of its oral-aural nature the radio is most suited to contentful presentation of the Biblical message, whereas television must be used with greater restraint.

In all of this the main point which the church needs to affirm is this: no medium, electronic of otherwise, can substitute for the worship of the local

---

[79] *Westminster Confession of Faith*, I.6.
[80] John Calvin, *Commentaries*. 1540-1563. Translation and reprint. Edinburgh: Calvin Translation Society. 1847. Reprint, vol. 18 (Grand Rapids: Baker Book House, 1969) 291, on Acts 7:39.

church, especially its preaching. Media such as the cassette tape, and the radio rebroadcast of the sermon, may augment the ministry of the Word. These too, however, must be used with great caution. For example, cassettes of the weekly sermon may be fruitfully distributed for the use of shut-ins, the sick, or others interested in the ministry. This medium becomes a problem when cassette listening is substituted for public worship. This is true of all electronic media.

When it comes to worship itself the amplifying system might be used to augment the voice of the preacher. Sound amplification is not necessary to preaching but may help extend the voice. Audience manipulation, by modulation during the act of preaching, however, should be avoided. One Reformed church of which I am aware has a sound system which can make the voice of the preacher sound as if it is coming from the rear of the auditorium, like the voice of God. This would seem to be a dangerous practice. McLuhan suggests, "the microphone, which makes it so easy for a speaker to be heard by many, also forbids him to exhort or be vehement. The mike is indeed a cool medium."[81] Overhead projectors directly interfere with the preaching by drawing attention away from the preacher, functioning as a kind of visual competition. Remember the hearers are not an audience to be entertained or a student body to be taught. They are worshippers in the presence of the living God, and in the presence of the pastor He has called to address His people in His name and with His Word.

While some of these benefits may tangentially aid our preaching none enhances the act of preaching itself. If they were necessary to preaching then God would have provided them at the outset. The electronic media are no surprise to the God who enabled us to create them.

Theological Education at a Distance

With everyone jumping on the bandwagon of "distance education," with computerized educational technology, we do well to ask ourselves some hard questions about the ways in which the electronic revolution will affect theological education. Such questioning must not begin with an analysis of technology itself, but rather of the nature, aims and means of historic theological education.

In an insightful address to a joint meeting of the Southeastern Pennsylvania Theological Library Association and the New York Area Theological Library Association in May 1998 Dr. Darryl G. Hart expressed grave concerns about the negative impact of educational technology on

---

[81] Marshall McLuhan, "Liturgy and the Microphone," in *The Medium and the Light: Reflections on Religion*, edited by Eric McLuhan and Jacek Szlarek (Toronto: Stoddart Publishing Co. Limited, 1999) [midway].

theological education. His concerns center on what he calls the "three R's of seminary education ... reading, writing and religious communities."[82]

Hart contends that "digitized text" and especially searchable Bible software lends itself to an "engineering hermeneutic." Word searches give the illusion of study, while obviating the kind of "deep reading" that cultivates thoughtfulness. "Would such a search produce real learning, or simply a lot of citations? ...The point of these questions, of course, is that the automation revolution at least indirectly promotes the hermeneutics of engineers rather than that of humanists, and this development is harmful for the kind of readers we should try to nurture at good theological schools."[83] While we should be alert to the dangers of which Hart warns, we should not minimize the enormous benefit which searching an electronic text of the Bible or even a classic theology text afford the assiduous student. I would argue that the time saved in searching for various grammatical constructions and word usages in the Biblical text may be used for the kind of deep reflection advocated by Hart. In reacting to the liabilities of electronic media, which many Christians seem to blithely overlook, the Christian must also be alert to the benefits of those media, which God has graciously allowed us to develop in common culture.

As goes reading, so writing. Internet education involves very little term paper writing. This is contrary to what used to be considered the "pinnacle of a good education, namely, the writing of a dissertation, the longest of research papers. So if technology makes it possible for students to stay home rather than come to campus, and if it tempts theological educators to offer an education that does not include library research and the writing of a term paper, then the automation revolution may not only be furthering poor reading skills but also rearing a generation of students who don't know how to write."[84] The use of the Internet and word processing, for the thoughtful user, may actually enhance writing and research in some significant ways, as long as the new efficiency is not used to sidestep the disciplines of thinking and writing. Perhaps learning to write without modern equipment is the best way to learn to use the new technology to its greatest advantage. This has certainly been the experience of the computer cross-over generation. It remains to be seen how the next generation will fare in this regard.

The most provocative question of all is: "Does information technology give students the skills they need to become a part of a religious community's conversation?" Hart answers a resounding "No!" The failure of community

---

[82] D. G. Hart, "The Three R's of Theological Education," *Nicotine Theological Journal* 2, no. 3 (1998): 1-4. Dr. Hart is the Librarian and an Associate Professor of Church History and Theological Bibliography at Westminster Theological Seminary in Philadelphia.
[83] *Ibid.*, 2.
[84] *Ibid.*, 3.

conversation is rooted in the neglect of the seminary's two greatest resources: its books and its faculty.[85] Sadly, those who raise such questions become the objects of ridicule, and are labeled "old fashioned" or "out of touch," a kind of "untouchable" caste in a technological society. A recent article titled "Computing the Sermon," ends with the patronizing statement, "If your church or pastor has not gotten into the computer age, the time has come!"[86]

"Distance" is the operative word in the new concept. Overcoming distance may, in some cases, be a great benefit. It will avoid the disruption of family life often associated with theological traditional education. The transfer of information and documents from all over the world enhances all forms of education. However, the decrease in face-to-face encounter, combined with the loss of the community of learning, is a clear liability of the new system. As Douglas Groothuis points out: "seminaries have traditionally 'disrupted' students' lives, and for good reason. To prepare for ministry, one must immerse oneself in biblical exegesis, theology, apologetics, ethics, practical ministry, and more. This requires a shift in one's whole life."[87] The rigors of seminary are only a prelude to the rigors of pastoral ministry. If habits of intense commitment are not developed in the community of pastor-scholars, where else will they be developed? Those on the avant-garde may end up being the ones who are "out of touch," after all.

Beyond this, Hart's warning about an "engineering hermeneutic," points to one of the greatest dangers of the "Information Revolution." Douglas Groothuis recalls the warning of Mark Noll that the church has tended since the nineteenth century to treat Scripture like a jig-saw puzzle. Bible software exacerbates this problem. Groothuis observes: "Users may end up dissecting the Bible into info-chunks instead of understanding the Scripture's context, historical setting, and overall theological significance."[88] Hard intellectual and spiritual work can easily seem unnecessary to the novice student armed with tons of software.

Steven Vanderhill, executive director of ministry resources at Westminster Theological Seminary, is completely enthusiastic about the advent of the "virtual classroom." Through electronic mail the student and the professor can "personally interact." He believes that "Internet assisted" seminary programs will enhance three "central concerns: interactivity, accountability, and community."[89] What is missing in this article is even a hint of appreciation of

---

[85] *Ibid.*, 3.
[86] John R. Tinsley, "Computing the Sermon," *New Horizons* (July 1997) 5.
[87] Douglas Groothuis, *The Soul in Cyberspace* (Grand Rapids: Baker Books, 1997, Reprint, Eugene, OR: Wipf and Stock, 1999) 152.
[88] *Ibid.*, 146.
[89] Steven Vanderhill, "The Internet Seminary," *New Horizons* (July 1997) 8, 9.

the potential liabilities of this new technology. The questions are not even being asked, much less answered.

I believe that due to the presuppositional nature of Christian criticism the Christian is in the best, and theoretically the only, position to pursue Media Ecology. One task for Christian Media Ecology is the inclusion of its discipline within existing Christian schools at every level. Most important will be the influence of a Christian Media Ecology in the homiletics departments of leading seminaries, and graduate schools. If we learn anything from the work and influence of Wilbur Schramm it is that training doctoral level academics is a key to pervasive academic, and eventually cultural, influence. A Graduate School of Christian Media Ecology should also be a goal.

The Power of Community

Without repeating what has been said at the end of the last chapter, the place of community in the church provides the most powerful fabric for resisting the idolatry of the world. The church also provides something which is fast disappearing in the world: community. "Culture watchers, social critics, politicians, clergy, theologians, philosophers, and just about everyone else within earshot have at least one thing in common today: They are all lamenting the loss of community and civility in American culture."[90] Just as the early church rescued the female infants from the flaming dumps of the Roman world, so the church has an unprecedented opportunity to demonstrate to the world what true community looks like. This should be one of the most enduring fruits of Christian Media Ecology. Negatively this requires the demonstration of wise restraint in our involvement with electronic media. Positively it calls us to cultivate the communion of saints already given to us as the Body of Christ. The church consists of an ecumenical diversity which is impossible for the world to attain, because it has no enduring basis for unity. The church's diversity is rooted in the person and work of the Head of the new humanity, Jesus Christ.

Ephesians 2:19-22 beautifully pictures this reality: "Now, therefore, you are no longer strangers and foreigners, but fellow citizens with the saints and members of the household of God, having been built on the foundation of the apostles and prophets, Jesus Christ Himself being the chief corner*stone*, in whom the whole building, being joined together, grows into a holy temple in the Lord, in whom you also are being built together for a dwelling place of God in the Spirit." The historical reality of the Incarnation is present in a world increasingly alienated and fragmented by electronic communication. The

---

[90] Groothuis, *The Soul in Cyberspace*, 121.

"Global Village" is being built at the expense of the real villages in which we live. At the heart of the village, which is the church, is a mandate to show the world the difference that the crucified and risen Christ makes in the daily lives of His people. The preaching of the Word stands at the center of this village to call the world, alienated from God to be reconciled through His amazing grace. Paul powerfully enunciates this mandate in 2 Corinthians 5:18-20: "Now all things *are* of God, who has reconciled us to Himself through Jesus Christ, and has given us the ministry of reconciliation, that is, that God was in Christ reconciling the world to Himself, not imputing their trespasses to them, and has committed to us the word of reconciliation. Now then, we are ambassadors for Christ, as though God were pleading through us: we implore *you* on Christ's behalf, be reconciled to God." The church is a haven in a heartless world, an embassy of truth and peace, in a battle-torn culture. The simplest elements of face-to-face personal interaction, taken for granted until recently, have the profoundest effects on people's lives. The church must work to cultivate the fellowship and community of the local church.

CONCLUSION

In conclusion, we have seen the naiveté of the church regarding the nature of the electronic media. The church has not done well in resisting the great temptation presented by the electronic environment to compromise its foundations. In cultivating the counter environment the church must be aware of the church's counter environmental purpose as such. The reason is that the environment of the world over against which the church stands is not simple a pantheon of idols, but the entire atmosphere of the temple in which they communicate their various aspects of the message of idolatry. The electronic media add to the cohesiveness of that environment, like smog to the dank air of a foggy city. "Christians should not fear the idols and myths of our day, as long as they have no reverence for them. But idols and myths can take the form of moods and sensibilities as well as stone and creed, and there are many disturbing signs that many contemporary Christians have made the limited and limiting sensibility of popular culture their own. ...But a sensibility, a consciousness, is much more evasive and subtle." [91] Consciousness is the totality of the broad concept of idolatry explained in chapter 5—the atmosphere of the idols. While each electronic medium may be used in various ways suggested throughout this chapter as a gospel witness no electronic medium is a

---

[91] Kenneth M. Myers, *All God's Children and Blue Suede Shoes: Christians and Popular Culture* (Westchester, IL: Crossway Books, 1989) 87, 181.

substitute for the worship, service and witness of the local church. Most importantly the live, pastoral preaching of God's Word has no electronic competitors. That is the burden of the remaining two chapters.

PART IV

TOOLS OF COMMUNICATION: AN ECOLOGY OF PREACHING

9

Tongues of Fire: God's Chosen Medium

But His word was in my heart like a burning fire shut up in my bones; I was weary of holding it back, and I could not. "...The prophet who has a dream, let him tell a dream; and he who has My word, let him speak My word faithfully. What is the chaff to the wheat?" says the LORD. "Is not My word like a fire?" says the LORD, "And like a hammer that breaks the rock in pieces?"

—Jeremiah 20:9; 23:28, 29

And suddenly there came a sound from heaven, as of a rushing mighty wind, and it filled the whole house where they were sitting. Then there appeared to them divided tongues, as of fire, and one sat upon each of them. And they were all filled with the Holy Spirit and began to speak with other tongues, as the Spirit gave them utterance.

—Acts 2:2-4

Faith cometh by hearing.
ἡ πίστις ἐξ ἀκοῆς

—The Apostle Paul, Romans 10:17

I do not look for any other means of converting men beyond the simple preaching of the gospel and the opening of men's ears to hear it. The moment the Church of God shall despise the pulpit, God will despise her. It has been through the ministry that the Lord has always been pleased to revive and bless His Churches.

—C. H. Spurgeon[1]

---

[1] C. H. Spurgeon, *C. H. Spurgeon: The Early Years, 1834-1859*, A revised edition of his autobiography, originally compiled by his wife and private secretary (London: The Banner of Truth Trust, 1962) v.

From the beginning to the end of the Bible, the Word is the principal means by which God communicates with His people and the world. At the outset we encounter God speaking all of creation into existence by the Word of His power. The entire creation continues to communicate the attributes of God to His image bearers. "The heavens declare the glory of God; and the firmament shows His handiwork. Day unto day utters speech, and night unto night reveals knowledge. *There is* no speech nor language *where* their voice is not heard. Their line has gone out through all the earth, and their words to the end of the world. In them He has set a tabernacle for the sun, which *is* like a bridegroom coming out of his chamber, *and* rejoices like a strong man to run its race. Its rising *is* from one end of heaven, and its circuit to the other end; and there is nothing hidden from its heat." (Psalm 19:1-6). The entire created cosmos is a continual sermon. The Psalmist continues from verses 7 through 14 to extol the virtues of the written word. The very fact of Scripture implies the centrality of the Word, written and preached, in the life of the church in all ages. Scripture calls the church to cultivate an ecology of preaching, a stewardship of God's Word.

As we saw in chapter 5, the three essential or natural forms of media interact in the life of the church: the written, the oral, and the visual. The written Word is *foundational* in the life and worship of the church. The Scriptures, the history of their interpretation and their confessional expression form the constitutional basis of the church's life and worship. The written Word informs both the oral Word and the visual Word. The oral is *central* in the life and worship of the church. Preaching is the primary means of grace and thus takes center stage as the living voice of the church's Savior and Lord. The visual dimension signifies and seals the written and preached word through the sacraments. Each of the three is never present alone. Preaching is an exposition and application of the written Word and is visual in the person and gestures of the preacher, but the oral predominates. Preaching is the burden of this chapter.

The striking images of *hammer* and *fire* are used by Jeremiah to indicate the inner pressure which the Word of God exerts on the heart of the true preacher, and the awesome effects that Word has in history, respectively. The hammer is a symbol of judgment, as Sisera found out at the hands of Jael (Judges 4:21; 5:26). Babylon is described by Jeremiah as a hammer of judgment against unfaithful Judah (Jer. 50:23). In Jeremiah 23 the unfaithful shepherds of Israel are addressed as those who "destroy and scatter the sheep..." (v.1). Anticipating the coming of the Branch of Righteousness in the New Covenant the LORD promises to replace them with shepherds who feed the flock (vs. 4ff). The prophet's lament for the unfaithfulness of the prophets of Jerusalem follows (vs. 9-24). The prophet's word is a hammer of judgment against the prophets of lies. In the New Covenant context Paul changes the metaphor to make the same point: "For we are to God the fragrance of Christ among those who are being saved and among those who are perishing. To the one *we are* the aroma of death *leading* to death, and to the other the aroma of life *leading* to life. And who *is* sufficient for these things? For we are not, as so many, peddling the word of God; but as of sincerity, but as from God, we speak in the sight of God in Christ" (2 Cor. 2:15-17).

The image of *fire* is much more pervasive as a Biblical metaphor. It is the LORD who causes the Word to be a fire in Jeremiah's heart and mouth: "Because you speak this word, Behold, I will make My words in your mouth fire, And this people wood, And it shall devour them" (Jer. 5:14). This too is a symbol of judgment, reflecting the holiness of God. Jeremiah is inwardly constrained to preach judgment to his own people. It is an onerous task, but poignantly teaches the covenant breaking people of their need of a Covenant Keeper.

Thus, in the New Covenant, the image of Paul is two sided. The fire of judgment has been quenched by the covenant keeping Second Adam. The ritual purification of the burning of sacrifices on the alter of the Tabernacle and Temple are fulfilled in the work of the Great High Priest, who bears the sins of God's people. Thus, the final epoch of redemption opens with "tongues of fire" resting prophetically on the disciples at Pentecost, as the church announces the God's victory over sin and death to the world; the beginning of a new creation. The preaching of Christ is "the aroma of life *leading* to life..." for those who are being saved. Who is adequate to be a herald of such a significant message? Only those called and equipped by God Himself, who gives the preacher victory in Christ. God alone can prevent us from becoming "peddlers" of religion, seeking our own profit, fame, power, and honor. He does so by teaching us the nature of our calling and our task. He does so by giving us "tongues of fire," tongues aflame with the purifying message of new life. In this chapter we will explore the primacy of our task as preachers. Then in the final chapter we will consider the nature of our office and its execution in the electronic context. This material is not meant to cover the traditional territory of homiletics, but to supplement it in light of our electronic situation.

THE PRIMACY OF PREACHING: A BIBLICAL OVERVIEW

The most cursory study of the Bible will lead even the impartial reader, who is honest with the text, to acknowledge the primacy of the preached word in the life and worship of God's people, and in the evangelistic project of God's spokesmen.

God's spoken Word was necessary even in the Paradise state to provide the meaning of creation and the purpose of man's existence to His people, as they learned to listen to His Word and use their own words as expressions of thinking "God's thoughts after Him."[2] Thus Adam communed with God, and exercised dominion through the prophetic function of naming the animals (Gen. 2:19). God revealed His covenant to Adam by speaking to him the terms of obedience which tested his allegiance and loyalty to the LORD (Gen. 2:16, 17). Because man is made in God's image, in fact he *is* God's image, he needs the special revelation of God's Word as a creature apart from sin.

The fall, as we have seen in chapter 1, involved the Serpent's insinuation of doubt as to the veracity of God's Word. In response to Adam's ensuing disobedience God gave His word of promise: "I will put enmity between you and the woman, and between your seed and her Seed; He shall bruise your head, and you shall bruise His heel" (Gen. 3:15). All of subsequent redemptive history is an outworking of this divine assertion.

Since the message of God's Word was relatively short in the Adamic and Patriarchal ages, and because memory is keen and accurate in an oral culture the *written* Word of God was not a necessity, as far as we can glean, until the Mosaic covenant was given. The sheer volume of communication that came from Mount Sinai demanded a written document. "The secret things belong to the LORD our God, but those things which are revealed belong to us and to our children forever, that we may do all the words of this law" (Deut. 29:29).

The Bible is *written* because it is a covenant document. It is clear, both by the existence of Scripture as well as the early importance of writing as a means of preserving and communicating God's Word, that written communication is an essential aspect of mans' fulfillment of his cultural calling. In this respect the Bible is similar to other covenant documents. Real estate ownership requires a written deed. Mortgages are written agreements. So are marriage licenses. *Important* documents are written to prevent the corruption of agreements and contracts in a fallen world. The more important an established relationship is the more critical is its being written. What John wrote at the end of *Revelation* applies to all inspired writings: "If anyone adds to these things (i.e. written in this book), God will add to him the plagues that are written in this book; and if anyone takes away from the words of the book of this prophecy, God shall take away his part from the Book of Life, from the holy city, and from the things that are written in this book" (Rev. 22:18,19; cf. Deut. 4:2; *WCF* I.1). Meredith Kline has observed that "the formation of the

---

[2] Cornelius Van Til, in many places in his writings.

Old Testament canon will be traced to its origins in the covenantal mission of Moses in the third quarter of the second millennium BC, providentially the classic age of treaty diplomacy in the ancient Near East." Kline has thus properly asserted that "canon is inherent in covenant."[3]

In his fallen state man especially needs God's Word. Without the Word of the covenant of grace he is hopelessly lost in sin. "For since, in the wisdom of God, the world through wisdom did not know God, it pleased God through the foolishness of the message preached to save those who believe" (1 Cor. 1:21). Paul reminded Timothy that from his youth he had "known the Holy Scriptures, which are able to make you wise for salvation through faith which is in Christ Jesus" (2 Tim. 3:15).

Our concern here, however, is with *the primacy of preaching*, i.e. the live communication of God's Word by His chosen spokesman to His people. In arguing for the primacy of preaching I am not diminishing the importance of the written Word, the other means of grace or the institution of the visible church. The primacy of preaching is only important and effective in its vital connection with the Bible, prayer and the sacraments, and in the context of the visible church. Since this primacy is central to the means of grace and the visible church, when it is undermined the integrity of these will also be seriously compromised.

It should be clearly noted at this point, therefore, that the primacy of preaching is not precisely the same as the primacy of Scripture. The primacy of preaching assumes the primacy of Scripture. As we shall see in the next section the reformed confessions are uniform in their assertion that the primary means of grace is not simply the Word of God, but the *preaching* of the Word of God. The message must have a spokesman. In the Old Testament era the need for men to communicate the Word prefigures the coming of the eternal Word incarnate, who is the Prophet of prophets and the Preacher of preachers. In the New Testament era the coming of the incarnate Word, the Prophet greater than Moses (Deut. 18:15-22), the final speech of God (Heb. 1:1-3), ushers in an epoch of world wide preaching of which we are a continuing part until the consummation of history at the Parousia of our Lord.

Old Covenant

Moses is the great preacher of the Old Covenant. Prior to him Enoch had prophesied against the worldly wisdom of his day (Jude 14); and Noah had been a "preacher of righteousness" (2 Peter 2:5) warning his generation of the

---

[3] Meredith G. Kline, *The Structure of Biblical Authority* (Revised Edition. Grand Rapids: William B. Eerdmans Publishing Company, 1975) 43.

deluvian judgment of God. The Patriarchs had been given the prophetic word which presaged the Mosaic era and the great redemptive act of God in the Exodus (Gen. 15:13). But Moses was given the nucleus of Old Testament revelation. As a prototype of the Coming Prophet, he became God's agent of the record and interpretation of the primary redemptive event of the Old Covenant. The Word which he was given interpreted the significance of the Exodus for present and future generations. The remainder of the Old Covenant is an amplification and application of the Mosaic deposit; and like the pre-Mosaic revelation looks forward to an epoch of ultimate fulfillment surrounding the Prophet greater than Moses who would in turn preach, act and send preachers to explain His act to the world.

Despite his hesitation, Moses responded to God's call to preach to Pharaoh and to the people of Israel. Although Aaron acted as Moses' press secretary, Moses is still the prophet. Significantly the LORD did not send a document but insisted on sending a man. Similarly at Sinai, the LORD did not send tablets or the rest of the revelation which Moses wrote, but rather He sent Moses with His message. "Come up to Me on the mountain and be there; and I will give you tablets of stone, and the law and commandments which I have written, *that you may teach them*" (Exod. 24:12, emphasis added).

Moses is called first to learn God's Word from God's mouth (Exod. 4:12, 15) and then to teach that Word to Israel *in person* (Exod. 18:20). He is also to appoint elders to apply the Word to the lives of God's people (Exod. 18:21, 22); and Levitical priests to teach the Word to the people (Lev. 10:11; Deut. 24:8). Apart from the advent of the school of the prophets during the monarchy these were the ordinary God-appointed preachers of the Old Covenant period.

Samuel was the most notable prophet to arise in the post-Mosaic period. The school associated with him (1 Sam. 10) formed the basis for the proliferation of the Mosaic model throughout the periods of the monarchy, exile and restoration. The initial phase of this development saw prophets who were given special occasional *oral* messages, especially calling kings to account in light of the Mosaic Law (1 Sam. 15:1ff; cf. 1 Chron. 10:13; 2 Sam. 12:25; 2 Chron. 10:15). These were always delivered *in person* by a man chosen and commissioned to speak for the LORD.

The prophetic careers of Elijah and Elisha in the ninth century BC ushered in a new era of prophetic preaching and writing. Performing signs and wonders reminiscent of Moses, Elijah and Elisha challenged the corruption of the northern tribes and its kings. They laid the groundwork for an emerging prophetic portrait of a new era ushered in by the true King, the Servant of the Lord, the original Preacher. Over the next four centuries the great reversal of the Exodus, the Exile, formed the backdrop for an imposing body of prophetic writings. The promise of return, of a Second Exodus, centering in the person and work of the Messiah, draws the consciousness of Israel into a hopeful future. Again God calls men to communicate His message to His people and the world (Isa. 1:10; 8:20; 55:11; 66:5; Jer. 1:2; Eze. 1:3). The audience is noticeably enlarged to include the nations. Jonah was sent to call Pagan Ninevah to repentance (Jonah 2:3), presaging the gracious message of the Great Commission. The foundation for the great era of preaching to the nations was being laid.

The final touch came at the end of the Old Testament prophetic era, which was as well the end of Old Testament written revelation, through the ministries of Ezra and Malachi. In re-establishing Jerusalem temple worship Ezra fulfills his Levitical office and teaches the returned remnant "the Book of the Law of Moses, which the LORD had commanded Israel" (Neh. 8:1). Then Ezra and thirteen leaders with the Levites "read distinctly from the book, in the Law of God; and they gave the sense, and helped *them* to understand the reading" (Neh. 8:8). This was notable an *oral event*, in the well established Biblical tradition of the Levitical priesthood's teaching function (Lev. 10:11; Deut. 24:8). This became the central feature of synagogue worship which characterized the Diaspora during the four centuries prior to our Lord's appearance. The centrality of preaching in the synagogue became the chief characteristic of the New Covenant community and its worship (cf. Luke 4:16ff.; Acts 13:14ff.).[4]

The Old Testament ends with the promise of the future coming of two preachers (messengers, מַלְאָכִי, LXX ἄγγελόν): one to prepare the way, after the model of Elijah, for the Messenger of the Covenant, and the other the Messenger Himself (Mal. 3:1), the Sun of Righteousness who will arise with healing in His wings (Mal. 4:2). It is the promise of the Messenger who will come with a message of salvation for which the faithful remnant wait. And then the primacy of preaching will make its mark like never before.

Hughes Oliphant Old has written a convincing first volume of his monumental history of the reading and preaching of the Scriptures in the worship of the Christian church.[5] In that volume he asserts and proves that the entire Old Covenant canon is essentially a preaching document, i.e. it is associated with the live reading and preaching of God's Word to God's people.

New Covenant

It is with the coming of the incarnate Word, Jesus Christ, that the primacy of preaching comes into its own. Not only does the New Testament record the

---

[4] Hughes Oliphant Old. *The Reading and Preaching of the Scriptures in the Worship of the Christian Church: Volume 1 - The Biblical Period* (Grand Rapids: Eerdmans, 1998) 102.
[5] Old. *The Reading and Preaching of the Scriptures*, vol. 1, 19-110.

preaching of Jesus and the apostles, but it may also be said that the documents of the New Testament are themselves "the result of preaching."[6] In the New Testament there are "more than thirty verbs that denote the activity of preaching."[7] It may truly be said that the New Testament is a book of preaching.[8]

The essence of the ministry of the forerunner, John the Baptizer, is summed up by Matthew: "In those days John the Baptist came *preaching* in the wilderness of Judea" (3:1, emphasis added). Then in a pivotal passage in Luke Jesus gives the gist of His earthly ministry by quoting from Isaiah: "The Spirit of the LORD is upon Me, Because He has anointed Me *to preach* the gospel to the poor; He has sent Me to heal the brokenhearted, To proclaim liberty to the captives And recovery of sight to the blind, To set at liberty those who are oppressed; to proclaim the acceptable year of the LORD." (4:18, 19, emphasis added). There in His hometown synagogue Jesus proclaimed Himself to be the Messiah (the Anointed One of Isaiah 61, the Servant of the LORD). The chief means by which He brings healing and restoration to Israel is through *preaching*. Later in that same chapter He said to His disciples, "I must *preach* the kingdom of God to the other cities also, because for this purpose I have been sent" (Luke 4:43, emphasis added).

Jesus is *The* Prophet-Preacher, who not only *is* the Message of the entire Bible, but as the eternal Second Person of the Trinity, the Word made flesh (John 1:1, λόγος), He was the Author of the Old Testament Scriptures and the One who spoke through all of the writers of Scripture. Peter tells us that the Spirit of Christ spoke through the prophets of the salvation embodied in His own suffering and glory as the Messiah (1 Pet. 1:7-12). He preached through Noah (1 Pet. 3:18-20) and all who preached in the Old Covenant. Now He comes not only as The Preacher, but as the Redeemer whose work on the cross and subsequent resurrection on the third day, form the core of the message He gave His disciples to spread among the nations. Even before the cross they are commissioned to preach: "And as you go, *preach*, saying, 'The kingdom of heaven is at hand'" (Matt. 10:7). After the accomplishment of redemption the Great Commission is issued: "repentance and remission of sins should be *preached* in His name to all nations, beginning at Jerusalem" (Luke 24:47, emphasis added). The very denouement of history depends on the completion of the task of *preaching* the gospel to the nations. At the conclusion of the Olivet discourse, in which Jesus predicts the completion of redemptive history

---

[6] Sinclair B. Ferguson, David F. Wright and J. I. Packer, eds., *New Dictionary of Theology* (Downers Grove: InterVarsity Press, 1988). S.v. "Preaching, Theology of," by Klaas Runia.
[7] Ibid.
[8] Old, *The Reading and Preaching of the Scriptures*, vol. 1, 111-250.

he declares, "And the gospel must first be *preached* to all the nations" (Mark 13:10, emphasis added). Preaching will usher in the end of history.

"Christianity has its own especially deep oral roots. In the Christian dispensation, the central activity for spreading the faith is the *kerygma*, the preaching of Jesus the Christ by his followers. The written text of the New Testament itself is ordered to this oral activity. The oral textuality here is related to the fact that in the New Testament the Son of God incarnate, Jesus Christ is himself God's Word. And in thinking of the Son as the divine Word, the Christian is conceiving of the divine Word by analogy with the human spoken word ..."[9]

An essential feature of Jesus' preparation of the disciples for the cross in the Upper Room is His prophecy of the work of His Spirit in completing the revelation of the Gospel. "But the Helper, the Holy Spirit, whom the Father will send in My name, He will teach you all things, and bring to your remembrance all things that I said to you... He will testify of Me. And you also will bear witness, because you have been with Me from the beginning... He will guide you into all truth; for He will not speak on His own *authority*, but whatever He hears He will speak; and He will tell you things to come" (John 14:26; 15:26, 27; 16:13). Before this final deposit of Covenantal revelation was inscripturated it was a *preached* message. It is inscripturated so that it may, in turn, be preached to each new generation. Preaching is primary because God has made orality primary to all human communication.

"The apostles, commissioned by the risen Lord, preached this message as the very Word of God (1 Thess. 2:13)."[10] When Paul refers to "the Word of God," "the Word of the Lord" or simply "the Word" in his letters he is most often referring to the *preached* Word. This word was so effective because it was the living message of God Himself. "In the apostolic message (the emphasis being always on *the content*) the voice of the living God is being heard."[11]

The entire Book of Acts is the story of preaching as the fundamental medium for building and edifying the church. Acts is *the* book of preaching. At Pentecost the fundamental miracle of the Spirit is not speaking in tongues but the salvation of 3,000 people through the *preaching* of the Gospel. Significantly, what was spoken miraculously in languages unknown to the speakers, was the gospel, "the wonderful works of God (Acts 2:11)." The linguistic dispersion of the Tower of Babel was reversed. It was preaching that caused persecution: the leaders of the temple were "greatly disturbed that they taught the people and preached in Jesus the resurrection from the dead" (Acts

---

[9] Walter Ong, Review: *Beyond the Written Word: Oral Aspects of Scripture in the History of Religion* (William A. Graham) in *America* (Mar. 4, 1989): 204.
[10] *Ibid.*
[11] *Ibid.*

4:2). Preaching was the chief activity of the Apostles: "And daily in the temple, and in every house, they did not cease teaching and preaching Jesus *as* the Christ" (Acts 5:42). So important was preaching that no activity, however worthy, was to interfere with it. "It is not desirable that we should leave the word of God and serve tables" (Acts 6:2). Persecution, rather than silence the preaching, fostered it: "Therefore those who were scattered went everywhere preaching the word" (Acts 8:4). The central activity in Paul's ministry, from the very beginning of his Christian life was preaching: "Immediately he preached the Christ in the synagogues, that He is the Son of God." (Acts 9:20). At the end of Acts we find him imprisoned, but "preaching the kingdom of God and teaching the things which concern the Lord Jesus Christ with all confidence, no one forbidding him" (Acts 28:31). The coming Prophet had come and would be present to the end of the age through the preaching of His Word to all the nations.

As we noted earlier the structure of synagogue worship placed the reading and preaching of the Scriptures at the center of the service. Thus, as we saw in Luke 4, visiting preachers were often asked to expound the Scriptures. Paul, as well as Jesus, took full advantage of this fact, and in so doing built the New Covenant church on the ruins of the old. Paul's preaching, in Pisidian Antioch on the first missionary journey, reveals the pattern of his method and message (Acts 13:13ff.). He exemplified the primacy of preaching, and used it as the primary means of addressing the synagogue with the message of the accomplishment of redemption in Jesus the Christ. Paul gives us a model of adapting the message to the audience without changing the message itself. In the synagogue he assumed the authority of special revelation in the Scripture and sought to prove from it that Jesus was the Christ. In the Pagan forum (Acts 17) he assumed the authority of general revelation and sought to prove that God calls all of His creatures to repentance from sin and faith toward God. From the beginning of his ministry to the end Paul is the preacher, *par excellence*.

The Epistles lay the groundwork for the continuing work of the church after the Apostolic Age, as it is built on the foundation of the inscripturated Word. Central to the continuing ministry of the church is the task of preaching. This is God's means of saving Jew and Gentile. "How then shall they call on Him in whom they have not believed? And how shall they believe in Him of whom they have not heard? And how shall they hear without a preacher? And how shall they preach unless they are sent? As it is written: 'How beautiful are the feet of those who preach the gospel of peace, Who bring glad tidings of good things!' But they have not all obeyed the gospel. For Isaiah says, 'Lord, who has believed our report?' So then faith *comes* by hearing, and hearing by the word of God" (Rom. 10:14-17).

For Paul the call to be a minister of the New Covenant is primarily a call to preach. "For if I preach the gospel, I have nothing to boast of, for necessity is laid upon me; yes, woe is me if I do not preach the gospel!" (1 Cor. 9:16). This call *per se* is not essentially apostolic. The call to preach has a validity reaching far beyond the foundation-laying epoch of the twelve. Thus we are not surprised at Paul's injunctions to Timothy and Titus near the end of his life. "Preach the word! Be ready in season *and* out of season. Convince, rebuke, exhort, with all long-suffering and teaching" (2 Tim. 4:2). Even with the inscripturated Word (canon) complete God still sends men with His message. It is incumbent upon that first ordinary post-apostolic generation of preachers to pass on that calling and office to each successive generation. The apostolic deposit is to be studied, believed, passed on to faithful men, who preach it. "And the things that you have heard from me among many witnesses, commit these to faithful men who will be able to teach others also" (2 Tim. 2:2; cf. 2 Tim. 2:15; 2 Tim. 3:14-17;). "Till I come, give attention to reading, to exhortation, to doctrine. Do not neglect the gift that is in you, which was given to you by prophecy with the laying on of the hands of the eldership. Meditate on these things; give yourself entirely to them, that your progress may be evident to all. Take heed to yourself and to the doctrine. Continue in them, for in doing this you will save both yourself and those who hear you" (1 Tim. 4:13-16). All that Paul enjoins upon Timothy has to do with the *public* ministry of the Word.

In light of the overwhelming Biblical evidence for the primacy of preaching it is no wonder that the subsequent history of the church reflects that emphasis.

THE PRIMACY OF PREACHING:
A CHURCH HISTORICAL OVERVIEW[12]

A brief survey of the church's history subsequent to the apostolic era, demonstrates the centrality of preaching, even by the negative example of periods when preaching reached a low ebb. Much like observing a sick person nurtured back to health by returning to a good diet, so the church, whenever it experienced reformation and revival, can be seen to have returned to the preaching of the message of the Bible.

---

[12] The preacher must avail himself of the first three volumes of Hughes Oliphant Old's definitive history of preaching noted above. *Volume 2 - The Patristic Age,* and *Volume 3 - The Medieval Church* (Grand Rapids: Eerdmans, 1998, 1998, 1999). Several more volumes are projected.

Ancient Church

The Ancient Church, despite all of its weaknesses, was a preaching church. It was the great classically-trained orators like Ambrose and Augustine who usually made the best preachers. They understood the power of speech. Ambrose asserted: "Everything we believe, we believe either through sight or through hearing. ...Sight is often deceived, hearing serves as guarantee."[13] During the first three centuries after the apostles the sermon developed from an informal homily into a structured sermon.[14]

The earliest extant example of what preaching was like in the late first, or early second century is actually a sermon, *The Second Epistle of Clement*, written to the Corinthians.[15] It is ethical, rather than doctrinal.[16] The *Didache*, a church order, probably from the same period, provides much indirect information about early post-apostolic preaching.[17] "The second-oldest Christian sermon which has come down to us is an Easter sermon preached by Melito of Sardis" (ca. 130-ca. 190). He gives a Gospel message in the context of the history of salvation as an example of an early attempt at explaining Old Testament typology.[18] Justin Martyr (ca. 100-ca. 165) provides a clearer example of preaching, as he left a description of worship. Notable is the dominance of orality. The Scriptures were read seriatim because the average person did not own a Bible. Prior to his conversion Martyr was a rhetorician, a philosopher, and a lecturer.[19] With Clement of Alexandria (ca. 150-215), we begin to see the unfortunate influence of the Alexandrian allegorical hermeneutic, as well as the important apologetic emphasis on Christianity's superiority to Pagan philosophy, which began with Justin Martyr.[20]

Bringing allegorical preaching to new heights, Origen (180-253) also brought an extensive Biblical knowledge from his Christian upbringing into the pulpit.[21] "Origen's preaching marks the change from the hortatory homily to the expository sermon..."[22] Tertullian (ca. 150-ca. 225), Cyprian (200-258)

---

[13] Walter Ong, *The Presence of the Word* (New Haven: Yale University Press, 1967. Reprint, Minneapolis, MN: University of Minnesota Press, 1981) 52.
[14] Harwood T. Pattison, *The History of Christian Preaching* (Philadelphia: The American Baptist Publication Society, 1903) 48.
[15] Old, *The Reading and Preaching of the Scriptures*, vol. 1, 278
[16] Pattison, *The History of Christian Preaching*, 49.
[17] Old, *The Reading and Preaching of the Scriptures*, vol. 1, 251-352. Old gives a full account of this period.
[18] *Ibid.*, 285ff.
[19] Pattison, *The History of Christian Preaching*, 50.
[20] *Ibid.*, 51, 52.
[21] *Ibid.*, 52f.
[22] Everett F. Harrison, ed., *Baker's Dictionary of Theology* (Grand Rapids, MI: Baker Book House, 1960) S.v. "Preach, Preaching," by Carl G. Kromminga.

exemplified the use of rhetorical training in expository preaching, the latter being known for his superb eloquence.[23] Athanasius (297-373) continued the emphasis on expository preaching, but with a strong doctrinal clarity, honed in the noble battle with the Christological heresy of Arianism. Excelling him in stylistic brilliance were his fellow defenders of the faith, and classically trained rhetoricians, Basil (330-379) and Gregory Nazianzen (330-390).[24] Ambrose of Milan (340-397) brought his considerable skills as politician and pleader to his preaching. The mantel of Ambrose was passed on to his justly more famous disciple Augustine of Hippo (354-430). An adult convert from Paganism, and a widely acclaimed orator, he subordinated all of his considerable natural gifts and worldly attainments to the service of his Savior. Noted as the greatest of ancient theologians, he was also the most popular and powerful preacher of his day.[25] His only equal in pulpit eloquence was Chrysostom (347-407). "John of the Golden Mouth" wrote the first extant treatise on homiletics. Notable is the directness of his application of Scripture to his congregation.[26]

The ancient world's love of rhetoric and the popular orator lead to excesses in the pulpit. It "often degenerated there into artificial rhetoric, declamatory bombast, and theatrical acting." Many came to church, not to worship, but to hear the celebrated orator. The sermon was often punctuated by applause.[27] If we think the temptation to cast worship in the entertainment mode is unique to the modern world, we are mistaken. We simply have superior tools with which to cultivate this diabolical tendency.

Augustine and Chrysostom have left us with a large volume of sermons, which have been an inspiration to every generation of preachers. The modern preacher would do well to mine these treasures of pre-Gutenberg orality. What they lacked in theology, from a Reformation perspective, they amply made up for in pulpit power. They used the potency of the tongue to persuade thousands to bow before their heavenly Master's throne. Of the primacy of preaching in the ancient church there can be no doubt. Preaching was the staple of the Christian life, and the public worship of the church, in an age where texts were rare and precious, and the Word was mainly received through ear gate.

---

[23] Pattison, *The History of Christian Preaching*, 54ff.

[24] *Ibid.*, 57ff.

[25] *Ibid.*, 62f.

[26] *Ibid.*, 63ff.

[27] Philip Schaff, *History of the Christian Church*, vol. 3, (1910, Reprint Grand Rapids: William B. Eerdmans Publishing Company, 1981) 473.

Medieval Church

With the passing of Augustine and Chrysostom, the sun seemed to set on effective preaching. While it is accurate to say that there was an eclipse of preaching in medieval times, we must never forget that our Lord's promise that the church built on the solid rock of apostolic confession will not be prevailed against even by hell itself. Thus, although the light of the Word grew dim, it was never entirely extinguished.[28] The upheaval caused by the fall of Rome brought a darkness to the culture in which the church lived, which is almost inconceivable to the modern mind. What replaced Roman civilization had more to do with the enervation of the pulpit than the upheaval itself. The church was Western civilization, and priestcraft grew to have little sense of the urgency of preaching. Such is the legacy of confusing cultus and culture.

In the wake of clerical ignorance King Charlemagne, with the help of Alcuin, commissioned the preparation of a book of vernacular homilies to be read in the churches.[29] This *Homiliarium* (ca. 780) was used widely in France. Augustine of Canterbury and Bede compiled similar books for the British church.[30] Ulfilas (311-381), Patrick (372-465), Columba (521-597), the Venerable Bede (673-735), and others like them, brought the Good News with great effect to their own pagan European tribes. "There are not lacking incidental evidences that preaching never lost its hold on the people. The rules for the art, drawn up by Gregory the Great (pope from 590-604) were in use two hundred years after his time at the court of Charlemagne, and a century later yet, ...they were translated for the benefit of clergy, by Alfred of England. In the estimation of Charlemagne, indeed, preaching seems to have been an essential part of the priest's office."[31] He promoted the study of Scripture. In 813 the Councils of Mayence and Arles insisted on the priestly duty of preaching in every parish.[32]

Bernard of Clairvaux (1090-1151), of noble birth and noble piety, confessed: "...this is constantly my highest philosophy, to know Jesus Christ and him crucified." Luther called him "the golden preacher," and Schaff pronounces him the "most brilliant luminary of the pulpit after the days of Gregory the Great."[33] "The sermons were not written out, but delivered from

---

[28] Old, *The Reading and Preaching of the Scriptures*, vol. 3. Here is a rich harvest covering the Medieval period, usually dismissed by Reformed students of preaching, by a Reformed scholar, who is appreciative without being uncritical.
[29] Schaff, *History of the Christian Church*, vol. 3, 77.
[30] Schaff, *History of the Christian Church*, vol. 4, 401.
[31] Pattison, *The History of Christian Preaching*, 89. Gregory the Great had said that teaching was "the art of all arts," 78.
[32] *Ibid.*
[33] Schaff, *History of the Christian Church*, vol. 5, 855

notes or improvised after meditation in the convent garden." The flavor of eternity, combined with "a vivid apprehension of the grace of God," a love for his hearers, an intimate knowledge of Scripture, and "a faculty of magnetic description," placed him in the first rank of preachers in all ages.[34] Among four surviving homiletical treatises of the period Guibert of Nogent's *What Order a Sermon Should Follow* gives familiar advice about the importance of study and prayer in sermon preparation. Alanus ab Insulis's *Art of Preaching* counsels the need for humility and useful instruction to the end that attention will be drawn to the message and not the messenger.[35]

The mendicant orders provided some of the best preaching of the Medieval period. Very interestingly, some of the greatest Scholastic minds of this period were known for their preaching, among whom are Albertus Magnus (ca. 1193-1280), Thomas Aquinas (ca. 1225-74), and Bonaventura (ca. 1217-74). Among the most acclaimed mendicants was Anthony of Padua (1195-1231). Preaching in the fields and public squares he preached to thousands of common people.[36] His first sermon was on the text "Christ became obedient unto death, even the death of the cross." He was noted for staying close to the text of Scripture, and exposing and rebuking sin with great effect. He was a friend of the poor and a thunderer from on high.[37] Francis of Assisi (1181-1226) embodies the best of the mendicant friar tradition. His gentle, giving and gracious ways gave wings to the words he preached. He founded a school of preachers, and spent his life seeking to win the world to Christ.[38]

Then near the end of a period of relative darkness shone a morning star presaging the dawning of a new day, John Wycliffe (1324-1384). His passion was to preach the glorious gospel to Everyman, and that he did with great effect. Along with translating the Bible into the vernacular he schooled and sent an order of preachers throughout the land.[39] Following in his noble train John Huss (1369-1415) and Jerome of Prague (1375-1415) who "loved not their lives unto death" for preaching the heavenly kingdom.[40]

Sadly, much homiletical energy was devoted to the Crusades of the eleventh, twelfth and thirteenth centuries. Schaff records that "probably one-half of the priests in Germany in the twelfth century did not preach."[41] However, the preaching of the Word never ceased.

---

[34] *Ibid.*, 855.
[35] *Ibid.*, 853.
[36] *Ibid.*, 856f. Dominic founded the "Order of Preachers" in the late twelfth century.
[37] Pattison, *The History of Christian Preaching*, 107ff.
[38] *Ibid.*, 102ff.
[39] *Ibid.*, 114ff.
[40] *Ibid.*, 118f.
[41] Schaff, *History of the Christian Church*, vol. 5, 852.

It is important to note that in the absence of widespread literacy, as learning retreated into the monastery, the tendency to use visual aids, in the place of preaching for communication in the church, led to a prevalent idolatry. Preaching, and the Book upon which it is founded, go hand in hand. Whenever the knowledge of the Bible recedes preaching will suffer, and vice versa. In the Providence of God the advent of printing in the mid fifteenth century laid the communications groundwork for the Reformation, and set the stage for a renaissance of interest in both preaching and the Book, first to be printed by Gutenberg.

Reformation Church

The Reformation restored preaching to its primacy in the life and worship of the church. This great movement of the Spirit of Christ was both caused by and characterized by a revival of preaching. "Both Luther and Calvin were convinced that, when the message of the gospel of Jesus Christ is being proclaimed, God himself is heard by the listeners."[42] In his commentary on Galatians Luther asserted the centrality of the Word in contrast to idolatry: "All the highest religious, the holiness and most fervent devotions of those which do reject Christ the Mediator, and worship God without his word and commandment, are nothing else but plain idolatry."[43] In order to deal with the ignorance of the clergy in the early days of the Reformation in England two *Book of Homilies* were prepared by Edward VI and Elizabeth, which reflected the doctrines of the Reformation.[44] The printing press proved a great blessing in providing good sermons to those who would otherwise have gone hungry. Significantly, these sermons were not printed for individual reading, but to be *read aloud*, in the oral tradition, in the churches.

From the fiery Florentine Savanarola (1452-1498), and one of his famous hearers John Colet (1466-1519), who "became the first and most eminent expounder of the Bible in the University of Oxford..."[45] to the army of Puritan preachers in the first half of the seventeenth century exists a mighty testimony to the centrality and power of the preached Word. Martin Luther (1483-1546), was, of course, one of the greatest Reformation preachers. Intense personal conviction, combined with keenness of mind and a down-to-earth rhetorical instinct, caused the common person to hear him gladly. "His choice of words

---

[42] Sinclair B. Ferguson and David F. Wright, eds., *New Dictionary of Theology* (Downers Grove, IL: InterVarsity Press, 1988) S.v. "Preaching, Theology of."
[43] Martin Luther, *A Commentary on Saint Paul's Epistle to the Galatians* (Reprint. 1891. Grand Rapids: Baker Book House, 1979) 526.
[44] Schaff, *History of the Christian Church*, vol. 4, 401.
[45] Pattison, *The History of Christian Preaching*, 129.

was fresh and natural; he had at command fancy, imagination, irony, sarcasm. ...he was a master of the plain speech needed for popular exposition."[46] His spiritual power came from an intense love of Scripture as the very Word of God.

Space does not afford more than a passing mention of the other master preachers of the Magisterial Reformation. Ulrich Zwingli (1484-1531) saw preaching as the central work of the pastor of souls in Zurich. John Calvin's (1509-1554) own view of the centrality of preaching is reflected in the *Ecclesiastical Ordinances*, which were framed under his influence: "The first part of the office of the pastor, says the *Ordinances*, is 'to proclaim the Word of God, to instruct, admonish, exhort and censure, both in public and in private.' ...Calvin will very frequently use the most definite language to assert that the preaching of the gospel is the Word of God. It is as if the congregation 'heard the very words pronounced by God himself'. A man 'preaches so that God may speak to us by the mouth of a man.'"[47] All of this is, of course, bounded by Scripture and the calling of the minister as an ambassador of Christ. So seriously did Calvin take this task that he frequently preached every single day of the week. He preached without notes and probably directly from the Hebrew and Greek texts.[48] Despite having a naturally reserved personality, he exercised rare freedom in the pulpit. "His manner of delivery was lively, passionate, intimate, direct and clear."[49] One could hardly ask for a better model of preaching. Like Luther he spoke in the vivid vernacular of the Genevese.[50] For Calvin the sermon itself was an act of worship as it engaged the congregation in the reality of redemption.[51]

No preacher is better remembered for his power in the pulpit than John Knox (1505-1572). He was utterly fearless in proclaiming Christ and humbling the princes, *and* princesses, of the realm. He was a model for countless other Scottish preachers of his day. In the best of times he thanked God that "the gospel of Jesus Christ is simply and truly preached throughout Scotland."[52] Near the end of his life, in a condition so weakened that he could barely climb into the pulpit of Saint Andrews it is said by one observer that "before he was done with his sermon he was so active and vigorous that he was like to ding the pulpit in blads [pieces], and fly out of it." When he made application of his text, "he made me so thrill and tremble that I could not hold

---

[46] *Ibid.*, 134.
[47] T. H. L. Parker, *John Calvin* (Tring/Batavia, IL/Sydney: Lion Publishing, 1987) 106.
[48] *Ibid.*, 108ff.
[49] *Ibid.*, 110.
[50] *Ibid.*, 111.
[51] *Ibid.*, 114.
[52] Pattison, *The History of Christian Preaching*, 147.

a pen to write."⁵³ Such was the primacy of preaching during the Reformation, that men like Knox saved their best, and often only energy, to preach. Hugh Latimer (1490-1555) was Knox's fearless counterpart in England.

The Puritans brought the primacy of preaching to its apogee. Pattison calls the seventeenth century "The Golden Age of English Preaching."⁵⁴ The ground for this noble generation was laid during the golden age of English literature under Elizabeth. Among the illustrious names who adorned the church of Jesus Christ, among Puritans and Anglicans, were: Thomas Hooker (1553-1600); the "silver tongued" Henry Smith (1550-1593); Lancelot Andrews (1555-1624); and the poet John Donne (1573-1631). Then there were Joseph Hall (1574-1656); Thomas Fuller (1608-1661); and the Puritan Thomas Adams (1585-1655) called the "Shakespeare of the Puritans."⁵⁵ Scotland produced some of the best preachers of this era. David Dickson (1583-16??) opened Scripture with great effect, as the comment of an English merchant shows: "That man showed me all my heart."⁵⁶ Samuel Rutherford (1600-1661) was "at the same time a son of thunder and consolation."⁵⁷ Then there were: John Livingstone (1603-1661); "the sweetest and saintliest of the Puritans;"⁵⁸ Robert Leighton (1611-1684), whose "very look ...was expressive of holy ardor and of tender piety;"⁵⁹ Thomas Goodwin (1600-1679); theologian preacher John Owen (1616-1683); pastor par excellence, Richard Baxter (1615-1691); the pilgrim preacher John Bunyan (1628-1688); Anglican Jeremy Taylor (1613-1679); and Puritans John Howe (1630-1705), and Isaac Barrow (1630-1677). Surrounding these who are known to history is an almost countless number of faithful heralds.

Nowhere is the primacy of preaching more clearly expressed than in the great confessions which grew out of the Reformation. The earliest Reformation creed, articulating Luther's theology in the craftsmanship of Melanchton, *The Augsburg Confession* (1530), in Article V "Of the Ministry of the Church," after stating the primacy of "the ministry of teaching the Gospel" for the "obtaining of faith," asserts: "For the Word and Sacraments, as by instruments, the Holy Spirit is given: who worketh faith, where and when it pleaseth God, in those that hear the Gospel..." The power of the keys according to Article VII "is put in execution only by teaching or preaching the Word and administering the Sacraments..." It is stated almost offhandedly that people are saved by

---

⁵³ *Ibid.*
⁵⁴ *Ibid.*, 163.
⁵⁵ *Ibid.*, 184.
⁵⁶ *Ibid.*
⁵⁷ *Ibid.*, 185.
⁵⁸ *Ibid.*, 186.
⁵⁹ *Ibid.*, 187.

hearing the gospel. Of course, in the first part of the sixteenth century literacy was still the exception, despite the revolution caused by Gutenberg's revolutionary invention.

"In chapter 1 of the *Second Helvetic Confession* (1566) Heinrich Bullinger, the successor of Zwingli, summarized the position of the Reformers in one terse, and rightly famous statement: *Praedicatio verbi Dei est verbum Dei* - 'the preaching of the word of God *is* the word of God.' In the next sentence he interprets this statement as follows: 'Wherefore when the word of God [Scripture] is now preached in the church by preachers lawfully called, we believe that the very word of God is proclaimed, and received by the faithful.'"[60]

The last of the great Reformation Protestant creeds, *The Westminster Confession of Faith* (1648, chapter I.10) declares: "The supreme Judge, by which all controversies of religion are to be determined, and all decrees of councils, opinions of ancient writers, doctrines of men, and private spirits, are to be examined, and in whose sentence we are to rest, can be no other but the Holy Spirit speaking in the Scripture (Matt. 22:29,31; Eph. 2:20; Acts 28:25)." The Scriptures are the inviolable foundation for what the church believes. But how is that Word communicated effectively to sinners? *The Westminster Shorter Catechism*, question #89 (cf. *The Westminster Larger Catechism* #155) similarly asserts: "How is the word made effectual to salvation? A. The Spirit of God maketh the reading, but especially the *preaching* of the word, an effectual means of convincing and converting sinners, and of building them up in holiness and comfort, through faith, unto salvation (Neh. 8:8; 1 Cor. 14:24,25; Acts 26:18; Ps. 19:8; Acts 20:32; Rom. 15:4; 2 Tim. 3:15-17; Rom. 10:17; Rom. 1:16, emphasis added)."

Despite certain liabilities of printing, which have been noted in chapters 5 and 7, we must never forget that it helped to restore a balance in the church's life between the written Word of Scripture and the visible Word of the sacraments. Printing also clearly helped foster the revival of preaching as it fostered the literacy of clergy and people alike. Certainly diminishment of the sacraments in many Protestant communions, as well as the individualizing tendency of the printed word, should alert us to the need for balance among the three primary or natural media. There should, however, be no doubt that printing has been an extraordinary blessing to the church.

---

[60] *New Dictionary of Theology*, S.v. "Preaching, Theology of."

Modern Church

From the Peace of Westphalia (1648) to the present preaching has continued to be a central concern of the church. We see this in the great revivals in England and New England during the Enlightenment. Jonathan Edwards (1703-1758), George Whitefield (1714-1770), and the Wesleys are a staple of the church's recollection of its homiletical past. They were each, above all, preachers. In the late eighteenth and nineteenth centuries the great missionary effort of the English speaking church was characterized by sending preachers, like William Carey (1761-1834), to the most distant unreached people groups of every continent.

Perhaps the most influential and widely known pastor of that century, Charles Haddon Spurgeon (1834-1892), was known primarily for his preaching. The fact that he wrote his sermons for publication on the Monday after he preached them is a testimony to the endurance of orality in the life of the church. While we must never over-estimate "famous" preachers, their presence in the historical memory is an indication of the importance of preaching in the popular mind. As we have noted in our survey, behind every notable preacher was usually a host of faithful men adorning the pulpits of the land in regular pastoral ministry. Thus, the paucity of notable preachers since Spurgeon should alert us to the fact there has been a decline in preaching since the advent of electronic communication.

Since the most well known preachers of the twentieth century are connected with television, I have chosen not to list them as notable, since their ministries have not been in the church, or directly connected with it. This is not to say that we could not learn much about preaching from the best of them, like Billy Graham. My intention, however, is to encourage pastoral and evangelistic preaching in the church. I have already mentioned the notable radio ministry of Joel Nederhood. A long list of excellent preachers, well known more within narrower denominational contexts could be named. J. Gresham Machen, Donald Gray Barnhouse, D. Martyn Lloyd-Jones, Francis Schaeffer, John Stott, Jay Adams and D. James Kennedy might be exceptions to this rule. The fact that many of these and a host of others may be listened to on tape will be of help to the preacher in search of models.

As we move now from the Gutenberg Galaxy to the Electronic Age, the preacher faces a new challenge. The reorganization of the sensorium, along with the reshaping of every institution in our culture, through the influence of the new electronic environment created by the electronic media, demands awareness of the nature and place of the electronic media in culture and its effect on the church and the task of the preacher. No one "could be more effected than the preacher by the changes in the structure of the human psyche and the shift in the areas of sensitivity within modern man's sensorium."[61] The new media do not tend to replace, but rather to envelop the old media, so that we have secondary orality and secondary literacy. Most important to the preacher is his own, as well as the church's and the culture's, assessment of the value of his preaching task. At the close of the century of the Electronic Revolution there is no want of testimony to the depressed state of preaching, and the failure of nerve among preachers, in the churches. Witness a small sample of homiletical titles: *As One Without Authority*; *Crisis in the Pulpit: The Pulpit Faces Future Shock*; *The Empty Pulpit*; *The Gagging of God: The Failure of the Church to Communicate in the Television Age*; *The Sermon Under Attack*. Because man as a sinner, the reality of the crucified and risen Christ, and the truth of His infallible Word have not changed, we must with renewed understanding and vigor preach the Christ of Scripture.

THE EXCELLENCIES OF PREACHING AS A MEDIUM

In light of the modern assessment of various media, particularly the visual media and their electronic associates, preaching has been deemed by many to be an inefficient anachronism. Because the focus on form instead of substance has been properly viewed as a modern problem, orthodox homileticians have tended to shy away from dealing with the form of preaching as a medium.[62] My proposal is to challenge modern media assessments of preaching along the lines of a Biblical assessment of preaching *as a* medium. Assuming the existence of a sovereign and omniscient God, modern media are no surprise to the One who ordained preaching to be the most effective medium to communicate His Word. Thus, we must never forget that preaching is, despite its lack of technology, a medium. Everything created, as we have seen, is, in a general sense, a medium, analogous to and revelatory of the glory of the Creator. A medium is a channel, instrument, means or agency through which a force acts or an effect is produced. We have also noted that communication media are both primary or natural and secondary or technological. Preaching is a natural medium raised to a new height and for a unique redemptive purpose by the supernatural power and definition of God. The agency includes the man, body and soul, his voice and his message. As we have seen in chapter 5 each

---

[61] Fred B. Craddock, *As One Without Authority* (Nashville: Abingdon Press, 1971) 9.

[62] Cornelius Trimp, "Preaching as the Public Means of Divine Redemption," translated by Nelson D. Kloosterman, *Mid-America Journal of Theology*, Theme Issue: Preaching, Vol. 10 (1999) 39-75. A powerful defense of the monologic nature of preaching, and a plea to view preaching not only as a complete event, but in the context of the church, the liturgy, and pastoral care.

medium has its unique grammar and environment. We will now explore the unique excellencies which making preaching without peer among media, and therefore irreplaceable as the center of the church's worship and life.

Preaching is God's Choice

This grand fact should be first and foremost in our consideration. We have proven the primacy of preaching from Scripture. The centrality of preaching in Scripture is, in itself, sufficient warrant for us to place it first among the means of grace. When God commands something in His infallible Word the believer understands by faith that the God who gives commandments to His beloved people is an all-wise Shepherd. Since none of God's commands is arbitrary, we expect to find Biblical reasons for them. While it is not illegitimate to search for the reasons for a particular commandment, the ground upon which the believer accepts and obeys that commandment is God's Lordship in his life. The quest for reasons is itself an act of faith. It is a believing reflection on the wisdom of God revealed in His Word. This is the grand motive force behind all theology in the church. Theology is never simple speculation, but rather a faithful explication of God's grandeur and glory through His Word in the present historical situation. God says: "Preach the Word!"

Preaching is an Authoritative Monologue

While we must not isolate the medium from its message or its context in the worship and life of the church, Scripture bids us consider the *nature of the medium* God has ordained.. When attention is drawn to the medium it is usually only negative in the sense that the importance of the medium is downplayed. While the *content* of the message is clearly at the center of the Bible's emphasis on preaching, and while the medium due to the fallenness of preachers as men is imperfect, we need to appreciate the suitableness of the medium itself to the message of the Gospel.

The Modern-Postmodern age, including many of its homileticians, elevates the dialogical and the interactive aspects of communication almost to the exclusion of the monologue.[63] The reason for this is not difficult to discover. Authority at every level has been repudiated. The very idea of authorship is perceived to be an instrument of oppression. Thus, the single voice of the monologue carries with it the idea of authority, and, therefore, oppressive hubris. This is entirely unacceptable to the contemporary mindset.

---

[63] Cf. Craddock, *As One Without Authority*, 19. Modern homiletics is filled with depreciation of the monological aspect of preaching.

The modern antipathy to preaching is reflected in the oft repeated assertion, "We don't want to preach to people," or the more colloquial "Don't preach at me!"

We should also remember that the monologue of preaching has never been acceptable to the autonomous mind. It is in the context of a culture itching for new ideas that Paul referred to the "foolishness of preaching" in his first letter to the Corinthian church. It is often thought by modern Evangelicals that this *foolishness* refers to the simplicity of the method of monological public speech. In Paul's day, however, rhetoricians were held in highest esteem. In more oral cultures the singer, the poet and the bard were purveyors of cultural tradition.[64] Despite the presence of widespread pre-Gutenberg literacy, orality was still highly respected in the first century. The Greeks would never have thought of the medium of public persuasion as "foolish." The context of Paul's statement reveals that what the Greeks thought foolish was the *message* of the gospel of the crucified Christ (1 Cor. 1:21, 23). The *New King James Version* clarifies this: "it pleased God through the *foolishness of the message preached* to save those who believe." (1 Cor. 1:21, emphasis added).

"Our word-weary generation sometimes forgets how our grandparents before the days of telecommunications considered it a great privilege to go into town to attend a public meeting at which someone would give a public address."[65] It is only in light of the sophistication of modern electronic media that the act of monological speech is thought by some to be foolish. We must not submit to this estimate. Since God has ordained preaching, we are foolish not to cultivate an appreciation for its excellencies *as a medium* of communication. Postmoderns dislike all monological speech because of its inherent authority. In addition, Gospel monologue is disliked because of the message, which claims to be the only true way of salvation. Preaching is hated above all because, at its best, it is the most authoritative kind of monologue conceivable. The electronic media, especially the visual, appeal to the immanentistic, multi-cultural agenda of Postmodernism. Postmodernism is, as we have seen above, autonomous man come into his own. There are no authors or authoritative texts; there is no reality under the surface of anything, much less the words of a man who claims to speak for God.

There is, of course, a real sense in which preaching *is* dialogical, but I hesitate to use the term due to the postmodern baggage with which it is presently freighted. Preaching is dialogical because it is *covenantal*. That is to say it evokes and demands a response from those to whom it is addressed. The spoken word is more personal, and thus evokes a higher level of trust than

---

[64] Eric A. Havelock, *The Muse Learns to Write: Reflections on Orality and Literacy from Antiquity to the Present* (New Haven: Yale University Press, 1986) 73ff. The entire book deals with this question.
[65] Old, *The Reading and Preaching of the Scriptures*, vol. 1, 82.

other forms of communication.[66] But preaching is not properly speaking dialogical, because the two parties of the dialogue are not at all on an equal footing, as in the modern egalitarian use of the term. Perhaps the term *interactive* is more appropriate, although that term too is freighted with postmodern baggage. There is also a pugnacity in some preaching, which is confused with authoritativeness, which bears little resemblance to the Biblical model, and should be eschewed by every true herald of the gospel.

The excellence of the monological nature of preaching is seen more clearly in its immediacy. "Sound ...advertises presentness."[67] For the preacher this is to be the presence of God Himself. As a living voice, preaching is not the same as the immediacy of the visual media in several respects. Because preaching is content heavy it is, as McLuhan has observed, *hot* communication. Furthermore, when spoken in the church, it is spoken in a context in which knowledge of the message of special revelation already exists. The church possesses the written Scriptures, in which it meditates day and night. The church's knowledge of Scripture allows it to search the Scripture like the Bereans even in the act of listening, as the church ransacks its memory in the preaching moment, as the church receives the preaching through the collective and individual grid of Scripture knowledge.

Furthermore, even the unbelieving audience, such as Paul encountered in Athens, brings knowledge of God from its own cultural texts to its hearing, despite its inherent tendency to reject that knowledge (cf. Rom. 1:18ff). The hope of every right thinking preacher is that the message will be discussed after the worship, and even raise questions. As we have seen, one of the strengths of the written word is its reflective nature. It invites dialogue with the reader; it seeks to change the reader's perception, and allows the reader to stop and reflect on the message as it impinges on his consciousness. Most importantly then, preaching reinforces and informs the Bible reading of the church, and vice versa. Thus the combination of various aspects of the media which function in the church, i.e. oral, written and visual, works together to accomplish God's goal in the giving of His Word. It never returns to Him empty (Isa. 55:11).

On the other hand, preaching has all the power of *cool* communication in its immediacy. For in as much as it is God's Word it is unarguable, and there is no space in the preaching event for argument. This is God's design. The Preacher is not distracted by the audience, but is able to address it with singularity of purpose and effect. Unlike the preaching which is transmitted on television the hearer cannot turn off the messenger with as much ease. As a

---

[66] Craddock, *As One Without Authority*, 29.
[67] Ong, *The Presence of the Word*, 101.

totally *cool* medium television lulls the watcher into mental and spiritual sleep. The preacher is not and cannot be a real part of the watcher's life. And he is, after all, just a *watcher*, not a listener. Even so-called "live" television is only an illusion of reality, a virtual reality. The truly live preacher demands and commands the listener's attention. "When we hear the Word of God spoken by the mouth of men, we are ready to confine our attention to the visible speaker."[68] The Scottish reformer John Knox asserted: "What efficacy hath the living voice above the bare letter read, the hungry and the thirsty do feel their comfort." [69]

While we have referred to preaching as a medium, there is clearly a difference between the direct experience of a speaker's presence and the mediated experience of the electronic image. One is historical reality; the other is only an appearance. As Knox pointed out, even the read word does not have the same effect that the living voice of the preacher has. Thus, the church is never addressed by the living God, in the way He intended, without the living presence of preaching in its midst. Iain Murray, in his biography of D. Martin Lloyd-Jones, observes that Lloyd-Jones's commitment to writing was quite secondary to that of preaching. Ministers "were called to be preachers, not writers. He did not view the readiness of contemporary Christianity to allow the pulpit to be overshadowed by other means of communication as a wise adjustment to modern conditions but as a loss of faith in *the* means to which God has attached the special promise of His power."[70]

Along with being direct and unarguable the monological nature of preaching is inescapable. The challenge it brings is ultimately from God Himself. True preaching is God's challenge to change. He confronts us with the need to repent and believe His Word. The grand errand of true preaching is the transformation of sinners. This should not leave the preacher with the idea that he is "six feet above criticism." Indeed, the priesthood of all believers should always place us in the position of Paul in Berea. The common call among sixties critics of preaching for "feedback" should alert us to the need for openness to and encouragement of questions from the congregation, after worship.[71] We do not need to cave in to egalitarianism to provide forums for discussion of God's Word. Properly understood this enhances, rather than diminishes, the authority of the ministerial office. The wise preacher will be

---

[68] George Lawson, The Life of Joseph (1807 Reprint. Edinburgh: The Banner of Truth Trust, 1972) 87.
[69] Quoted in Iain H. Murray, *David Martyn Lloyd-Jones: The Fight of Faith 1939-1981* (Edinburgh: The Banner of Truth Trust, 1990) 345 (John Knox, *The Works of John Knox*, 1895, Vol. 5, 519).
[70] *Ibid.*
[71] Cf. Clyde H. Reid. *The Empty Pulpit: A Study in Preaching As Communication* (New York: Harper and Row, 1967).

constantly aware of his congregation's response to his preaching, both during the act of preaching and in his other pastoral contacts.

When all is said and done the monological nature of preaching has been and will always be offensive to a fallen world, because it is in essence a resounding "Thus saith the LORD." In this sense there are, as Charles Dennison has aptly said, no *modern* preachers, only preachers.[72] Our understanding of unique factors in the modern world should only reinforce our commitment to the age-old task before us as heralds of the gospel. The Christ of Scripture has commissioned His ambassadors, not to "share" the gospel, though we are called to share many things, but to announce and proclaim it with authority, to give full force to the imperative "Repent and believe the gospel." While this message must be preached with great humility, it must in humility be preached with great authority, the authority of God Himself.

Preaching Is the Voice and Presence of the Great Shepherd

This obvious excellence of preaching is often referred to as the "Incarnational Principle." Unfortunately this principle has often been associated with the immanentism of Liberal and Process theology—a call to social activism. Because the Eternal Son came in the flesh, taking to Himself a complete human nature, except without sin, the presence of a live preacher, called and commissioned by the Lord as His ambassador, is the most suitable means of communicating God's Word. So the secular dilemma of coordinating transcendence and immanence is obviated, not only by the covenantal character of God's revelation, but by the Incarnation. The One Who inhabits eternity becomes a man and enters history. So in preaching the Transcendent Lord is immanent through the living announcement of His Gospel Word.

Joseph is the first type of the Shepherd in Scripture (Gen. 49:24). Moses and Joshua follow the pattern of the Shepherd-leader. Just prior to his death Moses is concerned "that the congregation of the LORD may not be like sheep which have no shepherd" (Numb. 27:17). The kingship is instituted after this model and the great Shepherd Psalms (Pss. 23; 80) are penned by the "sweet psalmist of Israel," David, who prefigures the ministry of the Good Shepherd in His royal capacity (2 Sam. 5:2; 7:7). The great failure of Israel's shepherd-kings points up the need for the True Shepherd of the sheep as Israel's kings serve themselves and leave God's people without a shepherd (1 Kings 22:17). How glorious are the words of Isaiah's prophesy of the coming of the Great Shepherd of the sheep: "He will feed His flock like a shepherd; He will gather the lambs with His arm, And carry *them* in His bosom, *And* gently lead those

---

[72] Charles Dennison, "Preaching and Application: A Review," *Kerux* 4:3 (December 1989) 52.

who are with young" (40:11). This Shepherd will build the temple of God (Isa. 44:28). He will feed the sheep of the Lord's flock: "I will establish one shepherd over them, and he shall feed them—My servant David. He shall feed them and be their shepherd." (Eze. 34:23).

When He comes he assures us: "My sheep hear My voice, and I know them, and they follow Me" (John 10:27). His words, which are the words of the entire Scripture (1 Pet. 1:10,11) are the food upon which His sheep feed. He appoints overseers to shepherd His people by the preaching of His Word: "Therefore take heed to yourselves and to all the flock, among which the Holy Spirit has made you overseers, to shepherd the church of God which He purchased with His own blood" (Acts 20:28). The Great Shepherd calls undershepherds to lead His people (1 Pet. 5:2, 4). The Word given to the apostles is the voice of the Good Shepherd after the ascension: "The words that I speak to you are spirit, and *they* are life." (John 6:63). At the heart of the ministry of His undershepherds, then, is the communication of the voice of the Shepherd to His sheep: "the sheep follow him, for they know his voice" (John 10:4). This is the task of preaching, as the resurrected Lord emphatically told Peter: "Feed My lambs" (John 21:15).

The One who has visited His people in history continues to visit them through His Word and Spirit in the person of the preacher. Nothing can replace that personal presence and that living voice. The preacher ministers to a people whom he knows personally by name, even as their Shepherd knows them (John 10:3). He preaches the One who laid down His life for His sheep (John 10:15; 1 Cor. 2:2). He impresses them with the reality of the kingdom of God. In his famous treatise *The Religious Affections* Jonathan Edwards notes the importance of preaching in this regard:

And the impressing divine things on the hearts and affections of men is evidently one great and main end for which God has ordained that His Word delivered in the holy Scriptures should be opened, applied, and set home upon men, in preaching. And therefore it does not answer the aim which God had in this institution, merely to have good commentaries and expositions on the Scripture, and other good books of divinity; because, although these may tend as well as preaching to give men a good doctrinal or speculative understanding of the things of the Word of God, yet they have not an equal tendency to impress them on men's hearts and affections. God hath appointed a particular and lively application of His Word to men in the preaching of it, as a fit means to affect sinners with the importance of the things of religion, and their own misery and necessity of a remedy, and the glory and sufficiency of a remedy provided; and to stir up the pure minds of the saints, and quicken their affections, by often bringing the great things of religion to their remembrance, and setting them before them in their proper colours, though they know them, and have been fully instructed in them already. [73]

The Presence of the Good Shepherd in the preaching of the pastor, who is by the nature of his office an under-shepherd of Jesus Christ, is indispensable to the life of the church. The television preacher never knows his audience by name. His is not a living voice. Nor can he exemplify the self-denying love of His Master. How often Paul set himself forth as a model to be imitated: "Imitate me, just as I also *imitate* Christ" (1 Cor. 11:1; cf. Col. 4:16, 17; Heb. 6:12). We cannot imitate an image on a screen, much less feel accountable to the man behind the image as the shepherd or pastor of our souls. "If preaching ever loses the support of personal affection fostered by pastoral care and the human touch, it is doubtful if it can carried by what engineers—who always have a sound concern for foundations—call sky-hooks."[74]

The importance of face-to-face encounter is clearly central to the Incarnation. The face, more than any other aspect of the physical nature, reveals the person. Thus John wanted more than any other means of communication to see his spiritual children "face to face" (2 John 12; 3 John 14). Even writing a personal letter could not replace personal encounter: "Having many things to write to you, I did not wish *to do so* with paper and ink; but I hope to come to you and speak face to face, that our joy may be full" (2 John 12).

The consummate reality for the Christian will be seeing the face of Jesus Christ in resurrection glory: "But we all, with unveiled face, beholding as in a mirror the glory of the Lord, are being transformed into the same image from glory to glory, just as by the Spirit of the Lord" (2 Cor. 3:18). Until then we see the reflection of that glory through the preaching of Christ from His Word, mediated by the revealing power of the Holy Spirit. Sinners cannot survive in the presence of the glorified Lamb (Rev. 20:11). Only when the believer is sinlessly perfected in the resurrection will be able to stand before the face of Jesus Christ (1 John 3:2).

The face-to-face presence of the preacher is a reminder of what is coming (Rev. 22:4). It is a downpayment on eschatological glory. In commenting on Haggai 1:12, Calvin says: "We may then conclude from these words, that the glory of God so shines in his word, that we ought to be so much affected by it, whenever he speaks by his servants, as though he were nigh to us face to

---

[73] Jonathan Edwards, *Religious Affections*. (The Works of Jonathan Edwards, edited by Perry Miller, vol. 2. Edited by John E. Smith. New Haven: Yale University Press, 1959) 115, 116.
[74] Gaius Glenn Atkins, *Preaching and the Mind of Today* (New York: Round Table Press, 1934) 30.

face..."[75] Preaching is the primary means by which the Good Shepherd visits His people in the interim. Paul saw the preacher, not as a doctrinal lecturer, but as a pastor, who imparted his very life to the flock: "So, affectionately longing for you, we were well pleased to impart to you not only the gospel of God, but also our own lives, because you had become dear to us. For you remember, brethren, our labor and toil; for laboring night and day, that we might not be a burden to any of you, we preached to you the gospel of God." (1 Thess. 2:8, 9). "It is the job of the preacher to make the Word of God, the Word of the prophets put into writing, a living reality for the congregation."[76]

A word needs to be added about the *locality* of live preaching. The personal presence of the preacher among God's people the church is accurately communicated by the English word for the local pastor: *vicar*. The word vicar comes from the root for *vicarious*, in the place of another. The pastor functions as an ambassador of his Master.

> Now all things *are* of God, who has reconciled us to Himself through Jesus Christ, and has given us the ministry of reconciliation, that is, that God was in Christ reconciling the world to Himself, not imputing their trespasses to them, and has committed to us the word of reconciliation. Now then, we are ambassadors for Christ, as though God were pleading through us: we implore *you* on Christ's behalf, be reconciled to God. For He made Him who knew no sin *to be* sin for us, that we might become the righteousness of God in Him (2 Cor. 5:18-21).

The purpose of His ascension was that from His exalted position He would send His Spirit (John 14:16ff; 16:7). This is the Biblical means of Christ being present with His ecumenical body, i.e. the church among the nations. The World Wide Web and other forms of electronic communication have inverted this reality. They seek to transcend and, at points, even to deny space and time. While these media may in one sense overcome the limits of space and time, they also forfeit the locality of personal presence which may never be transcended by creatures. In *Acts* we see the apostles employing the "footpower of the gospel." Novelist Larry Woiwode comments: "In order to deliver that gospel in our age, you have to walk up to somebody, even if you've arrived earlier on a Concorde, and there is no proof that the spirit a Christian carries, or the Spirit who applies the gospel to a congregation, is transmitted over television. In *Acts* the delivery of the gospel is a personal act."[77] D. Martin Lloyd-Jones put it well: "There is a unity between preacher and hearers and

---

[75] John Calvin, *Commentary on Haggai* (1540-1563. Translation and reprint. Edinburgh: Calvin Translation Society. 1847. Reprint. vol. 15. Grand Rapids: Baker Book House, 1969) 343. I owe this quotation to my friend and colleague Stephen Doe.
[76] Old, *The Reading and Preaching of the Scriptures*, vol. 1, 59.
[77] Larry Woiwode, *Acts* (New York: HarperCollins Publishers, 1993) 121.

there is transaction backwards and forwards. That, to me, is true preaching. And that is where you see the essential difference between listening to preaching in a church and listening to a sermon on the television or on the radio. You cannot listen to true preaching in detachment and you must never be in a position where you can turn it off.[78]

Throughout the History of Redemption, God has personally met His people locally in space and time. His ultimate condescension in this regard is the Incarnation. While the modern world has never been better "connected" electronically, it seems to be starving nearly to death for lack of personal and local connectedness. Thus the local church provides this reality in a way that no other institution can. At the center of this is God's speech in the preaching and presence of His appointed vicars. "Sound unites groups of human beings as nothing else does. ...human community is essentially a union of interior consciousnesses."[79] The private reading of Scripture is always also a communal reading, because the Scriptures are a covenant document uniting God's people in all ages. Preaching accents and cultivates this communion. The worst tendencies of mass culture will be overcome by the promotion of live pastoral preaching as the center of the church's life. There is no better antidote to the electronic dispersion of our day.

Preaching Is the Unique Power of a Living Voice

There is a concreteness and a power to the voice that reflects the power of God's voice in His created image, man (*imago Dei*). We note the effectiveness of orality when we read a poem aloud instead of just reading it silently on the page. So in prayer we have a sense of the reality of our communication with God when we pray aloud. "I cry out to the LORD with my voice; with my voice to the LORD I make my supplication" (Ps. 142:1). The Bible has much to say about the power of human speech. "There is one who speaks like the piercings of a sword, but the tongue of the wise *promotes* health." (Prov. 10:18). The old adage about sticks and stones is more at home in a materialistic age. Anyone who knows the pain inflicted by gossip will quickly prefer a stone.

William Graham in his *Beyond the Written Word: Oral Aspects of Scripture in the History of Religion* examines the oral nature of Martin Luther's approach to Scripture and preaching. Walter Ong describes his conclusion: "Graham brings out the sensory immediacy of the oral and its communal effectiveness. Hearing a speech unites an audience, individual

---

[78] D. Martin Lloyd-Jones, "Knowing the Times: Extracts from an Important New Book by Dr. Lloyd-Jones, *Banner of Truth Magazine* 317 (February 1990) 11, 12.
[79] Ong, *The Presence of the Word*, 122, 146.

reading of the speech fragments them."[80] Ong is at his best and most useful, as an apologist for the oral, in his book *The Presence of the Word* (1967). He begins: "Man communicates with his whole body, and yet the word is his primary medium. Communication, like knowledge itself, flowers in speech."[81] He goes on to say, "The word is not an inert record but a living something, like sound, something going on."[82] Despite Ong's often-too-negative assessment of the written, he rightly laments the absence of the "wingèd word" in modern life. Only by the living word may persons enter into the consciousness and life of others.[83] Ong hopes that electronic media will revive our appreciation for words as sound. It is not in literate culture, however, that we are imprisoned, as Ong suspects. We are rather imprisoned in our sinful propensity to pervert all media to idolatrous purposes. Only through preaching does the Word of God have wings to fly into the hearts of the people in our day.

There is in the power of the voice, of the spoken word, a mystery, which stands as a poignant testimony against the flatness of Modernism and the superficiality of Postmodernism. Horizontally, that mystery is accounted for in the spiritual dimensions of the human soul. Vertically, that mystery is accounted for in the omnipresence of God. The Word, which He promises will accomplish everything He sends it for (Isa. 55:11), is the power behind the change of heart referred to by Jesus as the new birth (John 3). The gospel message is equated by Paul with God's creative word spoken in Genesis 1: "For we do not preach ourselves, but Christ Jesus the Lord, and ourselves your bondservants for Jesus' sake. For it is the God who commanded light to shine out of darkness, who has shone in our hearts to *give* the light of the knowledge of the glory of God in the face of Jesus Christ" (2 Cor. 4:5, 6). The staccato commands of Genesis 1 demonstrate the power of God's spoken Word in the miraculous immediacy of His creative acts. Paul links the effect of God's spoken Word in creation with the power of preaching in the new creation. This is the nature of the sound of the human voice as a replica of God's voice.

At just this point the warning of Ong should be heeded: Spatialized "accounts of language which make it a phenomenon rather than a communication, tend to think of God himself as no longer a communicator, one who speaks to man, but as a Great Architect (a typical eighteenth century concept)..."[84] The Bible, of course, does not pit the idea that God is the craftsman of space over against His orality. The two go hand in hand. Proverbs 8:30 pictures the Eternal Son in His relationship to the created order

---

[80] Ong, Review: *Beyond the Written Word*, 204.
[81] Ong, *The Presence of the Word*, 1.
[82] *Ibid.*, 12.
[83] *Ibid.*, 15.
[84] *Ibid.*, 73.

as a master craftsman (אָמוֹן artificer or architect). He is the great Supervisor, Builder who superintends His creation project from beginning to end. His voice is the instrument of His control according to Psalm 29:4, 5: "The voice of the LORD *is* powerful; The voice of the LORD *is* full of majesty. The voice of the LORD breaks the cedars, yes, the LORD splinters the cedars of Lebanon." As Ong points out the Kantian distinction between *noumena* and *phenomena*, intended to preserve scientific epistemology, as well as religion, has tended rather to focus attention on appearances, and thus on the visual. But sound alone, Ong maintains, penetrates surfaces.[85] "One does not produce words in order to get rid of them but rather to have them penetrate, impregnate, the mind of another."[86] We are again brought face to face with the need not to pit space against time, sound against sight. God is the Author of them both. However, Ong's strength is found in his assertion of the primacy of speech. We wish to make a more fundamental assertion of the primacy of preaching, which is rooted in the Original Preacher, who inhabits eternity, and is incarnate in time.

The Biblical concept of teaching in its relation to the effect of the voice is captured in the word catechize (κατηχέω). It literally means *to sound around* or *re-sound*: "*to sound* a thing *in one's ears, impress it* upon one *by word of mouth.*"[87] This potency of voice is used to describe the activity of the teacher of the law (Rom. 2:18), and the preacher of the gospel (Gal. 6:6). The voice of the preached word is effective, as God blesses it through the illuminating power of His Spirit. Ong maintains that "early man" experienced words "as powerful, effective, of a piece with other actuality far more than later visualist man is likely to do. A word is a real happening, indeed a happening par excellence."[88] "[T]he word as sound establishes here-and-now personal presence. Abraham knew God's presence when he heard his 'voice.'"[89] This is why we refer to the act of preaching as the "preaching moment" or "event." Despite all the imperfections of the human messenger God is acting in the "acoustic event" of preaching.[90]

Ong's mistake in this context is to attribute "more reality" to the spoken as opposed to the written word, because the latter is visual.[91] He goes on to assert: "Sound is a special sensory key to interiority."[92] Ong insists that "the book takes the reader out of the tribe."[93] This dichotomy between written and

---

[85] *Ibid.*, 74.
[86] *Ibid.*, 98.
[87] Liddell and Scott, *A Greek-English Lexicon*. New York: Harper and Brothers, Publishers, 1853.
[88] Ong, *The Presence of the Word*, 111.
[89] *Ibid.*, 113.
[90] Clyde E. Fant, *Preaching For Today* (New York: Harper and Row, 1975) 157ff.
[91] Ong, *The Presence of the Word*, 111.
[92] *Ibid.*, 117.
[93] *Ibid.*, 135.

spoken is contrary to what the Bible clearly teaches about the complementary relationship between the two. David's meditation on the Word in Psalm 1, among dozens of other similar passages, demonstrates that private reading may also be a powerful vehicle for interiorizing, as Sven Birkerts has pointed out of reading in general. Furthermore, as we have seen the public reading and preaching of the written Word seals what is written on the corporate consciousness and memory of the church, which has been entrusted with the deposit of the written Scriptures (2 Tim. 3:15). As normative covenant document the Bible has a unique power to unite. Eric Havelock states that the Bible is unique among printed books in remaining immune to McLuhan's critique of the printed word.[94] However, Ong's concept of the word as event is very important to the preacher as he approaches the preaching moment, and considers the unique God-given power of the human voice, especially when it is used to communicate the message of God's written Word. "No other speech has the public and yet private nature of preaching."[95]

The concreteness of the spoken word has no peer among the media in general. It is the primary means of human communication, because it is God's primary way of communicating. Thus, preaching is His chosen way to address people in all ages precisely because it is unmediated by technology. Furthermore, Biblical preaching is God's chief antidote to idolatry. A people of the Word will accept no substitutes. The Word of God preached has no peer among spoken words. It is God's means of imprinting His Word on the hearts of His people.[96]

HEARTS OF FLESH: THE COMMITTED HEARER

As covenantal communication preaching is always two-way. The hearer is always to be a worshipper. It is never preaching *and* worship. Preaching is the supreme act of worship.[97] Along with the internal work of God's Spirit the effectiveness of preaching depends, in part, on the attitude of the listener. This section is a meant to help those who regularly hear the Word of God preached to take their covenant responsibilities more seriously. It also provides an outline of issues which the preacher should address in his preaching.

---

[94] Eric Havelock, *The Muse Learns to Write: Reflections on Orality and Literacy from Antiquity to the Present* (New Haven: Yale University Press, 1986) 49.
[95] Gerald Hamilton Kennedy, *His Word Through Preaching* (New York: Harper, 1947) 8.
[96] Cf. Fant, *Preaching For Today*, 162. Quotes Thomas Aquinas: "Therefore it is fitting that Christ, as the most excellent teacher, should adapt that manner of teaching whereby his doctrine would be imprinted on the hearts of his hearers."
[97] Old, *The Reading and Preaching of the Scriptures*, vol. 1, 7.

Dangers To Avoid

Every attentive hearer of God's Word must be on the lookout for idolatrous tendencies in the culture of which he/she is a part. The following themes are examples of some of the worst dangers to avoid.

Avoid Being a Consumer of Entertainment

Among other unBiblical expectations of the minister in our age, the preacher is expected to be an entertainer. Television and all of the visual media have, as we have seen, cast all of modern life in the entertainment mode. Neil Postman has described the medium as a metaphor: "Media-metaphors classify the world for us."[98] We have moved from the "Age of Exposition" to the ""Age of Show Business."[99] Thus we are a culture which is regularly engaged by talk show and game show hosts. Entertainers have become the role models and spokesmen for our culture. They lecture at colleges and universities. Their opinions on a variety of "serious" subjects are regularly sought. We have come to expect all of life to be entertaining. This may color the way you look at the preacher, as it does the way the preacher often looks at himself.

I have a book in my library which I received in a box from the library of a retired minister. I keep it with the spine turned toward the wall because it is titled: *The Preacher Joke Book: Religious Anecdotes from the Oral Tradition*.[100] I comfort myself with the thought that I do not recognize any of the names of the contributors. I recently attended a conference at which the main speaker began with a lengthy joke, obviously to loosen up the audience, and assure us that he is, after all, a "regular guy." Just before presidential elections the two candidates now do a comedy spot.

Humor is wonderful gift, but it strikes me that only in the Age of Entertainment would humor be an expected part of the preacher's repertoire. When we think of the tone which ought to be set in the act of preaching, especially in the Age of Entertainment, we must conclude that it should be one of extreme seriousness. As our culture entertains itself to death, we must attach to the preaching of the word, a solemnity which we rarely find in the modern world. The analogy of the ambassador gives us Biblical boundaries in this regard.[101] Preachers have been given a very serious message from the King of

---

[98] Neil Postman, *Amusing Ourselves To Death: Public Discourse in the Age of Show Business* (New York: Viking Penguin, Inc., 1985) 10.
[99] *Ibid.*, 63.
[100] Loyal Jones, *The Preacher Joke Book: Religious Anecdotes from the Oral Tradition*, (Little Rock, AR: August House, 1989).
[101] I owe the suggestion of this analogy to T. David Gordon.

kings. We are to communicate as His messengers. As we bring the message of reconciliation to sinners we must speak in the words and way of the King who sovereignly proffers amnesty. As we enter the very presence of our augustly holy God in worship, dealing with issues of life and death, we must labor to be as unlike the "house of mirth" as possible. Every faithful hearer must expect this, and thereby encourage the preacher with our expectation.

As a Christian you must never expect entertainment in worship or from the preacher. The proper mode of worship is the Holy presence of our Lord. The committed hearer will look for substantive exposition of the Word of God. Exposition, not entertainment, is the mode of the preacher. That is the point of our favorite verse to prove the inspiration of the Scripture. "All Scripture *is* given by inspiration of God, and *is* profitable for doctrine, for reproof, for correction, for instruction in righteousness, that the man of God may be complete, thoroughly equipped for every good work" (2 Tim. 3:16, 17). This is the profit we must seek from preaching in the Age of Entertainment.

Avoid Being a Personality or Managerial Cultist

The power of celebrity is a uniquely modern problem. As Boorstin notes, celebrity is manufactured fame. Instead of the hero, who was known for his extraordinary character and deeds, the celebrity is a product of the Graphic Revolution. "The hero created himself; the celebrity is created by the media. The hero was a big man; the celebrity is a big name."[102] The celebrity is known for being known. He has an impressive persona. This has created a great temptation for the church. If the celebrity has become the role model for the world, the preacher may be expected to be the same, an image of the modern leader—just an image. Thus, the church is at times almost as superficial in its expectations of the pastor as the world is of its celebrities, looking for the "nice" personality.

It has been observed that the two vocational heroes of our time are the manager and the therapist. As we have seen, the ideal of the "professional" has become an idol of modern culture. This is no less true of the ministry. David Wells observes: "technical and managerial competence in the church have plainly come to dominate the definition of pastoral service. ...[T]he minister's authority or professional status rides not on his ...character, ability to expound the Word of God, or theological skill in relating that Word to the contemporary world, but on interpersonal skills, administrative talents, and ability to organize

---

[102] Daniel J. Boorstin, *The Image or Whatever Happened to the American Dream?* (New York: Atheneum, 1962) 47, 61.

the community."[103] This is reflected in one of the premier journals for evangelical clergy, *Leadership*, launched by *Christianity Today* in 1980. David Wells observes that 80 percent of its articles from 1980 to 1988 dealt with problems encountered by ministers, and 13 percent were devoted to "techniques for managing the church... ...[L]ess than 1 percent of the material made any clear reference to Scripture..."[104] If the pastor is truly called to imitate his Lord, who is the Great Shepherd of the Sheep (1 Pet. 5:1-4), in ministry, one need only replace His title with the Chief Executive Officer, to get a sense of how out of accord with Scripture the modern conception is.

Your attitude, combined with the expectations of the rest of the congregation, will either tempt the minister to consider himself, and therefore act like, a celebrity or manager, or it will encourage him to be what God has called him to be: a minister of the Word. There can be little doubt that the professionalization of the ministry has led to a decline in preaching passion and skills. The less God-centered the church's view of the ministry and preaching, the more man-centered the sermons will tend to be.[105] What is worse, as the church expects the pulpit to meet its needs, the pulpit becomes simply "a sounding board from which the Church hears itself."[106]

The temptation to esteem the "famous" preacher is one of the greatest threats, among those who esteem preaching, to preaching today. The preacher who has made a name for himself on the conference circuit, even though that may not have been his motive, makes the everyday preacher look drab and dull. There is no glossy photo in the bulletin, no recognition beyond the local church. This undermines God's basic institution. What He has provided for His people in the local church week after week, through thick and thin, is the greatest blessing of all. How can celebrity recognition be important in light of the message of a Savior who was crucified as a despised and rejected criminal?

Avoid Looking for Therapy

In our age the Devil simply caters to an age-old addiction when he promotes the therapeutic. This same anthropocentrism was evident in Calvin's day. In seeking to bring a Biblical concept of the church to expression in Geneva he noted of his opposition: "they were entangled in so many errors, because they would not follow that form which God had appointed. ...The first difference between true worship and idolatry is this: when the godly take in hand nothing

---

[103] David F. Wells, *No Place for Truth or Whatever Happened to Evangelical Theology?* (Grand Rapids: Eerdmans, 1993) 233, 234.
[104] *Ibid.*, 113, 114.
[105] *Ibid.*, 251.
[106] *Ibid.*, 253.

but that which is agreeable to the Word of God, but the other think all that lawful which pleaseth themselves, and so they count their own will a law..." Instead they "forge to themselves a carnal and worldly god."[107]

How much of our modern attitude toward worship reflects this self-oriented pleasure quest? How many judge the preacher and his sermon in terms of the question: "Is it meeting my needs?" This is usually what the slogan "relevance" refers to. The market-driven church has as its motto: "Find a need meet it, find a hurt heal it."[108] The entire "self esteem" philosophy which permeates every cultural institution reverses the Biblical concern when it claims that loving our neighbor as ourselves is a call to first love ourselves. This falls hard on the central ethical implication of the cross: self denial. The Gospel message, from the modern perspective, is irrelevant by its very nature. It demands repentance from our self preoccupation, and a liberating call to a God centered life, rooted in the kingdom of heaven. As George Macdonald poignantly observed: "that need which is no need, is a demon sucking at the spring of your life."[109] Expect and pray for preaching which will challenge and root out such demons.

Avoid Being a Passive Listener

One of the great dangers of the entertainment and therapy modes is that they make us used to being passive. We are entertained, or have our problems solved for us. Our participation is simply to enjoy or feel better about ourselves. In the consumer mode we are "programmed" to view everything, every situation or person as a product or service to be consumed. We ask questions like: "What can this church do for *me*? How can this preacher make *me* feel better, or solve *my* problems?" So we tend to sit, waiting to be entertained, waiting for our *needs* to be met. This is not the mode, position or attitude of the true worshipper.

The cry for "participation" in worship is one of the most misdirected quests of worshipping communities. It is often motivated by the desire to share the spotlight "on stage," or to feel the excitement of an emotionally charged group experience. Covenantal participation, on the other hand, is first of all an inward reality. Outwardly it means being prayerfully engaged in every element the order of service. This is especially true of listening to the sermon.

---

[107] John Calvin, *Commentary on Acts* [7:44] (1540-1563. Translation and reprint. Edinburgh: Calvin Translation Society. 1847. Reprint. vol. 18. Grand Rapids: Baker Book House, 1969) 298, 299, 303.
[108] Os Guinness, *Dining with the Devil: The Megachurch Movement Flirts with Modernity* (Grand Rapids: Baker Books, 1993) 62-67.
[109] *Ibid.*, 67.

"Hearing a sermon correctly is an act of religious worship."[110] Physically you may be passive, but spiritually and intellectually you are called to listen for the voice of the Good Shepherd in the ministry of His Word. This takes an intense effort, which challenges the "couch potato" mentality of our day. Listen to Sietsma:

> Hearing God's Word is not only an activity of the first order but the only activity befitting humans in relationship to their God. A relation of equality never exists between God and His people; however that fact in no way detracts from the dignity or office of the believer. Therefore, when in the administration of the Word, this relationship between speaking God and listening man shines forth, then the office of believer is most beautifully displayed and exercised. Thus we are not called to find a liturgy in which preaching is minimized so that the congregation can be given a more obvious role. The congregation's duty is to listen. Rather, we are to practice improving and increasing our ability to listen, so that the congregation may listen to the Word with all its heart and souls and mind. That is not a slight task.[111]

Attitudes and Practices To Cultivate

Elizabeth Elliot speaks wise words about our attitude toward worship: "Hymns constitute a crucial part of worship, but not by any means the whole. In churches which use almost exclusively what are called 'praise songs', that part of the service is usually referred to as 'Worship,' as though prayer, preaching, offering, and listening were something else. May I lodge a plea to those who use overhead projectors to make sure that some great hymns are displayed in addition to the praise songs? Hymns will get you through the night. ....Everywhere I go I try to point out what a tragic loss is the disappearance of these powerful aids to spiritual stamina."[112]

The Larger Catechism (Question #160) gives hearers of the Word excellent instruction: "What is required of those that hear the word preached? A. It is required of those that hear the word preached, that they attend upon it with diligence, preparation, and prayer; examine what they hear by the scriptures; receive the truth with faith, love, meekness, and readiness of mind, as the word of God; meditate, and confer of it; hide it in their hearts, and bring forth the fruit of it in their lives." How seriously our forefathers took the

---

[110] T. David Gordon, "Presuppositions Regarding Preaching," unpublished manuscript, nd.

[111] K. Sietsma. *The Idea of Office*. Translated by Henry Vander Goot (Jordan Station, Ontario: Paideia Press, 1985) 99.

[112] Elisabeth Elliot, "Whatever Happened To Hymns?" [WWW document] URL http://www.banneroftruth.co.uk//articles/whatever_happened_to_hymns.htm

responsibilities of the listener. In light of the following suggestions meditating on the Scripture references provided by the authors of the *Larger Catechism* will be an important aid to becoming a better hearer: Prov. 8:34; 1 Pet. 2:1,2; Luke 8:18; Ps. 119:18; Eph. 6:18,19; Acts 17:11; Heb. 4:2; 2 Thess. 2:10; James 1:21; Acts 17:11; 1 Thess. 2:13; Luke 9:44; Heb. 2:1; Luke 24:14; Deut. 6:6,7; Prov. 2:1; Ps. 119:11; Luke 8:15; James 1:25.

Come Prayerfully Expectant to Worship

Prayer in preparation for worship is essential. It should be noted, as we will see below in connection with the Scriptures, that praying in the Bible, even in private, was with the voice. David in countless places in the Psalms says that he cried out to the LORD with his voice. The voice lends concreteness to our words and to God's Word. Paul pled with the Ephesian church: "praying always with all prayer and supplication in the Spirit, being watchful to this end with all perseverance and supplication for all the saints—and for me, that utterance may be given to me, that I may open my mouth boldly to make known the mystery of the gospel, for which I am an ambassador in chains; that in it I may speak boldly, as I ought to speak" (Eph. 6:18-20). As the *Larger Catechism* instructs, we are to come to attend to preaching with diligence, preparation and prayer. Certainly both diligence and prayer must be part of our preparation. Preparing with prayerful reading of God's Word, especially on the eve of the Lord's Day, will cultivate the diligence to hear when the public worship begins. We will come expecting to hear from our Good and Great Shepherd.

Be Engaged in Listening as a Reader

The regular habit of good reading will help prepare you to be a good listener to good preaching. The very act of reading helps us to think more clearly, logically and cogently. It helps the reader to develop depth through contemplating what is being read. It provides a counter environment to the simultaneity of the electronic media, which tend to bypass thought processes. The non-reader will be prepared only for content-light preaching. Like Bud Lite lightweight preaching is nonfattening, and will not build the soul in Christian faith. This, of course, is especially true of Bible reading. The disciplined Bible reader will bring a store of knowledge of Biblical concepts and teaching to their listening. They will also bring the art of worshipful meditation to the pew, which is a requirement for engagement in Biblical preaching. The Bereans profited from Paul ministry precisely because they were good readers of God's Word.

Listen for the Voice of the Good Shepherd

"The 'book religion" of the Hebrews, as Siegfried Morenz points out, lay in the Hebrew 'genius for hearing'."[113] In the modern world there are many other voices competing for our attention. This has always been the case since Adam and Eve listened to the wrong voice in the Garden. The environment of this world is cultivated by the voices of communication. The world now has a heightened ability to impose its environment of thought, one which is contrary to the Word of God, on the church.

Psalm 1 is instructive in this regard. The Psalmist frames his inspired poem in negative terms. The believer is distinguished by his opposition to the entire environment of unbelief. He does not walk in the counsel, stand in the way or sit in the seat of the scornful unbeliever. He has a whole different approach. The world is the environment into which he is born. That environment is the given. But as a person of the Covenant he is part of the LORD's invasion of history through the Seed of the woman. The Psalmist cultivates an "anti-environment" by meditating on the Word of God day and night. Through redemption the believer is to develop a completely different approach to God and to all of life. He is to work at the development of a Christian mind so that he can withstand the environment of this "present evil age," based on the written Word of God.

One of the elements of poetry in the Bible which is largely lost on contemporary people is that it was written to be read aloud. The correlation between the written and the spoken word in the Bible is essential to cultivating the anti-environment. Its writtenness protects the Word from the corruption of the fallen mind. But the individualizing tendency of writing/print, while important in its own way, needs to be balanced with the hearing of the word, as well as the seeing/touching/tasting of the Word in the sacraments. Along with preparation for hearing God's Word read and preached each Lord's Day, as we have outlined above, it is important to read the Word in private and family devotions. Remember, catechizing, in oral culture, meant to teach by "sounding in the ear." Oral instruction was the staple of ancient pedagogy. God has made us to know Him through all of the *natural* media of communication.

In listening for the voice of Jesus Christ the committed listener must cultivate respect for His ordained under-shepherds. Many in our day believe that reading the Bible on their own is sufficient. But if you believe Paul's great statement: "faith comes by hearing" (Rom. 10:17), you will recognize the

---

[113] Walter Ong, Review: *Beyond the Written Word: Oral Aspects of Scripture in the History of Religion* (William A. Graham) in *America* (Mar. 4, 1989): 204.

absolute necessity of the preacher in his office as minister of the Word. In fact, we would be hard-pressed to find instances of conversion through mere reading the Bible, *in* the Bible. What we find, rather, are people like the Ethiopian Eunuch, who need an interpreter, or preacher to explain its meaning. You should always take the position of the eunuch who, when asked "Do you understand what you are reading?" answered, "How can I, unless someone guides me?" (Acts 8:30, 31). Even the Scripture-searching Bereans received the gospel by *hearing* Paul (Acts 17:10, 11).

One of the dangers we have seen in the printed book as a medium is that there is a tendency to undermine the authority of the spoken word, and the authority of the speaker. This should never be the case in the church, because God has designed the means of grace, as well as the church itself, to overcome this democratizing, privatizing tendency. Long before printing this sinful tendency of the human heart was addressed by the writer of Hebrews: "And let us consider one another in order to stir up love and good works, not forsaking the assembling of ourselves together, as *is* the manner of some, but exhorting *one another*, and so much the more as you see the Day approaching" (Heb. 10:24, 25).

In hearing the voice of your Savior you should be prepared to obey all that *He says*. Whatever attitudes, ideas, words, and activities need to be repented of, changed, or practiced, be ready to respond in repentance and faith. Remember that the Biblical idea of "hearing" is obedient response to the Word of God, "Speak Lord for thy servant heareth." If He is the Lord of your life, this should be your *only* response to Biblical preaching. An unrepentant attitude tends to create bitterness toward preaching and the preacher (Heb. 12:14-17).

Worship, with its covenantal order, is meant to provide an anti-environment to the ordinary life of the fallen world. The Sabbath is God's antidote to idolatry, as it teaches us our connection with heavenly realities (Leviticus 26:1 2,). It is God's way of cultivating His call, in the life of God's people, to live connected with Christ. We are called to reenact the heavenly pattern of Lord's Day worship in everyday life. Careful attention to God's Word preached is meant to inculcate moment by moment hearing and heeding of the Word of God as the applied Scripture rings in our ears in everyday life. Our attitude as worshippers, and thus as hearers, is summed up by the hortatory refrain of the glorified Lamb to the seven churches: "If anyone has an ear, let him hear" (Rev. 13:9). The power of the electronic environment is no match for this Voice. The power of modern images in their tendency toward idolatry is nil for a people of the Word.

10

Trumpeter of God: The Effective Preacher

Cry aloud, spare not; lift up your voice like a trumpet;
tell My people their transgression, and the house of Jacob their sins.

—Isaiah 58:1

The contemporary preacher must project his message
into the teeth of the gale of the mass media. The air is full of voices.

—Merrill R Abbey[1]

Christian ministry functions on the borderline between
the cross and the resurrection, between heaven and hell.
This frontier is no place for the faint-hearted; those who have
little faith in their message and its power do not belong in the pulpit.

—James Daane[2]

Anybody who keeps in mind the goals which the Reformation once set
for itself can only be appalled at what has happened in the church of Luther
and Calvin to the very thing which its fathers regarded as the source and
spring of Christian faith and life, namely, preaching.

—Helmut Thielicke[3]

The most effective weapon in the arsenal of the church militant is the preaching of the Word. This is so because God has mandated it to be so in His Word. Moreover, we have seen something of the wisdom of His arrangement in the previous chapter. If unmasking and challenging idolatry is

---

[1] Merrill R. Abbey, *Preaching to the Contemporary Mind* (Nashville: Abingdon Press, 1963) 32.
[2] James Daane, *Preaching With Confidence: A Theological Essay on the Power of the Pulpit* (Grand Rapids: Eerdmans, 1980) 29.
[3] Helmut Thielicke, *The Trouble With The Church* (New York: Harper and Row, 1965) 1.

our best critical weapon in apologetics and evangelism, preaching is the central *formative* weapon in building the church to withstand the onslaught of the world. The preacher is the trumpeter of God, announcing the arrival of the Savior of the world in Whom sin and death have been judged, and before Whom all will one day stand on the Day of Judgment. The trumpet (שׁוֹפָר) is a symbol of the sharp, penetrating sound of God's holy voice of judgment on all covenant-breaking and sin. We first encounter its use at Mount Sinai. The people are stricken with fear at the sound (Exod. 19:16), and moved to recognize their need for a mediator, Moses, who is a type of the Christ. Thus the Mediator alone is able to hear the trumpet. "And when the blast of the trumpet sounded long and became louder and louder, Moses spoke, and God answered him by voice" (Exod. 19:19). The trumpet of judgment is sounded when the people enter the promised land to establish the typological kingdom of Israel at Jericho (Josh. 6). It was a call to battle against the unbelieving nations who threatened God's claim upon Canaan (Judges 3:27).

The trumpet is also a call to listen to God and celebrate God's sacrifice of Jesus the coming Mediator (Numb. 10:2-10). The New Covenant uses the trumpet symbol prefigured in the Day of Atonement (Lev. 25:9): "Then you shall cause the trumpet of the Jubilee to sound on the tenth *day* of the seventh month; on the Day of Atonement you shall make the trumpet to sound throughout all your land." The sound of God's judgment in the all-encompassing annual sacrifice for sin is a signal of the coming liberty to be found in the Lamb of God, and the consummate victory of God over all His enemies. In the Olivet discourse Jesus describes the decisive denouement of the last battle: "And He will send His angels with a great sound of a trumpet, and they will gather together His elect from the four winds, from one end of heaven to the other" (Matt. 24:31). The long awaited glory will be realized: "Behold, I tell you a mystery: We shall not all sleep, but we shall all be changed—in a moment, in the twinkling of an eye, at the last trumpet. For the trumpet will sound, and the dead will be raised incorruptible, and we shall be changed" (1 Cor. 15:51, 52). It is with His trumpet voice that the glorified Lord of the church reveals to John the unfolding of this last epoch of history in which we now live (Rev. 1:10).

It is thus with trumpet voice that the preacher is to announce the reconciliation of God in Christ to the nations. The electronic age seeks to drown out the sound of the preacher's voice, to mute the clarion call of the trumpet. It is God's gracious call to hear the message of the gospel. In the midst of the confusion of tongues in Corinth Paul asks: "For if the trumpet makes an uncertain sound, who will prepare himself for battle?" (1 Cor. 14:8). The uncertain sound emanating from the modern pulpit will only be clarified by men who know their calling before God and are committed to trumpeting the clear, powerful, penetrating Word of God to the nations.

REMEMBER YOUR OFFICE

The Idea of Office

If we expect to receive a proper conception of our office from our cultural context we are doomed to disappointment, because we live in the worst of times for such a conception. We have been spoiled by a cultural respectability which no longer obtains for the Western church. Egalitarianism represents a radical threat to the Biblical idea of office. The democratization of office has leveled the authority structure which was once assumed by Western Civilization all the way back to the Roman Empire in which the gospel was first preached.[4] If the past tendency of abuse was toward elitism and authoritarianism, the opposite is the case today. Now the individual is king, and personality rules. All claims to proper authority are characterized by elitism or "stuffiness," or worse, "patriarchy." Of course, the removal of all official distinctions, and thus God's authority structure, leaves a culture open to all kinds of veiled elitism and oppression. We have discussed various strands of this monumental problem in chapter 6 in terms of "individualism" and "narcissism." Modernity posits the seat of authority in the individual, as an inherent right, rather than as the sovereign disposition of God, which Paul asserts in Romans 13:1-7. Professionalism has replaced the idea of calling to office with an anthropocentric, arbitrary social construct, initiated, perpetuated, and realized by the individual. The preacher, however, must begin with God's conception of his role.

The conception of who we are as pastors directly affects both what we do and how we do it. We have already examined the primacy of preaching in the Bible, and in the history of the church. We have also considered the unique qualities of preaching which explain why God has chosen it as His preferred medium. Now we need to look more closely at the Biblical conception of the office of the minister, comparing and contrasting it with modern conceptions of the ministry. The title *Minister of the Word*, for all centuries since the Reformation, except the twentieth, has embodied the church's concept of the pastoral office. It is telling that in most Protestant churches today the title has disappeared. The concept disappeared long ago. The Word, as the entire

---

[4] Cf. Gregory Reynolds, "Democracy and the Denigration of Office," In *Order in the* Offices, edited by Mark R. Brown (Duncansville, PA: Classic Presbyterian Resources, 1993); Nathan O. Hatch, *The Democratization of American Christianity* (New Haven: Yale University Press, 1989).

subject of the minister's calling, has been supplemented, and in many cases almost entirely replaced, by a host of other managerial and "leadership" duties. *Minister of the Word* succinctly expresses the nature of the pastoral office, and it is from this vantage point that our discussion shall proceed.

After discussing the place of hymns and "praise songs" in the context of the present-day debate and confusion about worship, J. I. Packer makes an important assertion: "What will resolve this unhappy situation is a renewal of the kind of preaching that gives congregations a strong sense of God. Here I think we need to learn from the Puritans. The strong preaching of the majesty of God, of His holiness and awesomeness, will create a sense of how we ought to worship Him. I can't see a congregation ever agreeing on how to worship unless they become united in a deeper and stronger sense of the greatness and glory of God."[5] Packer points to the Puritans for a Biblical corrective to the present misconceptions about the role of the minister. What the Puritans can teach us is:

...the Puritan understanding of God as holy and almighty, great in awesome and fearful judgment as He is great in grace. You can't break up the truth about God. The church today has a scaled-down understanding of Him that is shallow, sentimental, and incoherent. Such inadequacy in our thoughts about God is causing a great deal of suffering among Christians. It's the legacy of liberal theology, which diminished God right from the beginning. God's holiness, His active judgment, and His sovereign providence began to be eaten away years ago. I fear the greater part of the Christian church has ingested this. People today don't stand in awe of God. They don't tremble at His Word. They believe God is great only in the sense of being a great pal. Even when preachers emphasize God's holiness the congregation often does not take them seriously. Out of the pulpit, few preachers enforce the awesomeness of God in their counseling, instructing of people in the faith, or directing the leadership of the congregation.

Too many preachers spend the majority of their planning time thinking about programs which will enlarge their church's membership or income; in America, no institution is thought healthy unless it is expanding. Practical performance is emphasized—how to manage your family, how to manage your budget, how to do anything and everything as a Christian. But all this centers on human relationships and the business of living with other people. It doesn't have much to do with

---

[5] J. I. Packer, "The Challenge of the Third Millennium," *RTS Reformed Quarterly* 18:2 (Summer 1999) [WWW document] URL http://www.rts.edu/quarterly/summer99/qa.html [April 29, 2000].

growing downwards, as Christians must do, in the knowledge and adoration of the Lord.

We should focus on our relationship with God in light of His greatness, holiness, and awesomeness. If we'd appreciate these qualities more, we'd be a humbler lot of people than we are. And our hearts and consciences would be more sensitive to God's glory.[6]

God has ordained that His majesty and glory should be known through preaching, for it is His speech. The vertical dimension of preaching, properly understood, and implemented by preachers who are faithful and passionate in their proclamation, is the only means of reclaiming the glory which has departed from the church's worship. Only by defining our office in terms of *ministering the Word* of the living God will we begin to recover the Biblical emphasis.

The minister of the Word is essentially a *servant* of the LORD, as Moses (עֶבֶד־יְהוָה Deut. 34:5), Joshua (Josh. 24:29), David (Ps. 18:1) were called. We are now ministers of the Great Servant of the LORD who has suffered in the stead of His people and is calling them into His glorious kingdom by the Gospel we preach. "He shall see the labor of His soul, *and* be satisfied. By His knowledge My righteous Servant shall justify many, for He shall bear their iniquities" (Isa. 53:11). And so we are to exemplify His ministry as Paul tells Timothy: "a servant of the Lord must not quarrel but be gentle to all, able to teach, patient" (2 Tim. 2:24).[7] Unlike the leaders of the unbelieving world, who rule by force and often by tyranny and deceit, the minister of the Word is to be a *servant* who imitates His suffering Savior in humility. Our Lord contrasted the two in his response to the Sons of Thunder: "You know that the rulers of the Gentiles lord it over them, and those who are great exercise authority over them. Yet it shall not be so among you; but whoever desires to become great among you, let him be your servant. And whoever desires to be first among you, let him be your slave—just as the Son of Man did not come to be served, but to serve, and to give His life a ransom for many" (Matt. 20:25-28).

Yet humility is not to be confused with a pandering or obsequious lack of authority. For the suffering Servant of the Lord, "taught them as one having authority, and not as the scribes" (Matt. 7:29). In both cases the word translated "authority" is ἐξουσίαν.[8] Servanthood is the way in which Biblical authority is to be exercised. The word *office* comes from the Latin *officium*, a

---

[6] *Ibid.*

[7] K. Sietsma, *The Idea of Office*, translated by Henry Vander Goot (Jordan Station, Ontario: Paideia Press, 1985) 19.

[8] The verb form is used in Matt. 20:25 (κατεξουσιάζουσιν), the root being the same as the noun used in Matt. 7:29.

work or service performed. Biblically, office is a position of specific duty assigned to a person by the Lord. Each believer has a calling to general office. The minister is called to be a servant of the Lord as His spokesman, a minister of His Word. Paul needed to remind Timothy of his office. "Till I come, give attention to reading, to exhortation, to doctrine. Do not neglect the gift that is in you, which was given to you by prophecy with the laying on of the hands of the eldership" (1 Tim. 4:13, 14).

The teaching office is God's gift to the church. It is also commanded. Sietsma asserts: "the essence of office depends on the divine mandate."[9] Years ago I asked an older Reformed minister how to deal with emotion in preaching at funerals. Without hesitating he responded with words I shall never forget, "Remember your office!" This is our calling from God Himself. Do not ever forget it. This alone will give you courage not only to preach with all your might, to spend some of the best hours of your life preparing and praying for your ministry in the pulpit, but also to count preaching among the greatest joys and privileges of your poor life in this lost world.

No wonder Paul writes with such passion and force when he tells Timothy: "I charge *you* therefore before God and the Lord Jesus Christ, who will judge the living and the dead at His appearing and His kingdom: Preach the word! Be ready in season *and* out of season. Convince, rebuke, exhort, with all long-suffering and teaching. For the time will come when they will not endure sound doctrine, but according to their own desires, *because* they have itching ears, they will heap up for themselves teachers; and they will turn *their* ears away from the truth, and be turned aside to fables. But you be watchful in all things, endure afflictions, do the work of an evangelist, fulfill your ministry" (2 Tim. 4:1-5). Our fable-filled culture is not conducive to or receptive to preaching the Word, but preaching is what God has called us ministers to do. We must know what we are about and cultivate it with all our might.

One clear implication of what we have said above is: *Study* the nature of your office. Every wise pastor will make it his business to regularly consider the qualifications for his office in such passages as 1 Timothy 3:1-7 and Titus 1:6-9. Along with these obvious classical texts, the ministries of Jesus and Paul, as well as every minister of the Old and New Covenants, should be mined for the Biblical conception of office. Every minister will command respect for his office as he exhibits what his ministry entails. But this *commanding* will also necessitate gently correcting misconceptions as they appear in the life of your congregation. The account of Jesus at Caesarea Philippi demonstrates the importance of the concept of Jesus' office as Messiah (Matt. 16:12-28). Every preacher ought to answer this same question: "Whom do men say that I am?"

---

[9] *Ibid.*, 24.

Some say a psychologist and a counselor, some a social coordinator, some a chief executive officer, some a fund raiser. Is the ministry a calling or a career? Are you a professional or a prophet? God *calls* you to be *prophet*, nothing else. Paul defended and defined his office regularly, especially in his Corinthian epistles.

In addition, we must regularly teach our congregations the proper conception of our office in the course of our preaching as we come to texts such as 1 Thessalonians 5:12, 13; Hebrews 13:7, 17. The *Book of Acts* shows the ministry of the Word in action. Feast regularly on a good diet of books describing the history of preachers, their biographies, such as C. H. Spurgeon's *The Early Years* and *Full Harvest*, Douglas Kelly's *Preachers with Power*, James Stalker's *The Preacher and His Models*, and Gardiner Spring's *Power in the Pulpit*. It is also important to read books of wise counsel for preachers and reflections on preaching, such as Samuel Miller's *The Christian Ministry*, Charles Bridges's *The Christian Ministry*, Spurgeon's *Lectures to My Students*, D. Martin Lloyd-Jones *Preachers and Preaching*, and James W. Alexander's *Thoughts on Preaching*. Of course, *Minister of the Word* itself does not limit the activity of our office to preaching alone. Rather it centers and focuses it. Every other activity of the ministry should be conceived of as an extension of our activity of the pulpit. Every time we visit the home of a Christian family we bring the Word of God. Every time we visit someone in the hospital we minister the Word. Every time we plan the order and content of worship we are planning to minister the Word. However, the point of this book is to focus on the chief exercise of the ministerial office in the public preaching of the Word.

A Minister of the Word: Focus on Preaching

As a corollary of the idea of office, the wise preacher will constantly cultivate his own understanding of his task by studying that task through various tools which focus on preaching as his central work.

Study the best homiletical texts such as Robert Dabney's *Sacred Rhetoric*; Jay Adams's *Preaching with Purpose*, Broadus's unabridged classic *On the Preparation and Delivery of Sermons*. Jay Adams once told a class that most books on homiletics are simply a rehash of Broadus's classic. Along with these the best printed sermons should be read, and from a wide variety of authors. Calvin's sermons, Geerhardus Vos's *Grace and Glory*, Spurgeon's *New Park Street Pulpit* and *Metropolitan Tabernacle Pulpit*, Henry Fish's *Masterpieces of Pulpit Eloquence, Ancient and Modern*, are among the best. Remarkably Spurgeon's sermons were written for publication on the Monday after he preached them. The danger of reading printed sermons, of course, is developing a conception of preaching which is literary and not oral. It is critical, therefore, for the preacher to carefully distinguish between the written productions of a preacher, and their oral presentation, as we shall see below.

Every preacher should also make it his business to study the best living homiletical models. Some may say that in our day they are not plentiful, but we may even learn valuable lessons from the simplest, least gifted, and least known among us.

When asked about the reason for their remarkable careers as the founders of the Mayo clinic, the Mayo brothers responded that they made it their business to learn something new about their medical profession every day of their lives. If that is so for ministering to mortal bodies, how much more true is this for the one who ministers to the eternal concerns of people made in God's image. Let nothing deter you from concentrating on this task.

TAKE HEED TO YOURSELF

If one of the central values of pastoral preaching, as we have seen in chapter 9 is the personal presence of Christ in His chosen messenger, or as it is often called the "Incarnational Principle," then we must own the maxim that nothing is as important to our preaching as following our Master in daily life and ministry. Make it your business to be an *authentic* communicator through cultivating a holy life and a sympathetic pastoral ministry. Augustine understood this: "However, the life of the speaker has greater weight in determining whether he is obediently heard than any grandness of eloquence."[10]

Exemplify Your Office

Take Paul as your example:
> For you yourselves know, brethren, that our coming to you was not in vain. But even after we had suffered before and were spitefully treated at Philippi, as you know, we were bold in our God to speak to you the gospel of God in much conflict. For our exhortation *did* not *come* from error or uncleanness, nor *was it* in deceit. But as we have been approved by God to be entrusted with the gospel, even so we speak, not as pleasing men, but God who tests our hearts. For neither at any time did we use flattering words, as you know, nor a cloak for covetousness—God *is* witness. Nor did we seek glory from men, either from you or from

---

[10] Augustine, *On Christian Doctrine*, translated by D. W. Robertson, Jr. (Indianapolis: Bobbs-Merrill Educational Publishing, 1958) 164.

others, when we might have made demands as apostles of Christ. But we were gentle among you, just as a nursing *mother* cherishes her own children. So, affectionately longing for you, we were well pleased to impart to you not only the gospel of God, but also our own lives, because you had become dear to us. For you remember, brethren, our labor and toil; for laboring night and day, that we might not be a burden to any of you, we preached to you the gospel of God. (1 Thess. 2:1-10).

There is nothing more needed in the modern world than men of character, who live what they preach. This is a Biblical given, which every good book on the subject of preaching emphasizes amply. The image media have fostered the performing preacher—the celebrity. How many are there whose performance in public is betrayed by the awful fact that they are not what they *appear* to be. The electronic age is filled with such performances. Helmut Thielicke's searching question should frequently be ours: "Does the preacher drink what he hands out in the pulpit?"[11]

I remember the awful feeling as a young Christian watching an Evangelical pastor conduct worship before a live television audience. It reminded me of Johnny Carson. Mike in hand, strutting around the stage in the conversational style of the talk show host during his monologue. This performance was not for the congregation. It was a performance for the television audience, and thus undermined the very integrity of which the world, in our celebrity-worshipping, scandal-ridden age, is in such dire need. I believe that this particular man was a man of real spiritual integrity. But his public life undermined his real identity, in a way of which I am sure he was quite unaware. The integrity of a holy life, then, must be exhibited in the very act of preaching. The way he preaches must not undermine this integrity. We must preach what we practice. There must be no discontinuity between his life in the pulpit and his life outside the pulpit. In word and deed, in the pulpit and out of the pulpit, he communicates God's truth. His secret devotional life with the Lord is always evident in public, especially over the long term. Without communion with the Lord and deep meditation on His message, there will be no spiritual power in his ministry.

The Larger Catechism is instructive in this regard: Question #159 "How is the word of God to be preached by those that are called thereunto? A. They that are called to labour in the ministry of the word, are to preach sound doctrine, diligently, in season and out of season; plainly, not in the enticing words of man's wisdom, but in demonstration of the Spirit, and of power; faithfully, making known the whole counsel of God; wisely, applying themselves to the necessities and capacities of the hearers; zealously, with

---

[11] Thielicke, *The Trouble With The Church*, 3.

fervent love to God and the souls of his people; sincerely, aiming at his glory, and their conversion, edification, and salvation."

In preaching "sound doctrine" the Westminster Divines used Titus 2:8 as a proof text: "in all things showing yourself *to be* a pattern of good works; in doctrine *showing* integrity, reverence, incorruptibility, sound speech that cannot be condemned, that one who is an opponent may be ashamed, having nothing evil to say of you." Integrity of speech and life go hand in hand. The detection of the least insincerity will mar the reception of the Word: "And my speech and my preaching *were* not with persuasive words of human wisdom, but in demonstration of the Spirit and of power" (1 Cor. 2:4). Genuine love for God and the congregation ought to be communicated by every element of the preachers life (2 Cor. 5:13, 14; 12:15). Sincerity stands out in the description of Biblical preaching as an attribute especially necessary in the age of advertising and televangelism. In 2 Corinthians 2:17 and 4:2 Paul teaches us the true nature of sincerity. "Unlike so many, we do not peddle the word of God for profit. On the contrary, in Christ we speak before God with sincerity, like men sent from God. ...But we have renounced the hidden things of shame, not walking in craftiness nor handling the word of God deceitfully, but by manifestation of the truth commending ourselves to every man's conscience in the sight of God." What you see is what you get.

Be Earnest

The earnestness of an authentic life must be evident in the act of preaching. Earnestness is, according to *Webster's New World Dictionary and* Thesaurus "serious and intense; not joking or playful; zealous and sincere." The earnest preacher believes every word he utters. Authenticity requires the message and its communication to dominate our concerns in the pulpit. Love for God, God's people and sinners will generate simple language, genuine style, gestures and emotion. The greatest impediment to earnestness is pride which draws attention to self. The professional attitude and tone of voice detracts from the authenticity of the preacher. The entire purpose of public worship, in which preaching is central, is to draw people into the presence of God Himself, in adoration and praise. The preacher who does anything less will tend to lack earnestness and will consequently exude inauthenticity. Preachers need to labor to have an "aura of authenticity," in a world which sees very little of it.[12] If the preacher acts outside the pulpit as if his preaching makes no difference in his life, he cannot expect his preaching to make any difference in anyone else's life.

---

[12] Joel Nederhood, "Effective Preaching in a Media Age," class notes, Westminster Theological Seminary in California, 1990.

A closely related word, and one which is often misunderstood, is *boldness* (παρρησίᾳ). It is used ten times in *Acts*, in connection with preaching the Word. Like *unction*, as we shall see, boldness, is not to be confused with volume of voice or forcefulness of delivery or personality. It denotes a fearlessness and courage which reflects absolute confidence in what is being spoken.[13] The Biblical focus is first of all on the *message* not the method. Boldness is the freedom which arises from the certainty that the gospel is true. "Now when they saw the boldness of Peter and John, and perceived that they were unlearned and ignorant men, they marveled; and they took knowledge of them, that they had been with Jesus" (Acts 4:13).

The ultimate test of this certitude was the willingness of the apostles to give up their lives, security and earthly happiness, for the announcement of this message. Paul lived with the threat of death from the beginning to the end of his ministry. Shortly after his conversion and call to the apostolic ministry we are told: "And he spoke boldly in the name of the Lord Jesus and disputed against the Hellenists, but they attempted to kill him" (Acts 9:29). At the conclusion of the *Book of Acts* we find Paul teaching the gospel in his rooms as a prisoner with this same boldness, only here it is translated "confidence": "preaching the kingdom of God and teaching the things which concern the Lord Jesus Christ with all confidence, no one forbidding him" (Acts 28:31). Paul was the genuine article, and everyone knew it from his life and from the confidence with which he preached in the midst of the fiercest opposition. In other words, his earnestness was evident in his life *and* in his preaching. His method was a simple reflection of his ultimate confidence in the message, which in turn grew out of confidence in the Messenger of the Covenant, Jesus Christ. "For our gospel came not unto you in word only, but also in power, and in the Holy Ghost, and in much assurance (πληροφορία); as ye know what manner of men we were among you for your sake" (1 Thess. 1:5).

Now you may ask, How does this translate into the *way* we preach? While Phillips Brooks's definition of preaching expressed in the pithy phrase, "truth through personality,"[14] is an inadequate definition, it does emphasize an important point: let God use *your* personality, which He gave you, to express His truth with passionate earnestness. Do not imitate another's style. The personal attributes and gifts with which God has provided you are to be cultivated. Augustine said it well: "that should not be called eloquence which

---

[13] παρρησίᾳ also refers to the "right of speech in Roman public assemblies" (T. David Gordon). Thus in God's providence Paul was free to preach. In the case of Peter and John (Acts 4 & 5) even when civil/religious authorities forbade preaching God gives the freedom to preach based on the historical veracity of the message.

[14] Phillips Brooks, *Lectures on Preaching: The Yale Lectures on Preaching* (1877, Reprint, 1907, Grand Rapids: Baker Book House, 1969) 5.

is not appropriate to the person speaking."[15] This appropriateness included the person's age, experience, and station in life, as well as his gifts. "Be yourself" is often enjoined upon young preachers. However, apart from the good idea of letting go of stiff formality, this injunction implies a lack of effort. Developing your own manner of preaching takes a great deal of conscious effort. "A good preaching style is plain (but not drab), unaffected (but not unstudied) style that gets in there and gets the job done without calling attention to itself. It is clear and appropriate at every point to the message. Content should control this style."[16] Whatever you do, do not try to imitate the satin smooth style of the media personality.

An excellent book on the subject of earnestness was written in the last century by John Angell James, titled: *An Earnest Ministry: The Want of the Times*. At the heart of the word *earnest* is the idea of "intense devotedness."[17] James defines earnestness under five headings. First it implies a single object of pursuit. For the preacher this is to herald the glad tidings of salvation to sinners. Second, this object must possess the mind and kindle the heart. Nothing less than a lifelong engagement in preaching the gospel can satisfy the true preacher. Third, the earnest preacher will use every available means at his disposal to accomplish the desired task of preaching. Everything else will be subordinated to this desired end. Finally, the preacher will energetically engage in preaching in season and out of season.[18] D. Martin Lloyd-Jones exemplified this sort of attitude toward preaching as exhibited in the effect on the hearers: "there is an element of compulsion in preaching, and people who are there are gripped and fixed. I maintain that if that is not happening, you have not got true preaching. That is why reading must never be a substitute for preaching. You can put the book down, or you can argue with it. When there is true preaching you cannot do that, you are gripped, you are taken up, you are mastered."[19] Whatever eloquence God grants us must not be aimed at but rather spring from a soul ardently committed to communicating God's Word.

In practice this means that extensive and laborious preparation will not be shirked. If earnestness and boldness derive from the message, then the message must be our primary concern. The quality of our preparation is always evident in the act of preaching week in and week out. The arduous work of studying the text in the original languages, scouring the best commentary and theology,

---

[15] Augustine, *On Christian Doctrine*, 123.
[16] Jay Adams, *Preaching With Purpose* (Phillipsburg, NJ: Presbyterian and Reformed, 1982) 105.
[17] John Angell James, *An Earnest Ministry: The Want of the Times* (1847. Reprint. Edinburgh: The Banner of Truth Trust, 1993) 28.
[18] *Ibid.*, 31ff, 41ff, 45ff, 49ff, 66ff.
[19] D. Martin Lloyd-Jones, "Knowing the Times: Extracts from an Important New Book by Dr. Lloyd-Jones, *Banner of Truth Magazine* 317 (February 1990) 12.

so that our exegesis brings out the Spirit's meaning and application, represent the only course for the earnest minister. In an age which lives on the surfaces of reality, which prides itself in superficiality, only deep penetration beneath the surface of the Bible will avoid the light weight homilies and sermonettes which we are relentlessly told the market wants. Avoiding the proverbial use of texts as pretexts does not occur easily. Probing the text through prayer, and meditating in the throne room of the Great King, will all tell in the pulpit. Without the presence of the God of the text, we will have only ourselves, and our opinions to present in the place of worship. Alas, the impulse of marketing the church has, as its stock in trade, immediate impressions. This is the secret of its "power." This is the assurance that earnestness will be absent. The unreflective immediacy of electronic "communication" is precisely the environment which we must counter, not imitate.

In all that we may say about the medium of preaching we must ever be aware of the danger of emphasizing technique. In a homiletics class in 1990 Jay Adams warned us of this danger with a story. Marjo was the Bible Belt preacher prodigy who was ordained at age four. The techniques of Pentecostal preaching were drilled into him, and he mesmerized crowds from the age of four. Later he became disenchanted and exposed the sham, pointing to the power of group dynamics. Adams observed, "artfully manipulated words influence people." Stay close to God or you will become a Marjo.[20] I have said all of this because we now turn our attention to several crucial elements of "technique." Properly understood they will not undermine, but enhance authenticity in the pulpit.

REMEMBER YOUR MEDIUM

Do not be intimidated by the vaunted superiority of modern media and their overestimated technologies, as much of the church seems to be. Many churches use the overhead projector and other "visual aids," as if they will lack cultural respect if they are not "up-to-date." The hidden message here is that given the proper techniques we will be able to effectively minister to modern people, and thus we do not need God with all of our technique. At best we ask Him to bless what we believe are the best means, without consulting His Word at the outset. The problem is that by accommodating people in this way, and making them feel that they are still in the world in which they live every day, we also lend credence to the world's assumptions about the power of the electronic media.

---

[20] Jay Adams, "Preaching with Purpose," class notes, Westminster Theological Seminary in California, 1990.

Do not be seduced by the audio-visual fad. Ong warns: "Audiovisuals are worst of all in their deception because in them the word is fitted exactly to the visual apprehension and deprived of the paradox and mystery essential to the word's dialogic setting."[21] Note the ploy of Zedekiah in using a visual aid to impress King Jehoshaphat, while Micaiah simply speaks the plain Word of God (1 Kings 22). But what of the God-ordained drama witnessed in the so called "acting prophets"? "As bearers of revelation, prophets participated in that 'many and various ways' in which God spoke to the world prior to the definitive word brought by Christ and his apostles. Prophets were not *expositors* of revelation but *bearers* of revelation; subsequent to their activity, all ministers of the word are expositors of revelation, explainers of revelation; not bearers thereof."[22]

Remember: no medium is better calculated by God Himself to communicate His Word to His image-bearing creatures than live pastoral preaching. 2 Corinthians 4:6 declares: "For it is the God who commanded light to shine out of darkness, who has shone in our hearts to give the light of the knowledge of the glory of God in the face of Jesus Christ." Professor B. B. Warfield said of Princeton Seminary's preacher-professor Dr. George Purves, reflecting on the fact that Purves had written few books: "We are, perhaps, prone to overestimate the relative importance of books: *Litera scripta manet.* But the 'winged word' of speech moves the world; and it is better, after all, to form characters than to compile volumes."[23] As necessary as books are in our preparation for preaching, they cannot replace preaching itself. Nor can the overhead projector, the video cassette, the television, or the Internet.

Preaching as Conduit, Grammar, and Environment

As the minister of the Word in your congregation you are the primary *conduit* of covenantal information from God; that is what *Westminster Shorter Catechism* question #3 sums up as "what man is to believe concerning God, and what duty God requires of man." The preacher more than any other member of the church must be a Media Ecologist, a good steward before God of the media of communication, especially the God-ordained medium of preaching. This is the reason we have traveled a rather long road in this book to come to the subject of preaching itself. In emphasizing that the medium is

---

[21] Walter Ong, Review: *The Humiliation of the Word* (Jacques Ellul) in the *Journal of Communication* (1986): vol. 36, no. 1, pp. 156-158.
[22] T. David Gordon, "Drama in Christian Public Worship: Preliminary Considerations," n.d., unpublished paper.
[23] David, B. Calhoun, *Princeton Seminary: The Majestic Testimony 1869-1929*, Volume 2 (Edinburgh: The Banner of Truth Trust, 1996) 186.

the message, we should never minimize the message itself. Although every medium forms a distinct and important part of every message, the content is central, and that is precisely why we are concerned about the medium. The two are inseparable. That is never more true than in preaching. We are stewards of the mystery of the Gospel (1 Cor. 4:1, 2; 1 Pet. 4:10). After describing the ordinary offices of the continuing church to Timothy Paul says: "*I write* so that you may know how you ought to conduct yourself in the house of God, which is the church of the living God, the pillar and ground of the truth. And without controversy great is the mystery of godliness: God was manifested in the flesh, justified in the Spirit, seen by angels, preached among the Gentiles, believed on in the world, received up in glory" (1 Tim. 3:15, 16). The message is absolutely *the* central thing in the existence and life of the church to which it is entrusted.

As the minister of the Word in your congregation the *grammar* of your preaching is a vital aspect of communicating the content of God's Word. How to conduct yourself in the church (ἀναστρέφεσθαι) is a major concern of Paul in the ministry of Timothy and the post-apostolic church. The minister and his congregation are the medium for the life-altering message of the Gospel presented to the world. The message is "incarnated" in the life of the congregation lived in holiness and love. We should consider the grammar of preaching in terms of the unique "elements of production," considered in chapter 5. The preacher faces the congregation with the open Bible in his hands. The raised central pulpit, characterizing church architecture since the Reformation, is part of this grammar. It says something about the place of the preached Word in the worship, as well as the authority of the One whose Word it is. While some might argue that these elements are not essential to preaching, I think they reflect visually and acoustically the position of the Word in the church. Our didactic emphasis often eclipses the important secondary matter of the aesthetics of our worship space. The body, facial expressions, hand movements, tone and volume of voice of the preacher, are all essential to the grammar of preaching. As we have seen any medium which mediates these elements, in addition to preaching itself, modifies them in significant ways.

As the minister of the Word in your congregation the *environment* created by your preaching produces a life-changing counter environment over against the ungodly environment of the world, the flesh and the devil. The text of Scripture, expounded and applied, forms the interface between the church and the heavenly realm of its Lord. It also connects the church which hears with the church that has heard and the church which will hear that Word. Preaching connects the church with the history of redemption. As Samuel Volbeda insists, in his book *The Pastoral Genius of Preaching*, true preaching in the church is the feeding of the Father's flock through the power of the written Word communicated to His blood-bought children (Acts 20:28). Evangelistic preaching outside the congregation is an extension of the Word as an intrusion into fallen history, extending the counter environment into the domain a fallen world (Acts 17). The entire fabric of heavenly reality impinges on earth through the preaching of the Word. In Ephesus this invasion caused quite a stir, because the Word challenged and restructured the lives, perceptions and relationships of those who repented and believed the gospel. Luke tells us that "...many of those who had practiced magic brought their books together and burned *them* in the sight of all." The business community, which was intimately entwined in the occult practices of the Ephesians, was up in arms (Acts 19:19, 24ff). The media of communication were altered significantly by the presence of the Word preached.

One of the important questions we must face as preachers is: To what degree must we accommodate the unique characteristics and especially the weaknesses of the communication media of our age? As we shall see, the preacher must take account of the electronic environment. But even as he refuses, on Biblical grounds, to forsake preaching itself, as the chief means of God's communication, his hearers in the church and in the world are affected by the electronic media. Thus, especially with those who are not nurtured in the Word-oriented community of the church, the preacher must accommodate his hearers in the way Paul did at Athens, beginning with the general revelation of God in the situation of the Athenians. Paul followed the accepted format for public speaking in the forum on Mars Hill. What we explore below will focus on enhancing the characteristics which have always been featured in good preaching, many of which we have allowed to decay.

Some Distinctions of Preaching Types and Emphases

In Presbyterian and Reformed churches we may identify at least four approaches to preaching: expository, Neo-Puritan, Redemptive-Historical, and theological or doctrinal.[24] These are not necessarily different types of sermons. "Good preaching, then, while emphasizing one of the three aspects, will always include all three. There will be a text (a *telic* unit as a preaching portion), a topic (whatever is the subject or teaching, of the preaching portion), and an exposition (the work of the preacher to demonstrate that the purpose he teaches is actually the Holy Spirit's purpose in the text, and that is the sole authority for

---

[24] Ross W. Graham, Personal E-mail, 12 September, 1999.

what he says). If your preaching doesn't include all three, as well as application and implementation of the truth, there is something lacking."[25]

Every sermon must be textual, or it is not a Biblical sermon. Textual sermons are not a type of sermon but must be the foundation and fountain of every sermon. As noted by Adams above, the same can really be said of "topical" preaching. Every text has a topic, but any topic which does not come from the text of Scripture is not suitable subject matter for a sermon. Even a Biblical topic, like regeneration, must be rooted in a particular text, even though a sermon based on this text must take into account what the whole Bible teaches on regeneration.

A false dilemma is often fostered by distinguishing between teaching and preaching. The difference between *kerygma* and *didache* in the New Testament has been exaggerated. In Matthew 11:1 we read: "Now it came to pass, when Jesus finished commanding His twelve disciples, that He departed from there to teach (διδάσκειν) and to preach (κηρύσσειν) in their cities." Romans 10:15 also uses two Greek words for preach: "And how shall they preach (κηρύξουσιν) unless they are sent? As it is written: 'How beautiful are the feet of those who preach (εὐαγγελιζομένων) the gospel of peace, who bring glad tidings of good things!'" In Acts 28:31 we read that Paul was in Rome "preaching (κηρύσσων) the kingdom of God and teaching (διδάσκων) the things which concern the Lord Jesus Christ with all confidence, no one forbidding him." These three verses demonstrate that the three major words used for communicating the gospel in the New Testament are used interchangeably. Thus, rather than indicating a distinction of tasks, they reveal the richness of the concept of preaching.[26] Proclaiming the message as a public herald of good news includes instruction. While teaching tends to focus on instruction, and preaching on the proclamation of the gospel, all Biblical communication of the Gospel includes both. As Augustine enjoins: "instruction should come before persuasion."[27]

Most commonly advocated, though not often practiced, in Evangelical and Reformed churches today is expository preaching. This involves the consecutive exposition, from pericope to pericope, of a book of the Bible. Calvin preached this way and presently many Reformed pastors do the same. Among its many excellent strengths is the fact that it follows the logic of Scripture itself, and inculcates Biblical content in its Biblical setting. Such

---

[25] Jay Adams, *Essays on Biblical Preaching* (Grand Rapids: Zondervan Publishing House, 1982) 8, in Douglas Van Allen Heck, *The ERS Basic: The Five Steps of Bible Exposition* (Tulsa, OK: Expository Resource Services, Inc., 1990) 20.

[26] Cf a very helpful study of the NT words for preaching in Klaas Runia, "What Is Preaching according to the New Testament?" *Tyndale Bulletin* 29 (1978): 3-48.

[27] Augustine, *On Christian Doctrine*, 137.

preaching covers the rich terrain of the phenomena of the Biblical text, and thus covers topics which might be awkward for a preacher to choose topically. The only weakness of this approach is that unless the books chosen are chosen with care, the preaching may not cover the whole counsel of God as a system of doctrine. For example, a preacher might preach through all four gospels, consecutively over a period of years, and neglect the Old Testament preparation for the incarnation, and the apostolic interpretation and application of these events. Expository preaching is a wise choice for the pastor, as long as he is willing to intersperse other sermons as occasion may demand in the life of his congregation. The broader idea of "expository" should be true of every sermon. In this sense, there is truly no such thing as a Biblical sermon which is not expository. Every sermon must expound, explain, and apply a portion of Scripture.

Another approach is the Neo-Puritan, which emphasizes application. Clearly the Bible itself teaches that Scripture is given to transform God's elect (Cf. Rom. 12:1,2). Application is the goal of Biblical communication. Every text of Scripture is relevant, because it is addressed to God's people, not because the preacher makes it so by "application." The commonest complaint about this sort of preaching is that it tends toward introspection. While that may be true in extreme cases, where conviction of sin is seen as almost the sole purpose of preaching, a more cogent criticism is in the area of the failure to engage the listener in the context of the text itself. It may also degenerate into endless "practical" points of "how-to," ending in mere moralism, or worse, triviality. There may in some cases be the tendency to preach a dozen sermons on one verse. D. Martyn Lloyd-Jones preached in this way, consecutively through entire books. This, however, is not truly expository, since it often draws many sermons from one single verse, and is thus more topical in its presentation. This is a distinct weakness of the Puritan approach. Jay Adams has pointed to the dangers of the Scholastic method of Puritan preaching: doctrine then use; lecture then every possible application.[28] Despite these weaknesses the best Puritans were expository, and "opened" the text of Scripture for the church to receive its application. The Puritan passion to engage saints and sinners with the Christ of Scripture is in the best tradition of Biblical preaching.

The Redemptive-Historical approach to preaching emphasizes the historical, covenantal context of every pericope. As in the textual sermon, every sermon must be redemptive-historical to be Biblical. Cornelius Trimp has demonstrated that it is a false dichotomy to set the redemptive-historical approach over against the "exemplaristic" approach as if redemptive-history

---

[28] Adams, "Preaching with Purpose," class notes.

has no application.[29] The most common criticism of redemptive-historical preaching is that every sermon gives the history of the entire Bible through a single theme without ever challenging the hearer to change. I have actually never heard such a sermon, but would not call it preaching if I did. On the other hand, I have heard plenty of exemplaristic or moralistic sermons. Joseph is our example of how to avoid adultery. Was this the point of the text? Clearly not! Joseph is a type of the faithful Deliverer, whose life of faith exemplifies holiness at every point, including the resisting the temptation to sleep with Potipher's wife. The obedience of the Second and Last Adam is the point of this text. Yes the crucified Servant of the Lord is our motivation to sexual purity. We shall further explore the importance of redemption history for preaching below. Let it suffice to say that we are not to preach Biblical theology *per se*, but must preach redemptive-historically.

Finally, theological, or doctrinal preaching is an emphasis which seeks to inculcate the system of doctrine taught in the Scriptures. The common criticism of this preaching emphasis is that it teaches timeless truths, not tied to the historical text, and that it tends toward theological lecturing, rather than preaching. Clearly, this is a danger, especially in reaction to the modern antipathy to doctrine. However, as with Biblical theology, while we must not preach doctrine *per se*, we must always preach doctrinally. After all what is "doctrine" but teaching. Our systematic formulations of the teaching of Scripture provide a marvelous map of the truth of Scripture. These must always inform the exegesis and content of preaching.

True preaching should be a synthesis of the best elements of these four emphases which avoids the weaknesses of each. If we stick to the Spirit-inspired purpose of each text in its context, and remember Paul's statement in Romans 15:4 "whatever things were written before were written for our learning," we will preach Biblically.

Classical Rhetoric[30]

The use of ancient rhetoric by the best homileticians is a recognition of the blessings of common culture in which the world has gained wisdom about the art of effective oral communication. Not to glean from this wisdom is as foolish as rejecting the rules of grammar because it were formulated by unbelievers. A quick survey of the parts of ancient rhetoric will quickly

---

[29] Cornelius Trimp, *Preaching and the History of Salvation*, translated by Nelson D. Kloosterman (Dyer, IN: Dr. Nelson D. Kloosterman, 1996).
[30] I owe much of the material in this section to Robert Godfrey's course on "Rhetoric," delivered at Westminster Theological Seminary in 1978; and his course "The History of Rhetoric," delivered at Westminster Theological Seminary in California in 1990.

convince the experienced preacher that the ancients can teach us a great deal about good public discourse. Having said this, good oratory is a necessary, but not a sufficient condition of good preaching. "Still good preaching is not oratory. It cannot be equated with mastery of Public Speaking 101. It does not hail, for instance, from the principles of Aristotle's *Rhetoric*, but from the revelations received by the Hebrew prophets."[31] In 1 Corinthians 1 and 2 Paul is eloquent in his warnings about the danger of elevating rhetorical skills above the humbling message of the crucified Christ. Today, the danger probably lies more in elevating electronic communication. A healthy dose of good classical rhetorical skills will be good tools for the preacher. Preaching is much more than good rhetorical skills and practice, but it must be nothing less. Hughes Oliphant Old demonstrates that the writers of Scripture, who were first preachers, used "rhetoric with great mastery and power."[32]

Let us consider for a moment the five parts of classical rhetoric. *Inventio* (discovery) is the business of gathering the raw material for a public discourse, along with determining the particular purpose of the oration (deliberative, forensic, etc.). For the preacher this means studying Scripture, especially in the original languages, meditating on the meaning of the text, scouring his library for commentary and all other helps in understanding the pericope. It also involves prayer and meditation in the act of gathering. It involves determining the *telos* or purpose of the text as inspired by the Spirit of God. *Dispositio* (arrangement) is the act of placing the material in its proper order for public presentation. It was considered barbaric for this structure to be obvious. For the preacher this means building an outline, or structure, natural to oral delivery, which proclaims the meaning and the God-given purpose (telos) of the text as God's Word to His people. *Elocutio* (style) pays attention to the particular forms of expression, vocabulary, phrases, figures of speech, narrative, forms of argument. Here the preacher focuses on the specific tools of good oral presentation of his message. *Memoria* (memory) is internalizing the material so that it may be presented in public from memory, not necessarily *verbatim*. For the preacher this means mastering the sermon so as not to be tied to notes. *Pronunciatio* (delivery) is the actual delivery of the speech. For the preacher this is the preaching moment.

These parts of ancient rhetoric come into their own when considered from the perspective(s) of the medieval media of education, namely the *Trivium* (grammar, rhetoric, and dialectic), and *Quadrivium* (arithmetic, geometry, music, and astronomy). The lost tools of learning, delineated by the Trivium,

---

[31] Charles G. Dennison, "Some Thoughts on Preaching," *Kerux* 11:3 (December 1996) 4.
[32] Hughes Oliphant Old. *The Reading and Preaching of the Scriptures in the Worship of the Christian Church: Volume 1 - The Biblical Period* (Grand Rapids: Eerdmans, 1998) 49, 50, 65.

should be prized by the preacher, but held in strictest balance, and in the order given: the knowledge of language, public persuasion, and logic. For example, logic alone leads to pure speculation. That is why the study of language, as it is found in texts, comes first. Rhetoric is not simply public speaking, but speaking in the context of citizenship. The wise orator was a leading citizen, persuading for the common good. It is not that logic comes after learning how to persuade—that would be impossible—but that logic is subordinated to tradition and truth imbedded in texts, and in the memory of the community, and to the interests of the commonwealth as they are publicly declared and inculcated.

As with the ideal of this Ciceronian model, learned by Augustine, and promulgated in his *De Doctrina Christiana*, the citizen of heaven, who is a herald of the King, must marshal these disciplines in His service. In *De Doctrina Christiana* Augustine, the great rhetor, or artist of the forensic use of language, brings his immense classical learning to bear on homiletics. The first three books deal with hermeneutics, or the grammar of Scripture interpretation. The fourth book is offered, with great diffidence, on homiletics. Augustine knew the abuses of his profession. For Augustine the text must speak first and foremost, lest the preacher become a mere Sophist—a persuader without truth, a charlatan. So grammar takes precedence. Rhetoric alone can be an instrument of either truth or falsehood.[33] It may be learned almost as a natural result of the study of language, and should not be emphasized in itself, but only in as much as it aids the teaching of the Scriptures. "For a man speaks more or less wisely to the extent that he has become more or less proficient in the Holy Scriptures."[34] Augustine goes to great lengths to demonstrate that preachers like Paul employed eloquence in the interest of truth. He never "followed" the art of eloquence.[35] Like the servants in a great house eloquence stays out of sight.

It should be of paramount concern that today the church often allows men to preach who have neither mastered good public speaking nor the ability to exposit a passage of Scripture clearly. The first should be a given, like piety; the second should be a high, and non-negotiable demand. The exposition of Scripture has fallen on hard times. If anything of value about the nature of media has been learned thus far we will conclude that this medium—preaching—is all about what God has to say in His infallible Word. Thus, whatever we helpfully glean from ancient rhetoric, the Hebrew prophet and not

---

[33] Augustine, *On Christian Doctrine*, 118.
[34] *Ibid.*, 122.
[35] *Ibid.*, 125.

the Greek orator, is our model for preaching. This was the oral tradition of Jesus and His apostles.[36]

CULTIVATE YOUR PREACHING

The Question of Relevance

Preaching is not simply a repetition of the Biblical message, or else the task of the preacher would be simply to read the Scriptures to the congregation. The message "must be actualized into the present. If preaching is to be true and relevant, the message of Scripture must be addressed to people in their concrete historical situation. The biblical message may not be *adapted* to the situation of today, but it must be 'accommodated' (Calvin) to the situation. As in Christ God stooped down to take upon himself our flesh, so in the preaching of the word the Holy Spirit stoops down to reach people in their situation. The preacher must therefore be an exegete of both Scripture and of his congregation, so that the living word of God for today will be heard at the intersection of text and situation."[37] But the goal is not to *make* the text relevant to the situation, but to *demonstrate* its relevance. The text is always relevant, because it reveals the true state of the church united to the crucified and risen Christ. Calvin's idea of accommodation is not that we must seek to overcome any supposed distance between then and now—between past history in Biblical times and today. It is rather that in God's condescension He speaks to fallible and blind humans by the illuminating power of His Spirit. For Calvin there is no dichotomy between "then and now."

The question of relevance is one of the profoundest questions under discussion in homiletics today. Charlie Dennison has astutely observed: "Whether conservative or liberal, Calvinist or Arminian, most preachers pursue their task to the text of the world."[38] The titles of hundreds of books and articles indicate that "relevance" or "application" is their chief concern. The question concerns the connection between the text and the hearer, or more properly the church. The problem is that, however laudable the quest of many preachers to communicate, the impression is left that the ancient text is culturally determined, and thus that application means *making* the text relevant to a very different culture—the modern world. This was the over-riding concern of Rudolph Bultmann's project of "Demythologizing." The "ancient

---

[36] Clyde E. Fant, *Preaching For Today* (New York: Harper and Row, 1975) 36, 37.
[37] Sinclair B. Ferguson, David F. Wright and J. I. Packer, eds., *New Dictionary of Theology* (Downers Grove: InterVarsity Press, 1988). S.v. "Preaching, Theology of," by Klaas Runia.
[38] Dennison, "Some Thoughts on Preaching," 7.

text must be 'delivered' in the interests of relevance. ...The modern preacher lives in a qualitatively different age than the Biblical figures."[39]

Trimp turns the tables nicely: "The church pulpit is not a platform for demonstrating a timeless system of truths, but the place which God Himself reserves for the proclaiming of His living Word which seeks the hearts of God's children in their concrete needs, temptations, and expectations. Thus preaching is by definition 'relevant'."[40] *Sola Scriptura* "carries with it the relevance of preaching."[41] The congregation is never a group of spectators. "The historic distance between our time and the days of the apostles and prophets is therefore not bridged by our human work of re-presentation, but by the faithfulness of God Himself. ...We do not draw old stories towards ourselves, but in the garb of the old stories God approaches us across the centuries and countries, and the Christ of Scriptures desires to dwell in our midst. ...*Christ is relevant*—the same Christ in whom God at one time expressed Himself totally and about whom the Scriptures of the Old and New Testaments testify. No relevance can ever surpass this relevance. ...This relevance breaks through the myopia of modern man, the shortsightedness of the minister of the Word, and through the narrow scope of human demands for relevance. ...All relevance which is not at the same time a preaching of the Christ of Scripture, is pseudo-relevance and falls below the mark of the ministry of the Word."[42]

When it comes to application this redemptive-historical approach is never a matter of merely reciting the history of redemption, as is often alleged. As Trimp has reminded us the Christ of Scripture, who as the crucified and risen Lord, is the same yesterday and today and forever, and therefore always relevant, but not always in the way demanded by many modern Christians. As Geerhardus Vos teaches: "...we know full well that we ourselves live just as much in the New Testament as did Peter, and Paul, and John."[43] Thus, "good preaching calls men and women, young and old, to repentance and faith in Jesus Christ so that they might be delivered from the present evil age. ...good preaching does not make the text meaningful for us in our contemporary situation; rather good preaching makes us and our contemporary situation meaningful in the text."[44] From the *Pesahim* tractate in the *Mishnah* we read: "In every age man is under obligation to regard himself as if he had been

---

[39] Charles Dennison, "Preaching and Application: A Review," *Kerux* 4:3 (December 1989) 51.

[40] Cornelius Trimp, "The Relevance of Preaching," *Westminster Theological Journal* 36, no. 2 (fall 1973): 1.

[41] *Ibid.*, 2.

[42] *Ibid.*, 25-29.

[43] Geerhardus Vos, *Biblical Theology: Old and New Testaments* (Grand Rapids: Eerdmans, 1948) 303, in Dennison, "Preaching and Application: A Review," *Kerux* 4:3 (December 1989) 51.

[44] Dennison, "Some Thoughts on Preaching," 5, 8.

delivered out of Egypt." Gustaf Wingren of the Free University in Amsterdam asserts: "We do not first speak of the objective event and then try to find a way of applying it to men, for the *kerygma* concerning Christ's death and resurrection is already present; the hearer is there in the passage when the minister opens the New Testament."[45] This presentness is not to be confused with the Neo-Orthodox idea of supra-historical: "The whole content of the Gospel message and proclamation flows from the real history of Jesus Christ."[46] "*The kerygma proceeds from conditions fulfilled in Jesus Christ. It does not offer an exposition and application of the story of Christ's redemptive work; it implicates the hearer in that story.*"[47] Preaching "is not only the proclamation of the saving event that once took place in the life, death and resurrection of Jesus Christ, but it is also the announcement to the listener that, when he believes in this Jesus Christ, he finds himself in the new situation of salvation brought about by Jesus."[48]

Preaching in the electronic situation is not qualitatively different, whatever differences there may be between the Areopagus and the World Wide Web, from the first century situation. The same call to repentance and faith is in order. The question is never application or no application, relevance or no relevance, but rather which text defines relevance and application, the world or the Word? The heavenly reality brought to earth through the Incarnation transcends and invades the cultural developments between the times in this New Covenant epoch. And thus in a real sense, "There are no 'modern' preachers; there are only preachers."[49]

In an atmosphere befogged by a wide assortment of definitions of the preaching task we do well to look at the Biblical conception. God's Word clears the fog. T. David Gordon takes his definition of preaching from 2 Corinthians 5:20, "we are ambassadors for Christ, as though God were pleading through us: we implore *you* on Christ's behalf, be reconciled to God."

> The role of the minister, when preaching, is *not* to amuse (though some may find it amusing), is *not* to provide pastoral advice (though some may find good advice therein), is *not* to give a religious speech (though some may think it was a good speech), is *not* to inspire people to live as Christians (though some may be so inspired); the role of the minister is to *declare to the conscience* of the hearer what God has declared. God, not the minister, is to speak to the hearer, *through* the minister.[50]

---

[45] Jacob Firet, *Dynamics in Preaching* (Grand Rapids: Eerdmans, 1986) 31, 32.
[46] H. Diem, *Dogmatics* 132, quoted in Firet, *Dynamics in Preaching* 34.
[47] Firet, *Dynamics in Preaching* 45.
[48] Klaas Runia, "What Is Preaching according to the New Testament?" *Tyndale Bulletin* 29 (1978): 19.
[49] Dennison, "Preaching and Application: A Review," 52.
[50] T. David Gordon, "Presuppositions Regarding Preaching," unpublished manuscript, nd.

Develop Orality

The principle of *Sola Scriptura* "devours every dilemma that one might want to place between oral and written transmission."[51] The preacher must develop the finest oral skills as a communicator. Engage people with the content of the Word, with a convincing earnestness, and a compelling directness. The original meaning of propaganda was to propagate an idea (Latin "to sow"). This is persuasion in a positive sense. Preaching is a form of persuasion which intends the good of its hearers, while propaganda is mass persuasion which intends the good of the persuader.

As a preacher you must learn to distinguish between oral and written. The written is for the eye, while the oral is for the ear.[52] The greatest problem for the seminary trained *preacher*—few men can do without such training—is that we have had rigorous literary training. We are book, text and lecture oriented. Lectures are content heavy and meant basically to inform, not to move or persuade. Listen to J. C. Ryle: "English composition for speaking to hearers and English composition for private reading are almost like two different languages, so that sermons that 'preach' well 'read' badly."[53] Perhaps there is some truth to the provocative statement that "people today are not tired of preaching, but tired of *our* preaching."[54] Thielicke observes that "the man who bores others must also be boring himself."[55]

Put the results of your study in an oral format. Homiletics is the art of translating the meaning of the text, in the context of systematic and biblical theology, into a form designed to transform God's people. Theology serves homiletics not vice versa. Think of your preparation as soil for the sermon, not the sermon itself. Don't bring your study into the pulpit. Bring the results; and bring them in oral form. *Extemporaneous preaching* is live preaching, fully prepared for, but exclusively oral not rooted in the manuscript itself. "The written text of the New Testament itself is ordered to ...oral activity."[56] It is critical to recognize that the structure of persuasive speech is critical to its effect of the memory and thus the heart of the hearer.

Thus, your sermon notes should be structured as a set of visual cues, not a manuscript to be read or memorized. Use two manuscripts, if necessary: one

---

[51] Trimp, "The Relevance of Preaching," 18.
[52] Fant, *Preaching For Today*, 162.
[53] Iain Murray, *D. Martyn Lloyd-Jones: The Fight of Faith* (Edinburgh: The Banner of Truth Trust, 1990) 345.
[54] John W. Doberstein, Introduction to Thielicke, *The Trouble With The Church*, viii, referring to a statement by Paul Althaus, emphasis added.
[55] Thielicke, *The Trouble With The Church*, 9.
[56] Walter Ong, Review: *Beyond the Written Word: Oral Aspects of Scripture in the History of Religion* (William A. Graham) in *America* (Mar. 4, 1989): 204.

is a written summary of your exegesis and application put in the order of your sermon; the other is a one page abbreviated form for the pulpit. Near the end of my first decade of ministry I had a young summer intern replete with the latest laptop computer. He had taken all of his seminary notes with this wondrous new device. I had just begun using a simple Apple 2C, which was a dinosaur compared to his. Of course, he prepared his sermon notes on his word processor and suggested I try the same. After some resistance my intern prevailed upon me to try word processing my sermons. I did so much to my regret. Hitherto I had religiously used my beloved Mont Blanc fountain pen to write my sermons in full five page outlines, highlighting the main points in yellow and red. I had learned early on not to be a slave to my notes.

My only experience with word processing had been creating documents to be read, not preached. Book reviews, along with essays, periodical articles and the like, require an attention to grammatical and structural detail which preparation for oral presentation does not. In fact, as I learned through my first painful experience, preparing for preaching with precise writing is deadly to oral delivery, if that is the manuscript brought into the pulpit. Word processing, of which electronic mail is a type, while it allows non-typists like myself to produce documents, has a tendency to encourage sloppiness of spelling, grammar, composition, and thought. The old handwritten manuscript and the more recent typewritten manuscript encouraged care and thoughtfulness, because revision was difficult. That was my approach to my first word processed sermon. Because I had put so much effort into composition I felt naturally tied to the manuscript. For written productions one must be, because that is the final medium of communication. After one awkward sermon I vowed never to use the computer again for sermons.

It was not until half a decade later that I made the attempt again. Meanwhile, since I began my doctoral work just after the first negative encounter with word processing sermons, I had reflected on the nature of orality and preaching in connection with the electronic media. On a much more sophisticated machine I realized the potential of putting an entire sermon on one page so that I could avoid turning pages in the pulpit. I began by rewriting old five page sermons in the one page format. This enabled me to pay attention to the manuscript as a vehicle of oral communication rather than as a written record of a sermon. The highlighting and underlining had saved me from becoming a slave to the paper. Now I reworked the outline with directness and oral impact in mind. Few complete sentences, fewer quotations, highlighting vivid phrases in italic bold; everything was aimed at affecting the congregation. The difference was monumental. The effect has been dramatic. But it really all began with my reflection on my use of media, in this case the printed word, the written word, the word processed word and the preached word. All of this was inspired by a passion to be a better preacher, a goal to which every preacher should never stop aspiring.

It is foolish to try extemporaneous preaching without careful preparation and experience. Richard S. Storrs's *Preaching without Notes* is a classic on the subject.[57] Extemporaneous preaching requires as much, if not more, careful preparation as does preaching with a manuscript, just a different kind of preparation. Clyde Fant's *Preaching For Today* (1975) is especially helpful in this department.[58] He deals with some of the unique mechanics of oral preparation. Write like you speak; do not speak like you write. If you have ever read a written transcript of one of your sermons, you will be horrified at how badly it reads. That is as it should be. Listening to your sermons on tape with manuscript you used is a helpful exercise. This does not mean that poor speech patterns of grammar is acceptable orally. While no single method is universally helpful for each preacher Fant's point is that, like charity, orality begins at home. In other words, we must prepare *orally*. This means preparing our sermons "out loud."[59] After exegesis and the discernment of the point of the text, begin communicating it out loud, and then write down the main points of the logic of what you have said. Fant calls this the "rough oral draft." Then go back after more reflection on exegesis and the rough draft and make a "final oral draft." From this he recommends a final one page "sermon" brief.[60] Those who use limited notes in the pulpit, or only pay attention to highlighted full notes, already practice something like this. Something similar to this is required to become an effective preacher.

Furthermore, each genre of Biblical literature requires a different approach, a varied use of outlines. The systematic announcement of "headings" may be helpful in preaching from the logically argued epistles of Paul, but the narrative of Judges will be better preached by following the story sequence and leaving the logical divisions "invisible" in the preaching moment. The distinction between oral and written logic should not be exaggerated in this discussion. No one can think, speak or write, without logic. But the logic of narrative and the logic of epistles are quite different. They require different ways of ordering our thoughts, not a logic different from the way we think. The text itself dictates this. Much more work needs to be done with this area of homiletics.

General preparation is crucial for extemporaneous preaching. Reading widely on a daily basis is the best fertilizer both for the soil of immediate exegesis and the blooming of the sermon itself. With all that we have said

---

[57] Richard S. Storrs, *Preaching without Notes* (New York: Hodder and Stoughton, 1875).
[58] Fant, *Preaching For Today*, 159-173.
[59] *Ibid.*, 165.
[60] *Ibid.*, 166-169.

about the importance of orality it needs to be emphasized that private reading, deep reading, broad reading, and constant reading of Scripture is absolutely essential to the development of the mind and spirit of the preacher. As Joel Nederhood counsels: "Be addicted to reading."[61] This does not contradict the need to distinguish between written and oral *in the pulpit*. Furthermore, being a good writer enhances logical and rhetorical skills in public speech.[62]

One of the best ways to develop oral skill is to read aloud and pay attention to the best oral presentation outside the pulpit. Baseball announcers are an excellent example of vivid speech which engages the listener. In a visual age their skills are tested to the limit. They are well paid to hold attention, with words which stimulate the imagination so that the hearer visualizes the game. These announcers were often English majors in college and former English teachers. "That hard grounder to the short stop ate him up. ...He roped one over the head of the second baseman into right field. ...He crushed that one and sent it into the stands in center field. ...He had a notion, but checked his swing. ...A one-two-three inning ending double play."

The preacher must cultivate a love for the English language, especially the spoken word. Ransack the best dictionaries. Above all *read aloud*. Choose the best poetry and prose and read it aloud. Read the Psalms, George Herbert, Dylan Thomas, Shakespeare, the essays and stories of G. K. Chesterton, Hillaire Belloc, Stephen Leacock, Christopher Morley, *aloud*! The *King James Version* is best suited to the practice of reading Scripture aloud, not because it is a perfect or even the best translation, but because it was produced in a golden age of orality, the Elizabethan Age of Shakespeare. In this period the literary and the oral were held in excellent balance. One thing is certain: the *Authorized Version* was translated to be read aloud in churches. The authorized title says: "appointed to be read in churches." Be assured this did not mean silent, private reading. Let the beauty of the best of the richest language in history sink into your oral memory. Words are your tools. Court them. Work with them to become a wordsmith. Fall in love with them. As McLuhan said, "language itself is the principal channel and view-maker of experience for men everywhere."[63] "The spoken word involves all the senses dramatically."[64] The preached Word is the most powerful "view-maker" of all, as it corrects the

---

[61] Nederhood, "Effective Preaching in a Media Age."
[62] Storrs, *Preaching without Notes*, 45ff.
[63] Marshall McLuhan, "Catholic Humanism and Modern Letters," in *The Medium and the Light: Reflections on Religion*, edited by Eric McLuhan and Jacek Szlarek (Toronto: Stoddart Publishing Co. Limited, 1999) [page 2 or 3].
[64] Marshall McLuhan, *Understanding Media: The Extensions of Man* (New York: McGraw-Hill Book Company, 1964) 77, 78.

idolatrous "view-making" propagated by the electronic media, and inculcates the redemptive "view-making" of the heavenly reality of the Incarnate Logos.

Often the *King James Version* is considered a stumbling block to modern understanding. I believe that is only partly true. When read aloud it has a vividness and an oral power unequaled by any translation except the *Geneva Bible*. Because the average person today has little sensibility for the beauty and power of Elizabethan English, jaded as we are by secondary orality, image media, and functional illiteracy, I believe we are wisest to use a modern translation like the *New King James Version*, in the pulpit, because it retains the accuracy and much of the orality of the *King James Version*, without most of its antique oddities. It may surprise some to learn that one of the great lessons of the *King James Version* as a translation is its use of vernacular. English, American or British, is an amazingly versatile language. It is always evolving. The preacher must pay careful attention to the language which people speak every day. The danger, of course, is the temptation to be trendy or vulgar. But one need not compromise grammatical correctness, or good taste, in order to use the people's English well.

We need to offset and counteract one of the negatives of the written/printed word. It privatizes the experience of the reader and impresses the visual memory. We need to reconnect the written and the oral if we are to be effective preachers. Memorizing Scripture, especially your preaching pericope, and the *Shorter Catechism* will help mold this connection, both for you and your hearers.

Take the greatest care in reading the Scriptures aloud. Hughes Oliphant Old has titled his mult-volume history of preaching: *The Reading and Preaching of the Scriptures in the Worship of the Christian Church*, because of the essential difference between the written and the preached Word of God. When we read the Scripture we are saying: This is the source of what we are about to preach.[65] We are reading the word of the King. The synagogue and the ancient church read the Scriptures through, seriatim, on a regular basis. Copies of the Scripture prior to the Gutenberg era, were rare and expensive. The average person did not have a copy to read privately. In the electronic age we must not assume that people are reading their Bibles regularly or at all. Even when they are, they may not be reading the "whole" of Scripture. Even then there is a unique value, as we have seen for God's people to hear the Word with their ears. The immediacy of the effect when Scripture is read properly has a unique place in the life of the church. But we must cultivate this. The way that we read Scripture aloud, as well as our entire demeanor surrounding the reading, will determine the attitude of our hearers, especially in their

---

[65] Old, *The Reading and Preaching of the Scriptures*, vol. 1, 52, 58.

reception of what we preach after we read. Remember the immediate power of the human voice in orality, especially when what is read aloud is the very Word of God. The power of Josiah's reform is attested by the writer of 2 Kings: "And the king went up into the house of the LORD, and all the men of Judah and all the inhabitants of Jerusalem with him, and the priests, and the prophets, and all the people, both small and great: and *he read in their ears* all the words of the book of the covenant which was found in the house of the LORD" (2 Kings 23:2, KJV, emphasis mine). Read to catechize, sounding in the ear! Imagine how the Word sounded after being lost in the Temple for so many years, heard for the first time (2 Kings 22:8). The Word read poorly in the ears of God's people is tantamount to its being lost in the church today.

In Nehemiah 8:8 we read: "So they read distinctly from the book, in the Law of God; and they gave the sense, and helped *them* to understand the reading." Acts 13:15: "And after the reading of the Law and the Prophets, the rulers of the synagogue sent to them, saying, 'Men *and* brethren, if you have any word of exhortation for the people, say on.'" 1 Timothy 4:13: "Till I come, give attention to reading, to exhortation, to doctrine." We normally consider this "reading" private, and silent. Its connection with exhortation militates against that individualistic interpretation. Consider Revelation 1:3: "Blessed *is* he who reads and those who hear the words of this prophecy, and keep those things which are written in it; for the time *is* near." This is public reading. The public reading of Scripture does not replace private reading or preaching, nor does preaching replace the reading of Scripture. Rather the public reading of Scripture demands the preaching of it. In both, the oral dimension is its special power. The immediate presence of God in the voice of the reader/preacher of His Word is subversive to the sinner's rebellious position in the First Adam, and represents a living call to repentance and faith in the Second and Last Adam.

The deep well from which true preaching comes is Biblical meditation. Our age does not provide either the atmosphere or the motivation for careful reflection. The "engineering hermeneutic," of which Darryl Hart warned in chapter 8, presents a special temptation at this point. The pragmatic bent tends to propel us into gathering information in a mechanical way, leaving the illusion of having "studied" a text. Word and phrase searches have a beguiling power over the student. While I am not advocating the abandonment of these useful tools, they are never a replacement for quiet meditation in thought and prayer. Take time to pray and think and pray some more before you switch on the machine.

Trust the Power and Presence of God

Trust the Holy Spirit in the preaching moment. The greatest folly of our age is trusting the means, the techniques of doing things. The means of preaching, unlike any other form of public speaking, is uniquely dependent on God's blessing. Reformed preachers know the folly of trusting the Spirit without preparation; but we need to deal with the equal folly of sticking slavishly to our manuscript in the act of preaching, and thus trusting our preparation without trusting the Spirit. Your special and general preparation will be used in the act of preaching in ways you will never be free enough to experience if you are a notes-slave. Pray for the only power that can make the medium you use effective: the power of God's presence in your preaching through the ministry of the Holy Spirit.

Unction is not a human attribute, it is the secret and mysterious influence that God's Spirit bestows on faithful preaching. Thus it is not a tone of voice or style of delivery. The Sovereignty of the influence is meant to move us to pray and depend humbly on God's power in our preaching. He alone has access to the secret recesses of the human hearts of your hearers. Eph. 6:18-20 "praying always with all prayer and supplication in the Spirit, being watchful to this end with all perseverance and supplication for all the saints—and for me, that utterance may be given to me, that I may open my mouth boldly to make known the mystery of the gospel, for which I am an ambassador in chains; that in it I may speak boldly, as I ought to speak." Prayer is no substitute for study, but it must also not be a *mere* article of our faith, unpracticed in our private preparations for the pulpit. The effectiveness of our preaching will always be directly related to our dependence on God's power through all of our studious, intellectual efforts in opening God's Word. The Spirit influences the hearer and the preacher alike. As Augustine insists the true preacher "is a petitioner before he is a speaker."[66]

As we have seen in the Reformation conception of preaching as witnessed in the *Second Helvetic Confession* "the preaching of the word of God *is* the word of God." Our Lord, the incarnate Word, has identified the preaching of His ordained spokesmen with His Word: "He who hears you hears Me" (Luke 10:16). Herman Hoeksema correctly insisted that the Greek of Romans 10:14 should be translated as the *American Standard Version* has it: "And how shall they believe in Him *whom* they have not heard?" as opposed to "Him *of whom* they have not heard?"[67] Thus it is "the preached Word rather than the written

---

[66] Augustine, *On Christian Doctrine*, 141.
[67] David H. Schuringa, "The Preaching of the Word As a Means of Grace: The Views of Herman Hoeksema and R. B. Kuiper." Th. M. thesis (Calvin Theological Seminary, 1985) 18-22. Later in chapter III (34-43) a convincing case for the grammatical correctness of this translation is made.

Word" which is the primary means of grace.[68] Christ is immediately present as the true Speaker in the preaching moment. "The implication is that Christ speaks in the gospel proclamation."[69] So Calvin comments on the same passage: "This is a remarkable passage with regard to the efficacy of preaching..."[70] Preaching is not speaking about Christ, but is Christ speaking. Haddon Robinson goes so far as to insist that even the inspired letters of Paul were no substitute in his ministry for the preached Word: "A power comes through the word preached which even the inerrant word cannot replace."[71]

In his biography of James I. Packer, Alister McGrath gives Packer's excellent definition of preaching: "'The event of God bringing to an audience a Bible-based, Christ-related, life-impacting message of instruction and direction from himself through the words of a spokesperson (sic).' Preaching was thus defined, not in terms of human performance or activity, but in terms of divine communication."[72] Paul said it clearly to the Thessalonian church: "when you received the word of God which you heard from us, you welcomed *it* not *as* the word of men, but as it is in truth, the word of God" (1 Thess. 2:13). The preacher should never be satisfied with anything less than a congregation that is "taught by God" (1 Thess. 4:9). While recognizing that he is a mere man like each of his congregants, and a sinful man at that, the preacher must have the confidence which God has connected with his preaching ministry. If, as an ambassador, he sticks to the message of his King, he may be assured that God's word, and not his own, is what the church receives. Calvin recognized God's condescension in this arrangement in commenting that God "deigns to consecrate to himself the mouths and tongues of men in order that his voice may resound in them."[73] The egalitarianism which favors dialogue does not favor faith, as Peter Berger notes: "Ages of faith are not marked by 'dialogue' but by proclamation."[74]

---

[68] *Ibid.*, 33.
[69] *Ibid.*, 43.
[70] *Ibid.*, 44, John Calvin, *Epistle to the Romans*, Vol. 19 of *Calvin's Commentaries*, 22 vols. (Grand Rapids: Baker Book House, 1979) 398.
[71] Haddon Robinson, *Biblical Preaching* (Grand Rapids: Baker Book House, 1980) 17, in Heck, *The ERS : The Five Steps of Bible Exposition*, 12. Cf. Old, *The Reading and Preaching of the Scriptures*, vol. 1, 52.
[72] Alister McGrath, *A Biography of James I. Packer: To Know and Serve God* (London: Hodder and Stoughton, 1997) 256.
[73] John Calvin, *Institutes*, IV.1, in James Daane, *Preaching With Confidence: A Theological Essay on the Power of the Pulpit* (Grand Rapids: Eerdmans, 1980) 15.
[74] In Daane, *Preaching With Confidence*, 16.

Open the Word

The Word alone nurtures true Christian piety. In this Postmodern world we must emphasize that God's Word is absolutely true. It is His infallible Word and it is thus to be believed because it is true; believed because God has spoken. Many Evangelicals claim that there is no absolute truth. So the idol of Tolerance has even infected the church. Furthermore, the Gospel is utterly unique; it is the only way of salvation. "Nor is there salvation in any other, for there is no other name under heaven given among men by which we must be saved." (Acts 4:12).

Although it may seem to contradict what we have said about the importance of orality in the preacher's life and ministry, the preacher must ever be a man of letters, a man saturated with the Word. McLuhan once observed that as the printed word has lost its monopoly as a channel of information "it has acquired new interest as a tool in the training of perception."[75] The preacher must not stand above the Bible as an analyst, but be absorbed by it as the environment into which the risen Lord draws us by His grace.[76]

Teach the Doctrines of the whole counsel of God (Acts 20:27). Using the Catechisms and Confessions of the church help people to see how the system of doctrine is rooted in and discovered in the texts of Scripture. Every sermon should be full of doctrine but not a doctrinal lecture. Without the Word the preacher has nothing to say.

Tell the Story of Redemption

As Charles Dennison has so aptly put it: "There are no 'modern' preachers; there are only preachers."[77] With Paul and John we are in the final, that is eschatological, epoch of redemptive history. However, this does not eliminate the challenges which the preacher faces in his unique cultural situation. The Biblical response to that challenge is exemplified by Paul in terms of his approach to the two different audiences in the synagogue, for example at Pisidian Antioch, and the pagans in Athens. The era of electronic communication media represents a unique challenge to the preacher in our new century. As with Paul our situation demands that we tell the story of redemption. The centrality of narrative in the Bible cannot be overemphasized. The Covenantal structure of the entire Bible places the narrative text in the context of God's plan and work of redemption. Every other Biblical genre is rooted in that covenantal narrative. Thus we should not be surprised to find

---

[75] Marshall McLuhan, *Counterblast* (London: Rapp & Whiting, 1969) 99.
[76] Nederhood, "Effective Preaching in a Media Age."
[77] Charles Dennison, "Preaching and Application: A Review," 52.

New Testament preaching focusing on the story of redemption, even when it is given to an audience which has only natural revelation at its disposal. Without the Gospel-Acts narratives, for example, the epistles are meaningless.

The importance of story-telling in the ancient world has been largely overlooked by reformed preachers. This reaction to evangelical anecdotal preaching has left a void which needs to be filled. In the more orally-aurally oriented culture of the ancient world, where personal possession of "books" was rare, story-telling was the primary means of propagating and transmitting tradition. This appears to have been the case during the millennia from Adam's fall to the Mosaic revelation. The increase of oral-aural sensibilities in the electronic age is a providential prod to call us to return to the power of the story of redemption to impress the souls of our hearers.

Those, like Neil Postman, who are seeking to fend off the purposelessness, atomizing, dumbing down and evacuation of public education affirm the transcendent value and necessity of the great narratives, of which Christianity is one. But the church itself has atomized Scripture by quoting prooftexts and taking Scriptures stories and examples and using them as if they came out of nowhere. We have eviscerated the Scripture by tearing apart the single story of redemption into little timeless pieces, used for moral lessons and successful living. The power of the Great Epochal Narrative of Redemption thus disappears. With Christ at its center every text has a location in that history. To call it a *story* does not imply fiction. It is a single history with a beginning and an end. It is full of characters and concrete detail, full of interest and told by the Great Raconteur, the Holy Spirit, in order to reveal the Original Character and Hero Jesus Christ. The narrative power of television as the great storyteller of our time can only be countered by the Story of Redemption in the Bible. The story line of the Bible is the structure of the whole. While the electronic media, especially television and film, narrate the stories of a lost world seeking transcendence apart from God, and thus disciple the world, the church needs to be discipling God's people in the story of salvation. God has spoken. God has entered history. The Christ of Scripture is His final Word to this present evil age.

"Biblical theology imparts a new life and freshness to the old truth by placing it in its original historic setting. The Bible is not a handbook of dogmatics: it is a historical book full of dramatic interest."[78] Biblical Theology represents the interface between the text of Scripture and our system of theology. It is after all God's way of accounting for His redemptive acts in history. Thus, far from being a threat to either systematic theology or

---

[78] Geerhardus Vos, "The Nature and Aims of Biblical Theology," *Kerux: A Journal of Biblical Theological Preaching* 14/1 (May 1999): 7. Originally from *The Union Seminary Magazine* 13/3 (February-March 1902): 194-99.

supernaturalism, Biblical Theology lends cohesiveness and coherence to the orthodox account of truth. Without systematic theology, Biblical Theology will tend toward immanentism; without Biblical Theology, systematic theology will tend toward mere abstraction.[79]

Immanentism in all of its forms, including evolutionary thought, and Process Theology's idea that God is himself developing, is best answered on its own grounds: the historical. The "history of special revelation" is the divinely given account of the way in which the absolutely transcendent Creator God has acted in history through the vehicle of His covenant. Ultimately all forms of immanentism fail to find meaning and direction in history for the very reason that, in seeking concreteness in the historical, it has no reference point from which to interpret the very history it investigates. Only the Covenant Theology of the Bible presents the Absolute One and history together. It "grants us a new vision of the glory of God. As eternal, he lives above the sphere of history. He is the Being, and not the becoming one. But, since for our salvation he has condescended to work and speak in the form of time, and thus to make his work and his speech partake of the peculiar glory that belongs to all organic growth, we must also seek to know him as the One that is, that was, and that is to come, in order that our theology may adequately perform its function of glorifying God in every mode of his self-revelation to us."[80]

For the preacher there is no other theology which will answer his practical purposes in the church. "The knowledge of God communicated by it [the historic character of revelation] is nowhere for a purely intellectual purpose. From beginning to end it is intended to enter into the actual life of man. Hence God has interwoven his revelation with the historic life of the chosen race, so as to secure for it a practical form in all its parts. This principle has found its clearest expression in the idea of the covenant as the form of God's self-revelation to Israel. The covenant is an all-comprehensive communion of life, in which every self-disclosure is made subservient to a practical end."[81]

And yet at once the practicality of this historical concreteness stands as a most needed corrective to the subjectivism of our age and of the church which has taken on too much of the world's mindset in this department. "Sacred history deals with the redemptive realities created by the supernatural activity of God. Biblical theology deals with the redemptive knowledge communicated in order to interpret these realities. ...Revelation is designed to prepare, to accompany, and to interpret the great objective redemptive acts of God, such as

---

[79] It should be noted that abstraction is a necessary part of the human thought process. It is when this process, in theological reasoning is not rooted in history, that it leads to the kind of abstraction with which I am concerned.

[80] Vos, "The Nature and Aims of Biblical Theology," *Kerux*, 8.

[81] *Ibid.*, 5.

the incarnation, the atonement, the resurrection. It is not intended to follow the subjective appropriation of redemption in its further course."[82] It is primarily by the work of the Holy Spirit through preaching that this "subjective appropriation of redemption" is carried on.

The faithful preacher will demonstrate from every text of Scripture the connection of his hearers to the history of redemption. "Practical" in this context is not to be understood as advocating the kind of "world catering" application to which many preachers give the same label. In our day "practical" often means meeting the so-called "needs" of people who are wedded to this world. In this construction the Gospel becomes another program for promoting self-help and self-esteem. The practical nature of the Covenant is found in its revolutionary altering of the entire orientation and framework of the believer, who is connected by Christ to heavenly reality. "Seek ye first the kingdom of God...." The world's order of concerns is reversed. The source of this reversal is the present historical situation in which the Christ has come and reigns from His heavenly thrown guiding history towards its consummation. The preacher will therefore avoid co-opting the Gospel for a surreptitiously idolatrous agenda in the church, which is being promoted with renewed vigor with the new electronic means.

The subject-object distinction of the Cartesian worldview tends toward logical sequential formulations in which discreet realities are abstracted from their context. The history of redemption, on the other hand, brings subject and object together, without the relativizing tendency of postmodern alternatives to the Cartesian model. Unlike the "metalanguages" of structuralism, post structuralism, deconstruction, and all earth-bound attempts to describe the world, the narrative of redemption functions as *the* metanarrative by which all others are to be interpreted and judged.

There are no Biblical-Theological preachers, only preachers. Preachers who do not tell the story of redemption are not preachers in the Biblical sense.

Be Simple and Direct: Preach with Purpose

The Larger Catechism (Q #159), as we have noted, tells the preacher to preach "plainly," using 1 Corinthians 14:19 as the proof text: "in the church I would rather speak five words with my understanding, that I may teach others also, than ten thousand words in a tongue." The Catechism enjoins preachers to apply "themselves to the necessities and capacities of the hearers." Paul took the ability of his hearers into account. "I fed you with milk and not with solid food; for until now you were not able *to receive it,* and even now you are still

---

[82] *Ibid.*, 4, 5.

not able." The Puritans, with all of their immense learning—and they were among the most learned men of their times—were known for their "plain speaking" in the pulpit.

We must take special care with the language of theology and common Christian parlance. Some approach this problem by avoiding the use of terms like "propitiation" or "regeneration" altogether. This is a grave mistake. But it is also a serious error to use these words without explaining them in a vivid and memorable way. Never assume, especially given the current level of Biblical illiteracy, that your congregation, or an evangelistic audience has a Biblical vocabulary. Best to assume that an evangelistic audience knows nothing except its culture; that the church knows a little more, but still not much, because there are always unbelievers or new Christians present. The call is not for sermon-lite, but for clarity. As Augustine counseled: "The speaker should not consider the eloquence of his teaching but the clarity of it."[83] With Cicero he advised a "studied negligence" of high sounding speech in the interest of clear communication. As ambassadors our goal is to be understood, not to impress people with our vocabularies or our learning.

Believing as we ought that preaching is God's direct communication to His church we must labor to *engage* people. Use the introduction as a porch that invites people in. Begin where people are, not where the text begins in history. Ask a challenging question or make a provocative statement. But be careful not try to "make the text relevant." This is not the purpose of a good introduction. The hook of the introduction is meant to draw the church out of the world in which they are absorbed and into the text of which the church is a part. "It is into the Bible world of eternal redemption, that the preacher must bring his people. This eternal world from whence Christ came is contemporary with every age. ...The only preaching which is up to date for every time is the preaching of this eternity, which is opened to us in the Bible alone—the eternal of holy love, grace and redemption, the eternal and immutable morality of saving grace for our indelible sin."[84] Peter used the questions, misinterpretation, and scoffing of the crowd, due to the phenomena of miraculously speaking an unknown foreign language by the disciples at Pentecost, to introduce his sermon. Paul used the statue to an "unknown god" in Athens to introduce his sermon on Mars Hill. The introduction should be directly related to the purpose of the sermon as these two Biblical examples demonstrate. It should make the congregation hungry, like an hors d'oeuvre, to know what God has to say to them. "Tell me more!" should be their response.[85]

---

[83] Augustine, *On Christian Doctrine*, 133.
[84] P. T. Forsyth, *Positive Preaching and the Modern Mind* (New York: Hodder and Stoughton, 1907) 32, 33.
[85] Adams, "Preaching with Purpose," class notes.

Conclusions should leave the congregation with the difference the sermon makes in their lives. "How shall we then live?" should be the question the conclusion answers. This is not the same as a "practical how to" at the end of every sermon. It leaves the hearer with the point of God's Word in the expounded text. The conclusion should be brief, memorable and done only once. Both introductions and conclusions are best constructed after everything else in a sermon has been determined, then studied with extreme care just before the preaching event.

An important aspect of simplicity is sermon length. As a young fan of the Puritans I used to believe that limiting sermon length was akin to heresy. I have learned the opposite. To tax people beyond their capacity, especially in an era of short attentions spans, lacks the compassion and wisdom of an undershepherd of Jesus. Better to hold people's attention for half an hour with a clear, well pointed message, than to lose people for an hour. When the point of the text has been made, stop! In a generation informed by sound bites anything extraneous is not appreciated. The preacher would do well to heed the advice of W. Somerset Maugham to playwrights in 1938: "It is very different now, and the difference has been occasioned, I suppose, by the advent of the cinema. Today, audiences, especially in English-speaking countries, have learnt to see the point of a scene at once and having seen it want to pass on to the next; they catch the gist of a speech in a few words, and having caught it their attention quickly wanders... His [the playwrights] dialogue must be a sort of spoken shorthand. He must cut and cut till he has arrived at the maximum of concentration."[86] Add excessive length to a lecture-like sermon and you will foster a new motto of communication: the tedium is the message.

On the matter of directness John Angell James enjoins: "Our hearers must be made to feel that they are not merely listening to the discussion of a subject, but to an appeal to themselves: their attention must be kept up, and a close connection between them and the preacher maintained, by the frequent introduction of the pronoun 'you;' so that each may realize the thought that the discourse is actually addressed to him."[87] Spurgeon used the apt analogy of shooting barbed arrows. Arrows without feathers fly nowhere, like most applications and many illustrations. And if they arrive without barbs they do not stick. *The Larger Catechism* (Q #159) uses the same archer's metaphor: "sincerely, aiming at his glory, and their conversion, edification, and salvation." When we aim we should ask if our target includes these elements. If we have no target in mind we will leave people wondering why we spoke. Aimless preaching is one of the reasons why critics say preaching is dead. Our aim is

---

[86] W. Somerset Maugham, *The Summing Up* (Garden City, NY: Doubleday and Company, 1938) 126.
[87] James, *An Earnest Ministry*, 117.

the God-given purpose of the text. We may think of the use of the second person as the feathers which direct the arrow of the sermon. The third person aims at no-one in particular. Many preachers are afraid to say YOU, because they feel that people will think they are arrogant. There is certainly value in including yourself when appropriate, but you are God's spokesman and He wants you to address His people directly. This directness must be reflected in your title, and main sermon headings of oral cues. Preaching is first of all His Word to the church. The barbs are the specifics of the application.

Let us consider Matthew 15:13-20 as an example. Notice our Lord's use of "you." "But He answered and said, 'Every plant which My heavenly Father has not planted will be uprooted. Let them alone. They are blind leaders of the blind. And if the blind leads the blind, both will fall into a ditch. Then Peter answered and said to Him, 'Explain this parable to us.' So Jesus said, 'Are *you* also still without understanding? Do *you* not yet understand that whatever enters the mouth goes into the stomach and is eliminated? But those things which proceed out of the mouth come from the heart, and they defile a man. For out of the heart proceed *evil thoughts, murders, adulteries, fornications, thefts, false witness, blasphemies*. These are *the things* which defile a man, but to eat with unwashed hands does not defile a man.'" Jesus does not leave it us to identify the specifics of what defiles man.

Make preaching that transforms people into the image of Jesus Christ the focus and soul of your pulpit ministry. Romans 12:1,2 "I beseech you therefore, brethren, by the mercies of God, that ye present your bodies a living sacrifice, holy, acceptable unto God, *which is* your reasonable service. And be not conformed to this world: but be ye transformed by the renewing of your mind, that ye may prove what *is* that good, and acceptable, and perfect, will of God."

A very helpful book on preaching with directness is Jay Adams's *Preaching with Purpose*.[88] Adams pleads with preachers to stick to the purpose (telos) of each text. This is not a simply summary or description of its meaning, but communication of God's purpose for His church in light of Paul's dictum in Romans 15:4: "For whatever things were written before were written for our learning, that we through the patience and comfort of the Scriptures might have hope.." Only when this purpose is kept clearly in mind will directness be the result. With the purpose in his sight the preacher will hit the target intended by his Master.

Here a word about "effectiveness" is in order. Joel Nederhood refers to preaching effectiveness as "the great temptation."[89] As Cornelius Trimp points out: "our age is characterized by a strong attraction to *observable* and

---

[88] Jay Adams, *Preaching With Purpose* (Phillipsburg, NJ: Presbyterian and Reformed, 1982).
[89] Nederhood, "Effective Preaching in a Media Age."

measurable events."[90] Evangelists brag about the number of decisions recorded as a result of their "revival" preaching campaigns. We are overly impressed by denominational statistics. Much of the "marketing the church" movement motivates churches and pastors to adopt its techniques based on statistics, and measurable results. Visible success becomes the proverbial bottom line. One of the subtle, but virulent, forces in this equation is the desire to join culture in its putative forward movement. We want to fit in and demonstrate to the world that we are not a bad as we have been painted. We are here to aid the progress of human culture, as any other social institution. This mentality means that our greatest fear is of being removed to the margins of our society. When we observe the results of New Testament preaching we see that it often caused social upheaval as in Jerusalem at Pentecost, and in Ephesus. To be faithful to our calling as heralds of the Head of the new humanity we must be prepared to preach without fear of the consequences and without discouragement that our message may not meet with great visible success. Faithfulness, as we have seen, is the hallmark of the herald.

Draw Attention with Word Pictures

The challenge of the preacher in an age in which words are cheap and devalued, due to the all-at-onceness of mass electronic media, is to "find ways to convey through the dynamics of his words and the interrelations of words the sensible realities embodied in such ancient 'carriers of meaning' as God, Christ, Holy Spirit, reconciliation, redemption, salvation, sacrament, heaven, hell, faith, hope, love. In order to reach with words a people accustomed to communication through total sensory stimuli enwrapped in the convincing and attractive environments of electronic media, we must be able to unwrap and enwrap in similarly convincing and attractive ways the great words in which our Christian tradition is stored."[91] While we must not concede, as Mehl seems to in this statement, that the Scriptures need to be *made* relevant, the point of the power of words should be well taken. The Hebrew word for "word" (דָּבָר dabar) "carries with it the dynamic connotation of 'event.' ...Words have evocative power. They can call things into existence, change the old, undo what was, bring forth the new." Hebrews 4:12 declares: "the word of God is living and active" (NIV).[92]

---

[90] Cornelius Trimp, "Preaching as the Public Means of Divine Redemption," translated by Nelson D. Kloosterman, *Mid-America Journal of Theology*, Theme Issue: Preaching, Vol. 10 (1999) 42.
[91] Duane Mehl, "Mass Media and the Future of Preaching," *Concordia Theological Monthly* 41 (1970): 210.
[92] Daane, *Preaching With Confidence*, 20, 21.

David Buttrick asks, "What will happen to a religion of book in an age dominated by the epistemology of the electronic media? Obviously the whole notion of biblical authority will not wash in an electronic age."[93] He advocates a "street smart" strategy of "visual logic."[94] Since Biblical religion has by definition always been a religion of the book, we should not panic. The answer is not in the electronic media but in the Bible itself. The visual, along with all the senses, and the metaphorical have always been a vital part of human knowing and communicating. Rather than signaling the demise of Biblical authority their use in preaching reminds us that we are God's creatures and live in His world. He has created the structures of experience, and word pictures and metaphors, both given in the Bible, and used to communicate Biblical truth are assertions of His Lordship over all of life.

Word pictures stimulate the imagination in a Biblical way. Jesus used metaphors and drew verbal pictures throughout His earthly ministry. Study and use the biblical model of vivid, concise language (stories, illustrations and metaphors) to capture the imaginations of your hearers, thus making the theme of your pericope stick to their souls. Use the images and metaphors of Scripture. From Jesus we also learn that images from our culture are effective means by which to make a point. He used soils. We may uses automobiles and computers. Notice that Scripture metaphors and images are inspired, and though at times requiring explanation in urban culture, they are universal. They involve finance, agriculture, family life etc. They engage people in the concreteness of their everyday lives in God's world. For example, the ungodly are "like the chaff which the wind drives away" (Ps. 1:4)

Spurgeon was a master of what Jay Adams calls "sense appeal." His book *Studies in Preaching: Sense Appeal in the Sermons of Charles Haddon Spurgeon* is stimulating in this regard.[95] Adams observes that most homiletics texts advocate vividness, which is an appeal only to sight. However, all the senses should be used in a Biblical model.[96] In an age of image media, it is especially important that preachers take full advantage of this Biblical resource. It is also an excellent antidote to the danger of icon worship, since the meaning of metaphors is interpreted by the written Word of God.

Our language, generally, ought to be the language of Scripture, and be calculated to arrest, awaken people to the awful danger of being outside of Christ, and the awesome glory of being His.

---

[93] David G. Buttrick, "Preaching to the 'Faith' of America," in *Communication and Change in American Religious History*, edited by Leonard Sweet (Grand Rapids: Eerdmans, 1993) 319.
[94] *Ibid.*, 310, 316.
[95] Jay Adams, *Studies in Preaching: Sense Appeal in the Sermons of Charles Haddon Spurgeon*, Vol. 1. (Nutley, NJ: Presbyterian and Reformed, 1976).
[96] Adams, *Preaching With Purpose*, 87.

Expose and Destroy the Idols

Challenge your congregation with a clear understanding of the nature and effects of modern media in order to overcome the naïveté of the evangelical church with respect to the electronic media; and teach them how to be better worshipers and sermon listeners in this cultural context by helping them understand the uniqueness, excellence and genius of preaching as a medium. We must break through, rather than imitate or accommodate, the electronic environment. We must challenge the idolatry which is woven into the fabric of our culture. 1 Thess. 1:9, 10 "For they themselves declare concerning us what manner of entry we had to you, and how you turned to God from idols to serve the living and true God, and to wait for His Son from heaven, whom He raised from the dead, *even* Jesus who delivers us from the wrath to come."

This means that the gospel of the cross and resurrection must be central to all of your proclamation. "I plead with you: Good preaching is Christ-centered, not morality or behavior-centered; Scripture-centered, not culture-centered; history of redemption-centered, not history of the world-centered."[97] Instead of pandering to the modern mindset with a Christ who is good for the sinner, who will help make him a successful or better person, the gospel must be proclaimed as God's radical call for repentance and faith. The Gospel in its utter uniqueness must be heralded, not as a fine system of behavior, but as God in the crucified and risen Christ reconciling Himself to the world. "The Jesus that offends no one is not the Jesus of the New Testament."[98] The Jesus Christ must be announced as the Savior of the world, not because he is a great psychologist or social worker, but because He is the Second and Last Adam, Who challenges this present evil age at the core of its existence in the First Adam. The message is to be presented with urgency because it is true, and because the offer of reconciliation will be followed by the coming Day of the Lord, when Jesus the Christ will come to claim the territory and the citizens which are His, earned with His obedience, purchased with His blood.

Preachers you need to help Christians develop their critical faculties. When you expose the nature of specific idols, demonstrate their destructive effects, your congregation will be transformed. Then they will never watch television the same again. They will never think about the Internet or their computers the same again. It's not that we want people to stop using technology. This is the Anabaptist-Luddite mistake. We need to help Christians develop sales resistance in an idolatrous culture. T. S. Eliot quipped

---

[97] Dennison, "Some Thoughts on Preaching," 6.
[98] Daane, *Preaching With Confidence*, 34.

that "paganism holds all the most valuable advertising space."[99] But the church has the preaching of the Word of God. The best place to take the magic out of idolatry is not in the newspaper, on the television, radio or the Internet, but *in the pulpit*. Hendrick Berkhof counsels, "When the Powers are unmasked, they lose their dominion over men's souls."[100] Only the Gospel of Jesus Christ can slay the idols.

We must aid the church in discerning the vanity in Vanity Fair. "False gods are highly catching! With good reason both Old and New Testaments abound with warnings against participating in Pagan cultures... 'world' complements 'flesh' to constitute monolithic evil: the manufacture of idols instead of the worship of the true God."[101]

Counselor David Powlison observes: "If we would help people have eyes and ears for God, we must know well what alternative gods clamor for their attention. These forces and shaping influences neither determine nor excuse our sins. But they do nurture, exacerbate and channel our sinfulness in particular directions. They are often atmospheric, invisible, unconscious influences."[102] The preacher is called to awaken people from their deadly slumbers. "The Biblical gospel delivers from both personal sin and situational tyrannies. The Biblical notion of inner idolatries allows people to see their need for Christ as a merciful Savior from large sins of both heart and behavior."[103] Roman Catholic McLuhan makes a remarkable comment in a 1977 interview with Edward Wakin: "That's one of the jobs of the Church—to shake up our present population. To do that you'd have to preach nothing but hellfire. In my life, I have never heard one such sermon from a Catholic pulpit."[104] In his usual hyperbole he has exaggerated, but the need to preach on the reality of heaven and hell is clearly present in the church tempted as it is to "moods of conciliation" by the electronic culture. Moralizing and psychologizing not only pervert the Biblical text, but they cannot penetrate the darkness of the Adamic soul; they only assuage it.

During the reign of Jehoshaphat idolatry was completely abolished. "Now the LORD was with Jehoshaphat, because he walked in the former ways of his

---

[99] Thomas Stearns Eliot, *Christianity and Culture: The Idea of a Christian Society and Notes Toward the Definition of Culture* (New York: Harcourt Brace Jovanovich, 1968) 18.

[100] Hendrik Berkhof, *Christ and the Powers*, translated by John Howard Yoder (Scottsdale, PA: Herald Press, 1962) 36-46, in Herbert Schlossberg, *Idols For Destruction: Christian Faith and Its Confrontation With American Society* (Nashville: Thomas Nelson, 1983) 308.

[101] David Powlison, "Idols of the Heart and Vanity Fair," (photocopy) 15.

[102] *Ibid.*, 15.

[103] *Ibid.*, 24.

[104] Marshall McLuhan, "Our Only Hope Is Apocalypse," in *The Medium and the Light: Reflections on Religion*, edited by Eric McLuhan and Jacek Szlarek (Toronto: Stoddart Publishing Co. Limited, 1999). Electronic copy.

father David; he did not seek the Baals, but sought the God of his father, and walked in His commandments and not according to the acts of Israel. ...And his heart took delight in the ways of the LORD; moreover he removed the high places and wooden images from Judah" (2 Chron. 17:3, 4, 6). It was not enough, however, to remove, or turn off the media of idolatry. He resisted and overcame the idolatry of Baal worship by sending prophets and Levites throughout the land to teach the truth of the covenant. "So they taught in Judah, and *had* the Book of the Law of the LORD with them; they went throughout all the cities of Judah and taught the people" (2 Chron. 17:9). It was not only the Word of God read by the people, but the written Word preached and taught by God's appointed spokesmen, which cultivated the only anti-environment capable of overcoming idolatry and winning people to become disciples of the LORD. Such is the task of the preacher today.

Be careful with all of your critical awareness, and with your trenchant challenge to the idols of our age, never to be a cynic. Be a critic sparingly, and make it count. Focus on the truth, hopefulness, and glory of the redemption which is in Christ Jesus.

Point Them to God

The ultimate object of all preaching is to bring people into contact with God Himself. "The sense of being an ambassador of God makes preaching a holier experience than any other kind of public speaking." Our inspiration and authority in preaching comes directly from God. "When so many are preaching to the times, let one brother speak eternity."[105] Jonathan Edwards beautifully depicts the glory of tasting heaven on earth. Good preaching should aim at this.

> Intellectual pleasures consist in the beholding of spiritual excellencies and beauties, but the glorious excellency and beauty of God are far the greatest. God's excellence is the supreme excellence. When the understanding of the reasonable creature dwells here, it dwells at the fountain, and swims in a boundless, bottomless ocean. The love of God is also the most suitable entertainment of the soul of man, which naturally desires the happiness of society, or of union with some other being. The love of so glorious a being is infinitely valuable, and the discoveries of it are capable of ravishing the soul above all other love.[106]

---

[105] Gerald Hamilton Kennedy, *His Word Through Preaching*, (New York: Harper, 1947) 10, 11. Dr. Ian Maclaren quoting an old Puritan.
[106] Jonathan Edwards, Sermon on Matthew 5:8, *The Works of Jonathan Edwards*, Edited by Edward Hickman. Vol. 1. 1834. Reprint (Edinburgh: The Banner of Truth Trust, 1974) 907.

Bring God's people into the presence of God. As preaching overcomes the secular dichotomy between transcendence and immanence, the preacher as God's spokesman does not leave the congregation or the evangelistic audience on the horizontal plane, but draws them through the Word of Christ into heavenly reality, into their spiritual relationship and status as new creatures, united with Christ. At the center of this homiletical trajectory is the only Mediator between God and man, the Lord Jesus Christ. As the heart and soul of every text He is the One who makes the hearts of His disciples burn within them.

It is this Word—evocative, dynamic, creative, saving, sin-annulling, death-defeating, healing, life-giving—which the church proclaims. This is the Word the pulpit must preach, and those in the ministry are summoned by God to proclaim.[107]

---

[107] Daane, *Preaching With Confidence*, 29.

Coda:
Keep Yourselves From Idols

The idol is the measure of the worshiper.

—James Russell Lowell[1]

Little children, keep yourselves from idols.

—Saint John, *1 John 5:21*

I am from New Hampshire, as McLuhan was from Canada. Missourians have nothing on us when it comes to being curmudgeons. The New Hampshire Primary tradition sums up the essence of the state's character. She is a political probe, an asker of hard questions, a nose tweeker. While McLuhan liked to think of himself, in this role of contrarian, as an artist, I prefer the concept of prophet. The prophets were great probers, constantly getting under the skin of God's people, for their good and God's glory.

Whether or not our present technological, electronic expertise leads us to the Epicureanism predicted by Huxley, or the Totalitarianism of Orwell, we cannot tell at present. What we are certain of is the eschatology of the New Testament, especially the compelling and rich Johannine portrait in the Apocalypse. Most importantly we cannot control the progress of history or culture. Nor need this concern us, for we know the One into whose hands the scroll of history has been placed. The promise of the Rainbow Covenant insures the continuation of common culture until the Second Coming. Within the context of this promise is the most significant promise for the church and the preacher. "And this gospel of the kingdom will be preached in all the world as a witness to all the nations, and then the end will come" (Matt. 24:14). Professor Englesma asserts: "Jesus makes a truly astonishing claim for the activity of preaching. He maintains that the end of the world and His coming again wait on the preaching. Until the gospel has been preached everywhere,

---

[1] in Daniel J. Boorstin, *The Image or Whatever Happened to the American Dream?* (New York: Atheneum, 1962) 74.

the end cannot come."[2] The eschatological purposes of God are wrapped up in the preaching of His Word.

In light of the Lamb's present rule, what we can do, as Christians, is significant. We can warn others of the dangers of idolatry, especially those dangers connected with the electronic media. We can demonstrate proper stewardship in our understanding and use of these technologies, helping others to see both the liabilities and the benefits of each medium. We can be involved as professionals in the development of various communication technologies, as well as in the academic assessment of the new media. We can train, encourage, and pray for preachers who understand their prophetic calling as ministers of the Word, and preach with tongues of fire and hearts aflame with love for their Master. We can take our part in cultivating the rich life of the church, participating as pilgrims and servants of the living God and His Christ. We can be ambassadors to a lost world, whose destiny without Christ is a black and Godless eternity. We can witness the eternal importance of the kingdom of God as it has been revealed in Jesus Christ, and as it functions as our final transcendent reference point. We can demonstrate the reality of that kingdom in our daily lives, and the hope which is not connected with the structures of this present world, which transcends the processes of history, even while it is rooted in history, the history of redemption.

Because of the God-ordained centrality of preaching and the God-given superiority of preaching as a medium for communicating His Word to the world and to the church, the preacher must renew his enthusiasm for his task. It is a glorious task, for a glorious Lord. The power of His Word and Spirit insures the effectiveness of our labors. Ours is to be faithful "as servants of Christ and stewards of the mysteries of God" (1 Cor. 4:1). For the faithful preacher and Christian the Word is worth a thousand pictures.

---

[2] David Englesma, "The Worldwide Preaching of the Gospel," *Standard Bearer* (December 1, 1994) 114.

Appendix: Principles for Preachers
Principles for Preachers in the Electronic Age

Preaching is the most effective medium to communicate God's Word.

1. Understand the uniqueness, excellence and genius of preaching as a medium: the difference between written and oral communication; and address God's people directly as God's spokesman and not as a lecturer or entertainer.
2. Cultivate confidence in your office as a Minister of the Word and in God's chosen medium of preaching through biblical and confessional study; and through the study of the history of preaching and ministerial biography.
3. Using the biblical concept of idolatry as a critical paradigm, study the culture in which you live in order to better apply God's Word to your congregation/audience.
4. Develop a clear understanding of the nature and effects of modern electronic media, especially the image media, both their benefits and liabilities. Understand their effect on your audience.
5. Do not be intimidated by the vaunted superiority of modern media and its overestimated technologies, as they tend to undermine your practice of preaching.
6. Challenge your congregation with a clear understanding of the nature and effects of modern media in order to overcome the naïveté of the evangelical church with respect to the electronic media; and teach them how to be better worshipers and sermon listeners in this cultural context by helping them understand the uniqueness, excellence and genius of preaching as a medium.
7. Study and use the biblical model of vivid, concise language (stories, illustrations and metaphors) to capture the imaginations of your hearers, thus making the theme of your pericope stick to their souls.
8. Make preaching that transforms people into the image of Jesus Christ the focus and soul of your pulpit ministry.
9. Be an authentic communicator through cultivating a holy life and a sympathetic pastoral ministry.
10. Pray for the only power that can make the medium you use effective: the power of God's presence in your preaching through the ministry of the Holy Spirit.

Annotated Bibliography

I list here all of the writings which I have encountered in my research and arranged them under the headings of *Media Theory and Criticism, Homiletics and Rhetoric, Biblical Commentary and Theology,* and *Cultural Criticism and Apologetics.* While not an exhaustive list, the entries are intended to aid future researchers in the given areas of my study. I have commented on most of the works which I have read. There are several works which as a whole are not pertinent to my subject, that are cited in footnotes, but which are not listed below. Writings in the areas of *Biblical Commentary* and *Theology* are listed only if they are cited extensively or have formed a large part of my thinking in my research. Several important works, which I have not read, since they are only tangential to my work, are described by other authors. Under *Homiletics* I have listed a wide range of works, some of which are grounded in theological convictions quite different from my own.

MEDIA THEORY AND CRITICISM

Abbey, Merrill R. *Man, Media and the Message.* New York: Friendship Press, 1960.
Abelman, Robert, and Stewart M. Hoover, eds. *Religious Television: Controversies and Conclusions.* Norwood, NJ: Ablex, 1990.
Abercrombie, Minnie Louie Johnson. *The Anatomy of Judgement: An Investigation into the Processes of Perception and Reasoning.* Harmondsworth: Penguin Books, 1969.
Adler, Richard. *Television as a Cultural Force.* New York: Praeger Publishers, 1976.
———, ed. *Understanding Television: Essays on Television as a Social and Cultural Force.* New York: Praeger Publishers, 1981.
Adorno, Theodor W. "Scientific Experiences of a European Scholar in America." In *Intellectual Migration: Europe and America, 1920-*1960, edited by Donald Flemming and Bernard Bailyn. Cambridge, MA: Harvard University Press, 1969.
———. "The Radio Symphony." In *Radio Research* 1941, edited by Paul F. Lasarsfeld and Frank N. Stanton. New York: Duell, Sloan and Pearce, 1941.
———. "On Popular Music." *Studies in Philosophy and Social Science* 9, no. 1 (1941):17-48.
Adorno, Theodor W., Else Frenkel-Brunswik, Daniel J. Levinson, and R. Nevitt Sanford. *The Authoritarian Personality.* New York: Harper and Brothers, 1950.
A groundbreaking early study of prejudice, reflecting on the atrocities of World War II, from neo-Marxist perspective, thus critical of many things dear to political conservatives.
———. "Scientific Experiences of a European Scholar in America." In *The Intellectual Migration: Europe and America, 1920-1960,* edited by Donald Fleming and Berbard Bailyn. Cambridge, MA: Harvard University Press, 1969.

Al-Hibri, A. and L. Hickman, eds. *Technology and Human Affairs*. London: The C. V. Mosby Company, 1981.

Allen, Robert C., ed. *Channels of Discourse: Television and Contemporary Criticism*. London: Methuen Press, 1987.

Altheide, David and Robert Snow. *Media Logic*. New York: Aldine de Gruyter, 1979.

⎯⎯⎯⎯. *Media Worlds in the Postjournalism Era*. New York: Aldine de Gruyter, 1991.

Anderson, James A. and Timothy P. Meyer. *Mediated Communication*. Newbury Park, CA: Sage Publications, 1988.

Ang, Ien. *Desperately Seeking the Audience*. London: Routledge, 1991.

Anshen, R. N. *Language: An Inquiry into Its Meaning and Function*. Science and Culture Series, vol. 3. New York: Harper and Row, 1957.

Armstrong, Ben. *The Electric Church*. Nashville: Thomas Nelson, 1979.
Former director of the National Religious Broadcasters. A good example of naive optimism among Christians regarding the benefits of the electronic media. Electronic technologies will bring "a revolutionary new form of the worshiping, witnessing church that existed twenty centuries ago." Quoted in Schultze, *Redeeming Television*, 30.

Arnheim, Rudolf. *Visual Thinking*. London: Faber, 1970.

Ashby, W. Ross. *An Introduction to Cybernetics*. London: Chapman & Hall, 1956.

Augustine, Saint. *The Greatness of the Soul; The Teacher*. In *Ancient Christian Writers*. Translated and edited by Joseph M. Colleran. Westminster, MD: The Newman Press, 1964.
A profound ancient discussion of communication. A Must read for Christian Media Ecologists.

⎯⎯⎯⎯. *On Christian Doctrine*. Translated by D. W. Robertson, Jr. Indianapolis: Bobbs-Merrill Educational Publishing, 1958.
Augustines doctrine of Scripture, including hermeneutics. Book 4 is an exposition on rhetoric for the preacher.

Bachman, John W. *The Church in the World of Radio-Television*. New York: Association Press, 1960.
Professor of homiletics at Union Theological Seminary in NYC. He characterizes Christian views of the radio and television as "daydreams," "nightmares," or "illusions." His option is "vision." Has read McLuhan and Innis, and thus sees the need to focus on more than content. Raises some important questions for religious broadcasting in his day, from an old-style Liberal Protestant perspective. Never really integrates media analysis into a truly Christian view of communication.

⎯⎯⎯⎯. *Media—Wasteland or Wonderland: Opportunities and Dangers for Christians in the Electronic Age*. Minneapolis: Augsburg Publishing House, 1984.

Barfield, Owen. *Saving the Appearances: A Study in Idolatry*. 1957. Reprint. 2nd ed. Hanover, NH: Wesleyan University Press, 1988.
A study of epistemology with reference to religion. Theologically unsound at points, Barfield is best at framing the problem with the epistemology of the "scientific revolution." His definition of modern idolatry is "literalness," the objectification of the phenomenal world, which evacuates everything of meaning. His soteriological universalism is his greatest weakness. Interesting insights into the uniqueness of Israel's epistemology and historical sense. Not an easy read.

⎯⎯⎯⎯. *The Rediscovery of Meaning, and Other Things*. Middletown, CT: Wesleyan Univiversity Press, 1977.

Barlow, Horace, Colin Blakemore and Miranda Weston-Smith, eds. *Images and Understanding*. Cambridge: Cambridge University Press, 1990.

Barnouw, Erik. *Mass Communication.* New York: Holt, Rinehart and Winston, Inc., 1956.
―――――, ed. *International Encyclopedia of Communications.* New York: Oxford University Press and University of Pennsylvania Press, 1989.
Barrett, William E. *The Illusion of Technique: A Search for Meaning in a Technological Civilization.* Garden City, NY: Doubleday, 1979.
―――――. *Death of the Soul: From Descartes to the Computer.* Garden City, NY: Doubleday, 1987.
Barthes, Roland. *S/Z.* Translated by Richard Miller. Oxford: Blackwell, 1974.
   A key work by a key figure in the literary critical school known as "Deconstruction."
Bartlett, Frederic C. *Remembering.* Cambridge: Cambridge University Press, 1932.
―――――. *Political Propaganda.* Cambridge: Cambridge University Press, 1940.
Batra, N. D. *The Hour of Television: Critical Approaches.* Metuchen, NJ: Scarecrow Press, 1987.
Baudrillard, Jean. *The Transparency of Evil: Essays on Extreme Phenomena.* Translated by James Benedict. New York: Verso, 1990.
―――――. *Simulacra and Simulation.* Translated by Sheila Faria Glaser. Ann Arbor, MI: University of Michigan Press, 1994.
Beaudoin, Thomas. *Virtual Faith: The Irreverent Spiritual Quest Of Generation X.* San Francisco: Jossey-Bass, 1998.
Benjamin, Walter. *Illuminations.* Translated by Harry Zohn. New York: Harcourt, Brace and World, 1968.
Berger, Arthur Asa, ed. *Television in Society.* New Brunswick, NJ: Transaction Books, 1986.
Berlo, David K. *The Process of Communication.* New York: Holt, Rinehart and Winston, 1960.
Berry, Wendell. *What Are People For?* New York: Farrar, Straus and Giroux, 1990.
   These are the essays of an articulte Luddite, who steadfastly refuses to use even a word processor. Berry is a Southern Agrarian with an incisive, and at times scathing, critique of everything modern.
Berman, Ronald. *How Television Sees Its Audience: A Look at the Looking Glass.* Newbury Park, CA: Sage Publications, 1987.
Bertalanffy, Ludwig von. *General Systems Theory: Foundations, Development, Applications.* New York: Braziller, 1968.
Bertman, Stephen. *Hyperculture: The Human Cost of Speed.* Westport, CT and London: Praeger Publishers, 1998.
Bettelheim, Bruno. *The Uses of Enchantment.* New York: Knopf, 1976.
Billingsley, K. L. *The Seductive Image: A Christian Critique of the World of Film.* Westchester, IL: Crossway Books, 1989.
Birkerts, Sven. *The Guttenberg Elegies: The Fate of Reading in an Electronic Age.* Winchester, MA: Faber and Faber, Inc., 1994.
   An insightful critique of the deleterious effects of the electronic media on the fine art of reading and the act of writing. Birkerts is an unashamed apologist for the written and printed word. He maintains that the dramatic increase in linkage and referentiality combined with the evanescent quality of electronic text expand us laterally and diminish our cognitive depth.

Birt, John. "There Is a Bias in Television Journalism. It Is Not Against Any Particular Party of Point of View—It Is a Bias Against Understanding." *TV Guide* (9 August 1975): 3-7.

Block, J. Richard and Harold F. Yuker. *Can You Believe Your Eyes?* London: Robson, 1992.

Bloomer, Carolyn M. *Principles of Visual Perception.* New York: Van Nostrand, 1976.

Bolter, J. David. *Turing's Man: Western Culture in the Computer Age.* Chapel Hill: The University of North Carolina Press, 1984.

_____. *Writing Space: The Computer, Hypertext and the History of Writing.* Hillsdale, NJ: Lawrence Erlbaum, 1991.

Boorstin, Daniel J. *The Image or Whatever Happened to the American Dream?* New York: Atheneum, 1962.
    A classic, seminal study of the influence of the "graphic revolution" on American culture, by one of our premier historians. Boorstin focuses on the nature and effect of advertising and celebrity as they relate to the creation of "pseudo-events".

_____. "Television." *Life Magazine* (10 September 1971): 36-39.
    Brilliant popular article lamenting the tendency of television to segregate people from other people, from the source of "communication," from the past, and from reality. The only hope he holds out is finding ways to overcome the segregation.

Boulding, Kenneth E. *The Image.* Ann Arbor, MI: University of Michigan Press, 1956.
    An exploration of the "image" as a conceptual model at various levels of thought and life in an effort to remove the distinction between "fact" and "value" (173). "The meaning of a message is the change which it produces in the image" (7). The image includes fact and value and is created by various messages. It is actually an organizing principle for the various sciences, "looking at processes of organization" (175). He proposes his thinking as a new discipline" "eiconics."

_____. *The Meaning of the Twentieth Century: The Great Transition.* Lanham: University Press of America, 1988.

Bowers, C. A. *Cultural Dimensions of Educational Computing: Understanding the Non-Neutrality of Technology.* New York: Teachers College Press, 1988.

Bradt, Kevin M., S.J. *Story as a Way of Knowing.* London: Sheed and Ward, 1997.

Brand, Stuart. *The Media Lab: Inventing the Future at MIT.* New York: Viking Press, 1987.

Broadcasting, Society and the Church. Report of the Broadcasting Commission of the General Synod of the Church of England. London: Church Information Office, 1973.

Brooks, Cleanth, Jr., and Robert Penn Warren. *Understanding Poetry: An Anthology for College Students.* New York, H. Holt and Company [1938]
    A major influence on McLuhan during his literary criticism days. "Interpreting literature in the style of the New Criticism was the vehicle by which a half-century of Americans gained access to the intellectual life." The were known as the Vanderbilt agrarians. *The Intercollegiate Review* 35:1 (fall 1999) 10.

Brown, Ray, ed. *Children and Television.* Beverly Hills: Sage Publications, 1976.

Bruce, Vicki and Patrick R. Green. *Visual Perception, Physiology, Psychology, and Ecology.* London and Hillsdale, NJ: L. Erlbaum, 1985.

Buhler, Curt. *The Fifteenth Century Book.* Philadelphia: University of Pennsylvania Press, 1960.

Bullock, Alan. *Hitler: A Study in Tyranny*. Rev. ed. New York: Harper and Row, Publishers, 1962.

Bury, John Bagnell. *The Idea of Progress: An Inquiry into its Origin and Growth*. New York: Dover Publications, Inc., 1932.

Campbell-Kelly, Martin, and Willaim Aspray. *Computer: A History of the Information Machine*. New York: BasicBooks, 1996.
> An excellent detailed history of the development of the computer, including the PC and the World Wide Web.

Carey, James W. "Harold Adams Innis and Marshall McLuhan." *Antioch Review* (Spring 1967): 5-39.

_____, ed. *Media, Myths and Narratives*. Newbury Park, CA: Sage Publications, 1988.

_____. *Communication as Culture: Essays on Media and Society*. Boston, MA: Unwin Hyman, 1989.
> Considered by many to be the living dean of media ecology. Served as dean of the College of Communications, University of Illinois at Urbana-Champaign, George Gallop Chair at the University of Iowa (1976-79), and editor of *Communication*. Makes a strong argument for understanding communication in its cultural context. Maintains that communication media reflect as well as cultivate cultural aspirations. Although not a history of communication this book contains much helpful historical information and analysis.

Carnell, Edward J. *Television: Servant or Master?* Grand Rapids: Eerdmans, 1950.
> A pioneer Christian assessment of television by a leading Evangelical theologian.

Carothers, J. C. "Culture, Psychiatry and the Written Word." *Psychiatry*, November 1959.

Carpenter, Edmund, and Marshall McLuhan, eds. *Explorations in Communication, An Anthology*. Boston: Beacon Press, 1960.
> A anthology of articles from *Explorations*, a journal, edited by McLuhan and Carpenter, which provided a forum for Culture and Communication seminar members in the 1950s. Some excellent articles by McLuhan, Carpenter, Northrop Frye, D. T. Suzuki, Sigfried Giedion, H. J. Chaytor, and Robert Graves. First generation Media Ecology.

Carpenter, Edmund. *They Became What They Beheld*. New York: Outerbridge & Dienstfrey, 1970.

_____. *Oh What a Blow that Phantom Gave Me!* New York: Holt, Rinehart and Winston, 1973.

Cater, Douglass. "The Intellectual in Videoland." *Saturday Review* (31 May 1975): 13.
> A good popular assessment of commercial television at its 25th anniversary. He asks many pertinent questions about the effect of television on our politics and cultural institutions, based on Tony Schwartz's insights re: the difference the "grammar" of television makes on the viewer's perception. He laments the lack of critical reflection on the effects of television. Oddly he never mentions McLuhan.

Chandler, Daniel. "The Purpose of the Computer in the Classroom." In *Technological Literacy and the* Curriculum, edited by John Beynon and Hughie Mackay. London: Falmer, 1991.

_____. "The Phenomenology of Writing by Hand." *Intelligent Tutoring Media* 2, no. 3 (1992): 65-74. [WWW document] URL http://www.aber.ac.uk/~dgc/tecdet.html, 1994 [13 July 1999].
> Fine survey of the subject.

_____. "Writing Strategies and Writers' Tools." *English Today* B9/B2 (1993): 32-8.

———. "Who Needs Suspended Inscription?" *Computers and Composition* (1994): 191-201.

———. "The Transmission Model of Communication." [WWW document] URL http://www.aber.ac.uk/~dgc/tecdet.html, 1994 [13 July 1999].
Excellent critique of the Shannon-Weaver model of communication theory.

———. *The Act of Writing*. Aberystwyth: UWA, 1995.

———. "Texts and the Construction of Meaning." [WWW document] URL http://www.aber.ac.uk/~dgc/tecdet.html, 1995 [13 July 1999].
Distinguishes between Objectivist, Subjectivist and his position Constructivist. Not convincing.

———. "Technological or Media Determinism." [WWW document] URL http://www.aber.ac.uk/~dgc/tecdet.html, 1995 [13 July 1999].
Excellent discussion of determinism. Media Ecologists will not agree with the conclusions.

———. "Cultivation Theory." [WWW document] URL http://www.aber.ac.uk/~dgc/tecdet.html, 1995 [13 July 1999].
Critique of theory that television watching has cumulative, negative effect on watchers.

Chaytor, H. J. *From Script to Print: An Introduction to Medieval Literature*. Cambridge, England: W. Heffer and Sons, Ltd., 1945.
Seminal study by a master on this subject. Often quoted by first generation Media Ecologists.

Cherry, Collin. *On Human Communication: A Review, A Survey, and a Criticism*. Cambridge: Technology Press of Massachusetts Institute of Technology, 1957.

Children and Television. Cambridge, England: Pye Limited, 1978.
A national survey among 7-17 year olds, commissioned by Pye Limited.

Christians, C. "Communication Technology: An Assessment of the Literature." In *Philosophy and Technology: Ethics and Technology*, edited by F. Ferreacute and C. Mitcham, vol. 9, 233-249. Greenwich, CT: JAI Press, 1989.

Clanchy, M. T. *From Memory to Written Record: England, 1066-1307*. London: Edward Arnold, 1979.

Clark, David G. and William B. Blankenburg. *You and Media: Mass Communication and Society*. San Francisco: Canfield Press, 1973.

Cleveland, H. "The Twilight of Heirarchy: Speculation on the Global Information Society." In *Information Technologies and Social Transformation*, edited by B. Guile, Washington, DC: National Academy, 1985.

Cobb, Jennifer. *Cybergrace: The Search for God in the Digital World*. New York: Crown Publishers, Inc., 1998.
Excellent example of CyberGnosticism, under the influence of Teilhard de Chardin. This book is an affirmation of the possibility of finding spiritual life in cyberspace, as part of the evolution of consciousness. "This book was born of my attempt to find spiritual wholeness in a computational world." Exploration of Celtic rites helped her understand the "sacred dimension of the universe."

Comstock, George A., Eli A. Rubinstein, and John P. Murray. *Television and Social Behavior*. vols. 1-4. Washington, DC: U. S. Department of Health, Education and Welfare, National Institute of Mental Health, 1972.

Condry, John. *The Psychology of Television*. Hillsdale, NJ: Erlbaum, 1989.

Conners, Tracy Daniel, ed. *Longman Dictionary of Mass Media and Communication*. New York: Longman, 1982.

Conrad, Peter. *Television: The Medium and Its Manners*. Boston: Routledge and Kegan Paul, 1982.

Cooley, Charles Horton. *Human Nature and the Social Order.* New York: Charles Scribner's Sons, 1902 and 1922.
⸻. *Social Organization: A Study of the Larger Mind.* New York: Charles Scribner's Sons, 1909.
⸻. *Social Process.* New York: Charles Scribner's Sons, 1918.
<small>A classic of the early Chicago School Progressive Theorists. Cooley was one of the founding Chicago sociologists who believed that mass communication was the key to solving social problems. He conceived the idea of "the looking glass self."</small>

Coren, Stanley, Lawrence M. Ward and James T. Enns. *Sensation and Perception.* Fort Worth, TX: Harcourt Brace, 1994.

Cornford, F.M. "The Invention of Space." In *Background to Modern Science: Ten Lectures at Cambridge Arranged by the History of Science Committee,* edited by Joseph Needham and Walter Pagel. New York: Macmillan/Cambridge, UK: The University Press, 1938.
<small>Cornford directed Havelock's doctoral work at Cambridge. A forerunner, like A. I. Richards, of media ecology.</small>

Cowen, Robert J. "A Note on the Meaning of Television to a Psychotic Woman." *Bulletin of the Menninger Clinic* 23 (1959): 202, 203.

Cross, Frank Moore. *From Epic to Canon: History and Literature in Ancient Israel.* Baltimore: Johns Hopkins University Press, 1998.

Cross, Nigel et al., eds. *Man-Made Futures.* London: Hutchinson, 1974.

Crowley, David and Paul Heyer, eds. *Communication in History: Technology, Culture, Society.* 2nd ed. White Plains, NY: Longman, 1995.

Cruz, Jon and Justin Lewis. *Viewing, Reading, Listening: Audiences and Cultural Reception.* Boulder, CO: Westview, 1994.

Czitrom, Daniel. *Media and the American Mind: From Morse to McLuhan.* Chapel Hill: University of North Carolina Press, 1982.
<small>A more balanced and informative approach to the history of communications study than Rogers. It is an intellectual history divided into two parts: the history of contemporary response to three modern media (telegraph, cinema, and radio); theorists of modern communication (pioneers, empirical, and radical).</small>

Dery, Mark. *Escape Velocity: Cyberculture at the End of the Century,* New York: Grove Press, 1996.

DeFleur, Melvin L. *Theories of Mass Communication.* New York: David McKay Company, Inc., 1966.

De Latil, Pierre. *Thinking by Machine.* Boston: Houghton Mifflin, 1957.

Dember, William N. and Joel S. Warm. *The Psychology of Perception.* 2nd ed. New York: Holt, Rinehart & Winston, 1979.

Dern, Daniel P. *The Internet Guide for New Users.* New York: McGraw-Hill, Inc., 1994.

Derrida, Jacques. *Of Grammatology.* Baltimore: Johns Hopkins University Press, 1976.
⸻. *Writing and Difference.* London: Routledge, 1978.
<small>Derrida is a key figure in the literary critical school known as "Deconstruction" along with Paul de Man. American disciples of this school are Stanley Fish and the Duke critics. Practically this school evacuates meaning from all texts, and posits all meaning as a reader construct.</small>

Dewey, John. *The Public and Its Problems.* Chicago: Swallow Press, 1927.
<small>A classic of the early Chicago School Progressive Theorists. Like colleagues Parks and Cooley, Dewey was an ardent social reformer who believed that the educated elite were responsible to</small>

direct social behavior and institutions through education and mass media in order to "socialize intelligence." One of the most influential educational theorists of this century. We are still living with the aweful results of his Empiricism. Education is not a matter of content but of method.

Diringer, David. *The Alphabet A Key to the History of Mankind*. New York: Philosophical Library, Inc., 1948.

Dominick, Joseph R. *The Dynamics of Mass Communication*. New York: McGraw-Hill, 1990.

Donnelly, William J. *The Confetti Generation: How the New Communication Technology Is Fragmenting America*. New York: Henry Holt, 1986.

Dreyfus, Hubert L. *What Computers Can't Do*. New York: Harper and Row, 1979.

Dreyfus, Hubert and Dreyfus Stuart. *Mind Over Machine*. Oxford: Blackwell, 1986.

Dudek, Louis. *Literature and the Press*. Toronto: The Ryerson Press, 1960.

Duncan, Hugh D. *Communication and Social Order*. New York: The Bedminster Press, 1962.

Dundes, Alan. *Holy Writ as Oral Lit: The Bible as Folklore*. Lanham, MD: Rowan & Littlefield, 1999.

Ebersole, Samuel. "Media Determinism in Cyberspace." [WWW document] URL http://regent.edu/acad/schcom/rojc/mdic.html, 1995.
An excellent discussion of the Internet from a Christian perspective.

Edwards, Bruce, Jr. "The Medium and the Mediator: Viewing TV Christianly." *Mission Journal* (May 1981): 6.

Eisenstein, Elizabeth L. *The Printing Press as an Agent of Change: Communication and Cultural Transformations in Early-Modern Europe*. 2 vols. Cambridge, UK and New York: Cambridge University Press, 1979.
Often quoted by Media Ecologists. Excellent historical material.

_____. *The Printing Revolution in Early Modern Europe*. Cambridge, UK/New York: Cambridge University Press, 1983.

_____. "Printing: Cultural Impact." In *International Encyclopaedia of Communications*, edited by Erik Barnouw. New York: Oxford University Press and University of Pennsylvania Press, 1989.
Helpful summary of this important subject.

Ellul, Jacques. *The Technological Society*. Translated by John Wilkinson. New York: Alfred A. Knopf, 1964 (first French edition, 1954).
A classic, seminal study of the nature and influence of technology on Western civilization from a French Reformed Christian perspective. Ellul was professor of History and Contemporary Sociology at the University of Bordeau. This is a demanding scholarly work. As a "media determinist" Ellul emphasized the tyranny of technology as a significant threat to Christian faith and freedom. He was especially concerned with a lack of reflection on the purposes and effects of technology by those who develop and promote it.

_____. *A Critique of the New Commonplaces*. New York: Alfred A. Knopf 1968.

_____. *Propaganda: The Formation of Men's Attitudes*. Translated by Konrad Kellen and Jean Lerner. New York: Vintage Books, 1965.
A unique critique of propaganda as a sociological phenomenon. Analyses the inadequate concepts of other propaganda theorists. Propaganda goes hand in hand with a technological society. Propaganda is not "one way" but depends on the willingness of the propagandee to receive the illusion or myth being propagated. "Thus, propaganda, by first creating pseudo-needs through 'pre-propaganda' and thus providing 'pseudo-satisfactions for them, is pernicious."

[Intro. by Konrad Kellen]. Relevant, unwittingly, to the problem of the 'church growth' movement.

_____. *The New Demons*. Translated by C. Edward Hopkin. New York: Seabury Press, 1975.

_____. *The Betrayal of the West*. New York: The Seabury Press, 1978.

_____. *The Technological System*. New York: Seabury Press-Continuum, 1980.
An update of *The Technological Society*. More systematic, interacts with more scholars.

_____. *In Season and Out of Season*. Translated by Lani Niles. New York: Harper and Row, 1982

_____. *The Humiliation of the Word*. Translated by Joyce Main Hanks. Grand Rapids: Eerdmans, 1985.
Penetrating, if somewhat exaggerated critique of the visual media. Focuses on the dangers of visual technologies for civilization and the church, especially the preached Word. Sees the immediacy of the visual image as its greatest problem. The visual image represents things as present in a closed system of reality. A must read for Media Ecologists.

_____. *What I Believe*. Grand Rapids: Eerdmans, 1989.

_____. *The Technological Bluff*. Grand Rapids: Eerdmans, 1990.

Emery, Fred, and Merrelyn Emery. *A Choice of Futures: To Enlighten or Inform?* Canberra: Centre for Continuing Education, Australian National University, 1975.
Australians who have done unique research on the neurological effects of television. Mander quotes them extensively.

Emery, Merrelyn. *The Social and Neurophysiological Effects of Television and Their Implications for Marketing Practice: An Investigation of Adaptation to the Cathode Ray Tube*. Ann Arbor, MI: University Microfilms, 1985.
Ph.D. dissertation for the University of New South Wales. Recommended by Eric McLuhan.

Emery, Glenn. "Virtual Reality's Radical Vision." *Insight on the News* (6 May 1991): 20-25.
Explores the emerging technology of the ultimate in interactive computing. Reports rather than analyzes. Timothy Leary is quoted as being completely enthusiastic about electronic technology generally because of what he believes is its inherent subversion of all centralized power.

Enzensberger, Hans M. *The Consciousness Industry*. New York: Seabury Press, 1974.

Epstein, Edward Jay. *News from Nowhere: Television and the News*. New York: Random House, 1973.
Describes how events, such a fighting during the Vietnam war, are often enacted for the camera. M. Muggeridge.

Esslin, Martin. *The Age of Television*. San Francisco: W. H. Freeman and Company, 1982.

Evans, Christopher. *The Mighty Micro*. London: Hodder and Stoughton, 1980.

_____. *The Micro Millenium*. New York: Viking Press, 1980.

Evra, Judith van. *Television and Child Development*. Hillsdale, NJ: Erlbaum, 1990.

Ewen, Stuart. *All Consuming Images: The Politics of Style in Contemporary Culture*. New York: Basic Books, 1988.

Farrell, Thomas. *Walter Ong's Contributions to Cultural Studies: The Phenomenology of the Word and I-Thou Communication*. Creskill, NJ: Hampton Press, 1999.
An Ong scholar who knows his subject, and is a media ecologist as the title indicates.

Fasching, D. *The Thought of Jacques Ellul: A Systematic Exposition*. New York: Edwin Mellen Press, 1981.

Febvre, Lucien and Henri-Jean Martin. *The Coming of the Book*. London: Verso, 1984.
Feenberg, Andrew. *Critical Theory of Technology*. New York: Oxford University Press, 1991.
Ferré, John P., ed. *Channels of Belief: Religion and American Commercial Television*. Ames, IA: State University Press, 1990.
Fink, Donald G., and David M. Lutyens. *The Physics of Television*. New York: Doubleday, 1960.
Finnegan, Ruth. "Communication and Technology." In *Open University Course D101: Making Sense of Society, Unit 8 of Block 3, Communication*. Milton Keynes: Open University Press, 1975.
_____. *Literacy and Orality: Studies in the Technology of Communication*. Oxford: Blackwell, 1988.
Fischer, Claude S. *America Calling: A Social History of the Telephone*. Los Angeles: University of California Press, 1992.
Fish, Stanley. *Is There a Text in this Class?* Cambridge, MA: Harvard University Press, 1980.
A key American disciple of the "Deconstruction" school of literary criticism.
Fiske, John. *Television Culture*. London: Routledge, 1987.
_____. *Introduction to Communication Studies*. London: Routledge, 1990.
Florman, Samuel C. *The Existential Pleasures of Engineering*. New York: St. Martin's Press, 1975.
_____. *Blaming Technology: The Irrational Search for Scapegoats*. New York: St. Martin's Press, 1981.
Fore, William F. *Image and Impact: How Man Comes Through in the Mass Media*. New York: Friendship Press, 1970.
_____. "The Church and the Electronic Media." *The Christian Ministry* (May 1981): 5-10.
Head of the Communications Commission for the National Council of Churches, Fore maintains that commercial TV undermines Christian values. Televangelism becomes commercial entertainment. While suggesting some healthy directions for the church to follow in dealing with TV he is essentially Neo-Orthodox in his outlook. He sees PBS, et. al. as models for reforming TV. Worth reading. Lacks understanding of media ecology.
_____. *Myth Makers: Gospel, Culture and the Media*. New York: Friendship Press, 1990.
Frankl, Razelle. *Televangelism: The Marketing of Popular Religion*. Carbondale, IL: Southern Illinois University Press, 1987.
Franzen, Jonathan. "Perchance to Dream: In the Age of Images, a Reason to Write Novels." *Harper's Magazine* 292 (April 1996): 35-54.
Freeman, Christopher. "The Case for Technological Determinism." In Ruth Finnegan et al., eds. *Information Technology: Social Issues*. London: Hodder & Stoughton, 1987.
Freire, Paulo. *Pedagogy of the Oppressed*. New York: Seabury Press, 1970.
Friendly, Fred W. *Due to Circumstances beyond Our Control*. New York, Random House, 1967.

According to Muggeridge, Friendly was a colleague of Edward R. Murrow. His media reminiscences include his favorite dictum: "Because television can make so much money doing its worst, it often cannot afford to do its best."

Fry, Tony, ed. *RUATV? Heidegger and the Televisual.* Sydney: Power Institute of Fine Arts, 1993.

Fuller, Buckminster. *Education Automation.* Carbondale, IL: Southern Illinois University Press, 1961.

The Future of Broadcasting. The Annan Report. London: H. M. S. O., 1977.

Gabler, Neal. *An Empire of their Own: How the Jews Invented Hollywood.* New York: Crown Publishers, 1988.

_____. *Life the Movie: How Entertainment Conquered Reality.* New York: Alfred A. Knopf, 1998.

_____. *Winchell: Gossip, Power, and the Culture of Celebrity.* New York: Alfred A. Knopf, 1994.

Gattegno, Caleb. *Toward a Visual Culture.* New York: Outerbreidge and Dienstfrey, 1969.

Gehlen, A. *Man in the Age of Technology.* New York: Columbia University Press, 1980.

Gerbner, George. *Communication in the Twenty-first Century.* New York: Wiley, 1981.

Gerbner, George and Larry Gross. "Living With Television." *Journal of Communication,* (spring 1967).

_____. "The Scary World of TV's Heavy Viewer." *Psychology Today* (April 1976): 41-89.

Gerbner, George, and W. H. Melody, eds. *Communications Technology and Social Policy.* New York: John Wiley, 1973.

Gibson, William. *Mona Lisa Overdrive.* New York: Bantom Paperback, 1989.

Giedion, Sigfried. *Mechanization Takes Command: A Contribution to Anonymous History.* New York: W. W. Norton and Company, 1948.

Gilder, George F. *Microcosm: The Quantum Revolution in Economics and Technology.* New York: Simon and Schuster, 1989.

_____. *Life After Television: The Coming Transformation of Media and American Life.* Knoxville, TN: Whittle Direct Books, 1990.

Gitlin, Todd. "Sixteen Notes on Television and the Movement." In *Literature and Revolution* by George White and Charles Newman. New York: Holt, Rinehart and Winston, 1972.

_____. *Inside Prime Time.* New York: Pantheon Books, 1985.

Gitlin, Todd, ed. *Watching Television.* New York: Pantheon Books, 1986.

Godfrey, David and Douglas Parkhill, eds. *Gutenberg Two.* Toronto: Press Porceptic Limited, 1985.

Goethals, Gregor T. *The TV Ritual: Worship at the Visual Altar.* Boston: Beacon Press, 1981.

A study of American iconography, especially of television. She seeks to demonstrate how the television has become a "substitute for the sacraments," as the symbolic center of meaning for American culture. The last chapter is of particular interest to the Media Ecologist.

_____. *The Electronic Golden Calf: Images, Religion and the Making of Meaning.* Cambridge, MA: Cowley, 1990.

Goffman, Erving. *The Presentation of Self in Everyday Life.* New York: Anchor Books, 1959.
Situational sociologist who provied Meyrowitz's with the conceptual link between McLuhan's "medium theory" and culture and behavior.

Goody, Jack, ed. *Literacy in Traditional Societies.* Cambridge: Cambridge University Press, 1968.

———. *The Domestication of the Savage Mind.* Cambridge: Cambridge University Press, 1977.
"An anthropologist whose research on orality and literacy supports the media ecology perspective, Goody adds a British perspective that includes some engagement with European cultural theories. This 1978 book is particularly noteworthy for its stress on the impact of writing in general, as opposed to the specific effects of the alphabet, allowing for a more universal, less Western-centered approach to media ecology." Lance Strate

Goold, G. P. "Homer and the Alphabet." *TAPA* 91 (1960): 272-91.

Gordon, Cyrus H. *Ugarit And Minoan Crete; The Bearing of Their Texts on the Origins of Western Culture.* New York: W. W. Norton, 1966.

———. *Homer and Bible: The Origin and Character Of East Mediterranean Literature.* Ventnor, NJ: Ventnor Publishers, 1967.

———. *Before the Bible; The Common Background of Greek and Hebrew Civilizations.* Plainview, NY: Books for Libraries Press, 1973.
Brandeis archeologist has spent his career demonstrating the common origin of Greek and Hebrew cultures in a common Mediterranean civilization, as well as the presence of phonetic literacy long before Greek civilization, thus challenging some fundamental tenets of Havelock.

Gordon, T. David. "Technophilia and Technophobia: Evaluating Our Technological Culture." *Contact* 22, no. 1 (summer 1993): 3-6.
A fine, concise plea for Biblical balance in the Christian assessment of technology.

Gordon, W. Terrence. *Marshall McLuhan: Escape into Understanding, A Biography.* New York: BasicBooks, 1997.
This is the authorized (by McLuhan's widow Corrine) biography. A throughly researched portrait of a great and influential man, who left an indelible mark on all who knew him. The McLuhan family gave Gordon access to diaries and personal correspondence which proved an invaluable resource.

Gould, Stephen J. *The Mismeasure of Man.* New York: W. W. Norton and Company, 1981.

Gotz, I. L. "On Children and Television." *Elementary School Journal.* (April 1975): 415-418.

Gozzi, Raymond, Jr. "Why General Semanticists Should Distrust Computers." *ETC.* 56, no. 1 (spring 1999): 76-83.
A provocative article by a Media Ecologist. Critical of the "Aristotelian" binary nature of computing. Not very convincing, unless you are convinced of General Semantics.

———. *The Power of Metaphor in the Age of Electronic Media.* Cresskill, NJ: Hampton Press, 1999.

Gowers, Sir Ernest. *The Complete Plain Words.* London: H. M. S. O., 1954.

Graff, Harvey J. *The Labyrinths of Literacy.* London: Falmer, 1987.

Graham, William A. *Beyond the Written Word: Oral Aspects of Scripture in the History of Religion.* Cambridge, UK and New York: Cambridge University Press, 1988.

The book covers "the significant oral roles of written sacred texts in the history of religion," asserting "the fundamnetal orality of scripture." Walter Ong review in *America* (Mar. 4, 1989): pp. 1-17.

Grassie, William. *Democracy and Technology*. New York and London: Guilford Press, 1995.

Gregory, Richard L. *The Intelligent Eye*. London: Weidenfeld & Nicolson, 1970.

———. *Eye and Brain: The Psychology of Seeing*. London: Weidenfeld & Nicolson, 1972.

———. *Concepts and Mechanisms of Perception*. London: Duckworth, 1974.

Greenfield, Jeffrey. "Risk and the Media." Lecture notes. State University of New York, Purchase, 1990.

Greenfield, Meg. "TV's True Violence." *Newsweek* (21 June 1993): 72.
"The greatest harm of all the gore on the tube is that it may dull our response to the real thing."

Gress, David. "The Prophet of a New Media Age." *Insight on the News* (7 August 1989): 62-63.
Comment on the resurgence of interest in McLuhan a decade after his death and two decades after his meteoric rise to popular fame in the sixties.

Griffin, E. *A First Look at Communication Theory*. New York: McGraw-Hill, 1991.

Groothuis, Douglas. *The Soul in Cyberspace*. Grand Rapids: Baker Books, 1997. Reprint, Eugene, OR: Wipf and Stock, 1999.
One of best—and there are not many—full length books by a Christian dealing with an aspect of electronic communication. He understands Media Ecology and thus critiques not only the content but the grammar and environment of cyberspace.

Gunter, Barrie, and Jill McAleer. *Children and Television: The One Eyed Monster?* London and New York: Routledge, 1990.

———. *Children and Television*. 2nd ed. London and New York: Routledge, 1997.

Hadden, Jeffrey K., and Charles E. Swann. *Prime Time Preachers: The Rising Power of Televangelism*. Reading, PA: Addison-Wesley, 1981.

Hanhardt, John G., ed. *Video Culture: A Critical Investigation*. Layton, VT: Gibbs M. Smith, 1986.

Hall, E. T. *The Silent Language*. Garden City, NY: Doubleday and Company, Inc., 1959.

———. *Basic Readings in Communication Theory*. Compiled by C. David Mortensen. New York: Harper and Row, 1973.

Harris, Louis. "But Do We Like What We Watch?" *Life Magazine* (10 September 1971): 40-44.
An interesting view from Harris poll data, demonstrating that after only two and a half decades of network televevision the trend toward "audience selectivity" was strong, and the concept of "mass programming" was bankrupt.

Hattemer, Barbara and H. Robert Showers. *Don't Touch that Dial: The Impact of the Media on Children and the Family* Lafayette, LA: Huntington House Publishers,1993.
Excellent content oriented critique of television. Focuses on effects of sex and violence with public policy recommendations.

Havelock, Eric. *The Crucifixion of Intellectual Man*. Boston: Beacon Press, 1950.

———. *The Liberal Temper of Greek Politics*. New Haven: Yale University Press, 1957.

———. *Preface to Plato*. Cambridge: Harvard University Press, 1963.

Explores new territory in asserting his hypothesis that Plato's entire philosophy was constructed as an attack on the oral tradition of Greek poetry. Greek culture had been stored in the oral memory. The invention of the phonetic alphabet radically altered the storage system and laid the basis of Western education and literacy. The eye replaced the ear as "the chief organ employed for this purpose. [Foreward]."

———. *Origins of Western Literacy*. Toronto: Ontario Institute for Studies in Education, 1976.
Covers the development of Western literacy and education on the basis of the shift from oral to written culture in Plato's time.

———. *The Greek Concept of Justice: From Its Shadow in Homer to Its Substance in Plato*. Cambridge: Harvard University Press, 1978.
According to media ecologist Lance Strate of Fordham University, Havelock "traces shifts in word use and meaning (i.e., from more concrete to abstract) as reflections of the shift from orality to literacy."

———. "The Coming of Literate Communication in Western Culture." *Journal of Communication* (winter 1980).

———. *The Muse Learns to Write: Reflections on Orality and Literacy from Antiquity to the Present*. New Haven: Yale University Press, 1986.
His most recent reflections on the "crisis that occurred in the history of human communication, when Greek orality transformed itself into Greek literacy." He acknowledges the influence of Walter Ong's *Orality and Literacy* (1982) which provided the foundation for his synthesis. The most accessible single book of Havelock's for students of media.

Hay, Denys. "Fiat Lux." In John Carter and Percy H. Muir, eds. *Printing and the Mind of Man*. London: Cassell, 1967.

Hayek, F. H. *The Counter Revolution of Science: Studies on the Abuse of Reason*. Indianapolis: Liberty Press, 1952.

Heck, Douglas Van Allen. "Is TV a Medium for the Gospel?" *These Expository Times* (May and June 1990): 1-3.
A rare example of a conservative Christian who appreciates that the problem of TV as a medium for the gospel is the medium itself.

Heidegger, Martin. *Being and Time*. (*Sein und Zeit*, 1927) Translated by J. Macquarrie and E. S. Robinson. New York: Harpers, 1962.

———. *The Question Concerning Technology and Other Essays*. Translated by William Lovitt. New York: Harper and Row-Torchbooks, 1977.

Heim, Michael. *Electric Language: A Philosophical Study of Word Processing*. New Haven, CT: Yale University Press, 1987.

———. *The Metaphysics of Virtual Reality*. New York: Oxford University Press, 1993.

Henderson, Katherine, and Joseph Mazzeo, eds. *The Meanings of the Medium: Perspectives on the Art of Television*. New York: Praeger, 1990.

Herschensohn, Bruce. *The Gods of the Antenna*. New Rochelle, NY: Arlington House Publishers, 1976.
"a carefully documented, blow-by-blow account of how, through the machinations of the media, the United States lost a war and a President—perhaps the Presidency, too." M. Muggeridge.

Heylighen, F. *Representation and Change: A Metarepresentational Framework for the Foundations of Physical and Cognitive Science*. Gent: Communication & Cognition, 1990.

Hill, George H. *Airwaves to the Soul: The Influence and growth of Religious Broadcasting in America.* Saratoga: R & E Publishers, 1983.
Himmelstein, Hal. *Television Myth and the American Mind.* New York: Praeger, 1984.
Hirsch, H. D. *Validity in Interpretation.* New Haven, CT: Yale University Press, 1967.
Hobart, Michael E., and Zachary S. Schiffman. *Information Ages: Literacy, Numeracy, and the Computer Revolution.* Baltimore: Johns Hopkins University Press, 1998.
Hochberg, Julian E. *Perception.* Englewood Cliffs, NJ: Prentice-Hall, 1964.
Hodge, Bob and David Tripp. *Children and Television: A Semiotic Approach.* Oxford: Blackwell, 1986.
Hodges, A. *Alan Turing: The Enigma.* New York: Simon and Schuster, 1983.
Holt, John. *Escape from Childhood.* New York: E. P. Dutton, 1975.
Horsfield, Peter G. *Religious Television: The American Experience.* New York: Longman, 1984.
Horton, Donald, and R. Richard Wohl. "Mass Communication and Para-Social Interaction: Observations on Intimacy at a Distance." *Psychiatry* 19 (1956): 215-229.
Hovland, Carl I., Irving Janis, and Harold Kelley, eds. *Communication and Persuasion: Psychological Studies of Opinion Change.* New Haven, CT: Yale University Press, 1953.
> Propounds a one way theory of persuasion in light of educational background and group attachment.

Howard, Jane. "Oracle of the Electric Age." *Life Magazine* (28 February 1966).
Hughes, James R. *The Church in Cyberspace: The Coming Impact of the Computer on the Church.* [WWW document] URL http://www.reformed.com/pub/cyber.htm [9 September 1999].
> A classic example of a naive assessment of media, by a Christian. Very interesting array of technical information on coming changes and what they may mean to the church.

Ihde, Don. *Technics and Praxis.* Boston Studies in the Philosophy of Science, Vol. 24. Dordrecht: Reidel, 1979.
Illich, Ivan. *Tools for Conviviality.* New York: Harper and Row-Colophon Books, 1973.
Inbody, Tyron, ed. *Changing Channels: The Church and the Television Revolution.* Dayton, OH: Whaleprints, 1990.
Inglis, Fred. *Media Theory.* Oxford: Blackwell, 1990.
Innis, Harold. *Empire and Communications.* London: Oxford University Press, 1950.
> A key figure in the school of media critics known by McLuhan's term "Media Ecology". Innis was a colleague of McLuhan at the University of Toronto and a strong influence on his early media reflections.

_____. *The Bias of Communication.* Toronto: University of Toronto Press, 1951.
_____. *Changing Concepts of Time.* Toronto: University of Toronto Press, 1952.
_____. *The Strategy of Culture.* Toronto: University of Toronto Press, 1952.
_____. *The Imagery of Power: A Critique of Advertising.* London: Heinemann, 1972.
Iser, Wolfgang. *The Act of Reading.* London: Routledge & Kegan Paul, 1978.
Jamieson, Kathleen Hall. *The Interplay of Influence.* Belmont, CA: Wadsworth Publishing Company, 1982

———. *Eloquence in an Electronic Age: The Transformation of Political Speechmaking.* Oxford: Oxford University Press, 1988.
Jensen, J. *Redeeming Modernity: Contradictions in Media Criticism.* Newbury Park, CA: Sage Publications, 1990.
Jenson, Robert W. "The Hermeneutics of the Electronic Church." *American Academy of Religion* (Dallas meeting, November 1980).
Jhally, Sut. "Communications and the Materialist Conception of History: Marx, Innis and Technology." [WWW document] URL http://www.aber.ac.uk/~dgc/tecdet.html, 1993 [13 July 1999].
Johnson, Nicholas. *How to Talk Back to Your Television Set.* Boston: Atlantic Monthly Press, 1970.
Jonas, Hans. *The Imperative of Responsibility: In Search of an Ethics for the Technological Age.* Chicago: University of Chicago Press, 1984.
Jones, Barry. *Sleepers, Wake! Technology and the Future of Work.* Melbourne: Oxford University Press, 1990.
Joyce, James. *Finnegan's Wake.* London: Faber and Faber, 1939.
<small>Had enormous impact on the literary and media perceptions of McLuhan and all Media Ecologists. McLuhan student Donald Theall says, "One of the first major poetic encounters with the challenge that electronic media present to the traditioanlly accepted relationships between (sic) speech, script, and print." Joyce saw the coming transformation of the book by electronic media.</small>
———. *Ulysses.* New York: Modern Library, 1934
Kaplan, Donald M. "The Psychpathology of Television Watching." *Performance* (July-August 1972): 21-29.
Kaplan, E. Ann. *Rocking Around the Clock: Music Television, Postmodernism, and Consumer Culture.* New York: Methuen, 1987.
Katz, Elihu, and Paul Lazarsfeld. *Personal Influence: The Part Played by People in the Flow of Mass Communication.* New York: Free Press, 1955.
<small>Observations on the place of personal influence, departing from the sociological approach of critics like C. Wright Mills who sought to use their observations to effect social change.</small>
Kelber, Werner. *The Oral and the Written Gospel.* Philadelphia: Fortress Press, 1983.
Kenner, Hugh. "McLuhan Redux." *Harper's* 269 (November 1984): 71-73.
<small>Perceptive portrait of the enigmatic character of McLuhan's thought.</small>
———. *The Mechanical Muse.* New York: Oxford University Press, 1987.
Kernan, A. *The Death of Literature.* New Haven: Yale University Press, 1990.
Kittler, Friedrich. *Discourse Networks 1800/1900.* Los Angeles: Stanford University Press, 1990.
———. *Gramophone, Film, Typewriter.* Los Angeles: Stanford University Press, 1999.
———. *Literature, Media, Information Systems.* Amsterdam: G+B International, 1999.
Klapper, Joseph T. *Effects of Mass Communication.* Glencoe, IL: Free Press, 1960.
Know, B. W. "Silent Reading in Antiquity." *Greek, Roman and Byzantine Studies* 19 (1968): 432-35.
Kowinski, William Severini. "Cyclops: Man with One Eye in the Land of the Blind." *TeleVISIONS* (October/November 1975).

Kroker, Arthur. *Technology and the Canadian Mind: Innis, McLuhan, Grant*. New York: St. Martin's Press, 1984.

Kroker, Arthur. "Digital Humanism: The Processed World of Marshall McLuhan." In *Digital Delirium*, edited by Arthur Kroker and Marilouise Kroker. New York: St. Martin's Press, 1997.

Krugman, Herbert E. "Brainwave Measures of Media Involvement." *Journal of Advertising Research* (February 1971): 3-9.

Kubey, Robert, and Mihaly Csikszentmihalyi, eds. *Television and the Quality of Life: How Viewing Shapes Everyday Experiences*. Hillsdale, NJ: Lawrence Erlbaum, 1990.

Lanham, R. *The Electronic Word: Democracy, Technology and the Arts*. Chicago: University of Chicago Press, 1993.

_____. *Literacy and the Survival of Humanism*. New Haven, CT: Yale University Press, 1983.

Lasswell, Harold. *Psychopathology and Politics*. New York: Viking Press, 1930.
Lasswell made his mark in the field of propaganda analysis. In this important book he explores two types of political leader: the agitator and the administrator, thus founding the field of political psychology. He was a pioneer in discovering the effects of mass communication.

_____. *Propaganda Technique in the World War*. New York: Knopf, 1927.

Lazarsfeld, Paul F., Bernard Berelson, and Hazel Gaudet. *The People's Choice: How the Voter Makes Up His Mind in a Presidential Campaign*. New York: Duell, Sloan and Pearce, 1944.
A revolutionary investigation of the impact of radio broadcasts on voters in Erie County during the 1940 presidential election which challenged the idea that Mass media has a one way influence. It was discovered that people were a great deal more influential than the mass media.

Lemann, Nicholas. "Lost in Post-Reality." *The Atlantic Monthly* (January 1999): 97-101.

Lessig, Lawrence. *Code: and Other Laws of Cyberspace*. New York: Basic Books, 1999.
Harvard law professor and former special master in the anti-trust suit against Microsoft, "technorealist" Lessig argues for extensive government control of the Internet, given the ineptitudes and motivations, of the marketplace, as he perceives them from his left-wing position.

Lesser, Gerald S. *Children and Television*. New York: Random House, 1974.

Levinson, Paul. *The Soft Edge: A Natural History and Future of the Information Revolution*. London: Routledge, 1997.

_____. *Digital McLuhan: A Guide to the Information Millennium*. London: Routledge, 1999.

_____. "Millennial McLuhan: Clues for Deciphering the Digital Age." [WWW document] URL http://chronicle.com/weekly/v46/i08/08b01001.htm (14 October 1999).
An excellent brief summary of McLuhan's main lines of thought.

Levy, Pierre. *Becoming Virtual: Reality in the Digital Age*, New York: Plenum, 1998.

Lewin, Kurt. *Die Sozialisierung Taylorsystems* (*The Socialization of the Taylor System: A Fundamental Investigation in Industrial and Occupational Psychology*). Berlin-Fichtenau: Verlag Gesellschaft und Erziehung, 1920.
The father of "Group Dynamics" argues for worker participation in manufacturing.

Lewis, Clives Staples. *Studies in Words*. Cambridge, UK: Cambridge University Press, 1960.

A brilliantly insightful study by a master writer, pointing to the central importance of historical and textual context in determining semantic meaning.

———. *An Experiment in Criticism*. Cambridge, UK: Cambridge University Press, 1961.
A brilliant exposition of literary criticism by a master wordsmith. Lewis explores the way to read a literary text and the effect we should seek and expect.

Leymore, Varda Langholz. *Hidden Myth: Structure and Symbolism in Advertising*. London: William Heinemann, 1975.
Contains an excellent summary of the structuralist tradition of linguistics as it relates to modern media.

Lichter, Linda S., S. Robert Lichter, and Stanley Rothman. *The Media Elite*. Bethesda, MD: Adler and Adler, 1986.

———. *Watching America: What Television Tells Us about Our Lives*. New York: Prentice-Hall Press, 1991.

———. *Prime Time: How TV Portrays American Culture*. Washington, DC: Regnery Publishers, 1994.

Lippmann, Walter. *Public Opinion*. New York: Harcourt Brace, 1922.
Lippmann was one of the most influential non-academic intellectual influences on communication study. This, his most significant book, distinguishes between an event ("the world outside") and the mass media depiction of the event ("pictures in our heads"). He explores propaganda in mass communication and the development of "stereotypes".

Liska, Jo and Gary Cronkhite. *An Ecological Perspective on Human Communication Theory*. Fort Worth, TX: Harcourt Brace, 1995.

Livingstone, Sonia M. *Making Sense of Television*. Oxford: Pergamon, 1990.

Lloyd, Barbara B. *Perception and Cognition: A Cross-Cultural Perespective*. Harmondsworth: Penguin Books, 1972.

Locke, John L. *The De-Voicing of Society: Why We Don't Talk to Each Other Anymore*. New York: Simon & Schuster, 1998.
"Locke argues that the newer technologies reduce communication to the transmission of information, which, he argues, is one of the least important purposes of human communication." T. David Gordon

Logan, Robert K. *The Alphabet Effect: The Impact of the Phonetic Alphabet on the Development of Western Civilization*. New York: St. Martin's Press, 1986.
"One more member of the Toronto School, Logan's 1986 book began as a collaboration with Marshall McLuhan, and surveys the impact of alphabetic writing across various Western cultures. Also of interest is the role of the alphabet in Hindu and Islamic societies, and Logan's comparison of Western alphabetic culture with Chinese ideography-based culture." Lance Strate

———. *The Fifth Language: Learning A Living In The Computer Age*. Toronto: Stoddart Publishing Co. Limited, 1995.

———. *The Sixth Language: Learning a Living in the Internet Age*. Toronto: Stoddart Publishing Co. Limited, 2000.

Lovitt, W. and H. Lovitt. *Modern Technology in the Heideggerian Perspective*. Lampeter, Wales: Edwin Mellen Press, 1995.

Lowe, Donald. *History of Bourgeois Perception*. Brighton: Harvester Press, 1982.

Lowery, Sharon A. and Melvi De Fleur, eds. *Milestones in Mass Communication Research: Media Effects*. London: Longman, 1983.

Luckiesh, Matthew. *Visual Illusions*. New York: Dover, 1965.

Luke, Carmen. *Pedagogy, Printing and Protestantism*. Albany: State University of New York Press, 1989.

Lumpp, Randolph. "Walter Jackson Ong, S J: A Biographical Portrait." *Oral Tradition* 2, no. 1 (1987):13-18.

Luria, A. R. *The Mind of a Mnemonist*. New York: Basic Books, 1968.

Lynd, Robert S. *Knowledge for What?: The Place of Social Science in American Culture*. Princeton: Princeton University Press, 1939.

Lyon, David. *The Silicon Society*. Grand Rapids: Eerdmans, 1986.

MacKenzie, David and Judy Wajcman, eds. *The Social Shaping of Technology*. Milton Keynes: Open University Press, 1985.

Mander, Jerry. *Four Arguments for the Elimination of Television*. New York: Morrow, 1978.

> The true confessions of a former high end advertising executive. Quite serious about his proposal, and with four very compelling reasons. He is a self-confessed countercultural progressive. Excellent insight, especially into the power of images to create identity, the danger of mediated reality, and the mdium's inherent biases. Television is "irredeemable," period.

Marc, David. *Demographic Vistas: Television in American Culture*. Philadelphia: University of Pennsylvania Press, 1984.

_____. "Understanding Television." *The Atlantic* (August 1984): 33-44.

Marchand, Philip. *Marshall McLuhan: The Medium and the Messenger*. Cambridge, MA: Massachusetts Institute of Technology Press, 1998.

> This edition (first 1989, NY: Tichnor and Fields) has a new foreword by Neil Postman.

Marin, Rick. "Wide-eyed Prophecy Out of Focus." *Insight on the News* (16 April 1990): 60.

> A critical book review of George Gilder's *Life after Television*.

Martin, Henri-Jean. "Printing." In Contact, edited by Raymond Williams. London: Thames & Hudson, 1981.

Martin, James. *The Wired Society*. Englewood Cliffs, NJ: Prentice-Hall, 1978.

Marvin, Carolyn. *When Old Technologies Were New: Thinking About Electric Communication in the Late Nineteenth Century*. New York: Oxford University Press, 1988.

Mayer, Martin. *About Television*. New York: Harper and Row, 1972.

> A good history of television. According to M. Muggeridge, Mayer believes television is "a projection of tabloid journalism." Mayer predicted the day when every home would have an "entertainment centre with up to a hundred channels ..." Muggeridge exclaims: "Good Lord, deliver us!"

_____. *Making News*. Boston: Harvard Business School Press, 1993.

Mayr, Ernst. *Animal Species and Evolution*. Cambridge, MA: Belhap Press of Harvard University Press, 1963

> Havelock has noted that Mayr's evolutionary observations have "pointed to language as the key to the specific humanity of our species." Havelock, *The Muse Learns to Write*, 26.

McGuire, Don. *The Day Television Died*. New York: Doubleday, 1966.

> Jerry Mander claims that this was the only book of 6,000 written about television by 1977 which contemplates its elimination.

McKie, Robin. "E-mail, Pagers Add to Killer Stress." *The Union Leader* (6 July 1999).

McLaughlin, Raymond W. *Communication for the Church*. Grand Rapids: Zondervan, 1968.

McLuhan, Eric. *Electric Language*. New York: St. Martin's Press, 1998.

McLuhan, Marshall. *The Mechanical Bride: Folklore of Industrial Man*. Boston: Beacon Press, 1951.

A popular sociological exposition of the industrial propaganda of contemporary American advertising, using a format designed to make the point, and which presaged as well as exemplified McLuhan's most famous work *The Medium Is the Massage*.

————. *The Gutenberg Galaxy: The Making of Typographical Man*. Toronto: University of Toronto Press, 1962.

A *tour de force* of literary scholarship of Renaissance proportions analysing calteration of culture and human consciousness which the printed word wrought in Western man.

————. *Understanding Media: The Extensions of Man*. New York: McGraw-Hill Book Company, 1964.

The classic study from the seminal period of radical-critical media studies exploring the nature and influence of modern media on epistemology and culture. This is the most quoted scholarly treatment of McLuhan's media criticism. McLuhan became the guru of media studies not becsue he was the first to think and write in this area, but because his scholarship is so insightful and he knew how to appeal to the media mentality in popularized versions of his thought. Postman acknowledges McLuhan to be his mentor and to have passed on his mantel to Postman. McLuhan believed Postman had a gift for organizing a school which he lacked. This book is definitely the first word on the subject of media and in some areas may turn out to be the last as well.

————. *The Interior Landscape: The Literary Criticism of Marshall McLuhan, 1943-1962*. Edited by Eugene McNamara. New York: McGraw-Hill Book Company, 1969.

Excellent selections of an aspect of McLuhan's training and orientation which few appreciate. This is the epistemological and pedagogical key to McLuhan's media criticism. Essential reading.

————. *Counterblast*. London: Rapp & Whiting, 1969.

A fine clear summary of McLuhan at his most explicit. Formatted in mosaic form of *The Medium Is the Massage* and *War and Peace in the Global Village*.

————. "At the Flip Point of Time - The Point of More Return." *Journal of Communication* (autumn 1975): 102-106.

————. *Culture Is Our Business*. New York: McGraw-Hill, 1970.

————. *Letters of Marshall McLuhan*. Edited by M. Molinaro, C. McLuhan, and W. Toye. Toronto: Oxford University Press, 1987.

————. *Essential McLuhan*. Edited by Eric McLuhan and Frank Zingrone. New York: BasicBooks, 1995.

————. *Marshall McLuhan Essays: Media Research: Technology, Art, Communication*. Edited by Michel A. Moos. Australia: G&B Arts, 1997.

A collection of McLuhan essays, some of which are available nowhere else outside of their original journal publication.

————. *The Medium and the Light: Reflections on Religion*. Edited by Eric McLuhan and Jacek Szlarek. Toronto: Stoddart Publishing Co. Limited, 1999.

A unique collection of McLuhan's religious writings, the most neglected area of his thought. Many pieces have never been printed before or have long been forgotten in journals.

McLuhan, Marshall and Quentin Fiore. *The Medium Is the Massage: An Inventory of Effects*. New York: Bantom Books, 1967.

Like *The Mechanical Bride* the very format is the message/massage. And the message is not a naive approbation of modern media, but a warning to look more closely at the message in each medium. Note the pun in the title. McLuhan was a wordsmith. Not only is the metaphor of massage meant, i.e. it fully involves us, but the word can also be divided thus: "Mass Age".

_____. *War and Peace in the Global Village.* New York: Bantom Books, 1968.
   Same genre as *The Medium Is the Massage*. A mosaic of Joycean perceptions demonstrating the "all-at-onceness" of the new electric environment of the "global village." Divided surreptitiously to make us look for patterns into "Our Global Village: / War as Education: / Education as War: / The Bore War: and ending with A Message to the Fish:. Joyce dominates the margins. How very McLuhanesque!

McLuhan, Marshall, Kathy Hutchon and Eric McLuhan. *City as Classroom: Understanding Language and Media.* Agincourt, Ontario: Book Society of Canada, 1977.

McLuhan, Marshall and Eric McLuhan. *Laws of Media: The New Science.* Toronto: University of Toronto Press, 1988.

McLuhan, Marshall, and Harley Parker. *Through the Vanishing Point: Space in Poetry and Painting.* New York: Harper and Row, 1968.

McLuhan, Marshall and Bruce R. Powers. *The Global Village: Transformations in World Life and Media in the 21st Century.* New York and Oxford: Oxford University Press, 1989.

McLuhan, Marshall, and Wilfred Watson. *From Cliché to Archetype.* New York: Viking Press, 1970.

McQuail, Denis. *Towards a Sociology of Mass Communication.* London: Collier-Macmillan, 1969.

_____. *Mass Communication Theory,* 2nd ed. London: Sage Publications, 1990.

McQuail, Denis and Sven Windahl. *Communication Models.* London: Longman, 1993.

Meerloo, Joast. "Television Addiction and Reactive Apathy." *Journal of Nervous and Mental Disease* 120 (1954): 290,291.

Melman, Seymour. "The Myth of Autonomous Technology." 1972. In *Man-Made Futures,* edited by Nigel Cross et al. London: Hutchinson, 1974.

Mellencamp, Patricia, ed. *Logics of Television: Essays in Cultural Criticism.* Bloomington, IN: Indiana University Press, 1990.

Menconi, Al. "Is Television Destroying Christianity?" *Media Update* 8 (1989): 1-5.
   Content oriented critique with excellent principles for controlled viewing.

Messaris, Paul. *Visual Literacy: Image, Mind and Reality.* Boulder, CO: Westview Press, 1994.

Meyrowitz, Joshua. *No Sense of Place: The of Electronic Media on Social Behavior.* New York: Oxford University Press, 1985.
   A synthetic work of great scope and insight combining the "medium theory" of McLuhan with the sociological "situationist" paradigm of Erving Goffman.

_____. "Where Have All the Children Gone?" *Newsweek* (30 August 1982): 13.

_____. "Where Have All the Heroes Gone?" *Psychology Today* 18, no. 7 (July 1984): 47, 48.

_____. "The 19-Inch Neighborhood." *Newsweek* (22 July 1985): 8.

_____. "Intimate Strangers." *Boston Sunday Globe* (8 December 1985).

_____. "We Became a Nation of TV Mourners." *The Hartford Courant* (31 January 1986).

_____. "Is TV Keeping Us *Too* Well Informed." *TV Guide* (9 January 1988): 5, 6, 8.

_____. "True or False, We Were There." *USA Today* (1-3 April 1988).

———. "Altered States: How Television Changes Childhood and Challenges Parents." *Media and Values* 52/53 (fall/winter 1990): 2, 3.
———. "First the Word . . . Now the Image." *Human Concerns* (fall 1991): 4, 5.
———. "Images of Media: Hidden Ferment—and Harmony—in the Field." *Journal of Communication* 43, no. 3 (summer 1993): 55-66.
  Discusses three underlying metaphors used in studies of media: medium as a conduit, medium as a language, medium as environment. Simplified version of "Multiple Media Literacies."
———. "Taking McLuhan and 'Medium Theory' Seriously:Technological Change and the Evolution of Education."Chapter 4 in *Technology and the Future of Schooling: Ninety-Fifth Yearbook of the National Society for the Study of Education*, edited by Stephen T. Kerr. Part II. Chicago: University of Chicago Press, 1996.
———. "Multiple Media Literacies." *Journal of Communication* 48, no. 1 (winter 1998): 96-108.
  Discusses three underlying metaphors used in studies of media: medium as a conduit, medium as a language, medium as environment.
———. "Understandings of Media." *ETC* 56 (Spring, 1999): 44-52.
  Discusses three underlying metaphors used in studies of media: medium as a conduit, medium as a language, medium as environment. Simplified version of "Multiple Media Literacies."
Meyrowitz, Joshua, and Karen Webster. "Whose Views Make News?" *Cable in the Classroom* (July/August 1995): 10, 11.
Miller, Jonathan. *McLuhan*. London: Fontana, 1971.
Miller, Mark Crispin. *Boxed In: The Culture of TV.* Evanston, IL: Northwestern University Press, 1988.
Mitcham, Carl. *Thinking Through Technology: The Path Between Engineering and Technology*. Chicago: University of Chicago Press, 1994.
Mitcham, Carl, and Robert Mackey, eds. *Philosophy and Technology: Readings in the Philosophical Problems of Technology*. 1972; rpt. New York: Free Press, 1983.
Mitcham, Carl, and Jim Grote, eds. *Theology and Technology: Essays in Christian Analysis and Exegesis*. Lanham, MD: University Press of America, 1984.
Monaco, James. *How to Read a Film: The Art, Technology, Language, History and Theory of Film and Media*. New York: Oxford University Press, 1977.
———. *Celebrity: The Media as Image Makers*. New York: Delta Books, 1978.
———. *Media Culture*. New York: Delta Books, 1978.
Monsma, Stephen V., ed. *Responsible Technology: A Christian Perspective*. Grand Rapids: Eerdmans, 1986.
  Excellent work by six authors coming from a Dooyeweerdian perspective. Useful annotated bibliography. While we may disagree, as I do, with the idea of "normativity" in the 15 aspects of reality or "modalities" of Dooyeweerd, they are certainly helpful in identifying the structures of reality within which the Christian must work to apply the infallible norm of Scripture to all of life.
Moores, Shaun. *Interpreting Audiences: The Ethnography of Media Consumption*. London: Sage Publications, 1993.
Moos, Michel A. *Media Research: Technology, Art, Communication*. .
  A collection of essays by McLuhan
Muggeridge, Malcolm. *Christ and the Media*. Grand Rapids: Eerdmans, 1977.

An trenchant critique of the visual media, especially television, in which Muggeridge had so much experience, contrasting the "imaginary" reality of the image media with the incarnation. He perceptively addresses the question: "Is there any redeeming value in such media?" His answer is a loud, "No, not much". He is a "media determinist".

_____. "Muggeridge on Media." Interview by Steve Turner. *Radix* (May 1975): 7.

Muller, Herbert J. *The Children of Frankenstein: A Primer on Modern Technology and Human Values.* Bloomington, IN and London: Indiana University Press, 1970.

Mumford, Lewis. *Technics and Civilization.* New York: Harcourt, Brace and World, 1934.

A classic in communication study. A history of the development of technology in its relationship to culture. The second half of the book assesses the influence of modern technology on our culture in a far too optimistic way. The comprehensive "List of Inventions" and bibliography are useful reference tools, though quite outdated.

_____. *The Myth of the Machine: Technics and Human Development.* New York: Harcourt, Brace and World, 1966.

A more sober and pessimistic view of the effects of modern technology than his earlier *Technics and Civilization.* He attempts to account for man's spiritual dimension which he believes has been neglected in most modern accounts of man's uniqueness. Man's creativity is not merely a matter of survival but of higher aspirations. Mumford's evolutionary assumptions undermine his quest for meaning. He is left only with man's ability for self-transformation which the present commitment to technology seems to be eclipsing.

Munson, Eve Stryker and Catherine A. Warren, eds. *James Carey: A Critical Reader.* Minneapolis: University of Minnesota Press, 1997.

Mulholland, Thomas B. "Training Visual Attention." *Academic Therapy* (fall 1974): 5-17.

Nederhood, Joel. "The Back to God Hour: Mission Television Report," *Christian Reformed Church Synod Report.* Report 1:A, Supplement, 1977.

An extremely thoughtful reflection on the use of television for Christian broadcasting. Nederhood faces the difficult questions from an articulate reformed position. He has really understood the nature and influence of the visual media, especially television.

_____. "Communication: Is it Possible," *The Evangelical Roundtable*, 1987. Eastern College

_____. Interview by Gregory E. Reynolds. Transcript. Westminster Theological Seminary in California, 1990.

_____. "The Pre-eminence of Christ in the Westminster Confession of Faith." In *To Glorify and Enjoy God*, edited by John L. Carson and David W. Hall. Edinburgh: Banner of Truth Trust, 1994.

_____. *This Splendid Journey.* Grand Rapids: Board of Publications of the Christian Reformed Church and Nutley, NJ: Presbyterian and Reformed, 1998.

Negri, Antonio. *The Savage Anomaly*, Minneapolis: University of Minnesota Press, 1991.

Negroponte, N. *Being Digital.* New York: Alfred Knopf, 1995.

Nelson, Jenny. "Eyes Out of Your Head: On Television Experience." *Critical Studies in Mass Communication* 6, no. 4 (December 1989): 387-403.

Nevitt, Barry. *Communications Ecology: Re-Presentation vs. Replica.* Toronto: University of Toronto Press, 1982.

Newcomb, Horace, ed. *Television: The Critical View.* 3rd ed. Oxford: Oxford University Press, 1982.

O'Donnell, James J. *Avatars of the Word: From Papyrus to Cyberspace,* Cambridge, MA: Harvard University Press, 1998.
Olson, Alan M., Christopher Parr, and Debra Parr, eds. *Video Icons and Values.* Albany: State University of New York, 1990.
Ong, Walter J. *Ramus, Method, and the Decay of Dialogue.* 2 vols. Harvard University Press, 1958.
    ———, ed. *Darwin's Vision and Christian Perspectives.* New York: Macmillan, 1960
    ———. *The Barbarian Within, and Other Fugitive Essays and Studies.* New York: Macmillan, 1962.
    ———. *The Presence of the Word.* New Haven: Yale University Press, 1967. Reprint, Minneapolis, MN: University of Minnesota Press, 1981.
A foundational study of the primacy of the oral/aural and the radical nature of the change in the human sensorium which printing and the electronic media have initiated. Some of the best insights into the power, immediacy and effect/affect of the oral in divine and human life, by a Jesuit who interacts with Scripture. Ong is somewhat Neo-Orthodox and takes his cue from Teilhard de Chardin's evolutionary perspective on redemptive history.
    ———. "Worship at the End of the Age of Literacy." In *Worship* 43 (1969): 474-487. Reprinted in vol. 1 of Ong's *Faith and Contexts.*
    ———. Review: *Unfinished Man and the Imagination: Toward an Ontology and Rhetoric of Revelation* (Ray L. Hart). In *Biblica* 51 (Rome 1970): 253-258.
    ———. *Rhetoric, Romance and Technology.* New York: Cornell University Press, 1971.
    ———. *Interfaces of the Word: Studies in the Evolution of Consciousness and Culture.* Ithaca, NY: Cornell University Press, 1977.
    ———. "Literacy and the Future of Print." *Journal of Communication* 30 (winter 1980):1.
    ———. *Orality and Literacy: The Technologizing of the Word.* New York: Methuen, 1982.
    ———. Review: *The Humiliation of the Word* (Jacques Ellul) in the *Journal of Communication* 36, no. 1 (1986): 156-158.
    ———. Review: *Beyond the Written Word: Oral Aspects of Scripture in the History of Religion* (William A. Graham) in *America* (Mar. 4, 1989): 203-204.
    ———. *Media, Consciousness, and Culture: Explorations of Walter Ong's Thought.* Edited by Bruce E. Gronbeck, Thomas J. Farrell and Paul A. Soukup. Newbury Park, CA: Sage Publications, 1991.
    ———. *Faith and Contexts.* Edited by Thomas J. Farrell and Paul A. Soukup. Atlanta: Scholars Press, 1992.
    ———. "Digitization Ancient and Modern: Beginnings of Writing and Today's Computers." In *Communication Research Trends* 18, no. 2 (1998).
O'Sullivan, Tim et al. *Key Concepts in Communication Studies.* London: Routledge, 1983.
Owen, Virginia Stem. *The Total Image: Selling Jesus in the Modern Age.* Grand Rapids: Eerdmans, 1980.
Ozbekhan, Hasan. "The Triumph of Technology: *Can* Implies *Ought.*" 1968. In Nigel Cross et al., eds. *Man-Made Futures.* London: Hutchinson, 1974.

Pacey, Arnold. *The Culture of Technology.* Oxford: Blackwell, 1983.
Packard, Vance. *The Hidden Persuaders.* New York: David McKay Company, Inc., 1957.
> A thoughtful analysis of American advertising as it uses motivational research to identify and create market need. Analysis of early television programming and the profit motive.

Paglia, Camille. "She Wants her TV! He Wants his Book!" *Harpers* (March 1991).
> A witty exchange between Camille Paglia and Neil Postman.

Papanek, Victor. *Design for Human Scale.* New York: Van Nostrand Reinhold, 1983.
_____. *Design for the Real World.* 2nd ed. New York: Van Nostrand Reinhold, 1984.
Papert, Seymour. *Mindstorms: Children, Computers and Powerful Ideas.* Brighton: Harvester, 1980.
Park, Robert E. *The Immigrant Press and Its Control.* New York: Harper, 1922.
> Historian Rogers calls Park the "first theorist of mass communication". This, his only book, depicts mass communication as a "social-psychological process" in which humans connect on the basis of instinct rather than moral reason.

Park, Robert E. and Ernest W. Burgess. *Introduction to the Science of Sociology.* Chicago: University of Chicago Press, 1924.
> Pioneering study of the influence of the press on society. Rogers says it was considered the bible of sociology in its day.

Parker, Everett C., David W. Barry, and Dallas W. Smythe *The Television: Radio Audience and Religion.* New York: Harper, 1955.
Pattison, Robert. *On Literacy: The Politics of the Word from Homer to the Age of Rock.* New York: Oxford University Press, 1982.
Patterson, Graeme. *History and Communications: Harold Innis, Marshall McLuhan, and the Interpretation of History* Toronto: University of Toronto Press, 1990.
Patterson, Thomas E., and Robert D. McClure. "Political Campaigns: TV Power Is a Myth." *Psychology Today* (July 1976): 61-90.
Peace, Richard V. "The New Media Environment: Evangelism in a Visually-Oriented Society." *Journal of the Academy for Evangelism in Theological Education* 1 (1985-86): 36-45.
Perrolle, Judith A. *Computers and Social Change: Information, Property and Power.* Belmont, CA: Wadsworth, 1987.
Peters, John Durham. *Speaking into Air: A History of the Idea of Communication,* Chicago: University of Chicago Press, 1995.
Pickstock, Catherine. *After Writing: On the Liturgical Consummation of Philosophy.* Oxford: Basil Blackwell, 1998.
Pierce, J. R. *Symbols, Signals and Noise: The Nature and Process of Communication.* New York: Harper and Row, Publishers, Inc., 1961.
_____. *Communications Technology and the Future.* New York: Harper and Row, Publishers, Inc., 1966.
Pirsig, Robert M. *Zen and the Art of Motorcycle Maintenance: An Inquiry into Values.* New York: Bantam Books, 1974.
Postman, Neil. *Teaching as a Subversive Activity.* New York: Dell, 1969.
_____. *Teaching as a Conserving Activity.* New York: Dell, 1979.
_____. *The Disappearance of Childhood.* London: Allen, 1983.
> An analysis of the concept of childhood in western history, with a critique of its disappearance due to media influence.

---. *Amusing Ourselves To Death: Public Discourse in the Age of Show Business.* New York: Viking Penguin, Inc., 1985.
A groundbreaking critique by McLuhan's successor. Postman critiques the pervasive influence of the visual media, especially television, on all areas of culture, demonstrating that intelligent, substantive public discourse is thereby severely diminished. He believes that the genius of the image media is entertainment and that it makes entertainment out of everything it touches. Postman applies the second commandment to the modern use of images.

---. *Conscientious Objections: Stirring Up Trouble About Language, Technology and Education.* New York: Knopf, 1988.
A collection of witty essays by a master wit on the range of subjects described in the subtitle. There is much excellent material here on media ecology.

---. "Learning By Story." *Atlantic* (December 1989): 119-124.

---. Interview by Gregory E. Reynolds. Transcript. New York University, 1990.

---. *Technopoly: The Surrender of Culture to Technology.* New York: Vintage, 1993.
Postman traces the development of technology from tool making to technocracy to technopoly. He demonstrates the present monopoly that electronic media have in every area of American life. This monopoly is a mass delusion that radically undermines the humanity of our culture. Postman offers a cogent, if inadequate, humanistic solution.

---. *The End of Education.* New York: Knopf, 1995.
Postman challenges contemporary educators to wrestle with the question of the purpose of education. He critiques a host of inadequate notions of purpose and offers his own. His view that the "narratives" that give form and purpose to culture are relatively "true" is in itself inadequate. He posits the narrative of civil religion as the most hopeful prospect of unity in public education. Education is his church. He asks many of the right questions; points out the weaknesses of modern pedagogy; and offers some stimulating alternatives. As usual his insights into the relation of the media to education are incisive.

---. *Building a Bridge to the Eighteenth Century: How the Past Can Improve Our Future.* New York: Knopf, 1999.
The title reveals the most fundamental problem with Postman: he is an Enlightenment Modernist with a twist. He is a transcendental relativist, who believes the metanarratives or ultimate truths are each "in some way true." As in all of his other writings his analysis of the particular issues as well as his proposed solutions have much merit. He is truly a craftsman of thought and word.

Powers, Bruce R. *The Global Village: Transformations in World, Life and Media in the 21st Century.* New York: Oxford University Press, 1989.

Ravetz, Jerome R. *Scientific Knowledge and Its Social Problems.* New York: Oxford University Press, 1971.

Rechtien, J. G. "The Structural Significance of Sola Scriptura." *Centerpoint* 2 (1976): 7-19.

---. "The Visual Memory of William Perkins and the End of Theological Dialogue." *Journal of American Academy of Religion* 45, Supplement D (1977b): 69-99.

---. "John Foxe's Comprehensive Collection of Commonplaces: A Renaissance Memory System for Students and Theologians." *Sixteenth Century Journal* 9 (1978a): 83-89.

---. "The Transmission of Oral Culture in the Style of Thomas Stapleton." *Style* 12 (1978b): 258-273.

_____. "Logic In Puritan Sermons In The Late 16th Century And Plain Style." *Style* 13 (1979): 237-258.

_____. "The Ramist Style of John Udall: Audience and Pictorial Logic in Puritan Sermon and Controversy." *Oral Tradition* 2 (1987): 188-213.

Richards, I. A. *The Philosophy of Rhetoric*. New York and London: Oxford University Press, 1936.
His method of literary criticism had a seminal influence on McLuhan. Richards directed McLuhan's doctoral dissertation at Cambridge.

_____. *The Principles of Literary Criticism*. London: K. Paul, Trench, Trubner, & Co., Ltd. and New York: Harcourt, Brace & Co., 1924, 1925.

_____. *Science and Poetry*. London: K. Paul, Trench, Trubner & Co., 1926.

_____. *Practical Criticism: A Study of Literary Judgment*. London: K. Paul, Trench, Trubner & Co., 1929.

_____. "The Spoken and Written Word." *The Listener*, 37 (October16, 1947): 669-670.

Richards, I. A. and Charles Kay Ogden. *The Meaning of Meaning: A Study of the Influence of Language upon Thought and of the Science of Symbolism*. London: K. Paul, Trench, Trubner & Co. and New York: Harcourt, Brace, 1923.
Very influential on McLuhan while at Cambridge.

Robins, Kevin and Frank Webster. *The Technical Fix*. London: Macmillan, 1989.

Rogers, Everett. *Communication Technology: The New Media in Society*. New York: The Free Press, 1986.

_____. *A History of Communication Study: A Biographical Approach*. New York: The Free Press, 1994.
This encyclopedic work covers the general history of communication study with an emphasis on the sociological and scientific dimensions of the broad field. While it provides a helpful general background it is extremely thin in the area of media ecology. Innis and McLuhan get only passing mention, while Ellul, Ong and Postman are omitted altogether. The bibliography is extensive, covering over fifty pages.

Rosenthal, Raymond, ed. *McLuhan: Pro and Con*. Baltimore: Penguin Books, 1968.
Excellent critical essays by a wide range of authors, including a scathing "write-off" of McLuhan by Theodore Roszak.

Roszak, Theodore. *The Cult of Information*. Cambridge: Lutterworth Press, 1986.

Rybczynski, W. *Taming the Tiger: The Struggle to Control Technology*. New York: Penguin Books, 1983.

Sacks, Oliver. *An Anthropologist on Mars*. New York: Vintage, 1995.

Salomon, Gavriel. *Interaction of Media, Cognition and Learning*. San Francisco: Jossey-Bass, 1979.

Sanderson, George and Frank Macdonald, eds. *Marshall McLuhan: The Man and His Message*. Golden, CO: Fulcrum, 1989.
An informative montage consisting of writers describing, reflecting on, and interacting with Marshall McLuhan. Includes fourteen essays and articles by McLuhan, and two interviews. This is one of the best introductions to McLuhan that I know. The interview with Hubert Hoskins titled "Electronic Consciousness and the Church"is unique and especially pertinent for the Christian.

Schiller, Herbert I. *Mass Communication and American Empire*. New York: Kelley, 1969.

_____. *The Mind Managers*. Boston: Beacon Press, 1973.

Schramm, Wilbur Lang. *Communications in Modern Society*. Urbana: University of Illinois Press, 1948.

_____. *The Process and Effects of Mass Communication*. Urbana: University of Illinois Press, 1954.
Studies the effects of mass communication rather than on the nature of media themselves.

_____. *Mass Media and National Development*. Stanford: Stanford University Press, 1964.

_____. *Men, Messages, and Media: A Look at Human Communication*. New York: Harper and Row, 1973.

Schramm, Wilbur Lang, Jack Lyle and Edwin B. Parker. *Television in the Lives of Our Children*. Stanford: Stanford University Press, 1961.

Schultze, Quentin J. *Television: Manna From Hollywood?* Grand Rapids: Zondervan, 1986.
A popular critique of television, focusing on content analysis. Everything said here is better said in his later work.

_____, ed. *American Evangelicals and the Mass Media*. Grand Rapids: Zondervan, 1990.

_____, proj. coord. and Roy M. Anker, ed. *Dancing in the Dark: Youth, Popular Culture and the Electronic Media*. Grand Rapids: Eerdmans, 1991.
This is a wide ranging scholarly critique of youth and popular culture in relation to the electronic media from a Christian perspective by six members of the Calvin College faculty who have expertise in a variety of disciplines. The strength of this book is in its exploration of the socio-cultural context of the electronic media. No analyisis of the media *per* se. The comparison of George Whitefield to Boy George, along with the imprimatur of Bill Moyers should raise the reader's critical antennae.

_____. *Televangelism and American Culture: The Business of Popular Religion*. Grand Rapids: Baker Book House, 1991.
Helpful sociological analysis, with a little about the grammar of television. Excellent advice regarding the taming of televanglelism, including the need to educate the church to "address the implications of living in a television age," but no analysis of the ways in which the technology changes us and our institutions.

_____. *Redeemimg Television: How TV Changes Christians - How Christians Can Change TV*. Downers Grove, IL: InterVarsity Press, 1992.
A well informed look at television from a Christian viewpoint. Schutze's best book to date. Perhaps too sanguine an assessment. He takes issue with Postman et. al. Helpful in developing the positive dimension of television. Lots of inside information about the production of programming and the motivations behind the programming. Excellent analysis of conspiracy theories and development of content and sociological analysis. very good discussion of television as story teller. No general theory of media analysis. Combines progressive and scientific theory, viewing media essentially as conduits, occasionally as languages, never as environments.

_____. *Communication through the Eyes of Faith*. Grand Rapids: Baker Book House, in press.

Schumacher, E. F. *Small Is Beautiful*. New York: Harper and Row, 1973.

Schuurman, Egbert. "A Confrontation with Technicism as the Spiritual Climate of the West." *The Westminster Theological Journal* 58, no. 1 (spring 1996): 63-84.
Thoughtful Dooyeweerdian critique of "technicism," or the worship of technology with a "redemptive motive."

———. *Reflections on the Technological Society*. Toronto: Wedge, 1977.
———. *Technology and the Future: A Philosophical Challenge*. Translated by H. D. Morton. Toronto: Wedge, 1980.
Schwartz, Tony. *The Responsive Chord*. Garden City, New York: Anchor Books, 1973.
> Keen analysis of the difference between Gutenberg and Electronic man. Creator of ill-famed atomic bomb commercial during the 1964 presidential campaign, which showed a child in a field picking daisies as a countdown for atomic disaster. He concludes that "truth" is a child of print and does not apply in the electronic media. Thus a new set of questions need to be raised in order to deal with television. Cf. Cater, "The Intellectual in Videoland."

———. *Media: The Second God*. New York: Random House, 1981.
Scribner, Sylvia and Michael Cole. *The Psychology of Literacy*. Cambridge, MA: Harvard University Press, 1981.
Searle, John. *Minds, Brains and Science*. Cambridge, MA: Harvard University Press, 1984.
Segal, H. P. *Technological Utopianism in American Culture*. Chicago: University of Chicago Press, 1985.
———. *Future Imperfect: The Mixed Blessings of Technology in America*. Amherst, MA: University of Massachusetts Press, 1994.
Segall, Marshall H., Donald T. Campbell and Melville J. Herskovits. *The Influence of Culture on Visual Perception*. Indianapolis, IN: Bobbs-Merrill, 1966.
Siegel, Alberta E. "Communicating With The Next Generation." *Journal of Communication* (autumn 1975).
Seiter, Ellen et al., eds. *Remote Control*. London: Routledge, 1989.
Sekuler, Robert and Randolph Blake. *Perception*. 3rd ed. New York: McGraw-Hill, 1994.
Selfe, C., and S. Hilligoss, eds. *Literacy and Computers: The Complications of Teaching and Learning with Technology*. New York: Modern Language Association, 1994.
Senden, M. von. *Space and Sight*. London: Methuen, 1960.
Shallis, Michael. *The Silicon Idol*. Oxford: Oxford University Press, 1984.
Shannon, Claude, and Warren Weaver. *The Mathematical Theory of Communication*. Urbana: University of Illinois Press, 1949.
> The composite of two journal articles written for Bell Labs explaining his famous "source-message-channel-receiver" concept of information theory. While Shannon intended the theory for application to communications engineering it has been extensively applied to all forms of human intentional communication.

Shenk, David. *Data Smog: Surviving the Information Glut*. San Francisco: Harper Edge, 1997.
———. *The End of Patience: Cautionary Notes on the Information Revolution*. Bloomington, IN: Indiana University Press, 1999.
Shlain, Leonard. *The Alphabet Versus the Goddess*. New York: Viking Press, 1998.
Shulman, Milton. *The Ravenous Eye: The Impact of the Fifth Factor*. London: Cassell, 1973.
> TV producer and critic, Shulman refers to the "fifth factor," the effect of violence and sin on young audiences. M. Muggeridge.

———. *The Least Worst Television in the World*. London: Barrie and Jenkins, 1973.

Silverstone, Roger. *The Message of Television: Myth and Narrative in Contemporary Culture*. London: Heinemann Educational Books, 1981.
———. *Television Myth and the American Mind*. New York: Praeger, 1984.
Silverstone, R and E. Hirsch, eds. *Consuming Technologies: Media and Information in Domestic Space*. London: Routledge, 1992.
Skornia, Harry J. *Television and Society*. New York: McGraw-Hill, 1965.
Slater, Philip. *The Pursuit of Loneliness*. Boston: Beacon Press, 1971.
Smith, Frank. *Reading*. Cambridge, UK: Cambridge University Press, 1978.
———. *Understanding Reading*. Hillsdale, NJ: Erlbaum, 1988.
Smith, Robert Rutherford. *Beyond the Wasteland: The Criticism of Broadcasting*. Urbana, IL: ERIC, 1976.
Snow, C. P. *The Two Cultures and the Scientific Revolution*. New York: Cambridge University Press, 1959.
Snow, Robert. *Creating Media Culture*. Newbury Park, CA: Sage Publications, 1983.
Sommerville, C. John. *How the News Makes Us Dumb: The Death of Wisdom in an Information Society*. Downers Grove, IL: InterVarsity, 1999.
"Following in Boortsin's steps, Sommerville argues that pre-occupation with contemporary and insignificant events prevents us from attaining that wisdom that could be attained from the historical evaluation of significant events. Sontag, Susan. *Against Interpretation*. New York: Dell, 1961." T. David Gordon.
Sontag, Susan. *Against Interpretation*. New York: Dell, 1961.
Spengler, Oswald. *Man and Technics: A Contribution to a Philosophy of Life*. Translated by Charles Francis Atkinson. New York: Knopf, 1932.
Spoehr, Kathryn T. and Stephen W. Lehmkuhle. *Visual Information Processing*. San Francisco: Freeman, 1982.
Standage, Thomas. *The Victorian Internet: The Remarkable Story of the Telegraph and the Nineteenth Century's On-line Pioneers*. New York: Walker, 1998.
History of the telegraph.
Stanley, Manfred. *The Technological Conscience: Survival and Dignity in an Age of Expertise*. Chicago: University of Chicago Press, 1978.
Stavins, Ralph L., ed. *Television Today: The End of Communication and the Death of Community*. Washington, DC: Communication Service Corp., 1969.
Stearn, Emanuell. *McLuhan: Hot and Cool*. New York: Signet Books, 1967.
Stearn, Gerald E., ed. *McLuhan Hot and Cool*. Harmondsworth: Penguin Books, 1968.
Stein, Ben. *The View From Sunset Boulevard: America As Brought to You By the People Who Make Television*. New York: Basic Books, 1979.
Stephens, Mitchell. *The Rise of the Image, the Fall of the Word*. Oxford: Oxford University Press, 1998.
Stevenson, Nick. *Understanding Media Cultures: Social Theory and Mass Communication*. London: Sage Publications, 1995.
Stoll, Clifford. *Silicon Snake Oil: Second Thoughts on the Information Highway*. New York: Doubleday, 1995.
A sober reflection on the value of the Internet and the computer by a veteran user. A true iconoclast Stoll explodes myths left and right with all the credibility of an insider. While acknowledging the benefits of the online and computer worlds, as an astronomer, he articulates grave reservations concerning the overblown claims of promoters. He challenges conventional

assumptions at a pragmatic level, especially debunking myths about vaunted educational uses of computing and the Internet.

Strate, Lance. "Post (modern) Man." *ETC* 51, no. 2, 1994.

_____. "An Overview of Communication Analysis." *Antenna: Newsletter of the Mercurians, in the Society for the History of Technology* 10, no. 2 (May 1998): 4-8.
An excellent overview of the history of communication studies by a media ecologist.

_____. *Understanding Media Ecology.* Forthcoming.

Strate, Lance, Ron Jacobson, and Stephanie Gibson, eds. *Communication and Cyberspace.* Creskill, NJ: Hampton Press, 1996.

Street, Brian V. *Literacy in Theory and Practice.* Cambridge, UK: Cambridge University Press, 1984.

Sweet, Leonard, ed. *Communication and Change in American Religious History.* Grand Rapids: Eerdmans, 1993.

Taylor, Frederick W. *The Principles of Scientific Management.* New York: Norton, 1967.
Postman and Ebersole point to this book as signalling a dramatic and dangerous shift in thinking about technology in business. Postman maintains that this is the beginning of "Technopoly". Taylor announces "in the past man has been first, in the future the system must be first" (7).

Taylor, George Rogers. *The Transportation Revolution, 1815-1860.* Edited by H. David et al. New York: Harper, 1968.

Tenner, Edward. *Why Things Bite Back: Technology and the Revenge of Unintended Consequences.* New York: Alfred Knopf, 1996.

Theall, Donald F. *The Medium is the Rear View Mirror: Understanding McLuhan.* Montreal: McGill-Queens Univerity Press, 1971.
An insightful, sometimes scathing, critique of McLuhan by McLuhan's first doctoral student at Toronto. One of the few critics who really understands McLuhan and appreciates his best insights. He puts his finger on some real weaknesses in McLuhan, and is himself equally well read. McLuhan's failure to develop a coherent philosophy of communication is the most telling.

_____. *Beyond the Word: Reconstructing Sense in the Joyce Era of Technology, Culture and Communication.* Toronto: University of Toronto Press, 1995.

_____. *The Virtual McLuhan: Poetry, Prophecy, Piety and Technology.* Montreal: McGill-Queen's University Press. Forthcoming.

Thomas, Gordon L. "A Study of the Effects of Certain Elements of Oral Style on the Intelligibility of Informative Speeches." Unpublished dissertation, Northwestern University, 1952.

Tinsley, John R. "Computing the Sermon." *New Horizons* (July 1997) 5.
An uncritical plug for the use of the PC in sermon preparation.

Tostengard, Sheldon A. *The Spoken Word.* Minneapolis: Fortress Press, 1989.

Turner, Frederick. "Escape from Modernism: Technology and the Future of Imagination." *Harper's* 269 (November 1984): 47-55.

Turner, Tim. "Effective Counseling in a Media Age." *The Biblical Counselor* (September 1991).
Very content oriented critique. Helpful in terms of culture reflecting and changing content.

Umble, Diane Zimmerman. "The Amish and the Telephone: Resistance and Reconstruction." In *Consuming Technologies*, edited by R. Silverstone and E. Hirsch. London: Routledge, 1992.

Helps correct misconceptions and stereo-types regarding the way in which Anabaptists deal with electronic technology.

Vanderhill, Steven. "The Internet Seminary." *New Horizons* (July 1997) 8, 9.
An uncritical promotion of "virtual" seminary education.

Vernon, M. D. *Perception Through Experience*. London: Methuen, 1970.

_____. *The Psychology of Perception*. Harmondsworth: Penguin Books, 1971.

Vico, Giambattista. *The New Science of Giambattista Vico* with "Practic of the New Science." 1744, 3rd ed. Reprint. Translated and edited by Thomas Goddard Bergen and Max Harold Fisch. Ithaca: Cornell University Press, 1984.
"One of the few works of authentic genius in the history of social theory." [blurb] Instead of beginning with empirical observation as Francis Bacon, Vico begins with the Providence of God, and investigates the Providential development of social institutions from ancient times to 1725. He was a professor of rhetoric at the University of Naples. Philosopher of history, who had a great influence on James Joyce and thus on McLuhan.

Walhout, Clarence. "Christianity, History, and Literary Criticism: Walter Ong's Global Vision." *Journal of the American Academy of Religion* 62 (1994): 435-459.

Wark, McKenzie. "Sprit Freed From Flesh: Cultural Technologies and the Information Landscape." *Intervention* 21/22 (1987): 89-96.

_____. *Virtual Geography: Living with Global Media Events*. Bloomington, IN: Indiana University Press, 1994.

_____. *The Virtual Republic: Australia's Culture Wars of the 1990s*. St. Leonards, NSW: Allen & Unwin, 1997.

_____. *Celebrities, Culture and Cyberspace*, Sydney: Pluto Press, 1999.

Watson, James and Anne Hill. *Dictionary of Communication and Media Studies*. London: Arnold, 1989.

Wegerer, Michael. *Scanning 'Star Trek: The Next Generation'*. Aberystwyth: Dept. of Education, UWA, 1995.

Weiner, Richard. *Webster's New World Dictionary of Media and Communications*. New York: Simon and Shuster, 1990.

Weizenbaum, Joseph. *Computer Power and Human Reason: From Judgment to Calculation*. New York: W. H. Freeman, 1976.

White, Lynn. *Medieval Technology and Social Change*. Fair Lawn, NJ: Oxford University Press, 1962.

Wiener, Norbert. *Cybernetics: Or Control and Communication in the Animal and the Machine*. Cambridge: MIT Press, 1948.
Weiner, the brilliant mathematician sets forth his famous theory of self-regulating systems, which can be applied to physics, closed systems, or the interelationships of human systems.

_____. *The Human Use of Human Beings: Cybernetics and Society*. Boston: Houghton Mifflin, 1950.
Interesting mid-century reflection on the social implications of cybernetics and the rise of modern science in general. Wiener's chief fear is the totalitarian use of communication technology. He sees totalitarianism present in the Communist Party, Roman Catholic Church, and American business and government. A good popular introduction to Wiener's cybernetics theory.

_____. *God and Golem, Inc.: A Comment on Certain Points Where Cybernetics Infringes on Religion*. Cambridge: MIT Press, 1964.

Wiens, John. "Television: Friend and Foe." *The Covenant Companion*. Reprint. Chicago: Covenant Publications, 1987.

A tract sounding the standard content warnings of conservative Christendom.

Williams, Raymond, ed. *Television: Technology and Cultural Form.* 2nd ed. London: Routledge, 1970.

———, ed. *Contact: Human Communication and its History.* London: Thames and Hudson, 1981.

Williamson, G. I. "Entering Cyberspace." *New Horizons* (July 1997) 3, 4.
An uncritical assessment of the value of computing for the church.

Willmott, Glenn. *McLuhan, or Modernism in Reverse.* Toronto: University of Toronto Press, 1997.

Winn, Marie. *The Plug-in Drug.* Rev. ed. New York: Viking Penguin, 1985.
An engaging, articulate, popular critique of television from a moderately Liberal perspective, first published in 1977. Compares television watching to an addiction. Appeals to a large quantity and variety of research to strengthen her case. Focuses on the nature of television rather than content. Anecdotal and parent oriented. First section on television itself is most helpful to Media Ecologist.

Winner, Langdon. *Autonomous Technology: Technics-Out-Of-Control as a Theme in Political Thought.* Cambridge, MA: MIT Press, 1977.

———. "Mythinformation: Romantic Politics in the Computer Revolution." In P. Durbin, ed. *Philosophy and Technology*, vol. 7. Greenwich, CT: JAI Press, 1984.

———. "Who Will Be in Cyberspace?" [WWW document] URL http://communication.ucsd.edu/pagre/tno/september-1995.html#who [13 July 1999].

———. "Computers and Hope in an Urban Ark." [WWW document] URL http://www.rpi.edu/~winner, 1997 [13 July 1999].

———. "Cyberlibertarian Myths and the Prospects for Community ." [WWW document] URL http://www.rpi.edu/~winner, 1997 [13 July 1999].

———. *The Handwriting on the Wall: Resisting Technoglobalism's Assault on Education.* Marita Moll, ed. Ottawa: Fernwood Pub., 1997. [WWW document] URL http://www.rpi.edu/~winner, 1997 [13 July 1999].

———. "How Technomania Is Overtaking the Millennium." *Culture Watch* (23 November 1997) B06. [WWW document] URL http://www.rpi.edu/~winner, 1997 [13 July 1999].

Woiwode, Larry. "Television: The Cyclops That Eats Books." *Imprimis* 21, no. 2 (February 1992): 1-3.
Pulitzer Prize winning novelist and Orthodox Presbyterian warns of the television's centrality as mentor. Focuses more on content and baleful effects of the medium than the medium itself. Influenced by Mander, Postman, and Muggeridge. TV eats children, books, and ultimately reality itself. Beautifully and convincingly written.

Wolf, G. "The Wisdom of Saint Marshall, the Holy Fool." *Wired* 4.01: 124-125, 182-186.

Worsley, T. C. *Television: The Ephemeral Art.* London: Ross, 1970.
"A sensitive, perceptive analysis of the craft and craftiness of television practitioners..." M. Muggeridge.

Zimmerman, Michael. *Heidegger's Confrontation with Modernity: Technology, Politics, and Art.* Bloomington, IN: Indiana University Press, 1990.

HOMILETICS AND RHETORIC

Abbey, Merrill R. *Preaching to the Contemporary Mind*. Nashville: Abingdon Press, 1963.
   Neo-Orthodox. Interesting and suggestive at points, but weak on inspiration—subjective.
_____. *Communication in Pulpit and Parish*. Philadelphia: The Westminster Press, 1973.

Adams, Jay. *Studies in Preaching: Sense Appeal in the Sermons of Charles Haddon Spurgeon*. Vol. 1. Nutley, NJ: Presbyterian and Reformed, 1976.
   An excellent study of the importance of the "sensual" element in effective preaching.
_____. *Preaching With Purpose*. Phillipsburg, NJ: Presbyterian and Reformed, 1982.
   Adams effectively challenges the preacher to communicate with the goal of transforming hearers. He shows us how to apply the point of the text from the beginning to the end of the sermon, avoiding getting stuck in the "way back then," in the third person and in the lecture style.
_____. *Sermon Analysis: A Preacher's Personal Improvement Textbook and Workbook*. Denver, CO: Accent Publications, 1986.
   Unique and helpful study of sermons from Origen to the present (Graham and Nederhood) designed for analysis to help the preacher.

Alexander, James W. *Thoughts on Preaching: Being Contributions to Homiletics*. 1864. Reprint. Edinburgh: The Banner of Truth Trust, 1975.
   A feast from the experience of one of the better nineteenth century Presbyterian preachers and a Princeton TS professor. Rich potpouri of inspiration and interest.

Aristotle. *The Rhetoric of Aristotle*. Translated by Lane Cooper. New York: Appleton-Century-Crofts, 1932.
   First of the ancients to write on the subject of rhetoric. An essential classic which has influenced rhetoric and homiletics for over two millennia.

Atkins, Gaius Glenn. *Preaching and the Mind of Today*. New York: Round Table Press, 1934.
   Neo-Orthodox. Some good insights. Pits lyrical against creedal. Preaching is a quest rather than a proclamation. Hopelessly Romantic in outlook.

Augustine, Saint. *On Christian Doctrine*. 427 AD. Reprint. Indianapolis: Bobbs-Merrill Educational Publishing, 1958.
   Excellent ancient discussion of Christian epistemology as it focuses on hermeneutics. Book 4 is Augustine's rhetoric, based on his classical training, especially in Cicero, he masterfully applies it to homiletics.

Barth, Karl. "The Doctrine of the Word of God" (Prolegomena to Church Dogmatics, being Vol. I, Part I). Translated by G. T. Thomas. Edinburgh: T. & T. Clark, 1936.
   Despite serious flaws in his Neo-Orthodox view of the Scriptures Barth places preaching at the center of the church's life. The "event of real proclamation is the life-function of the Church which conditions all the rest." Otherwise not very helpful.

Baumann, J. Daniel. *An Introduction to Contemporary Preaching*. Grand Rapids: Baker Book House, 1972.
   Applies Shannon-Weaver (S-M-C-R) communication model to homiletics. Interacts with McLuhan, but really doesn't understand him or Media Ecology.

Beecher, Henry Ward. *Yale Lectures on Preaching*. New York: J. B. Ford and Company, 1872.
   Pastor of Plymouth Congregational Church (1847-1874), son of Lyman Beecher. Most influential "pulpiteer" and writer during Civil War and beyond. Favored evolution. Rejected Calvinism along with eternal punishment. These 1872 Yale lectures were interestingly taken

from "Phonographic Reports." Very interesting reading in the context of his "new theology," which sought to adapt the message to changing times. Helpful advice on some subjects, and a very good example of what Reformed preachers do not want emulate.

Bergsma, Derke P. "Preaching for Modern Times." Photocopied. Escondido, Ca: Westminster Theological Seminary in California, 1989.
Summary of weaknesses of contemporary theology. Good case set forth for expository preaching.

Blackwood, Andrew W. *The Fine Art of Preaching.* Grand Rapids: Baker Book House, 1976.
Most influential American homiletician early to mid twentieth century. Presbyterian and Professor of homiletics at Princeton TS (1930-1950). Practical help, especially to beginners. No interaction with Media Ecology or any communications studies. Views sermon as a work of art.

Bridges, Charles. *The Christian Ministry.* 1830. Reprint. Edinburgh: The Banner of Truth Trust, 1967.
Nineteenth century classic on ministry by an orthodox Anglican. Part IV covers homiletics. Excellent part on ministerial character. A must read for Reformed ministerial students and pastors.

Broadus, John A. *A Treatise on the Preparation and Delivery of Sermons.* 1870. New (25th) edition. Edited by Edwin Charles Dargan. New York: A. C. Armstrong and Son, 1902.
According to Jay Adams little has been added to homiletical texts since this definitive edition of this classic nineteenth century work. The Dargan edition is the best edition ever published. Adams himself has amplified a Broadus topic in his own *Preaching with Purpose.* The entire question of preaching as a medium is untouched by Broadus. Of course he was for the most part pre-electronic. Thus the question of assessing electronic media, and applying the conclusions to homiletics is a subject barely touched by twentieth century homiletics.

Brooks, Phillips. *Lectures on Preaching: The Yale Lectures on Preaching, 1877.* 1907. Reprint. Grand Rapids: Baker Book House, 1969.
Broadus considers this the most valuable of the Yale lecture series. Evanglical Episcopalian of broad sympathies. Pastor of Trinity Church in Boston for much of his ministry. One of the most notable American preachers of his day. Deep pastoral concern. Positive, energetic, valuable.

Buttrick, David G. *Homiletic.* Philadelphia: Fortress Press, 1987.

_____. "Preaching to the 'Faith' of America." In *Communication and Change in American Religious* History, edited by Leonard Sweet. Grand Rapids: Eerdmans, 1993.
A plea for change in homiletical method in light of the simultaneity of the electronic media environment. Caves in to many of the worst aspects of the electronic media. Counsels using the logic of consciousness, rather than the linear sort, the logic of narrative, rather than the outline. Some valuable insights here, despite my caveat. But, be careful of reactions to "left hemisphere" thinking, they can be deadly to normative truth.

Campbell, George. *Lectures on Systematic Theology and Pulpit Eloquence.* Edited by Henry J. Ripley. Boston: Lincoln and Edmands, 1832.
Broadus comments: "judicious and useful."

Chapell, Bryan. *Christ-Centered Preaching: Redeeming the Expository Sermon.* Grand Rapids: Baker Book House, 1994.

Cicero. *De Oratore, Orator, Brutus.*
Greatest Roman orator. Lived in first century before Christ. His concepts and practice of rhetoric form the great classical ideal of oratory.

Clowney, Edmund P. "Preaching the Word of the Lord: Cornelius Van Til, V.D.M." *Westminster Theological Journal* 46 (1984): 233-253.

An excellent appreciation of Van Til's commitment to preaching the Christ of Scripture, in contrast with the Barthian idea, corrupted as it is with Post-Kantian epistemology. Van Til's preaching shaped his apologetics. Preaching must always be God-centered and Christ-centered, as the whole counsel of God is exegeted and expounded. Van Til preached to the end of his long life.

_____. *Preaching and Biblical Theology*. Nutley, NJ: Presbyterian and Reformed, 1973.
One of the best books on this important and oft misunderstood subject. "The text must drive us to the pulpit" (19). The text, that is in its infallible, epochal character. A must read and reread for Reformed preachers.

Colquhoun, Frank. *Christ's Ambassadors, The Priority of Preaching*. Grand Rapids: Baker Book House, 1965.
Evangelical Anglican writing with great clarity and persuasiveness. Apart from several idosyncracies of Anglican forms this is a fine apologia for the primacy of preaching the gospel without compromise with many ringing assertions and practical instructions for the preacer.

Cowen, Arthur A. *The Primacy of Preaching*. New York: Charles Scribner's Sons, 1955.
Neo-Orthodox, but engaging at points.

Craddock, Fred B. *As One Without Authority*. Nashville: Abingdon Press, 1971.
Neo-Orthodox Lutheran, who typically pits oral against written, which he considers a "lifeless record." Some good insights into orality, sounding like Ong.

Daane, James. *Preaching With Confidence: A Theological Essay on the Power of the Pulpit*. Grand Rapids: Eerdmans, 1980.
Refreshingly clear and unashamed call to make preaching the first task of the church, with a solid array of Biblical reasons for doing so. Demostrates the uniqueness and indispensibleness of Biblical preaching.

Dabney, Robert L. *Sacred Rhetoric or A Course of Lectures on Preaching*. 1870. Reprint. Edinburgh: The Banner of Truth Trust, 1979.
The best of classical rhetoric applied passionately and intelligently to Reformed preaching by a one of the great Southern Presbyterian churchmen.

_____. *Discussions: Evangelical and Theological*. 1891. Vol. 1, "The Gospel Idea of Preaching", pp. 595-601; Vol. 3, "Simplicity of Pulpit Style", pp. 80-90. Reprint. Edinburgh: The Banner of Truth Trust, 1967.
The best of nineteenth century thought on preaching by a premiere homiletician.

Dargan, E. C. *A History of Preaching*. Grand Rapids: Baker, 1959.

De Jong, Jacobus. "User Friendly Evangelism." *Lux Mundi* 17:1 (March 1998): 2-4.
Excellent critique of Hybels and Willow Creek.

Dennison, Charles G. "Preaching and Application: A Review." *Kerux* 4:3 (December 1989) 44-52.
A very insightful critical review of Greidanus's *The Modern Preacher and the Ancient Text*, demonstrating the folly seeking to bridge the ancient text and the modern audience. Makes a plea for the redemptive historical realization that we are in the NT epoch now. "There are no modern preachers, only preachers." Superb article.

_____. "Some Thoughts on Preaching." *Kerux* 11:3 (December 1996) 3-9.
A brief, terse description of what "good" preaching is. Excellent thoughts on relevance.

Dodd, C. H. *The Apostolic Preaching and Its Developments*. 2nd ed. New York and London: Harper & Brothers, Publishers, 1944.
Professor at Oxford and Cambridge. One of the most influential NT scholars during the mid twentieth century. Put forth controversial concept of "realized eschatology." Despite his Liberal presuppositions regarding infallibility he demonstrates the *kerygmatic* character of the entire NT, and delineates the essential features of the single message of the apostolic gospel.

Eby, David. *Power Preaching for Church Growth: The Role of Preaching in Growing Churches*. Fearn, UK: Christian Focus Publications, 1996.
> Excellent positive presentation of a Reformed approach to church growth with preaching at its center. Helpful critique of the Church Growth Movement. This is a WTSC D. Min. project.

Engelsma, David. "The Worldwide Preaching of the Gospel." *Standard Bearer* (Decemeber 1, 1994) 114-117.
> Excellent article defending the primacy of preaching based on Jesus' statement in Matt. 24:14 "And this gospel of the kingdom shall be preached in all the world for a witness unto all nations; and then shall the end come."

Englund, Harold N. "Observations on Preaching Since 1950." *Reformed Review* (autumn 1986): 51-56.
> Enjoins us to keep preaching relevant by imitating television as a medium. He has read McLuhan but got the wrong message about the medium. Robert Schuller fan—relationships not metaphysics. Part of the problem not the solution.

Eslinger, Richard L. *A New Hearing: Living Options in Homiletic Method*. Nashville: Abingdon Press, 1987.
> Discussion of recent changes in homiletic theory.

Fant, Clyde E. *Twenty Centuries of Great Praching: An Encyclopedia of Preaching*. 13 vols. Waco, TX: Word Books, 1972.

_____. *Preaching For Today*. New York: Harper and Row, 1975.
> Generally helpful. Argues convincingly that preaching has always been controversial, with its share of critics, and that there has never been a "Golden Age of Preaching," even in the nineteenth century. Chapter 10 "Out of the Gutenberg Galaxy," is especially insightful on the use of orality, suggesting a useful method for oral preparation. Critical of both Fundamentalism and Neo-Orthodoxy. Tends to quote the latter more often and more favorably. Chides those who speak of Scripture being "inspired in the autographs" as "extreme objectivism."

Farmer, Herbert H. *The Servant of the Word*. London: Nisbet, 1941.
> Much quoted Neo-Orthodox Cambridge homiletician. "Whoso says Christianity, says preaching" (18).

Fenelon, M. de. *Dialogues concerning Eloquence in General; and Particularly that Kind which is Proper for the Pulpit*. Edited by Henry J. Ripley. Boston: Lincoln and Edmands, 1832.
> Broadus comments: "very readable, and excellent at some points."

Fish, Henry C. *Masterpieces of Pulpit Eloquence, Ancient and Modern, with Historical Sketches of Preaching in the Different Countries Represented, and Biographical and Critical Notices of the Several Preachers and Their Discourses*. 2 vols. London: Hodder and Stoughton; New York: M. W. Mead, 1856.
> An excellent compendium of some of the best sermons from the widest variety of preachers to be found in any two volumes.

Frei, Hans W. *The Eclipse of Biblical Narrative: A Study of Eighteenth and Nineteenth Century Hermeneutics*. New Haven: Yale University Press, 1974.
> According to David Buttrick this work helped revive interest in narrative preaching.

Firet, Jacob. *Dynamics in Preaching*. Grand Rapids: Eerdmans, 1986.
> Dutch theologian. Stimulating study of the pastor's role as minister of the word. Expounds the word as a form of the Lord's presence, the revelation of the name, the revelation of the truth, etc.

Ford, D. W. Cleverly. *Preaching Today*. London: Epworth, 1969.

_____. *The Ministry of the Word*. Grand Rapids: Eerdmans, 1979.
> Seeks to demonstrate the uniqueness of the sermon in the modern world. Liberal Anglican, assumes Documentary Hypothesis and other higher critical theories in his summary history of

preaching in the OT. Good summary of the history of preaching since the NT. Lacks note of authority of the message of the infallible Word.

Forsyth, P. T. *Positive Preaching and the Modern Mind*. New York: Hodder and Stoughton, 1907.
English Congregational pastor and professor of the late nineteenth and very early twentieth century. This book is the 1907 Lyman Beecher Yale Lectures. One of the most quoted books on homiletics since published. Very rich in thought, but theologically deficient. Useful to the careful student. All of his insights into rejecting some of the worst of modern thinking, and promoting a positive power in preaching would only have been strengthened by a stronger orthodoxy.

Gold, Philip. "Getting the Word to a Mass Market." *Insight on the News*, 17 December 1990, 44-48.
Informative picture of Evangelical publishing and music in 1990. Not encouraging. The trend is overwhelmingly toward "Chrisianity is a life, not a doctrine." Self-help prevails.

Graham, Billy. "The Future of T.V. Evangelism." *TV Guide* 31 (1983): 10.

Greidanus, Sidney. *Sola Scriptura: Problems and Principles in Preaching Historical Texts*. Toronto: Wedge, 1970.
Deals with the historical differences between moralism or exemplaristic preaching as over against redemptive-historical preaching. Makes a strong case for the latter being more Biblical. Excellent.

_____. *The Modern Preacher and the Ancient Text*. Grand Rapids: Eerdmans, 1988.
A clear statement against the moralistic preaching against which Dutch theologian Klaas Schilder stood earlier in the twentieth century. A dense student manual by a Reformed scholar in the Redemptive-Historical tradition. Seeks to bridge the supposed distance between the ancient text and the modern world. In so doing he separates faith from history, in a way similar to Bultmann. "For both, the ancient text must be 'delivered' in the interests of relevance." From review by Charles Dennison, *Kerux* 4:3 (December 1989). Useful with the caveat in mind.

_____. *Preaching Christ from the Old Testament: A Contemporary Hermeneutical Method*. Grand Rapids: Eerdmans, 1999.

Gritters, Barry L. "The Participating Pew." *The Standard Bearer* 74 (15 January 1998): 187-192.
Excellent Reformed exposition of true participation in worship by a Protestant Reformed Pastor.

Hall, Thor. *The Future Shape of Preaching*. Philadelphia: Fortress Press, 1971.
Lutheran professor at Duke, who proposes a "new homiletic" based on a "new hermeneutic." Calls for an entirely different conception of the church and the ministry. Counsels taking full account of the new communication studies, especially of McLuhan and Ong. One of the few homileticians who is thoroughly familiar with Media Ecology, and thirty years ago. However, his solution for preaching is an ecumenical accommodation along the lines of Langdon Gilkey's *How the Church Can Minister to the World without Losing Itself* and the World Council of Churches. The church is not a counter environment but a social catalyst for Universalism. Undermines the centrality of preaching. Takes McLuhan in a direction largely unintended by the conservative Catholic. Well worth reading, but with discernment.

Heck, Douglas Van Allen. *The ERS Basic: The Five Steps of Bible Exposition*. Tulsa, OK: Expository Resource Services, Inc., 1990.
Articulate apologia for expository preaching. Quotes Postman, Muggeridge, Marie Winn, as well as many well known Reformed authors, favorably. While not a Media Ecologist, Heck's emphasis on preaching as over against electronic competitors and the "Pop Church," is excellent. Good Scriptural argument for expository preaching.

Henderson, David W. *Culture Shift: Communicating God's Truth to Our Changing World*. Grand Rapids: Baker Books, 1998.

Analysis of Postmodern American culture. Henderson falls prey to the old "then and now" problem of relevance, thus caving into the very subjectivism which plagues our culture.

Herbert, George. *A Priest to the Temple or The Country Parson, His Character and Rule of Holy Life*. 1652.

Horne, Charles Sylvester. *The Romance of Preaching*. New York: Fleming H. Revell, 1914.

Horne, Chevis F. *Crisis in the Pulpit: The Pulpit Faces Future Shock*. Grand Rapids: Baker Book House, 1975.
    Better at describing the crisis than proposing a solution.

Hyde, T. Alexander. *Ecce Orator! Christ the Orator or Never Man Spake Like This Man*. Boston: Arena Publishing Company, 1893.
    An interesting example of late Victorian Romantic Liberalism. Explores Jesus' power as an orator. Already he notes a decline in the influence of the pulpit. Sadly the Christ he preached was not the Christ of Scripture, but the great teacher of a beautiful moral life.

James, John Angell. *An Earnest Ministry: The Want of the Times*. 1847. Reprint. Edinburgh: The Banner of Truth Trust, 1993.
    Powerful, convincing exposition of the specific characteristics of authentic gospel ministry. Loaded with Scripture and church historical references. Exemplified what he wrote, as one of the notable pastor-preachers of early nineteenth century England (Birmingham).

Jones, E. Winston. *Preaching and the Dramatic Arts*. New York: Macmillan Company, 1948.
    Already in the early postwar era a feeling of desparation over the decline of preaching was setting in. Interesting exploration of the place of emotion in preaching. Prelude of things to come.

Jowett, J. H. *The Preacher: His Life and Work*. New York: C. H. Doran, 1912.

Keller, Timothy. "Preaching to the Secular Mind." *The Journal of Biblical Counseling* 14, no.1 (fall 1995): 54-62.
    Helpful reflections on the postmodern situation and how it is a challenge to preachers.

Kelly, Douglas F. *Preachers With Power: Four Stalwarts of the South*. Edinburgh: The Banner of Truth Trust, 1992.
    An excellent inspiration for preachers from the lives of four of the best Southern Calvinists, by a sympathetic and skillful biographer. He emphasizes their imitable strengths. Note the reference to the visual media in my prologue.

Kennedy, George A. *Classical Rhetoric and Its Christian and Secular Tradition from Ancient to Modern Times*. Chapel Hill, NC: The University of North Carolina Press, 1980.
    A rich resource on the history of rhetoric up to and including the Enlightenment. Strongest in ancient rhetoric and homiletics.

Kennedy, Gerald Hamilton. *His Word Through Preaching*. New York: Harper, 1947.
    Defines preachers as ambassadors of Christ. Appears to be a Barthian. Defends the centrality of preaching in church and ministry. Some very stimulating material.

Killinger, John. *The Centrality of Preaching in the Total Task of Ministry*. Waco, TX: Word Books, Publishers, 1969.
    Neo-Orthodox homiletician who maintains that what the world is tired of is not preaching but "non-preaching." Commendable passion for preaching, but not the Christ of Scripture.

Knox, John. *The Integrity of Preaching*. New York: Abingdon Press, 1957.

Kooienga, William H. *Elements of Style for Preaching*. Grand Rapids: Zondervan, 1989.

Litvin, A. Duane. and Robinson, Haddon W., eds. *Recent Homiletical Thought, An Annotated Bibliography.* Vol. 2, 1966-1979. Grand Rapids: Baker Book House, 1983.

Lloyd-Jones, D. Martyn. *Preachers and Preaching.* Grand Rapids: Zondervan, 1971.
Thoroughly delightful popular book on preaching by one of the best expository preachers of the twentieth century. Reformed in doctrine and passionate in the pulpit. The best of the Welch preaching tradition. A must read for Reformed preachers. Excellent chapter on the "Primacy of Preaching."

Logan, Samuel T., Jr., ed. *The Preacher and Preaching.* Phillipsburg, NJ: Presbyterian and Reformed, 1986.
Excellent anthology of essays in three categories: the man, the message, and the manner, by twentieth century Reformed writers, all of whom are preachers.

Lowry, Eugene. *The Homiletical Plot.* Atlanta: John Knox Press, 1980.
Advocating narrative preaching inspired by Frei's *The Eclipse of Biblical Narrative.*

_____. *Doing Time in the Pulpit.* Nashville: Abingdon Press, 1985.

Macleod, Donald. *The Problem of Preaching.* Philadelphia: Fortress Press, 1987.
Professor of Preaching and Worship in Princeton TS. Neo-Orthodox. Interacts with McLuhan and especially Ong. Counsels "re-presentation." Some good material for the discerning.

Marcel, Pierre Ch. *The Relevance of Preaching.* Edited by William Childs Robinson. Translated by Rob Roy McGregor. Grand Rapids: Baker Book House, 1963.
French Reformed pastor and theologian. Clear apologia for the centrality and importance of preaching. Well worth reading.

McNeil, Jesse Jai. *The Preacher-Prophet in Mass Society.* Grand Rapids: Eerdmans, 1961.
Another Neo-Orthodox proponent of preaching. Baptized existentialism with no antithesis.

McWilliam, Stuart W. *Called to Preach.* Edinburgh: St. Andrew, 1969.

Mehl, Duane. "Mass Media and the Future of Preaching." *Concordia Theological Monthly* 41 (1970): 206-213.
Excellent article which deals with problem of the devaluation of words by the electronic media.

Mid-America Journal of Theology. Theme Issue: Preaching. Vol. 10 (1999).
Fine volume of articles from an explicitly Reformed perspective.

Miller, Calvin. *The Empowered Communicator.* Nashville, TN: Broadman & Holman, 1994.

_____. *Spirit, Word, and Story: A Philosophy of Preaching.* Grand Rapids: Baker Books, 1989.
The best of the Miller books. Has some stimulating ideas about the nature of the word, especially the spoken word, and the importance of story telling. His wide reading of good writers such as Chesterton and Lewis tames his reaction to his repudiated Fundamentalist upbringing. Miller is an excellent writer, who engages even when you disagree, as I often did.

_____. *Marketplace Preaching: How to Return the Sermon to Where It Belongs.* Grand Rapids: Baker Books, 1995.
Reads like a television. Perfect example of letting the electronic environment set the agenda for the pulpit. A must read for preachers, who want a good taste of the Evangelical homiletical climate.

Miller, Donald G. *Fire in Thy Mouth.* Nashville: Abingdon Press, 1954.
Much quoted Presbyterian homiletician who calls preachers back to the text of the Bible. Suggestive material: "In a real sermon, then, Christ is the Preacher. The Preacher speaks through the preacher" (17). Affirms historical "third day" resurrection as at the heart of the kerygma, but sounds Neo-Orthodox in places.

Murphy-O'Connor. *Paul on Preaching.* New York: Sheed and Ward, 1964.
: Roman Catholic scholar. Biblical study seeking a renewal of preaching in the RC church.

Murray, Iain H. *David Martyn Lloyd-Jones: The First Forty Yeras 1899-1939.* Edinburgh: The Banner of Truth Trust, 1982.

_____. *David Martyn Lloyd-Jones: The Fight of Faith, 1939-1981.* Edinburgh: The Banner of Truth Trust, 1990.
: One of best biographies of a modern Reformed preacher in print. The better part of his ministry was spent at Westminster Chapel in the heart of London.

Nash, Thomas. *The Christian Communicator's Handbook.* Wheaton, IL: Victor Books, 1995.

Nederhood, Joel. "Effective Preaching in a Media Age." Lecture notes. Westminster Theological Seminary in California, 1990.

_____. Interview by Gregory E. Reynolds. Transcript. Escondido, CA, 1990.

Nichols, J. Randall. *The Restoring Word: Preaching As Pastoral Communication.* San Francisco: Harper and Row, 1987.

Old, Hughes Oliphant. *The Reading and Preaching of the Scriptures in the Worship of the Christian Church: Volume 1 - The Biblical Period, Volume 2 - The Patristic Age,* and *Volume 3 - The Medieval Church,* Grand Rapids: Eerdmans, 1998, 1998, 1999.
: Rich historical resource with excellent commentary, and extensive bibliography and indexes. More than a history of preaching, loaded with Biblical and historical wisdom for the preacher.

Pack, Frank and Prentice, Jr., Meador. *Preaching To Modern Man.* Abilene, TX: Biblical Research, 1969.

Packer, James Innis. "The Challenge of the Third Millenium." *RTS Reformed Quarterly* 18:2 (Summer 1999) [WWW document] URL http://www.rts.edu/quarterly/summer99/qa.html. [April 29, 2000]
: Engaging plug for the majesty of God in worship. Points to Puritan example.

Pattison, T. Harwood. *The History of Christian Preaching.* Philadelphia: The American Baptist Publication Society, 1903.
: A scholar of broad sympathies, deals more with style and influence than doctrinal content. He observed of the sermons of Unitarian Wilaim Ellery Channing, "Defective on their doctrinal side, his sermons rose above the level of his time in their ethical emphasis" (363). Despite a lack of theological discernent this is one of the few to cover two millennia of preahing in a single refernece volume. Divides preachers into four groups: orators, thinkers, messengers, and teachers. Cf. Dargan, *A History of Preaching.*

Perkins, William. *The Art of Prophesying, with The Calling of the Ministry.* Reprint 1606, 1605. Edinburgh: The Banner of Truth Trust, 1996.
: A fine Puritan classic by one of the most powerful preachers of the late sixteenth century in Cambridge. Lots of simple practical advice. Clear standard work.

Perry, Lloyd M. *Biblical Preaching For Today's World.* Chicago: Moody Press, 1973.

Quintilian (Quintilianus, Marcus Fabius). *The Institutes of Rhetoric (Institutio Oratoria).* Translated by H.E. Butler. London: W. Heinemann; New York: G.P. Putnam's Sons, 1921-36.
: Born within a decade of the Crucifixion, Quintilian held first publicly endowed chair of rhetoric in Rome. Chief purveyor of ancient rhetoric right up to the nineteenth century.

Read, David H. C. *The Communication of the Gospel: The Warwick Lectures for 1951* London: S. C. M. Press, 1972.
: Chaplain to the University of Edinburgh. Neo-Orthodox.

_____. *Sent From God: The Enduring Power and Mystery of Preaching*. Nashville: Abingdon Press, 1974.

Reid, Clyde H. *The Empty Pulpit: A Study in Preaching As Communication*. New York: Harper and Row, 1967.
Communication scholar at Boston University School of Theology. Interacts extensively with McLuhan. Suggests a new egalitarianism with "feedback." Critical of the message pulpits and monologues send. No concept of office or Biblical authority. Interesting example of sixties ecclesiology.

Reid, Gavin. *The Gagging of God: The Failure of the Church to Communicate in the Television Age*. London: Hodder and Stoughton, 1969.

Reynolds, Gregory. "Democracy and the Denigration of Office." In *Order in the Offices*, edited by Mark R. Brown. Duncansville, PA: Classic Presbyterian Resources, 1993.
Study of the negative effects of the Egalitarian ideal on the structure of Biblical authority.

Robinson, Haddon W. *Biblical Preaching: The Development and Delivery of Expository Messages*. Grand Rapids: Baker Book House, 1980.
Evangelical expository homiletician. Professor of homiletics at Dallas TS and Gordon-Conwell. Standard textbook. Defends the centrality of preaching, as well as exposition of an infallible Bible. Takes Greidanus, Stott view of "relevance."

Rowe, Gary. "The Living Room Pew." *The Christian Ministry* 12:3 (May 1981):11-15.
Classic example of a clergyman "sold" on TV as a means of ministry, despite being aware of MCLuhan and himself stating that television doesn't lend it self well to the sermon. "Television does not convert: it seduces." Some good suggestions for television presentations other than worship or preaching.

Runia, Klaas. "What Is Preaching according to the New Testament?" *Tyndale Bulletin* 29 (1978): 3-48.
A rich study of preaching through a survey of the homiletical vocabulary and commentary of the NT. Summarized in *The Sermon Under Attack*. A vigorous defense of the necessity and centraility of preaching. Distances himself clearly from Barth's subjectivism.

_____. *The Sermon Under Attack*. Greenwood, SC: The Attic Press, Inc., 1983.
A fine exposition of the centrality and relevance of redemptive historical preaching. He asks the right questions, and gives Biblical answers. He interacts extensively and critically with Karl Barth. The Appendix on "Women in the Pulpit?" is untenable and is out of place with most of what he says in the text.

Schellings, Mary. "Homiletics." Working Paper: no. 4. London: Centre for the Study of Communication and Culture, November, 1980.
Roman Catholic consideration of the place of communication studies in homiletics. Accepts use of mixed media, but concludes with a suggestive statement: "There is no doubt that a very profound connection exists between (sic) liturgy, homiletics, and ecclesiology" (5).

Schuringa, H. David. "The Preaching of the Word As a Means of Grace: The Views of Herman Hoeksema and R. B. Kuiper." Th. M. thesis, Calvin Theological Seminary, 1985.
Excellent exposition of the centrality of preaching in the writings of these two twentieth century preachers, who were also influential Reformed homileticians. Fine discussion of Rom. 10:14 as a definitive text in identifying preaching with Christ's living presence in the preaching moment. This stands in contrast to Kuiper's more general notion that the Word of God is the means of grace, not necessarily preaching the Word.

Shedd, William G. T. *Homiletics and Pastoral Duties*.

Sietsma, K. *The Idea of Office*. Translated by Henry Vander Goot. Jordan Station, Ontario: Paideia Press, 1985.
: A crisp and profound Reformed corrective for a democratic culture in which office is not respected, much less understood.

Spring, Gardiner. *The Power of the Pulpit: Thoughts Addressed to Christian Ministers and Those Who Hear Them*. 1848. Reprint. Edinburgh: The Banner of Truth Trust, 1986.
: Pastor of the Brick Presbyterian Church in NYC. Longest pastorate in American history, 62 years. Enduring power in the pulpit for the better part of the nineteenth century. Classic work.

Spurgeon, Charles Haddon. *An All-Round Ministry*. 1900. Reprint. London: The Banner of Truth Trust, 1960.
: Really an extension of *Lectures to My Students*. Lively, memorable, vivid and fresh as if he were alive today. Spurgeon is always worth reading. His method of preaching from a different text each Sunday is not recommended.

_____. *Lectures To My Students*. n.d. Reprint. Grand Rapids: Zondervan, 1972.
: See above.

_____. *Encounter With Spurgeon*. Edited by Helmut Thielicke. Grand Rapids: Baker Book House, 1975.
: Excellent inroduction to Spurgeon by a surprising admirer.

Stalker, James. *The Preacher and His Models*. New York: Hodder and Stoughton, 1891.
: Scottish minister, professor, and writer in the United Free Church, late ninteenth, early twentieth centuries. Uses topical models, such as man of the word, and thinker to cover the homiletical territory. Powerful Christ-centered preacher who effected many lives for Christ in his day.

Steimle, Edmund A., M. J. Niedenthal, and Charles L. Rice, eds. *Preaching the Story*. Philadelphia: Fortress Press, 1980.
: Advocating narrative preaching inspired by Frei's *The Eclipse of Biblical Narrative*.

Storrs, Richard S. *Preaching without Notes*. New York: Hodder and Stoughton, 1875.
: An excellent treatment of the art of extemporaneous preaching.

Stott, John R. W. *Between Two Worlds: The Art of Preaching in the Twentieth Century*. Grand Rapids: Eerdmans, 1982.
: Evangelical Anglican. Discusses what he calls the "Cybernetics Revolution." A popular attempt to bridge the supposed distance between the ancient text and the modern world: "Preaching as Bridge-building." Useful, at points insightful, but otherwise bland and dsiappointing Cf. Greidanus above.

Theremin, Francis. *Eloquence a Virtue; or, Outlines of a Systematic Rhetoric*. Rev. ed. Translated with an introductory essay by William G. T. Shedd. Andover: Warren F. Draper, 1860.
: Broadus says it "may be read with great profit." Very concise and useful.

Thielicke, Helmut. *The Trouble With The Church*. New York: Harper and Row, 1965.
: German Lutheran theologian and university professor has strong, clear words against homiletical innovators, and favoring the centrality and importance of engaging and passionate preaching.

Tizard, Leslie James. *Preaching: The Art of Communication*. New York: Oxford University Press, 1959.

Trimp, C. "The Relevance of Preaching." *Westminster Theological Journal* 36, no.2 (fall 1973): 1-30.
: Demonstrates the absolute connection between relevance and *sola scriptura*, over against RC tradition and higher critical "re-presentation." The "distance" between then and now is bridged not by re-presentation but by God's covenant faithfulness. The message of the infallible Scripture

breaks through the blindness of modern man. All relevance is based on the Christ of Scripture, not an analysis of the modern situation. Excellent redemptive-historical study.

_____. *Preaching and the History of Salvation*. Translated by Nelson D. Kloosterman. Dyer, IN: Dr. Nelson D. Kloosterman, 1996.
An excellent exposition and critique concerning the Dutch debate over "redemptive-historical preaching". He interacts extensively with B. Holwerda, M. B. van't Veer and K. Schilder. He corrects many of the extremes in that school, demonstrating the proper place for "example" and personal application.

Volbeda, Samuel. *The Pastoral Genius of Preaching*. Grand Rapids: Zondervan, 1960.
Excellent Biblical presentation of the uniqueness of pastoral preaching by a Dutch theologian.

Wallace, Ronald S. *Calvin's Doctrine of the Word and Sacrament*. Edinburgh: Oliver and Boyd Ltd., 1953.
An excellent sourcebook for Calvin's doctrine by a Neo-Orthodox scholar, whose respect for his subject usually leads him to give an accurate picture.

Walters, Gwyn. *Home Again To Wales: The Reflections of a Visitor on the Religion and Culture of Wales, 1986-87*. Aberystwyth: Gwasg Cambria, 1987.
Useful and interesting observations on Welch preaching in the mid nineteen eighties.

_____. *Towards Healthy Preaching: A Manual for Students, Pastors and Laypreachers*. Danvers, MA: Bradford and Bigelow, 1987.
Another unique workbook, full of ideas and challenges to better preaching in a unique format by former professor of ministry at Gordon-Conwell. Eclectic Evangelical approach.

Wedel, Alton E. *The Mighty Word: The Power and Purpose of Preaching*. St. Louis: Concordia, 1977.

Welsh, Clement. *Preaching in a New Key: Studies in the Psychology of Thinking and Listening*. Philadelphia: United Church Press, 1974.

Willimon, William H. "The Importance of Preaching." *The Christian Ministry* 12 (May 1981): 3.
Interesting brief article witnessing the continued importance of preaching in the ministry of a United Methodist pastor. Wrote *Intergrative Preaching: The Pulpit at the Center*, 1981.

_____. *Peculiar Speech: Preaching to the Baptized*. Grand Rapids: Eerdmans, 1992.

_____. *The Intrusive Word: Preaching to the Unbaptized*. Grand Rapids: Eerdmans, 1994.

Wingren, Gustaf. Translated by V. C. Pogue. *The Living Word: A Theological Study of Preaching and the Church*. London: SCM, 1960.

BIBLICAL COMMENTARY AND THEOLOGY

Augustine, Saint. *The Greatness of the Soul; The Teacher*. In *Ancient Christian Writers*, translated and edited by Joseph M. Colleran. Westminster, MD: The Newman Press, 1964.
Excellent ancient discussion of Christian epistemology as it relates to teaching.

Calvin, John. *Commentaries*. 1540-1563. Translation and reprint. Edinburgh: Calvin Translation Society. 1847. Reprint (22 vols.). Grand Rapids: Baker Book House, 1969.

_____. *Institutes of the Christian Religion.* 1559. Reprint (1 vol. in 2). The Library of Christian Classics, vol. XX. Edited by John T. McNeill. Translated by Ford Lewis Battles. Philadelphia: The Westminster Press, 1960.

_____. *Selected Works of John Calvin: Tracts and Letters.* 16C. Translation and reprint (7 vols.). Edited by Henry Beveridge and Jules Bonnet. Translated by Henry Beveridge, David Constable and Marcus Robert Gilchrist. Edinburgh: Calvin Translation Society, 1844. Reprint. Grand Rapids: Baker Book House, 1983.

Charnock, Stephen. *The Existence and Attributes of God.* 1797. Reprint. Minneapolis, MN: Klock and Klock Christian Publishers, 1977.

Currid, John. "The Message of Israel's Plagues: Worshiping Idols Does Not Pay." *RTS Reformed Quarterly* (fall 1996).

Douglas, J. D. *The New Bible Dictionary.* Grand Rapids: Eerdmans, 1962. S.v. "Idolatry," by J. A. Motyer.

Edwards, Jonathan. *Religious Affections.* The Works of Jonathan Edwards, edited by Perry Miller, vol. 2, edited by John E. Smith. New Haven: Yale University Press, 1959.

Kline, Meredith G. *The Structure of Biblical Authority.* Revised Edition. Grand Rapids: Eerdmans, 1975.

_____. "Creation in the Image of the Glory-Spirit." *Westminster Theological Journal* 39, no. 2 (spring 1977): 250-272.

_____. "Investiture with the Image of God." *Westminster Theological Journal* 40, no. 1 (fall 1977): 39-62.

_____. *Kingdom Prologue.* South Hamilton, MA: Meredith G. Kline, 1993.

Lawson, George. *The Life of Joseph.* 1807. Reprint. Edinburgh: The Banner of Truth Trust, 1972.

Luther, Martin. *The Table Talk of Martin Luther.* 1952. Reprint. Edited by Thomas S. Kepler. Grand Rapids: Baker Book House, 1979.

Miller, Perry. *The New England Mind: The Seventeenth Century.* New York: Harper and Row, Publishers, 1939.

Miller, Perry and Johnson, Thomas H., eds. *The Puritans: A Sourcebook of Their Writings.* 2 vols. New York: Harper and Row, Publishers, 1963.

Owen, John. *The Works of John Owen.* Vol. 1. Edited by William H. Goold. 1850-53. Reprint. Edinburgh: The Banner of Truth Trust, 1965.

Schaff, Philip. *History of the Christian Church,* 8 vols. 1910. Reprint. Grand Rapids: Eerdmans, 1981.

Vos, Geerhardus. *Biblical Theology: Old and New Testaments.* Grand Rapids: Eerdmans, 1948.
It is doubtful that anyone will ever become skilled at telling the story of redemption without mastering this masterpiece.

Wallace, Ronald S. *Calvin's Doctrine of the Word and Sacrament.* 1953. Reprint. Tyler, TX: Geneva Divinity School Press, 1982.

_____. *Calvin's Doctrine of the Christian Life.* 1959. Reprint. Tyler, TX: Geneva Divinity School Press, 1982.

Williamson, G. I. *The Heidelberg Catechism: A Study Guide*. Phillipsburg, NJ: Presbyterian and Reformed, 1993.

CULTURAL CRITICISM AND APOLOGETICS

Adler, Mortimer J. *Reforming Education*. Edited by Geraldine Van Doren. New York: Macmillan, 1988.
An articulate advocate of classical education based on the Great Books curriculum. Sees a liberal education as essential to the preservation of democracy. Naive about the effect of the electronic environment on education. Asserts Aristotle's ethics as the only adequate basis for moral teaching. This is one of the reasons McLuhan abandoned the Great Books effort at the University of Chicago back in the 1940s. A must read for the Christian educator.

Adler, Mortimer J. and Van Doren, Charles. *How to Read a Book*. 1st ed., rev. New York: Simon and Schuster, 1972 [1940].
A classic on the importance of reading, especially developing skills in being a "good" reader. Carson (*The Gagging of* God) notes the change from 1st ed. in the assessment of the objectivity of historical knowledge (p. 25). The first ed. assumes that knowledge may be learned, as opposed to mere opinion. The revised edition asserts that historical fact is "one of the most elusive things in the world."

Allen, Diogenes. *Christian Belief in a Postmodern World*. Louisville, KY: Westminster and John Knox Press, 1989.
Professor of Philosophy in Princeton Theological Seminary. A stimulating and articulate defense of reasonable Christian faith against the Enlightenment pretensions of modern science by a Postmodernist Neo-Orthodox theologian. Equipped with a profound knowledge of both philosophy and historic Christianity, focuses on the uniqueness of the Christian faith in the pluralist culture of Postmodernism.

Arendt, H. *Eichmann in Jerusalem: A Report on the Banality of Evil*. New York: Penguin Books, 1977.

Bahnsen, Greg L. "The Crucial Concept of Self-Deception in Presuppositional Apologetics." *Westminster Theological Journal* 57, no. 1 (spring 1995): 1-31.
Bahnsen at his best. On the noetic effects of the fall in its relationship to apologetics.

_____. *Always Ready: Directions for Defending the Faith*. Edited by Robert R. Booth. Atlanta, GA: American Vision,1996.
An excellent cogently written summary of the essential tenets of Van Til's apologetic. As a compilation of material from Bahnsen, it is sometimes repetitive.

_____. *Van Til's Apologetic: Readings and Analysis*. Phillipsburg, NJ: Presbyterian and Reformed, 1998.
A comprehensive analysis of Van Til's thought. Cf. John Frame's *Cornelius Van Til: An Analysis of His Thought*.

Barzun, Jacques. *The Teacher in America*. Boston: Little, Brown and Company, 1944, 1945.
"Barzun fought a heroic struggle against the Germanization of the American university." *The Intercollegiate Review* 35:1 (fall 1999) 9. Barzun was a university professor and provost at Columbia Univeristy.

_____. *Darwin, Marx, Wagner: Critique of a Heritage*. Boston: Little, Brown and Company, 1941.

A masterful intellectual critique of a powerful and influential Romantic trinity: the scientist, the sociologist, and the artist, who helped set the intellectual tone of the twentieth century. Barzun has no answers to the barbaric trends he sees developing.

———. *The House of Intellect*. New York: Harper and Brothers, Publishers, 1959.
A profound discussion of the state of the intellect in the mid twentieth century. He predicts that appreciation for intellect will decline with the rise of the egalitarian ethos. The democratic spirit breeds hatred to whatever is superior.

———. *Science: The Glorious Entertainment*. New York: Harper and Row, Publishers, 1964.
A witty and trenchant critique of the dominance of modern science in modern thinking. Barzun challenges the notion that the scientific method and outlook is applicable to every department of the academy and culture.

———. *Critical Questions: On Music and Letters, Culture and Biography, 1940-1980*. Bea Friedland, ed. Chicago: University of Chicago Press, 1982.

———. "An American Commencement." *Columbia* (June 1988): 49-51.
A witty apologia for the value of reading by one of America's premier intellects. Barzun's commencement speech for the 1988 Columbia University graduation.

———. *The Culture We Deserve*. Edited by Arthur Krystal. Middletown, CT: Wesleyan University Press, 1989.
Despite, and perhaps because of the specialization of modern life, Barzun opines that "in the qualitative, honorific sense, culture—cultivation—is declining." These essays propose a multitude of reasons for the decline and some very compelling solutions.

Bauman, Zygmunt. "The Self in Consumer Society." *Echoes* (winter 1998): 27-30.

Bellah, Robert N. *Beyond Belief: Essays on Religion in a Post-Traditional World*. New York: Harper and Row, 1970

Bellah, Robert N., Richard Madsen, William N, Sullivan, Ann Swidler, and Steven, M. Tipton, *Habits of the Heart: Individualism and Commitment in American Life*. New York: Harper and Row, 1985.
Classic sociological analysis of the American heart, or what aspirations give shape to American institutions, culture and behavior. Focuses on the theme of individualism as it is expressed in various arenas of American life. Profoundly disturbing and informative for the Christian who seeks to understand his world. No solutions are offered due to relativistic stance of the authors.

Berger, Peter L. *The Precarious Vision: A Sociologist Looks at Social Fictions and Christian Faith*. Garden City, NY: Doubleday, 1961.

———. *A Rumor of Angels*. Garden City, NY: Doubleday-Anchor, 1969.
A brilliant sociological study of the relativising trend in Christian theology. Berger challenges the relativizing tendency of sociology by insisting that the same critical light may be shined on the sociologist, who has his own "plausibility structure". "The relativizers are relativized" (53). Berger, however, ends up foundering on the same relativistic rocks in the shape of ecumenism.

———. *Facing Up to Modernity: Excursions in Society, Politics and Religion*. New York: Basic Books, 1977.

———. *The Heretical Imperative: Contemporary Possibilities of Religious Affirmation*. Garden City, NY: Doubleday, 1980.

———. *A Far Glory: The Quest for Faith in an Age of Credulity*.

Berger, Peter L., Brigitte Berger, and Kellner Hansfried. *The Homeless Mind: Modernization and Modern Consciousness*. New York: Random House, 1979.

Berkhof, Hendrik. *Christ and the Powers*. Translated by John Howard Yoder. Scottsdale, PA: Herald Press, 1962.

_____. *Christ the Meaning of History*. Translated by Lambertus Buurman. Richmond: John Knox Press, 1966.

Berman, Marshall. *All That Is Solid Melts into Air: The Experience of Modernity*. New York: Simon and Schuster, 1982.

Berry, Wendell. *What Are People For?* New York: Farrar, Straus and Giroux, 1990.
A trenchant criticism of the industrialization of American life. As a farmer, poet and writer Berry challenges the assumptions of technological progress and effectively maintains that community, meaning and humanity are being destroyed while all of our institutions acquiesce to the pillage which has reduced life to productivity and profit. Few contemporary writers are as crisp, cogent and important.

Blamires, Harry. *The Christian Mind*. New York: The Seabury Press, 1963.
A classic treatment of the importance of developing an intelligent Christian worldview by learning to think and articulate Christianly in the face of modern anti-intellectualism and scientism.

_____. *Recovering the Christian Mind: Meeting the Challenge of Secularism*. Downers Grove, IL: Inter Varsity Press, 1988.
An update of *The Christian Mind*. Not the equal of the classic.

Bledstein, Burton J. *The Culture of Professionalism: The Middle Class and the Development of Higher Education in America*. New York: W. W. Norton and Company, 1976.
An illuminating classic study of the Pragmatic foundation and direction of American education, as it bears on the concept of professionalism and its ramifications for modern life. Not a pretty picture; also not the whole picture, but by a scholar of excellent insight, like Bellah and Lasch. Preachers should read it along with David Well's "The New Disablers," in *No Place for Truth*.

Bloom, Allan. *The Closing of the American Mind: How Higher Education Has Failed Democracy and Impoverished the Souls of Today's Students*. New York: Simon and Schuster, 1987.
A scathing critique of modern higher education by a master teacher. He gives a cogent argument for return to the "Great Conversation" offered by the classical curriculum, or "Great Books." The inadequacy of his proposal does not mitigate the power of his criticism.

Boorstin, Daniel. *Democracy and Its Discontents: Reflections on Everyday America*. New York: Random House, 1971.
A thoughtful series of essays by one of America's premiere historians on what we might call the downside of democracy. Chapters on over-communication, opinion and television are particularly germane to my thesis. Boorstin has his finger on the pulse of one of the great paradoxes of American democracy: individualism and conformity. He brilliantly applies this Tocqueville observation to the trends of modernity.

_____. *The Americans: The Democratic Experience*. New York: Random House, 1973.

Brittan, Arthur. *The Privatised World*. London: Routledge and Kegan Paul, 1977.

Brown, Norman O. *Life against Death: The Psychoanalytical Meaning of History*. Middletown, CT: Weslyan University Press, 1959.

Calinescu, Matei. *Faces of Modernity: Avante-garde, Decadence, Kitsch*. Bloomington, IN: Indiana University Press, 1977.

Carson, D. A. *The Gagging of God: Christianity Confronts Pluralism*. Garnd Rapids: Zondervan, 1996.
A *tour de force* on the subject of pluralism. The first section on the hermeneutics and epistemology of pluralism will be most helpful to the Christian Media Ecologist, and that combined with chapter 4 on pluralism within Evangelicalism for the preacher

Clouser, Roy. *The Myth of Religious Neutrality*. Notre Dame: University of Notre Dame Press, 1991.

Colson, Charles, and Ellen Santilli Vaughn. *Against the Night: Living in the New Dark Ages*. Ann Arbor: Servant Publications, 1989.
<blockquote>A fine popular treatment of the spiritual decline of American civilization by a man who has been at the center of political power and been wonderfully humbled by God's grace.</blockquote>

Connor, Steven. *Postmodern Culture: An Introduction to Theories of the Contemporary*. Oxford: Basil Blackwell, 1989.

Cox, Harvey. *The Secular City*. Rev. ed.. New York: The Macmillan Company, 1966.
<blockquote>"Argued that 'death of god' was the inevitable and permanent future for modern man just before the contemporary boom in 'spirituality.'" *The Intercollegiate Review* 35:1 (fall 1999) 5.</blockquote>

_____. *Religion in the Secular City: Toward a Postmodern Theology*. New York: Simon and Schuster, Inc., 1984.
<blockquote>An unwashed fan of ecumenism who sees Postmodernism as the perfect context in which a "carnival" of theologies may join. Some perceptive comments on Modernity and television.</blockquote>

Davis, Joseph E. "Healing the Fragmented Self." *Echoes*, Winter (1998) 23-26.

Dawson, Christopher. *Religion and the Rise of Western Culture*. Garden City, NY: Doubleday, 1958.
<blockquote>"An essential work of European history that shows how the rise of Christianity altered civilization in the West." *The Intercollegiate Review* 35:1 (fall 1999) 10.</blockquote>

Debord, Guy. *Society of the Spectacle*. Detroit: Black and Red, Box 9546, 1973.

D'Souza, Dinesh. *Illiberal Education: The Politics of Race and Sex on Campus*. New York: The Free Press, A Division of Macmillan, Inc., 1991.
<blockquote>An insider assessment of multi-culturalism on the American campus, by a scholar who did battle in the environment of Dartmouth College as the maligned editor of a conservative student newspaper. Essentially a Neo-Rationalist like Bloom.</blockquote>

Dewey, John. *Democracy and Education: An Introduction to the Philosophy of Education*. New York: Macmillan, 1916.
<blockquote>"Dewey convinced a generation of intellectuals that education isn't *about* anything; it's just a method, a process of producing democrats and scientists who would lead us into a future that 'works.' Democracy and Science (both pure *means*) were thereby transformed into the moral *ends* of our century..." *The Intercollegiate Review* 35:1 (fall 1999) 4.</blockquote>

Dooyeweerd, Herman. *In the Twilight of Western Thought*. Philadelphia: Presbyterian and Reformed, 1960.
<blockquote>Penetrating analysis of the state of western thought in the mid twentieth century.</blockquote>

Edgar, William. "No News Is Good News: Modernity, The Postmodern, and Apologetics." *Westminster Theological Journal* 57, no. 2 (fall 1995): 359-82.
<blockquote>A brilliant article from the Van Til perspective analysing Postmodernism as the irrationaist pole of the secular "rationalist-irrationalist" dialectic.</blockquote>

_____. *Reasons of the Heart: Recovering Christian Persuasion*. Grand Rapids: Baker Books, 1996.
<blockquote>A fine piece of popular apologetics in the presuppositional tradition.</blockquote>

Eliot, Thomas Stearns. *Notes toward the Definition of Culture*. New York: Harcourt, Brace and Company, 1949.

_____. *Christianity and Culture: The Idea of a Christian Society and Notes Toward the Definition of Culture*. New York: Harcourt Brace Jovanovich, 1968.
<blockquote>Two classics in one volume by one of the great literary thinkers of the twentieth century. On the relationship between Christianity and culture Eliot is certainly the place to begin. His Anglican</blockquote>

perspective and lack of exegesis of Scripture warns us that his ideas are not the place to complete our own thinking. Cf. Schilder, C. Van Til, Myers, H. Van Til, *et al.*

Ferguson, Harvie. "Glamour and the End of Irony." *Echoes* (winter 1998): 5-9.

Foster, Hal, ed. *The Anti-Aesthetic: Essays on Postmodern Culture.* Port Townsend: WA: Bay Press, 1983.

Frame, John M. *The Doctrine of the Knowledge of God.* Phillipsburg, NJ: Presbyterian and Reformed, 1987.
> An excellent treatment of Christian epistemology from the Van Tillian perspective. His perspectival approach is a helpful means of analysing and applying Christian knowledge.

_____. *Apologetics to the Glory of God: An Introduction.* Phillipsburg, NJ: Presbyterian and Reformed, 1994.
> A comprehnsive summary with frank discussion of points of weakness and disagreement.

_____. *Cornelius Van Til: An Analysis of His Thought.* Phillipsburg, NJ: Presbyterian and Reformed, 1995.
> A comprehensive summary of Van Til's thought by one who does not dsiagree at all with Van Til. Cf. Greg L. Bahnsen, *Van Til's Apologetic: Readings and Analysis.*

Franklin, R. William and Joseph M. Shaw, *The Case for Christian Humanism.* Grand Rapids: Eerdmans, 1991.
> A stimulating piece on an important topic. Chapter 9 "Worship and Work in the Machine Age" is an interesting historical survey, which calls the church to reconsider the place of the Lord's Supper in the worship and community of the church. The centrality of the Lord's Supper is an emphasis which is at odds with the New Testament. The mixture of Roman Catholic and high Anglican flavor of the book weakens its over message.

Frye, Northrop. *The Modern Century.* Toronto: Oxford University Press, 1967.

Gablik, Suzi. *Has Modernism Failed?* London: Thames and Hudson, 1984.

Gans, Herbert J. *Popular Culture and High Culture: An Analysis and Evaluation of Taste.* New York: Basic Books, 1974.

Gardner, Martin. *The Ambidextrous Universe.* New York, Basic Books, 1964.

Gergen, Kenneth J. "The Self: Death By Technology." *Echoes* (winter 1998): 10-15.

Gilkey, Langdon. *How the Church Can Minister to the World Without Losing Itself.* New York: Harper and Row, 1964.
> Raises many of the most important questions regarding the church in culture. His answers are not satisfying from the Reformed Protestant. As a Liberal ecumenists he is good at discerning ways in which modernity has influenced the church, but has little to offer since his theology is part of the problem. All of his books are most helpful in the area of the sociology of religion. They are also useful in helping us understand the contradictions in the Liberal Protestant mind.

_____. *Naming the Whirlwind: The Renewal of God-Language.* Indianapolis and New York: The Bobbs-Merrill Company, 1969.

_____. *Society and the Sacred: Toward a Theology of Culture in Decline.* New York: Crossroad, 1981.

Gitlin, Todd. "Hip-Deep in Post-modernism." *The New York Times Book Review* 6 (November 1988).

Gold, Philip. "Getting the Word to a Mass Market." *Insight on the News* (17 December 1990): 41-48.
> Good insight into the perils of tele-evangelism.

Graff, Harvey J. *Literacy and Social Development in the West: A Reader.* New York: Cambridge University Press, 1981.

Greeley, Andrew M. *God in Popular Culture.* Chicago: Thomas More Press, 1988.

Grudin, Robert. *Time and the Art of Living*. Cambridge, MA: Harper & Row, 1982.

Guinness, Os. *The Dust of Death: A Critique of the Establishment and the Counter Culture - and a Proposal for a Third Way*. Downers Grove, Il: InterVarsity Press, 1973.
   A thoughtful apologetic for Christianity in light of the sixties counter culture. Guinness analyses the bankruptcy of counter cultural humanism. His best work.

_____. *The Gravedigger File: Papers on the Subversion of the Modern Church*. Downers Grove, Il: InterVarsity Press, 1983.

_____. *Dining with the Devil: The Megachurch Movement Flirts with Modernity*. Grand Rapids: Baker Books, 1993.
   A penetrating popular critique of the Church Growth Movement which analyzes the church's uncritical acceptance of marketing and managing techniques in building the church.

_____. *The American Hour: A Time of Reckoning and the Once and Future Role of Faith*. New York: The Free Press, 1993.

_____. *Fit Bodies Fat Minds: Why Evangelicals Don't Think and What to Do About It*. Grand Rapids: Baker Books, 1994.
   A trenchant application of Blamire's *The Christian Mind* to contemporary culture. Guinness chronicles the damage that anti-intellectualism has done to evangelicalism for over two hundred years of its recent history. A thoughtful sociological analysis of the church's assimilation of cultural characteristics which are inimical to its mission.

_____. *God in the Dark: The Assurance of Faith Beyond a Shadow of Doubt*. Wheaton, Il: Crossway Books, 1996.

Guinness, Os and John Seel, eds. *No God But God: Breaking with the Idols of Our Age*. Chicago: Moody Press, 1992.
   A bold challenge to modern idolatry. The first chapter, by Richard Keyes, sets forth the paradigm for cultural criticism: idolatry. Various authors offer applications of this biblical principle.

Habermas Jürgen. *Toward a Rational Society*. Boston: Beacon Press, 1971.

_____. "Modernity—An Incomplete Project." In *The Anti-Aesthetic: Essays on Postmodern Culture*. Translated by S. Ben-Habib. Edited by Hal Foster. Port Townsend: Bay, 1983.
   Student of Adorno in the Frankfurt School. Seeks to revive Enlightenment rationality by meeting the challenge of Postmodernism head on in Neo-Kantian fashion. Believes in an indestructable core of modernity which will prevail through the defense of reason.

_____. *The Philosophical Discourse of Modernity*. Cambridge: Polity Press, 1987.

Hardison, O. B. *Disappearing Through the Skylight: Culture and Technology in the Twentieth Century*. New York: Viking Press, 1989.

Hart, D.J. "Evangelicals on the Durham Trail." *Calvin Theological Journal* 30, no. 2 (Nov. 1995).
   A scathing and penetrating critique of the evangelical penchant for "contemporary worship." Hart maintains that such a penchant is an inherent contradiction to Protestantism's historic nature.

Harvey, David. *The Condition of Postmodernity*. Cambridge, MA: Basil Blackwell, 1989.

Hatch, Nathan O. *The Democratization of American Christianity*. New Haven, CT: Yale University Press, 1989.

Hauerwas, Stanley, and William Willimon. *Resident Aliens: A Provocative Christian Assessment of Culture and Ministry for People Who Know That Something Is Wrong.* Nashville: Abingdon Press, 1989.
Henry, Carl F. H. *The Christian Mindset in a Secular Society.* Portland, OR: Multnomah Press, 1984.
Hirsch, David H. *The Deconstruction of Literature: Criticism after Auschwitz.* Hanover, NH: Brown University Press, 1991.
Hofstadter, Richard. *Anti-intellectualism in American Life.* New York: Vintage Books, 1966.
This is an instructive study of American intellectual, social and religious history. For all of his anti-Christian bias Hofstadter singles out the Puritans for their devotion to the life of the mind.
Hoffer, Eric. *The Ordeal of Change.* New York: Harper and Row, 1952.
_____. *The True Believer.* 1951. Reprint. New York: Time Incorporated, 1963.
A classic study of mass movements, but not at all friendly to Christianity. Fanaticism was a Judeo-Christian invention. Some good insights into mass psychology.
Horton, Michael, ed. *The Agony of Deceit.* Chicago: Moody Press, 1990.
An excellent content oriented critique of televangelism from a Reformed perspective. Missing, however, is an analysis of the medium itself, even in the chapters by Quentin Schultze, and Joel Nederhood. Presumably they wrote on assigned topics. Horton missed a perfect opportunity.
_____. *Power Religion: The Selling Out of the Evangelical Church.* Chicago: Moody Press, 1992.
Hunter, James Davison. *American Evangelicalism: Conservative Religion and the Quandary of Modernity.* New Brunswick, NJ: Rutgers University Press, 1983.
Hutchison, William R. *The Modernist Impulse in American Protestantism.* Cambridge: Harvard University Press, 1976.
_____, ed. *Between the Times: The Travail of the Protestant Establishment in America, 1900-1960.* Cambridge, MA: Cambridge University Press, 1989.
Huxley, Aldous. *Brave New World.* New York: Modern Library, 1946.
Classic fictional depiction of the dangers of a totalitarianism of pleasure.
_____. *Brave New World Revisited.* New York: Bantam Books, [1958] 1960.
Classic fictional depiction of the dangers of a totalitarianism of pleasure.
Illich, Ivan, et al. *The Disabling Professions.* New York: Marion Boyars, 1978.
Jencks, Charles. *What Is Postmodernism?* London: Academy Editions; New York: St. Martin's Press, 1989.
Traces the downfall of modern architecture, and analyses the distinctive features of postmodern architecture. "Double coding" is the combination of modern technique and efficiency with an eclectic use of the past which is openended with multiple meanings. Edgar [*No News*...373].
Jones, Peter. *Spirit Wars: Pagan Revival in Christian America.* Mukilteo, WA: WinePress Publishing and Escondido, CA: Main Entry Editions, 1997.
An in-depth popular study of the relationship between ancient Gnostic texts and the modern revival of Gnosticism in the church today. Jones demonstrates convincingly that the religious syncretism of the sixties counter-culture has become the religion of mainstream culture.
Kearney, R. *The Wake of Imagination: Toward a Postmodern Culture.* Minneapolis: University of Minnesota Press, 1988.
Koestler, Arthur. *The Sleepwalkers.* New York: The Macmillan Company, 1959.
_____. *The Ghost in the Machine.* Chicago: Henry Regnery Company, 1967.

Koster, John P., Jr. *The Atheist Syndrome.* Brentwood, TN: Holgemuth and Hyatt, Publishers, Inc., 1989.

Kroker, Arthur. *Panic Encyclopedia: The Definitive Guide to the Postmodern Scene.* New York: St. Martin's Press, 1989.

Kuhn, Thomas. *The Structure of Scientific Revolutions.* Chicago: University of Chicago Press, 1962, 2nd ed., enlarged, 1970.
> A masterful study of the epistemology of science. He defines a paradigm as, not a single hypothesis or theory, the dominant worldview asumed by scientists. But when too much evidence challenges that worldview a crisis occurs. Thus as crisis gives way to a new or revised paradigm it again takes on the characteristics of what Kuhn calls *normal science*. Good presuppositionalism within the limited domain of science.

Kuyper, Abraham. *Lectures on Calvinism.* 1931. Reprint. Grand Rapids: Eerdmans, 1978.

Lacey, Michael J., ed. *Religion and Twentieth Century American Intellectual Life.* Cambridge, MA: Cambridge University Press, 1989.

Lasch, Christopher. *Haven in a Heartless World: The Family Besieged.* New York: Basic Books, Inc., 1975.

_____. *The Culture of Narcissim: American Life in an Age of Diminishing Expectations.* New York: Warner Books, 1979.
> A penetrating account of the cult of self in American culture.

_____. "The Politics of Nostalgia: Losing History in the Mists of Ideology." *Harper's* 269 (November 1984): 65-70.

Lawhead, Stephen R. *Turn Back the Night: A Christian Response to Popular Culture.* Westchester, IL: Crossway Books, 1985.

Lears, Jackson. *No Place for Grace: Antimodernism and the Transformation of American Culture, 1880-1920.* New York: Pantheon Books, 1981.

Lewis, Clives Staples. *The Abolition of Man or Reflections on Education with Special Reference to the Teaching of English in the Upper Forms of Schools.* New York: Macmillan Company, 1947.
> A classic account of the dehumanizing effect of the modern secular philosophy of education. "We make men without chests and expect of them virtue and enterprise. We laugh at honour and are shocked to find traitors in our midst. We castrate and bid the geldings be fruitful" (p. 16).

_____. *Miracles.* New York: Macmillan, 1947.
> Beautifully articulated defence of Christian Supernaturalism, as compared and contrasted with the Naturalism, with which Lewis was persoanally all too famililiar.

_____. *An Experiment in Criticism.* Cambridge, UK: Cambridge University Press, 1961.
> A unique and brilliant exposition of how to enter into a work of literature.

Lints, Richard. "Modernity: Friend or Foe?" *Contact* 22, no. 1 (summer 1993): 7-9.
> A fine, concise plea for Biblical balance in the Christian assessment of technology.

Lloyd-Jones, D. Martyn. *Knowing The Times.* Edinburgh: The Banner of Truth Trust, 1989.
> A good example of how a leading twentieth century preacher addressed issues facing the modern church. Lloyd-Jones was an advocate of knowing history in order to better "know the times."

Lundin, Roger. *The Culture of Interpretation: Christian Faith and the Postmodern World.* Grand Rapids: Eerdmans, 1993.

Lyotard, Jean-François. *La condition postmoderne: rapport sur le savoir*. Paris: Editions de Minuit, 1979.

———. *The Postmodern Condition: A Report on Knowledge*. Minneapolis: University of Minnesota Press, 1984.
One of the original purveyors of the word and idea of "postmodernism." The rationalistic universalizing project of Modernism is, according to Lyotard, finished. Cf. William Edgar.

———. *The Postmodern Explained*. Minneapolis and London: University of Minnesota Press, 1992.

MacDonald, Dwight. *Against the American Grain: Essays on the Effects of Mass Culture*. New York: Da Carpo Press, 1952.

Machen, J. Gresham. "Christianity and Culture," *Princeton Theological Review* (1913) 11:1-15.
Originally delivered as an address titled "The Scientific Preparation of the Minister," at the opening of the 101st session of Princeton Theological Seminary, September 20, 1912. A masterful essay on this theme.

Marsden, George M. *Fundamentalism and American Culture: The Shaping of Twentieth Century Evangelicalism, 1870-1925*. New York: Oxford University Press, 1980.
Marsden's first major attempt to explore the uneasy relationship between American Fundamentalism and American culture. Groundbreaking historiography by a committed Evangelical scholar.

———, ed. *Evangelicalism and Modern America*. Grand Rapids: Eerdmans, 1984.

———. *The Soul of the American University: From Protestant Establishment to Established Nonbelief*. New York and Oxford: Oxford University Press, 1994.
Excellent history of the development of American higher education, with a nuanced critique of the Christian failure to develop a Christian mind.

———. "The Collapse of American Evangelical Academia." In *Reckoning with the Past*. Edited by D. G. Hart. Grand Rapids: Baker Books, 1995.

Martin, David. *The Religious and the Secular: Studies in Secularization*. New York: Schoken Books, 1969.

———. *A General Theory of Secularization*. New York: Harper, 1978.
W. Edgar in "No News ..." [366] calls this a masterful tracing of three types of topography of secularization: monopolistic (ala Russia), pluralistic (ala America) and mixed (ala Britain).

Mascall, E. L. *The Secularization of Christianity: An Analysis and Critique*. New York: Holt, Rinehart, & Winston, 1965.

McNamara, Mary. "Therapy Is All the Rage, But Is It Helping?" *The Union Leader* (22 January 2000) B2.

Miller, David Leroy. *The New Polytheism: Rebirth of the Gods and Goddesses*. New York: Harper and Row, 1974.

Miller, Perry. *The New England Mind: The Seventeenth Century*. New York: The Macmillan Company, 1939.
A master of American intellectual history, and a pioneer in reappreciating the Puritan contribution to the American mind. His major weakness is in understanding and assessing covenant theology.

———. *The Life of the Mind in America: From the Revolution to the Civil War*. New York: Harcourt, Brace & World, 1965.

Molner, Thomas. *The Pagan Temptation*. Grand Rapids: Eerdmans, 1987.

Mumford, Lewis. *The Story of Utopias*. New York: Boni and Liveright, 1922.

_____. *The Culture of Cities.* New York: Harcourt, Brace, 1938.
_____. *The Transformations of Man.* New York: Harper and Brothers, 1956.
Myers, Kenneth M. *All God's Children and Blue Suede Shoes: Christians and Popular Culture.* Westchester, IL: Crossway Books, 1989.
  An arresting and incisive analysis of American popular culture from a Christian perspective. As a former producer and editor for National Public Radio, Myers brings an insider's insight to his criticism. He makes a cogent historical case for the unique ascendency of popular culture over folk and high culture in our generation. He also argues convincingly for the superiority of high culture as a more sympathetic purveyor of transcendent values.
Nash, Ronald. *The Closing of the American Heart: What's Really Wrong With America's Schools.* Dallas, TX: Probe Books, 1990.
  A thoughtful critique of American education by a Christian scholar who teaches philosophy at a major secular university (Western Kentucky). His suggestions for reform, especially for Christian schools, is excellent, including a suggested secondary school curriculum.
Nederhood, Joel. *The Church's Mission to the Educated American.* Grand Rapids: Eerdmans, 1960.
Newbigin, Lesslie. *Foolishness to the Greeks: The Gospel and Western Culture.* Grand Rapids: Eerdmans, 1986.
_____. *The Gospel in a Pluralistic Society.* Grand Rapids: Eerdmans, 1989.
Niebuhr, H. Richard. *Christ and Culture.* New York: Harper and Row, Publishers, 1951.
  Classic discussion of the various approaches to this Gordian Knot.
Noll, Mark A. *The Scandal of the Evangelical Mind.* Grand Rapids: Eerdmans, 1994.
  From the same perspective as Marsden, Noll laments the agenda setting role of secularism in American education, critiques Christians for their failure and offers suggestions for turning the tide.
Oden, Thomas C. *After Modernity ... What?: Agenda for Theology.* Grand Rapids: Academie Books, 1990.
  Evangelical theologian, professor of theology at Drew University, converted to Evangelicalism, ordained Methodist minister. Excellent historical perspective. Sees Postmodernism as a new opportunity for Christian faith.
_____. *Two Worlds: Notes on the Death of Modernity in America and Russia.* Downers Grove, IL: InterVarsity Press, 1992.
Orwell, George. *Animal Farm.* New York: Harcourt, Brace and Company, 1946.
  Classic fictional depiction of the dangers of a totalitarianism of pain.
_____. *1984.* New York: Harcourt, Brace and Company, 1949.
  Classic fictional depiction of the dangers of a totalitarianism of pain.
Powlison, David. "Idols of the Heart and Vanity Fair." photocopy.
  An excellent seminal treatment of the relationship between idolatry and counseling.
Pratt, Richard L., Jr. *Every Thought Captive: A Study Manual for the Defense of Christian Truth.* Phillipsburg, NJ: Presbyterian and Reformed, 1979.
  An excellent short treatment of Van Tillian presuppositional apologetic.
_____. "Pictures, Windows, and Mirrors in Old Testament Exegesis." *Westminster Theological Journal* 45 (1983): 156-167.
  Excellent short study of Biblical hermeneutics. Useful metaphor for reading all texts.
Read, H. *To Hell with Culture and Other Essays on Art and Society.* New York: Shocken Books, 1963.
Reif, Philip. *The Triumph of the Therapeutic.* Chicago: University of Chicago Press, 1987.

_____. *The Feeling Intellect*. Chicago: University of Chicago Press, 1990.

Reventlow, Henning G. *The Authority of the Bible and the Rise of the Modern World*. Translated by John Bowden. Philadelphia: Fortress Press, 1984.

Rice, John Steadman. "The Therapeutic Ethic and the Self." *Echoes* (winter 1998): 16-22.

Rosenau, Pauline Marie. *Post-Modernism and the Social Sciences: Insights, Inroads and Intrusions*. Princeton, NJ: Princeton University Press, 1992.
    An very informative overview of postmodernism from a secular perspective. This is a must read because Rosenau packs an enormous amount of postmodern thought into a small space.

Roszak, Theodore. *The Making of a Counter Culture: Reflections on the Technocratic Society and Its Youthful Opposition*. Graden City, NY: Anchor Books, 1969.
    A harbinger of the Postmodern reaction to scientific rationalism. Marcuse disciple. Seeks wisdom from the East and the primative past to help formulate a critique of "technocratic manipulation." An apologist for the counter-culture.

Schaeffer, Francis A. *The God Who Is There: Speaking Historic Christianity into the Twentieth Century*. Downers Grove, IL: Inter-Varsity Press, 1968.
    One of the first books to speak to the sixties counter-culture. More rationalistic than Van Til's presuppositionalism, but applies apologetics to modern culture rather than just philosophy.

_____. *Escape from Reason*. Downers Grove, IL: Inter-Varsity Press, 1968.
    A warning against the irrational epistemology of the sixties.

_____. *The Church at the End of the Twentieth Century*. Downers Grove, IL: Inter-Varsity Press, 1970.
    A warning to the church in light of the student revolution and the relentless onslaught of modernity. A plea for the church to be authentic in a dying culture.

_____. *He Is There and He Is Not Silent*. Downers Grove, IL: Inter-Varsity Press, 1972.
    The third in the trilogy of *The God Who Is There* and *Escape from Reason*. An argument for God's revelation to modern man.

Schlossberg, Herbert. *Idols For Destruction: Christian Faith and Its Confrontation With American Society*. Nashville: Thomas Nelson, 1983.
    A profound apologetic which analyses and criticizes American intellectual culture from the perspective of idolatry. He analyses the idols of history, money, nature, power and religion.

Seel, John. "Reading the Post-Modern Self." *Echoes*, Winter (1998) 35-40.

Solzhenitsyn, Alexander. *One Word of Truth*. New York: Farrar, Strauss and Giroux, 1970.

Stringfellow, William. *An Ethic for Christians and Other Aliens in a Strange Land*. Waco, TX: Word, 1973.

_____. *A Simplicity of Faith: My Experience in Mourning*. Nashville: Abingdon, 1982.

Thiselton, Anthony. *Two Horizons*. Grand Rapids: Eerdmans, 1980.

Tocqueville, Alexis. *Democracy in America*. 1835. Reprint. New York: Anchor Books, 1969.

Toffler, Alvin. *Future Shock*. New York: Bantam Books, 1971.
    McLuhan opined, "FUTURE SHOCK ...is 'where it's at.'" Pioneer in developing a "sociology of the future." Focuses on assessing and dealing with the increasing rate of sociological change.

Toulmin, Stephen. *Cosmopolis: The Hidden Agenda of Modernity*. New York: Free Press, 1990.

Toynbee, Arnold J. *A Study of History*. London: Oxford University Press, 1948.
   "Made the possibility of a divine role in history respectable among serious historians." *The Intercollegiate Review* 35:1 (fall 1999) 9.
_____. *An Historian's Approach to Religion*. New York: Oxford University Press, 1956.
   Chapter 16, "The Idolization of the Invincible Technician," is well worth reading. Toynbee counsels a universal syncretism, based on religious tolerance.

Vahanian, Gabriel. *No Other God*. New York: George Braziller, 1969.

Van Til, Cornelius. *The Defense of the Faith*. 3rd edition. Nutley, NJ and Philadelphia: Presbyterian and Reformed, 1967.
   Presents the essential presuppositional apologetic theory of Van Til. Van Til has mounted the most comprehensive and penetrating theoretical challenge to post-Kantian thought of any Christian apologist. His "transcendental" approach exerts positive pressure on the idolatrous presuppositions of the unbeliever, taking his cue from the Pauline epistemology of Paul in Romans 1. This book represents Van Til's doctrine. What follows is his commentary on that position.

_____. *Paul at Athens*. Philadelphia: Presbyterian and Reformed, 1954.
   Gives an exegetical basis for Van Til's presuppositional approach from Acts 17.

_____. *A Survey of Christian Epistemology*. Vol. 2 of *In Defense of the Faith/Biblical Christianity*. Nutley, NJ: Presbyterian and Reformed, 1969.
   Critical analysis of epistemology in the history of philosophy as the historical foundation for presuppositionalism.

_____. *A Christian Theory of Knowledge*. Nutley, NJ: Presbyterian and Reformed Publishing Company, 1969; Grand Rapids: Baker Book House, 1969.
   Sets forth a Christian epistemology with critical analysis of the history of apologetics and philosophy.

_____. *The Reformed Pastor and Modern Thought*. Nutley, NJ: Presbyterian and Reformed, 1971.
   Critical essays on modern theology, philosophy and apologetics.

_____. *Common Grace and The Gospel*. Nutley, NJ: Presbyterian and Reformed, 1972.
   A collection of essays on common grace as it relates to apologetics. Helpful in developing a theology of culture.

_____. *The New Modernism: An Appraisal of the Theology of Barth and Brunner*. Phillipsburg, NJ: Presbyterian and Reformed, 1972.
   Demonstrates the post-Kantian nature of the thinking of two prominent Neo-Orthodox theologians.

_____. *An Introduction to Systematic Theology*. Vol. 5 of *In Defense of the Faith/Biblical Christianity*. Nutley, NJ: Presbyterian and Reformed, 1974.
   Deals with contemporary developments in Neo-Orthodox and Neo-Evangelical theology from the perspective of the Reformed Doctrine of revelation (special and general) and inspiration. sets forth the basis of Christian epistemology in the context of propadeutics, which is the introduction to the study of systematic theology.

_____. *Christian Apologetics*. Phillipsburg, NJ: Presbyterian and Reformed, 1976.
   A good summary of Van Til's thought written by Van Til himself.

Van Til, Henry R. *The Calvinistic Concept of Culture*. Grand Rapids: Baker Book House, 1959.

A thoughtful exposition of a Reformed theology of culture. Borrowing the best from Augustine, Calvin, Kuyper and Schilder, Van Til calls for cultural transformation under the Lordship of Christ. If not *the* it certainly is *a* very fine treatment of the subject.

Veith, Gene Edward, Jr. *Loving God with All Your Mind: How to Survive and Prosper as a Christian in the Secular University and Post-Christian Culture.* Westchester, IL: Crossway Books, 1987.
A fine popular guide for Christian undergraduates in secular institutions.

_____. *Postmodern Times: A Christian Guide to Contemporary Thought and Culture.* Wheaton, IL: Crossway Books, 1994.
An excellent popular description of and response to Postmodernism.

Voegelin, Eric. *New Science of Politics: An Introduction.* Chicago: University of Chicago Press, 1987; translation *Die Neue Wissenshaft der Politik: Eine Einfuehrung* Muenchen: Karl Alber, 1991.
Marshall McLuhan said of this book: it "is a denunciation of the Gnostic sects from Joachim of Flora [*sic*] Marx." in *Letters*, 237. "Here, one of the century's most learned political philosophers powerfully critiques the modern quest for secular salvation." *The Intercollegiate Review* 35:1 (fall 1999) 13.

_____. "Political Science and the Intellectuals." A Paper presented at the 48th Annual Meeting of the American Political Science Association, 26-28 August 1952. Transcribed by Geoffrey L. Price. *Voegelin-Research News*, 5, no. 1 (January 1999): 1-20

_____. "Necessary Moral Bases for Communication in a Democracy." In *Problems of Communication in a Pluralistic Society*. Milwaukee, Wisconsin: Marquette University Press, 1956, pp. 53-68.

Wacker, Grant. "Uneasy in Zion: Evangelicals in Postmodern Society." In *Reckoning with the Past*. Edited by D. G. Hart. Grand Rapids: Baker Books, 1995.

Walhout, Clarence and Leland Ryken, eds. *Contemporary Literary Theory: A Christian Appraisal*. Grand Rapids: Eerdmans, 1991.

Waugh, Patricia, ed. *Postmodernism: A Reader.* Cambridge, MA: Basil Blackwell, 1989.

Webb, James. *Occult Establishment*. La Salle, IL: Open Court, 1976.

Wells, David F. *No Place for Truth or Whatever Happened to Evangelical Theology?* Grand Rapids: Eerdmans, 1993.
Cuts a wide and deep swath through the socio-epistemology of the modern church. Tracing the influence a variety of cultural trajectories Wells demonstrates their corruption of evangelical thinking at its foundation.

Whitehead, Alfred North. *Science and the Modern World.* New York: The Macmillan Company, 1925.
A ground breaking classic work of the philosophy of science. While maintaining the importance of religion in relationship to science Whitehead asserts the centrality of a Christian worldview to the scientific enterprise.

_____. *Modes of Thought*. New York: The Macmillan Company, 1938.
Six lectures delivered in Wellesley College, Massachusetts, and two lectures in the University of Chicago. Postman points out that this is the first work to point out "the need for a thorough study of the effects of changes in media on the organization of the sensorium." (*Amusing Ourselves to Death*, 166) McLuhan and Ong would later repeat and expand upon this theme.

Will, George. "30 Minutes? Nah, Fame Is 30 Seconds." *The Standard Star*, July 1990.

Williams, Michael A. *Rethinking 'Gnosticism': an Argument for Dismantling a Dubious Category*. Princeton, N.J: Princeton University Press, 1996.

Williams, Peter W. *Popular Religion in America: Symbolic Change and the Modernizing Process in Historical Perspective*. Urbana, IL: University of Illinois Press, 1989.

Wilson, Bryan R. *Contemporary Transformations of Religion*. Oxford: Oxford University Press, 1976.

———. *Religion in Secular Society*. Baltimore: Penguin Books, 1969.

Wilson, John. *Religion in American Society: The Effective Presence*. Englewood Cliffs, NJ: Prentice-Hall, 1978.

Wuthnow, Robert. *The Restructuring of American Religion: Society and Faith Since World War II*. Princeton: Princeton University Press, 1990.

———. *The Struggle For America's Soul: Evangelicals, Liberals and Secularism*. Grand Rapids: Eerdmans, 1989.

Yorks, Cindy Lafavre. "Gimme That New Time Religion." *U. S. A. Weekend* (13-15 April, 1990): 4-7.

Index of Subjects[1]

A

absolute truth · 171, 173, 209, 211, 214, 293, 386
Absolute Spirit (Hegel) · 73
academia · 66, 81, 97, 100, 213
   autonomous · 67
   Christian participation · 51
Acadia University · 107
advertising · 90, 105, 111, 175, 204, 220, 291
   celebrity image · 125, 223
   creates needs · 222
   image · 221, 267
   images idealized ·
   narcissism · 221-223, 225
   television · 252, 255, 265, 293, 363
   theology and ethics · 266, 396
   trivializes · 253
   visualization · 265
   See also consumerism, commercialism
Alcoholics Anonymous · 219
alphabet · 106-108, 117, 142, 194, 197, 199, 254, 258. *See* phonetic alphabet
Amish: telephone · 157
Anabaptist · 395
ancient church · 382
   preaching · 324-325
Anglican preaching · 330
Annenberg School of Communications · 131
anthropology. *See* man
   Biblical · 158, 182
Anti-Christ · 3, 270
anti-historicism · 225-228
anti-intellectualism · 28, 51, 74, 228-231
   definition · 228
   electronic environment · 229, 269
   narcissism · 229
   public discourse · 229
   revivalism · 228
antinomianism · 205, 286
anti-Semitism · 76, 92
antithesis · 28, 41. *See also* apologetics
Apis, ox god · 6

Apollo · 59, 117
apologetics · 26-61, 65, 162
   church · 25, 28
   culture and cultural criticism · 29, 29n, 42
   deconstruction · 236
   defense · 46
   God-centered · 31
   Holy Spirit, work of · 44
   neutral ground · 54
   paradigm for communication · 54, 162
   personal · 43
   philosophical · 46
   popular culture · 46
   preacher · 28, 307, 355
   reasoning · 44
   relativism · 80, 209
   reasoning · 44
   See also idolatry
Apple · 144, 145, 146
Apple Computer Inc · 144
   Apple II and Macintosh · 144
architecture
   International Style · 210, 226, 239
   Postmodern · 210
Areopagus · 17
Arianism · 325
Arminianism · 28
   electronic communication · 291
Asherah · 6
Ashtoreths · 8
Assumption College · 110
atheism · 32, 71
Athens · 32, 42, 44, 53, 369, 386, 390
   Paul confronts idolatry · 17
   Stoicism and Epicureanism · 38
atomism · 38, 67
AutoCAD · 242, 259
automobile
   benefits and liabilities · 244
   horseless carriage · 187
autonomy · 196, 211. *See also* idolatry, man
   man · 2, 3, 5, 8, 11, 13, 24, 35, 36, 37, 55, 72, 75, 209, 235, 238, 239, 335

---

[1] Names of Deity, pagan gods, and places are listed here.

reason · 34-36, 205, 214
technology · 55, 132, 137, 235, 237
axiology · 38, 56

B

Baal worship · 6, 13, 23, 31, 41, 222, 397
Babel, Tower of · 3, 54, 57, 181, 182, 238, 321
Babylon the Great · 238
Back To God Hour · 177, 304
baptism · 195, 196, 202. *See also* sacraments
bardic tradition · 107
Barna Poll: absolute truth · 211
Barna Research Group · 282
Bauhaus movement · 76
BBC · 141, 173
beast, image of the · 182
Beliefnet · 290-292
Bell Labs · 96, 97, 142
Bennington College · 129
Bennington Writing Seminar · 129
Berlin, University of · 68, 73, 79, 82, 84
Bible. *See* Scripture
Bible software · 306
Biblical Theology · 66
  historical concreteness · 388
  practical · 388
  preaching · 372, 378, 386-389
  subject-object distinction · 389
  See redemptive history
bi-cameral mind · 36
Bologna, University of · 68
Bonn, University of · 73, 74
book · 49, 112, 129-130, 157, 253, 255, 259, 267, 272-276, 281, 290, 298, 307, 328, 339, 344, 45, 352, 353, 360, 365, 367
  printing · 68, 121, 193, 226, 261, 274
  rationality and logic · 260, 378
  tradition and history · 200, 260, 387, 394
Book of Common Prayer · 301
Book of Homilies · 328
Book of the Covenant · 9
Book of the Law · 12
Boolean logic and mathematics · 96, 142
Bordeaux, University of · 122
British Broadcasting Corporation · 141, 173
Broadcast Education Association · 132
Brown University · 249
Bureau of Applied Social Research at Columbia University · 90

C

calling: Christian concept of · 49, 158, 180, 201, 206, 220, 222, 223, 233, 315, 316, 323, 329, 356-366, 393, 400

California at Los Angeles and Santa Barbara, University of · 147
Calvin College · 172, 175, 177
Calvin Theological Seminary · 177
Calvinism: rationality · 48
Cambridge University · 68, 94, 107
  Balliol College · 125
  Trinity College · 125
  Trinity Hall · 109
capitalism · 73, 207, 220
Cartesian logic · 34
Cartesian rationalism · 41, 59, 200
cassette tape: sermons · 305. *See video*
catechize · 344
cathode ray tube (CRT) · 141, 144, 258
  immediacy of image · 221
  neurological effect · 251
Catholicism · 161, 202. *See* Roman Catholicism
celebrity · 125, 216, 223, 292, 293, 347
Center for Understanding Media · 119
Centre for Culture and Technology · 110, 119, 126
Charismatic Movement
  electronic communication · 291
Chicago Federation of Churches · 280
Chicago School · 81-85 105, 125
  decline · 85
  influence of German research institutions · 81
  interdisciplinary · 85
Chicago school of sociology · 72
Chicago, University of · 77, 81, 82, 84, 87, 104, 111, 112, 125, 135
choice: apotheosis of · 217
Christ. *See* Jesus Christ
  Anointed One · 320
  antidote to idolatry · 14
  Author of all Scripture · 198
  Author of OT Scripture · 320
  Covenant Keeper · 315
  culture · 47
  cyberspace · 287
  eternal Word · 195
  Great High Priest · 315
  healing power · 218
  incarnate Word · 319
  Last Adam · 238
  Logos · 54
  media balance · 197
  media model · 197

INDEX OF SUBJECTS

Mediator exegetes Father · 195
Messenger of the Covenant · 319
Messiah · 42, 195, 319, 320
  place of written Word in ministry · 198
  Preacher · 61, 315, 318
  presence in sacraments · 202
  resurrected, defeats the idols · 17
  resurrection · 53, 163, 198, 232, 289, 320, 354, 377, 389, 395
  Second Adam · 315
  Servant of the Lord · 318
  Shepherd · 338
  Son of God · 22, 195, 218, 321, 322
  Son of Man · 21, 22, 198, 358
  Spirit of · 320
  teaching ministry · 195
  true Mediator · 18
  unites word and creation · 194
Christian counseling · 218
Christian counter environment
  balanced sensorium · 271
  community · 271
  conversation · 275
  conservative and progressive · 158
  cultivating · 270, 271
  cultivating both orality and literacy · 275
  cultural and media determinists · 158
  developing critical intelligence · 275
  future development, outline for · 179
  graduate education, need of · 308
  heavenly pattern · 271
  importance of theology · 270
  intellectual renewal · 271
  letter writing · 272, 275
  means of grace · 271
  preaching · 277
  reading aloud · 275, 381, 382
  reading and writing · 272
  Scripture · 276
  transcendental narrative · 273
  wide reading · 274
  worship and community · 276
Christian education · 230
Christian media criticism
  content oriented · 279
  media naiveté · 279-281
Christian Media Ecology · 43, 131, 132, 137
  aesthetic questions · 247
  Anabaptist tendency · 157
  anthropology · 184
  appreciates verbal and visual · 246
  Biblical paradigm of idolatry · 1-61, 159
  church community · 308
  communication: covenantal · 180, 181
  communication: Trinitarian · 180, 181
  communication, definition of · 179
  conceptual structure · 183
  consecrating media · 296-298
  cultural criticism · 205
  definition of · 182
  ecology of preaching · 313-398
  electronic media and worship · 304
  Ellul · 161
  epistemological questions · 247
  epistemology · 195
  Frame's perspectivalism · 195
  inadequacy of secular definition · 180
  Incarnation embodies triad · 195
  Incarnation in media criticism · 194
  Luddite · 157
  means of grace · 194
  media balance · 190, 191
  media context · 188
  media critic · 53, 55
  mediated orality · 192
  medium and content · 184
  medium is the message · 184
  Meyrowitz's media metaphors · 186
  multimedia triad · 191-203
  Nederhood's five categories of influence · 190
  oral word · 201
  perception · 183
  personal responsibility · 158
  preacher · 367
  primary media · 191, 195
  response to the debate · 157
  secondary media · 192
  seminary homiletics · 308
  soft and hard determinism · 158
  stewardship · 180
  substantial and ritual theories of technology · 159
  technological media · 195
  technophobes and techophiles · 157
  unmediated orality · 192
  visual word · 201-203
  written word · 197-201
  See Media Ecology
Christian mind · 31, 40, 43, 51, 59, 134, 137, 157, 159, 172, 204, 228, 264
  classics of Christian faith · 230
Christian nurture: images inimical to · 293
Christian theology
  antidote for information overload · 270
Christian thinker · 31, 40, 43, 51, 59, 134, 137, 157, 159, 172, 204, 228, 264
Christian tradition · 215

Christian warfare · 58
Christian worldview · 134, 137
Christianity
   culture · 206
   intellect · 53
   life not doctrine · 288
Chrysler Building · 141
church. *See also* preaching
   anti-institutionalism · 157
   body of Christ · 299
   building an audience · 285
   community · 308
   compromise · 28, 31, 47, 56, 222, 286, 317
   counter environment · 298-310
   cultural compromise · 1
   doctrinal compromise · 282
   electronic environment · 167
   electronic media: communication competitors · 243
   embassy · 309
   Gnosticism · 286
   historic worship · 300
   idolatry · 15
   images · 293
   institution · 299
   marketing · 230, 282-285, 286, 349, 366, 393
   marketing and self denial · 283
   media restraint · 308
   mega-church · 284
   message and medium go together · 285
   naive attitude toward media · 280-281
   naiveté re: cyberspace · 281
   need to debate electronic media · 281
   new humanity · 308
   positive use of Internet · 290
   pragmatism · 285
   propaganda · 297
   relevance · 349
   resisting idolatry · 308
   spiritual nature of · 58, 136
   temple · 339
   television · 178
   transformed by electronic media · 279
   visible · 317
church growth · 282-286
   ads · 283
   easy believism · 44
   electronic media affirmed · 283
   marketing · 53, 282, 284, 349, 393
   narcissistic · 284
   pragmatic · 284
   preaching · 283
   undermines truth · 285
   use of unorthodox media · 285
   user friendly goal · 284
   worship · 303
Church Growth Movement · 282
cinema · 66, 84
City of God · 135, 206, 238
City of Man · 135, 206, 238
City University of New York · 132
classical rhetoric · 372-375. *See* rhetoric
   five parts · 373
   protocol of the Areopagus · 17
closure, laws of media · 187
cognitive dissonance · 52
cognitive majority · 52
cognitive minority · 52
coherence theory · 59
Colby College · 82
Columbia Broadcasting System · 141
Columbia University · 78, 81, 94, 126, 274
   School of Journalism · 99
   sociology · 92
   Teachers College · 169
commercialism · 106
common culture · 5, 19, 25, 28, 158, 184, 190, 233, 237, 238, 306, 372, 399
   common blessing · 245
   development of writing · 193
   idolatry · 238
   media · 243
   recreation · 245
common grace · 19, 21, 28, 30, 31, 50, 58, 152, 153, 189, 192, 271
   covenant of · 158, 181
communication
   communion of persons · 203
   computer-mediated · 154
   definition of · 156, 179, 180, 268
   face-to-face · 192
   history of · 134
   imagination · 245
   individualizing · 268
   mechanized · 107
   nonverbal · 72
   patterns of · 103
   personal · 130
   privatizing · 268, 269
   Shannon-Weaver model · 55
   symbolic · 179
   Trinity · 179
   visual and verbal · 246
   See communication study and theory
communication effects
   two-step flow' model · 91

communication media. *See* media
  magical art forms · 268
  media balance · 197
communication study
  academia · 66
  American context · 81
  critical theorists · 101-137
  critical theorists introduce mediating factors · 102
  cultural criticism · 67
  doctoral level · 97-100, 99, 308
  effects of mass media · 87
  empirical research · 86
  epistemology · 67
  European intellectual roots · 68-80
  Federal government · 135
  group dynamics · 92-93
  history of · 65-148
  humanities · 67
  influence of literary criticism · 101
  information theory · 96
  intelligence community · 66
  interdisciplinary influence · 78-79, 85, 99, 105, 107
  interpersonal · 99, 100, 101
  interpretive approach · 85
  journalism · 98
  landmarks · 138
  marketing research · 87
  mass communication effects · 89
  mass persuasion · 378
  Media Ecology · 101-137
    cultural and literary criticism · 102
    uniqueness of · 102
  nature of media · 103
  one way communication · 88
  origin of mass communication study in departments of journalism · 101
  origin of Media Ecology in departments of English literature · 101
  persuasion · 91, 94, 136, 335
  progressive and scientific theorists · 65, 81-100
  progressive theorists · 81-85
  public opinion research · 87
  quantitative analysis · 66, 67, 85, 87, 88, 99, 102, 234, 236
  schools of journalism · 99
  scientific paradigms · 89
  scientific theorists · 86-100
  sleeper effect · 94
  social psychology · 87
  social science paradigm · 67
  social sciences · 66, 69, 81
  sociology · 134
  statistical · 67, 69, 72, 85, 88, 99, 128, 143, 293
  World War I · 66
  World War II · 66
  See communication theory
communication systems
  channel capacity · 97
communication theory
  cultivation theory · 131
  media metaphors (conduit, grammar, environment) · 132-134, 186-187
  medium theory · 133
  Shannon-Weaver Model · 131
  SMCR model (source-message-channel-receiver) · 97
  symbolic representation · 105
  transmission model · 97, 131
  See communication study
community: counter environment · 308
computer · 57, 58, 128, 130, 142-148, 166, 258-260
  8086 16-bit Intel chip · 144
  Altair 8800 · 144, 148
  analogue · 146
  Apple II · 145
  ARPA Information Processing Techniques Offices · 146
  BASIC software programming system · 144
  binary digit · 142
  central processing unit (CPU) · 144
  Commadore PET · 144
  Compaq · 145
  Complex Number Calculator · 143
  critical analysis · 258-260
  cultural naiveté · 242
  DEC VAX · 144
  Defense Calculator, IBM 701 · 143
  Disk Operating System (DOS) · 145
  early · 142
  educational benefits · 243
  electromagnetic memories · 143
  ENIAC (Electronic Numerical Integrator and Computer) · 143
  first all-electronic binary · 143
  first commercial · 143
  first electromechanical machine · 143
  first electronic digital computer · 143
  first graphic user interface (GUI) · 144
  first integrated circuits · 143
  first large-scale automatic digital · 143
  first memory, *memex* · 146

first microprocessor-based computer, Altair 8800 · 144
first Microsoft Windows operating system · 146
first-generation, vacuum tube · 143
graphic user interface (GUI) · 145
history of · 142-148
hypertext · 146, 262, 263, 268
IBM Acorn · 145
IBM OS/2 · 146
IBM System/360 series · 143
IBM-compatibles · 145
icons, menus, and windows · 144, 145
impermanence · 231
Intel 80286 processor · 146
Libraries of the Future · 146
Lisa · 145
Macintosh · 145, 146
magnetic-core memory · 143
mainframe technology · 144, 145
Mark II, relay computer · 143
mechanical · 96
microchip · 144
mouse · 144
MS-DOS · 145
PDP-1 (Programmed Digital Processor) · 143
personal · 130, 142, 144, 145, 148, 158-260, 258, 263
    CD-ROM · 258
    critical analysis · 258-260
    ephemeral screen text · 259
    history of · 142-148
    Internet · 258
    screen reading · 259
personal, first · 144
propaganda · 242
punch cards · 142, 143, 144
Radio Shack Tandy · 144
random access memory (RAM) · 144
silicon chip · 143
transistor · 143
ultra-tiny · 242
UNIX system · 145
user-friendly · 145
Windows 1.0, 2.0, 3.0, 95, and 98 · 146
word processor · 145
Xerox Alto · 144
Xerox Star · 145
computer literacy · 243
computer programming · 97
    logical skills · 260
consciousness
    moral · 47

consumerism · 28, 220-222, 223, 291
    therapy · 220
content, definition of · 185
contingency: meaningless · 48
coordination theory · 60
Cornell University · 69, 92
correspondence theory · 59
Councils of Mayence and Arles · 326
counter environment · 196, 271-277, 298-309
counterculture · 209
    happenings · 116
    McLuhan · 115
covenant breaking · 2, 3, 6, 13, 181, 196, 214, 315
covenant keeping · 181, 315
covenant lawsuit · 9, 11
Covenant of Grace · 9, 20, 317
    as counter environment · 196
covenant sanctions · 11
Covenant Theology · 388
covenantal commitment · 214
covenantal relationship · 49
creation · 343
    ex nihilo · 189, 198
    medium of revelation · 24, 196, 265
    potentialities of · 22, 55
    recreation · 245
creativity: further reading · 247
Creator
    Author of imagination · 245
    goodness · 214
    Original Communicator · 180
    revealed in creation · 196
Creator-creature distinction · 35, 167, 212
critical theorists · 89, 101-137
    critique of empirical approach · 102
    empirical research · 79
    interdisciplinary · 78-79
    literary criticism · 79
    religious views · 159-172
critical school, Frankfurt · 77, 78-79
    neo-Marxists · 78
Crusades · 327
Cult of Divine Kings · 3
cultural anthropology · 282. *See* anthropology
cultural criticism · 4, 27, 28, 30, 46-54, 67, 131, 209. *See also* culture
    complexity · 208
    distinction between Modernism and Postmodernism · 204
    electronic media · 206
    needed by pastors and church · 28
    paradigm · 27
    preaching · 206

INDEX OF SUBJECTS

cultural determinism · 158
cultural development · 34
cultural environment: media · 152
cultural instinct · 49, 53
cultural mandate · 49, 179, 181
culture · 46-54. *See also* cultural criticism
    Christ · 47
    Christianity · 206
    communication technology, place of · 158
    consecrated · 51, 247
    cultus · 49, 326
    definition of · 49
    deification of · 194
    electronic media · 53
    fatalism · 158
    formation · 5, 107, 154
    Fundamentalism · 245
    gift of God · 206
    glory of God · 49
    God's dominion · 50
    God's gift · 49
    Holy Spirit · 50
    matrix of influences · 132
    mechanized · 86
    nature of · 157
    Noahic covenant · 49
    patterns in building · 60
    popular · 29, 47, 109, 210, 247, 255, 302, 309
Culture and Communication Seminars · 113, 114
cyberchurch: visual image · 287
cyberecclesiology · 288
Cybergnosticism · 57, 263
cybernetics · 77, 94, 95, 114, 136, 261
    etymology · 95n
    social sciences · 95
cyberspace · 286, 288, 291. *See* Internet
    church · 58
    education · 130
    final extension of man · 260
    First Church in Cyberspace · 58
    magic · 288
    undermines theology · 287
    Utopianism · 57, 263

D

Dagon · 8
Dartmouth College · 85
Darwinism · 72, 73, 84
    Positivism · 72
Day of Atonement · 355
Day of Judgment · 214, 355
Day of the Lord · 3
Death of God Movement · 123
Decalogue · 4
Deconstruction · 211-214, 389
    denial of absolutes · 237
    epistemology · 213
    narcissism · 216
    oppression · 213
    relativism · 211, 212, 213
decontextualizing information · 140
Defense Department research · 146-148
dehumanizing · 23, 42, 182
Deism · 36
demythologizing · 375
Denver Seminary · 172
Department of Agriculture
    Division of Program Surveys · 98
determinism: fatalism · 158, 160, 168
dial-a-prayer · 286
dialectical historical method · 73
dialectical theology · 123, 159
Diana, goddess of the Ephesians · 18
Diaspora · 319
Didache · 324, 370
differential analyzer machine · 96
Digital Equipment Corporation · 143, 144
Dionysian mysteries · 75
Dispensationalism · 238
DNA chemistry · 236
Doctor of Ministry: professionalism · 224
doctrine · 46
    of revelation · 48
    Reformed · 28
dominion
    devil's · 61
    new humanity · 245
Dooyeweerdian · 173
Drake University · 175
Duke University · 211

E

earth worship · 235
Eastern mysticism · 217
Ecclesiastical Ordinances, Geneva · 329
ecology, definition of · 152
Eden, Garden of · 151, 181
    holy culture · 50
education. *See also* seminary education
    alleged benefits of computer literacy · 243
    anti-intellectualism · 230
    computer programming · 260
    distance · 305
        benefits and liabilities · 307
        community · 306
        impact on writing · 306
        theological · 305-307
    Internet · 306

negative effects of technology · 305
egalitarian · 83, 229, 336, 337, 385
  preaching · 356
Egyptian hieroglyphics · 199
electric media, history of · 139-148
electronic church · 279-296, 286
electronic communication
  unreflective immediacy · 366
electronic dispersion · 342
electronic environment · 252, 275, 332, 353
  belief · 30
  illusion · 265
  relativism · 192
  simultaneity · 116
electronic highway · 281
electronic icons: mediators of value · 253
electronic mail
  benefits · 262
  liabilities · 262
    disenfranchisement · 263
    literacy and grammar · 262
    no sense of place · 262
electronic media · 106, 153, 156, 283, 343
  alters social structures · 133
  anti-intellectualism · 229, 269
  anti-social · 268
  benefits · 244-248
  benefits and liabilities · 241-277, 242, 304
  Christian assessment · 297. *See* Part III
  Christian consecration · 51, 247, 257, 296
  church use · 172-179, 278-310
  cultural control · 27
  cultural naiveté · 242
  cultural vernacular · 281
  efficiency · 272
  humanity · 264
  idolatry · 31, 222, 235, 268, 400
  illusion · 264
  information overload · 269
  liabilities · 271
  liabilities and limits, distinction · 243
  means of salvation · 235
  messianic mediation · 268
  monologue · 335
  narcissism · 217
  orality · 192, 335
  overestimated · 366
  pragmatism · 229
  preaching · 369
  privatizing · 215, 268, 269
  public naiveté · 280-281
  ratings · 250
  relativism · 213
  restructures consciousness · 229
  sensory balance, effect on · 251, 332
  simultaneity · 351
  social behavior · 133
  stewardship · 248
  teaching nature of · 254
Electronic Revolution · 137
  key dates · 148
Elizabethan Age: golden age of orality · 381
Elizabethan England · 106, 190
Emerson College · 129
Emerson School of Oratory · 108
empirical investigation · 51
empirical research
  communications · 59, 66, 79, 82, 86-87, 91, 102, 104
  quantitative and qualitative · 66-67
  scientific · 51, 82, 84
Empiricism · 34-35, 59
encounter groups · 93
English literature · 101, 330
English Populism · 111
Enlightenment · 34, 36, 40, 59, 79, 148, 197, 205, 207, 214, 227, 230, 235, 237, 245, 258, 332
  irrationalism · 34-36, 209
  metanarratives · 210
  rationalism · 34-36, 272
entertainment · 128, 191, 292
  benefits · 247
  culture · 226, 255
  edification · 247, 304
  liabilities · 247
  recreation · 245, 247
entropy · 96
Ephesus · 18
Epicurean · 38, 39, 399
Episcopalian liturgy · 301
epistemology · 35, 41, 56, 192, 252, 344
  ethics · 38
  existential perspective · 196
  Kantian · 29
  know truly but not exhaustively · 60
  modern man · 209
  normative perspective · 196
  perspectivalism · 195, 198
  philosophical · 209
  Post-Kantian · 103
  situational perspective · 196
  systems theory · 77
eschatology · 30, 50, 237, 400
  kingdom · 22
  new heavens and new earth · 56
  progress · 235
Eucharist · 156

INDEX OF SUBJECTS   469

evangelism. *See also* apologetics
   prayer · 44
   television and radio · 304
evolution · 1, 69-72, 86, 122, 132, 236, 388
   of consciousness · 193
Existentialism · 35, 103, 122
existential perspective · 196-197
Exodus, the · 8, 50, 318
   idolatry · 7
   Second · 318
experimental psychology · 81, 82, 93
extension, laws of media · 187

F

face-to-face interaction · 133, 185, 232, 264
   childhood development · 274
   television · 231
faith: inductive · 52
Faith 20 television · 177
fall, the. *See* man
   culture · 18, 25
   human nature: narcissism · 221
   man, condition of · 34
   noetic effects of · 24, 28
   power of the visible · 8
Fascism · 75, 76, 78, 81, 90, 92, 269, 290.
   See Hitler
Federal government · 134-135
feminism · 36, 289
Field Theory · 92
figure-ground distinction · 55, 118, 185
film · 54, 94, 134
First Church of Cyberspace · 286-291
First Commandment · 4, 21
flood judgment · 238
forbidden fruit · 2
Ford Foundation · 113
Fordham University · 107, 119
   Center for Communications at Fordham · 119
Frankfurt Institute for Social Research · 79
   critique of empirical approach · 102
Frankfurt School · 81, 126
   Fascism · 78
Frankfurt, University of · 68
Free University of Amsterdam · 177
freedom
   boundaries · 117
   idol of autonomy · 35, 36, 205, 206, 220
   pulpit · 329, 364
   technology · 123, 134, 137
Freiburg, University of · 103
French resistance · 123
French Structuralism · 212
Fuller Theological Seminary · 282, 283

Fundamentalism · 53

G

gatekeepers · 89
General Electric · 141, 142
Geneva Bible · 382
gestalt psychology · 92
global village · 57, 117, 140
   community · 308-309
   preliterate · 122
glory of God · 314, 388
   revealed in creation · 24
Gnosticism · 122, 135, 137, 164, 166, 176, 287, 288, 289. *See also* Utopianism
   definition · 56
   self-illumination · 57
   transcendence of space and time · 286
God. *See also* transcendence, Trinity
   aseity (*aseitas*) · 17, 199
   immanence · 11, 37, 38
   mystery · 35
   omnipresence · 165
   ontological · 180
   re-imagining · 36, 57-58
   self-revelation · 190
   self-revelation in Scripture · 35
   Sovereign over history · 17
   space and time · 344
   transcendence · 11, 38, 160
   transcendent and immanent · 17, 38
goddess spirituality · 290
gods · 11, 16, 208, 220. *See* idols
golden calf · 6, 7, 11, 39, 55, 293, 304
Gospel Communications Network · 175
Gospel message ("good news") · 43, 44-46
Göttingen, University of · 68, 94
Graphic Revolution · 347
Great Books · 111
Great Commission · 319, 320
great narratives · 128, 171-172, 387.
   See meta-narrative
group dynamics · 92-93, 366
Gutenberg Galaxy · 117, 332

H

handwriting · 275, 379
Harvard University · 68, 84, 88, 94, 98, 107, 112, 121, 125, 129, 143, 235
Harvard Divinity School · 292
Harwood Pajama Factory · 93
hearing the Word preached. *See* preaching
   dangers to avoid · 346
   entertainment · 346
   managerial cult · 347
   passive listener · 349
   personality cult · 347

therapy · 348
practices to cultivate · 350
   listening for Christ · 352
   prayerful expectancy · 351
   reading · 351
heart · 358. *See* man
   definition · 46
   distinct from head · 46, 230
   fallen and sinful · 14, 34, 37, 214
   intellect · 51
   meditation · 273
   strengthened in worship · 276
heart-head dichotomy · 46, 230
Heaven's Gate cult · 57
hedonism · 209
Hegelian dialectic · 78
Heideggerians, Parisian · 211
Heidelberg Catechism
   danger of images · 296
   definition of idolatry · 23
Heidelberg, University of · 68
Hellenism · 28
hermeneutic: engineering · 306, 307, 383
hermeneutics
   allegorical · 324
   constructivist and objectivist · 211
   relativism, subjectivist · 210-211
Hermes · 16
hidden ground · 55, 103
history. *See also* redemptive history
   Christian view · 226
   concept of · 200
   redemptive purposes · 50
history of communication study · 65-148
   importance to Media Ecology · 65
history of redemption. *See* Biblical theology, redemptive history
history of technology · 86
Hollerith (IBM) card · 97, 143
Holy Spirit · 20, 21, 25, 43, 45, 60, 170, 202, 230, 246, 265, 298, 299, 308, 313, 328, 330, 339, 341, 344, 351, 362, 363, 393
   Giver of culture · 50
   illumination · 166, 330-331, 340
   inspiration of Scripture · 216, 321, 369, 372, 387
   minimized in cyberspace · 288
   preaching · 198, 288, 321-323, 331, 375, 384-385, 387, 389, 400
   regeneration · 44
   resisted · 17
holy war · 7
Hoover Institution on War, Revolution, and Peace · 88

Hot Air Club · 98
Hull House · 83
human potential · 136
humanistic studies. *See also* education
   dialectics · 110
   grammar · 110
   rhetoric · 110
hypertext · 146, 172, 213, 261, 263, 268. *See also* text, preaching, sermon
hypnotism · 77
hypostatic union · 20

I

IBM · 143, 144, 146, 148
   model 5100 · 145
iconography · 34
icons · 32
   locus of meaning · 266
Idealism · 73
idol factory · 19, 39
idols, idolatry · 1-25, 30, 44, 46, 129, 179, 328. *See* image
   Adamic · 1, 2
   allegiance · 33
   antidote · 9-11, 14, 20, 25, 345, 353
   anthropocentric · 32
   apologetics · 31, 60, 208
   autonomous man · 2, 14
   autonomous use of media · 8
   Babel, tower of · 54
   Babylon · 13
   Biblical concept · 1, 27
   Biblical warnings · 278
   broad concept · 14, 32, 34
   business · 221
   captivity fit Israel's sin · 11
   chief temptation of church · 25
   chief temptation of OT Israel · 6
   Christ the antidote · 7
   Christian deconstruction · 236
   commands to flee · 20
   concept of · 1, 2, 4, 5, 23-25, 28, 30
      broad and narrow · 34
   constructed · 32, 61
   consumerism · 220, 253
   control, idol of · 39
   control of God · 5
   counterfeit attributes of God · 39
   counterfeit mediators · 18, 25, 39
   covenant with gods · 39
   creature worship · 2, 18, 19, 32, 33, 137
   critical paradigm · 158, 206, 214
   cultural · 18, 34, 204, 214-236
   cultural criticism · 27, 206
   defeated by Christ's resurrection · 17

INDEX OF SUBJECTS

definition in *Heidelberg Catechism* · 23
dehumanizing · 23, 42, 182
destruction of · 8, 14, 43, 54, 230
discipleship · 13
distinction between god and image · 5
Eden, originated in · 19
Egyptian · 6
electronic image · 267
electronic media · 25, 31, 400
Elijah's challenge · 6
enslaves · 13
entertainment · 253
epistemological tendency · 37
epistles · 18-21
epitomized by Jezebel · 23
exchanging truth for a lie · 19
existential ramifications · 39
Exodus · 7-9
fallen culture · 19, 25
fallen human nature · 2
far · 37-39
final destruction · 23
First and Second Kings · 9
first Biblical reference · 3
first NT reference · 15
foolish · 13, 41
Former Prophets · 9
futile · 12, 40, 41, 42
Genesis · 2-4
God re-imagined · 11, 36, 57-58, 286
goddess worship · 289
heart desire · 265
host of heaven · 15
household · 4
human constructs · 32, 61
illusion · 265
imagination · 246
immorality · 22, 24
impermanence · 233
intentional · 55
irrationalism · 37
Jehoshaphat's reform · 396
Jeroboam · 7
Jerusalem Council · 16
Levitical responsibility · 12
magic · 6
manufacturing gods · 19, 39
marketing · 230
Mars Hill · 17
matter of heart · 15, 33, 45
media balance · 194
media of · 43, 44
Modernity · 52
morality · 21

Mosaic legislation · 4-7
narcissism · 214-235
narrow concept · 34
near · 37, 38
near and far · 37-39
Nebuchadnezzar · 13
Neo-Animism · 235
New Testament · 14-23
novelty, idol of · 225, 266
Old Testament · 2-14
ontological tendency · 37
pantheon of · 35, 36
Paul · 17
Paul at Lystra · 16
PCUSA · 36
perception · 33
Pharisees · 14
philosophical · 208-214
philosophical relativism · 209
plagues of Exodus · 7
pleasure, idol of · 38
post-exilic Israel · 6n
preaching · 203
presuppositions · 31, 208
pre-technological world · 55
prophets · 11-14
psychology · 230
rationalism · 37
rationalizations · 37
re-imagining God · 11, 36, 57-58, 286
religious alternative · 2
repentance · 20
Revelation, Book of · 21-23
Satanic · 21
self worship · 217
slavery · 34
silicon · 58
sinful affections · 24
sociology · 230
spiritual warfare · 58
subtlety in NT Israel · 14
summary of Biblical concept · 23-25
suppression of truth · 19
symbolic representation · 5
tabernacle/temple as antidote · 9-11
technique · 234
technological prowess · 59
television · 178
television worship · 293
therapy, idol of · 219
toppling · 8, 14, 40-43, 54, 230
transcendence, quest for · 207
ultimate loyalty · 14
unmasked · 40

vigilance of church · 278
visible media · 196
visual · 24, 202, 222
visual image, seductive power of · 24
warnings to Israel · 8
witchcraft · 8
wooden · 13, 23
work of the flesh · 21
worship · 300, 301, 348
worthless · 13, 16
Illinois, University of · 69, 136, 174, 176
   Department of Speech and Dramatic Arts · 99
   first degree granting academic unit called communication · 99
   Institute of Communications Research · 138
image and images · 8, 12, 14. *See* idol
   artistic · 287
   beguiled Eve · 2, 264
   beguiling · 2, 264, 274
   Biblical usage · 2
   carved · 4
   dangers · 161
   golden, in Daniel · 13
   heavenly glory, symbolic of · 9
   immediacy · 264
   Incarnate Son · 20
   manipulation · 265
   mediated · 337
   Narcissus · 215
   non-idolatrous use of · 56
   not debatable · 281
   perception · 265
   positive use of · 245
   primitive power · 265
   seductive · 2
   television · 174
   redemptive revelation, media of · 9
   Revelation, used in Book of · 21
   tabernacle/temple, use of · 9
   visual · 38
   wood · 13, 23
image media. *See also* television
   discipling power · 14
   temptation · 264
image of God. 2, 36, 41, 45, 59, 132, 158, 169, 179, 183, 194, 199, 212, 273, 274, 314, 316, 342. *See* man
imagination · 166, 245
   definition · 246
   gift of God · 241, 245, 265
   idolatry · 265
   illusion, opposite of · 241

   metaphor · 246
   occult visualization · 265
   perception · 265
   images, positive use of · 245
   reading · 274
   serve loyalties · 46
   sinful · 13, 14, 15, 21, 24, 35, 40, 46, 245
   television · 267
   verbal and visual · 246
immanence · 36, 37, 338
immanentism · 122, 205, 338
immanentism and Biblical Theology · 388
impermanence · 231-233
   electronic media · 231
   ministry · 233
   narcissism · 231
   novelty · 233
   technology · 233
Incarnation · 22. *See* Christ, Jesus Christ
   community · 308
   conquers idolatry · 42
   final medium of revelation · 20
   sacraments · 202
   topples idols · 43
individualism · 202, 205, 209, 211, 225, 235
   competitive · 215
   tradition · 215
   victimization · 218
individualizing media · 68, 157, 268, 277. *See* privatizing media
Industrial Revolution · 76, 79, 111, 128, 153, 163, 223, 226, 236
industrialization · 135
information highway · 130, 147
information overload · 140, 269, 271
   decrease of meaning · 270
Institute for Advanced Studies in Princeton · 79
Institute for American Values · 219
Institute for Social Research in Frankfurt · 78
Institute of Church Growth · 282
intellectual history · 66
intelligence community · 66
intelligent design · 236
interdisciplinary influence on communication study · 78-79, 85, 99, 105, 107
International Congress of Psychology at Yale · 92
Internet · 54, 130, 142, 144, 260-264, 287
   advertising · 291
   America On-line · 147
   anonymity · 237
   Arpanet · 146, 147, 148
   author/readers · 213

INDEX OF SUBJECTS 473

benefits · 261
BITNET ("Because it's Time") · 147
CERN High-energy Physics Laboratory · 147
Christian assessment · 260-264
Christian use · 290
CompuServe · 147
critical analysis · 260-264
CSNET · 147
culturally pervasive · 255
cybernetics · 261
education · 306
electronic commerce · 220
electronic mail · 147, 262
Ethernet · 147
first became public · 147
first electronic publishing · 147
first retrieval system, Gopher · 147
gateway-network packets concept · 147
Genie · 147
history of · 142, 146-148
imagination · 267
IMP (Interface Message Processor) · 146
information access · 261, 304
interactive · 255
LAN · 147
liabilities: pornography · 264
marketing · 57
medium of media · 260
Milnet · 147
ministry · 286
modems · 147
naive use · 288
pantheism · 57
Postmodernism · 235
Prodigy · 147
relativism · 260
sensorium, new synthesis of · 263
superficiality · 263
theological education · 305-308
universality · 263
World Wide Web · 147, 148, 154
See cyberspace
Interpretive School · 85
Iowa Child Welfare Research Station · 92
Iowa State University · 143
Iowa Writers' Workshop · 98
Iowa, University of · 98, 136, 138
School of Journalism · 98, 99
irrationalism · 34-36, 37, 38, 48, 205, 209, 237
Israel · 6
restoration · 320
typological kingdom · 194, 199

I-thou relationship · 48
Ivy League · 68
J
Jacksonian populism · 282
Jesus Christ. *See* Christ
antidote to idolatry · 14, 20, 25
center of history · 43
express image of God · 20
Incarnation: condescension · 342
Judge · 43
Lord of media · 44
Mediator · 178
Prophet-Preacher · 320
Servant of the LORD · 358
Johns Hopkins University · 69
journalism · 98, 100, 105
origin of mass communication study · 101
sociology · 99
teaching of · 99
See also newspaper
Jubilee · 355
judgment of God · 3, 30, 214, 238, 318, 355
Jupiter · 16
K
Kate Smith War Bond drive · 91
KDKA radio, Pittsburgh · 90
kerygma · 370, 377
Keynesian economics · 99
King James Version
reading aloud · 275, 381, 382
L
L'Abri Fellowship · 29, 209
language · 57, 77, 104, 121, 179-181, 185, 186, 259, 263, 264, 266, 295, 343,
ancient · 197, 199
Christian concept · 179-181
metaphor · 246
preaching · 363, 374, 381, 382, 390, 394
ultimate immutable referent · 212
law of non-contradiction · 35
laws of media · 187-188
Lazarsfeld-Stanton Program-Analyzer · 90
learning: Moses in Egypt · 274
Leipzig, University of · 74, 82, 98
letter writing · 275
Levitical priests · 318
teaching function · 319
Liberal naturalism · 136
Liberal rationalism: bankruptcy · 217
Liberal theology · 36, 122, 136, 338
Liberalism: political · 110, 205
Librarian of Congress · 98, 125, 255
computers · 261
Library of Congress, 262

Experimental Division for the Study of
  War-Time Communication · 87
mass communication study, origin of · 98
Office of Facts and Figures · 98
literacy · 192-194, 222, 253
  absence in Medieval world · 328
  Bible fosters · 230
  constitutional republic · 255
  electronic mail · 262
  Greeks not first · 194
  Havelock · 107-108
  illiteracy · 382, 390
  McLuhan · 168
  Ong · 170, 175, 190, 192-194
  orality · 108
  phonetic alphabet · 106-108, 117, 142, 194, 197, 199, 254, 258
  preaching fosters · 331
  pre-Gutenberg · 335
  preservation · 272, 275, 298
  secondary · 333
  sixteenth century · 331
  social interaction enhanced · 268
  television · 253, 254
  text and nontextual media · 253
  word processing · 259
  See also book, reading
literary criticism · 104
  communication study · 79, 101, 110, 170
  Deconstruction: relativism · 211
liturgy · 170, 301, 350
Logos: divine · 54
Lord's Day · 201, 351, 352
  antidote to idolatry · 353
Lord's Supper · 16, 196
  senses · 202
  idol feasts · 20

M

ma'at · 7
machina sapiens · 86
machine: new messiah · 280
Macy Foundation Conferences · 95, 114
Madison Avenue · 8, 125, 134, 295
magic rituals · 5
man
  autonomous · 2, 14, 35, 36, 67, 205, 206, 220, 237, 239, 335
  creatively constructive · 54, 179
  cultural calling · 316
  deification of · 182
  fallen · 5, 42
  finite · 45
  heart · 45, 183
  idolatrous: creates God-substitutes · 24

image of God · 36, 41, 45, 59, 132, 158, 169, 179, 183, 194, 199, 212, 273, 274, 314, 316, 342
  intuitive and rational · 192
image of God distorted by idols · 42
image of God: wider sense · 47
intellectual capacities · 45, 46, 191
mind-body relationship · 219
ontological nature · 183
rationality · 45, 46, 191
receptively reconstructive · 54, 179
redeemed to conform to Christ's image · 20
self-salvation · 234
sense of deity (*sensus deitatis*) · 40
soul · 45
transcendence, need for · 183
vice-gerent · 3, 198
will · 45
Manchester, University of, Institute of Science and Technology · 270
Manitoba, University of · 109
Marburg, University of · 103
Marconi Wireless Telegraph · 141
Marietta College · 97
market research · 87, 90, 92, 100, 134
marketing · 53, 145, 230, 282-285, 286, 366, 393. *See also* advertising, commercialism
  Internet · 57
  television · 254, 255
marketing the church · 230, 282-285, 286, 349, 366, 393. *See also* church growth
Mars Hill · 17, 45, 165, 369, 390
Mars Hill Audio · 29
Marxism · 57, 73, 83, 123, 159
mass communication · 87, 207, 269, 270
  effects · 89-92, 100, 102
  information messiah · 270
  manipulating a mass audience · 91
  Medieval image · 291
mass communication research · 82, 84, 90-94, 98, 99, 101, 132, 175
mass media · 73, 177, 299
  celebrity · 216
  commercialism · 135
  conformity · 267
  democratizing · 210
  effect on church · 297
  empirical research · 102
  establishment control · 78
  gatekeepers · 89
  image, primacy of · 221
  images · 125
  interpersonal relationship · 91

INDEX OF SUBJECTS

Lippmann · 88
media agenda · 89
media formats · 207
narcissism · 221
personal influence · 102
pluralizing · 210
propaganda · 124, 269
pseudo-event · 89
public opinion · 85, 89
sense of community · 82, 83
social institutions · 207
two way · 91
mass-society: concept of · 102
Masterpiece Theatre · 175
materialism · 78
materialistic science · 74
mathematics · 59, 66, 90, 95, 96
Mayo clinic · 361
McCombs-Shaw content analysis · 89
McMaster University · 104
Me Generation · 215
means of grace · 166, 198, 271, 298, 299, 317, 353. *See also* church, sacraments
   counseling · 218
   media balance · 190, 194, 195
   preaching: primary · 201, 314, 317, 334, 385. *See* preaching
   Roman Catholic view · 170
mechanized culture · 86
media. *See* medium, media theory
   benefits and liabilities · 241-277, 242, 281
   bias · 204
   chosen by God for special revelation · 25
   commercial · 135
   conduits of information · 103, 114, 156, 176, 206
   content · 117
   content analysis · 89
   context · 117
   determining culture
      conservative and progressive · 152
      hard and soft determinism · 152-153
   environment ·115, 116
   just tools · 58
   natural · 314
   nature of · 91, 107, 115, 117, 118, 131, 157, 168, 174, 210, 279, 304, 374
      transmission and ritual theories · 156
   neutral tools · 281
   presuppositions · 298
   primary · 190, 191, 195, 203
   social context · 11, 117, 188, 190, 207
   social structure · 154

   theory and criticism · 65, 101-137, 151-203
   violent content · 251
media consciousness · 208
media criticism · 47, 101-137, 107, 129, 151-203, 185
   McLuhan paradigm · 118
   synthetic approach · 134
   types of · 153
media culture · 208
media determinism · 105, 131, 153, 154, 158, 172
   conservative and progressive · 153
Media Ecology · 96, 97, 101, 119, 131, 132, 182. *See* Christian Media Ecology
   anthropology · 184
   Christian assumptions · 125, 134, 137, 179-203
   contemporary voices · 126-137
   critical of writing and print · 200
   definition · 152, 180
   founders · 103-126
   lack of a unified theory · 137
   Lippmann · 89
   media balance · 191-193, 251
   media criticism · 159
   nature of media · 103
   religion · 151, 159-179
   social context · 103
   stewardship · 152
Media Ecology Association · 119
Media Ecology Program at NYU · 127, 139
media fantasy. *See* media
   antidote to · 151
media theory · 131, 151-158. *See* media
   Christian view · 157
   conservative and progressive · 152-153
   determinism: hard and soft · 152-153
   grammar shapes perception · 186
   instrumental and substantive theories · 152, 154
   social context · 11, 117, 188, 190, 207
   social structure · 185, 189
   technophobes and technophiles · 152
   transmission and ritual theories · 152, 156
mediating institutions · 218
Mediator · 14, 178, 238, 328, 355, 398
   alternative image · 20
   counterfeit · 18, 25, 39, 253
   exegetes Father · 195
   Lord of media · 44
   medium · 298
   threefold office · 194
   See Christ, Jesus Christ

Medieval church · 68, 194
   preaching · 326-328
   rise of the university · 68
medium. *See* media
   classical rhetoric · 61
   closely associated with message · 24
   conduit, grammar, environment · 132-134, 185-187
   context · 188
   definition · 333
   inherent tendencies of · 157
   metaphor · 346
   nature of · 296
   shapes perception · 55
   technology · 55
mega-church · 284
Mercury · 16
Messiah · 16, 42, 43, 195 319, 320
   counterfeit · 270, 280
   office of · 359. *See* Christ
metalanguages · 389
metanarratives · 207, 210, 389
metaphor · 111, 134, 160, 182, 185, 186-187, 199, 238, 246, 248, 315, 346, 391, 394. *See also* symbol
Metropolitan Community Church of San Diego · 284
Michigan State University · 69
Michigan, University of · 96, 129
Micro Instrumentation Telemetry Systems · 144
micro-narratives · 207
Microsoft · 144, 146
Middle Ages: image · 291
Millennium Bug, Y2K · 158
mind: renewing · 46, 271, 392
minister of the Word · 177, 201, 220, 348, 353, 356-361, 367, 368, 376
   idea of office · 356-361
   OT opposition to idolatry · 13
   See preacher
ministry · 195, 198, 305, 309, 313-398
   congregational expectations · 224
   impermanence · 233
   marketing techniques · 282
   professionalism · 223-225, 233
   television and Internet · 280, 292, 305
Minnesota, University of · 69, 147
missions: Third-World · 282
MIT · 92, 95, 96, 114, 136
modern literature · 110
modern science · 41, 48. *See* science
Modernism · 36, 204, 209, 214, 220, 343
   hubris · 239

   International Style · 210
   rationalism · 205, 212
Moloch · 15
monotheism · 57
Montpellier, University of · 122
Morrill Act · 69
Mosaic covenant · 4, 316, 318
   codified in writing · 194
   visual media · 203
   idolatry · 4
Mother of Harlots · 22, 23
Mount Holyoke College · 129
movies · 141, 148. *See* cinema
   history of · 139
multimedia triad · 191-203
mystery · 35, 52
   elevation of · 41
   ultimacy of · 38, 39

N

narcissism · 209, 214-233, 291
   anti-historicism · 225
   anti-intellectualism · 228-231
   consumerism · 220-222
   impermanence · 231-234
   novelty · 225-228
   pragmatism · 234
   professionalism · 222-225
   progress · 226
   psychotherapy · 217
   relationships · 233
   relativism · 215
   rise of electronic media · 227
   therapy · 217-220
Narcissus · 4, 215, 216
narrative
   great · 128, 171-172, 387
   meta · 207-208, 210, 389
   micro · 207
   preaching · 380
   redemptive · 200, 273, 276, 386-390
National Association of Broadcasters · 132
National Broadcasting Company · 141
National Museum of History and Technology · 125
National Public Radio · 29
National Sales Executives · 220
National Socialism · 79
natural revelation · 387. *See* revelation
naturalism · 209
Nazism · 79, 90, 92
Neilson ratings · 293
Neo-Conservativism · 207, 214, 217
Neo-Enlightenment · 217
Neo-Orthodoxy · 36, 122, 123, 159, 160

INDEX OF SUBJECTS 477

Neo-Paganism · 222, 289
Neo-Platonism · 36, 166
New Age · 111, 217, 219, 265, 287
New Covenant · 9, 314, 315, 319
   final intrusion of Mediator · 238
   visible media, sacraments · 196
New Criticism · 108, 109
New Hampshire, University of · 69, 119, 132
New Hermeneutic · 210, 226
   challenges Modernist rationalism · 212
   relativism · 211
New Jerusalem · 21
New School for Social Research · 81, 85, 119
New Testament · 25, 33, 151, 170, 173, 280, 288, 291, 317, 370, 376, 377, 378, 387, 393, 395, 396, 399
   final revelation · 195
   idolatry · 14-23
   preaching: primacy · 319-323
   orality of text · 321
new tribalism · 108
New York University · 119, 127, 132, 139
   Department of Culture and Communication · 119, 127
news as entertainment · 173
newspaper · 79, 82, 83, 84, 140, 187, 210, 248. *See also* journalism
   entertainment · 255
Newtonian physics · 41, 59
nihilism · 40, 74-76
Noahic covenant · 190, 206, 238, 243, 264
noosphere · 122
normal science · 89
normative perspective · 195-196
novelty · 42, 225-228, 263, 269, 301
   anti-historicism · 225-228
   idol of · 266
   impermanence · 233
   intellectual · 43
   rhetoric · 226
   television · 227
Now Generation · 225

O

occult · 18, 56, 265
   challenged by preaching · 369
   motifs of modernity · 208
   rediscovering tradition · 230
   waning of modernity · 230
office (church): definition · 359. *See* preacher
Office of Radio Research at Columbia University · 90
Office of Radio Research at Princeton University · 90
Office of War Information

Surveys Division · 98
Old Covenant · 20, 317, 318, 320
   craftsmanship · 246
   place of written Word · 198
   typology · 324
   visible media · 196
Old Testament · 21, 23, 25, 32, 42, 126, 171, 195, 267, 287, 280, 299, 320, 324, 371
   idolatry · 2-14
   preaching: primacy · 317-319
   orality of text · 319
Olivet discourse · 320
ontology · 41, 56, 103
oral cultures · 192, 194, 316, 352
oral memory · 107, 381
oral tradition · 106, 107, 328, 375
   primacy of · 200
orality · 121, 170, 171, 190, 193, 321, 332
   ancient church · 324, 325
   ancient world · 335
   catechizing · 344
   electronic media · 192
   insures fixity · 201
   literacy · 108, 192, 275
   preaching · 321, 378-383, 386
   pre-Gutenberg · 325, 335
   primacy of · 192, 197
   primary and secondary distinction · 191n, 192, 333, 258
   space · 343
   voice · 342
original sin · 135. *See also* man
Orthodox Presbyterian Church · 290
overhead projectors · 366. *See also* preaching
   preaching and worship · 202, 305, 350
Oxford University · 68, 328
   Balliol College · 125
ox-god, Canaanite · 6, 7

P

Padua, University of · 68
pagan culture · 53
   Egypt · 7
paganism · 6, 38, 222. *See also* idol
   rebirth in modern culture · 75, 222
Pagan/Wiccan Religion · 291
Palo Alto Group · 77, 95
pantheism · 57
Paradise · 37, 135, 235, 239, 316
Paris, University of · 68, 122
patterns of access · 133
Pennsylvania, University of · 131, 143
Pentecost · 315, 321

perception · 2, 25, 33, 35, 41, 55, 92, 117, 118, 169, 176, 178, 183, 186, 191, 196, 229, 249, 260, 265, 271, 336, 386
  imagination · 246
persuasion research · 94
phenomenology · 103, 122
philosophy. *See also* apologetics
  post-Kantian · 40
  problem of unity and diversity · 35
philosophy of history · 30
  Augustinian · 226, 237, 238
philosophy of technology · 68
phonetic alphabet · 117, 199,
  balance of sensorium · 106, 107, 258
  Canaanite and Phoenician origins of · 108
  Greek origin of · 108, 142, 194, 197, 254
  See alphabet, text, writing
Pisidian Antioch · 322
plagues of Egypt · 7, 8, 21
Plato's cave · 267
plausibility structures · 52, 53, 208, 214
pluralism · 52
polls and surveys: public-perception · 89, 100
polytheism · 74
Pontifical Institute of Medieval Studies · 164
popular culture · 29, 47, 109, 210, 309
  dominance · 247, 255
  worship · 302
Positivism · 70, 71, 72, 78, 81, 230
Post Structuralism · 389
post-Kantian thought · 74, 103, 172, 289
  immanentism · 57
Postmillenial eschatology · 140
Postmodernism · 35, 36, 51, 204-240, 343
  anti-historicism · 200
  architecture · 210
  communication, end of · 213
  counterculture · 204
  culture · 130
  cynicism · 227
  dehumanizing · 235
  epistemological challenge · 34
  epistemology · 210, 214
  Internet · 263
  irrationalism · 205, 209
  metanarratives, end of · 210
  narcissism · 217
  reactionary · 235
  Romanticism, roots in · 205
  Scripture · 288
  tolerance · 266
Pragmatism · 82, 83, 84, 134, 136, 229, 234, 235, 296
  narcissism · 234-236

Pragmatism, French · 70
Prague, University of · 79, 327
prayer · 11, 25, 108, 159, 189, 262, 285, 298, 301, 317, 327, 400
  evangelism · 44
  hearing preaching · 349-351
  preaching · 342, 359, 366, 373, 383-385
  reasoning · 44
  worship · 351
preacher · 313-398. *See* preaching, sermon
  ambassador of Christ · 329, 338, 341, 346, 377, 390
  celebrity · 292, 293, 347, 348, 362
  Christian Media Ecologist · 367
  criticism · 337
  entertainer · 346
  herald · 315, 330, 336, 338, 365, 370, 374, 393
  integrity: moral and spiritual · 361-365
    scandal · 295, 362
  office of minister · 356-361, 359
  pastoral care · 337
  pastoral presence · 340
  professionalism · 223-225, 356
  pulpit freedom · 329, 364
  servant of the Lord · 201, 318, 338-342, 343, 353, 358, 372, 374, 400
  television eliminates presence · 294
  trumpeter of God · 354-355
  undershepherd · 339, 391
  vicar · 341
preaching · 313-398. *See* preacher
  acoustic event · 344
  acting prophets · 367
  allegorical · 324
  ambassadors point to God · 397-398
  antidote to idolatry · 203, 345, 394
  apologetics and evangelism · 355
  apostolic · 321-323
  application · 216, 238, 314, 325, 329, 339, 366, 370-379, 389, 391, 392
  architecture: church · 368
  audiovisuals · 202, 305, 350, 366, 367
  authenticity · 363
  authority · 334-338
  autonomous mind · 335
  Biblical Theology · 386-389
  body: use of · 333, 343, 368
  boldness · 364-365
  centrality of cross and resurrection · 395
  classical rhetoric · 372-375
  cool communication · 336
  conduit, grammar, and environment, preaching as · 367-368

INDEX OF SUBJECTS

counter environment · 203, 270-277, 298-310, 368, 369
covenantal · 335
cultivation of · 375-398
cultural criticism · 206
cultural situation · 386
dangers of Scholasticism · 371
deconstructing idols · 237, 395-397
Deconstruction · 212
depressed state of · 333
dialogue · 334, 335
didache · 370
doctrinal · 369, 372
earnestness · 363-366
ecology of · 314, 313-398
effectiveness · 392
Egalitarianism · 356
electronic competitors · 367
electronic situation · 1, 369, 377
environment, preaching as · 368
eschatological · 340, 386-389
evangelistic · 369
excellencies as medium · 333-345
   authoritative monologue · 334-338
   God's choice · 334
   power of living voice · 342-345
   presence of Christ · 338-342
exemplaristic · 371
expository · 369, 370
extemporaneous · 378-380
foolishness of · 335
freedom in pulpit · 329, 364
glorifies God · 340, 358
grammar, preaching as · 368
hearing · 345-353
Holy Spirit · 331, 372, 375, 384-385, 387, 389, 400
hot communication · 336
humor in pulpit · 346
idolatry: challenge to · 225, 354, 395
idolatry: warning of · 238
image · 203
imagination · 381, 394
immediacy · 201, 336, 342-345, 384-385
imprinting Word on heart · 345
Incarnational principle · 338, 340, 361
Internet · 341
Word of God, is the · 331, 385
Jesus' · 321
John the Baptist's · 320
jokes · 346
kerygma · 321, 370, 377
life-altering message · 368, 392
language · 363, 374, 381, 382, 390, 394

literacy: fosters · 331
majesty of God · 357
marketing · 230, 248-258, 279-295, 366, 393. *See also* technique
medium · 179-203, 321, 333-345, 366
medium and message · 285, 334, 374
medium: God's choice · 356, 367
medium: natural · 333
mendicant orders · 327
message of the cross · 179
message, centrality of · 364
monologue · 334-338
moralism · 372
multi-media triad · 191-203, 198
mystery · 343, 367
narrative · 386-389
   transcendental · 273
neo-Puritan · 369, 371
opening the Word · 386
oral skills, developing · 378-383
oral and written: distinction · 201, 378
oral preparation · 378-380
orality · 334-345, 378
orality: use of notes · 378-380
overhead projector · 202, 305, 350, 366
pastoral care · 360
Paul's · 322-323
perception · 336, 369
personality · 364
persuasion · 370, 378
physical aspects · 333, 343, 368
Postmodernism · 335
power and presence of Holy Spirit · 331, 372, 375, 384-385, 387, 389, 400
prayer · 342, 359, 366, 373, 383-385
preaching moment · 344, 393
preparation, general · 274, 380
preparation, importance of · 365
primacy of · 315-333
   Biblical overview · 315-323
   church historical overview · 323-333
   marketing, threatened by · 283
   Medieval Church · 326-328
   medium · 197
   Scripture · 317
   Ancient Church · 324-325
   Modern Church · 332-333
   Reformation Church · 328-331
   Reformation confessions · 330
primary means of grace · 201, 203, 314
primary orality · 192
printing · 328
Puritans · 357
purpose · 389

radio · 342
reading: importance of · 274, 380
reading of Scripture: public · 382, 383
rationalizations, exposing · 214
Redemptive-Historical · 369, 371, 386-389
relevance · 178, 371, 375-378
repentance · 319, 320, 322, 343, 349, 353, 376, 377, 395
scandal · 295, 362
Scripture · 200, 276, 321, 386
Scripture memory · 382
second person: use of · 391
simplicity · 389-393
story of redemption · 386-389
superiority as a medium · 333-345, 400
supreme act of worship · 345
teaching and preaching: distinction · 370
technique · 366, 393. *See also* marketing
technological competition · 366
television · 248-258, 336, 341, 342
television audience · 362
telic unit · 369
text of Scripture · 368. *See* text
therapy · 218
tongues of fire · 315
topical · 370
transcendence and immanence · 398
transformational · 368, 392
types and emphases · 369-372
unction · 364, 384
unites community · 276
unmediated by technology · 345
unmediated experience · 337
view-maker · 381
visual aids · 202, 305, 350, 366
visual elements · 201-203, 333, 343, 368
weapon of church: primary · 354
word as event · 344, 393
word pictures: use of · 393
worship: central to · 363
Word of God: preaching is · 321, 329, 331, 384-385
written word: relation to · 193, 197-201
See also Scripture, sermon, text
pre-Raphaelites · 165
Presbyterian · 290, 392
  intellect · 228
Presbyterian, Orthodox · 290
Presbyterian Church in the USA · 36, 58, 136, 286
presuppositional apologetics · 1, 26-46, 29, 31, 34, 35
  idolatry · 31

presuppositions · 171
  Christian · 42, 48
  exposing · 42
  idolatry · 208
  inconsistent in unbeliever · 49
  fool · 41
Princeton Theological Seminary · 47, 71, 136, 228
principle of coherence · 32
print. *See also* alphabet, text, writing
  democratizing · 201
  fixity · 199
  normativity · 196
  mechanized writing · 261
  privacy, privatizing · 200-201, 268, 269
printing · 54, 68, 105, 106, 191, 196, 200, 226, 280, 331, 353, 368
  authority of spoken word · 353
  cultural effects · 280
  democratizing · 280
  first mass medium · 200
  liabilities · 331
  linear logic · 191
  moveable type · 118
  preaching · 328
printing press · 117, 174, 226, 280, 328
privatizing media · 268, 269.
  See individualizing media
Process Theology · 36, 338, 388
professionalism · 222-225
  career · 223
  Christian ministry · 223, 225
  Doctor of Ministry programs · 224
  preaching · 224, 356
  televangelism · 224, 295, 363
Progressivism · 81-86, 102, 125, 135, 153, 163, 176, 226, 239, 296. *See* Utopianism
Promised Land · 8, 39, 355
propaganda · 85-90, 98, 105, 215, 251, 297
  analysis: World Wars I and II · 86-88, 136
  analysis: Laswell · 87-88
  analysis: Lippmann · 88-89
  computer: benefits of · 242
  de-Christianization · 297-298
  definition of · 87, 87n, 378
  government control · 269
  Ellul · 124, 222, 239, 269, 297-298
  Goebbels and Hitler · 90, 269
  mass media · 124, 269
  military and intelligence · 135n
  technological society · 239
  television · 251
prophets · 182, 198, 320
  false · 8, 37

INDEX OF SUBJECTS

idolatry exposed · 6, 9, 11-14, 42
school of · 318
spokesmen and writers · 195
true · 37, 55
unfaithful · 314
Protestant work ethic · 222
Proto-Sumerian · 199
Prussian Academy of Sciences · 79
pseudo-Gemeinschaft · 91
psychoanalysis · 77
psychology
   disease model · 219
   experimental · 81, 82, 93
   materialism · 219
Public Broadcasting: commercialism · 220
public opinion · 82, 85, 87-89
Public Service Company of New Hampshire · 221
Puritanism · 37, 163, 166, 222, 371
   intellect · 228
   physician of the soul · 218
   preaching · 328, 357
   primacy of preaching · 330
   Regulative Principle · 246, 304
   sermon length · 391
   simplicity in preaching · 390
   work, view of · 222
Pythagorean · 35

Q

quadrivium · 373
Queens College · 132, 134
Quill and Scroll Society · 99

R

radio · 66, 90, 96, 113, 141, 148, 175, 258, 261
   audience impact · 91
   audience research · 92
   commercialism · 220
   consecrated use · 296
   content oriented · 304
   evangelism · 304
   history of · 139
   imagination · 267
   impermanence · 231
   preaching · 332
   sermons · 305, 177
radio ministry · 305, 177
Radio Research Project · 90, 136
Rainbow Covenant · 399
rationalism · 34-36, 37, 38, 40, 48, 59, 200, 205, 209, 217, 235, 245, 258
   exhaustive · 48
   idolatry · 237
   irrationalism · 34-36
   scientific · 45, 51, 71, 200
   Utopian · 227
rationality · 47, 59, 260, 272
   communication · 54
   established by God · 42, 191-192
   social and individual · 269
   television · 257
reading · 121, 129-130, 187, 246, 272-275, 306, 380, 381. *See also* literacy
   aloud · 12, 201, 275, 328, 342, 352, 381-383
   benefits · 272
   childhood development · 249, 253, 256, 274
   expands soul · 273
   imagination · 274
   important for worship · 351
   interiority · 129, 193, 345
   media balance · 191
   privacy of · 157, 193, 200, 352, 360, 365, 378
   reflective · 272
   Scripture · 193, 200, 201, 319, 322, 323, 329, 336, 342, 351, 353, 359, 382, 383
reason, reasoning · 39, 41, 44, 46, 59, 84, 143, 205, 209, 211, 214, 227, 237
   prayer · 44
recreation · 245
   entertainment · 247
   gift of God · 245
redemption: narrative of · 200
redemptive history · 200, 316, 320
   preaching · 386-389
   See Biblical Theology
Reformation · 123, 294, 330, 331, 354, 356
   intellectual renaissance · 230
   preaching · 202, 328-331, 384
   printing · 280
   restoration of the gospel · 328
   Word: emphasis on · 202, 368
Reformed Presbyterian Church of North America · 281
Reformed Theological Seminary · 282
Regent College · 172
Regulative Principle · 202-203, 300 303-305
   electronic media · 303
   prevents idolatry · 203, 246
re-imagining God · 11, 36, 57-58, 286
relativism · 52, 74, 125, 128, 129, 130, 134, 172, 209-211, 213, 215
   Deconstruction · 211
   narcissism · 215
   popular culture · 210

Theory of Relativity · 80
transcendental · 210
religion: debunking of · 60
Religious Communication Association · 175
Religious Speech Communication Association · 175
Remphan · 15
Renaissance · 68, 106, 110, 190
Renaissance literature · 110
repentance · 20, 33, 44, 61, 219, 225, 319, 320, 322, 349, 353, 376, 377,383, 395
Research Center for Economic Psychology · 90
Research Center for Group Dynamics at MIT · 92
Research Center of the University of Newark · 90
resurrection · 21, 321, 340
    Christ's' · 53, 163, 198, 232, 289, 320, 354, 377, 389, 395
retrieval, laws of media · 188
reversal, laws of media · 187
revelation · 20, 183, 190, 201, 271, 274, 338
    general · 2, 10, 19, 24, 35, 40, 41, 44, 48, 52, 54, 60, 182, 196, 236, 265, 322, 369, 387. *See also* Scripture
    general and special · 48, 191, 213
    images, positive use of · 246
    intelligent design · 236
    natural · 19, 54
    redemptive · 41, 50, 246
    special · 7, 10, 12, 13, 25, 35, 48, 192, 193, 194, 195, 196, 197, 316, 318, 321, 322, 336, 367, 387, 388
    verbal and non-verbal · 191
    written · 198, 199, 319
revelation, history of · 196
revivalism: anti-intellectual · 228
rhetoric · 100, 109, 110, 226, 381
    ancient church · 324, 325
    Areopagus · 17
    ancient Corinth · 335
    classical in preaching · 61, 335, 372-375
    Elizabethan · 109
    manipulative power · 76
    Reformation · 328
    sophistic · 295
rituals · 32, 49
Rockefeller Communication Seminar · 136
Rockefeller Foundation · 90, 136
    Institute of Human Relations · 94
Rockefeller Foundation Seminar on Mass Communication · 87
Rockhurst College · 121

Roman Catholicism · 161. *See* Catholicism
    emphasis on sacraments · 168, 170, 202
Roman Empire · 22, 28
romantic philosophy · 74
Romanticism · 205, 227
Royal Friedrich-Wilhelms University of Berlin · 92

S

sacraments · 12, 25, 168, 170, 196, 246, 253, 298, 317, 330, 393. *See* means of grace
    baptism · 202
    idolatry · 202
    Incarnation · 202
    signs and seals of Word · 199, 202, 314, 331, 352
Saint Andrews University · 329
Saint Louis, University of · 109
Saint Michael's College · 110
salvation · 8, 18, 44, 45, 89, 171, 179, 198, 229, 230, 231, 301, 317, 319, 320, 331, 335, 363, 365, 377, 386, 388, 391, 393
    corporate reality · 179, 321
    god within · 217, 219
    historical plan of · 57, 324, 387
    idolaters · 22, 56, 234, 235
sanctification · 299
    idolatry · 21
Scholastic · 327, 371
science, scientific · 1, 41, 55, 68-72, 86, 106, 269. *See also* sociology
    deification of · 128, 135-136, 218, 239
    communication study · 66-68, 79, 85, 86-100, 102, 115, 133, 135, 147, 159, 176, 210
    empirical · 35, 59, 78, 83
    foundation: Biblical revelation · 48
    Kuhn: revolutions · 89
    materialism · 74, 77, 200
    method · 48, 80, 110, 344
    rationalism · 36, 45, 51, 71, 123
Scopes Trial · 70
Scripture · 32, 35, 41, 44, 48, 56, 108, 121, 170, 181, 197-201, 214, 326, 338, 372, 375, 385, 392. *See* Word of God
    application · 59, 225, 325, 339, 353, 389
    atomized · 387
    authority of text · 195, 196, 263
    canon · 199, 271
    centrality · 314, 317
    Christ's Word · 14, 320, 339
    corporate consciousness · 345
    counter environment · 179, 352
    covenantal · 182, 199, 316
    culture · 49, 54

INDEX OF SUBJECTS

Deconstruction · 213
demolishes false reasoning · 58
element of worship · 203
eschatological · 199
exegesis: careful · 61
heavenly pattern revealed · 271
hermeneutics · 307, 387
hermeneutics of narcissism · 216
historical medium · 200
hypertext: undermined by · 263
idolatry: antidote to · 12, 14, 43, 123, 179, 212, 274
images and metaphors, use of · 166, 394
inspiration · 216, 347
knowledge of God · 59
media balance · 202
meditation · 273
medium: foundational · 199, 201, 314
medium: written · 193, 334
multi-media triad · 191-203
normative covenant document · 196, 345
orality · 193, 196, 201, 314
Postmodernism · 288-289
preaching · 317, 319, 322, 329-334, 348, 350-351, 373, 374, 381-383, 395
primary Author, Holy Spirit · 216
principal means of divine communication · 314
private-communal reading · 174, 342, 352
private reading · 174, 273-274, 342, 352, 376
public reading of · 12, 198, 201, 324, 328, 342, 352, 375, 382, 381-383
relevance · 178, 230, 375-378, 393
songs · 302-304
stability · 193, 197, 200
text · 230, 273, 276, 288, 299, 327, 358, 370, 371, 386
visual analogues · 202
visual image · 199, 201-203, 314.
See visual
written · 122, 170, 193, 197-201, 316, 317, 331, 336, 345
bounds oral · 200
power of · 386
reflects eternity · 200
See also preaching, sermon, text
Seattle Computer Products · 145
Second Coming · 238, 399
Second Commandment · 4, 5, 9, 25, 33, 129, 171, 174, 203, 265, 276
misinterpreted · 246
Second Helvetic Confession · 331
on preaching · 384

secondary orality · 192, 258, 333, 382
secularization · 30, 52, 135, 190, 237, 299
seed of the Serpent · 41
Seed of the woman · 41, 352
self-awareness movement · 215
self-esteem · 219, 389
love of neighbor · 219
self-image · 215, 221
seminary education · 305-307
See theological seminary
sensibility · 273
sensitivity training · 93
sensorium · 183, 257
balance · 107, 117, 133, 197, 271, 276
reorganized by electronics · 263, 332-333
sensus deitatis · 40
separatist · 53
sermon · 14, 171, 284, 295, 314, 348, 366, 386, 394, 396. *See also* preacher (ing)
act of worship · 329
application · 59, 225, 325, 339, 353, 371, 389, 390-392. *See also* preaching, text
church history · 324-329, 332, 333
computer, use of · 307, 379
conclusion · 391
cyberspace · 286-290
electronic media · 305, 342
expository · 324, 370, 371
hearing · 275, 345-353, 395
introduction · 390
length · 391
notes, use of · 378-380
preparation · 360, 372-375, 380-383
printing · 328, 378
redemptive-historical · 371-372, 386-389
telos of text · 373, 392
textual · 370, 371
topical · 370
types and emphases · 369-372
Sermon on the Mount · 14, 295
sexuality, mysteries of · 75
Shannon-Weaver Model · 55, 131
Shinar · 15, 22
Sinai, Mount · 6, 197, 316, 318
trumpet · 355
situationist sociology · 133, 134, 154-156, 186-188, 191, 192, 195, 206, 207, 231, 232. *See also* social sciences
situational perspective · 195-196, 232
sleeper effect · 94
SMCR model (source-message-channel-receiver) · 97, 131
Smithsonian Institution · 125
social activism · 338

Social Darwinism · 72, 73
social engineers · 34, 135
social evolution · 73
social improvement · 136
social place · 133, 188, 231-232
social sciences, sociology · 86, 136, 197
　Chicago school · 70-73, 78, 82, 84, 134, 136
　Comte: father of · 70
　Columbia University · 92
　Darwinian evolution · 72
　communication study · 66, 67, 69, ,87, 90, 90, 93, 95, 99, 100, 106, 122, 134, 175, 206
　European influence · 81
　knowledge: sociology of · 52
　qualitative analysis · 67
　quantitative analysis · 66, 67, 85, 87, 88, 90, 99, 102
　religion · 52, 230
　religion: sociology of · 52
　Simmel · 81
　social behavior: electronic media · 133
　social context: electronic media · 82, 103, 116, 117, 188, 190
　social structure · 105, 154, 185, 189, 249, 280
　See also situationist sociology
Society for General Systems Research · 95
Society of Jesus · 121
sola scriptura · 376, 378
Son of God · 22, 218, 321, 322.
　See Jesus Christ, Christ
Son of Man · 21, 22, 198, 358.
　See Jesus Christ, Christ
Sophia, goddess · 36
Sophists · 38
Sorbonne · 125
Southern Agrarianism · 111, 136
space-biased media · 106, 190, 192, 227
Spirit. See Holy Spirit
spirituality: commercialized · 290
spoken word · 118, 124, 170, 190, 195, 199, 275, 321, 335, 342-345, 352
　authority · 353
　concreteness · 345
　creation · 316, 343
　mysterious · 343
　power · 76, 201
　preaching · 342-345, 381
　recreative power · 3
St. Louis University · 119, 121
St. Stanislaus Seminary · 121

Stanford's Center for Advanced Study in the Behavioral Sciences · 93
Stanford Research Institute · 145
Stanford University · 88, 93, 99, 138, 144
　Department of Communication and Journalism · 99
　Institute for Communication Research · 99
　Institution for Communication Research · 138
State University of New York, Fredonia · 126
Stoics · 38, 39
story-telling · 377, 380, 386-389
　ancient world · 387
Strasbourg, University of · 122
Structuralism · 212, 389
suzerainty treaties ANE · 199
symbol · 5, 6, 7, 8, 9, 15, 54, 87, 110, 128, 142, 155, 156, 171, 179, 180, 199, 220, 238, 239, 252, 253, 266, 275, 280, 281, 314, 315, 355. *See also* metaphor
symbolic interactionism · 84, 156
symbolic logic · 96
symbolic manipulation · 221
symbolic representation · 105
synagogue · 44, 319, 320, 383, 386
　public reading of Scripture · 382
　worship · 322
syncretism · 7, 11, 56, 136
Syracuse University · 270
systematic theology · 387
Systems Theory · 77
　entropic · 95
　negentropic · 95

T

tabernacle · 7, 9-11, 15, 16, 25, 196, 271, 315. *See also* temple
　creativity of Bezalel and Aholiab · 246
Tabulating Machine Company · 143
Taylor's "time-and-motion" theory · 93
technicism
　technological eradication of sin · 235
technological autonomy · 132
technological determinism · 66, 116, 117, 123, 132, 154, 236
　critics of · 116, 131
　definition · 116
　fatalism · 116
　hard and soft · 116
　media determinism · 131
technological snobbery · 266, 307
technological society · 123, 124, 236, 239
technological theory · 152-153, 154-156
　instrumental and substantive · 154, 155
　neutrality · 155

INDEX OF SUBJECTS 485

Chandler · 131-132
Ellul · 122-124, 159-161
Technological University of Eindhoven · 173
Technological University of Delft · 173
technology · 65, 68, 76, 122, 123, 124, 154, 159, 160, 166, 188, 194, 207, 210, 220
    assessment · 54, 59, 85-86, 104, 151-203
    Christian view · 151-203, 229, 244, 395
    common grace · 57-58
    communication · 105, 153, 176
    consecrated to God · 59, 157, 299
    culture · 22, 25, 27, 35, 128, 158
    definition · 177, 208
    deification of · 22, 25, 27, 128, 234
    determinism: hard and soft · 116, 117, 131, 132, 154, 168
    electronic · 57, 117, 118
    environmental · 106
    glory of God · 58
    historical context · 105
    history · 85-86, 114, 139-148
    idolatry · 5, 55, 57, 234, 237, 239
    Luddites · 152, 243
    managers of · 135
    medium · 55
    Mumford, historian of · 85-86
    negative educational impact · 254, 258, 270, 305-308
    neutrality of · 156
    novelty · 153, 232, 256
    overwhelms · 117, 128, 270
    preaching · 333, 345
    spirituality · 286, 289
    technophiles · 152, 153, 174
    technophobes · 152, 154, 174
    threefold sociological effect [Innis] · 280
    unintended consequences · 244
    Utopianism · 57, 140, 235, 242
    See technological theory
telegraph · 66, 68, 79, 139, 140, 142, 147, 148, 156, 248, 261
    annihilation of time · 140
    history of · 139
    impermanence · 231
    liability · 272
    naive reception · 280-281
    wireless · 141
telemarketing · 286
telephone · 84, 92, 97, 142, 258, 275
    Amish response · 157
    commercialism · 221
    computing · 143
    impermanence · 231
    novelty · 227

televangelism · 224, 295, 363
television · 131, 136, 141-142, 148, 248-258
    addiction · 250, 257, 267, 269
    advertising · 220, 254, 264, 293
    anti-historical · 257
    benefits · 175, 257, 387
    catechizing power · 253
    categories of influence · 178, 190-191
    cathode ray tube · 141, 144, 221, 251, 258
    celebrity · 174, 216
    childhood development · 256, 267, 275
    color image · 251
    conduit · 248
    conformity · 267
    consecrated use · 296
    critical analysis · 173, 190-191, 248-258
    dehumanizing · 297
    educational effects · 128, 253, 254
    effect on print culture ·
    eliminates transcendence · 292
    Empire State Building · 141
    entertainment · 27, 128, 176, 178, 247, 255, 292, 346
    environment · 187, 206, 249
    epistemological effect · 191, 252
    evangelism · 304
    existential effect · 254
    experiential influence · 191
    fantasy · 57, 173
    fragmentation · 227
    grammar · 186, 248
    history of · 141-142
    illusion · 231, 264, 266, 294, 340
    intimacy · 231, 294, 340
    image · 250
    images, black and white · 251
    imagination · 256, 267
    Internet · 254
    journalism · 173
    literacy · 178, 251, 254, 255
    logic · 252, 257
    modalistic influence · 191
    naive reception · 280-281
    narrative power · 175, 257, 387
    neurological effect · 190, 249, 250, 258
    novelty · 227
    passivity · 256
    perception · 178, 249
    preaching: decline of · 332
    privatizing · 268, 269
    propaganda · 269
    pseudo-environment · 179
    quick flash technique · 190, 252
    religion · 177, 178, 292-293

secularism · 293
sensory bombardment · 252
sex and violence · 186
sociological effect · 133, 188, 191, 231, 249, 252, 255, 256, 294
tradition, truth · 258, 292, 293, 295
ubiquity of · 229
temple · 7, 12, 14, 25, 196, 198, 246, 271, 298, 308, 315, 319, 321, 322, 339, 383.
  idol temples · 8, 10, 13, 15, 17, 19, 22, 23, 222, 236, 288, 309
  idolatry: antidote · 9-11
  redemptive revelation · 10, 246
  See tabernacle
Ten Commandments · 21, 197
Tenth Commandment · 21
text, texts · 68, 108, 127, 170, 236, 253, 258, 26, 262, 274, 276, 306, 336.
  literary · 109, 118
  relativism · 211-214, 216, 237, 285, 287, 288, 289, 335
  Scripture · 54, 181, 198, 201, 216, 230, 231, 235, 263, 273, 274, 276, 277, 299, 306, 321, 325, 327, 329, 365, 366, 368-378, 380, 383, 386, 387, 389, 390-396, 398
  See also hypertext, preaching, sermon
T-groups · 93
The Augsburg Confession · 330
theological seminary
  distance education · 305-307
  intellect · 51
  See theological seminary
theophany · 37, 55
theosophy · 166
therapy · 215, 217-220
  alternative religion · 219
  blameshifting · 219
  consumerism · 220
  idolatry · 219
  self-centered · 219
Third Reich · 213
Thomism · 184
time-biased media · 106, 190, 192, 227
tolerance · 28, 266
  idol of · 386
Toronto, University of · 105, 108, 110, 113, 117, 119, 126
  Centre for Culture and Technology · 138
  Program in Culture and Technology · 119
  theological schools · 164
total depravity · 28
totalitarianism · 27, 134, 399
transcendence · 2, 59, 93, 122, 183, 292, 338

culture of · 47, 273
God · 11, 17, 38, 49, 160, 263, 388, 400
idolatrous quest · 2, 27, 36-38, 52, 55, 57, 135, 169, 206-207, 210, 215, 232, 258, 286, 387
values · 215, 387
See also Gnosticism, God, idols, man, Utopianism
transcendence-immanence dilemma · 36, 338, 398
transcendental argument · 43
Trinity · 137, 180-182, 234, 320
  communication · 56, 179, 190, 197
  eternal communication · 54, 181, 182
  Nicene doctrine · 181
  opera ad intra · 182
  Second Person · 195
Trinity Evangelical Divinity School · 177
trivium · 114, 373
trumpet · 354, 355
  preaching · 355
Tufts University · 94
type (Biblical): definition · 16
typewriter · 145
  literacy · 259
tyranny of experts · 136, 137
U
U.S. Army, Research Branch of the Division of Information and Education · 98
Ugarit · 108
unction, in preaching · 364, 384
unintended consequences · 80, 97, 244
Union Theological Seminary · 289
universals · 59
university · 68, 69, 81-85. *See also* education
unknown god: Athens · 39
Unmoved Mover · 59
urbanization · 135, 207
user friendly gospel · 44, 282, 284, 293, 295
Utah, University of · 145, 147
Utopianism · 57, 136, 227, 235, 239
  communication technology · 135, 153, 242, 263, 288
  Progressivism · 125, 153
V
vacuum tube · 141, 143, 292
values clarification · 215
Vanity Fair · 396
vicar · 341
Victoria College · 107
Victorian · 81, 121, 217
Victorian Christianity · 74
video cassettes · 247, 287, 301, 367
video games: privatizing · 268-269

INDEX OF SUBJECTS 487

Vienna · 76, 89
Vienna Circle of Logical Positivists · 76
Vienna, University of · 77, 79, 90
Vietnam War protesters · 115
virtual classroom · 307
virtual reality · 130, 234, 264, 266, 268, 299, 337
visual · 5, 27, 55, 117, 181, 185, 190, 222, 231, 245, 253, 258, 261, 274, 275, 280
   image · 8, 11, 124, 160, 275
   literacy and logic · 175, 394
   seductive power · 2, 24-25, 35, 38, 112, 160, 221, 265, 295
   Word and worship · 191-203, 246, 276, 305, 314, 328, 333, 335, 344, 346, 366-368, 378, 381, 382
   See also idolatry, image
Vorticism · 113

W

Wales, Aberystwyth, University of · 131
Walkman: privatizing · 268-269
War-Time Communications Project · 136
Western intellectual tradition · 137
Westminster Confession of Faith · 316, 331
Westminster Larger Catechism · 331
   hearing the Word · 350
   preaching · 362, 389, 391
Westminster Shorter Catechism · 331, 367, 382
Westminster Theological Seminary · 29, 172, 307
Westminster Theological Seminary in California · 177
Willow Creek Community Church · 284
Windsor, University of · 110
Wisconsin, University of · 69, 109
   first school of journalism · 99
witchcraft · 8
Word of God. *See* Scripture
   foundational · 199, 201, 314
   inscripturated · 322
   oral · 193, 196, 201, 314
   visual · 199, 201-203, 314
   fire · 315
   hammer · 314
   medium · 191-203, 343
   Multimedia Triad · 191-203
   Paradise · 316
   written · 122, 170, 193, 197-201, 316, 317, 331, 336, 345
word processor · 213
   better typewriter · 260
   literacy · 259
   writing and research · 306

World War I · 80, 104
   propaganda research · 86-88
World War II · 122, 244
   propaganda research · 66, 87, 88, 94-96
worship · 1-25, 199-203, 276-277, 300-305
   antidote to idolatry · 353
   anti-formalism · 301
   audiovisuals · 202, 305, 350, 366
   compromise · 1-25, 279-296, 299
   contemporary · 36, 279-295, 300-302
   counter environment · 12, 195, 199-203, 276, 298-305, 351
   electronic media · 203, 303-305
   entertainment · 292-296, 303, 325, 349
   glory of God · 276
   hearing the Word · 345-353
   historic · 300-303
   hymns and songs · 300-302, 303, 350, 357
   idolatry · 1-25, 36-43, 300, 301, 348
   images: danger of · 2, 296
   individualism · 214-236, 303, 349
   media balance · 203, 276
   medium and message · 5, 55, 302
   natural media · 314
   participation · 349
   popular culture · 302
   prayer · 351
   preaching · 329, 351, 363, 368
   Presbyterian · 300, 301
   primary media · 195
   public · 195, 199, 276, 298, 299, 363
   public reading of Scripture · 383
   purpose and meaning · 298
   Regulative Principle · 202, 246, 300, 303-305
   sacraments · 202
   Scripture: centrality · 199, 201, 304, 314
   Scripture warrant · 4, 5, 9, 25, 171, 246
   television · 248-258, 292-295, 362
   See also church, preaching
writing · 259, 272-276. *See also* alphabet
   origin · 108, 142, 191, 194, 197, 199, 254

X

Xerox PARC · 144, 145

Y

Yale Communication Research Project · 136
Yale Institute of Human Relations · 136
Yale University · 107, 121

Z

Zeus · 16
Ziggurat · 54
Zurich, University of · 79

Index of Authors and Persons[1]

A

Abbey, Merrill R. · 354
  Man, Media and the Message · 138
Adam, communication · 54, 181, 316
Adams, Henry · 27
Adams, James Truslow · 272
Adams, Jay · 332
  Scholasticism in preaching · 371
  preaching text · 370
  Preaching with Purpose · 360, 392
  Sense Appeal in the Sermons of Charles Haddon Spurgeon · 394
  warning about technique · 366
Adams, Thomas · 330
Adler, Margot · 290
Adler, Mortimer · 255
Adorno, Theodor · 78, 90, 91, 98, 126
  Lazarsfeld · 102
  The Authoritarian Personality · 78
Aiken, Howard H. · 143
Alanus ab Insulis · 327
Albertus Magnus · 327
Alcuin · 326
Alexander, James W.
  Thoughts on Preaching · 360
Alfred of England · 326
Allen, Paul · 144
Altheide, David · 207
  media formats · 207n
Ambrose of Milan · 324, 325
Andrews, Lancelot · 330
Anthony of Padua · 327
Aquinas, Thomas · 166, 327
Arendt, Hannah · 126
Aristotle · 59, 163, 184
  Rhetoric · 373
Atanasoff, John B. · 143
Athanasius · 325
Augustine · 180, 265, 324, 325, 326
  Christ the Wisdom of reason · 183
  classical rhetoric · 374
  De Doctrina Christiana · 374
  De Magistro · 180
  audibles and visibles · 183
  importance of teaching preaching · 370
  personality in preaching · 364
  philosophy of history · 238
  preaching · 384
  simplicity of preaching · 390
  Trinity · 195
Augustine of Canterbury · 326

B

Babbage, Charles · 142
Bach, J. S. · 302
Bacon, Francis · 235
  first philosopher of technology · 68
Bahnsen, Greg
  Van Til's Apologetic: Readings and Analysis · 29
Baird, John L. · 141
Baker, Jim · 292
Barlow, John Perry · 57
Barna, George · 282
Barnhouse, Donald Gray · 332
Barnouw, Erik: *Mass Communication* · 138
Barrow, Isaac · 330
Barth, Karl · 122, 123, 159
  utter transcendence · 122
Barth, Roland · 211
Barzun, Jacques · 28, 205, 215
  cultural criticism · 27
  information overload · 270
  reading · 274
  Science: The Glorious Entertainment · 115
Basel, University of · 74
Basil · 325
Bateson, Gregory · 95, 136
  Communication: The Social Matrix of Psychiatry · 77, 114
  Steps to an Ecology of Mind · 77
Baudrillard, Jean: information overload · 270
Baxter, Richard · 330
Bede, the Venerable · 326

---

[1] Names of Deity and pagan gods are listed in the Index of Subjects.

INDEX OF AUTHORS AND PERSONS

Bellah, Robert: *Habits of the Heart* · 216
Belloc, Hillaire · 381
Benjamin, Walter · 78, 294
Berger, Peter · 53, 93, 385
   A Rumor of Angels · 52
   pluralism · 52
   sociology of religion · 52
Bergman, Ingmar: *The Silence* · 40
Berkeley, George · 59
Berkhof, Hendrick: idolatry · 396
Berlo, David K.
   The Process of Communication · 97, 138
Bernard of Clairvaux · 326
Berry, Wendell: television education · 254
Bertalanffy, Ludwig von
   General Systems Theory · 95
Bettelheim, Bruno
   television and imagination · 267
   The Uses of Enchantment · 267
Birkerts, Sven · 129-130, 241, 345
   apologist for written word · 129
   church as guardian of literacy · 298
   electronic media · 129
   electronic superficiality · 263
   Guttenberg Elegies, The · 129, 139
   interiority · 157, 193
   interiority of reading · 129
   inwardness · 273
   literacy · 298
   literary criticism · 129
   Luddite · 129
   medium shapes the message · 129
   reading · 272
Bissel, Claude · 117
Blake, William · 151, 164
Blamires, Harry: *The Christian Mind* · 228
Blankenhorn, David · 219
Bledstein, Burton
   The Culture of Professionalism · 223
Bleyer, Willard G. "Daddy" · 99
Bloom, Allan · 211
   metanarratives · 210
   The Closing of the American Mind · 51
Bonaventura · 327
Boorstin, Daniel J. · 125-126, 156, 227, 255
   advertising · 125, 267
   Americans, The · 125
   cultural criticism · 27
   Graphic Revolution · 125, 347
   Image, The · 125, 138
   Lippmann · 125
   power of celebrity · 125, 347
   pseudo-event · 89, 125
   relativism · 125

   television · 256
Borg, Marcus · 290
Boulding, Kenneth E. · 95
   The Image · 138
Bradley, F. H. · 48
Bramson, Leon
   history of theory of mass society · 102
Bridges, Charles
   The Christian Ministry · 360
Broadus, John A.
   On the Preparation and Delivery of Sermons · 360
Bronfenbrenner, Urie · 256, 257
Brooks, Phillips: definition of preaching · 364
Brooks, Van Wych · 140
Brücke, Ernst · 77
Bryant, William Jennings · 70
Bullinger, Heinrich · 331
Bultmann, Rudolph · 103, 123, 159, 375
   demythologizing · 235
Bunyan, John · 330
Burgess, Ernest W. · 84
Bush, Vannevar · 96, 146
Buttrick, David: electronic media and the authority of the book · 394

C

Caesar · 74
Calvin, John · 162, 293, 328, 329, 340, 354
   accommodation of the Word · 375
   doctrine of God · 29
   efficacy of preaching · 385
   expository preaching · 370
   idol factory · 246
   idolatry · 9n, 19, 24, 33, 39
   idolatry in the church · 15
   idolatry in worship · 304, 348
   images in OT cultus · 9
   invention of the arts · 50
   power of the visual · 265
   preaching as condescension of God · 385
   relevance of preaching · 375
   sensus deitatus · 18
   sermons · 360
   spectacles of Scripture · 54
   worship · 300
Carey, James · 66, 88, 156
   definition of communication · 180
   technology in culture formation · 208
Carey, William · 332
Carnegie, Dale · 222
Carpenter, Edmund S. · 119
   McLuhan · 114
Carson, D. A. · 211
   The Gagging of God · 210

Carter, Stephen · 211
Cater, Douglass · 248
Cerf, Vint · 147
Chandler, Daniel · 116, 131-132, 153
  critical of McLuhan and Postman · 131
  technocentrism · 154
  technological-media determinism · 131
  text and reader · 211
Charlemagne · 326
Charnock, Stephen: idolatry · 37
Chesterton, G. K. · 115, 120, 162, 163, 165, 245, 381
  apologetics · 60
  imagination · 241
  What's Wrong with the World · 111, 161
Chrysostom · 325, 326
Cicero · 128, 374, 390
Clark, Gordon
  presuppositional apologetics · 31
Clarke, Sir Arthur C. · 242
Clement of Alexandria
  The Second Epistle of · 324
Cobb, Jennifer · 289
Colet, John · 328
Colson, Charles: *Against the Night* · 209
Columba · 326
Comte, Auguste · 81, 134
  father of sociology · 70
Cooley, Charles Horton · 82
  Hawthorne studies · 102
  Human Nature and the Social Order · 82
  looking glass self · 82
  Social Organization: A Study of the Larger Mind · 82
  Social Process · 82
Cooper, Cary · 270
Coover, Robert · 261
Copernicus · 68
Cox, Harvey · 292
Crick, Francis · 236
Culkin, John · 119
Cyprian · 324
Cypriote Zeno · 38
Czitrom, Daniel · 67, 79, 86, 105, 113, 135, 141
  history of electric technology · 139
  intellectual history · 66
  Media and the American Mind: From Morse to McLuhan · 66
  radical theorists · 101
  student of Innis and Carey · 66

D

D'Souza, Dinesh: *Illiberal Education* · 213
D'Vinci, Leonardo · 239

Daane, James · 354
Dabney, Robert: *Sacred Rhetoric* · 360
Darwin, Charles · 69-72, 73, 74, 281
  atheistic system · 71
  Chicago school of sociology · 72
  Descent of Man, The · 72
  Expression of the Emotions of Men and Animals, The · 72
  On the Origin of Species · 70
  radical restructuring of natural science · 72
David · 8, 338; opposition to idolatry · 9
Dawson, Christopher · 165
De Forest, Lee · 141
de Man, Paul · 211, 213
de Saussure, Ferdinand · 212
Democritus · 38
Dennison, Charles · 338, 386
Derrida, Jacques · 211, 213
  meaning and difference · 212
Deutsch, Karl · 114
Dewey, John · 82-83, 84, 88, 94, 134
  Education and the Social Order · 83
  Great Community · 83
  Pragmatism · 235
  public school for social transformation · 83
  The Public and Its Problems · 83
Dickson, David · 330
Dionysius · 59, 117
Dionysius the Areopagite · 44
Donne, John · 330
Du Mont, Allen B. · 141
Durkheim, Emile · 82
  The Rules of Sociological Methods · 81

E

Ebersole, Samuel · 116, 153, 172, 296
  media determinism · 154
Eby, David: Church Growth Movement · 283
Eckert, Presper · 143
Edgar, William · 207, 210, 214, 234
  immanence · 36
Edward VI · 328
Edwards, Jonathan · 332
  preaching · 397
  Religious Affections, The · 339
Edwards, Richard H. · 141
Einstein, Albert · 79-80
  relativism · 80
  theories of relativity · 79
  theory of gravitation · 90
Elijah · 318, 319
  challenging idolatry · 31, 40
Eliot, T. S. · 110, 112, 161, 270, 395
  Christianity and Culture · 47, 247
Elisha · 318

INDEX OF AUTHORS AND PERSONS

Elizabeth, Queen · 328
Elliot, Elizabeth: worship · 350
Ellul, Jacques · 66, 67, 117, 122-124, 126, 137, 155, 158, 159-161, 176, 183, 194, 246
   Barth · 123
   Christian faith · 159, 160
   cultural criticism · 124
   determinism · 160
   dialectical theology · 123
   distrust of technology · 159
   efficiency, worship of · 124
   eschatological time · 159
   human freedom · 123
   human responsibility · 160
   Humiliation of the Word, The · 139, 160
   Marxism · 123, 159
   media determinist · 153
   metaphysics of technology · 234
   Neo-Orthodox theology · 159
   overview of history of technology · 139
   propaganda · 124, 222, 239, 269, 297
   Propaganda: The Formation of Men's Attitudes · 124
   propaganda and the church · 297
   technique · 132, 234
   technique, definition of · 123
   technological determinism · 123
   technological society · 123
   technological tyranny · 123
   technology and media · 124
   technology for human ends · 236
   Technological Society, The · 116, 123, 127, 138
   transcendence · 160
   visual image · 124, 160
   Word of God · 160
Emerson, Ralph Waldo · 140
Emery, Merrelyn · 251
   cathode ray tube · 258
   Social and Neurophysiological Effects of Television, The · 259
   television education · 254
Engelbart, Doug · 145, 146
Engels, Friedrich · 73
Englesma, David: preaching · 399
Epicurus · 38, 39, 71, 73
Evans, David · 145
Ezra · 319

F

Fallwell, Jerry · 292, 293
Fant, Clyde: *Preaching For Today* · 380
Farnsworth, Philo T. · 141
Farrell, Thomas
   analogues of intellection · 201
Fasching D. · 123
Feenberg, Andrew
   Critical Theory of Technology · 154
   Heidegger · 155
Festinger, Leon
   Cognitive Dissonance · 93
   father of experimental psychology · 93
Feuerbach, Ludwig · 73, 78
Fiore, Quentin · 139
Fish, Henry
   Masterpieces of Pulpit Eloquence · 360
Fish, Stanley · 211
   interpretive community · 212
Foerster, Heinz von · 95
Foucault, Michel · 211
Frame, John
   Cornelius Van Til: An Analysis of His Thought · 29
   Doctrine of the Knowledge of God, The · 29
   idolatry · 31
   perspectivalism · 195
   Van Til's transcendental argument · 43
Francis of Assisi · 327
Freud, Sigmund · 60, 69, 76-78, 80, 87, 89, 94, 217, 218
   influence on communication study · 77
   Interpretation of Dreams, The · 77, 88
   Jung · 77
   psychoanalysis · 77
   rejected Judaism and Christianity · 77
   religion a projection · 60
   theory of the unconscious · 77
   wish fulfillment · 77
Friedson, Eliot · 102
Fromm, Eric
   Art of Loving, The · 78
   Eros and Civilization · 78
   Zen Buddhism and Psychoanalysis · 78
Frye, Northrop · 164
Fuller, Thomas · 330
Gadamer, Hans-Georg · 210, 212
Gallup, George H. · 99
Galton, Sir Francis · 72
Gannett, Ezra S. · 140
Gates, Bill · 144
George VI · 141
Gerbner, George · 126, 131, 207, 267
Gideon · 41
Giedion, Sigfried · 131
   Mechanization Takes Command · 114, 138
Gill, Eric · 165

Goebbels, Josef · 90
Goethals, Gregor · 253, 258
   visual icons · 266
Goffman, Erving · 206
   "backstage" and "onstage" social settings · 133
   situational geography · 133
   situationist sociology · 133
   social roles · 134
Goodwin, Thomas · 330
Gordon, Cyrus
   challenge primacy of Greek literacy · 194
Gordon, T. David
   definition of preaching · 377
Gordon, W. Terrence · 162
Gozzi, Raymond
   The Power of Metaphor in the Age of Electronic Media · 160
Graham, Billy · 293, 332
Graham, William
   Beyond the Written Word: Oral Aspects of Scripture in the History of Religion · 121, 342
Graves, Robert · 166
Greeley, Andrew · 290
Gregory Nazianzen · 325
Gregory the Great · 326
Groothuis, Douglas · 260
   distance theological education · 307
   Soul in Cyberspace, The · 172
Gropius, Walter · 76, 210, 239
Gross, Larry · 267
Grudin, Robert
   Time and the Art of Living · 275
Guibert of Nogent · 327
Guinness, Os · 28, 31, 57, 172, 218, 219, 222, 268
   anti-intellectualism · 228
   critique of Church Growth · 282
   Dining with the Devil · 282
   Fit Bodies Fat Minds: Why Evangelicals Don't Think and What to Do about It · 51
   No God But God: Breaking with the Idols of Our Age · 30, 244
   television · 257
   therapy · 217, 219
Gutenberg, Johann · 226, 280, 325, 328, 331
   invention of printing press · 68

H

Habermas, Jürgen · 78
Hall, Joseph · 330
Hart, Darryl · 34, 288, 305, 306, 307
   dangers of computer in learning · 383
   electronic church · 286
   idolatry as a paradigm · 32
   worship · 300
Harth, Eric · 270
Hatch, Nathan
   The Democratization of American Christianity · 228
Havelock, Eric · 107-108, 129, 192, 194, 202, 345
   McLuhan · 108
   oral tradition · 107
   Origins of Western Literacy · 107
   phonetic alphabet · 117
   Preface to Plato · 107
   primary and secondary orality · 191n
   The Greek Concept of Justice · 107
   The Muse Learns to Write · 108
Hegel, G. W. F. · 59, 70, 167
   Absolute Spirit · 73
   relativism · 209
   Universal Mind · 73
Heidegger, Martin · 103-104, 155, 160, 210, 211, 212, 213
   Being · 104
   literary criticism · 104
   mass-man · 103
   ontology · 103
   Question Concerning Technology and Other Essays, The · 104
   Sein und Zeit (Being and Time) · 103
   technology · 104
Henderson, Charles · 287
Henderson, Katherine · 288
Henslow, John · 69
Heraclitus · 39
Herbert, George · 381
Hertz, Heinrich · 141
Hilkiah · 12
Hitler, Adolph · 78, 81, 90, 92, 290
   magic power of the spoken word · 76
   mass media · 75
   Mein Kampf · 75
   propaganda · 269
Hodge, Charles: criticism of Darwin · 71
Hoff, Marcian "Ted" Jr. · 144
Hofstadter, Richard: *Anti-intellectualism in American Life* · 228
Hollerith, Herman · 143
Hooker, Thomas · 330
Hopkins, Gerard Manley · 110, 112, 119, 121, 161
Horkheimer, Max · 78
Hoskins, Hubert · 165
Hovland, Carl · 94, 98, 136

one-way communication · 94
persuasion research · 94
Hovland, Carl I. · 77
How, W. W. · 302
Howe, John · 330
Hughes, James
   Church in Cyberspace, The · 58
   media naiveté · 281
Hull, Clark · 83, 92, 93, 94, 136
Humbard, Rex · 293
Huss, John · 327
Husserl, Edmund · 103
Huxley, Aldous · 71, 134, 135, 399
   Brave New World · 26
   Brave New World Revisited · 26
   cultural criticism · 27
   totalitarianism of pleasure · 27
Huxley, Thomas · 71
Hybels, Bill: church growth · 284

I

Innis, Harold · 66, 101, 104-107, 116, 131
   Bias of Communication, The · 105, 113, 138
   communication, history of · 105
   communication study · 105
   cultural criticism · 106
   electronic media · 106
   Empire and Communication · 138
   Empire and Communications · 105
   History of the Canadian Pacific Railroad, The · 105
   holistic and radical media theory · 104
   influence on McLuhan · 107, 113
   interdisciplinary · 105
   McLuhan · 113n
   mechanization of knowledge · 106
   media criticism · 107
   media determinism · 105
   oral tradition · 106
   political economics · 105
   present-mindedness · 106
   sociology · 106
   space-biased media · 106, 190, 192, 227
   technology, sociological effects · 280
   time-biased media · 106, 190, 192, 227
   Toronto Seminar · 113n
   Veblen · 105n
Issachar, cultural criticism · 27

J

James, John Angell
   An Earnest Ministry · 365
   definition of earnestness · 365
   directness in preaching · 391
James, William · 82, 84, 88, 116, 134
   Pragmatism · 235
Jenkins, Charles Francis · 141
Jobs, Steve · 144, 145
Wycliffe, John · 327
Joseph: type of Christ · 372
Joshua · 338
Josiah: opposition to idolatry · 9, 12
Joyce, James · 110, 112, 161, 250, 260, 263
Jung, Carl G.
   The Psychology of the Unconscious · 77
   theory of the unconscious · 77
Jünger, Ernst · 234
Justin Martyr · 324
Kahn, Bob · 147
Kahn, Genghis · 238
Kant, Immanuel · 40, 57
   epistemology · 29
   heuristic principle · 172
   noumena and phenomena · 344
   relativism · 209
Kapp, Ernst: first use of term "philosophy of technology" · 68
Katz, Elihu · 91
Kelly, Douglas: *Preachers with Power* · 360
Kennedy, D. James · 293, 332
Keyes, Richard · 26, 31, 32
   apologetics · 60
   idolatry · 265
   near and far idols · 37
   No God But God: Breaking with the Idols of Our Age · 30
Kierkegaard, Søren · 123, 159
Klapper, Joseph · 102
Kleinrock, Leonard · 146
Kline, Meredith G. · 238, 316, 317
   Genesis history · 30
   on Genesis 6 · 3
   on woman in Zechariah 5 · 22
Knox, John
   preacher · 329
   preaching as living voice · 337
   worship · 300
Koppel, Ted: television · 257
Kroker, Arthur, disappearing ego · 233
Kuhn, Thomas: *The Structure of Scientific Revolutions* · 89

L

Lama Surya Das · 290
Lamarck, Jean-Baptiste de Monet de · 69
Lamech · 2
Lasch, Christopher · 220, 226
   The Culture of Narcissism · 215
Lasswell, Harold D. · 77, 87-88, 89, 98, 124, 134, 136

content analysis · 87
definition of propaganda · 87
development of policy sciences · 88
political psychology · 87
propaganda analysis · 87
psychoanalysis · 87
Psychopathology and Politics · 87
social psychology · 87
Latimer, Hugh · 330
Lazarsfeld, Paul F. · 81, 89-92, 98, 134
   Adorno · 102
   focus groups · 91
   market research · 90, 92
   mass communication effects · 89
   one-way effects of mass media · 92
   People's Choice, The · 91
   Personal Influence: The Part Played by People in the Flow of Mass Communication · 91
   Radio and the Printed Page · 92
   radio audience research · 90
   Radio Research Project · 91
   sociological methodology · 90
Leacock, Stephen · 381
Leary, Timothy: electronic realities · 268
Leavis, F. L. · 109
Leibniz, Gottfried Wilhelm · 59
Leighton, Robert · 330
Leonard, John · 255
Levinson, Paul · 250
Lewin, Kurt · 81, 92-93, 98, 136
   concept of cohesion · 93
   Field Theory · 92
   concept of gatekeepers · 93
   group dynamics · 92
   individual perception · 92
   one of founders of social psychology · 92
Lewis, C. S. · 245, 266
   An Experiment in Criticism · 247
   chronological snobbery · 226
   formal worship · 301
   novelty · 233
   reading · 274
   warm and *cold* sins · 38
Lewis, Corinne · 110
Lewis, Wyndham · 110
Licklider, J. C. R. · 145, 146
Lippmann, Walter · 88-89, 125
   agenda setting · 89
   commercialism in media · 221
   intellectual influence on communication study · 88
   Phantom Public, The · 89
   "pictures in our heads" · 88

   pseudo-environment · 89
   Public Opinion · 88, 138
   "stereotypes" · 89
Livingstone, John · 330
Lloyd-Jones, D. Martin · 332, 337, 341
   earnestness in preaching · 365
   Preachers and Preaching · 360
Lowell, James Russell · 399
Lowenthal, Leo · 78
Luce, Claire Booth · 250
Lud, Ned · 152
Luddite · 128, 129, 152, 157, 174, 194, 235, 236, 243, 395
Luther, Martin · 73, 136, 302, 326, 330, 354
   commentary on Galatians · 328
   love of Scripture · 329
   on printing · 280
   Scripture and preaching · 342
Lyell, Charles · 69
Lynd, Robert · 102
Lyotard, Jean-François
   The Postmodern Condition · 210

M

Macdonald, George · 349
Machen, J. Gresham · 137, 332
   consecrating culture · 59
   intellect · 51, 53
   on culture · 47
   tyranny of experts · 136
MacLeish, Archibald · 98
Maguire, John · 170
Malachi · 319
Malthus, Thomas: *Essays on the Principle of Population* · 69
Mander, Jerry · 176
   danger of X-radiation in television · 251
Mannheim, Karl, sociology of knowledge · 52
Marjo · 366
Marsden, George: *The Soul of the American University* · 228
Marshall, John · 90
Maruyama, Allen · 165
Marx, Karl · 60, 69, 73, 78, 80, 87, 88, 123, 159
   Communist Manifesto, The · 73
   dialectic of class conflict · 73
   religion as opiate of masses · 73
Mattingly, Terry · 284
Mauchly, John W. · 143
Maugham, W. Somerset: brevity · 391
Mayo brothers · 361
McGavran, Donald · 282
McGrath, Alister: J. I. Packer biography · 385
McLuhan, Eric · 164, 250, 251, 259

INDEX OF AUTHORS AND PERSONS

laws of media · 187
limiting electronic media · 275
literacy · 275
Medium and the Light, The · 167
McLuhan, Herbert · 109
McLuhan, Marshall · 30, 66, 67, 101, 108-120, 121, 126, 128, 129, 131, 132, 137, 158, 161-170, 174, 176, 178, 183, 194, 196, 203, 229, 236, 241, 242, 260, 261, 280, 281, 386
   acoustic and visual space · 55, 117, 190
   advertising · 111
   all-at-onceness · 227
   artist · 399
   Buddhism and Hinduism · 165
   Calvin · 162, 163
   Calvinism · 163
   Carpenter, Edmund · 114
   Catholicism · 163
   Center for Understanding Media · 119
   change of social scale · 188
   Chesterton · 161, 162, 162n
   Christ is medium and message · 166
   Christian communication theory · 170
   Christian view of man · 157, 168, 184
   Christianity in his media criticism · 164
   church · 167, 170
   church and electronic environment · 167
   Ciceronian ideal · 110
   computer · 57, 166, 258
   concepts · 166
   conservative · 115
   content analysis · 185
   conversion to Catholicism · 161
   cool medium · 305
   counter culture · 115
   counter-environment · 299
   Creator-creature distinction · 167
   Culture and Communication Seminars · 113
   cybernetics · 114, 114n
   determinism · 168
   discarnate man · 55, 57, 169, 254, 286
   early religious life · 162
   education · 112, 169, 254
   electric technology · 118
   electronic extension of human consciousness · 167
   electronic illusion · 270
   English literature · 109, 166
   Eucharist · 168
   Explorations in Communication · 114
   extensions of man · 55, 68, 107, 118, 127, 184
   faith · 161n, 164
   figure-ground distinction · 55, 118, 185
   Fordham University · 119
   founder of Media Ecology · 119
   global village · 57, 117, 122, 140
   Gnosticism · 166
   God · 165
   Great Books · 111
   Gutenberg Galaxy, The · 68, 117, 118, 122, 168
   historical concreteness of Christianity · 165
   history of communication · 114
   holistic and radical media theory · 104
   hot communication · 336
   humanistic studies · 110
   ideas and concepts · 162
   idolatry · 4, 5
   Incarnation · 165
   Incarnation and resurrection · 163
   information overload · 271
   Innis, Harold · 107, 113n, 113
   instant communication · 101
   intellectual detective · 112
   intellectual life · 162
   lack of theoretical foundation · 120
   language as view-maker · 381
   laws of media · 55, 187
   Lewis, C. S. · 161n
   library of C and C Seminar · 114n
   literacy · 168
   literary criticism · 110
   literary symbolism · 110
   love of books · 275
   Luther, Martin · 163
   magic in media · 267
   man as image of God · 169
   mass media · 111, 169
   Mechanical Bride, The · 111, 138, 167
   mechanization of human sensorium · 257
   media, nature of · 107
   media and education · 189
   media bias · 204
   media criticism and the church · 164
   media determinist · 153
   media ecology · 102
   media education · 169
   media naiveté · 279
   Medium Is the Massage, The · 139
   medium is the message · 54, 120, 184, 302, 368
   microphone · 305
Ong, Walter · 119
orality · 201

participation in electronic environment · 275
pattern recognition · 271
Pentecostal condition · 57
percept · 165
perception · 169
percepts and concepts · 166
Place of Thomas Nashe in the Learning of his Time, The · 109
Plato · 163
point of view · 120; circulating · 112
popular culture · 109
preaching · 396
Preface to Plato · 108
print culture · 168
printed word · 345
probes · 118
Protestantism · 163
Puritanism · 163, 166
Ramist logic · 109n
rear view mirror · 187
religion · 109, 161
religion and culture · 164
religion and media ecology · 165
religious upbringing · 108
retribalization · 133
rhetoric · 109
rhetorical pattern · 110
Scripture · 170
secret societies · 166
shift from visual to acoustic space · 261
somnambulist · 118; public · 112
technological determinist · 116
Teilhard's cosmic evolution · 167
television · 250
television, light through quality of · 250
television and dyslexia · 256
television viewing · 256
Theall, Donald · 113
theoretical foundation · 183
Thomism · 163
Toronto Seminar · 113n
trivium · 114n
Understanding Media · 57, 117, 118, 127, 138
universal gnosticism · 166
War and Peace in the Global Village · 139
Wiener, Norbert · 114n
written word, detribalizing · 276
Mead, George Herbert · 83, 84, 105
symbolic interactionism · 84
Mead, Margaret · 95
Mehl, Duane · 278

Merriam, Charles · 87
Merton, Robert
pseudo-Gemeinschaft · 91
Metcalfe, Robert · 147
Meyrowitz, Joshua · 117, 120, 132-134, 137, 176, 186-187, 192
determinism · 133
disappearance of childhood · 231
education and television · 253
electronic situations · 133, 207
integration of media metaphors · 187
media and education · 189
media and social settings · 206
media criticism · 185
media metaphors · 134, 186
media theory · 132
medium and structure of social situations · 188
medium as a conduit · 186
medium as a language/grammar · 186
medium as an environment · 186
medium theory · 185
No Sense of Place · 133, 231
patterns of access
group identity · 188
hierarchies · 188
patterns of access to information · 188
socialization · 188
Postman · 119
print situations · 133, 207
relativism · 134, 189, 232
relativism of social identity · 189
role triad · 188
social place · 231
synthetic approach · 134, 154
Miller, Samuel: *The Christian Ministry* · 360
Mills, C. Wright: *The Power Elite* · 91
Mitcham, Carl · 68, 160
Morenz, Siegfried · 352
Morley, Christopher · 381
Monsma, Stephen V. · 172
value-ladenness of technology · 156
Morse, Samuel F. B. · 139, 140, 280
idea of electric communication is not debatable · 281
Moses · 199, 318, 338
servant of the Lord · 358
type of Christ · 355
written covenant · 317
Muggeridge, Malcolm · 173-174, 176, 278
Christ and the Media · 139, 151, 173
Christian faith · 173
criticism of television · 173
cult of consumption · 174

ignorance of McLuhan · 174
Jesus Christ, antidote to television · 174
journalist · 173
London Lectures in Contemporary
    Christianity · 173
media ecology · 174
Socialism · 173
television journalism · 173
word and image · 174
Mumford, Lewis · 85-86, 114, 126, 132, 142,
    264, 280
  eotechnic · 86
  list of inventions · 139
  megamachine · 86
  monotechnic · 86
  myth of the machine · 238
  Myth of the Machine, The · 86, 138
  neotechnic · 86
  paleotechnic · 86
  polytechnic · 86
  Technics and Civilization · 85, 127, 138
Murray, Iain · 337
Myers, Kenneth · 29, 176, 205, 227, 309
  *All God's Children and Blue Suede
    Shoes: Christians and Popular
    Culture* · 247
  critique of popular culture · 247
  cultural criticism · 47
  description of culture · 49
  television · 252

N

Napier, John · 142
Napoleon · 74
Nash, Ronald · 213
  The Closing of the American Heart · 51
Nashe, Thomas · 109, 114n; trivium · 114
Nebuchadnezzar · 21, 22
Nederhood, Joel · 177-179, 190-191, 254,
    256, 274, 296, 297, 304, 332
  categories of influence · 249
  *Christian Reformed Church Synod
    Report*, on television ministry · 178
  *Church's Mission to the Educated
    American, The* · 177, 228
  effectiveness in preaching, snare of · 392
  five · 178
  five categories of influence · 190
  homiletician · 177
  importance of reading · 381
  preaching · 178
  radio ministry · 177
  Reformed Broadcaster · 177
  salvation, church oriented · 179

television as a technique/delivery system ·
    178
  television criticism · 178
  television ministry · 177
Nelson, Ted · 146
Neumann, John von · 143
Neurath, Otto · 76
Newman, Cardinal · 165
Niebuhr, H. Richard: *Christ and Culture* · 47
Niebuhr, Reinhold · 32, 123, 159
Nietzsche, Frederich · 40, 74-76, 77
  attacks on Christianity · 74
  autonomy of man · 75
  Beyond Good and Evil · 75
  Gay Science, The · 75
  God is dead · 75
  idols · 75
  pagan revival · 222
  superman · 74
  Thus Spoke Zarathustra · 74
  Twilight of the Idols, The · 75
  will to power · 74, 80, 206
  Will to Power, The · 75
Nipkow, Paul · 141
Noah · 317, 320
Noll, Mark · 307
  academia · 51
  Scandal of the Evangelical Mind, The ·
    228
Nylen, Bob · 290
Nystrom, Christine · 96

O

Oden, Thomas · 226, 229
Old, Hughes Oliphant · 319
  classical rhetoric · 373
  *Reading and Preaching of the Scriptures
    in the Worship of the Christian
    Church, The* · 382
  worship · 301
Olsen, Ken · 143, 144
Ong, Walter · 66, 67, 120, 121-122, 124,
    126, 129, 137, 166, 170-171, 194, 229,
    342
  audio-visual fad · 367
  Darwinism · 170
  elevation of the oral · 122
  evolving sensorium · 183
  Greek philosophy · 201
  *Interfaces of the Word: Studies in the
    Evolution of Consciousness and
    Culture* · 170
  interiority · 273
  literacy · 193
  literacy, critique of · 193

McLuhan · 119
oral and visual · 344
orality · 170; nature of · 121
Orality and Literacy · 108, 121, 139
orality: primacy of · 192
orality undermined by print · 258
Presence of the Word, The · 138, 343
primary and secondary distinction · 191n
print, critique of · 200
print media · 168n
Ramism · 121
Ramist logic · 109n
Ramus Method, and the Decay of Dialogue · 121
Scripture and alphabet · 197
Scripture, stability of · 197
shift from orality to literacy · 190
Teilhard de Chardin · 121, 122, 122n, 170
text and Holy Spirit · 170
Trinity · 190
visual · 201
visual analogues · 201
visual, critique of · 344
word, man's primary medium · 343
word as event · 345
written and printed word · 121, 171
Origen · 324
Orwell, George · 88, 134, 135, 173, 399
1984 · 26
Animal Farm · 26
cultural criticism · 27
totalitarianism · 27
Owen, John · 330
Owens, Judith · 249
Owens, Virginia Stem · 176

P
Pacey, Arnold · 155
Packard, Vance
symbolic manipulation · 221
The Hidden Persuaders · 138
Packer, James I.
definition of preaching · 385
worship · 357
Pagels, Elaine
Gnostic Gospels · 58
Paglia, Camille · 222
Park, Robert E. · 84-85, 105
crowd and public · 84
first academic student of mass communication · 84
human ecology · 84
Immigrant Press and Its Control, The · 84
Introduction to the Science of Sociology, The · 84

referential and expressive communication · 84
separated research from applied sociology · 84
Pascal, Blaise · 142
Patrick, Saint · 326
Pattison, T. Harwood · 330
Paul · 315
confronts idolatry · 17
letters are Scripture · 198
Paul Goodman: *New Reformation* · 65
Pavlov · 92, 93, 94
Pearson, Karl · 72
Peirce, C. S. · 83
Pragmatism · 235
Piaget · 92
Plato · 32, 36, 59, 107, 184
Poe, Edgar Allan · 96, 112, 120, 168
Popper, Karl
falsifiability criterion · 79
law of unintended consequences · 80, 97
Postman, Neil · 4, 26, 66, 67, 96, 119, 126-129, 131, 132, 134, 137, 143, 158, 171-172, 176, 177, 203, 229, 241, 272, 281
Age of Exposition · 346
Age of Show Business · 346
Amusing Ourselves to Death · 27, 127, 128, 139, 255
Building a Bridge to the Eighteenth Century · 172
computer · 128, 142
computer literacy · 243
cultural criticism · 27
danger of amusement · 247
Disappearance of Childhood, The · 279
education · 254
End of Education, The · 127, 230
Enlightenment epistemology · 172
epistemology: Post-Kantian · 172
great narratives · 171, 387
great symbol drain · 128
idolatry · 4, 5, 129
Jewish faith · 171
loving resistance fighters · 128
McLuhan · 119, 126, 127, 128
media criticism · 171
media determinist · 153
media education · 128
medium as metaphor · 346
metanarratives · 210
Old Testament · 171
presuppositions · 171
printing and common language · 280
reading · 272

INDEX OF AUTHORS AND PERSONS 499

relativism · 128, 129, 172
Second Commandment · 129, 171
technology: sociological effects · 279
Technopoly · 126, 128, 139, 266
television · 128, 292
television and education · 267
television and worship · 292
television as entertainment · 346
television critique · 292
television religion · 295
worship · 171
worship and culture · 171
Pound, Ezra · 110, 112, 196
Powlison, David · 31, 214
idolatry · 39, 396
idolatry and perception · 33
idolatry in counseling · 30
Pulitzer, Joseph · 99
Purves, George · 367
Q
Quetelet, Adolphe · 69
R
Ramus, Petrus · 121, 109n
Reusch, Jurgen · 114
Richards, I. A. · 109, 111
Roberts, Larry · 146
Roberts, Oral · 292, 293
Robertson, Pat · 292, 293
Robinson, Haddon: preaching · 385
Rockefeller, John D. · 136
Rogers, Everett M. · 67, 68, 70, 72, 79, 88, 100, 105, 116, 117, 135
A History of Communications Study: A Biographical Approach · 66
Roosevelt, Franklin Delano
first televised president · 141
radio broadcasts · 90, 98
Rorty, Richard · 211
Rose, Lance · 291
Rose, Stephen · 288
Roszak, Theodore
Cult of Information, The · 139
Rowe, Gary: naiveté re television · 280
Russell, Bertrand · 94
Rutherford, Samuel · 330
Ryle, J. C.: oral and written · 378
Samuel · 9, 318
opposition to idolatry · 8
Sarnoff, David · 141
Sartre, Jean-Paul · 103
Savanarola · 328
Schaeffer, Francis · 28, 46, 204, 332
cultural criticism · 209
epistemology · 60

Escape from Reason · 209
God Who Is There, The · 209
line of despair · 209
presuppositional apologetics · 31
relativism · 209
Van Til's apologetics · 29
Schaff, Phillip · 326
Schlick, Moritz · 76
Schlossberg, Herbert · 31
atheism · 32
idolatry: paradigm for cultural criticism · 27, 30
Idols For Destruction: Christian Faith and Its Confrontation With American Society · 30
McLuhan · 30
Schoenberg, Arnold · 76
Schopenhauer, Arthur
materialistic science · 74
Schramm, Wilbur · 66, 67, 97-100, 136, 175, 186, 308
communication study · 97
English literature · 98
first communication textbooks · 99
first Ph.D. degrees in communications · 99
founds first doctoral program in mass communications · 138
journalism · 98
Keynesian economics · 99
Mass Media and National Development · 100
OFF's educational director · 98
Process and Effects of Mass Communication, The · 100
Television in the Lives of Our Children · 100
Schuller, Robert · 292
Schultze, Quentin · 172, 174-177, 175, 176, 246
absence of Media Ecology · 177
assessment of Media Ecologists · 176
distinction between portrayal and point of view · 175
McLuhan · 176
Postman · 177
Redeeming Television: How TV Changes Christians - How Christians Can Change TV · 175, 177
Reformed media scholar · 174
Schramm · 175
technology a tool · 176
television evaluation · 257
television: narrative power · 257
work in radio and television · 175

Schuurman, Egbert
    Reflections on the Technological Society · 173
    technicism · 235
    Technology and the Future · 173
Seashore, Carl · 98
Seyle, Hans · 117
Shakespeare · 381
Shannon, Claude · 96-97, 98, 114, 142
    binary digit, concept of (bit) · 97
    concern about uses of his model · 97n
    first full communication theory · 97
    information theory · 96
    Mathematical Theory of Communication, The · 96, 138
Sheen, Bishop Fulton
    naiveté re: television · 280
Sietsma, K.: office, idea of · 350, 359
Sills, David · 91
Simmel, George · 82, 84
    abstract social forms · 207
    co-founder of modern sociology · 81
Small, Albion W. · 82
Smith, Adam · 82
    Wealth of Nations · 69
Smith, Henry · 330
Snow, Robert
    media formats · 207n
    media logic · 207
Solomon: opposition to idolatry · 11
Spence, Kenneth · 92
Spencer, Sir Herbert: Social Darwinism · 72
Spinoza, Benedict · 59
Spong, Bishop John Shelby · 290
Spring, Gardiner: Power in the Pulpit · 360
Spurgeon, Charles Haddon · 332
    centrality of preaching · 313
    Early Years, The · 360
    Full Harvest · 360
    Lectures to My Students · 360
    Metropolitan Tabernacle Pulpit · 360
    New Park Street Pulpit · 360
    sense appeal, use of · 394
Stalin, Joseph · 78
Stalker, James
    The Preacher and His Models · 360
Stanton, Frank · 90
Stephen: opposition to idolatry · 15
Stibitz, George R. · 143
Stock, Brian · 164
Stoddard, George · 99
Stoll, Clifford · 130
    near Luddite · 130
    Silicon Snake Oil: Second Thoughts on the Information Highway · 130
Storrs, Richard S.
    Preaching without Notes · 380
Stott, John · 332
Strasser, Otto · 76
Strate, Lance · 107
Sutherland, Ivan · 145
Swaggart, Jimmy · 292

T
Tarde, Gabriel: Laws of Imitation · 81
Taylor, Jeremy · 330
Teilhard de Chardin, Pierre · 121, 190, 289
    cosmic evolution · 122
    Gnosticism · 122
    McLuhan · 166
    noosphere · 122
    Phenomenon of Man, The · 122
Telushkin, Joseph · 290
Tertullian · 324
Tesler, Larry · 145
Thales · 69, 154
Theall, Donald · 114, 119, 164, 183
    Innis · 113n
    McLuhan · 113, 119
Thielicke, Helmut · 354, 362
    preaching · 378
Thomas, Dylan · 381
Thompson, Francis
    The Hound of Heaven · 1
Thoreau, Henry David · 140
    contextless information · 270
Tillich, Paul · 103, 123, 159
Tocqueville, Alexis de
    American individualism · 215
Toffler, Alvin
    information overload · 269
    neurological effects of television · 252
Trimp, Cornelius · 371
    idolatry · 5
    relevance in preaching · 376
    results in preaching · 392

U
Ulfilas · 326

V
Van Til, Cornelius · 26, 29, 31, 34, 35, 38, 41, 43, 55, 205
    antithesis · 50
    borrowed capital · 56, 159, 172, 214
    epistemology: Christian · 29
    idolatry · 17, 37, 55
    liturgy · 301
    presuppositional apologetics · 29, 31
    rationality · 47

INDEX OF AUTHORS AND PERSONS

relativism · 209
Van Til, Henry: definition of culture · 49
Vanderhill, Steven · 307
Veblen, Thorstein · 116
  influence on Innis · 105n
  Theory of the Leisure Class · 105
Veith, Gene Edward · 176
  apologetics · 236
  Postmodern Times · 209
Venturi, Robert · 210
Volbeda, Samuel
  The Pastoral Genius of Preaching · 368
Vos, Geerhardus
  definition of idolatry · 5
  Grace and Glory · 360
  relevance of Scripture · 376

W

Wakin, Edward · 279, 396
Warfield, Benjamin Breckenridge
  classical apologetics · 31
  preaching, importance of · 367
Weaver, Warren · 96, 114
  popularized Shannon model · 96n
Weber, Max · 82, 123
  The Protestant Ethic and the Spirit of Capitalism · 81
Wells, David · 224, 225, 234
  congregation as customer · 285
  content of preaching · 348
  electronic analgesic · 229
  No Place for Truth · 228
  preacher and professionalism · 347, 348
Wesleys · 332
Whitefield, George · 332
Whitehead, Alfred North · 94, 98
Whitman, Walt · 140, 205
Wiener, Norbert · 94-96, 98, 136, 114n
  Cybernetic Theory · 95
  Cybernetics: Or Control and Communication in the Animal and the Machine · 94, 95, 114, 138
  feedback · 95
  God and Golem, Inc.: A Comment on Certain Points Where Cybernetics Infringes on Religion · 95
  Human Use of Human Beings: Cybernetics and Society · 95, 127
  Systems Theory · 95
  technology, warning re: · 242
Wiersbe, Warren
  religious television · 292
Wilberforce, Bishop · 70
Wilde, Oscar · 279
Wilkinson, John · 116, 234

Williams, R. Vaughan · 302
Wingren, Gustaf · 377
Winn, Marie · 264
  television addiction · 250
  television and drug use · 250, 252
  television and reality · 266
  The Plug-in Drug · 139
Wittgenstein, Ludwig von · 210
  Tractatus Logico- philosophicus · 77
Woiwode, Larry · 341
Wong, Eric · 242
Wozniak, Steve · 144
Wundt, Wilhelm · 84, 98
  experimental psychology · 81

Y

Yeats, William Butler · 110, 112, 239
  The Second Coming · 204
Zeno, Cypriote · 39
Zwingli, Ulrich · 329, 331
Zworykin, Vladimir · 141

Index of Scripture References

Genesis
Book of · 2
1 · 198, 343
1:1 · 181
1:19 · 3
1:26, 27 · 2
1:28 · 49
2:16, 17 · 316
2:19 · 202, 316
3 · 2, 3
3:15 · 316
4 · 2
4:19 ff · 50
6 · 3
9:1-17 · 49
9:16 · 181
11 · 3
11:4 · 182
15:13 · 318
28 · 288
31:19 · 3
49:24 · 10, 338

Exodus
3:14 · 3
4:12, 15 · 318
18:20 · 318
18:21, 22 · 318
19:16 · 355
19:19 · 355
20:4-6 · 4
20:25 · 10
21:6 · 3
22:8, 9, 28 · 3
23:32 · 39
24:12 · 318
31:3-5 · 246
31:18 · 197
32:1, 23 · 6
32:9 · 7, 15

Leviticus
10:11 · 318, 319
25:9 · 355
26:30 · 6
26:41 · 15

Numbers
10:2-10 · 355
27:17 · 338

Deuteronomy
4:2 · 316
4:15 ff. · 8
7:25, 26 · 19
12 · 8, 10
12:11 · 10
18:9-22 · 8
18:15-22 · 317
24:8 · 318, 319
28:36 · 22
29:14-19 · 12
29:29 · 316
30:10 · 199
32:15 ff · 8
32:17 · 8
34:5 · 358

Joshua
6 · 355
24:29 · 358

Judges
3:27 · 355
4:21 · 314
5:26 · 314
6 · 8
16:28-31 · 8
17:5 · 8

1 Samuel
10 · 318
15:1ff · 318
31:9 · 8

2 Samuel
5 · 8
5:2 · 338
7:7 · 338
12:25 · 318

1 Kings
12 · 7
16:31ff · 23

18:1 ff · 23
18:20 ff · 6
18:21, 24 · 31
18:27 · 40
21:25, 26 · 23
22 · 367
22:17 · 338

2 Kings
9:30 ff · 23
17:8, 15 · 11
22:8 · 383
23:2 · 383

1 Chronicles
10:9 · 8
10:13 · 318
16:26 · 9
22:5 · 10
22:19 · 10

2 Chronicle
3:10 ff. · 10
6:14, 18 · 11
10:15 · 318
17:3, 4, 6 · 397
17:9 · 397
29 · 12
29:25 · 12
30:22 · 12
34:8 ff · 12
34:14 · 9
34:21 · 12
35:26 · 13
36:7, 14 · 13
36:19 · 13
36:21 · 13

Nehemiah
8 · 12
8:1 · 319
8:8 · 319, 331, 383

Job
38:35 · 140

Psalms
1 · 193, 200, 345, 352
1:4 · 394
2 · 13, 42
4:4 · 273
11:9 · 182
18:1 · 358
19:1-6 · 314
19:7-14 · 314
19:8 · 331
23 · 338
29:4, 5 · 344
34:8 · 202
36:9 · 202
49:6, 11 · 3
51:6 · 273
52:9 · 294
75:1 · 182
77:12 · 273
80 · 338
82:6 · 3
90 · 10
91 · 10
91, fn · 16
95:2 · 294
115 · 4
115:4-7 · 6
115:8 · 11, 24
135:15-17 · 6
138:1 · 3
138:2 · 182
142:1 · 342

Proverbs
5:12 · 13
6:23 · 13
8:30 · 10, 343
10:18 · 342
13:24 · 13
26:4 · 41
26:5 · 41

Isaiah
1:10 · 319
2:8 · 6
2:18, 20 · 12

502

INDEX OF SCRIPTURE REFERENCES

3:4, 5 · 228
6:10 · 15
7:9 · 183
8:20 · 319
10:10, 11 · 12
17:8 · 12
28:16 · 10
31:7 · 11
40:11 · 339
40:18 · 6
41:21-29 · 12
42:8 · 12
44:8 · 6
44:9-20 · 12
44:18 · 6
44:28 · 339
45:16 · 12
45:20 · 12
46:1-7 · 12
46:6 · 6
48:5 · 12
53:11 · 358
55:11 · 319, 336
57:1-13 · 12
58:1 · 354
61:1 · 320
66:1,2 · 15
66:3 · 12
66:5 · 319

Jeremiah
1:2 · 319
2:30 · 13
3:17 · 13
5:3 · 13
5:14 · 315
7:28 · 13
9:13 · 13
10:2 · 13
10:5,6 · 37
10:8 · 12, 13
16:12 · 13
18:12 · 13
20:9 · 313
23 · 314
23:23, 24 · 12
23:28, 29 · 313
32:33 · 13
50:23 · 314
51:17, 47, 52 · 12

Ezekiel
1:3 · 319

6:4 · 6
14:3 · 12
34:23 · 339
44:10, 12 · 12

Daniel
2 · 13, 22
4 · 13, 22
5:5ff · 197
7 · 21
11:36, 37 · 3

Hosea
8:4 · 30

Amos
5:25-27 · 15

Jonah
2:3 · 319

Habakkuk
2:18-20 · 11

Haggai
1:12 · 340

Zechariah
5 · 15, 22
10:2 · 12
13:1, 2 · 14

Malachi
3:1 · 319
4:2 · 319

Matthew
2:19-22 · 10
3:1 · 320
6:24 · 14
7:29 · 358
10:7 · 320
10:20 · 296
11:1 · 370
12:34 · 46
15:13-20 · 392
16:12-28 · 359
18:20 · 276
20:25-28 · 358
22:15-22 · 14
22:29, 31 · 331
24:14 · 399
24:31 · 355

Mark
3:26 · 22
7:21 · 46
13:10 · 321
14:58 · 10, 15

Luke
1:4 · 196
1:51 · 46
4 · 322
4:16ff · 319
4:18, 19 · 320
4:43 · 320
9:47 · 46
10:16 · 384
10:27 · 45
16:14 · 15
20:47 · 15
24:47 · 320

John
1 · 60
1:1 · 181, 320
1:9 · 54
1:18 · 195
2:19 · 15
3 · 343
3:3 · 202
4:21-23 · 171
5:20 · 181
5:39 · 195
6:63 · 339
10:3 · 339
10:4 · 339
10:15 · 339
10:27 · 339
14:9 · 20
14:16ff · 341
14:26 · 321
15:26, 27 · 321
16:7 · 341
16:13 · 321
17:4, 8 · 181
21:15 · 339

Acts
2:2-4 · 313
2:11 · 321
4:2 · 322
4:12 · 386
4:13 · 364
5:42 · 322
6:2 · 322
6:13, 14 · 15

7 · 15, 16
7:39, fn · 304
7:42, 43 · 15
7:48-50 · 15
7:51 · 15
8:4 · 322
8:30, 31 · 353
9:20 · 322
9:29 · 364
13:13ff · 322
13:14ff · 319
13:15 · 383
14:12 · 16
15:29 · 16
17 · 322, 369
17:10, 11 · 353
17:16-34 · 17
17:23 · 17
17:27, 28 · 182
17:30, 31 · 45
19:19, 24ff · 369
19:20 · 18
19:37 · 19
20:27 · 386
20:28 · 339, 369
20:32 · 331
25:19 · 53
26:8 · 53
26:18 · 331
28:25 · 331
28:31 · 322, 364, 370

Romans
1 · 14, 17, 18, 40
1:16 · 230, 331
1:18 · 2
1:18, 20 · 19
1:18-20 · 182, 236
1:18-32 · 18, 36
1:18ff · 336
1:20 · 24, 40
1:21 · 19
1:21-23 · 42
1:23 · 20
1:24, 26-32 · 19
1:25 · 2, 18, 19, 33
2:18 · 344
6:6 · 33
7:23 · 202
8:29 · 20

503

10:3 · 14
10:14 · 384
10:14-17 · 322
10:15 · 370
10:17 · 313, 331, 352
12:1, 2 · 230, 371, 392
12:2 · 46, 271
12:11 · 33
15:4 · 331, 372, 392
16:17, 18 · 33

1 Corinthians
1 & 2 · 373
1:21 · 317, 335
1:21, 23 · 335
1:23 · 183
2:2 · 339
2:4 · 363
2:13 · 285
3:16 · 288
4:1 · 400
4:1, 2 · 368
5:10, 11 · 21
6:9, 10 · 21
8:4, 7, 10 · 21
9:16 · 323
10:14 · 20
10:14-22 · 20
10:20 · 21
10:23-31 · 56
10:28 · 21
11:1 · 340
12:2 · 21
14:8 · 355
14:19 · 389
14:24 · 279
14:24,25 · 331
15:49 · 21
15:51, 52 · 355

2 Corinthians
2:15-17 · 315
2:17 · 363
3:6 · 200
3:18 · 20, 340
4:2 · 363
4:4 · 20
4:5, 6 · 343
4:6 · 367
4:16 · 273
5:13, 14 · 363

5:18-20 · 309
5:18-21 · 341
5:20 · 377
6:16 · 21
10:3-5, fn · 236
10:3-6 · 58
10:4-6 · 42
11:6 · 279
12:15 · 363

Galatians
4:3 · 21
4:9 · 33
5:20 · 21
6:6 · 344

Ephesians
1:10 · 158
2:19-22 · 10, 308
2:20 · 331
2:21 · 298
4 · 272
4:15, 16 · 294
4:17 · 42
6:7 · 33
6:18-20 · 351, 384

Colossians
1:15 · 20
3:5, 10 · 20, 21
4:16, 17 · 340

1 Thessalonians
1:5 · 364
1:9 · 20, 44
1:9, 10 · 395
2:1-10 · 362
2:4, 5 · 295
2:5 · 224
2:8, 9 · 341
2:13 · 321, 385
4:9 · 385
5:12, 13 · 360

1 Timothy
3:1-7 · 359
3:15, 16 · 299, 368
4:13 · 383
4:13, 14 · 359
4:13-16 · 323

2 Timothy
1:13 · 271
2:2 · 323
2:15 · 323
2:24 · 358
3:14-17 · 323
3:15 · 193, 317, 345
3:15-17 · 331
3:16, 17 · 347
4:1-5 · 359
4:2 · 323

Titus
1:6-9 · 359
2:7 · 271
2:8 · 363
3:3 · 33

Hebrews
1:1-3 · 317
1:3 · 20
4:12 · 393
6:12 · 340
9:11 · 10
10:1 · 20
10:24, 25 · 353
13:7, 17 · 360

James
3:1-12 · 184

1 Peter
1:7-12 · 320
1:10,11 · 339
2:5 · 298
3:15 · 44, 46
3:18-20 · 320
4:10 · 368
5:1-4 · 348
5:2, 4 · 339

2 Peter
2:5 · 317

1 John
3:2 · 340
5:21 · 20, 399

2 John
12 · 340

3 John
14 · 340

Jude
14 · 317

Revelation
Book of · 238
1 · 21
1-3 · 61
1:3 · 383
1:10 · 355
2:18 · 22
9:20 · 22
9:20,21 · 21
9:21 · 22
13:9 · 353
13:15 · 182
14 to 18 · 22
14:9, 11 · 23
15:2 · 23
17:16 · 22
18:3 · 23
18:23 · 22
20:4 · 23
20:11 · 340
21:8 · 21, 22
21:22 · 10
22:4 · 340
22:15 · 21, 22
22:18,19 · 316

Colophon

This book is set in AGaramond for the title page and chapter headings, and the text is set in New Times Roman.

AΩ

www.ingramcontent.com/pod-product-compliance
Lightning Source LLC
Chambersburg PA
CBHW071220290426
44108CB00013B/1232